Roman
Homosexuality

IDEOLOGIES OF DESIRE
David M. Halperin
Series Editor

The Female Thermometer
Eighteenth-Century Culture and the Invention of the Uncanny
TERRY CASTLE

Gide's Bent
Sexuality, Politics, Writing
MICHAEL LUCEY

The Erotic Imagination
French Histories of Perversity
VERNON A. ROSARIO II

Roman Homosexuality
Ideologies of Masculinity in Classical Antiquity
CRAIG A. WILLIAMS

Roman Homosexuality

Ideologies of Masculinity
in Classical Antiquity

CRAIG A. WILLIAMS

New York • Oxford

Oxford University Press

1999

Oxford University Press

Oxford   New York
Athens   Auckland   Bangkok   Bogotá   Buenos Aires   Calcutta
Cape Town   Chennai   Dar es Salaam   Delhi   Florence   Hong Kong   Istanbul
Karachi   Kuala Lumpur   Madrid   Melbourne   Mexico City   Mumbai
Nairobi   Paris   São Paulo   Singapore   Taipei   Tokyo   Toronto   Warsaw

and associated companies in
Berlin   Ibadan

Published by Oxford University Press, Inc.
198 Madison Avenue, New York, New York 10016

Oxford is a registered trademark of Oxford University Press

Library of Congress Cataloging-in-Publication Data
Williams, Craig A. (Craig Arthur), 1965–
Roman homosexuality : ideologies of masculinity in classical
antiquity / Craig A. Williams.
p.   cm.—(Ideologies of desire)
Revision of thesis.
Includes bibliographical references and index.
ISBN-13 978-0-19-511300-6; ISBN-13 978-0-19-512505-4 (pbk.)
ISBN 0-19-511300-4; ISBN 0-19-512505-3 (pbk.)
1. Homosexuality, Male—Rome—History.   2. Homosexuality, Male, in
art.   3. Homosexuality, Male, in literature.   4. Rome—Social life
and customs.   I. Title.   II. Series.
HQ76.2.R6W56   1999
306.76'62'0945632—dc21   97-51843

7 9 8 6

Printed in the United States of America
on acid-free paper

ACKNOWLEDGMENTS

My first debt of gratitude is owed to Ralph Hexter, my teacher and friend, who encouraged me to write the dissertation that has grown into this book: I have relied on his warm support and shrewd advice for more than a decade. My dissertation also benefited from the characteristic acumen of my other advisor, Gordon Williams, and I thank him again here.

Over the past six years I have entirely rewritten my dissertation, and the result is a very different (and, I hope, better) book. I have been grateful to David Halperin for his friendly encouragement and keen insights throughout this process; they have helped shape this book into what it is. Both he and Ralph Hexter have read and commented on the entire manuscript, as has Daniel Selden, and I offer all three of them my warm thanks here. Their contributions have strengthened my book just as their astuteness has saved me from embarrassment on a number of occasions, although it goes without saying (and so, like everything that goes without saying, will be said anyway) that the blame for any errors, infelicities, or wrongheaded conclusions lies with me alone. I also wish to thank Randolph Trumbach, who read parts of the manuscript and with whom I have had many helpful conversations on the history of sexuality.

Finally, I would like to acknowledge the help of Oxford University Press's anonymous readers, who pulled no punches, and to express my warm gratitude for the support and advice of various friends over the years: Panayotes Dakouras, Lee Elliott, Mario Erasmo, Marco Formisano, Debra Hamel, Edward Harris, and Ned Lochaya.

CONTENTS

ABBREVIATIONS

Abbreviations for ancient texts generally follow standard practice (see *OLD* and LSJ for lists). The following abbreviations are used for certain collections of ancient texts or works of modern scholarship.

ANRW	Temporini, Hildegard, ed. *Aufstieg und Niedergang der römischen Welt: Geschichte und Kultur Roms im Spiegel der neueren Forschung*. Berlin, 1972– .
CGL	Goetz, Georg, ed. *Corpus Glossariorum Latinorum*. Amsterdam, 1965.
CIL	*Corpus Inscriptionum Latinarum*. Berlin, 1893– .
CLE	Buecheler, Franz, ed. *Carmina Latina Epigraphica*. Leipzig, 1895. (Vol. 2 of *Anthologia Latina, sive Poesis Latinae Supplementum*, ed. Franz Buecheler and Alexander Riese.)
Ernout-Meillet	Ernout, Alfred, and Antoine Meillet, *Dictionnaire étymologique de la langue latine*. 4th ed. Paris, 1959.
GLK	Keil, Heinrich, ed. *Grammatici Latini*. Leipzig, 1857–1870.
ILS	Dessau, Hermann, ed. *Inscriptiones Latinae Selectae*. Berlin, 1892–1916.
Lewis and Short	Lewis, Charlton T., and Charles Short. *A Latin Dictionary*. Oxford, 1879.
LSJ	Liddell, Henry George, and Robert Scott. *A Greek-English Lexicon*. Revised by Sir Henry Stuart Jones and Roderick McKenzie. 9th ed. Oxford, 1940.
OLD	Glare, P. G. W., ed. *Oxford Latin Dictionary*. Oxford, 1982.

RAC   *Reallexikon für Antike und Christentum*. Stuttgart, 1950– .
RE   *Paulys Realencyclopädie der classischen Altertumswissenschaft*.
          Munich, 1894–1980.
TLL   *Thesaurus Linguae Latinae*. Leipzig, 1904– .
Walde-Hofmann   Walde, Alois, and Johann Baptist Hofmann. *Lateinisches
          etymologisches Wörterbuch*. 3rd ed. Heidelberg, 1938–1956.

Roman
Homosexuality

Introduction

Ancient Romans lived in a cultural environment in which married men could enjoy sexual relations with their male slaves without fear of criticism from their peers; in which adultery generally aroused more concern than pederasty; in which men notorious for their womanizing might be called effeminate, while a man whose masculinity had been impugned could cite as proof of his manhood the fact that he had engaged in sexual relations with his accuser's sons; in which men who sought to be sexually penetrated by other men were subjected to teasing and ridicule, but were also thought quite capable of being adulterers. These scenarios highlight some obvious differences between ancient and modern ideologies of masculine sexual behavior, and one of the central aims of this study is to explore those differences.

But how can we make such claims concerning an ancient culture, or indeed any culture? What precisely is the nature of these claims? What was the relationship between the ideological environment just outlined and the realities of living as a man in ancient Rome? What are the implications for us today of perceiving differences rather than continuities? These are basic questions implicated in any discussion of gender and sexuality in ancient cultures, and in this introduction I attempt to provide some preliminary responses to them, at the same time defining my terms and describing the conceptual framework within which I am working, and pointing to some of the problems involved in this kind of a study. Here I lay the foundations for the book as a whole, in which I will flesh out the cartoon figures of Roman men just sketched.

This study examines prevalent ideologies of masculinity among Romans by focusing on the representations and, when possible, the realities of men's sexual practice in general and sexual practices between males in particular. That formulation calls for expansion. When I speak of *ideologies* I refer to the systems of norms, values, and assumptions that were bequeathed to Roman men as part of their cultural patrimony and that enabled them to describe and evaluate individual experience in public contexts—in other words, to give public meaning to private acts. These ideologies were "prevalent" in the sense that, while different belief systems surely existed, these particular systems claimed the publicly pledged allegiance of the men who wielded power in ancient Roman culture and whose writings not coincidentally constitute nearly all of the surviving source material; a rejection of these ideologies was tantamount to the abrogation of power, to submission.[1] *Masculinity* refers to a complex of values and ideals that can more profitably be understood as a cultural tradition than as a biological given: the concept refers to what it is to be fully gendered as "a man" as opposed to merely having the physical features held to signify "a male."[2] The phrase *sexual practices* alludes to the realm of human existence that concerns stimulation of the genital organs and the desire for engaging in such stimulation; the practices described here almost always end up involving a man's penis, but I am consciously replicating Roman phallocentric paradigms so as to interrogate them.[3] Finally, while our definitions of "Roman" culture are increasingly being interrogated,[4] for my purposes Roman culture comprises those individual men and groups of men, mostly living in Rome or Italy, who looked to the city of Rome as their cultural center and wrote in Latin within a self-identified Roman literary tradition.[5] Roman cultural and literary traditions stood in a complex and often agonistic relationship with those of Greece, and throughout this study I will be pointing to similarities and differences between Roman and Greek ideologies of masculine sexual practices.[6]

Homosexuality, Heterosexuality, and Bisexuality

I begin with a central paradox. To judge by the sources left to us, homosexuality turns out not to have been an important issue for Romans. Nor, for that matter, was heterosexuality. It is one of the fundamental premises of this book—one that it aims to justify—that Roman men were not encouraged by their cultural heritage to categorize, much less evaluate or judge, sexual acts and agents on the basis of whether only males or males and females were involved. (We will see that sexual acts between females were treated rather differently.) A study of Roman homosexuality would seem as incomplete and as peculiar to an ancient Roman as would a study of Roman heterosexuality. An impulse to explore Roman attitudes toward homosexuality or toward heterosexuality derives, I would argue, less from an instinctive recognition of an objective, transcendent truth than it does from a culturally conditioned predisposition: it is something like an intellectual Pavlovian response.

And yet this book circumscribes Roman homosexuality as its subject. The paradox is intentional. I apply the concepts of homosexuality and heterosexuality heuristically, in order to expose their historical specificity and their inadequacy as categories of analysis in a description of Roman ideological traditions. In other words, I am reifying these conceptual entities only temporarily and for strategic purposes. For modern readers of the ancient material, homosexuality and heterosexuality may seem unavoidable terms; but by putting historical pressure on them, I aim to challenge them.[7] Consequently, my entire project, and not least its title, implies a certain ironic distance: a book titled "Roman Heterosexuality" would illustrate the point equally well.[8]

It may deserve emphasis that in its insistent problematization of the category "homosexuality," my study differs from nearly all previously published work on ancient Rome. Certainly homosexuality is very much alive in recent scholarship. In a 1991 study of *stuprum*, Elaine Fantham speaks of an ancient accusation of "homosexual promiscuity," mentions an ancient "homosexual rapist," and describes a Juvenalian satire as an "invective against homosexuals."[9] Amy Richlin argues in a 1993 article that there were men who were identified in antiquity as "homosexual" and were thus the victims of "homophobia."[10] Rabun Taylor's 1997 essay arguing for the existence of a "homosexual subculture" in Rome, while admitting that "ancient Mediterraneans would doubtless regard the aggregate of behaviors categorized as 'homosexual' to be somewhat arbitrary," nonetheless speaks of men in ancient texts who "openly flaunt their homosexuality," describes others as "confessing their homosexual inclination," and posits among Romans a "gradual recognition of male homosexuality as an institution and lifestyle rather than simply an aberrant act."[11]

Nor do the existing monographs specifically dedicated to the question of Roman "homosexuality" or "bisexuality" seriously interrogate those categories. Eva Cantarella, who promisingly begins her 1988 book (published in English translation in 1992) by acknowledging "how imprecise and misleading it is to speak of 'homosexuality' with reference to the ancient world,"[12] in practice constantly makes assertions about "homosexuality" in ancient Rome that could just as well be made about "heterosexuality," such as the following: "Homosexuality, then, was at the same time a social manifestation of the personal power of a citizen over slaves, and a personal reconfirmation of his virile potency."[13] Likewise, Saara Lilja's 1983 monograph offers the following summary of "moral aspects of homosexuality" in antiquity:

> Homosexual relations with slaves seem to have been generally accepted, provided that the slave acted as the passive partner. The same sharp distinction between passive and active roles also determined the general attitude towards homosexual relations between freeborn citizens: while the active partner was accepted or at least tolerated, the passive partner's submissive role was ridiculed. Bisexuality seems to have been considered as a normal phenomenon, but again only if the male in a homosexual contact acted as the active partner as he did in a heterosexual contact.[14]

These are also "moral aspects of heterosexuality": everything she says about homosexual relations with slaves and with freeborn citizens is equally true of heterosexual relations.[15] This is indeed what her last sentence seems to be saying, and the confusion created by the invocation of the concept of "bisexuality" reveals the problems of conceptualization. If we impose our own conceptual categories X and Y upon the ancient material and set out to investigate ancient attitudes to X, we will come to the conclusion that X is approved in contexts A and B and disapproved in contexts C and D, but that Y is also approved in A and B and disapproved in C and D. Clearly we need to discard X and Y and examine A, B, C, and D directly if we are to arrive at any useful insights. But enough of algebra: for X read "homosexuality," for Y "heterosexuality"; "bisexuality" equals X + Y.[16]

This conceptual problem has its linguistic reflex. Since language plays so crucial a role in the process by which culture shapes individual experience (that experience being given public meaning precisely through the representational medium of language), words matter a great deal—both the words used by ancient Romans and the words that we use as we attempt to describe ancient cultures and their discourses. Here we run into the basic difficulty confronting both the translator and the ethnographer: how to describe one culture in another's language. On the one hand, it has often been noted that Latin has no words identical in meaning to "homosexual" or "heterosexual" (or, I would add, "bisexual").[17] On the other hand, many of the terms that Romans did use are untranslatable: *stuprum* and *pudicitia* are far more specific than "debauchery" and "chastity," and *cinaedus* is not the same as "faggot," neither is *fellator* identical to "cocksucker" (see chapters 3 and 5). Since I seek to reconstruct ancient discourses on their own terms as far as possible, I refrain from translating such words as *stuprum* or *cinaedus*, nor will I offer "homosexual" or "heterosexual" as an English rendering of any Latin word.

Yet, conditioned from birth to speak and think in terms of heterosexuality and homosexuality, we are probably incapable of entirely discarding these concepts as analytic tools, or of purging them from our conceptual and linguistic systems. The dilemma appears inescapable, but as with the analytical categories "homosexuality" and "heterosexuality," which I deploy only strategically and with a certain ironic distance, so with English words. The abstract nouns "homosexuality," "heterosexuality," and "bisexuality" will only appear in my discussion as heuristic devices: quotation marks are to be imagined around every occurrence of the words. I never use "homosexual" and "heterosexual" as nouns referring to persons (e.g., "Juvenal criticizes homosexuals"), but I have found them occasionally useful as adjectives referring to acts or combinations of sexual agents (e.g., "heterosexual anal intercourse"). As such, however, the words should be understood merely as referring to observable phenomena and as making no assumptions regarding any deeply seated identities (see chapter 5 for this concept).[18] Similarly, I employ the adjective "homoerotic" and the phrase "same-sex"—as one might use "heteroerotic" and "opposite-sex"—to refer to acts or the desire that leads to those acts.

All of this linguistic usage reflects a central assumption of my work: while describing a sexual *act* as taking place between males, between males and females, or between females, can be a statement with relatively low ideological content, to speak of a *person* as "homosexual," "heterosexual," or "bisexual" is precisely to trumpet an ideology. As we will see, Roman texts certainly show an awareness that just as there are males and females, men may engage in sexual practices with males or with females or with both; and that just as males and females exhibit physical differences, so sexual practices between persons of the same sex may be compared or contrasted with such practices between persons of different sexes.[19] But the ancient sources quite consistently fail to suggest that these practices are significantly and essentially different. Rather, they are portrayed as two sides of one coin, differing mainly in surface detail. Some men were clearly more interested in one side of the coin than in the other, or even in one side exclusively; but in general, Roman men do not appear to have been inclined to focus on the obvious fact that the coin had two sides. If we emphasize precisely that fact, we will be importing a preoccupation that is alien to the Roman sources.

Indeed, according to widespread contemporary conceptions, every human being can meaningfully be pigeonholed as heterosexual or homosexual, with an intermediate category, bisexual, serving to handle intractable cases.[20] The ancient sources, though, offer no evidence for a widespread inclination to assign individuals an identity based on their sexual orientation as homosexual, heterosexual, or bisexual in the way that Western cultural discourses came to do later, above all after the emergence of the discipline of psychology in the late nineteenth century. That thesis is often associated with Michel Foucault, but he is hardly alone. Mary McIntosh's pioneering 1968 study of "the homosexual role" distinguishes between individual behaviors and social roles, beginning with the argument that "the vantage-point of comparative sociology enables us to see that the conception of homosexuality as a condition is, in itself, a possible object of study," observing that the role of "the homosexual" does not occur in all human societies, and arguing that it did not emerge in England until the late seventeenth century.[21] Jeffrey Weeks, in his landmark 1977 study of homosexual politics in Britain, makes this observation:

> Homosexuality has existed throughout history. But what have varied enormously are the ways in which various societies have regarded homosexuality, the meanings they have attached to it, and how those who were engaged in homosexual activity viewed themselves. . . . As a starting point we have to distinguish between homosexual behavior, which is universal, and a homosexual identity, which is historically specific.[22]

Similarly, in his 1988 volume *The Construction of Homosexuality*, David Greenberg observes that in some civilizations, "although homosexual roles may be recognized, mere involvement in a sexual relationship with someone of the same sex does not become the basis for classifying someone as a distinct type of person."[23] And a growing number of scholars have supported such claims with evidence from cultural environments ranging from ancient Greece to Renaissance Florence to early modern Japan to certain Native American and Melanesian peoples and even to early-twentieth-century New York City.[24] It is one of the central arguments of this book that ancient Rome belongs on that list.[25]

Roman assumptions about masculine identity rested, as we will see, on a binary opposition: *men*, the penetrators, as opposed to everyone else, the penetrated. The penetrated *other* included women, boys, and slaves; adult Roman men who displayed a desire to be penetrated were consequently labeled deviants and anomalies. This hierarchical structure, in which sexual practices are so clearly implicated in broader issues of power, reflects a worldwide tendency according to which acceptable sexual partners for adult men of the dominant class never belong to the same social grouping as themselves; they are either females or males who are in turn either boys or men not fully gendered as "men." Some scholars thus speak of "transgenerational" and "transgenderal" paradigms, evident not only in ancient Rome but also in such other settings as medieval Japan, whose samurai might have relationships with adolescent males or with young kabuki actors; in certain Native American cultures, where a man might legitimately have sexual relations with a person (today conventionally called *berdache*) who was identified at birth as a male but who in the course of his life came to be assigned to a third gender, no longer fully a man nor yet a woman; in some Melanesian societies, where in order to become fully gendered men, all boys must be inseminated by men; and indeed in ancient Greece, where publicly recognized relations between citizen males and adolescent males were a prominent feature of the cultural landscape.[26] In all of these cultures, Rome included, what was lacking was a so-called egalitarian model for sexual relations; in these traditions, men's publicly acceptable partners are always marked as significantly *different*, even if they are of the same biological sex—a consideration which obviously challenges the very concepts of homosexuality and heterosexuality, resting as they do upon the assumption that the only significant sameness or difference lies in the biological sex of the participants in a sexual act.[27]

In this regard, another preliminary point deserves to be made. There is a noticeable disparity between Roman representations of sexual practices between males and those of sexual practices between females.[28] The poetry of Ovid incisively illustrates the point. In his *Metamorphoses*, a compendium of Greek mythology designed for a Roman audience, Ovid has Iphis, a girl smitten with desire for another girl, expostulate on the bizarre nature of her passion, plaintively considering the animal world: cows do not yearn for cows, she observes, nor mares for mares (*Met.* 9.726–34). But the same poem offers no such objections to the existence of sexual attraction between males. On the contrary, it represents male homoerotic passion as an unexceptionable feature of human and indeed divine experience. Ovid includes the tales of Apollo and Hyacinth (a pederastic couple) and Narcissus (a young man who fell in love with another young man, who happened to be himself) in the same work that contains a tortured rejection of female homoerotic desire.[29] In a passage from his *Ars Amatoria (Art of Love)*, the same poet observes in passing that he prefers women on practical and admittedly altruistic grounds, but his phrasing is significant: "I hate couplings that do not give pleasure to both partners; that is why I am touched by the love of a boy less" (*Ars* 2.683–4: *odi concubitus qui non utrumque resolvunt; / hoc est cur pueri tangar amore minus*). He does not feel it necessary to disclaim all interest in boys (note that he writes "less" rather than "not at all"), neither does he attempt any general problematization of sexual practices between males. Indeed, in the programmatic introduction to his collection of love poems called the *Amores*, Ovid alludes to the proper subject matter for Roman love elegy (written from the perspective of the desiring male subject) as "either a boy or a girl adorned with long hair" (*Amores* 1.1.20: *aut puer aut longas compta puella comas*). In short, to this poet, as to his readership, there seem to have been no significant parallels, no meaningful common ground, between sexual practices between men and boys on the one hand and between women on the other: they did not both constitute embodiments of the overarching concept *homosexuality*, with the subsets *male* and *female*.

Representation and Reality

As my opening formulations suggest, the relationship between representation and reality is crucial to this inquiry. Of course, the two terms are not strictly antithetical: for one thing, it can be argued that all reality is mediated through representation in the same way that human experience is mediated through language.[30] Still, the terms are useful provided one bears in mind their limitations. By *reality* I mean the actual day-to-day experiences of real Roman men (for example, that on a certain day one man anally penetrated another), whereas *representation* refers to the ways in which Roman men as a group publicly portrayed the experiences, whether real or imagined, both of themselves and of others (for example: gossip reported by a historian to the effect that a certain man had been penetrated in his youth; love poetry in which the persona proclaims his love for a young man; or graffiti crudely proclaiming that a certain man performs fellatio). When we consider ancient representations we are looking for the shared language of words, concepts, prejudices, and preconceptions concerning masculinity and men's sexual behavior that is detectable in the surviving sources: the discourse of masculinity.[31]

It is of course the representations that are the most easily apprehensible for us today, since, unlike anthropologists studying contemporary cultures, we cannot interview native informants, neither do we have direct access to the realities of living as a man in ancient Rome. Thus we inevitably come to the question of how the representations that have been left to us relate to the historical realities of living in ancient Rome. In his poetry, Gaius Valerius Catullus was willing to cast himself in the role of the lover of a young man named Juventius; the biographer Suetonius tells us that Julius Caesar was mocked for having had in his youth an affair with the Bithynian king Nicomedes in which he played the receptive or "passive" role in sexual intercourse. These are examples (and, as we shall see, typical examples) of Roman representation. But what was the reality that lay behind or within them? In these two particular cases, we simply cannot know. Catullus may have been indulging in poetic fancy, and Caesar's enemies may have been spreading malicious but groundless gossip; on the other hand, Catullus may have really had an affair with Juventius, and Caesar with Nicomedes. We have the representations, but the realities are lost to us.

Yet the representations can be richly rewarding in themselves. For one thing, they tell us a lot about what a self-respecting Roman man would have publicly endorsed as acceptably masculine behavior (for example, erotically pursuing a beautiful young man), as well as what he and his peers would have considered to be a basis for accusation (for example, playing the receptive role in anal intercourse with a foreign king). We cannot be certain what the particular experiences of a given man were, but we can learn a great deal about larger and perhaps more rewarding questions.[32] In the arena of public interactions between men, which sexual practices were held to be acceptable and which were not? How did these practices affect a man's masculine status? How were these practices categorized, labeled, and evaluated, and what sorts of conceptual interrelationships existed between them?

Here the concept of the persona is obviously important, especially in texts that use a first-person narrative. It should go without saying that when I speak of Catullus,

Martial, and Cicero, I refer to the persona projected by each of those writers, which may or may not reflect the actual desires and preoccupations of the men themselves. And the same holds true for other people described by those authors. Thus, when I speak of Martial or a character in one of his epigrams—or of Cicero or a character in one of his speeches—who "wants" or "says" or "does" something, it should not be thought that I am reifying these characters, as if, for example, Martial's Hyllus was a real man who actually wanted to be penetrated. But the point is that as far as Martial's Roman readers were concerned, he *could* have been. In fact, ancient writers easily made the jump from persona to person, breezily disregarding occasional protests against the practice.[33] In a passage from a philosophical work to which we shall return, Cicero preaches on the dangers of sexual passion, and in so doing he discusses the love poets:

> quid denique homines doctissimi et summi poetae de se ipsis et carminibus edunt et cantibus? fortis vir in sua re publica cognitus quae de iuvenum amore scribit Alcaeus! nam Anacreontis quidem tota poesis est amatoria. maxume vero omnium flagrasse amore Reginum Ibycum apparet ex scriptis. (Cic. *Tusc.* 4.71)

> In short, what do those most learned men and greatest of poets reveal about themselves in their poems and songs? Consider what Alcaeus—recognized as a hero in his native land—wrote concerning the love of young men. All of Anacreon's poetic oeuvre, of course, is about love. But it is obvious from his writings that Ibycus of Regium burned with love more than anyone else.[34]

Cicero moves effortlessly between poetry and poets, and indeed he makes no bones about it: poetry reveals the man. In a world of Ciceros, a poet would have to be very bold indeed to assign to his persona attitudes or behaviors with which he would be ashamed to be associated.

Still, although we must deal in representations, we cannot ignore historical realities. Reality and representation interpenetrate: on the one hand, real individual experiences can only be given public meaning by being passed through the filter of representation; on the other hand, representations are representations of *something* and are understood as such by those who create and disseminate them. There are moments, even in the relatively limited body of Roman source material left to us, in which we get a fleeting glimpse through the representations to realities that may or may not harmonize with them. Thus, while this study focuses on the social script inherited and passed on by Roman men, it will also, where possible, consider to what extent the actors actually read from that script in their day-to-day existence.[35]

One feature of the Roman cultural landscape concisely illustrates the complexities of the relationship between representation and reality: the crucial importance of *appearances* for masculine identity. We shall see that one fundamental rule of masculine behavior was that a self-respecting man should play the insertive ("active") role in penetrative sexual acts, and never the receptive ("passive") role. But if a certain man actually played the receptive role in the majority of his sexual encounters, yet managed to keep that fact a secret known only to himself and his partners, and otherwise maintained the appearance of a fully masculine man, then practically speaking he *was* a fully masculine man in the all-important arena of public discourse, despite the fact that he actually was breaking the rules behind closed doors. By contrast, if there were persistent rumors to the effect that a man liked to play the receptive role in intercourse, even if the man himself had never actually been penetrated, he was *ipso facto* a marked man, metaphorically "fucked" even though not literally so. We will return to this point in chapter 5.

The Question of Diachronic Change

What kinds of sources are available for this kind of inquiry? Physical artifacts (wall paintings, statues, and the like) are of central importance, and I will discuss relevant objects whenever possible, but the majority of our sources are textual in nature, ranging from what we would call literary works to such subliterary texts as graffiti and inscriptions, written between the second century B.C. and the second century A.D.[36] Ancient texts, like statues and paintings, are artifacts produced by and for members of a particular culture and class and suffused with a common language, a shared network of meanings and values. Although the body of texts that I am considering spans four centuries of Roman history and embraces a considerably broad range of genres, each with its own traditions and strategies, all of these works—from comedy and obscene epigrams to courtroom speeches and rhetorical handbooks—were created by Roman men for an audience principally consisting of Roman men. As cultural artifacts, they simultaneously reflected and reinforced certain normative standards to which both writer and audience claimed allegiance.[37] One of my goals is to demonstrate that if we consider all of the sources as an ensemble, looking for what they commonly assail and what they commonly suppress, a consistent picture emerges. Such texts as a speech of Cicero, an epigram of Martial, a biography of Suetonius, or graffiti scratched on a wall come equipped with an impressive array of cultural baggage, and I wish to begin the process of unpacking. (See appendix 3 for an overview of the ancient sources used in this study.)

Of course, since our sources span four centuries of Roman history, diachronic change looms as a distinct possibility. Indeed, a number of scholars have assumed or even explicitly argued that there were significant changes in Roman traditions, especially over the course of the transition between Republic and Empire which took place approximately halfway through this central period. Saara Lilja, for example, imposes the death of Augustus in A.D. 14 as a chronological limit on her study *Homosexuality in Republican and Augustan Rome* because after that point, she submits, "foreign influence from different sources grew to an extraordinary extent, not least in the sphere of sex."[38] The influence of foreign (i.e., Greek) traditions on Roman sexual mores, long a shibboleth among classicists, is considered in my first two chapters, where I argue that only the specific practice of *paiderastia*, or sexual and romantic relations between citizen men and freeborn adolescent males, was considered by Romans to be a "Greek" practice; never was it thought that male homoerotic practices in general were a Greek borrowing. As for the general assumption that the Empire was significantly different from the Republic, I aim to demonstrate that the traditional codes governing sexual behavior, and the

conceptual systems informing those codes, underwent no alterations in the transition from Republic to Empire during the first centuries B.C. and A.D.[39]

There may indeed have been some fluctuations in practice, such as in the
open display of luxury or in the extent to which Romans felt free to admit to behavior considered nontraditional and decadent. For example, it is often suggested
that close contact with Greece in the second century B.C. helped create an atmo-
sphere that encouraged an open enjoyment of such traditionally disapproved practices as the courtship of married women or freeborn boys, and that the reign of
Vespasian (A.D. 69–78) witnessed a puritanical vogue.[40] Eva Cantarella has also
argued that the first century A.D. saw a marked increase in nontraditional practices. In particular, she suggests that more and more men were openly flaunting
their predilection for being penetrated:

> The ideology, then, has not changed: a man is only a real man if he is gloriously active.
> But the facts show that real Roman males are getting rarer and rarer. Even allowing
> for the exaggerated description of current practices, offered both by Martial and by
> Juvenal, passive behaviour has kept on spreading in a worrying fashion. And as we
> shall see, it goes on spreading. Here is the great, intolerable novelty.[41]

But this theory of a significant change in practices rests on tenuous foundations.
As Cantarella herself points out, Martial and Juvenal indulge in hyperbole, and it is
hazardous to draw conclusions about how widespread certain practices may have
been solely on the basis of their poems; thus it is not at all clear that "the facts"
show anything in this regard. Indeed, Cantarella's conclusion is based on an argument from silence: we simply do not have sources comparable to Martial and Juvenal
from the second or early first centuries B.C.[42] If we did, we might well have an image
of Roman practices during that period that would be strikingly similar to that which
is provided by Martial and Juvenal for the first and second centuries A.D.[43]

In fact, there are texts from the second and first centuries B.C. that decidedly
weaken any theory of an explosive growth of "passive behavior" in the first century
A.D. Commenting on Juvenal's portrayal of a man who accepts gifts, even money, to
sexually penetrate a man and his wife, Cantarella writes:

> The interest and novelty of this satire is obvious. Male prostitution, as we know, had
> always been widespread in Rome. But in the old days, boys sold themselves to be
> subjected to sex like women. Their paymaster was still a real man. Now, everything has
> changed. Naevolus is an active homosexual. The Romans have sunk to such a level of
> depravity that they no longer pay to put somebody else underneath them—they now
> pay someone to go on top.[44]

Her language is imprecise: Naevolus can hardly be called a "homosexual" as he not
only services both his male patron and his wife but also expresses an interest in
girls (*puellas*, 9.128); and it was certainly not the case that Roman men "no longer"
paid prostitutes whom they penetrated. Above all, though, the idea that a man
might pay a prostitute to play the insertive or penetrative role was hardly a novelty.
In the early first century B.C. Pomponius staged an Atellan farce called *The Prostitute (Prostibulum)* whose main character was a male prostitute who makes it bru-

tally clear that he penetrates his male clients (see chapters 1 and 2 for further discussion of this play). Any theorizing about significant changes in Roman men's sexual practices must be viewed with great caution.[45]

In the end, Cantarella reminds us that what never changed is the *ideology*, and that is precisely the main concern of my study. Even if we accept the unprovable hypothesis that during the Empire more men openly broke the rules (flaunting, for example, their indulgence in such illicit behaviors as adultery or their desire to be penetrated), the rules themselves never changed. Adultery was still adultery, and to be penetrated was still thought incompatible with a fully masculine image. The ideological traditions that were either affirmed or violated by individual Romans over the course of time remained intact throughout the period studied in this book.[46]

Past and Present

No attempt at describing the past—especially a past that is thought to have played such a crucial role in the formation of the present—can be entirely disinterested. The fact that, any paradox notwithstanding, I have designated my book as a study of Roman homosexuality as it relates to ideologies of masculinity reveals my interest in the contemporary project of exploring the ways in which sexual practices between males have been given meaning over the course of human history. But I refrain from using terms like "gay history" for reasons that should already be clear: a historical inquiry into "homosexuality" or "gay people" is thwarted by the fact that the very concept of what a "homosexual" or a "gay person" *is* is notoriously disputed. Yet feminist scholars like Amy Richlin have directed our focus to certain fundamental continuities in discourses of gender and sex, reminding us of the unbroken tradition of oppressive patriarchal structures in Western cultures.[47] To be sure, Western patriarchy has a long history, and there are some obvious continuities between ancient Rome and contemporary Western cultures with regard to sexual practices: male human beings both then and now have consciously experienced desire for others, both male and female, and have sometimes embodied those desires in specific acts, and the basic forms that the physical consummation of those desires has taken are finite and familiar (the practices most often described in the Roman sources, at any rate, are vaginal and anal penetration, fellatio and cunnilinctus).[48] Beyond mere physical encounters, men have desired to form lasting bonds with sexual partners both male and female, and the spectrum of emotional states involved in pursuing and maintaining those relationships seems to have remained basically the same. But what has changed, and indeed what generally varies over time and between cultures, is the way in which men have been encouraged by their cultural heritage to categorize and evaluate these acts and actors, relations and relationships. That is precisely my interest in this book. In probing the gaps between antiquity and modernity with regard to ideologies of masculinity in general and sexual practices between males in particular, and by historicizing modern discourses on heterosexuality and homosexuality, my study will, I hope, shed light on both ancient and contemporary ideologies of masculinity, and perhaps also on the mechanisms by which culture molds individual experience.

The Script of Masculinity

These are the kinds of issues that shape my exploration of the ways in which Roman masculinity was performed. The actors, the script from which they read, and the performance itself are all objects of this inquiry (whether the actors always followed the script is another question, about which we can only speculate).[49] Of these, it is the script that is most accessible to us today, and it is around the script that this book is organized. Thus I structure my inquiry not around an opposition between homosexual and heterosexual, nor in terms of a homosexual/heterosexual/ bisexual triad, but instead around the relevant Roman concepts. Chapters 1 and 2 are concerned above all with the relationship between Rome and Greece; I argue that, independently of any Greek influence, Roman moral traditions always provided for an acceptance of sexual practices between males in certain configurations and contexts; that what Romans saw as "Greek" in this area was the particular social practice of pederasty (*paiderastia*); and that there are certain characteristics of Roman representations of masculine sexual behavior (most outstandingly, a value placed on unusually generous phallic endowments) that are strikingly different from corresponding Greek representations. The next three chapters are structured so as to reveal some of the basic organizing principles of Roman scripts for masculinity: first, the opposition between freeborn Romans and everyone else (slaves in particular) that protected the sexual integrity of free persons of both sexes and generally disregarded the distinction between heterosexual and homosexual acts (chapter 3); second, an opposition between masculine and effeminate traits or behaviors that was not aligned with the distinction between heterosexual and homosexual acts and that relied instead on the association of masculinity with concepts of dominion and control (chapter 4); and third, a conceptual system concerned with the role played in sexual acts that was fundamentally structured around the antithesis between the insertive or penetrating role and the receptive or penetrated role, and that was related to issues of *gender identity* rather than *sexual orientation* (chapter 5). A concluding discussion looks both backward and forward, offering a recapitulation and suggesting future avenues of inquiry.

Roman Traditions

Slaves, Prostitutes, and Wives

Some of the most fascinating problems in the study of Roman cultural traditions arise from the complex interactions between Rome and Greece that resulted in what is often called Greco-Roman culture, a term that points to the extraordinary influence exerted by Greece, nominally the captive nation, on Rome. Roman writers were themselves fully aware of this phenomenon. The poet Horace's lapidary phrase, although concerned specifically with literary influences, is often cited as a typical perspective on the relationship between the two civilizations: "Captive Greece captured its barbarian conqueror."[1] In recent times the project of teasing out the native Roman from the imported Greek threads in the fabric of Greco-Roman culture (or, alternatively, of denying the utility or even possibility of such an attempt) has engaged scholars interested in the history and nature of the Roman literary tradition and in the more general development of a Roman cultural identity in opposition to the established traditions of the Greeks.[2]

In view of the much-discussed Hellenic tradition of pederasty,[3] the question of Greek versus Roman becomes especially important for inquiries into Roman ideologies of masculinity and sexual experience. Scholarly focus on Greek traditions has generally resulted in a belief that, whether in historical reality or in ancient perceptions of that reality, native Roman ideals of masculinity before the advent of the corrupting influence of Greek customs encouraged an exclusive heterosexuality. According to this view, the acceptance of homosexuality—more

extreme proponents imply even its practice—was one of the cultural items borrowed by Rome from Greece, one ingredient in the package of extravagance and
luxury that was the conquered race's insidious gift to its conquerors, as if it were a
type of sexual Trojan horse. L. P. Wilkinson and Ramsay MacMullen offer two
especially vigorous expositions of the view:

> In the early Republic the Romans' attitude to homosexuality was that of most non-
> Greeks; it was a Greek idiosyncrasy which they despised. . . . But in the second cen-
> tury BC, when captured Greece captivated its rude conqueror, there was an increase in
> homosexual practices; and at some time a *Lex Scantinia* was passed against them.[4]

> The Greek origin of "Greek love" among the Romans is suggested by its appearance
> disproportionately in Greek dress in early Roman literature. . . . It seems safe to con-
> clude that "the man in the street," or at least the man in the forum and law courts who
> constituted the ordinary audience for political statements, could be assumed to be the
> foe of male homosexuality.[5]

There have always been dissenting opinions,[6] and two articles by Paul Veyne and
one book by Eva Cantarella directly argue against the conclusions suggested by
Wilkinson and MacMullen:

> It is not true that "Greek" love was, at Rome, of Greek origin: like more than one
> Mediterranean society even today, Rome never opposed the love of women to the love
> of boys. It opposed activity to passivity: to be active is to be a male, whatever the sex of
> the passive partner.[7]

> Rome did not have to wait for hellenization to allow various forms of love between
> males. . . . This is the world of heroic bravado, with a very Mediterranean flavour,
> where the important thing is to be the ravisher, never mind the sex of the victim.[8]

> To sum up, homosexuality in itself was neither a crime nor a socially reproved form of
> behavior. Carrying on with a slave (so long as he did not belong to someone else) was
> accepted as normal behavior, as was paying a male prostitute. The only thing that was
> not acceptable was to make love to a young free Roman citizen.[9]

But the views set forth by Veyne and Cantarella have hardly gained universal acceptance among classicists. Indeed, the complex of beliefs suggested by Wilkinson and
MacMullen, although rarely so trenchantly expressed, is still widespread among classicists: that native Roman cultural traditions were uncomfortable with or even hostile to sexual experience between males; that only the philhellenizing upper classes
adopted Greek perspectives on that experience, and thus tolerated or even celebrated
affairs between men and boys; and finally that, whatever the historical realities may
have been, Romans themselves associated male homosexuality with Greece.[10]

The tenacity of such views is no doubt partially due to the cultural milieu to
which contemporary European and American scholars themselves belong, a milieu
that encourages them to categorize and evaluate human beings as sexual subjects
on the basis of the sex of their preferred partners and thus has induced many
scholars to look for "Roman attitudes toward homosexuality." But, as I suggested

in the introduction, to inquire into Roman attitudes toward homosexuality and their relation to Roman attitudes toward Greece means also inquiring into Roman attitudes toward heterosexuality and their relation to Roman attitudes toward Greece. Traditional Roman standards of acceptably masculine sexual behavior included, as we will see, provisions for sexual experience with both males and females in certain contexts (notably with one's own slaves and with prostitutes). Moreover, we will see that those sexual practices that could be represented as somehow "Greek" were primarily those involving freeborn boys openly courted in accordance with the Hellenic traditions of pederasty—and not all sexual relations between males—and that relations with fancy female prostitutes could also be given a "Greek" coloring. In the following two chapters I discuss the evidence for this view (which has been espoused by other scholars), but I also ask how "Greek" the practice of pederasty actually was: How large did pederastic traditions actually loom in Roman images of Greek culture, and to what extent were pederastic relationships in a Roman context actually colored as Greek? Chapter 2 then proceeds to explore certain specifically Roman features of the cultural landscape detectable in the ancient sources.

The Protocols of Masculine Behavior

Scholarly inquiry into human sexual behavior worldwide, from the earliest times to the present, has made one thing clear: apart from the modern social formation conventionally called "Western culture," very few cultures have issued a blanket condemnation of sexual practices between males as being in and of themselves objectionable.[11] While there are always restrictions and qualifications—this kind of sexual behavior is only acceptable in certain contexts—the same is true of *all* human sexual practices, which are generally among the most intensely scrutinized and policed of behaviors. As we will see, the sources left to us from ancient Rome make it abundantly clear that Roman traditions fell squarely in line with the worldwide trend: homosexual behavior was not condemned per se, and a citizen male could admit to sexual experience with males in certain contexts and configurations without fear of ridicule or reprisal, without the threat even of a raised eyebrow.[12]

By saying "certain contexts and configurations" I imply that there existed restrictions; but restrictions were placed even on a man's behavior with his legitimate wife. One ancient anecdote reveals something of the character of Roman traditions regarding publicly acceptable conduct. We will have several occasions to consider the figure of Marcus Porcius Cato. Consul in 195 B.C., and censor in 184 B.C., Cato has regularly been held by both ancients and moderns to be the very embodiment of traditional Roman standards, unswerving in his dedication to the *mos maiorum* or "ways of the ancestors" and unremitting in his attacks on decadence and luxury.[13] During his tenure as censor, renowned for its strictness, he exercised one of the privileges of his office by expelling from membership in the Senate a man named Manilius. What was Cato's cause for complaint? The man had kissed his wife in broad daylight in the presence of their daughter. According to Plutarch, the censor observed that he himself only fell into his wife's embrace when startled by loud thunder, jokingly adding that he was a lucky man when it thundered. Of course the second comment undermines the first one, as Cato is slyly admitting that kissing one's wife has its pleasures. But there was a time and a place for everything, and Manilius had apparently gone too far.[14]

But what were the traditional protocols[15] governing sexual practices between males among Romans? As was argued in the introduction, to ask this question is really to ask about sexual protocols in general, as the most fundamental rules regulating men's sexual behavior were in effect regardless of whether their partners were male or female. Another crucial point made in the introduction, and that will be discussed in more detail in chapter 5, deserves to be reiterated. What was at stake was less a man's actual behavior and more the *appearance* he gave and the *image* he had; how he was seen and talked about by his peers more than what he actually did in the privacy of his bedroom. With these important qualifications in mind, we now consider the basic rules of the game evident in the ancient texts surveyed in this book.

First and foremost, a self-respecting Roman man must always give the appearance of playing the insertive role in penetrative acts, and not the receptive role: to use popular terminology often unfortunately replicated in the language of contemporary scholarship, he must be the "active," not the "passive," partner.[16] This can justly be called the prime directive of masculine sexual behavior for Romans, and it has an obvious relationship to broader structures of hierarchical male power. For according to this scheme, penetration is subjugation (in the sense that the act is held simultaneously to be a figure for, and to effect, subjugation), and masculinity is domination. The conceptual system informing this prime directive, along with ancient modes of representing various sexual acts and agents, are taken up in detail in chapter 5; for now it will suffice to note that a similar protocol for masculine sexual behavior can be found in many other cultural settings, from ancient Greece to early modern Japan to certain Polynesian and Native American cultures to some contemporary Islamic societies.[17] In a Roman setting, this paradigm can handily be called a Priapic model of masculinity.[18] First worshipped in the Greek town of Lampsacus, the god Priapus, a fertility deity whose outstanding attribute was his prodigiously large penis, became extraordinarily popular among Romans, and a number of Roman texts, blending poetic conceit with folk beliefs, explore the notion that a statue of the god, with a sickle in one hand and his characteristic member jutting out from his crotch, would protect a garden by raping thieves, whether male or female.[19] Priapus' popularity in the Roman world is suggestive. He can be seen as something like the patron saint or mascot of Roman machismo, and his vigorous exploits with women, boys, and men indiscriminately are clearly a mainstay of his hyper-masculine identity.[20] Like this phallic deity, a Roman man was ideally ready, willing, and able to express his dominion over others, male or female, by means of sexual penetration. By contrast, men who willingly played the receptive role in penetrative acts were imagined thereby to have abrogated their masculine privilege, to have assimilated themselves to the inferior status of women, and were thus liable to ridicule and scorn.

A second protocol governing men's sexual behavior concerned the status of their partners, and here too the rule applied regardless of their partners' sex: apart from his wife, freeborn Romans both male and female were officially off-limits sexual partners for a Roman man (this protocol is explored in chapter 3). As always, it is worth bearing in mind that the existence of rules implies their violation, but here we are not concerned with what men actually did as much as we are with what they were *supposed* to do. According to the rules, freeborn Roman males and females were excluded as acceptable partners, thus leaving slaves, prostitutes, and noncitizens of either sex as persons (other than his wife) with whom a Roman man could have sexual relations without causing eyebrows to rise—provided always, of course, that the man observed the prime directive of maintaining the appearance of playing the insertive role in these sexual encounters.[21]

The next protocol did not constitute a restriction on men's sexual practices in the same way that the first two did. As we will see, the violation of the first rule by being penetrated damaged one's masculine identity (chapters 4 and 5), and the violation of the second rule by having relations with a freeborn Roman of either sex had certain moral and legal consequences (chapter 3). The third protocol did not have comparable consequences, and is less of a rule than a tendency pervading the ancient sources: a noticeable proclivity toward smooth young bodies, such that, on the one hand, old women were the object of sometimes blood-curdling invective and, on the other hand, when the sources conceive of the kind of male partner who will normally arouse men's desires, they regularly picture a smooth youth. Men's normative sexual partners as represented in the textual tradition are therefore usually divisible into two classes: women or girls (*feminae* and *puellae*) on the one hand—treated indifferently as a group, but clearly excluding women thought to be disgustingly past their prime—and young men or boys (*pueri*, *adulescentuli*, or *iuvenes*) on the other hand, excluding mature men (*viri*).[22] Although we will see in chapter 2 that this last restriction was not always observed, still, the ideal male partner, the *youth* or *boy* of our sources, belonged to the age-group roughly equivalent to what is now called adolescence. For Romans, this period's beginning was marked by the onset of puberty (generally held to occur between the twelfth and fourteenth years and to be marked by the maturation of the genitals and hence the arrival of sexual maturity, as well as by the appearance of a light down on the cheeks) and its end was marked by what they saw as the completion of the process of maturation, most notably the arrival of the full, manly beard (which is attested usually to have occurred somewhere around the twentieth year).[23] In between those two extremes lay the golden years, the "flower of youth" (*flos aetatis*), when boys were no longer prepubescent children, but not yet men; when they were at the peak of desirability and thus of vulnerability. (See chapter 2 for the ancient evidence and further discussion.)

Boys and Girls

A conceptual system that gives rise to the prime directive of masculinity outlined above—that a man should appear to play the insertive role with his partners, whether they are male or female—necessarily includes an understanding that it is normative (natural and normal, we might say) for a man to desire sexual contact with male and female bodies alike.[24] Such a perspective is evident in sources from the earliest to the latest times, in all genres of writing from graffiti to *belles lettres*. As we turn to the evidence, moreover, it should be borne in mind that nowhere do we find a suggestion that the protocols or behavioral codes, or the morality informing them, owe anything to the influence of Greek culture. It is true that the great majority of the surviving contemporary evidence dates from after the second century B.C.: after, that is, the wave of Greek influence had swept over Rome. Still, Roman writers were acutely aware of that influence and were quick to point out the ways (almost entirely pernicious, as they would have it) in which contact with Greece had affected the Roman cultural landscape, and they never suggest that the basic understandings of masculine identity sketched above had been taken over from the Greeks. What they do suggest, as we will see in chapter 2, is that Greek influence resulted in increased licentiousness, as witnessed, for example, by an increased indulgence in prostitutes.

Graffiti from Rome, its port city Ostia, Pompeii, and elsewhere throughout the Roman world—messages scratched on walls by people (almost entirely, it would seem, men) of various backgrounds—offer a valuable insight into discourses of Roman masculinity in a context and format presumably less susceptible to the influences of Greek literary traditions; and these graffiti attest to the prevalence of the Priapic model for masculinity. A number of them boast of sexual conquests of males and females alike in bluntly penetrative terms. The following, for example, were scratched on the walls of Pompeii:

> hic ego cum veni futui, deinde redei domi (Diehl 614)
> hic ego me memini quendam futuisse puellam (Diehl 616)
> Secundus pedicavd pueros lucle [. . .] utis (Diehl 622)
> futui coponam (Diehl 1087)

> When I came here, I fucked. Then I went back home.
> I remember fucking some girl here once.
> Secundus butt-fucked [. . .] boys.
> I fucked a bar-maid.

A metrical graffito found in Spain and probably dating from the first century A.D. makes this blunt boast: "Surianus, who wrote this, butt-fucked Maevius."[25] Similarly proud messages can be found scattered around the Roman world: one man claims, "I butt-fucked Nisus ten times,"[26] while another man shows himself to have been slightly more restrained: "I butt-fucked six times."[27] Other graffiti similarly redolent of macho prowess range from an untranslatable pun describing the anal penetration of a male[28] to the considered opinion that it is better to penetrate a hairy vulva than a smooth one[29] to an only partially decipherable boast scribbled on the wall of a building in Ostia that seems to specify multiple modes of penetration of a male.[30] Less coarse but equally typical is a metrical graffito found on a wall of Nero's Domus Aurea in Rome that offers this opinion, possibly making a naughty pun in the process:

> quisquis amat pueros, etiam sin(e) fine puellas,
>   rationem saccli non h(a)bet ille sui.

Whoever loves boys as well as girls without end, takes no account of his pouch.[31]

The fact that a closely similar graffito was found in Remagen in Germany—on the fringes of the Roman world—suggests that the sentiment was something of a commonplace, maybe even a tag.[32] Finally, the so-called *glandes Perusinae*, or lead sling-bullets dating from the siege of Perugia by Octavian's troops during the winter of 41/40 B.C., are inscribed with various messages, some of which direct a nakedly phallic aggression against both male and female opponents: "I seek Octavian's asshole"; "Loose Octavius, sit on this"; "Greetings, Octavius: you suck dick"; and, representing the other side, "Bald Lucius Antonius and Fulvia, open up your asshole" and "I seek Fulvia's clitoris."[33] Since these bullets are of a shape that might well be described as phallic, and since the Latin word for sling-bullet, *glans* (originally meaning "acorn"), has been used by medical writers both ancient and modern to describe the tip of the penis, one might say that the *glandes Perusinae* evoke the image of the penis both visually and verbally.[34] These physical artifacts incisively symbolize the Roman male sexual persona in its most elemental form: the phallus, ready, willing, and able to assert its penetrative power at the expense of another, female or male.

In the literary sources, this paradigm is most obviously embodied in representations of the phallic god Priapus standing guard over the gardens assigned to his care. A Roman poet or poets produced (probably in the first century A.D.) a collection of poems on the subject of this deity, now known as the *Carmina Priapea*,[35] and they often give the god a voice as he stands ready to protect his turf from thieves. And he does not mince words:

> Percidere, puer, moneo; futuere, puella;
>   barbatum furem tertia poena manet. (13)

> Femina si furtum faciet mihi virve puerve,
>   haec cunnum, caput hic, praebeat ille nates. (22)

> Per medios ibit pueros mediasque puellas
>   mentula, barbatis non nisi summa petet. (74)

> I warn you, boy, you will be screwed; girl, you will be fucked; a third penalty awaits the bearded thief.

> If a woman steals from me, or a man, or a boy, let the first give me her cunt, the second his head, the third his buttocks.

> My dick will go through the middle of boys and the middle of girls, but with bearded men it will aim only for the top.[36]

Consider, too, this slightly more decorous prayer from a verse dedication to Priapus made at Tibur (modern Tivoli), probably in the late first century A.D., by the freedman Julius Agathemerus:

... da mihi floridam iuventam,
da mihi ut pueris et ut puellis
fascino placeam bonis procaci
lusibusque frequentibus iocisque
dissipem curas animo nocentes
nec gravem timeam nimis senectam. (*CIL* 14.3565.2–7; *CLE* 1504)

Grant me a flowering youth; grant that I may please good boys and girls with my naughty prick, and that with frequent fun and games I may chase away the worries that harm the soul, and that I may not fear old age too much.

This prayer, whether pious or parodic, relies on the assumption that Priapus is the god par excellence of youthful masculine vigor, and that that vigor will express itself in penetrative sexual relations with boys and girls.[37] Finally, it is worth noting that when Tibullus imagines a Roman man calling upon Priapus for advice in matters erotic, the specific concern is how to catch a beautiful boy.[38]

Surviving quotations from second-century B.C. statesmen such as Cato the Elder, Scipio Aemilianus, and Gaius Gracchus provide helpful glimpses into contemporary popular morality during the period when the influence of Greece was beginning to make itself felt on a large scale. Not only do these fragments offer evidence for what Romans of the time actually did, but they suggest a great deal about the kinds of perspectives that orators felt comfortable espousing in the public arena, and thus ultimately about the assumptions and values they expected their audiences to endorse. In other words, we can assume that their speeches reflect a traditional Roman morality; public figures in a society renowned for its conservative moral and political traditions would hardly have subscribed to new-fangled notions recently arrived from Greece. That is, even if Greek traditions eventually caused significant changes in native Roman paradigms (I am arguing that they did not), it seems highly unlikely that any such changes could have become so entrenched in the course of the second century B.C. as to be fully incorporated into the moral systems shared by politicians of that period and their audiences.

When, in 124 B.C., C. Sempronius Gracchus returned from his quaestorship in Sardinia, he delivered a speech before the people that has been partially preserved by Aulus Gellius. In a surviving portion of the speech (fr. 27 Malcovati), Gracchus makes this proud claim:

biennium fui in provincia; si ulla meretrix domum meam introivit aut cuiusquam servulus propter me sollicitatus est, omnium nationum postremissimum nequissimumque existimatote. cum a servis eorum tam caste me habuerim, inde poteritis considerare quomodo me putetis cum liberis vestris vixisse. (Gell. 15.12.3)

I spent two years in the province; if any [female] prostitute came into my home or if anyone's slave-boy was accosted for my sake, you can think of me as the basest and most worthless person in the world. . . . Considering that I so chastely kept myself from their slaves, you can reflect on how you think I treated your children.

The assumptions regarding male desire that shape Gracchus' rhetoric are telling. First, it is significant that he says nothing about his treatment of his own slaves; what he did with them was presumably not a matter for public discussion. Second, one can perceive an unspoken understanding between Gracchus and his audience: even if Gracchus had been unable to keep his hands off prostitutes and other men's slaves, his transgression would not have been particularly reprehensible; consequently, his actual conduct has been extraordinarily restrained. This implication is in fact a mainstay of Gracchus' rhetoric, for his ultimate goal is to head off any accusations of misbehavior with the freeborn young Romans in his province, a more serious offense. In any event, Gracchus obviously shares with his audience the understanding that an important man like himself might well be susceptible to the charms of attractive young men, and there is no hint of any blame attached to such desires.[39] The issues important for Gracchus and his audience are not an opposition between homosexual and heterosexual behavior but rather the distinction between slave and free, as well as the manner in which a Roman official in the provinces should treat the young citizens under his authority.

Scipio Aemilianus, consul in 147 B.C. and censor in 142, issued this attack against a certain P. Sulpicius Galus:

> nam qui cotidie unguentatus adversus speculum ornetur, cuius supercilia radantur, qui barba vulsa feminibusque subvulsis ambulet, qui in conviviis adulescentulus cum amatore cum chirodota tunica inferior accubuerit, qui non modo vinosus sed virosus quoque sit, eumne quisquam dubitet quin idem fecerit quod cinaedi facere solent?
> (fr. 17 Malcovati; Gell. 6.12.5)

> For the kind of man who adorns himself daily in front of a mirror, wearing perfume; whose eyebrows are shaved off; who walks around with plucked beard and thighs; who when he was a young man reclined at banquets next to his lover, wearing a long-sleeved tunic; who is as fond of men as he is of wine: can anyone doubt that he has done what *cinaedi* are in the habit of doing?

This man displays various effeminate characteristics in his style of clothing and deportment (see chapter 4); he reclines at banquets with his male lover; he is crazy not only for wine but also for men (here Scipio indulges in a bit of word-play: *vinosus/virosus*). The conclusion, Scipio would have us believe, is obvious: the man has done "what *cinaedi* are in the habit of doing." The circumlocution, while euphemistic, drives the point home quite effectively: the man has been sexually penetrated.[40] The fragment nicely illustrates the mechanisms of men's gossip, along with some possible topics of sexual innuendo, and we note that the criticism is directed entirely at the effeminate, receptive partner (whose effeminacy is linked to moralizing notions of luxury: see chapter 4), and that no attack is made on his lover.

In short, there seems to have been a traditional understanding among Roman men that, while effeminacy might lay a man open to abuse, it was perfectly normal for a man to desire and pursue boys as well as girls or women. In fact, the game of comparing the two types of partners seems to have amused audiences of Roman men from the earliest times. The audience of Plautus' *Truculentus*, for example, was treated to a miniature debate on the virtues and vices of boy prostitutes as opposed to their female counterparts. Bantering with the slave-girl of a female prostitute whose favors he has enjoyed, a young man named Diniarchus pointedly observes that he is looking for "a small piece of land to plow." The slave-girl retorts

that if he wants to plow he would be better off going after boys, and there ensues
a set piece on the differences between professional women and their young male
colleagues:

> AS. non arvos hic, sed pascuost ager: si arationes
> habituris, qui arari solent, ad pueros ire meliust.
> hunc nos habemus publicum, illi alii sunt publicani.
> DI. utrosque pergnovi probe.   AS. em istoc pol tu otiosu's,
> quom et illic et hic pervorsus es. sed utriscum rem esse mavis?
> DI. procaciores esti' vos, sed illi peiiuriosi;
> illis perit quidquid datur neque ipsis apparet quicquam:
> vos saltem si quid quaeritis, exbibitis et comestis.
> postremo illi sunt inprobi, vos nequam et gloriosae. (Plaut. *Truc.* 149–57)

> AS. There is no field for plowing here, but instead a pasture. If you yearn to plow, it's
> better to go to the ones who are usually plowed: boys. This field that we have is public
> land, but those guys are public contractors.   DI. I know both types quite well.   AS.
> Right; that's why you are a man of leisure, since you went astray both here and there.
> But which ones do you prefer to do business with?   DI. You are more impudent, but
> they are liars. Whatever is given to them disappears, and you can't see it on them; but
> you, at least, if you ask for something, you drink it and eat it up. In short, they are
> shameless, you are naughty and proud.

We will return later to the question of the value of Plautus' comedies as a source
for Roman belief systems (the trouble is that they were based on Greek originals).
Here it will suffice to observe that in the monologue immediately preceding this
scene the same slave-girl, complaining about how young men often abuse the gen-
erosity of female prostitutes, saucily reminds the audience that some of them can
vouch for what she is saying.[41] In this metatheatrical moment a direct link is made
between the nominally Greek prostitutes of the play and the real experiences of
the Roman men sitting in the audience, and that link is surely still in place when
Diniarchus complacently draws on his experience with prostitutes of both sexes to
weigh their relative merits.

Diniarchus' main concern seems to be of a financial nature; he says nothing
about any physical traits that might distinguish boys from women. By contrast, a
line from Lucilius that compares sexual relations with males and females is emphatically rooted in the body: "She bloodies you, but he on the other hand beshits
you."[42] This line, like so many from Lucilius' poetry, and indeed from most early
Roman literature, is preserved without a clue as to its original context. We can only
conjecture, but it is nonetheless clear that the speaker of this line—whoever he
was, whoever his addressee, whatever the dramatic situation—is commenting on
the potential drawbacks of vaginal and anal penetration respectively (we will return later to the language of defecation in conjunction with descriptions of anal
intercourse). Lucilius' readership, like Plautus' audience, is being drawn into a
consideration of the relative merits of female and male sexual partners as the objects, or rather recipients, of men's phallic desires.[43]

The interchangeability of boys and women as erotic objects must also lie behind a fragment from Lucilius in which the speaker's praise of a lovely young woman

culminates with the assertion that she is like a boy.[44] A certain androgynous quality could occasionally elicit praise from Roman men (Ovid lauds the virginal Atalanta as having a "face that you could truthfully call girlish on a boy, boyish on a girl"),[45] and Lucilius' line gives us a remarkable glimpse at one man's publicly espoused tastes: this speaker can apparently find no better way to argue for a woman's desirability than to liken her to a boy. Another fragment likewise refers to women's bodies:

> quod si nulla potest mulier tam corpore duro
> esse, tamen tenero maneat, qui sucus lacerto,
> et manus uberi<bus>, lactanti in sumine, sidat. (Lucil. 174–6 Marx)

> If no woman can have as firm a body, nonetheless she remains with a soft one, with sap in her arm, and a hand rests on her breasts, her milky udder.

There are serious textual difficulties here, but the phrase *tam corpore duro* ("as firm a body") clearly implies a comparison ("as firm as . . .", *tam corpore duro quam . . .*): surely to boys.[46] Yet another line speaks of a "beautiful boy" who is "worthy" of the addressee; in fact, since Nonius Marcellus, the ancient source that preserves the line, tells us that it comes from the fourth book of Lucilius' poetry, like the lines concerning a woman's body just quoted, it is generally thought that both fragments come from some kind of comparison between male and female sexual partners.[47] Another fragment seems to refer to yet another point of contrast: "They [masc.] will both ask for less and give to you much more properly and without disgrace [*flagitium*]." Since Nonius cites the lines from Lucilius as an illustration of the archaic use of the noun *flagitium* to refer to a "wrong-doing inflicted upon a maiden," the most likely interpretation of the Lucilian lines is that the speaker is indicating the advantages of using boy prostitutes as opposed to having one's way with a young Roman woman (*virgo*).[48] Indeed, according to one interpretation, the entire seventh book of Lucilius' satires consisted of a discussion of the pros and cons of various sexual arrangements: with married women, female prostitutes, and boys.[49]

It is interesting to hear a character from an Atellan farce by Novius claiming that "everyone knows that a boy is superior to a woman, and how much better is one whose voice is breaking [*cuius vox gallulascit*], whose branch is just growing [*cuius iam ramus roborascit*]."[50] The man avows a preference for boys who have just reached puberty,[51] and his jingling, alliterative evocation of an adolescent's freshly burgeoning penis (observe not only the alliteration in *ramus roborascit* but also the homoioteleuton in *gallulascit . . . roborascit* together with the parallelism in *cuius . . . cuius*) is intriguing. Elsewhere boys and women are represented almost exclusively as objects or receptacles (see, for example, Lucretius' Epicurean theory of desire [4.1052–7]). Here, although we have been deprived of the passage's full context and thus face many unanswerable questions (What kind of character uttered the lines? Is he being mocked? How did his interlocutor[s] respond to his comment that "everyone knows" that a boy is better than a woman?), nonetheless we see that Roman audiences did occasionally face the fact that boys have penises, and that those penises might even be of interest, however passing.[52] In any case, it is clear that the relative merits of women and boys as the objects of men's phallic attentions intrigued third- and second-century B.C. Roman audiences. Thus it is quite likely that, besides Plautus, Lucilius, and Novius, other writers whose work is now lost to us engaged in the debate; certainly later texts show that the question continued to interest Roman readers into the second century A.D. at least.[53]

The attractive quality of boys, conventionally held to fade with the arrival of body hair and the beard, serves as the raw material for numerous jokes in early Roman texts. A line from one of Novius' Atellan farces spells out the implications of the appearance of body hair with typically Roman straightforwardness: "As long as they will be able to be submissive [*pati*], before their butts become hairy."[54] The meaning is unmistakable, even crude: boys are capable of being sexually penetrated (*pati*) only as long as their buttocks are hairless (for this implication of *pati*, see chapter 5). Perhaps the most celebrated writer of *togatae* (a genre of Roman drama which, unlike the comedies of Plautus and Terence, was not based on Greek originals and thus brought Roman and Italian realities directly to the stage) was Afranius. Although we now possess only tattered remnants of his oeuvre, a comment offered by Quintilian makes it clear that among the themes treated by Afranius' plays were sexual intrigues with boys.[55] One of the surviving fragments of Afranius most likely belonged to such a context: "What's more, my body is just now beginning to get hairy."[56] The speaker is obviously an adolescent boy, and as a conjecture one might suggest that his words constitute an attempt to fend off the unwelcome advance of an older man; or he might be lamenting his fading desirability; or, like the speaker in Martial 11.39, he might be boasting of his newly achieved manhood. In any case, all this fuss about body hair was no mere literary convention. The elder Pliny recommends the application of ants' eggs to boys' armpits so as to prevent the growth of unsightly hairs, and he adds that dealers in slave-boys, in order to keep their merchandise as marketable as possible, used blood from the testicles of castrated lambs to delay the growth of the beard.[57] Elsewhere the same writer gives a dazzling catalogue of depilatory substances (bats' brains, fried viper, gall from hedgehogs, the milk of a bitch who has given birth to her first litter, and so on), beginning with the remark that bats' blood will not work on boys' armpits unless followed by an application of copper rust or hemlock seeds.[58] It seems that a good deal of energy was expended on the obviously important problem of adolescent boys' body hair.

Not surprisingly, the practice of using boys as men's sexual partners seems to have left traces in the colloquial language of the Romans. In his dictionary of Republican Latin, Festus tells us that the noun *pullus*, literally denoting a young animal in general or chick in particular, was used by the men of old (*antiqui*) as a term of endearment for a boy who was loved by a man, and he illustrates the usage with an anecdote that is as amusing as it is revealing. Q. Fabius Maximus, consul in 116 B.C. and censor in 108 B.C., was given the cognomen Eburnus (Ivory) because of his fair complexion, but after having suffered the misfortune of being struck by lightning on his buttocks, he was further nicknamed "Jupiter's chick" (*pullus Iovis*), as if having been anally raped by the king of the gods.[59] The ironic, even campy humor characterizing that nickname suggests a comfortable, long-standing familiarity with certain facts of sexual behavior among Fabius' contemporaries. There is evidence, too, that during roughly the same period, Lucilius drew on this use of *pullus.* In an epigram by the fifth-century A.D. poet Ausonius, we read of a man so fond of anal intercourse with boys that a member of the Pythagorean sect, subscribing to a belief in the transmigration of souls, concludes that he will be reincarnated as a dung beetle. In the course of his description of this man, one of the speakers in Ausonius' epigram cites some terms that he attributes to Lucilius: *subpilo* (plucker) and *pullipremo* (chick-squeezer).[60] Festus tells us, moreover, that in Plautus the right hand is called *pullaria*: we might conjecture that this was because the right hand, like a boy, might be used to stimulate a man's penis to orgasm.[61]

Turning to poetry from the first centuries B.C. and A.D., we note that the poems of Catullus and Martial, among others, present a palpably Priapic persona who is interested in both boys and girls: though usually with less violence than Priapus himself, this poetic persona willingly imposes his manhood on both male and female partners and does not hesitate to tell the world about it.[62] In one of his poems, Martial addresses his "wife"[63] who has found him anally penetrating a boy. To her nagging observation that she can provide him with the same kind of pleasure the poet responds with a catalog of mythological *exempla* illustrating the point that anal intercourse is more pleasurable with boys than it is with women, and he concludes with a harsh dismissal: "So stop giving masculine names to your affairs, and think of it this way, wife: you have two cunts." In other words, while he is perfectly willing to penetrate his wife anally, her anus is not a boy's anus, but only a second vagina.[64] A subtler but no less telling profession of a desire to penetrate both women and boys is found in an epigram that consists of a single couplet:

> Uxorem nolo Telesinam ducere. quare?
>   moecha est. sed pueris dat Telesina. volo. (Mart. 2.49)

> I don't want to marry Telesina.—Why not?—She is an adulteress.—But Telesina puts out for boys.—I want her.

Disinclined to marry Telesina because she is given to adulteries, he instantly changes his opinion upon learning that she bestows her favors upon boys (*pueri*).[65] His sudden eagerness is explained by what Martial elsewhere calls the "boyish punishment" (*supplicium puerile*, 2.60.2),[66] one of the traditional modes of revenge allowed a cuckolded husband: anal rape of the adulterer. In other words, if he were to catch Telesina in the act with a boy, he would have the right to exact his (obviously sweet) revenge on the young adulterer.[67] Another poem portrays the poet in the act of anally penetrating a young man named Hedylos. The latter, rapidly approaching orgasm, gasps an encouragement to his partner: "I'm coming! Do it if you're going to do it!"[68] We can make no claims that Marcus Valerius Martialis actually had such an encounter with a boy named Hedylos, but the crucial point is that he was willing to let his Roman readership imagine him doing so.

Literary texts of a less blunt nature are likewise permeated by the assumption that a normal Roman man will openly seek to have sexual relations with persons of either sex. Prose writers such as Livy and Valerius Maximus imagine a Roman past in which men desired women and girls as well as boys,[69] while the love poetry of Catullus, Horace, and Tibullus presents the persona of a man experienced in the exquisite joys and hardships accompanying affairs with both women and boys.[70]

Even the personae projected by Propertius and Ovid, while clearly drawn to women, hardly reject the love of boys out of hand: in one poem Propertius opines that affairs with boys are easier than those with women, and Ovid claims that he is "less" (*minus*) interested in boys than he is in women.[71] The idealized rural land-scape of Roman pastoral poetry follows the same pattern: its shepherds pine for both boys and girls.[72] Finally, Roman writers sometimes present the image of a man who has been deprived of the pleasures of sex, and these pleasures include relations with both boys and women or girls. One of the *Priapea*, for example, has the god issue this dramatic curse on a thief: may he burst with an erection while being deprived of boys and women. In lyric vein, Horace sadly observes his lack of interest in the erotic pleasures of youth ("I now find pleasure neither in woman nor in boy") and in the vivid prose of Petronius, Encolpius, afflicted with impo-tence due to the wrath of Priapus, is said to be "unable to sell his goods, whether to a boy or to a girl".[73] These men confirm by their misfortune the normative status of what is no longer theirs.

Passages taken from the work of two widely different yet equally Roman poets, Lucretius and Ovid, provide a helpful summary. Ovid's programmatic introduction to his collection of love poems known as the *Amores* describes the proper subject matter of love elegy, produced by and for Roman men, as "either a boy or a girl adorned with long hair."[74] Lucretius' poem *On the Nature of Things*, a vigorous attempt to make Epicurean philosophy meaningful and appealing to a readership of Roman men, includes this image of those who are most likely to arouse sexual passion among his readers:

> sic igitur Veneris qui telis accipit ictus,
> sive puer membris muliebribus hunc iaculatur
> seu mulier toto iactans e corpore amorem,
> unde feritur, eo tendit gestitque coire
> et iacere umorem in corpus de corpore ductum. (Lucr. 4.1052–6)

> Thus he who is struck by the weapons of Venus—whether it is a boy with feminine limbs who takes aim at him, or a woman casting forth love from her entire body—heads for the origin of his wound and is eager to mingle with it and to cast into a body the liquid derived from a body.

The theory expounded here is that beautiful boys and women stir up desire in the men who gaze upon them; that desire in turn causes a build-up of semen within the men, who then yearn to expel the built-up semen, preferably into the very body that stimulated its creation. The underlying assumptions are beautifully clear: men's desires are normally aroused by boys and women, who function simulta-neously as stimulant, object, and receptacle.[75]

Dirty Jokes

Lucilius' crude imagery for anal penetration in a line cited earlier—where the speaker opines that vaginal intercourse "bloodies" the penis while anal intercourse "beshits" it (1186 Marx)—brings us to another significant characteristic of Latin literature from the earliest times on: a readiness to indulge in an unabashed description of the physical realities of sexual practices, including those between males. Such jokes hardly come across as nervous references to suspect "Greek" practices: this is home-grown humor.

Marx's interpretation of Lucilius' line deserves mention. Prostitutes, he imagines the speaker to be saying, are so avaricious that they will take on customers even when they ought to excuse themselves: if they are female, when menstruating; if they are male, when suffering from diarrhea.[76] Certainty is of course impossible, since the line has been shorn of its context, but the reading is ingenious and quite possibly correct. Indeed, nearly two centuries later, the epigrams of Martial unambiguously make the point that diarrhea can interfere with the enjoyment of anal intercourse. In one mischievous poem we read of a certain Charisianus who complains that he has been unable to indulge in this practice—as the insertive partner, he claims—for quite some time; when asked why, he complains that he is suffering from diarrhea, thereby unintentionally revealing that he must in fact be playing the receptive rather than the insertive role.[77] In a couplet intended to accompany a gift of sorb-apples, the poet observes that this is a gift especially appropriate to one's slave-boy, since they bind up loosened bowels, which could be an inconvenience for both slave and master.[78] Such may be the context in which Lucilius' line ought to be placed, although it is still possible that the speaker of the line is simply alluding to the fact that whether one penetrates a male or a female, there is always a potential for messiness, apart from the problem of diarrhea.[79]

Lucilius' language, in all its coarseness,[80] belongs to a longstanding tradition in Roman literature. Earthy depictions of anal penetration appear elsewhere in Lucilian fragments: "if he has shoved a thick water-snake with a head into your butt";[81] "to penetrate into a hairy bag";[82] "Hortensius, the wrestling-ground of the anus was made for that thing."[83] A fragment from the farce *Pappus Praeteritus* by Novius offers this crass joke: "As long as you invite those supporters, father, you will put your butt on a sword-hilt before you put it in the magistrate's chair."[84] With their reference to *suffragatores* (supporters of a candidate for political office) and the *sella curulis* (the official seat used by certain magistrates), together with the metaphorical use of *capulus* ("sword-hilt") to refer to the penis, these lines are utterly Roman in tone, as is their hearty humor at the expense of a man who is, figuratively at least, being anally penetrated.

Allusions to anal penetration were also a part of the repertoire of another writer of Atellan farces, Pomponius. In one of his plays (called *Pistor*) a man gives voice to this heartfelt wish: "Unless someone [masc.] suddenly comes up to me now to bend over, so I can plant my boundary-post in a safe place."[85] The hearty gusto that obviously characterized Pomponius' sexual humor erupted in a play whose loss is truly to be regretted. Called simply enough *Prostibulum* ("The Prostitute"), this farce was dedicated to a male prostitute (whom Frassinetti identifies with the stock character Bucco), and the scattered lines that survive give a hint at the rowdiness of the whole. One thing is clear: this professional services men. At one point someone, surely the title character, protests in mock-innocence, "I haven't butt-fucked a single citizen by deceit—only when he himself came up to me begging to bend over."[86] Elsewhere someone warns him that his services will be in great demand, and again we are reminded that it is not just men but specifically Roman citizens who are interested in enjoying his assets: "Right away they'll run up to you, arranged by voting-group, looking for a penis."[87] Pomponius also deploys the language of defecation in conjunction with anal penetration. The prostitute refers to his customers in a boisterously alliterative line: "I'm looking for some-thing to eat; they [fem.] are looking for something to shit out; it's just the oppo-site."[88] What they are looking to "shit out" is apparently a penis, and on this inter-pretation, the speaker's point is that while he is trying to scrape together just enough to feed himself, there are some effeminate citizens who are looking to satisfy the cravings of another orifice. Despite his dismissal of these customers of his as wom-anish (he uses the feminine form of the demonstrative pronoun), the tight balance of the line reflects a deeper mutuality. He has just the thing for them, and since they are willing to pay him for it, the arrangement must have been satisfactory all around.[89]

The receptive partner in anal intercourse seems elsewhere to be said to "shit out" the penis of his partner. The speaker of a line from Novius swaggeringly ob-serves that "There's nothing for you to eat, but if you want something to shit out, there's plenty!" (i.e., he will fill their anuses with his substantial member), and in one of the *Priapea* the phallic god warns a potential thief that if he is considering stealing from his garden, he should consider "how heavy a load of dick you will have to shit out."[90] The imagery is fascinating, for not only does it evoke the physi-cal realities of anal penetration with characteristically Roman bluntness, but it seems also to represent the sensations of the receptive partner as his insertive partner withdraws. This is not an image, one might argue, that would have been used by men who had never had the experience of being anally penetrated. Perhaps, then, we see here a chink in the armor of masculine identity: a reminder that the same men who swear allegiance to the ideal of impenetrability were once those very boys whose penetrability made them so desirable.[91]

Slaves, Male and Female

Clearly an assumption prevalent among Romans was that, as a group, men nor-mally experience desire for both female and male bodies, and that any given man might act out those desires with persons of one or the other sex, or both. As long as he followed the protocols reviewed at the opening of this chapter, he would be immune from criticism. We now turn to the second of these protocols—that free-born Romans of both sexes were off-limits—and especially its corollary: that one's own slaves were fair game. Indeed, in the eyes of the law slaves were property pure and simple, and in general neither the law nor popular morality had anything to say about how a man used his own property (Cato, for example, blandly recom-mended selling old or sick slaves along with old cows and plows).[92] Thus slaves' bodies were entirely at their masters' disposal, and from the earliest of times it seems to have been understood that among the services that Roman men might expect their slaves to perform was the satisfaction of their sexual desires.[93] And, as we will see both in the earliest contemporary sources and in later references to the distant past, it seems always to have been assumed that the master would make such use of his slaves of both sexes.[94]

This understanding, a gentlemen's agreement among slave-owning Romans, is hardly surprising in view of the evidence we have been considering, and this protocol stands in a close relationship with the other two. On the one hand, the most desirable male slaves were generally represented as boys, although we will see later that this was more of a guideline than a rule and was not always followed. On the other hand, the distribution of physical roles was supposed to be aligned with the power-differential between master and slave: the master must be seen as playing the active role and the slave the passive role. There are scattered allusions to a reversal of roles (Seneca writes of a slave who is "a man in the bedroom, a boy in the dining room" and Martial pointedly observes that a certain man's anus is as sore as his slave-boy's penis),[95] but Seneca is scandalized and Martial is teasing, and the scenarios they describe are precisely inversions of the expected pattern. Even as they remind us that not everyone followed the rules, these texts reconfirm what the rules were.

A comprehensive catalogue of Roman texts that refer to men's sexual use of their male and female slaves would be massive. Here I offer a sampling, by way of illustrating not only the ubiquity of the practice but also the way in which it was simply taken for granted that this kind of freedom (or rather, dominion) was one of the many perquisites of being a Roman slave owner. The earliest relevant texts are the comedies of Plautus, but in view of the special problems attending their interpretation, I will return to them after having surveyed the other, impressively widespread, evidence.

In his treatise on agriculture, chock full of advice to landowners, Columella urges his reader to refrain from appointing as overseer (*vilicus*) "one of those slaves who provide pleasure with their bodies." He is of course speaking of male slaves, and his advice seems proffered with the voice of experience.[96] Catullus' epithalamium or wedding song for Manlius Torquatus and Junia (to which we will return later in this chapter) alludes to the groom's use of a male slave as his concubine (*concubinus*), somewhat complacently observing that this was perfectly acceptable behavior in a young, unmarried man.[97] More naughtily, Martial mentions a *concubinus* as a valuable item that a son might inherit and indeed take possession of the first night after his father's death.[98] In Petronius' *Satyricon,* the *nouveau riche* freedman Trimalchio, recalling his early years as a slave, unabashedly refers to his role as his master's "darling" (*deliciae*): after all, he adds, "what the master orders is not shameful," and he then observes with a show of modesty that he served his mistress as well.[99]

This kind of assumption about men and their slaves informed the ethical stance adopted by Roman men in a variety of situations. The Augustan orator Haterius, defending a client in court, used as a mainstay of his defense the apparently axiomatic principle that the loss of one's sexual integrity (*impudicitia*), while a matter of "reproach" for the freeborn and a matter of "duty" for freedmen, is a matter of "necessity" for slaves.[100] Valerius Maximus tells of a man who was condemned for having killed a domesticated ox to gratify the whim of a slave-boy whom he loved. Valerius' pithy summation is revealing: the man was "innocent, had he not been born in such ancient times."[101] The nature of the man's offense is brought out by other sources. In his treatise on agriculture, Columella observes that killing an ox used to be a capital offense of the same magnitude as killing a Roman citizen, and the elder Pliny relates the story of the same man and his slave-boy (whom Pliny calls his *concubinus*) by way of illustrating the great value placed by the Romans of old on oxen: the man was sent into exile, Pliny notes, as if he had killed one of his farmhands.[102] Needlessly killing an ox was a crime in the olden days; making sexual use of one's own slave never was.

Valerius Maximus also tells the tale of one Calidius of Bononia who, having been caught one night in a married lady's bedroom, wriggled out of a tight spot by claiming that he was only there for a tryst with a slave-boy—a truly eloquent defense.[103] In an interesting variation on the theme, a slave appears as a sexual pawn in a case cited by the elder Seneca in his collection of *Controversiae*. A husband charged his wife with adultery, having found a handsome young slave in her bedroom. The defense counsel argued that in fact the husband had called for the slave in order to have a ménage à trois—as one advocate put it, the slave had been summoned to satisfy his master's lust—but when the wife refused the husband took his revenge by crying adultery.[104] Horace's satires open a window not only onto the foibles of humanity but also onto commonly held beliefs about right behavior. In one of them Horace recommends to his readers that if they want to play it safe, they will vent their sexual energies on their own slaves; he speaks of male and female slaves indifferently:

> num, tibi cum faucis urit sitis, aurea quaeris
> pocula? num esuriens fastidis omnia praeter
> pavonem rhombumque? tument tibi cum inguina, num, si
> ancilla aut verna est praesto puer, impetus in quem
> continuo fiat, malis tentigine rumpi?
> non ego; namque parabilem amo venerem facilemque. (Hor. *Sat.* 1.2.114–9)[105]

> Now really, when your throat is parched with thirst, you don't ask for golden goblets, do you? When you're hungry, you don't turn your nose up at everything but peacock and turbot, do you? When your crotch is throbbing and there is a slave-girl or home-grown slave-boy ready at hand, whom you could jump right away, you don't prefer to burst with your hard-on, do you? I certainly don't. I like sex that is easy and obtainable.

The chatty style and appeals to the three basic appetites for food, drink, and sex give a common-sense feeling to his argument. The language itself, with its insistent repetitions of the interrogative particle *num* in tricolon crescendo, seems designed to make an urgent appeal to his readership, to convince them of something that should in any case be obvious to them, that men's slaves are meant to be used and can be used without fear of repercussions.[106]

The epigrams of Martial give us a clear view of a cultural landscape in which the availability of beautiful slave-boys as sexual companions for their masters was a prominent feature. This was a world in which a man who paid an exorbitantly high price for a beautiful boy could be simultaneously congratulated and envied for his purchase (1.58).[107] Martial's own persona ruefully contrasts his impoverished condition with that of his friend Candidus: while the rich man enjoys gorgeous clothing, elegant furniture, and a band of slave-boys worthy of being compared to Jupiter's own Ganymede (the beautiful Trojan prince whom Zeus took as his cupbearer and concubine: see discussion later in this chapter), poor Martial must content himself with wretchedly cheap clothes and furniture, and instead of finding sexual release in the ministrations of lovely young slaves, Martial is reduced to taking matters into his own hand (2.43). Contrasting with this self-pitying stance, plenty of other epigrams show Martial not only fantasizing about but actually enjoying the company of compliant slave-boys, and these range from the lyrical:

> O mihi grata quies, o blanda, Telesphore, cura,
>   qualis in amplexu non fuit ante meo . . . (Mart. 11.26.1–2)

> O delightful peace, O winsome care, Telesphorus: such as I have never before had in my arms . . .

to the blunt:

> Cum me velle vides tentumque, Telesphore, sentis,
>   magna rogas—puta me velle negare: licet?—
> et nisi iuratus dixi "dabo," subtrahis illas,
>   permittunt in me quae tibi multa, natis. (Mart. 11.58.1–4)

> Telesphorus, when you see that I want it and feel me bulging, you ask for much (imagine that I *want* to deny you: can I?) and unless I swear an oath that I will give it to you, you withhold that butt of yours, that gives you so much power over me.

Poems such as the latter display the bawdiness for which the epigrammatic tradition was infamous—and cherished—but the topic of beloved slave-boys in and of itself was clearly not considered indecent.[108] One of Martial's more soft-edged pieces on the slave-boy Diadumenos (3.65, extolling his kisses) comes *before* the point at which he warns his readership that his epigrams will from now on contain obscenity: up to this point his poems are suitable for matrons, but from here on they will be X-rated (3.68). Likewise another poem on Diadumenos and his kisses (5.46), as well as an epigram on the love of Martial's friend Aulus Pudens for his slave Encolpos (5.48; cf. 1.31, where their relationship is also celebrated, and 4.13, where Pudens' marriage to Claudia Peregrina is likewise celebrated), are found in a book of epigrams that proclaims itself as suitable reading for decent people (married ladies, boys, and girls: 5.2). G-rated poetry in Martial's world included the celebration of men's love for their male slaves.

Indeed, an ancient biography of Virgil reveals that a marked predilection for boys, along with an alleged relationship with a woman, was not incompatible with receiving a reputation for virginal modesty: the poet was nicknamed Parthenias ("The Maiden") by the Neapolitans.[109] The same biography tells us that one of the slaves to whom Virgil was most devoted was a lad named Alexandrus, given as a gift by Asinius Pollio, and that he was the inspiration for the character of the desirable young Alexis in Virgil's second eclogue.[110] Martial was later to use Alexis as a figure for the perquisites of a poet's privilege or source of his inspiration,[111] and in one poem Martial hints that he could use some inspiration of that kind: neither Ovid's nor Virgil's hometowns would reject me as their poet, he writes, if I can find a

Corinna or an Alexis.[112] This poem, too, is contained in a book that Martial dedicates in fulsome terms to the Emperor Domitian, noting that he has not allowed the epigrams of this book to "speak as wantonly as they usually do."[113]

Having such slaves was one of the benefits of being rich and powerful. Most powerful among Roman men was, of course, the emperor. Augustus himself acquired the reputation of an avid womanizer,[114] but he also was said to have kept male slaves as his *deliciae* or "darlings," one of whom, named Sarmentus, is mentioned in passing by Plutarch.[115] Funerary inscriptions from the imperial household under Augustus and Tiberius reveal that among the different positions filled by slaves in the palace were those of *glaber ab cyatho* (a smooth boy who served wine), *glabrorum ornator* (a male slave who served as beautician for the smooth boys), and *puerorum ornatrix* (a female beautician for boys).[116] Vitellius began his brief reign as emperor in A.D. 69 by publicly honoring a freedman of his named Asiaticus, with whom he had had a stormy affair when Asiaticus was a young slave of his.[117] We read that Trajan kept *delicati*, and this detail is dropped in such a way as to suggest that this was a standard feature of the imperial household.[118]

But above all we hear a great deal about Domitian's beloved eunuch Earinos, in the words of poets like Martial and Statius, desperate to flatter the emperor.[119] One technique—unsubtle but probably effective—was to compare the boy to Ganymede (Martial 8.39, 9.16, 9.36). Both Martial and Statius celebrate the occasion on which Earinos dedicated a lock of his hair to Asclepius: Martial dedicates three epigrams to the subject (9.16, 17, 36) and Statius writes an especially servile poem in which, in a tour de force of abject flattery, he proclaims that Earinos is not merely comparable to Ganymede but is actually superior to Jupiter's beloved because, whereas Juno fiercely rejects the beautiful Trojan youth whom she has to see every day, Earinos enjoys the affection of both Domitian and his wife Domitia.[120] Later Statius goes so far as to proclaim that Earinos' castration must have been performed by Asclepius, the god of healing, himself: Earinos suffered no pain and was left with no scar.[121]

It is interesting to contrast Statius and Martial's fulsome flattery of Earinos with their treatment of one of Domitian's sexual experiences that, unlike his relationship with Earinos, violated traditional moral standards: an alleged affair with his niece Julia that resulted in her pregnancy and subsequent death as a result of a botched abortion.[122] Understandably enough, the two poets pass over the whole affair in silence. Martial refers to Julia only after her death, in one poem invoking her—surely with a straight face, though for us the irony is pungent—as a goddess benignly watching over the child soon to be delivered by Domitian's wife Domitia (6.3; cf. 6.13, 9.1). But once Domitian was safely dead, Juvenal savagely attacks him precisely for his relationship with Julia (2.29–33).

Slaves in Plautus

I have postponed discussion of the plays of Plautus, even though they provide the earliest contemporary evidence for the sexual role of slaves, because of a special problem in their interpretation. Plautus' plays, though written in Latin and staged for a Roman audience, are based on Greek originals and set in Greek cities, and the characters wear Greek dress and have Greek names. Thus it might be argued that their references to men's relations with male slaves reflect a Roman view of Greek practices, just as the plays present a Roman perspective on Greek culture generally.[123] The question of the relationship between Greek and Roman in Plautus is complex, and has been treated by a number of scholars, but for the purposes of this discussion it will suffice to observe that Plautus' plays are pervaded with references to things Roman, anchoring the stage securely in Rome: hence the frequent references to senators, triumphs, and the like.[124] Representative of the striking blend of Greek and Roman in Plautus' plays is a scene from the *Curculio* to which we will return later in this chapter. The play is nominally set in the Greek city of Epidaurus, yet when the Producer steps on stage and delivers a monologue describing the setting to his audience, the city he describes is unmistakably Rome, complete with its Forum, Velabrum, and Vicus Tuscus (466–86)[125]—as if a contemporary American film set in Paris were suddenly to include jokes about Times Square, Greenwich Village, and Harlem. The technique is characteristic: although his plays are set in Greek locales with Greek characters, Plautus constantly Romanizes them, sometimes subtly, sometimes—as here—baldly. It is an obvious fact, but one worth recalling, that Plautus wrote to draw laughs from a Roman audience, and it is their perspective on the world that his characters so often adopt.[126]

Perfectly in keeping with this Roman perspective are numerous jokes at the expense of slaves that make unkind reference to their sexual subjugation. These are usually found in scenes that constitute Plautine expansions upon the Greek originals: typically, the playwright brings the action to a screeching halt for the sake of some slapstick humor at the expense of slaves, sometimes using Latin puns that are obviously not taken from the Greek original, and sometimes leaving other textual traces of his activity.[127] Since humor surrounding the sexual subjugation of slaves seems not to have played an important role in the Greek New Comedy that served as Plautus' inspiration, it is all the more likely that the jokes constitute the playwright's own contribution, aimed at getting a laugh from his Roman audience.[128]

In the *Pseudolus* a pimp and an old man shower Harpax, slave of the soldier Polymachaeroplagides, with a torrent of insults capped off by this outrageous slur: "When the soldier went out at night on guard duty and you went with him, did his sword fit into your sheath?"[129] The *Asinaria* includes a scene of comic reversal in which a slave forces his master to assume an equine hands-and-knees position ("like you used to do when you were a boy") while the slave mounts him.[130] In the *Casina*, a slave secretly observes his master making an advance on another of his male slaves and offers a crass aside to the audience ("My God, I do believe this guy wants to dig up his bailiff's bladder!") and then recalls that he himself was once in the same position as his fellow-slave is now.[131] In the *Rudens* one slave smugly observes to another that *his* master, at least, does not force himself upon his slaves;[132] at *Epidicus* 66 a slave asks another whether their master is in love with a captive girl and receives the taunting reply, "He loves her more than he ever loved you!" ("plusque amat quam te umquam amavit")—a zinger that prompts a curse in reply ("Iuppiter te perduit!"). The *Mostellaria* contains a song (*canticum*) between the two slaves Pinacium and Phaniscus in which Pinacium petulantly claims that

Phaniscus' arrogance is due to the fact that "the master loves you"; shortly thereafter Phaniscus himself smugly notes "the master knows me," thus providing the
feed-in for his sidekick's punchline: "Sure, of course he knows his own mattress!"[133]
At *Persa* 284–6 Paegnium replies to another slave's insulting remark that he had
been "mounted" by breezily admitting it (a tried and true way of deflating an
opponent's rhetoric), but he is unable to resist adding his own barb:

> SAG. video ego te: iam incubitatus es.   PA. ita sum. quid id attinet ad te?
> at non sum, ita ut tu, gratiis.   SAG. confidens.   PA. sum hercle vero.
> nam ego me confido liberum fore, tu te numquam speras. (Plaut. *Pers.* 284–6)

> SAG. I see you: you've been mounted.   PA. Yes, that's true. But what does that mat-
> ter to you? At least I haven't done it for nothing, like you.   SAG. Confident, aren't
> you?   PA. I sure am confident—that I'll be free someday, while you don't expect that
> you'll *ever* be.

Paegnium's implication is that because of his sexual services to his master he will
someday earn his freedom, whereas the unfortunate Sagaristio has to perform his
services without the hope of any such reward.[134]

The Roman character of these jokes about slaves is confirmed by Plautus' use
of Latin puns on the subject that cannot have been translated from anything Greek
(and are indeed untranslatable into English). In the midst of an insult-match between two slaves appears this brief exchange: "Restrain him.—No, restrain *him*:
he has been taught how to provide that service!" ("Comprime istunc.—immo istunc
qui didicit dare!" *Casina* 362). The first slave asks his master to "restrain"
(*comprimere*) the other, that is, make him shut up, and his opponent retorts by
punning on other meanings of the verb: "squeeze" or "copulate with." His point is
that this slave, like Phaniscus the "mattress," is quite accustomed to being "restrained." And he caps off his retort with another pun: the verb *dare* (translated
above as "provide that service") can also mean "to provide sexual favors," that is,
"to put out." This cluster of puns is purely Latin.[135] So too is an exchange from the
Curculio:

> CU. . . . quaeso ne me incomities.
> LY. licetne inforare, si incomitiare non licet?
> CU. non inforabis me quidem, nec mihi placet
> tuom profecto nec forum nec comitium. (Plaut. *Curc.* 400–3)

> CU. . . . Please don't insult me (*incomities*).   LY. Well, if I can't insult you (*incomitiare*),
> may I dig at you (*inforare*)?   CU. You certainly will not dig at me (*inforabis*); I don't
> like your "Forum" *or* your "Comitium"!

Lycus makes, and Curculio dutifully echoes, a wicked pun on the words *incomitiare*
("to insult as one might in a public assembly") and the Comitium (the place of
public assembly itself) on the one hand, and *inforare* ("to bore into," a handy sexual
metaphor) and the Forum on the other. But of course the Forum and Comitium
are found in the heart of Rome, and the pun is only possible in Latin.[136] These lines
must be purely Plautine invention.

In sum, Plautine humor draws on the realities of sexual experience with slaves in a comfortable, knowing way precisely because those realities were a fact of life familiar to his Roman audience: as familiar as the references to Roman food, topography, military and political themes, and indeed heterosexual practices that permeate his plays. Rather than poking fun at bizarre foreign practices, Plautus' earthy jokes about buggering slaves invite knowing chuckles.[137] Plutarch supports his suggestion that at Rome "it was neither disreputable nor shameful for the men of old to love male slaves in the bloom of youth" by citing the evidence precisely of comedy,[138] but as we have seen, the validity of Plutarch's comment is amply confirmed by a wide range of Roman sources. Those sources illustrate the normative status of men's sexual use of male slaves, as well as a disinclination to evaluate such experience any differently from the sexual use of female slaves, and they assume the same situation to have obtained from the earliest of times. When Cicero likens Mark Antony to "a slave-boy bought for the sake of lust" (*Phil.* 2.45; see further discussion later in this chapter) he is making reference to a familiar feature of the social landscape.

Slaves and Luxury

The possession of slaves, and the possibility that their master might make sexual use of them, was an unquestioned Roman tradition. Moral censure did come into play, however, when slave owners gave the appearance of excess or luxury. Slaves both male and female, especially those acquired in foreign lands, often appear in catalogues of the accoutrements of a luxurious lifestyle, in the company of silver and gold, clothing and furniture.[139] Juvenal writes bitterly of an affluent host who drinks the best wine served in golden goblets by an exquisite Asian slave while his guests are served cheap wine in pottery vessels by surly African slaves (5.24–106); elsewhere, commenting on the power of wealth, Juvenal refers to a hitherto unsuccessful lawyer who wishes to give the appearance of wealth by traveling about in a litter shopping for slave-boys, silver, vases, and villas, while a man wishing to hire a lawyer first asks if he has "eight slaves, ten companions, a litter behind you and clients at your feet."[140] Corresponding to these negative paradigms of luxurious slave-owning are some examples of decent behavior. In another Juvenalian satire the speaker himself boasts that at his own respectably restrained dinner parties, the slaves are neither foreign nor intended to provide the guests with sexual thrills (11.136–82). Nepos approvingly observes that Atticus had slaves who were not only beautiful but useful, but they were all either born or raised in his home. Representing a blend of the aesthetic and the practical, these slaves were a sign of their master's self-control and diligence.[141] In the same way, Gaius Gracchus, upon his return from Sardinia (see discussion earlier in this chapter) proudly claimed that in his provincial headquarters he had neither a disreputable tavern (*popina*) nor "slave-boys of outstanding appearance"; no female prostitutes came to his home, and he never laid hands on other men's slave-boys.[142] And what of Cato, the patron saint of Roman austerity? Plutarch reports that Cato himself claims to have observed the cardinal principle of moderation, not only with regard to food, drink, and clothing but also with regard to his human possessions: he looked for slaves who were good workers rather than delicate, beautiful young things who would be of no use in the fields, and he advised selling slaves when they became useless, whether from old age or from illness.[143] In short, for Cato slaves, food, and clothing should all be acquired with an eye to filling basic needs; pretty packaging was an unnecessary luxury that often precluded practical utility.

Finally, apart from the question of luxury, a man who went beyond the mere physical use of his slaves and actually became emotionally involved with them ("fell in love," we might say) could, like any lover, be subject to teasing and might consequently want to keep quiet about it.[144] But none of this took away from the fact that Roman men with sufficient financial means always had their slaves as a sexual option. If they were married, they might have their wives' jealousy to contend with (see discussion later in this chapter), but neither the law nor society in general took exception to Roman men's sexual use of their own slaves. If they were not married, Roman men's freedom in this regard was only qualified by the need to maintain the appearance of moderation. In the end, what is especially important for our purposes is that nowhere is the use of male slaves condemned *qua* homosexual. Any limitations on men's freedom to make sexual use of their slaves applied to male and female slaves alike.

Prostitutes, Male and Female

Apart from his slaves, a Roman man might turn to prostitutes—persons who were not his own slaves and for whose services he paid—for sexual pleasure.[145] These prostitutes were often themselves slaves owned by masters (*lenones*, "pimps") who sold their services to others,[146] but the jurist Ulpian notes that a pimp could also ply his trade with free persons,[147] and there must have been some self-managing freeborn prostitutes as well. Prostitutes themselves were always regarded with suspicion, distaste, or worse, and the whole business was thought to be unsavory: brothels and public latrines could be mentioned in the same breath,[148] and cheap taverns and brothels could be described as features of the urban landscape alien to the simpler, purer lifestyle of the country.[149] When the speaker in a Juvenalian satire exhorts his readership to be careful not to pass on their vices to their children, he cites female prostitutes as a characteristic sign of a decadent lifestyle:

> nil dictu foedum visuque haec limina tangat
> intra quae pater est. procul, a, procul inde puellae
> lenonum et cantus pernoctantis parasiti. (Juv. 14.44–6)

> Let the threshold within which there is a father not be touched by anything shameful to say or see. Away, away with pimps' girls and with the song of the parasite who stays up all night.

And when Nepos writes of the Sicilian tyrant Dionysius' corruption of Dion's young son, he includes an indulgence in whores among the "shameful desires" with which Dionysius imbued the boy.[150] Finally, among Romans as among others before and since, prostitution could be used as a forceful metaphor: an auctioneer is said to have prostituted his voice, a corrupt age to have prostituted the hallowed traditions of friendship.[151]

Still, provided they maintained at least the appearance of moderation, Roman men felt free to indulge in occasional visits to prostitutes, and it seems always to have been assumed that the services of prostitutes of both sexes would be in demand.[152] Indeed, one of the most common (and pejorative) words denoting a prostitute was *scortum*, a neuter noun that could be used of both males and females.[153]

Among the pieces of nonliterary evidence testifying to the existence of professionals of both sexes is a calendar found at Praeneste in Latium and thus known as the *Fasti Praenestini*. This inscription informs us that on April 25, a day marked by a festival called the Robigalia in honor of the spirit of blight or grain mildew, Romans also observed a holiday for "pimps' boys" (*pueri lenonii*), and the inscription adds a brief but revealing explanation: "because the previous day is a holiday for female prostitutes [*meretrices*]."[154] The causal connection is noteworthy: both types of professionals were thought worthy of some kind of communal reward. But of course the festivals came only once a year. Graffiti from the walls of Pompeii specify the kind of individual reward sought by these workers on a day-to-day basis. We read, for example, that a woman or girl named Lais would fellate for two *asses* (not a great deal of money), while a man or boy named Felix would provide the same service for only one *as*.[155] Rather less crass are the advertisements for Eutychis and Menander, a female and a male respectively, each of them endowed with "charming manners" and each of them available for two *asses*.[156] Finally, a law inscribed on a bronze tablet found in the southern Italian town of Heraclea, and usually identified as the *lex Julia municipalis* of 45 B.C., stipulates that among the classes of men forbidden from participating in the governing councils of small towns are thieves, debtors, gladiatorial trainers, actors, pimps, and "he who has made a living with his body," in other words, male citizens who have prostituted themselves.[157]

The earliest literary evidence for the availability of prostitutes of both sexes comes from Plautus. In the speech from the *Curculio* mentioned above, we hear that among the characters haunting the Roman Forum, along with perjurers, liars, braggarts, spendthrifts, and other types, were prostitutes, evidently of both sexes.[158] It is interesting to observe how comfortably these prostitutes are integrated into the urban landscape, and that the Vicus Tuscus, the section of the Forum specified by Plautus' speaker as the area where one can find "the people who sell themselves," retained this association well into the first century B.C.[159] In Plautus' *Pseudolus* a young boy prostitute delivers a pathetic soliloquy in which he laments his inability to find a male customer, and the playwright takes the opportunity to raise some laughs at the boy's expense. In his inexperience, he worries about the discomfort "they say" comes with the role he will be expected to play (after all, it is accompanied by a great deal of groaning), but true to his profession, he bravely resolves to endure it all for the sake of cold, hard cash:

si quispiam det qui manus gravior siet
quamquam illud aiunt magno gemitu fieri
comprimere dentes video posse aliquo modo.[160] (Plaut. *Pseud.* 785–7)

If someone were to give me something to make my hand heavier, even though they say it causes a great deal of groaning, I'm sure I can manage to grit my teeth.

In a scene from the *Truculentus* discussed earlier in this chapter, a female prostitute's slave-girl, complaining of the inconsiderate behavior of the young men who come to visit her mistress, saucily observes that "some of you spectators know perfectly well that I'm not lying" and then encourages a young man to compare prostitutes of both sexes; the young man speaks from experience.[161] This scene, with its typically comic address to the audience, clearly speaks to the experiences and perspectives of Roman men. Indeed, in the same play's opening monologue, Diniarchus bitterly comments on the female prostitute's scheming plans to "Greek it up" with another man:[162] a helpful reminder of the connections that might be made by Romans between Greek ways and luxurious, decadent behavior of any kind.

Plautus' comedies hardly constitute the only literary evidence for Roman men's use of male prostitutes during the Republican period. Lucilius writes of his relations with the boys Gentius and Macedo, and while they may have been his own slaves, one fragment seems to imply that Lucilius shared Gentius, at least, with another man; if that is so, the figure of Gentius recalls the girls of comedy, hired out to one man after another, and sometimes shared.[163] Valerius Maximus reports an incident from the early third century B.C. in which a man named Gaius Cornelius, accused of having had sexual relations with a freeborn youth, defended himself by claiming that the boy had openly prostituted himself.[164] The defense did not work, but more significant for our purposes is the fact that Valerius Maximus, or his source, imagined that young men, both freeborn and slaves,[165] were selling their favors to men even in the days of old, before the onslaught of luxurious Greek ways. Certainly there is contemporary evidence for the practice from the early second century B.C., just before that onslaught began in earnest: Cato the Elder refers to the Senate's conviction that freeborn men who "openly earn a living with their bodies or who have hired themselves out to pimps" have forfeited their claim to the physical inviolability that was the normal privilege of the freeborn.[166] And we have already seen that Pomponius dedicated an entire comedy, the *Prostibulum*, to the topic of a man who sold his favors to Roman citizens.

That freeborn Romans themselves might engage in the world's oldest profession, willingly or not, always loomed as an especially shocking possibility. Valerius Maximus writes of a scandalous incident of 52 B.C. in which a Roman man set up a brothel in his own home where he sold the services of two well-born ladies and a noble boy.[167] Tacitus reports that in A.D. 19 the Senate passed a decree prohibiting the granddaughter, daughter, or wife of a Roman knight (*eques Romanus*) from working as a prostitute, and the decree clearly came in response to existing practices.[168] A rhetorical exercise by Calpurnius Flaccus imagines a young Roman man falling into a life of prostitution and later committing suicide, while Seneca ponders a moral dilemma: What should you do if you have been kidnapped and the only person offering to pay the ransom is a man (implicitly a citizen) who has prostituted himself?[169] Among the outrageous characters whose presence in Rome provokes the stinging abuse of Juvenal's persona are men who cheat their young male wards out of their inheritance, forcing them to turn to prostitution,[170] while the principal character of Juvenal's ninth satire (discussed further in chapter 2) is a free but impoverished man who makes a living off his apparently quite marketable genital endowment.

We earlier alluded to the fact that Roman moral traditions fostered a distinct bias against prostitutes; thus men who made use of them to excess could be subject to moral criticism, and to surround oneself with whores could be interpreted as a sign of decadence, along with overindulgence in drinking, eating, and gambling. Cicero observes of Catiline's followers that "if amidst their wine and dice they were only interested in carousing and whoring, we would certainly despair of them, but we would still put up with them";[171] in fact, he adds, they are guilty of plotting to overthrow the government. In a speech attributed to Sallust, we read of luxurious young men who live in fancy houses, indulge in extravagant dinners, and spend every night in the company of whores.[172] A stock figure in Roman comedy is the father distressed by his whoring son, and Horace as well as various declaimers expound upon the moral issues raised by a young man's excessive involvement with prostitutes, one of the more important of which was a concern for fiscally responsible behavior.[173] An excessive indulgence in prostitutes could also be held to be incompatible with military discipline: as part of a rigorous program for restoring austerity and discipline among his troops, Scipio Aemilianus expelled as many as two thousand prostitutes (perhaps of both sexes) and pimps from his camp in Numantia in 134–3 b.c.[174]

Cicero, trying to paint a lurid picture of Publius Clodius Pulcher's disgraceful lifestyle, claims that he was in the habit of surrounding himself with prostitutes of both sexes.[175] In the world of invective the principle of "like father like son" often held: Valerius Maximus writes that P. Clodius Pulcher the Younger was infamous for an affair with a common (female) whore.[176] Among the countless shocking actions reportedly taken by the emperor Elagabalus was a decision to grant special privileges to pimps and to prostitutes of both sexes.[177] Interestingly, the profession of actors was often assimilated to prostitution, the assumption apparently being that if someone takes money to entertain audiences by performing on stage, she or he might just as well engage in more private, but no less mercenary, forms of entertainment.[178] This sexual availability was associated with actors of both sexes: Sulla and Maecenas both were reputed to have been involved with male actors (Metrobios and Bathyllos, respectively), and Cicero tweaks Antony for his fondness of the company of both male and female mime-actors.[179] The polymath Pliny the Elder, whose curiosity seems to have known no bounds, provides a catalogue of those who experienced sudden death ("the greatest blessing of life") that includes the following men: "Cornelius Gallus the former praetor and Titus Hetereius, a Roman knight, died in the act of love, as did in our own lifetime two men of the order of knights, [who died] with the same pantomime actor, Mysticus, an outstanding beauty of his day."[180] These two unnamed men made quite a catch, but at an unexpected cost.

There was moreover a long tradition of slandering prostitutes (whether slave or free, male or female) not only as vaguely disreputable but also as greedy, venal, and untrustworthy. Two sententious lines from Publilius Syrus sum up the stereotype: "a [female] prostitute is the instrument of insult," and "a [female] prostitute is merciful because of gifts, not tears."[181] Writing of Verres' favorite Chelidon, Cicero condescendingly observes that "she responded in a not inhumane way, considering her profession."[182] Rather more compassionately, Livy describes Hispala, the likeable prostitute who played a crucial role in the Bacchanalian scandal of 186 B.C., as "not worthy of her profession" (*non digna quaestu*, 39.9.5). In general (unless one was a Verres), one would not want to be seen in the presence of a known prostitute in a public setting. The law cited above, prohibiting men who had prostituted themselves from holding certain public offices, also stipulates that such characters may not sit with the local officials at public games, neither may anyone knowingly allow them to take part in a public banquet.[183]

Not surprisingly, prostitutes provided fuel for the fires of Roman invective, both in the courtroom and out, and an accusation of prostitution was a handy weapon to use against both male and female opponents. As we shall see, Cicero's defense of Caelius bluntly makes the argument that Clodia has lived the life of a whore. On other occasions he calls her brother, his own arch-enemy Clodius, both a "whore for the masses" (*scortum populare*, *Dom.* 49) and a more specialized "whore of wealthy men-about-town" (*scurrarum locupletium scortum*, *Sest.* 39)[184]— Cicero covered his bases well—and elsewhere he asserts that in his youth Mark Antony was nothing but a "common whore":

> sumpsisti virilem, quam statim muliebrem togam reddidisti. primo vulgare scortum; certa flagiti merces nec ea parva; sed cito Curio intervenit qui te a meretricio quaestu abduxit et, tamquam stolam dedisset, in matrimonio stabili et certo conlocavit. nemo umquam puer libidinis causa tam fuit in domini potestate quam tu in Curionis.
>
> (*Phil.* 2.44–45)

> You assumed the man's toga and then immediately turned it into a loose woman's toga. First you were a common whore, the price for your shame being fixed and not small. But Curio soon intervened, rescuing you from your profession as prostitute and, as if he had given you a matron's robe, settling you down in a lasting and stable marriage. No boy purchased for sex was ever under his master's control as much as you were under Curio's.

Cicero's language[185] is echoed nearly a century later in a scene from Petronius' *Satyricon*. The central character, Encolpius, has been abandoned by his boyfriend Giton for another man, and he lashes out against the boy in a soliloquy teeming with self-pity and abuse:

> quid ille alter? qui die togae virilis stolam sumpsit, qui ne vir esset a matre persuasus est, qui opus muliebre in ergastulo fecit, qui postquam conturbavit et libidinis suae solum vertit, reliquit veteris amicitiae nomen et, pro pudor, tamquam mulier secutuleia unius noctis tactu omnia vendidit. (Petr. *Sat.* 81.5)

> And what about that other one? On the day he should have assumed the man's toga he put on the matron's gown; he was persuaded by his mother not to be a man; he did woman's work among the chain-gangs; after he went bankrupt and became an emigrant in lust, he abandoned the name of an old friendship and (the shame of it!) sold everything for one night of groping, like a loose woman.

Both Cicero and Encolpius pointedly liken the objects of their invective to women in sexual terms, and both add the further taint of prostitution. The dynamics are worth noting: the imagery of prostitution is invoked in order to disparage the ones who prostitute themselves, the whores, rather than their clients. Indeed, with prostitutes of either sex there was a double standard firmly in place: a man who publicly hurled epithets like *scortum* by day might not think twice about giving himself the pleasure of the services of a hired companion, male or female, by night.[186]

As usual, ancient images of the monumentally conservative Cato give us a glimpse at the dynamics of traditional Roman morality. Significantly enough, Cato was said to have approved of the use of prostitutes within certain limits. Horace relates this anecdote:

> quidam notus homo cum exiret fornice, "macte
> virtute esto" inquit sententia dia Catonis;
> "nam simul ac venas inflavit taetra libido,
> huc iuvenes aequom est descendere, non alienas
> permolere uxores." (Hor. *Sat*. 1.2.31–5)

> When a certain well-known man was coming out of a brothel, the godly judgment of Cato said, "Well done, sir; for as soon as foul lust swells the veins, it is right for young men to come here, and not to grind away at other men's wives."

Cato's unsolicited advice (whose pompousness Horace mischievously undercuts with his use of the rather inelegant *permolere* ["grind away at"]) combines a certain uneasiness in the face of sexual desire as a whole (*taetra libido*) with a more practical awareness that these troublesome urges young men have cannot be ignored and are best deflected away from other men's wives and into the safe obscurity of the brothel. But the ancient commentary on Horace attributed to Acro adds a significant detail to the story. After Cato saw the same young man coming out of the same brothel on a number of occasions, Cato's smug approval transformed itself into reproof: "Young man, I commended you on the understanding that you were coming here occasionally, not living here!" ("adulescens, ego te laudavi tamquam huc interdum venires, non tamquam hic habitares"). Cato's criticism places his earlier praise in its proper context. Visits to prostitutes are perfectly acceptable (note Cato's *laudavi*), as long as they are only occasional (*interdum*) and thus give the appearance of moderation.[187] And this moderation was generally conceived of in both financial and more broadly moral terms: a young Roman ought not to squander his resources on whores.[188]

Indeed, according to Polybius, Cato was distressed at the number of young Romans who, under the influence of Greek laxity in this regard, had been wasting their money on prostitutes of both sexes as well as extravagant dinner parties. Cato took offense at this and on one occasion complained to the people that beautiful boys were now fetching more than fields, smoked fish more than ox-drivers.[189] His remark betrays his ideological commitments to austerity, fiscally responsible behavior, and the virtuous life of agriculture and soldiery: Cato himself wrote that "the bravest men and most strenuous soldiers are born from farmers," and it was precisely this belief that was being disregarded by an alarming number of young Romans.[190]

The Catonian view of men's relationships with prostitutes is perhaps most famously demonstrated by an incident involving L. Quinctius Flamininus, a distinguished nobleman whom Cato expelled from the Senate during his celebrated tenure as censor in 184 B.C. We begin with the summary of the scandal offered by Livy, who had access to the text of a speech made by Cato against Flamininus. According to Livy, among the reproaches that the censor leveled against Flamininus was the fact that, while serving as proconsul in Gaul, he had summoned from Rome (at no small expense) a young prostitute named Philippus.[191] But Philippus had left Rome to fulfill his professional obligations to Flamininus before he could see a gladiatorial contest, and one evening in Gaul, Flamininus grandly offered to make it up to Philippus. Referring to a local nobleman who had sought asylum in the Roman governor's headquarters, Flamininus asked his companion if he would like to see the Gaul die, since he had missed out on the gladiatorial show. Philippus nodded half-seriously, whereupon Flamininus seized a sword and killed the Gaul.[192]

It is worth noting that Cato's use of this incident as a reason for expelling Flamininus from the Senate has nothing to do with a homophobic intolerance of Flamininus' sexual partner. Livy paraphrases the conclusion of the censor's attack on Flamininus: if he did not deny the incident, Cato thundered, "did he think that anyone would be sorry at his being disgraced, seeing that he had made sport of human life at a banquet, while out of his mind with wine and love?"[193] Cato's phrase "out of his mind with wine and love" is telling. He is not pointing a censorial finger at Flamininus' homosexuality, but rather at the fact that he allowed the pleasures of wine and sex to dictate his behavior. And if M. Porcius Cato the censor did not take the opportunity to deliver himself of a homophobic comment on this occasion, it is difficult to believe that any other Roman would have done so.[194]

In fact, a number of ancient writers believed that Flamininus' paid companion was not a boy but a woman. Livy himself indicates that there is an alternative tradition followed by the writer Valerius Antias, according to which the prostitute was "an infamous woman" (and the victim, rather than a local nobleman, was a condemned criminal), and that is the tradition that both Valerius Maximus and Seneca the Elder unquestioningly follow. Another ancient reference to the incident fails to specify the prostitute's sex, simultaneously making quite clear the issue thought to have been most important to Cato: lust.[195] The double tradition reveals that to Romans looking back on the incident, the prostitute's sex simply did not matter.[196] Thus the anonymous treatise *De Viris Illustribus* ("On Outstanding Men"), giving a précis of the story, notes that Cato expelled Flamininus from the Senate "because while in Gaul Flamininus had, for the entertainment of a certain whore, ordered a certain man to be cast out of prison and killed at a banquet"; the writer, giving the bare essentials of the story, uses the neuter noun *scortum* to refer to the prostitute, thus revealing how unimportant his or her gender was.[197] When Livy himself notes the existence of the alternative tradition, he tellingly describes the version with the female prostitute as "another narrative, but similar in its lust and cruelty" ("aliud argumentum, simile tamen et libidine et crudelitate"). Perhaps because of this conviction that there was no significant difference between the two versions of the incident, Livy, despite the evidence from Cato's own speech to the effect that the prostitute was male, seems to leave open the other possibility:

> facinus sive eo modo quo censor obiecit sive ut Valerius tradit commissum est, saevum atque atrox: inter pocula atque epulas, ubi libare diis dapes, ubi bene precari mos esset, ad spectaculum scorti procacis in sinu consulis recubantis mactatam humanam victimam esse et cruore mensam respersam. (Livy 39.43.4)

> Whether it was done in the way for which Cato criticized him or as Valerius hands down, the deed was harsh and cruel: that, amidst drinking-cups and banquets, where it was the custom to make libations to the gods along with the proper prayers, a human victim was offered in sacrifice and the table spattered with blood, all to entertain a wanton whore who lay in a consul's arms.

The image of a blood-drenched banquet was clearly a shocking one, and equally offensive was the public flaunting by a Roman official of his paid companion (note Livy's focus on the image of a whore lying in the consul's embrace), as well as the fact that he allowed his actions to be influenced by his companion's desires, displaying a callous disregard for proper procedure.[198]

The orators whose comments on the incident are preserved by the elder Seneca (they assume that the prostitute was female, and the victim an already condemned criminal) make exactly those arguments as they accuse Flamininus of the crime of *maiestas*, or damaging the dignity of the Roman state.[199] Some of these comments include revealing remarks about the use of prostitutes. One orator notes that the argument could be made that simply having a girlfriend or paid companion is not an actionable offense in a provincial governor, nor is summarily executing a criminal. But those arguments could be met by counterarguments based on notions of propriety. There is a time and a place for everything, and a Roman official must be careful about how he uses his privilege:

> "puta, amicam habet proconsul: ideo maiestatis damnabitur? quod amplius est dico: puta, matronam corrumpit dum proconsul est: adulterii causam dicet, non maiestatis. singula," inquit, "aestima quae obicis. si tantum amicam habuisset, numquid accusares? si animadvertisset in aliquem nullo rogante, numquid accusari posset?" (Votienus Montanus *apud* Sen. *Contr.* 9.2.13–14)

> "licet ire in lupanar; si praecedentibus fascibus praetor deducetur in lupanar, maiestatem laedet, etiamsi quod licet fecerit. licet qua quis velit veste uti; si praetor ius in veste servili vel muliebri dixerit, violabit maiestatem." deinde illam fecit quaestionem: an hoc facere ei licuerit. "non licuit," inquit, "illo loco aut illo tempore aut ex illa causa occidere. quaedam quae licent tempore et loco mutato non licent."
> (Pompeius Silo *apud* Sen. *Contr.* 9.2.17)

> "Imagine that a proconsul has a girlfriend: will he be condemned for *maiestas* on that account? Furthermore, imagine that he corrupts a married lady while proconsul: he will be tried for adultery, but not for *maiestas*." He continued, "Evaluate individually the things of which you accuse him. If he had simply had a girlfriend, you wouldn't be accusing him, would you? If he had punished someone when no one had asked him to do so, surely he couldn't be accused?"

"It is permissible to enter a brothel; but if a praetor is escorted into a brothel with the insignia of his office borne before him, he will be guilty of *maiestas*, even though he has done something that is permissible. It is permissible to wear whatever clothing one wishes to wear; but if a praetor conducts legal proceedings while wearing the clothing of a slave or a woman, he will be guilty of *maiestas*." Then he proposed this line of inquiry: whether in fact it was permissible for him to do what he did. He said, "It was not permissible for him to kill the man in that place, at that time, for that reason. There are certain permissible things that are not permissible at a different time or place."

The passing comments that it is permissible to enter a brothel or that a proconsul cannot be tried just for having a girlfriend point to a certain understanding among men. Occasional visits to a prostitute, or even keeping a paid companion by one's side, need not cause any offense; but there were important questions of propriety and moderation that needed to be taken into account, especially by one exercising the authority of a magistrate.

Seneca's orators imagine a female prostitute, but we must not forget that, according to Livy, Cato himself understood the prostitute to be a young man named Philippus. Whether Flamininus paid for the favors of a woman from Placentia or a young man from Carthage, and indeed whether any Roman man paid for the favors of a "pimp's boy," a "pimp's girl," a "professional woman" (*meretrix*), or a male "prostitute" (*prostibulum*), the issues were the same. Prostitutes were untrustworthy, disreputable people; brothels were hardly decent places. But, like latrines, they had their function, and no one would have suggested dismantling them.[200] The existence of prostitution as an institution, and the availability of both male and female prostitutes for men's use, was never questioned.

Indeed, there seems to have been a fairly widespread belief that prior to settling down in marriage, young men should be allowed to sow their wild oats—in the appropriate fields, of course.[201] The most celebrated exposition of this indulgent belief is found in Cicero's defense of the twenty-six-year-old Marcus Caelius Rufus in 56 B.C. Caelius had been slandered for loose living, particularly for his affair with the rich widow Clodia, and Cicero's defense on this score is, in brief, that boys will be boys. His argument deserves a closer look. First he imagines that some might question the moral standards implied in his indulgent views, but he replies by suggesting that a life utterly devoid of pleasures of any kind may have characterized some of the greatest of the austere Romans of days gone by, but simply does not speak to the contemporary realities of life in Rome (39–40). And perhaps that is as it should be:

> quam ob rem si quem forte inveneritis qui aspernetur oculis pulchritudinem rerum, non odore ullo, non tactu, non sapore capiatur, excludat auribus omnem suavitatem, huic homini ego fortasse et pauci deos propitios, plerique autem iratos putabunt. ergo haec deserta via et inculta atque interclusa iam frondibus et virgultis relinquatur. detur aliqui ludus aetati; sit adulescentia liberior; non omnia voluptatibus denegentur; non semper superet vera illa et derecta ratio; vincat aliquando cupiditas voluptasque rationem, dum modo illa in hoc genere praescriptio moderatioque teneatur. (Cic. *Cael.* 42)

> Therefore, if perchance you come upon someone who does not deign to look upon the beauty of things, who is not taken in by any smell, any touch, any taste, who excludes all sweetness from his ears, I and a few others shall perhaps think that the gods have

been gracious to him, but most people will think the gods are angry with him. So then let this deserted road, no longer kept up and now blocked by leaves and bushes, be abandoned. Let some playfulness be granted to youth; let the years of youth be somewhat free; let not everything be denied the pleasures; let not reason, true and straightforward, always win out; let desire and pleasure sometimes triumph over reason, provided that this precept of moderation be followed.

He then enumerates some of the features of the prescribed "moderation": not squandering one's inheritance and not bringing disgrace on other households, which means keeping one's hands off freeborn Romans.[202] This refers of course to the second of the protocols for sexual behavior discussed at the beginning of this chapter, and, as we have seen, it is accompanied by the assumption that one's own slaves and prostitutes are fair game. This is precisely Cicero's interest—in particular, the question of prostitutes—for his defense of Caelius' morality rests upon a frontal attack on Clodia herself, in the form of a claim that she has lived the life of a whore rather than that of a decent Roman widow.

Consequently, Caelius' affair with Clodia is to be judged precisely as one judges a visit to a prostitute. Could anyone fault the young Caelius for that? Apparently his accusers implied that indeed one could. Here is Cicero's sly response:

> verum si quis est qui etiam meretriciis amoribus interdictum iuventuti putet, est ille quidem valde severus—negare non possum—sed abhorret non modo ab huius saeculi licentia verum etiam a maiorum consuetudine atque concessis. quando enim hoc non factitatum est, quando reprehensum, quando non permissum, quando denique fuit ut quod licet non liceret? (Cic. *Cael*. 48)

> But if there is someone who thinks that young men should be forbidden even from engaging in affairs with prostitutes, he is, to be sure, very strict indeed (that I cannot deny), but he is at variance not only with the permissiveness of our own era but also with what our ancestors practiced and allowed. For when was this not commonly done? When was it criticized? When was it not permitted? When, in short, was it the case that what is licit was illicit?

First admitting that such a belief displays an admirable commitment to Roman traditions of austerity, he then plays his trump card, arguing that not even the austere men of old excluded the occasional use of prostitutes. He concludes with a commanding tetracolon crescendo (*quando . . . quando . . . quando . . . quando . . .*) that insistently pressures the audience into admitting that the occasional use of prostitutes has always been licit. A denial of that freedom would constitute a restriction that is not only unnecessary, but one that was never made even by the famously austere ancestors.[203] Here we recall the anecdote concerning Cato's comments to the young man emerging from the brothel: perfectly fine—within limits, of course.

Men and Their Wives

There was thus a long-established understanding among Roman men: a man's own male and female slaves were attractive and available sexual objects, and their use

was one of the perquisites of ownership and of Roman manhood that would cause
no eyebrows to rise in disapproval or surprise (except, as we will see, those of the
man's wife, who might well disapprove but would probably not be surprised). So
too an occasional visit to a prostitute of either sex was unobjectionable, although if
a man persisted in such behavior he ran the risk of censure for overindulgence.

But there were other attitudes to be found among Romans. After all, traditional
morality placed great value on austerity and looked suspiciously upon overindulgence; and, as we will see, representing a strand of the Roman tradition that became
increasingly influential between the second and fourth centuries A.D., certain schools
of thought inspired by Greek philosophical traditions—those of the Stoics most notably—encouraged an ascetic approach to sexual practices that condemned anything
other than intercourse between husband and wife for the purpose of producing
children. But even apart from the influence of Greek philosophy, the austere, even
puritanical, strand of Roman morality has led one scholar to summarize traditional
Roman views with these ironic words: "Real Romans only had sex with their wives
and even then not too often."[204] How accurate is this assessment?

To be sure, it serves as a useful reminder of traditional Roman asceticism: this
was, after all, a culture in which *amator* ("lover") could be hurled as an insult,[205]
and we are reminded of Cato's condemnation of a senator for kissing his wife in
broad daylight, in front of their daughter (see earlier in this chapter). But we must
also remember Cato's joking comments on that same occasion: that he himself
only embraced his wife when it thundered loudly, and that he was a happy man
when it did thunder—a wry admission of the fact that enjoying one's wife is not
such a terrible thing after all, as long as one does it with the appropriate discretion
and decorum. Furthermore, the notion that "real Romans only had sex with their
wives" speaks, of course, only to Roman men who *had* wives, and a man did not
have to be married to qualify as a "real Roman." While the pressure to marry and
beget legitimate children was certainly considerable,[206] some men managed perfectly well to avoid succumbing to that pressure: Catullus, Propertius, Tibullus,
and Horace all project the persona of the carefree, unmarried man about town
(according to Suetonius' biography Horace, for one, in fact never married), but
their reputations never seem to have suffered for it.[207]

But if a Roman man did marry, would he have been encouraged by traditional
morality to restrict his sexual experience to his wife alone? To be sure, Roman
wives themselves did not always sit back and meekly allow their husbands to exercise their sexual freedoms without resistance on their part. In the course of a bitter
tirade against women, the speaker in Juvenal's sixth satire notes that one of the
countless hardships of the married life is an irascible, suspicious wife:

> semper habet lites alternaque iurgia lectus
> in quo nupta iacet; minimum dormitur in illo.
> tum gravis illa viro, tunc orba tigride peior,
> cum simulat gemitus occulti conscia facti:
> aut odit pueros aut ficta paelice plorat . . . (Juv. 6.268–72)

The bed in which there lies a bride forever witnesses fights and mutual recrimination;
you can hardly sleep there. She is harsh with her husband, worse than a tigress bereft

of her cubs, when she fakes sighs, aware of her own guilty secret: either she hates the slave-boys or she weeps because of a made-up girlfriend.

The speaker's characteristically vitriolic point is that the wife has her own guilty secrets that she is trying to cover up by means of her nagging accusations of infidelity with made-up partners of both sexes. In this particular case, the accusations are said to be unfounded (*ficta paelice*), but it is clear that countless Roman wives had every reason to be suspicious, especially when it came to slaves. Petronius' *Satyricon*, for example, dramatizes a brawl that breaks out between Trimalchio and his wife Fortunata when Trimalchio shows too much interest in a pretty young slave-boy.[208] Scenarios like these only sharpen the point of a poem of Martial's in which he tries to scare off a woman who wants to marry him by making a series of demands that he knows she will refuse: she must provide a enormous dowry; she must expect no sex from him, not even on their wedding night; and she must allow him free enjoyment not only of his own slaves, male and female, but also of hers.[209]

This is of course a fantasy scenario; other texts show us the other side of the coin, imagining wives who succeed in asserting their wishes. After Tibullus has relayed Priapus' advice on how to catch and keep a boy, he adds:

> haec mihi, quae canerem Titio, deus edidit ore:
>   sed Titium coniunx haec meminisse vetat.
> pareat ille suae: vos me celebrate magistrum,
>   quos male habet multa callidus arte puer. (Tibull. 1.4.73–6)

> These are the things that the god uttered to me, that I might recite them to Titius. But Titius' wife forbids him to remember them. Let him obey his wife; you men who are mistreated by a boy clever with his great skill—*you* celebrate me as your teacher.

Titius' wife was not amused by her husband's request for advice on how to hunt for boys, and she put her foot down. Yet not all wives were as rigorous, or as perceptive, as Titius'. Indeed, after leaving Titius to his wife, Tibullus addresses other men who need Priapus' advice, and these are presumably not just unmarried men but also include men blessed with an agreeable, or ignorant, wife. In fact, the pleasures of getting away with it fairly suffuse Plautine comedy: the action of the *Casina*, for one, is set in motion by Lysidamus' desire to enjoy the lovely young slave-girl after whom the play is named. But his wife finds out and sets her own counterplot in motion; hilarity ensues and the husband is finally beaten into submission. But lest we leave the theater with the mistaken belief that wives always have the last laugh, at the play's end an actor steps out of character to deliver the traditional request for applause:

> nunc vos aequomst manibus meritis meritam mercedem dare:
> qui faxit, clam uxorem ducet semper scortum quod volet;
> verum qui non manibus clare quantum poterit plauserit,
> ei pro scorto supponetur hircus unctus nautea. (Plaut. *Cas.* 1015–8)

> Now it is only fair that you give us our deserved payment with your deserved applause. Whoever does this will always bring home unbeknownst to his wife the whore that he wants; but whoever does not clap his hands as loudly as he can will find underneath him, instead of a whore, a he-goat smeared with bilge-water.

The blessing wished for the men in the audience is appropriate enough for this play, in which a husband fails to pull the wool over his wife's eyes, but one has the distinct impression that this was considered a blessing by Roman men in general, not just those watching a performance of the *Casina*. Even the repulsive alternative called down upon those who fail to applaud sufficiently still rests on the apparently axiomatic assumption that married men will stray.

The fact that it could be considered a blessing to enjoy a whore *without* one's wife knowing about it reminds us that many married men must have felt the need to weigh their own urges against a respect for their wives' wishes—or, more pragmatically, a desire to keep their wives quiet. One way in which this balancing act could be successfully achieved was by observing a certain discretion, along with the appearance of moderation; failing discretion, a husband could try reasoning with his wife. Martial, for one, is able to advance some arguments apparently designed to appease wives who have caught their husbands red-handed with the slave-boys:

> Cum tibi nota tui sit vita fidesque mariti
>   nec premat ulla tuos sollicitetve toros,
> quid quasi paelicibus torqueris inepta ministris,
>   in quibus et brevis est et fugitiva Venus?
> plus tibi quam domino pueros praestare probabo:
>   hi faciunt ut sis femina sola viro;
> hi dant quod non vis uxor dare. "Do tamen," inquis,
>   "ne vagus a thalamis coniugis erret amor."
> non eadem res est: Chiam volo, nolo mariscam:
>   ne dubites quae sit Chia, marisca tua est.
> scire suos fines matrona et femina debet:
>   cede sua pueris, utere parte tua. (Mart. 12.96)

Since your husband's way of life and faithfulness are known to you, and no woman weighs down or disturbs your conjugal bed, why are you foolishly tormented by slave-boys as if they were your rivals? Venus is brief and fleeting in them. I will prove that the boys actually give more to you than they do to their master. They see to it that you are the only woman your husband has; they give him what you, his wife, refuse to give. You say, "I'll give it anyway, as long as my husband's love does not stray from our bedroom." But it's not the same thing. I want a [succulent] Chian fig, not a [big and cheap] *marisca*. Lest you be in doubt as to which one the Chian is: yours is the *marisca*. A matron and a woman ought to know her limits. Yield to the boys when it comes to their part, and make use of your own.

As so often with Martial, the humor, however hyperbolic, reveals something about the readership to which it appealed. His argument runs as follows: if we men indulge our fancy with our slave-boys, you wives really ought to be happy, since these affairs are destined to be short-lived. After all, the boys will mature, whereas if we were involved with girls or women, you would have more to worry about; furthermore, they are providing us with the pleasures of anal intercourse, which you refuse to give us. When the wife then insists that she would grant even this pleasure if it would keep her husband from wandering, the poet squelches any further resistance by stating outright that boys offer a kind of physical pleasure that girls and women simply cannot and that boys' anuses are preferable to women's.[210] This is no doubt somewhat facetious—and certainly comes across as the posturing of a man eager or perhaps desperate to have his cake and eat it too, to keep his wife pacified while enjoying his slave-boys. But it must also be drawing on some biases, predilections, and ideologies circulating among Martial's readership: though it may be unfair to their wives, men will be men, and women should just make the best of it.[211] As Mark Antony wrote in a letter to Octavian (later Augustus), referring to his own scandalous relationship with Cleopatra, "Does it make any difference where or in which woman you get it up?"[212] These were the cocky words of one married man to another. More than a century later, Aelius Verus, heir-apparent of the emperor Hadrian, reportedly met his wife's complaint about his sexual peregrinations by telling her that she would have to put up with them and that in any case being a wife had more to do with status than with pleasure.[213] Such were the attitudes that Roman wives were up against.

And yet we can also find evidence for the existence of an ideal of mutual fidelity, of sexual exclusivity between husband and wife. But in this case, as often, between ideal and reality there existed a considerable gap; indeed, the very ways in which the ideal is expressed suggest that it did not enjoy widespread support, and the very texts that subscribe to the ideal often undercut it at the same time. Ultimately, I argue that if we approach those texts with a willingness to read between the lines, we will see that this marital ideal failed to supersede the Priapic model, according to which the prime directive of masculine sexual behavior was to assert one's sexual dominion over others, whether one was married or not.[214]

To begin, it should be noted that, while we occasionally hear of married women who asserted the same sexual freedoms as their husbands,[215] they were clearly fighting against an entrenched double standard: husbands could stray without fearing the kinds of repercussions that adulterous wives had to contend with.[216] This arrangement, so convenient for Roman men, had the considerable weight of tradition behind it. Cato himself once laid bare the double standard with breathtaking clarity:

> in adulterio uxorem tuam si prehendisses, sine iudicio impoene necares; illa te, si adulterares sive tu adulterarere, digito non auderet contingere, neque ius est.
>
> (Cato fr. 222 Malcovati)
>
> If you caught your wife in adultery, you could kill her with impunity and without a trial; but if you committed adultery, or if you were adulterated, she would not dare to lay a finger on you, nor is it legally permitted [for her to do so].

The language that Cato uses to describe a husband's extramarital activity is evidently designed to be comprehensive in its use of the active and passive forms of the verb *adulterare*. The references must be, respectively, to those situations in which a husband is the insertive partner and to those in which he is the receptive partner, an interesting glimpse at the complex possibilities of extramarital affairs.[217] But those possibilities existed only for the husband; as Cato reminds us, if the wife strayed in any way, there were all sorts of legal and moral repercussions: it was *adulterium*, and the husband had grounds for divorce at the very least.

This double standard shines through several texts. We have seen that Roman men, married or not, were always free to make sexual use of their own slaves; an affair with a female slave did not constitute *adulterium*. By contrast, if a married Roman woman engaged in sexual relations with one of her male slaves, she was guilty of *adulterium* and her actions could bring considerable disgrace upon herself. Thus in Livy's narrative of the rape of Lucretia, Tarquinius' final threat to the matron—the one that so terrified her that she at last capitulated to his advances— was that he would kill both her and a male slave, and leave the two naked bodies together, "that she might be said to have been slain in a foul adultery" (*ut in sordido adulterio necata dicatur*, 1.58.4). Similarly, in Tacitus' *Annals* (6.40) we read that a married woman named Aemilia Lepida was formally accused of adultery with a slave (*ob servum adulterum*) and, in view of her obvious guilt, committed suicide without even attempting a defense. Later, at *Annals* 14.60, we read that Poppaea accused Octavia of an affair with an Egyptian slave (*servilis amor*) in order to force Nero to divorce her. (Octavia was found guilty and banished to Campania for a while, but eventually forced to commit suicide after being subjected to another charge of adultery, this time with Anicetus.) Not only were slaves useful tools in the sexual intrigues of freeborn Romans, but they were expendable: the Digest notes that a husband has the right to kill a slave who is the *adulter* of his wife.[218]

But if it was a question of a married man and his slave-girl, things were quite different. Quintilian offers as an example of a false or misleading analogy the following propositions: "If a relationship between a mistress and a male slave is disgraceful, then one between a master and a female slave is disgraceful; if pleasure is the goal for dumb animals, then the same is true for human beings." Quintilian clearly expects his readership to find both of these claims to be nonsense, and he offers a counterargument from contraries (*ex dissimilibus*): "It is not the same thing for a master to have relations with a female slave as it is for a mistress to have them with a male slave; nor, if pleasure is the goal for dumb creatures, is it the goal for reasoning creatures as well."[219] To argue that an affair between a free woman and her male slave is the same as one between a free man and his female slave is as silly as the suggestion that human morality should be defined with reference to animals (see Appendix 1).

Nonetheless, despite this obvious double standard, some Roman men did pay allegiance to an ideal of mutual fidelity within marriage. Perhaps the most sustained meditation on the notion comes, not surprisingly, from an epithalamium, or wedding hymn, composed by Catullus to honor the marriage of Manlius Torquatus and Junia Aurunculeia. The poem includes some remarkable statements about the benefits and function of marriage. For example, addressing Hymen, the god of marriage, the poet claims:

> nil potest sine te Venus,
> fama quod bona comprobet,
> commodi capere: at potest
> te volente. quis huic deo
>   compararier ausit? (Catull. 61.61–5)

Without you, Venus can obtain no benefit that public opinion will approve of; but she can if you are willing. Who would dare to be compared with this god?

The sentiment is of course in direct contradiction to everything else we have seen. One need only think of Horace's allusion to sexual relations with one's own slaves as "easy and obtainable" and much preferable to pursuing a married lady (*Satires* 1.2.114–9), or indeed the persona elsewhere adopted by Catullus himself: hardly a servant of Hymen and apparently quite proud of it. Here it is worth recalling the generic context of Catullus' comment. This is a poem not only in honor of the new couple but also in honor of the god Hymen himself, and the question he asks above ("Who would dare to be compared with this god?") in fact forms a refrain, repeated at the end of the next two stanzas (69–70, 74–5). The hyperbolic strategy recurs in another question:

> quis deus magis est ama-
> tis petendus amantibus?
> quem colent homines magis
> caelitum, o Hymenaee Hymen,
>   o Hymen Hymenaee? (Catull. 61.46–50)

> Which god is more to be sought by those who love and are loved? Which of the heavenly ones will humanity worship more, O Hymenaeus Hymen, O Hymen Hymenaeus?

Cupid and Venus are two answers to the rhetorical questions that come to mind, neither of them necessarily linked with marriage. The hyperbole reflects the extravagant language of the whole: in one stanza the bride is extolled as the most beautiful woman in the entire world (84–6), and three stanzas later it is categorically stated that her husband will not fall into the arms of any adulteress (97–105).

Any reader of Roman literature will easily recognize this passage as a striking instance of wishful thinking at least partly conditioned by the poem's generic requirements. Interestingly enough, the poem itself seems to suggest this very thing ten stanzas later, when it undermines its own ideological stance, or at least shows its hollowness, with this blunt piece of advice to the bride:

> nupta, tu quoque quae tuus
> vir petet cave ne neges,
> ni petitum aliunde eat. (Catull. 61.144–6)

> Bride, you too must be careful not to deny what your husband will seek from you, lest he go to seek it from some other source.

With these words an assumption underlying Roman concepts of marriage becomes brutally clear. It is the wife's responsibility to keep her husband sexually satisfied; otherwise he will simply go elsewhere. It is never suggested that the husband should try to limit his urges.

The gap between a heartwarming idealism and the realities of Roman married life is further emphasized by the poem's final images. Once again the burden of seeing that the ideal is lived up to falls squarely upon the wife: after a touching description of the infant son that Junia will no doubt provide her husband, the poet expresses the hope that the baby will resemble Manlius, thereby proving the identity of his father and the chastity of his mother, who is implicitly compared to the paradigmatically faithful Penelope (214–23). The hymn thus climaxes with praise of the wife's chastity; as for the husband, he will simply go elsewhere if his wife does not fulfill his sexual requirements. All of this puts the fulsome praise of the marriage god in a clear context. Ultimately, even in a hymn in his honor, Hymen bows before Priapus.[220]

But there are some texts that more directly advocate the position that husbands should be held up to the same standard as their wives. The elder Pliny pointedly observes that among doves, both mates are faithful: "adulterous affairs," as he puts it, "are known to neither of them."[221] His comment simultaneously reveals a longing for an ideal situation (if only humans were like doves) and a realization that the ideal is not in fact followed in practice. Similarly the jurist Ulpian comments on the injustice involved in holding wives to standards to which husbands are not subject, but he is obviously speaking of well-entrenched practices.[222] Valerius Maximus includes among his roster of outstandingly self-controlled men (in his chapter "De Abstinentia et Continentia") one who had sexual relations with his wife and with no one else—a truly exceptional character:

> Drusum etiam Germanicum, eximiam Claudiae familiae gloriam patriaeque rarum ornamentum, et quod super omnia est, operum suorum pro habitu aetatis magnitudine vitrico pariter ac fratri Augustis duobus rei publicae divinis oculis mirifice respondentem, constitit usum veneris intra coniugis caritatem clausum tenuisse.
>
> (Val. Max. 4.3.3)
>
> Concerning Drusus Germanicus—that outstanding glory of the Claudian family and rare ornament of his country, who (most outstandingly of all) in the greatness of his accomplishments measured up quite splendidly, considering his age, to his stepfather as well as his brother (both of them emperors, both of them the divine eyes of the State)—it is agreed that he kept his sexual experience strictly confined to conjugal affection.[223]

Valerius obviously reports Drusus' behavior precisely because it was abnormally austere. Such an unusual display of self-denial seemed worthy of being included in a rhetorical roster of the champions of abstinence, and its very rarity is what is most eloquent.[224]

Above all, the belief that men should, like Drusus, keep their sexual experience within the confines of marriage was the province of philosophers.[225] Occasionally their advice to restrict one's sexual experiences to one's spouse is accompanied by an exhortation to engage in intercourse with one's wife only for the purpose of procreation, a qualification that reveals what may be the basic impulse behind these philosophers' urgings: sex is something that should be distrusted, restricted to the bare essentials. The Roman philosopher who makes the point most baldly is the first-century A.D. Stoic teacher Musonius Rufus. While it is true that Musonius Rufus, like Seneca, moved on the highest levels of Roman society, it is important to consider the ways in which their philosophical teachings—for example, on the questions of slavery and sexual abstinence—sometimes, even often, advocated stances that were distinctly at variance with what we might call popular morality.[226] Seneca, for example, argued that slaves were as fully human as their masters and thus deserved equal treatment (*Epist.* 47). The very fact that Musonius lectured in Greek rather than Latin may be taken to signal a certain distance from popular discourse among Romans. In any case, the central point of one of his lectures is that men should restrict all sexual behavior to intercourse with their wives that was aimed at the begetting of children. Any other sexual practices, *even within marriage*, should be avoided.

χρὴ δὲ τοὺς μὴ τρυφῶντας ἢ μὴ κακοὺς μόνα μὲν ἀφροδίσια νομίζειν δίκαια τὰ ἐν γάμῳ καὶ ἐπὶ γενέσει παίδων συντελούμενα, ὅτι καὶ νόμιμά ἐστιν—τὰ δέ γε ἡδονὴν θηρώμενα ψιλὴν ἄδικα καὶ παράνομα, κἂν ἐν γάμῳ ᾖ. (Muson. Ruf. 86.4–8 Lutz)

Those who do not live licentiously, or who are not evil, must think that only those sexual practices are justified which are consummated within marriage and for the creation of children, since these practices are customary. But [such people must think that] those [sexual practices] which hunt for mere pleasure are unjust and illicit, even if they take place within marriage.

Musonius here advocates an extreme asceticism, following in the footsteps of, and perhaps even surpassing, Greek philosophers like Plato (particularly in his last work, the *Laws*, whose language Musonius here echoes) and certain Stoics.[227] I have been arguing that the limitation of a man's sexual practices *to his wife* was implicitly represented by popular Roman morality as an unusually ascetic response; Drusus Germanicus is cited by Valerius Maximus as an extreme example of self-discipline for doing precisely that. Musonius goes even further, advocating the restriction of sexual practices between husband and wife only to those which are aimed at procreation. It would seem that only vaginal intercourse when the wife was fertile met with Musonius' approval.

The extent to which Musonius condemns behaviors that were usually accepted without question is made even clearer when he emphasizes (with a parenthetic oath) that a virtuous man should avoid sexual relations even with his own slave-woman:

ὡς μετά γε σωφροσύνης οὔτ᾽ ἂν ἑταίρᾳ πλησιάζειν ὑπομένειέ τις, οὔτ᾽ ἂν ἐλευθέρᾳ γάμου χωρὶς οὔτε μὰ Δία θεραπαίνη τῇ αὑτοῦ. (Muson. Ruf. 86.12–4 Lutz)

If one is to behave moderately, one would not dare to have relations with a courtesan, nor with a free woman outside of marriage, nor, by Zeus, with one's own slave-woman.

Later, returning to the question of relations with one's slave woman, he observes that "some consider this behavior to be entirely blameless, since every master is thought to have absolute power to treat his own slave however he wishes" (it is worth pointing out that Musonius uses a generalizing masculine form to refer to the slaves over whom masters are thought to have absolute authority).[228] But we must not let the rhetoric mislead us: the belief that Musonius Rufus attributes to "some" in fact characterizes the overwhelming majority of the sources left to us, the only exceptions being ascetic philosophers such as himself.

Indeed, the paradigm of marital exclusivity almost always yielded to the more pressing needs of the Priapic man. We return to the persona Martial sometimes presents, that of a married man whose wife puts up with his dalliances with boys: she complains, but nothing changes. Then there is Antony's letter to the married Octavian in which he asks if it really matters who his sexual partners are: a truly rhetorical question. These give us more realistic perspectives than the idealized proclamations of wedding hymns or the fervent opinions of ancient jurists or philosophers. In the end, the conviction that a married man should ideally have sex only with his wife was an ideal more preached than practiced, and even when it was preached, it was often drowned out by the voice of the Priapic man, ready to exercise his prerogative whether he was married or not. In all its macho bravado, that was the voice of those who ultimately called the shots, regardless of any objections by the less powerful or the more considerate.

Jupiter and Ganymede

One of the more striking characteristics of the cultural interaction between Greece and Rome is that Greek mythic traditions were adopted nearly wholesale by the Romans and integrated into, or grafted onto, native Italian traditions: Jupiter became assimilated to Zeus, Venus to Aphrodite, Mars to Ares, and so on. In view of the evidence reviewed so far, it should come as no surprise that Greek myths involving pederastic relations between gods and young men—such as the stories of Apollo and Hyacinth, Hercules and Hylas, and others—were readily adopted by the Romans.[229] But above all, Roman audiences seem to have found something appealing in the tale of Ganymede, the stunning young Trojan prince who caught Zeus' eye and was carried off by the god's eagle (or, in some versions, by Zeus himself disguised as an eagle) to serve him eternally on Olympus as cupbearer and concubine.[230]

The figure of Ganymede as an archetype of the agelessly beautiful young man literally swept off his feet by an older male lover seems to have caught on fairly early among Romans: at some point before the late third century B.C. his name underwent a transformation (mediated by the influence of the Etruscans, who called him *Catmite*) from *Ganymedes* to *Catamitus*, just as *Odysseus* had become *Ulixes*.[231] An indication of how early, and how well, the story became known among Romans is a reference in one of Plautus' plays to paintings depicting the abduction of Ganymede (*Catamitus*) by the eagle and of Adonis by Venus,[232] and while the play is set in Greece, the use of the young man's Romanized name reminds us that these images obviously meant something to the Roman audience. At the beginning of the first century B.C. Varro composed a Menippean satire entitled *Catamitus*, now unfortunately lost to us. A further indication of the extent to which Ganymede/Catamitus was naturalized at Rome is found in the opening lines of Rome's national epic, the *Aeneid*, where Virgil includes among the causes of Juno's unceasing wrath at the Trojans her jealousy of the honors given to Ganymede.[233] Another sign of the Romanization of Ganymede can be found in a poem of Propertius, who cites as examples of Jupiter's amorous escapades Semele, Io, and Ganymede: his point is that since even Jupiter succumbed to sexual temptation, the all-too-human poet cannot resist.[234] This same poet elsewhere proudly claims to have wedded Greek form and Roman content (3.1.3–4), and his use of Ganymede as a prime example of what men desire constitutes a perfect illustration of that blend. Indeed the figure of Ganymede appears throughout Roman literature as the archetype of the beautiful, sexually desirable male slave as perquisite of wealth and privilege: Martial, Statius, and Juvenal specifically focus on the image of rich men being served at their dinner tables by young men comparable in their beauty to Ganymede.[235] Likewise Catamitus appears in a funerary inscription as the name of a former slave, just as Hylas appears as a name for a desirable young slave boy in Martial's poetry.[236]

That Romans generally assumed Ganymede's service to Jupiter to have had its sexual aspects is made clear by various texts. Cicero pointedly asks, "Who has any doubts as to what the poets mean when they speak of the abduction of Ganymede, or who does not understand what Euripides' Laius [who similarly abducted Pelops' son Chrysippus for sexual motives] is speaking of and what he desires?"[237] Festus, duly noting in his dictionary of republican Latin that Ganymede was also called Catamitus, blandly adds that he was "Jupiter's concubine."[238] Martial makes the same point with his characteristic blend of wit and obscenity. In one poem he woefully contrasts his own poverty with that of his rich friend: while his friend is surrounded by beautiful young slave-boys who rival Ganymede in their charms, Martial himself is compelled to use his hand instead of a Ganymede. Elsewhere we find him flattering one young slave by saying that he could take Ganymede's place in Jupiter's bed, or asking another for his sexual favors: Give me what I want, he pleads, and "I would say that Jupiter has it no better with Ganymede." More crassly still, he observes that just as he anally penetrates his boyfriends despite his wife's offers to provide the same service, so Jupiter sleeps with Ganymede despite Juno's remarks that she too has an anus. Pursuing the same irreverent motif, he elsewhere imagines that before Ganymede's arrival on Olympus, Juno served "as a Ganymede" for Jupiter (the sexual meaning is clear, given his comment in the same poem that Cornelia, Julia, and Porcia all allowed their husbands to penetrate them anally).[239] In one of the *Priapea*, the god comes up with clever ways of asking a beardless youth to allow him to penetrate him anally, including a reference to what Jupiter received from "the one who was carried off by the sacred bird."[240] It is also worth noting that *catamitus* came to be used not as a proper name but as a noun referring to a beautiful young man in his role as the subordinate sexual partner of a man.[241] Augustus, one late source gossips, used to sleep in the midst of twelve *catamiti* and as many girls,[242] and Cicero uses the word to insult the adult Marcus Antonius as well as some other man whose identity is now lost to us.[243]

With all this in mind, it is interesting to observe that the story of Ganymede (unlike more lurid tales such as that of Myrrha, involving father-daughter incest)[244] was never said to be shockingly alien or fundamentally incompatible with Roman *gravitas*. On the contrary: Horace begins an ode that solemnly invokes the eagle as a flattering image for Augustus' stepson Drusus by observing that it was an eagle with whom Jupiter entrusted the task of carrying away Ganymede, while the anonymous poet of the *Laus Pisonis*, seeking an appropriate image for the majestic relaxation in which Jupiter indulges after a hard day's work of hurling thunderbolts, comes up with a banquet at which Ganymede serves.[245] Such, it seems, were the appurtenances befitting the king of the gods. We have already seen that when the emperor Domitian fancied himself a god on earth, poets like Martial and Statius obligingly compared his eunuch Earinos to Ganymede.

Images of the beautiful young Trojan, usually in the presence of the eagle, dotted the Roman landscape. Juvenal refers to a statue of Ganymede placed in Vespasian's Forum of Peace as something of a landmark, and the Christian writer Lactantius notes that images of Ganymede and the eagle were to be found in temples to Jupiter and were "worshipped equally with him."[246] He is of course exaggerating for lurid effect, but his exaggeration would have had the desired effect only if based on some sort of observable reality. Certainly the image of Ganymede was extremely popular in Roman art.[247] Surviving depictions range from images of Ganymede being approached by the eagle to scenes of the eagle actually grasping the youth or carrying him aloft, and the variety of media in which the mythic paradigm of the beautiful youth swept off his feet by a male lover appears is impressive: Ganymede and the eagle graced wall paintings, mosaics, jewelry, coins, and even sarcophagi all over the Roman world; statuary groups of the pair survive in abundance.[248] Martial seems to have a visual representation of the pair in mind when he compares the spectacle of the emperor Domitian's lions, who allowed hares to play safely in their mouths, to the way in which Jupiter's eagle tenderly carried the young Ganymede aloft:

> Aetherias aquila puerum portante per auras
>   illaesum timidis unguibus haesit onus:
> nunc sua Caesareos exorat praeda leones
>   tutus et ingenti ludit in ore lepus.
> quae maiora putas miracula? summus utrisque
>   auctor adest: haec sunt Caesaris, illa Iovis. (Mart. 1.6)

> As the eagle carried the boy through the breezes of the sky, the burden clung uninjured to the timid talons: now Caesar's lions are won over by their own prey, and the hare plays safely in the immense mouth. Which miracle do you think greater? Each one has the highest cause: the one is Caesar's and the other Jupiter's.

The analogy is clear: Domitian, the lion, and the hare correspond to Jupiter, the eagle, and Ganymede.[249] And it relies on an image obviously familiar to Martial's Roman audience (we note that Martial does not need to name names: references to "the eagle" and "the boy" suffice). Indeed, even as they looked up to the nighttime skies above them, Roman men might see Ganymede, and the eagle with him: many people considered the constellation Aquarius, over which swooped the Eagle (the constellation Aquila), to represent Ganymede.[250]

In connection with Martial's image of the eagle tenderly grasping Ganymede, it is interesting to observe that in a number of ancient depictions of the pair (whether we are to imagine the eagle as being Zeus in disguise or merely his emissary) the interaction between the two is characterized by a markedly relaxed, even tender tone. Often we see Ganymede giving the bird a drink from his cup;[251] sometimes the two are standing comfortably together, apparently enjoying each other's company (Plate 1).[252] While in some of the scenes where the eagle carries Ganymede away the youth appears to be resisting (as in a second- or third-century A.D. mosaic [Plate 2]),[253] in others this is hardly the case: in an architectural relief from around A.D. 200 Ganymede reaches up to caress the eagle's neck,[254] and in a statuary group from the same period he turns to look into the eagle's eyes as he is borne aloft

(Plate 3).[255] One statue, thought to be closely based on the famous group by the Greek sculptor Leochares (Plate 4),[256] reads more as an elegant erotic dance than as a violent rape. These images remind us of the Roman textual tradition's occasional acknowledgment of the fact that young men were not always entirely passive in the processes of flirtation and courtship (see chapter 5). And the sexual implications of the depiction of the eagle grasping a nude young Ganymede from behind (see, for example, Plates 2 and 3)[257] would surely not have been lost on a Roman viewer.

The myth of Ganymede was integrated into Roman literary and artistic traditions with an obvious ease, and his image was pervasive. Why this was so seems clear: Ganymede, a foreigner abducted by a potentate in order to be his slave, corresponded perfectly to real role among Romans. Indeed, the Roman textual tradition conveniently elides the fact that Ganymede was a prince in his own country and emphasizes instead his role as servant: Martial for one calls him Jupiter's *minister* ("servant") or, irreverently, his *cinaedus* (an untranslatable term to which we will return in chapter 5; it invokes his sexual service to the god).[258] The visual representations frequently emphasize his foreign birth by depicting him wearing a distinctive cap of Asian peoples. These are not coincidental details. To represent Ganymede as a non-Roman and a slave was to make him compatible with the standard sexual paradigm (a Roman man and his slave) and to differentiate as much as possible the relationship between Jupiter and Ganymede from the problematic paradigm of *stuprum* (relations with freeborn Romans). Thus the king of the gods, enjoying the services of his beautiful young slave, a captive from Asia Minor, is the stereotypical Roman man writ large. There is of course a touch of fantasy in the detail that Ganymede remains conveniently young for all eternity, while the way in which Roman texts imagine Juno's reaction to her husband's favorite reflects the Roman reality discussed earlier in this chapter: she complains bitterly and resents his presence, but ultimately she has no choice but to put up with the arrangement.[259]

Finally, it is interesting to note that in Apuleius' *Metamorphoses*, an old hag ironically refers to her male lover—hardly a boy—as her "dear Endymion" (another beautiful boy of Greek myth, loved by the moon goddess Selene) and as her "Catamitus."[260] This passage reminds us of the risks of imposing modern preconceptions on the ancient material: while we might be tempted to think of Ganymede as an outstanding emblem of homosexual love, he seems instead to have been an icon of a youthful male beauty that might attract either male or female admirers. It is not coincidental that in his catalogue of beautiful young men in Greek myth, Hyginus lists both those who found female lovers (including Adonis and Endymion) and those who found male lovers (including Hyacinth and Ganymede).[261] Likewise, Juvenal notes that being a gladiator makes a man supremely desirable in the eyes of women: "this turns them into Hyacinths."[262] In other words, even such mythic figures as Hylas, Hyacinth, and Ganymede, all of them loved by male heroes or gods, were not pinup boys of homoeroticism, but were rather conceived of as beautiful youths who might attract admirers of either sex. It is their ravishing beauty rather than their participation in homosexual experience that is the fundamental characteristic of these mythic paradigms of youthful male desirability.

Hadrian and Antinous

Another figure worth considering is as historical as Ganymede is mythical: indeed, we might think of him as a real-life counterpart to Jupiter's cup-bearer. This is the beautiful young Bithynian named Antinous, beloved of the emperor Hadrian.[263] Very little is known about his origins: he may have been a slave, or he may have been born free, but the one clear fact is that he died under mysterious circumstances in A.D. 130 while on a trip to Egypt with Hadrian; he was about twenty years old. But whatever Antinous' background was, he did not live as a freeborn Roman, and because of that crucial fact there seems to have been no scandal surrounding his relationship with the emperor. Nor should we be surprised. Had Hadrian taken up with a freeborn Roman, male or female, things would certainly have been different.[264]

To be sure, Christian writers took offense at the relationship between the two,[265] and even certain pagan writers of the third and fourth centuries A.D., a period of ever-increasing asceticism, raise an eyebrow at Hadrian's hedonism and Antinous' "infamous" service to him.[266] But otherwise, the relationship does not seem to have given rise to the kind of stinging gossip that we see directed against other emperors' sexual proclivities: for oral sex, for example, or for playing the receptive role in anal intercourse;[267] for a scandalous desire for well-endowed men;[268] for formally marrying males, either as bride or as groom;[269] for marrying a niece;[270] for incestuous relations with a sister or mother.[271] No emperor was ever maligned for taking a beautiful young foreigner as his concubine.

Indeed, the principal criticism leveled against Hadrian by his contemporaries was not for his relationship with Antinous in itself, but instead for his intense reaction to the youth's death: he "wept like a woman,"[272] named a city in Egypt after his beloved, caused his statues to be erected throughout the Empire, and finally had him deified.[273] One source reports that Hadrian was ridiculed for so excessive a response (people asked why he had not reacted in a similar way to the death of his own sister),[274] and there certainly was mystery and gossip concerning the manner of Antinous' death: some said, for example, that he had offered up his own life when Hadrian was told by his astrologers that if he wished to live long another life had to be given (one thinks of the mythic Alcestis, who agreed to die in the place of her husband Admetus).[275]

But if, as I have suggested, a parallel can be drawn between Hadrian's relationship with Antinous and Jupiter's with Ganymede (itself, as we have seen, already appropriated by Roman poets interested in flattering Domitian and Earinos), we should not expect to find indications to the effect that Antinous' deification met a great deal of resistance. Indeed, it is just possible that some Romans besides obsequious poets considered themselves to have been witnesses of a real-life Ganymede, added, like the mythical Trojan prince, to the company of the gods while in the bloom of his youth. Antinous was strikingly beautiful and safely foreign, and since youthful male beauty was a culturally acceptable topic for celebration (see chapter 2), many must have envied Hadrian's success in snagging the young Bithynian. So too they must have admired Antinous' image, which was dispersed after his death throughout the Roman world in sculpture, coins, medallions, and other media. In some of these numerous representations he appears simply as a beautiful young man (see, for example, Plates 5 and 6), while in others we find him in the guise of various gods, such as the Greek Dionysus (Plate 7), the Roman Vertumnus or Silvanus, or the Egyptian Osiris.[276]

We are told that poets composed works (unfortunately lost to us) on the subject of Antinous, and inscriptions in Antinous' honor have been found in Rome and elsewhere.[277] One of them, from Tivoli, was dedicated by a certain Quintus Siculus and may originally have accompanied a statue of Antinous. The text compares Hadrian's beloved to the foreign god Belenus, who was himself held to be analogous to the eternally youthful Apollo: "If Antinous and Belenus are alike in age and beauty, why should Antinous also not be what Belenus is?"[278] The question reads as a contribution to an ongoing debate about Antinous' deification, and if in fact these verses accompanied a statue of the new god, the dedicator is making a strong statement in favor of the deification. He is, to be sure, engaging in flattery of the emperor, but I would suggest that Roman men's flattery need not always have been perfunctory in the case of the lovely young Antinous.

Finally, the parallel between Antinous and Ganymede raises an interesting question for us: if Juno provides a divine paradigm for the bitter, jealous wife who nonetheless puts up with her husband's behavior, what was Hadrian's wife Sabina's reaction to all this? The ancient sources are not explicit on the point, but they rather plainly suggest that the marriage was one of convenience. Hadrian is reported to have said that were he not emperor he would divorce her, so difficult and unpleasant could she be; for her part, Sabina was thought to have been unbecomingly intimate with various men in the court, including the biographer Suetonius.[279] But in the end, like Jupiter and Juno, Hadrian and Sabina, and no doubt any number of Roman couples, stayed together in an arrangement that must often have been made more bearable for the husband and more exasperating for the wife by the presence of charming young men like Ganymede and Antinous.

2

Greece and Rome

According to the second of the basic protocols outlined at the beginning of chapter 1, freeborn Romans of either sex apart from their wives were officially off-limits as Roman men's sexual partners. Their own slaves of either sex were fair game, and an occasional visit to a male or female prostitute would provoke no censure; and while a married man had his wife's claims to reckon with, as well as an occasionally sanctioned ideal of sexual exclusivity within marriage, I have suggested that those concerns were usually overshadowed by the imperatives of the Priapic model. Still, sexual relations with freeborn Romans other than one's wife met with the disapproval of traditional moralists and were often represented as instances of *stuprum*, a word that originally meant "disgrace" (see chapter 3 for further discussion). Thus adultery constituted a variety of *stuprum*, as did relations with freeborn unmarried women, girls, and widows. So too, of course, did relations with freeborn Roman men and boys, and it is here that we come to perhaps the most important distinction between Greek and Roman paradigms for the public representation of male sexual experience. The Greek tradition of pederasty, whereby citizen males might openly engage in romantic and sexual relationships with freeborn adolescent males who would one day be citizens, in Roman terms was *stuprum*; it was a disgraceful, illicit behavior. Thus a situation like that obtaining in Athens, where a statuary group of the pederastic couple Harmodios and Aristogeiton was erected in the agora in recognition of their role in overthrowing the last tyrant of

Athens, would be impossible in Rome.[1] Yet this was not because
male[2] but because both parties were freeborn; equally impossib
public celebration of the relationship between a freeborn Roman
older lover. Indeed, we have already seen that same-sex relations
freeborn Roman youth were in fact capable of being publicly a(
even celebrated, as was the case with Domitian's Earinos, flatteringly compared to
Ganymede, and Hadrian's Antinous. In short, it is not *homosexuality* but specifically *pederasty* in the Greek sense of publicly acknowledged romantic and sexual
relationships between adult citizen males and freeborn adolescent males (future
citizens) that constituted what from a Roman perspective was peculiarly Greek in
matters erotic;[3] precisely this erotic configuration will be the referent of the term
pederasty throughout this study.

In this chapter I first discuss the evidence supporting the conclusions just outlined, also considering the extent to which the Roman sources actually associate
pederasty with the influence of Greece; then I turn to Roman traditions regarding
men's sexual practices that stand in illuminating contrast with those of Greece.

"Greek" Love: Pederasty and the Gymnasium

The great majority of the ancient sources that explicitly or implicitly identify a
sexual practice as "Greek" pertain to the public courtship and pursuit of freeborn
young men, often in such places as the gymnasium and palaestra, and they regularly point to one or more of the characteristic features of the Greek practice.
Thus, among the Greek customs that Cornelius Nepos enumerates in the preface
to his collection of biographies of foreign leaders is the fact that "it is considered a
matter of praise in Greece for young men to have had as many lovers as possible"[4]
and the same writer elsewhere reports that in his youth Alcibiades was "loved by
many, according to the custom of the Greeks."[5] In the fifth book of his *Tusculan
Disputations*, Cicero cites Dionysius, tyrant of Syracuse, as an example of a man
who was profoundly unhappy because unable to trust any of those whom he loved,
even though he was lucky enough to have enjoyed many friends and "had, according to the custom of Greece, certain young men joined to him in love."[6] In a fragment of the fourth book of Cicero's *Republic*, we find the observation that "it was
a matter of reproach for young men if they did not have lovers,"[7] and the next
piece of text presents the words of Scipio, associating the Greek gymnasia with
sexual encounters involving young men.[8] Cicero makes a connection with Greek
gymnasia in another passage from the *Tusculan Disputations*, where he speaks of
relationships to which he gives the curious label "love of friendship" (*amor
amicitiae*): "This practice seems to me to have its origin in the gymnasia of the
Greeks, where such love-affairs are freely allowed."[9] All of these comments, however urbane their tone, imply a certain distance between Roman and Greek customs: these love affairs occur "according to Greek custom" (*more Graeciae* or *more
Graecorum*); they are freely permitted in Greek gymnasia. Indeed, Nepos explicitly observes that the Greek practices he cites—of which pederasty is one—are
accounted notorious, undignified, or dishonorable among Romans.[10]

But it is clear that these writers are not addressing the entire question of sexual practices between males, but only the particularly Hellenic tradition of pederastic relations with freeborn young men. On the question of age each of the texts explicitly refers to "youth" (*iuventus, adulescentes, adulescentuli,* or *adulescentia*). As for the issue of status, Alcibiades was of course freeborn, and in the passage from the *Republic*, Scipio makes explicit reference to the freeborn (*ingenui*).[11] Cicero's discussion of the *amor amicitiae* associated with gymnasia incorporates an approving citation of a line from Ennius, and the line is specifically concerned with the behavior of citizens: "Nudity amongst citizens is the beginning of disgrace"[12]— "amongst citizens," not "amongst men." The remaining passages (Nepos' preface and Cicero's reference to Dionysius' love affairs with young men) do not explicitly designate that the younger partners are freeborn, but it is clear that Roman readers would have made that assumption. Firstly and most importantly, a Roman writer would have no cause to represent sexual relations between men and male slaves as a Greek custom since, as was argued in chapter 1, such practices constituted an accepted fact of Roman life from the earliest times. Secondly, the Greek tradition to which Nepos refers in his preface (commending young men who have had numerous lovers) is without a doubt the same Greek custom (*mos Graecorum*) that he mentions in his life of Alcibiades (2.2), according to which Alcibiades was courted by a number of adult male lovers, and these lovers were as freeborn as was Alcibiades himself. Similarly the practice (*consuetudo*) whose origin Cicero locates in Greek gymnasia (*Tusc.* 4.70) is precisely the Greek custom (*mos Graeciae*) to which he refers later in the same treatise (*Tusc.* 5.58) in his discussion of Dionysius of Syracuse. Finally, the gymnasia to which Cicero makes pointed reference were patronized by free men and not by slaves, who were in Athens barred from them by laws attributed to Solon.[13]

No ancient source ever claims that indulgence in or approval of male homoerotic desires or activities *tout court* was learned, borrowed, or imported by Romans from Greece; the only practice that was associated with Greece was the peculiarly Hellenic tradition of relations with freeborn youth. The practice born in the Greek gymnasia to which Cicero refers is not homosexuality but *paiderastia*, the courtship of free youths by older males, and the central issue was status rather than gender. The distinction is crucial, although often blurred or simply disregarded in modern scholarship.[14] If the Greek cultural heritage had included, for example, a tradition of publicly courting other men's wives, and if Romans had displayed an awareness of that tradition, it would be pointless for us to speak of a Roman association between Greece and heterosexuality. Equally groundless is the assumption that Romans understood homosexuality to be Greek.[15]

How "Greek" Was Pederasty?

The wave of Greek influence that swept over Rome in the second and first centuries B.C. effected great changes in both practices and attitudes among Romans, no doubt especially among the aristocracy.[16] In view of the fact that pederasty formed an important part of Greek traditions, it is a reasonable enough supposition that among the results of Greek influence was an increase in the acceptance and practice among Roman aristocrats of romantic relationships with freeborn youth. Indeed, whereas Catullus, writing in 60s and 50s B.C., assumed the persona of a man in love with the freeborn youth Juventius,[17] less than a century earlier a certain Valerius Valentinus had been condemned by public opinion for having written a poem on his relationships with a freeborn boy and a freeborn girl.[18]

But the writer who reports this story, Valerius Maximus, offers no hint to the effect that Valentinus' relationship with the boy was thought to be any more "Greek" than his relationship with the girl, and alongside Catullus' poems on Juventius stand the more famous poems on an affair with the married woman whom he calls Lesbia.[19] Likewise, Aulus Gellius (19.9.10–4) preserves a selection of love poems composed by Valerius Aedituus, Porcius Licinus, and Q. Lutatius Catulus (all of whom were active in the late second and early first centuries B.C.); one of them is addressed to a female and one to a male partner, each with Greek names (Aedituus writes to a Pamphila and Catulus addresses verses to a Theotimus). But the object of Licinus' poetic attention is of unspecified gender, and the imprecision is revealing. All of this love poetry is inspired by Greek models, and all of it has a Greek feel, whether the beloved is male or female. The same-sex, and most likely pederastic, love affair of Catulus' poem is not singled out as being any more indebted to Greek traditions than are the others.

In the previous chapter, it was noted that the work of such other Roman love poets as Horace, Tibullus, Propertius, and Ovid reflects a cultural environment in which men might openly express desire for both boys and girls: here it is worth noting that nowhere do they suggest that one type of erotic experience was more "Greek" in inspiration than the other. Indeed, one poem by Propertius proclaims that his elegies are Greek in form but anchored in Roman realities (3.1.3–4), and that blend characterizes all of his work, whether it is on the subject of Cynthia or of a young man, figured as Hylas, loved by Gallus (1.20). It is interesting to read a poem addressed to Cynthia in which the poet cites as examples of the irresistible (and often destructive) power of love Jupiter's passions for Semele, Io, and Ganymede (2.30.27–32). All three myths are Greek, but the distinction between homosexual and heterosexual is obviously irrelevant, and the Ganymede myth is not represented as being somehow more Greek than the others. That a Roman poet should evoke the myth of Jupiter and Ganymede in a poem dedicated to his girlfriend shows both the extent to which Greek myth was naturalized among Romans and the extent to which Roman poets of love were disinclined to make certain distinctions.

One thing is clear: in this poetry, the joys and heartbreaks of loving a boy have no more and no less to do with Greece than do the joys and heartbreaks of loving a girl. When Martial provides an overview of Roman love poets and the sources of their inspiration (8.73: Propertius and Cynthia, Gallus and Lycoris, Tibullus and Nemesis, Catullus and Lesbia, Ovid and Corinna, Virgil and Alexis), only Virgil's beloved is male, but all of them have Greek pseudonyms; the homoerotic relationship is not singled out as being any more or less Greek than the others.

The persona of a poet like Catullus is flaunting his disregard for traditional standards of sexual behavior, openly proclaiming his love for a freeborn boy and for a married woman. But even those texts that present a more traditional Roman viewpoint on pederastic relationships (by, for example, condemning them as instances of *stuprum*) avoid representing such relationships as being in any way more Greek than other illicit sexual practices. A passage from Polybius cited in chapter 1, in which the Greek historian describes what he sees as a crucial turning point in the development of Roman public morality in the second century B.C., is especially illuminating:

οἱ μὲν γὰρ εἰς ἐρωμένους τῶν νέων, οἱ δ᾽ εἰς ἑταίρας ἐξεκέχυντο, πολλοὶ δ᾽ εἰς ἀκροάματα καὶ πότους καὶ τὴν ἐν τούτοις πολυτέλειαν, ταχέως ἡρπακότες ἐν τῷ Περσικῷ πολέμῳ τὴν τῶν Ἑλλήνων εἰς τοῦτο τὸ μέρος εὐχέρειαν. (Polyb. 31.25.4)

For some of the young men had given themselves over to boyfriends, others to female prostitutes, and many to musical entertainments and drinking parties and the extravagance that goes along with them, having swiftly adopted the permissiveness of the Greeks in this regard during the war with Perseus.

The "Greek permissiveness" to which Polybius alludes gave rise to indulgence in expensive prostitutes, both male and female,[20] along with luxurious drinking parties. Hellenism is here evoked as a figure not for the acceptance of pederasty but for the kind of self-indulgence and extravagance that led young Romans to pay as much as a talent for boy prostitutes, thereby provoking the ire of Cato the Censor:

καὶ τηλικαύτη τις ἐνεπεπτώκει περὶ τὰ τοιαῦτα τῶν ἔργων ἀκρασία τοῖς νέοις ὥστε πολλοὺς μὲν ἐρώμενον ἠγορακέναι ταλάντου, πολλοὺς δὲ ταρίχου Ποντικοῦ κεράμιον τριακοσίων δραχμῶν. ἐφ᾽ οἷς καὶ Μάρκος ἀγανακτῶν εἶπέ ποτε πρὸς τὸν δῆμον ὅτι μάλιστ᾽ ἂν κατίδοιεν τὴν ἐπὶ τὸ χεῖρον προκοπὴν τῆς πολιτείας ἐκ τούτων, ὅταν πωλούμενοι πλεῖον εὑρίσκωσιν οἱ μὲν εὐπρεπεῖς παῖδες τῶν ἀγρῶν, τὰ δὲ κεράμια τοῦ ταρίχου τῶν ζευγηλατῶν. (Polyb. 31.25.5)

So great a lack of self-control with regard to such things had fallen upon the young men that many of them bought a boyfriend for a talent, or a jar of smoked fish from the Black Sea for three hundred drachmas. Greatly upset at this, Cato once said before the people that they could most clearly perceive the country's turn for the worse from these events, when pretty boys fetched more on the market than fields, jars of smoked fish more than ox-drivers.

Other Greek writers describing this incident specify the object of Cato's displeasure: Plutarch observes that Cato was out to "attack extravagance" and Diodorus says that Cato was launching an assault on the luxurious lifestyle that increasingly took hold of Rome, while Athenaeus reports that Cato complained of the importation of "foreign luxury" into Rome.[21] To use Athenaeus' terms, what Cato saw as foreign (that is, Greek) was neither homosexuality nor pederasty but the luxury exemplified by indulgence in expensive delicacies, boy prostitutes, female prostitutes, and the like.[22] Neither Cato nor the later writers describing his reaction mention pederasty in the strict sense of the term (relations with freeborn boys), some of them even fail to mention boys, and the use of costly male prostitutes is cited as only one among several characteristics of the "Greek permissiveness" that gradually took hold among philhellenizing Romans.[23]

Another report of Cato's attacks on the increasingly luxurious lifestyles of the Romans of his day has him pointing a finger in the direction of Greece and Asia, and even sounding the theme of *Graecia capta*, but we look in vain for any specific reference to pederasty.[24] Indeed, among Roman writers who describe the influx of luxury from the East in the second century B.C., some make no reference to sexual issues (focusing instead on things like furniture and fancy chefs),[25] but even those who do so fail to focus on pederasty. Sallust, for example, writes of *stuprum* in general and two particularly outrageous embodiments of the offense: men playing the receptive role in intercourse, and women being free with their favors.[26]

In his second Catilinarian, delivered to an assembly of the Roman people in 63 B.C., Cicero condemns Catiline as a lover of freeborn youth:

> iam vero quae tanta umquam in ullo iuventutis inlecebra fuit quanta in illo? qui alios ipse amabat turpissime, aliorum amori flagitiosissime serviebat, aliis fructum libidinum, aliis mortem parentum non modo impellendo verum etiam adiuvando pollicebatur.
> (Cic. *Cat.* 2.8)

> Has there ever been so great an enticement for young men as there is in him? He himself loved some of them most disgracefully; served the love of others most shamefully; promised to some the fulfillment of their lusts, to others their parents' death—not only encouraging them but also assisting them.

While the consul's scandalized words convey an imposing sense of moral outrage, he does not point a finger at "Greek custom." Similarly, various Roman allusions to the wartime rape of freeborn boys, girls, and women (see chapter 3) make no attempt to single out the rape of young men as having any special relationship to "Greek ways." When Valerius Maximus narrates a series of incidents illustrating the value placed by Roman morality on the sexual integrity (*pudicitia*) of the freeborn of both sexes, several of these incidents involve sexual relations between men and freeborn youth (e.g., 6.1.7, 6.1.10), but nowhere does Valerius allude to the corrupting influence of Greece. Likewise, when Livy writes of the Bacchanalian scandal of 186 B.C. (39.8–19), he portrays Roman anxiety concerning the initiation of young men under twenty years of age by means of sexual penetration, and xenophobia contributes a great deal to the outrage and anxiety that Livy describes. But the historian sees no link between the two factors: the anti-Greek sentiment in his account is directed not toward the sexual initiation of young men but toward the importation of foreign religious rites.[27] One scholar claims that "what is offered as the principle [*sic*] charge, somewhat muffled for decency's sake, was aimed against male homosexuality which characterized the meetings and had become their main purpose of recent years";[28] but this is an untenable interpretation. The sexual exploitation of young male initiates is never singled out as an aspect of the cult's foreignness any more than is the same exploitation of female initiates. All of it is illicit and disgraceful behavior (*stuprum*), none of it particularly Greek.[29] Indeed, over the years the Bacchanalia became a symbol for a drunken licentiousness antithetical to Roman traditions of discipline and austerity, but they do not seem to have had any particular association with illicit sexual practices between males.[30]

Tacitus tells of how the emperor Tiberius, freed from the restraining influence of his mother Livia upon her death in A.D. 29, openly attacked his adopted grandson, Germanicus' son Nero Caesar, accusing him in a letter not of sedition but of "love affairs with young men and unchastity".[31] But Tiberius did not make any arguments to the effect that his grandson's alleged pursuit of young men was somehow un-Roman. We may contrast this with the same emperor's reaction to a proposal made seven years earlier that a decree proclaiming special honors for Nero Caesar's brother Drusus be engraved in the Senate House in gold lettering: according to Tacitus, Tiberius condemned the proposal as being "not in accordance with ancestral traditions."[32] Love affairs with young men could equally have been described as foreign or *contra patrium morem*, but Tiberius seems not to have found it useful to deploy that rhetoric.

The complex attitudes toward Greeks and Greek culture evident in Roman texts have been the subject of a good deal of scholarly work,[33] and one clear fact that emerges from those studies is that preeminent among the biased beliefs expressed by Roman writers was a conviction that Greeks were excessively self-indulgent and inordinately fond of a life of luxury. One might have expected Roman writers to make use of pederasty as a major weapon in their assault against Greek cultural traditions, but they quite noticeably fail to do so. While we might conjecture that the influence of Greek culture encouraged an increased tolerance of pederastic relationships, ancient writers themselves give us little reason to do so, for they most often associate the influence of Hellenism with an increased tolerance of traditionally discouraged heterosexual practices, such as the poetic celebration of adulterous affairs or a luxurious overindulgence in female prostitutes. Thus the verb *graecari* ("to act like a Greek") and its compounds, far from suggesting pederasty, evoke a hedonistic indulgence in food, drink, and love, often in the company of female prostitutes; Festus, for example, defines *pergraecari* as "being devoted to banquets and drinking-parties."[34] Likewise, in one after another condemnation of Greek decadence we hear not of pederasty but of a general *levitas*, hedonism, or luxuriousness.[35] Roman writers often use the contemptuous diminutive *Graeculi* to belittle Greeks, but references to these frivolous, shifty, pleasure-loving "Greeklings" never imply that pederastic pursuits were one of their defining characteristics.[36] The unflattering diminutive was used as a nickname for the emperor Hadrian, famous for his philhellenic tastes and, indeed, for the lavish honors he bestowed upon his beloved Antinous after his death (see chapter 1). But the ancient biography informing us that Hadrian was called *Graeculus* connects the nickname not with his fondness for boys but rather with his devotion to Greek studies in general; there is no mention of Antinous.[37] Juvenal's third satire is an especially prodigious monument in the history of Roman bigotry, but even here pederasty is not singled out as a Greek vice. Rather, we read of their suspect versatility (3.73–80), their talents for flattery, acting, and toadying (3.86–108), and their selfish monopoly of patrons to the detriment of native Romans (3.119–25). In the midst of this catalogue Juvenal does cite Greek men's sexual behavior (3.109–12), yet the outstanding characteristic of the *Graeculus* is not his interest in young men but rather his uncontrolled sexual appetite: he will pounce on matron and maiden, bridegroom and son, or, failing these outlets, even his patron's grandmother.[38] On another occasion Juvenal refers to those who "make love in Greek" (*concumbunt Graece*), but these are women who use Greek terms of endearment in order to sound sexy to men.[39]

Even Roman images of the gymnasia and palaestrae, which, as we have seen, could be associated with pederastic pursuits, in fact fail to place emphasis on pederasty as un-Roman or characteristically Greek. It is true that one surviving source speaks of a Roman identification of pederasty as one sign of the general inferiority of Greek culture (ironically enough, this was a Greek writer describing Roman traditions). According to Plutarch, Romans considered the gymnasia and palaestrae to be the primary source of Greek weakness:

τὸ γὰρ ξηραλοιφεῖν ὑφεωρῶντο Ῥωμαῖοι σφόδρα, καὶ τοῖς Ἕλλησιν οἴονται μηδὲν οὕτως αἴτιον δουλείας γεγονέναι καὶ μαλακίας ὡς τὰ γυμνάσια καὶ τὰς παλαίστρας, πολὺν ἄλυν καὶ σχολὴν ἐντεκούσας ταῖς πόλεσι καὶ κακοσχολίαν καὶ τὸ παιδεραστεῖν καὶ τὸ διαφθείρειν τὰ σώματα τῶν νέων ὕπνοις καὶ περιπάτοις καὶ κινήσεσιν εὐρύθμοις καὶ διαίταις ἀκρίβεσιν, ὑφ' ὧν ἔλαθον ἐκρυέντες τῶν ὅπλων καὶ ἀγαπήσαντες ἀνθ' ὁπλιτῶν καὶ ἱππέων ἀγαθῶν εὐτράπελοι καὶ παλαιστρῖται καὶ καλοὶ λέγεσθαι. (Plut. *Rom. Ques.* 40.274D)

The Romans used to be very suspicious of anointing, and they believe that nothing has been as responsible for the slavery and softness of the Greeks as the gymnasia and palaestrae, which give rise to a great deal of ennui and idleness, mischief, pederasty, and the ruin of young men's bodies by sleeping, strolling about, performing rhythmic exercises, and following strict diets. Influenced by these things, they have unconsciously left behind their weapons and prefer to be called not good warriors and knights, but rather nimble, beautiful athletes.

But the unemphatic position of the reference to pederasty in the midst of a catalogue of enervating practices associated with the gymnasia is significant. The overall thrust of the passage is aimed not at pederasty as a corrupt, foreign sexual practice but rather at a self-indulgent method of training young men that is hardly conducive to the kind of endurance engendered by the tough life of farming and soldiery so idolized by traditionalist Romans, and that could not compare to traditional Roman exercises of swimming, horseback riding, and javelin throwing.[40] Pederasty is merely one symptom among many of a deeper disorder.

Scholars speak of a Roman suspicion of the nudity associated with Greek gymnasia, sometimes implicitly connecting it to anxieties concerning pederasty; one commentator has noted that "the Romans regarded them as hot-beds of immorality because nudity was usual in them."[41] But one thing is clear: this distrust of gymnasia can hardly have stemmed from homophobic anxieties. Plutarch's biography of Cato the Elder reports that Cato observed that his son's presence encouraged him to speak as decently as if he were in the presence of Vestal Virgins, and that he refused to bathe with his son. Plutarch adds that this was a tradition among Romans of old, such that even fathers-in-law avoided bathing with their sons-in-law. Clearly, the concern evident in the behavior of Cato and his compatriots cannot be described as homophobic. On the one hand, they were not worried about the potential for sexual relations between fathers and sons; on the other hand, Plutarch adds that once this traditional restriction on nudity was relaxed under

Greek influence, the Romans went even further than the Greeks, bathing in the presence of women as well.[42] The resistance among traditional Romans to nudity (apparently an uphill battle) was not connected to questions of acceptable or unacceptable sexual desires but rather to more general questions of decent behavior among Roman citizens. We recall the line from Ennius: "it is the beginning of disgrace to strip bodies amongst citizens" (Cic. *Tusc.* 4.70).

When in A.D. 60 Nero instituted Greek-style stage competitions at Rome, he met with some resistance, and Tacitus' summary of the objections implies a connection between Greek gymnasia and "disgraceful love affairs." The passage deserves quotation at length, for the reference to these love affairs needs to be put in its context:

> spectaculorum quidem antiquitas servaretur, quotiens praetores ederent, nulla cuiquam civium necessitate certandi. ceterum abolitos paulatim patrios mores funditus everti per accitam lasciviam, ut quod usquam corrumpi et corrumpere queat in urbe visatur, degeneretque studiis externis iuventus, gymnasia et otia et turpes amores exercendo, principe et senatu auctoribus, qui non modo licentiam vitiis permiserint, sed vim adhibeant ut proceres Romani specie orationum et carminum scaena polluantur. quid superesse nisi ut corpora quoque nudent et caestus adsumant easque pugnas pro militia et armis meditentur? an iustitiam auctum iri et decurias equitum egregium iudicandi munus expleturos, si fractos sonos et dulcedinem vocum perite audissent? noctes quoque dedecori adiectas ne quod tempus pudori relinquatur, sed coetu promiscuo, quod perditissimus quisque per diem concupiverit, per tenebras audeat.
>
> (Tac. *Ann.* 14.20)

Let the old-fashioned practice with regard to spectacles be maintained, they argued, whenever the praetors put on shows; no citizen should be compelled to compete. But now ancestral customs, gradually abandoned, were being completely overturned by an imported licentiousness, so that whatever was capable of corrupting or being corrupted could now be seen in the city, and the young men were becoming degenerate in their foreign pursuits, indulging in the gymnasia and idleness and disgraceful love affairs. And this was happening with the blessing of the emperor and the Senate, who not only had granted permission for vice but were even forcing Roman noblemen to be polluted by the stage under the pretext of oratory and poetry. What next? Would they strip their bodies, too, and pick up boxing gloves, considering combat of that sort to be a substitute for military service? Did they really think that justice would be increased and the members of the equestrian order would fulfill their well-known duty as jurors if they honed their skills by listening to affected sounds and sweet voices? Nighttime, too, they argued, was added to the disgrace, so that no time of day might be left safe for decency; instead, whatever the most corrupt people desired during the day they could dare to undertake at night in a mixed gathering.

We might view this passage in light of Plutarch's comments on Roman views on the gymnasia and as a result understand these love affairs to be pederastic.[43] If so, again we observe the subordinate role that pederasty plays in the argument, and that the emphasis is placed, as in Plutarch, less on issues of sexual behavior per se and more on questions of discipline and dignity commensurate with status: compare Tacitus' *otia* ("leisurely activities") with Plutarch's μαλακία ("softness").[44] While traditionalists may have objected to pederastic affairs as "disgraceful," the erotic pursuits of decadent young men are only a side issue. The real issue here is the Roman bias against stage performance, a bias that Nero himself shockingly disregarded.[45] Neither is the condemnation of pederastic affairs apparently reported here significantly harsher than other moralizing responses to illicit sexual practices; the phrase *turpis amor*, for example, is used by other writers to describe disgraceful affairs between men and women.[46]

Thus it would be imprecise and indeed misleading to describe Roman suspicions of Greek gymnasia and of male nudity as deriving from a xenophobic, let alone homophobic, anxiety regarding pederastic pursuits. Moreover, other practices and values held to be Greek provoked a more vocal resistance among Romans. In this regard Nepos' discussion of Greek cultural traditions is especially illuminating. First, it is important to note that he expects that his Roman readership will not necessarily be thoroughly acquainted with Greek literature and that they will approach his biographies of Greeks with a pronounced Roman bias. They may well be surprised, for example, at the prominence given to musical training among Greeks:

> non dubito fore plerosque, Attice, qui hoc genus scripturae leve et non satis dignum summorum virorum personis iudicent, cum relatum legent quis musicam docuerit Epaminondam, aut in eius virtutibus commemorari, saltasse eum commode scienterque tibiis cantasse. sed hi erunt fere qui expertes litterarum Graecarum nihil rectum, nisi quod ipsorum moribus conveniat, putabunt. hi si didicerint non eadem omnibus esse honesta atque turpia, sed omnia maiorum institutis iudicari, non admirabuntur nos in Graiorum virtutibus exponendis mores eorum secutos. (Nepos, pr. 1–3)

> Atticus, I am sure that there will be many who consider this type of writing to be trivial and unworthy of the image of great men, when they read the name of Epaminondas' music teacher or when they see mentioned among his virtues the fact that he danced well and skillfully sang to the accompaniment of the flute. But these will likely be readers who have no experience of Greek literature and who consider nothing to be right except what is in accordance with their own customs. If these people learn that the same things are not considered honorable or disgraceful by everyone, but rather that everything is judged by the standards of ancestral tradition, they will not be surprised that when writing about the virtues of Greek men I have followed their own customs.

Having opened his work with this forceful expression of his commitment to cultural relativism, how does Nepos handle Greek pederastic traditions? Far from passing over the custom in a shocked or censorious silence, he includes it, as we have seen, in his prefatory discussion as one among several Greek customs[47] and later makes incidental reference to the practice in his biographies of Pausanias and Alcibiades.[48] Nepos' casual treatment of this Greek custom stands in marked contrast to his discussion of music and dancing. It is precisely the value placed on these very pursuits that provides the occasion for the sermon on cultural relativism just quoted, and he insistently reasserts this doctrine in the first sentence of his biography of Epaminondas:

de hoc priusquam scribimus, haec praecipienda videntur lectoribus, ne alienos mores ad suos referant, neve ea, quae ipsis leviora sunt, pari modo apud ceteros fuisse arbitrentur. (Nepos, *Epam.* 1.1)

Before I write about this man, it seems to me that I ought to remind my readers that they should not compare foreign customs to their own, and that they should not imagine that what is trivial to them is seen the same way by other people.

In both passages Nepos adopts a preachy tone that never characterizes his allusions to pederastic relationships. Clearly he expects his Roman readership to be more troubled by Greek mores concerning the role of music and dance in the education of the upper classes than by Hellenic traditions of pederasty. Two other Greek traditions that Nepos feels obliged to explain to his readership are the value placed on *scribae* (*Eumenes* 1.5) and the Athenian tradition of allowing marriage between half-brother and half-sister (pr. 4, *Cimon* 1.2); it is instructive to contrast his careful explanation of the latter with his passing reference to pederasty at *Alcibiades* 2.2–3.[49]

In sum, ancient writers, both Greek and Roman, display no preoccupation with pederasty as a distinguishing characteristic of Greek culture or as a particularly alien threat to Roman moral traditions. Eva Cantarella claims that "for the Romans, pederasty was 'the Greek vice,'" but no such phrase is attested in any ancient source.[50] Instead, when *vitium* is attributed to Greeks, we read not of pederasty but of such things as stylistic flaws or the unnecessary and luxurious uses to which that decadent nation has put such gifts of nature as olive oil.[51] Neither do the surviving texts preserve any phrase like "Greek love."[52] Even more neutral phrases like "Greek custom" or "the Greek way" (*mos Graeciae, mos Graecorum*) are never deployed as a code for pederasty, instead being used to describe a wide variety of specifically Greek practices, ranging from the habit of drinking a toast at symposia, to the exclusion of honorable women from dinner parties, to the use of olive branches in supplication, to the holding of deliberations in theaters, to certain types of tombs, torture devices, and games, to stylistic and orthographical conventions such as the use of double negatives or writing double consonants.[53] This lack of focus on pederasty as a characteristically Greek practice can easily be related to the absence among the writers and readers of Roman texts of an impulse to condemn homosexual behavior in and of itself. As a result, there was little incentive for Roman writers to represent pederasty, simply because it was homosexual, either as essentially distinct from any other kind of *stuprum* or as an outlandish practice. "Greek love" is a modern invention.

The Appeal of Youth

One important effect of Greek pederastic traditions was a tendency to dichotomize the publicly acceptable objects of male desire not into females and males generally but specifically into women and boys.[54] As discussed in chapter 1, the same tendency characterizes many Roman sources, and there was a related inclination to privilege certain physical traits specific to male adolescence, most outstandingly the absence of fully developed hair on the face and body. The beardless "pinup boys" so prevalent in Attic vase-painting are blessed with a smooth, sleek muscularity that clearly appealed to the tastes of the Athenian male public.[55] Their Roman counterparts had a taste for smooth young bodies as well. I earlier cited a verse from Novius' Atellan farce *Exodium* that takes a practical view of the advantages of hairless buttocks;[56] more generally, the adjective *glaber* ("hairless") was used to describe young men, usually slaves, who were considered sexually attractive because of their smoothness, whether natural or artificially attained by depilation. In his poem on the wedding of Manlius Torquatus, Catullus notes that the bridegroom has shown a marked penchant for such partners: "Perfumed husband, they say you have a hard time keeping your hands off your hairless boys."[57] Seneca, expressing a Stoic disgust at the ways in which Roman men mistreat and abuse their slaves, makes reference to a man who enjoys the company of his *glaber*—whose hairlessness, however, represents an artificial attempt to prolong the slave-boy's youthfulness.[58] And we saw in chapter 1 that the imperial household in the time of Augustus and Tiberius included slaves called *glabri*.

Consequently, just as in the Greek textual tradition, the arrival of a full beard often appears in Roman texts as a distinct signifier: once a boy grows a full beard, he is no longer a boy but a man and thus no longer generally desirable to other men. Such an understanding informs Horace's ode on the cruel young Ligurinus (4.10), as it also does two charming epigrams by Martial on the subject of the relationship between his friend, the centurion Aulus Pudens, and the latter's slave-boy Encolpos.[59] Indeed, there is an assumption pervading the Roman sources that beardless young men, blessed with the "flower of youth" (*flos aetatis*), stand at the acme of physical desirability.[60] This period was generally held to end with the arrival of the full beard, and the ceremony that came to be observed to mark that event (the *depositio barbae*, in which clippings from the beard were offered to the gods) seems most often to have been held in the twentieth year or later.[61] The composer of an epitaph for a young man who died in his twenty-first year used the fact that he had not yet grown his full beard to especially poignant effect:

Laet[i]lio C. [f.] Ga[ll]o de[c(urioni)] qui vixit annos XX m. VII d. VII Laetilia T. f. Custa filio carissimo atq(ue) pient(issimo) mater infel[ix]

Dum c[u]pidus i[u]venis urbem voluisse videre,
inde regrediens incidi febribus acris.
at pres[s]us graviter omisi cun flore i[u]vent[a]m,
quoniam [in]iqua meam sic fata voca[ru]nt,
intonsamque tuli [in ipso fu]nere barbam
infelix nec potui p[e]rfer[r]e vota meorum.
f]unere acerbo iace[o] sedibus istis,
et misera mater abet in corde dolorem,
cottidie fletus dat, et in pectore palmas. (*CLE* 629 = *CIL* 5.8652)

Laetilia Custa, daughter of Titus, unhappy mother, [dedicates this] to her most beloved and dutiful son, . . . Laetilius Gallus, son of Gaius, the *decurio*, who lived twenty years, seven months, and seven days.

Eager to see the city as a young man, I fell victim to a harsh fever as I was coming back. Thus overwhelmed, I lost my youth together with its flower, since my unjust fates have thus called me, and I bore an unshaven beard when I met my death, nor was I able to fulfill my family's wishes. I lie in this resting-place in bitter death, and my wretched mother has pain in her heart, weeps daily, and [has] her hands on her breast.

The language of flowering youth frequently appears in funerary inscriptions for young men who died in their teenage years or even in their early twenties; the imagery obviously had a broad appeal.[62] One such epitaph is noteworthy for its evocation of youthful beauty among other traditional Roman virtues:

> Hic Aquilae cineres miserabilis urna sepultos
>   contegit et fatis exproperata nimis.
> occidit infelix coepto modo flore iuventae,
>   quem finit annus septimus et decimus.
> formonsus frugi doctus pius a patre maesto
>   accepit tumulos quos dare debuerat. (*CLE* 1151 = *CIL* 11.3163)

Here a pitiful urn, too quickly brought by the fates, houses the buried ashes of Aquila. Unhappy, he died when the flower of his youth had just begun; his seventeenth year brought him to an end. He was beautiful, decent, learned, and dutiful, and he received from his grieving father the tomb that he ought to have given him.

Another evidently prevalent assumption was that as long as young men enjoyed the flower of youth they were the most vulnerable, even susceptible, to men's sexual advances. In Livy's narrative of the Bacchanalian scandal of 186 B.C., the informant Hispala explains to the consul that for the preceding two years, no one over the age of twenty had been initiated because young men of that age were susceptible to being led astray,[63] and her language (*stupri patientes*) has the clear implication that they were sexually penetrated in the initiatory rites. When the consul addresses the people, he obliquely cites this practice, noting the young men's age with a show of pity and horror:

> si quibus aetatibus initientur mares sciatis, non misereat vos eorum solum, sed etiam pudeat. hoc sacramento initiatos iuvenes milites faciendos censetis, Quirites? (Livy 39.15.13)

If you were to know at what ages the males are initiated, you would not only have pity on them but you would be ashamed as well. Citizens, is it your judgment that young men initiated with this oath should be made soldiers?

The reference to their age is calculated. Cicero makes similar rhetorical use of a young man's age in the course of his acerbic attack on Clodius' adoption by the twenty-year-old Fonteius, broadly hinting that Clodius was the younger man's lover:

> nego istam adoptionem pontificio iure esse factam: primum quod eae vestrae sunt aetates ut is qui te adoptavit vel fili tibi loco per aetatem esse potuerit, vel eo quo fuit.
>   (Cic. *Dom.* 36)[64]

> I assert that this adoption was not performed in accordance with pontifical law: first, because your respective ages are such that the man who adopted you could, on account of his age, be related to you either as a son or as he actually was related to you.

A mere allusion to Fonteius' youth suffices to suggest a perversion of roles: that Clodius was his adoptive father's older lover. In his biography of the playwright Terence, Suetonius reports rumors to the effect that the handsome young playwright had used his physical charms as a means of gaining an entrée into the upper circles of Roman society, in particular Scipio Aemilianus and his friend Laelius. But he also reports that at least one writer gave no credence to those rumors, because he believed that Terence was actually older than either Scipio or Laelius. That consideration alone was apparently enough for this writer to rule out any erotic entanglements.[65]

It is in light of such assumptions regarding the vulnerability of male adolescence that oratorical references to a man's misspent youth (*aetas* or *pueritia*) take on a special point.[66] The first part of Cicero's defense of Caelius is an extended effort to defend his handsome young client's reputation for sexual integrity (*pudicitia*) from his sixteenth to nineteenth years[67]—in other words, to show that he was not the sort of youth as the one attacked by Scipio Aemilianus, reclining at banquets with his male lover, as fond of wine as he was of men (see chapter 1). Juvenal makes the preconception baldly explicit when he suggests that parents might want to think twice about praying for a beautiful son:

> filius autem
> corporis egregii miseros trepidosque parentes
> semper habet: rara est adeo concordia formae
> atque pudicitiae. (Juv. 10.295–8)

> But a son blessed with a remarkable body always has wretched, fearful parents: so rare a thing it is to find beauty and chastity joined together.

He goes on to spell out the implications: a beautiful boy runs the risk of being castrated or raped, and may well end up becoming an adulterer, with all the risks that that entails (10.298–345).

In such an environment, there was reasonably enough some concern about finding men suitable for teaching Roman youths who were at the ripest and most alluring time of life. When, for example, Pliny responds to his friend Corellia Hispulla's request for a recommendation for someone to tutor her adolescent son, he makes a special point of observing the youth's beauty and the dangers that it might entail:

> adest enim adulescenti nostro cum ceteris naturae fortunaeque dotibus eximia corporis pulchritudo, cui in hoc lubrico aetatis non praeceptor modo sed custos etiam rectorque quaerendus est. videor ergo demonstrare tibi posse Iulium Genitorem.
>
> (Plin. *Epist*. 3.3.4)

> Indeed, our young man is endowed not only with the gifts of nature and fortune but also with an outstanding physical beauty, and at this slippery point in his life we need

to find him not only an instructor but a guardian and guide. Consequently I believe I can recommend Julius Genitor to you.

Not only teachers but also their older classmates posed a potential threat to beautiful boys. In language as decorous as Pliny's, Quintilian recommends segregation:

> pueros adulescentibus permixtos sedere non placet mihi. nam etiamsi vir talis, qualem esse oportet studiis moribusque praepositum, modestam habere potest etiam iuventutem, tamen vel infirmitas a robustioribus separanda est, et carendum non solum crimine turpitudinis verum etiam suspicione. (Quint. *I.O.* 2.2.14)[68]

> I do not at all recommend that boys sit together with young men. For even if the kind of man who ought to be put in charge of their intellectual pursuits and moral development can keep even the young within the bounds of decency, nonetheless the weak ought to be kept apart from the stronger; and not only should there be no charge of immorality, but there should not even be the suspicion of it.

Quintilian's veiled apprehensions clearly have to do with the fact that some older students might be tempted to take advantage of their younger schoolmates. Juvenal, as usual, does not beat around the bush, writing of teachers who sexually use their male students (the poet once describes a phenomenon that occurs in great quantity as being equal to "the number of students whom Hamillus bends over"),[69] and of sexual horseplay among students.[70] One of Pomponius' plays (*Maccus Virgo*) contains a joke on the same topic: "As he walked by he saw Dossenus in school not respectfully teaching his fellow student but 'scratching' his butt."[71] Underlying all of these texts is the assumption that if young men (Hispala specifies those below twenty years) are placed in potentially compromising situations with men, they are likely to be led astray. Significantly, it is the youths' vulnerability that is held up for comment; older men's desires for them are generally neither questioned nor challenged. Even when Quintilian portrays those desires as worrisome, his tone suggests that they are only to be expected, a normal human weakness in need of policing.

The notion that the years of male adolescence are the most appropriate period for being the object of men's sexual attentions is also reflected by a tendency to deploy the language of boyhood in descriptions of the consummation of those attentions in an act of anal penetration. The basic obscenity denoting the act, *pedicare*, is said to be derived from the Greek *paidika* ("boyfriend"): thus "to do what one does to one's boyfriend" is to anally penetrate.[72] Martial refers to the anal penetration of a woman as *illud puerile* ("that boyish thing," 9.67.3) and to the anal rape of an adulterer as *supplicium puerile* ("the boyish punishment," 2.60.2); the narrator in Apuleius' *Metamorphoses* describes the added pleasure of anal intercourse with a woman as *puerile corollarium* ("the boyish bonus," Apul. *Met.* 3.20). And in three poems of the *Priapea* cited in chapter 1, the god provides a neatly arranged distribution of the punishment that he will so gleefully mete out to those who would steal from his garden: women or girls he will penetrate vaginally; men he will penetrate orally; and boys he will penetrate anally.[73]

Thus we see some distinct overlaps between Greek and Roman traditions: adolescent males are represented as highly desirable sexual objects, their desirability often explicitly being connected with their youth and hairlessness. But while such tastes among Romans must have been influenced to some extent by Greek pederastic traditions, they must also be understood in the context of a general valorization of youth and of young bodies that was connected with an aesthetic preference for smooth bodies and faces; after all, both *puella* ("girl") and *puer* ("boy") could be used to refer to a man's sexual object regardless of his or her actual age, and also to his slave.[74] And these tendencies bear no necessary relationship to Greek influence (consider the comparable valuation placed on youth in the urban culture of seventeenth-century Japan), neither are they restricted to sexual behavior between males. A number of poets allude to women's appreciation of hairless or beardless young men,[75] and Martial describes a certain Chloe as being enamored of a "smooth Lupercus" (*tener Lupercus*); he calls her a *glabraria*.[76] The same poet writes of a certain Labienus, who depilates his chest, legs, arms, and pubic region to please his girlfriend (2.62). Statius imagines Venus proclaiming that Domitian's beloved eunuch, Earinos, will surpass in his beauty some legendarily gorgeous young men: Endymion, Attis, Narcissus, and Hylas—the first two of whom were loved by goddesses.[77] And the fabulist Hyginus includes all four of these in a list of "most beautiful ephebes" and their lovers, both male and female.[78] It is interesting to note in this regard Juvenal's observation that being a gladiator turns a man into a Hyacinth in women's eyes: there was apparently nothing anomalous in citing Apollo's boyfriend as archetype for a beautiful, desirable young man pursued by women. In the same way an old woman in Apuleius' *Metamorphoses* hyperbolically describes her male lover as her "dear Endymion" and her "Catamitus," the latter (as discussed in chapter 1) being another form for Ganymede's name.[79]

It seems, in short, that the bodies of smooth young men were generally thought to be attractive to men and women alike, and ancient texts display no inclination to separate out the pederastic erotic configurations involving such young men from the heterosexual ones or to identify the former as being more Greek than the latter.

Mature Males as Sexual Objects

Obviously there was a premium placed by Roman culture on youthful beauty, both male and female. But I have suggested that this tendency need not be related to the influence of Greek pederastic traditions. In fact, since Rome lacked a pederastic tradition encouraging the courtship of freeborn adolescent males, one might expect to find in the sources slightly less pressure to dichotomize men's erotic objects into women and boys, and less of a tendency to focus specifically on boys as the only acceptable male objects of men's phallic desires, than we find in the Greek sources. We have already seen in chapter 1 that Roman men inherited a cultural patrimony that permitted, even encouraged, them to make sexual use of their slaves of whichever sex: might these not also be of any age? Certainly, while Greek men's cultural inheritance allowed, even encouraged them to pursue romantic relationships with freeborn boys, Roman men's upbringing predisposed them to seeing anyone—girl or woman, boy or man—as an object that might potentially be subordinated to their phallic dominion. Again the figure of Priapus is instructive, and his aggressively penetrative stance (see chapter 1) includes a suggestive point of divergence between Greek and Roman traditions. Priapus will indiscriminately inflict his phallic punishment on women, boys, and men, even bearded ones.[80] The allusions to Roman men who followed in Priapus' footsteps in this regard are fairly neutral in tone, presumably because, although their partners were no longer in the hairless bloom of youth, these men were still observing the prime directive of masculinity by seeking to penetrate their partners.

The scenes from Plautine comedy to which we earlier alluded, where the sexual subjugation of slaves fuels slapstick humor, sometimes raise the possibility that a lustful master might make an advance on a male slave even after he is no longer in the bloom of youth. This notion forms the raw material for a scene in the *Casina* that is particularly revealing not least because it shows a number of signs of being strictly Plautine material, an expansion upon the Greek original (Diphilos' *Kleroumenoi*, now lost to us) that spoke to the prejudices and expectations of a Roman audience. In this scene, the slave Chalinus, working for his master's wife, spies upon a meeting between his master Lysidamus and his fellow-slave Olympio, who has been helping his master obtain the beautiful slave-girl Casina. Olympio ingratiates himself to Lysidamus:

> OL. ut tibi ego inventus sum opsequens! quod maxume
> cupiebas, eiius copiam feci tibi.
> erit hodie tecum quod amas clam uxorem. (Plaut. *Cas*. 449–51)

> How obliging I've turned out to be to you! I've given you the means to obtain what you wanted most. Today you'll have what you love, and your wife will have no idea.

Suddenly, though, the master expresses his desire not for Casina but for Olympio himself, and Chalinus delivers hilarious asides to the audience commenting on this surprising new erotic tension:

> LY. tace.
> ita me di bene ament ut ego vix reprimo labra
> ob istanc rem quin te deosculer, voluptas mea.
> CH. quid, deosculere? quae res? quae voluptas tua?
> credo hercle ecfodere hic volt vesicam vilico.
> OL. ecquid amas nunc me?   LY. immo edepol me quam te minus.
> licetne amplecti te?   CH. quid, 'amplecti'?   OL. licet.
> LY. ut, quia te tango, mel mihi videor lingere!
> OL. ultro te, amator, apage te a dorso meo!
> CH. illuc est, illuc, quod hic hunc fecit vilicum:
> et idem me pridem, quom ei advorsum veneram,
> facere atriensem voluerat sub ianua.
> OL. ut tibi morigerus hodie, ut voluptati fui!
> LY. ut tibi, dum vivam, bene velim plus quam mihi.
> CH. hodie hercle, opinor, hi conturbabunt pedes:
> solet hic barbatos sane sectari senex. (Plaut. *Cas*. 451–66)

> LY. Quiet! So help me God, I can barely restrain my lips from kissing you, my darling, because of that business.   CH. [aside] What do you mean, "kissing"? What "busi-

ness"? What do you mean, your "darling"? By Hercules, I do believe he wants to dig up his bailiff's bladder.   OL. Do you really love me now?   LY. God, yes, more than I love myself. May I embrace you?   CH. [aside] What do you mean, "embrace"?   OL. You may.   LY. Ah! Touching you, it's like I'm licking honey!   OL. Back off, lover boy—off my back!   CH. [aside] *That's* why he made this guy his bailiff! Once when I ran into him, he wanted to make *me* his doorman right there under the door.   OL. How compliant to you I've been today, how delightful!   LY. How, as long as I live, may I wish you as well as I wish myself!   CH. [aside] It seems to me, by Hercules, that these guys are going to lock legs today: the old guy really goes for the bearded ones.

Then, just as suddenly, Lysidamus redirects his desires and the audience's atten-tion to their original object, Casina, and Chalinus exclaims that he now has evi-dence for Lysidamus' designs on Casina:

> LY. ut ego hodie Casinam deosculabor, ut mihi
> bona multa faciam <clam> meam uxorem!   CH. attatae!
> nunc pol ego demum in rectam redii semitam.
> hic ipsus Casinam deperit. habeo viros.
> LY. iam hercle amplexari, iam osculari gestio. (Plaut. *Cas.* 467–71)

> LY. Ah, how I'll kiss Casina today! How I'll do all sorts of nice things without my wife's knowing it.   CH. [aside] Aha! Now, finally, I'm back on the right track. The master himself is dying for Casina. I've got them!   LY. Now, by Hercules, I'm really hot to hold her, to kiss her.

And so the scene continues on its way, as if the sexual horseplay between master and male slave had never occurred—or, rather, as if it had been inserted by Plautus for the sake of a few laughs from his Roman audience. Certainly it comes out of nowhere, since the overriding theme of the scene and indeed the play is Lysidamus' passion for Casina and his machinations to obtain her. There are, moreover, some textual signs of Plautine tinkering with the Greek original. Lysidamus' *tace* (451) abruptly initiates his advance on Olympio, which just as abruptly ends with an exclamation by Chalinus (*attatae*, 468); and at the beginning and end of the inter-vening material Lysidamus closely parallels Olympio's words concerning Casina (*erit hodie tecum quod amas clam uxorem*, 451; *ut mihi / bona multa faciam <clam> meam uxorem*, 467–8). It is also worth noting that, again at the beginning and end of the erotic interlude between master and slave, Lysidamus uses *deosculer* of his desire to kiss Olympio (453) and of his plans for Casina (467). This virtual duplica-tion of words and images constitutes a type of seam that characteristically marks Plautine insertions, just as the abrupt appearance of coarse, farcical humor in the middle of a scene is also a favorite Plautine device.[81] It is suggestive that Chalinus marks the return to the original theme (Lysidamus' passion for Casina) by noting that he is "back on the right track" (*in rectam redii semitam*, 469). This might even be a joking indication by the playwright of his own tinkering with his original: the scene had been brought to a sudden halt for the sake of some broad sexual humor of a type that seems especially to have appealed to Roman audiences and is now just as abruptly brought back on track.

It is my suggestion that what makes the humor of this routine particularly Roman is not only the master-slave dynamic, but also the fact that the slave is no longer a boy. When Chalinus observes that his master Lysidamus "really goes for the bearded ones" (*solet hic barbatos sane sectari senex*, 466) his words hardly express shock or confusion at some unexpected behavior. Rather, by proposition-ing a slave of his, Lysidamus is exhibiting behavior typical of a Roman man—and Chalinus himself should know, since Lysidamus had earlier made a move on him (461–2).[82] Like nearly all of Plautus' characters, Lysidamus is nominally Greek, but I would argue that he acts like a Roman in his open pursuit of his slaves even after they have left behind the golden bloom of youth.

Nor was Lysidamus alone. When two other Plautine characters insinuate, in a scene cited in chapter 1, that the slave Harpax has served as the sheath for his master's sword (*Pseud.* 1180–1), there is no indication that Harpax is a beardless youth. In the *Mercator*, a lustful father has made an advance on his son's girlfriend, and the clever slave Acanthio, clearly no longer a boy, reports this unwelcome development to the son Charinus:

> AC. . . . sed scelestus subigitare occepit.   CH. illamne, opsecro?
> AC. mirum quin me subigitaret. (Plaut. *Merc.* 203–4)
>
> AC. . . . But the damn guy began to feel her up.   CH. Oh, no, *her*?   AC. It's surpris-
> ing he didn't feel *me* up!

The line is a throwaway and quite possibly, like the lines from the *Casina*, a Plautine addition designed to elicit a chuckle from a Roman audience predisposed to imag-ine that a lustful master's desires would hardly limit themselves to boys and women. In a passage from the *Miles Gloriosus* or *Braggart Soldier*, the title character Pyrgopolynices is compared to a stallion who services both males and females, but the comment is provoked when the soldier, having been told that his concubine's sister has recently arrived, lecherously inquires after both the sister and the cap-tain of her ship (*nauclerus*), who is surely no longer a boy:[83]

> PA. . . . sororem germanam adesse et matrem dicito,
> quibu' concomitata recte deveniat domum.
> PY. qui tu scis eas adesse?   PA. quia oculis meis
> vidi hic sororem esse eiius.   PY. convenitne eam?
> PA. convenit.   PY. ecquid fortis visast?   PA. omnia
> vis obtinere.   PY. ubi matrem esse aiebat soror?
> PA. cubare in navi lippam atque oculis turgidis
> nauclerus dixit, qui illas advexit, mihi.
> is ad hos nauclerus hospitio devortitur.
> PY. quid is? ecquid fortis?   PA. abi sis hinc, nam tu quidem
> ad equas fuisti scitus admissarius,
> qui consectare qua maris qua feminas.
> hoc age nunc. (Plaut. *Mil.* 1102–14)
>
> PA. Say that her sister and mother are here and that she can travel home with
> them.   PY. How do you know they're here?   PA. Because I saw her sister here with
> my own eyes. PY.   Has she visited her?   PA. Yep.   PY. So, did she look hot?   PA.

You want everything! PY. Where did the sister say their mother was? PA. The ship captain who brought them here told me that she was lying in bed on the ship, her eyes inflamed and runny. The captain is staying as a guest with these people. PY. What about him? Did *he* look hot? PA. Get out of here! You've sure been a talented stud for the mares, chasing after both males and females. Pay attention now.

The dynamics are worth noting. The slave is ostensibly flattering his master on his masculine potency, but at the same time succeeds in mocking him, just as he later refers to him in an aside to the audience with the unflattering term *moechus* ("womanizer" or "adulterer" [1131]). But he does not single out Pyrgopolynices' expression of lustful interest in the captain as any more or less worthy of teasing than his interest in his concubine's sister. Moreover, as in the scene from the *Casina*, the entire routine bears all the signs of a Plautine addition to the Greek original: it could be entirely excised from the scene without any loss of continuity; the slave's impatient "Pay attention now" (*hoc age nunc*, 1114), like Chalinus' "Now, finally, I'm back on the right track" ("nunc pol ego demum in rectam redii semitam," *Cas.* 469), might signal a return to the original sequence. Fraenkel has even suggested that the soldier's randy interest in both males and females was itself a particularly Roman motif added by the playwright.[84]

Neither is the evidence for this pattern confined to the fictional characters of Roman comedy. Suetonius records that the emperor Galba was particularly fond of men who were "very hard and grown up,"[85] and it is worth noting that Galba's fondness for mature men seems to have caused no eyebrows to rise, presumably because he was observing the two basic protocols of masculine sexual comportment: maintaining the appearance of an appropriately dominating stance with his partners and keeping himself to his own slaves and to prostitutes. Suetonius does observe with an implied tone of reproach that when Galba heard the news of Nero's death from one of his male concubines named Icelus, he welcomed him and kissed him in public, then taking him aside for a sexual encounter;[86] but this seems to be a question of the same traditional standards of decorous public behavior that were violated, in Cato's eyes, by a senator who kissed his wife in front of their daughter (chapter 1). Otherwise, Galba seems to have enjoyed a generally good reputation with regard to his alleged sexual experiences. As seen in chapter 5, Suetonius reports audience reactions to lines from dramas (creative misreadings, we might say) that played off of rumors about Augustus' and Tiberius' sexual experiences (the former as having been penetrated, the latter as being fond of cunnilinctus);[87] in his biography of Galba, he reports a similar incident, but the line that was reinterpreted by the audience was taken to refer not to any of the emperor's alleged sexual experiences but to his infamous stinginess.[88] It is also instructive to contrast the generally negative image of Otho in the ancient sources as an effeminate with Galba's evidently unsullied masculine image (see chapter 4). In short, Suetonius' allusion to Galba's tastes for mature males is far removed in tone from his explicitly moralizing condemnation of Tiberius' shocking sexual use of very young boys (what he did is "wrong to be mentioned or heard, let alone believed"); the comment on Galba is more readily comparable to the biographer's matter-of-fact description of Claudius' exclusive taste for women or Virgil's predilection for boys.[89]

Two Greek writers attribute to well-known Romans this distinctly non-Greek practice of taking their sexual pleasure from males who had passed the bloom of adolescent youth, and the way in which these writers make their point reminds us that such practices were not in accordance with traditional Greek images of proper masculine behavior. Plutarch claims that Sulla loved the actor Metrobios even when the latter was fully adult (ἔξωρος), and that Sulla made no attempt to hide the fact—a comment that thinly veils the suggestion that perhaps he ought to have made the attempt.[90] Dio reports that Seneca was fond of mature males (he, too, uses the word ἔξωροι to describe them), and that he even taught Nero to share his tastes.[91] The same historian puts a speech in the mouth of the British queen Boudicca, who led a rebellion against the Romans in A.D. 61, in which she constructs a contrast between the manly Britons, led by herself, and the decadent, effeminate Romans, led by Nero, who was no man (see further, chapter 4). The Romans, she sneers, live in luxury, drinking unmixed wine, anointing themselves with perfume, taking warm baths, and "sleeping with lads, and out-grown ones at that"; she notes with equal scorn and parallel syntax that the Romans were slaves to an emperor who was "a lyre-player, and a bad one at that."[92] The parallelism suggests that in Boudicca's (and perhaps Dio's) eyes, sleeping with lads and being enslaved to a musician were bad things in themselves, made worse by the fact that the lads were grown up and the musician untalented. But what was wrong with sleeping with lads? It is probably significant that Dio has her speak of Roman men literally sleeping with them (καθεύδοντας) in a phrase immediately preceded by a reference to their luxurious sleeping habits in general (μαλθακῶς κοιμωμένους): in other words, Boudicca's slur is not primarily directed against the fact that Roman men had sexual encounters with lads, or even with out-grown ones, but that they wasted their time lolling about in bed with them, just as they enervated themselves with warm baths, perfumes, and wine.

In any case, these words are mere invective against Roman practices attributed to a barbarian queen by a Greek historian; but Priapus' lack of discrimination in his victims (boys, girls, women, and men will all do), along with the hints offered by the Plautine jokes and by Suetonius' passing allusion to Galba's tastes, suggest that this invective may have been based on some real practices among Romans. Certainly it is reasonable to assume that the Greek writers Plutarch and Dio Cassius frame their allusions to such practices the way they do precisely because those practices would seem alien to their Greek readership. Although erotic configurations other than those in accordance with the pederastic model no doubt did occur among Greek males, the nearly complete absence of such configurations from the surviving textual record constitutes an eloquent silence: the notion that a man might display sexual interest in male partners beyond the bloom of youth is rarely attested in a value-neutral tone in the Greek sources.[93] Whereas Greek men paid homage to the cultural icon of the smooth young man, ripe for courtship and a potential object of romantic and erotic attention, Roman men had before them a different figure, not an object of desire but a source of identification: the god Priapus, prodigiously erect, ready, willing and able to penetrate boy, woman, or man.

Exoleti

A further point of divergence between Greek and Roman sexual ideologies concerns male prostitutes. While the assumption universally informing Greek references to male prostitutes is that they are boys hired to play the receptive role in intercourse,[94] and while, as seen in chapter 1, Roman men made similar use of boys whom they called *pueri meritorii* ("professional boys") or *pueri lenonii* ("pimps' boys"), there is clear evidence that the Roman market also included male prostitutes who were hired to penetrate their male customers, as well as those who, regardless of the sexual role they were expected to play, had passed the bloom of youth. While male prostitutes like these may well have plied their trade in classical Athens, it is significant that their existence is missing from the surviving textual record, whereas the Roman sources mention them quite openly.

There is fairly early evidence for prostitutes who were paid to penetrate their male customers in the fragments of Pomponius' Atellan farce on precisely that theme (the *Prostibulum*, discussed in chapter 1). A play that included such lines as "Right away they'll run up to you, arranged by voting-district, looking for a penis" and "I haven't butt-fucked a single citizen by deceit—only when he himself came up to me begging to bend over"[95] obviously pulled no punches, taking mischievous delight in confronting the audience with the arresting image of Roman citizens begging to be anally penetrated. Nearly two centuries later, Juvenal's ninth satire features a man named Naevolus who services both his patron[96] and his patron's wife, and the text leaves no room for doubt—Naevolus is paid to penetrate:

> an facile et pronum est agere inter viscera penem
> legitimum atque illic hesternae occurrere cenae?
> servus erit minus ille miser qui foderit agrum
> quam dominum. (Juv. 9.43–6)

> Do you think it's an easy or straightforward thing to shove a proper dick into his guts, there to run into yesterday's dinner? The slave who has plowed the field will be less miserable than the one who has plowed the master.

To be sure, Naevolus is no street whore from the Vicus Tuscus, and is perhaps best described not as a prostitute but as an impoverished client who provides sexual services to his patron.[97] Still, Juvenal's language recalls Pomponius on a number of occasions,[98] and it is quite possible that the character of Naevolus may be partially based on Pomponius' prostitute. In any case, Naevolus, who receives financial rewards in exchange for "plowing" men, has a long line of predecessors and cannot have been alone in his own day, and what he does perhaps only metaphorically (prostituting himself) other men must have done quite literally.[99]

Indeed, male prostitutes who had passed the hairless bloom of youth clearly formed a part of the Roman cultural landscape, to such an extent, in fact, that there existed a technical term for them, *exoleti*. A participle of the verb *exolescere* (to grow up, to grow old), *exoletus* literally means "grown up" or "outgrown" and thus can be contrasted with *adolescens*, "growing up."[100] In that sense *exoletus* appears as an adjective throughout the entire range of our source material, from Plautus' reference to an *exoleta virgo* (grown-up maiden)[101] to Firmicus Maternus' reference to a *senex exoletus* (outgrown old man).[102] Seneca uses the term to describe obsolete words (*exoleta verba*), while Quintilian writes of outdated authors (*exoleti auctores*).[103] Plautus twice uses the participle as an adjective modifying the noun *scortum* ("whore"),[104] and it is presumably based on such a usage that the participle came to be used substantively, as a technical term denoting a mature male prostitute.[105] Thus Cicero makes the point that Clodius was always to be found in the company of prostitutes of both sexes (*scorta, exoleti,* and *lupae*); Martial naughtily writes of a married woman who shares a bed and an *exoletus* with her husband; and the biographer of Elagabalus reports that the emperor surrounded himself with prostitutes both male and female (*meretrices* and *exoleti*) as well as pimps and madams.[106]

It has been suggested that the term designated prostitutes who specialized in playing the insertive or penetrative role with their customers, like Pomponius' character.[107] But while some references to *exoleti* do imply that they play the insertive role,[108] others unambiguously cast an *exoletus* in the receptive role. A rhetorician quoted by Seneca the Elder imagines decadent men castrating their *exoleti* "so that they might be suitable for a longer submission to unchastity [*impudicitia*]"— a euphemistic but, as seen in chapter 5, unambiguous way of saying that the *exoleti* will be used as the penetrated partners in phallic acts.[109] It seems, in short, that the term had no specific relation to the question of role. When Tacitus mentions that on one occasion Nero had his *exoleti* arranged by age and by their *scientia libidinum* (that is, their specialty in bed),[110] those specialties surely included a wide variety of sexual pleasures, only some of which involved the use of their penises.

Interestingly, Nero's arrangement of his *exoleti* by age as well as specialty also implies that they represented a certain range in years. Similarly, in the midst of a description of a rich man's luxurious surroundings, Seneca refers to *exoleti* who are marked with the preeminent sign of adolescence: down on their cheeks.[111] Thus it seems that the term *exoletus* could occasionally be used of a male prostitute who was not yet *exoletus* in the literal sense ("grown up"), but still in fact *adolescens*. In these instances the term's euphemistic character is being stretched: as "adult" materials today may include images of adolescents and may be used by adolescents, or as "marital" aids are not always employed in the pursuit of conjugal bliss, so *exoleti* need not always be fully mature men.

In sum, the term *exoletus* denoted a male prostitute past the age of adolescence, who might well be called upon to play the insertive role in penetrative acts with his male clients, but who might just as well also play the receptive role. His distinctive feature was not his sexual specialty, but rather his age, although sometimes even that was not a definitive characteristic, as the word seems in some contexts to refer to a male prostitute of any age.

To be sure, the term *exoletus* makes reference to an ideal standard of youthfulness: *exoleti*, being "outgrown," have passed the prime. And yet the very existence of the term also implies that there was a Roman market for male prostitutes who could no longer be called boys or adolescents, and this constitutes a cultural reality without parallel among ancient Greeks. Perhaps the closest linguistic equivalent for Latin *exoletus* is the Greek adjective *exôros* (ἔξωρος: "past the prime"). Although never used as a calque for the technical term *exoletus*, the word is occasionally used to describe a male as object of men's sexual desires, and it is notable that in those references to Roman men who were involved with postadolescent males that are made by Greek writers, it is precisely the word *exôros* that we find employed in such a way as to establish a tone of surprise.

As we have already seen, Plutarch makes the point that Sulla felt no need to deny his love for Metrobios even when the latter was *exôros* and Dio's Boudicca raises a disdainful eyebrow at the Romans' habit of sleeping with lads who are precisely *exôroi*. Two other instances of the use of the term in a Greek setting illustrate how different the word is from the Latin *exoletus*. In the course of Aeschines' denunciation of Timarchus for having sold his body and spent his inheritance, the orator notes that even when Timarchus had become *exôros*, his corrupt nature continued to govern his behavior: although, in view of his mature age, "reasonably enough, no one was giving him anything anymore," he continued to "desire the same things," namely to be penetrated.[112] In a piece of sexual invective from a courtroom scene between a priest and a man named Thersander in Achilles Tatius, we encounter a contrast between *hôraioi* (ὡραῖοι: boys "in the prime," who are appropriate sexual objects for men) and *exôroi* (ἔξωροι: those "past the prime," who are undesirable and inappropriate sexual objects for men). Having summarized Thersander's youthful man-chasing, the priest turns to the latest stage in his opponent's sexual career:

> ταῦτα μὲν οὖν ὡραῖος ὤν – ἐπεὶ δὲ εἰς ἄνδρας ἧκε, πάντα ἀπεκάλυψεν, ἃ τότε ἀπέκρυπτε. καὶ τοῦ μὲν ἄλλου σώματος ἔξωρος γενόμενος ἠμέλησε, μόνην δὲ τὴν γλῶτταν εἰς ἀσέλγειαν ἀκονᾷ καὶ τῷ στόματι χρῆται πρὸς ἀναισχυντίαν, ὑβρίζων πάντας, ἐπὶ τῶν προσώπων φέρων τὴν ἀναίδειαν, ὃς οὐκ ᾐδέσθη τὸν ὑφ᾽ ὑμῶν ἱεροσύνῃ τετιμημένον οὕτως ἀπαιδεύτως βλασφημεῖν ὑμῶν ἐναντίον. (Ach. Tat. 8.9.5)

> Now, all of that was while he was blessed with the beauty of youth ["while he was *hôraios*"]. But when he became a man, he revealed everything that he had previously kept concealed. Having become too old [*exôros*] with regard to the rest of his body, he no longer took care of it, now sharpening only his tongue for licentiousness and making use of his mouth for disgraceful purposes, insulting everyone, displaying his shamelessness on his face. Why, he was not ashamed to slander in your very presence (and how crudely he did it!) one whom you have honored with a priesthood.

Although on the surface the priest is describing Thersander's outrageous slander of himself, the narrator had prefaced this speech by observing that it betrayed the influence of Aristophanic humor and was filled with innuendo about Thersander's depraved sexual habits.[113] Indeed, the contrast that the speaker draws between the rest of Thersander's body, now unattractive because past its prime, and his tongue, employed in the pursuit of disgraceful purposes, makes a clear, nasty implication. Now that the bloom of youth has left him, he is unable to attract lovers to penetrate him anally and must gratify them orally.

The assumption informing both Greek texts is clear. Once a youth is past his prime, having left adolescence behind him, he cannot expect to attract lovers. As Aeschines puts it, it is only reasonable (εἰκότως). But whereas for Greek writers *exôroi* are positively undesirable sexual objects, at Rome *exoletus* is a technical term for an evidently marketable type of prostitute,[114] and the Latin term thus serves as an index of an important gap between Greek and Roman sexual ideologies. Among Romans, who lacked a pederastic tradition that channeled men's publicly acceptable desires into precisely two classes of normative erotic objects (women and boys), and thus excluded mature males as such objects, there was presumably less pressure than among Greeks to elide the presence of male-male configurations other than the pederastic scheme of bearded man and beardless youth participating in a public, romantic relationship. This seems especially likely in view of the fact that the Priapic model encouraged Roman men to represent sexual relations in fairly direct terms of phallic domination, particularly of slaves of any age. Although Roman men certainly paid tribute to the special desirability of adolescent male bodies and associated the receptive role in anal intercourse with boys, there was some room in the arena of Roman public discourse not only for beautiful boys but also for fully mature males as objects of men's phallic desires: as prostitutes known as *exoleti* who might be penetrated by their male customers; as bearded slaves who might be compelled to yield to their masters' advances; or as thieves who might be forced to submit to the imaginary phallic dominion of that hypermasculine divinity, Priapus.

The Example of Priapus: The Bigger the Better

The fact that Priapus' most notable attribute is his impressive genital endowment suggests a further point of divergence between Greek and Roman sexual ideologies. The god was far more popular among Romans than among the Greeks with whom he originated, and his image was diffused by means of countless statues and paintings. Whereas the sleek, muscular boy with a small, tidy penis may justly be termed a cultural icon among classical Athenian men,[115] Priapus constitutes the most salient Roman icon: the mature male, amply capable of asserting his masculinity by penetrating others with his impressive member. There is of course an important difference between the two, which can be described in terms of the contrast between desire and identification: Athenian men circulated images of smooth, discreet boys as objects of desire, while Roman men looked to the figure of the well-endowed, hypermasculine Priapus as a source of identification.[116] We will see that the Priapic male also functioned as an object of desire among Romans, but those who were imagined to *desire* penises of unusually large size were, not surprisingly, either women or effeminate men, in either case imagined as willingly submitting to the raw power of the phallic male. But whether the well-endowed male functioned as an object of desire or as a source of identification, whether the oversized phallus was coveted as an instrument of pleasure or admired as an embodiment of masculine supremacy, the principle is clear: the bigger the better.[117]

A considerable variety of ancient writers attest to the existence of Romans, both men and women, who openly displayed a sexual interest in amply endowed men. Not surprisingly, the poet or poets responsible for the *Priapea* dwell on the

god's well-known endowments on a number of occasions. In one display of brutal
machismo, Priapus boasts that his "scepter" will subjugate anyone who attempts to
steal from the gardens under his tutelage, and he complacently cites the widely
based appeal that his massive member holds:

> hoc sceptrum, quod ab arbore est recisum
> nulla et iam poterit virere fronde,
> sceptrum, quod pathicae petunt puellae,
> quod quidam cupiunt tenere reges,
> quoi dant oscula nobiles cinaedi,
> intra viscera furis ibit usque
> ad pubem capulumque coleorum. (*Priap.* 25)

This scepter, cut off from a tree and no longer able to grow green with foliage, the
scepter that pathic girls seek, that certain kings desire to hold, that well-known *cinaedi*
kiss—this scepter will enter the thief's guts all the way up to the hair and the hilt of my
balls.[118]

The writers of the biographies of the emperors Commodus and Elagabalus report
that they displayed a weakness for well-endowed men. Commodus was especially
fond of a well-provided man—probably a slave—whom he lovingly called his donkey and rewarded with both money and priestly office.[119] So too Elagabalus is said
to have promoted to political office certain men recommended to him for their
genital endowments, and to have sought out especially virile men from throughout
the city, but especially from among sailors.[120]

While these anecdotes may be apocryphal and are certainly meant to be scandalous, it is clear that, whether or not these particular emperors displayed such
tastes, many Romans did.[121] Juvenal's Naevolus complacently notes that his impressive equipment provokes admiration from the likes of Virro, although that
does not necessarily guarantee financial success: poor Naevolus is stuck with a
cheap patron who refuses to compensate him adequately, neglecting his hard-work-
ing stud and on the lookout for "another two-legged donkey."[122]

> nam si tibi sidera cessant,
> nil faciet longi mensura incognita nervi,
> quamvis te nudum spumanti Virro labello
> viderit et blandae adsidue densaeque tabellae
> sollicitent, αὐτὸς γὰρ ἐφέλκεται ἄνδρα κίναιδος. (Juv. 9.33–7).

For if the stars are against you, the unheard-of dimensions of your lengthy tool will do
you no good, even though Virro foams at the mouth when he sees you nude, and
flattering letters of solicitation come to you fast and furious (it is, you see, the *cinaedus*
who draws the man to himself).

Naevolus' assumption that his assets will find many admirers is, satirical hyperbole
aside, an interesting commentary on the Rome of Juvenal's day. Elsewhere Juvenal's
satiric persona himself grimly observes a type of legacy-hunting that he finds especially revolting, and that is indeed one of the reasons why he cannot help but
compose satire:

> . . . cum te summoveant qui testamenta merentur
> noctibus, in caelum quos evehit optima summi
> nunc via processus, vetulae vesica beatae?
> unciolam Proculeius habet, sed Gillo deuncem,
> partes quisque suas ad mensuram inguinis heres. (Juv. 1.37–41)

[How can you not be outraged] when you are pushed aside by those who earn their place in wills at night: those who are lifted to the skies on the easiest path to success these days, a rich old lady's crotch? Proculeius has a mere twelfth of the estate, but Gillo eleven twelfths, each of them inheriting his share in proportion to the measurement of his groin.

This rich old lady has rewarded Proculeius and Gillo in direct proportion to the size of their services to her.

Her tastes were shared by a certain Hostius Quadra, who lived in the time of Augustus and whose sexual exploits are reported by Seneca in a passage notable for its combination of moralizing outrage and thinly veiled prurience (see further discussion in chapter 5). Not only did Hostius anticipate both Elagabalus and Commodus by recruiting sexual partners on the basis of the size of their genital equipment (Seneca tells us he made the rounds of the baths), but, not satisfied with their already hefty endowments, he was in the habit of setting up magnifying mirrors so as to derive pleasure from looking at the artificially enlarged reflection of the penises of his "studs" (admissarii) as they serviced him from behind.[123]

Men gifted with sizeable members make appearances in the graffiti scratched on the walls of Pompeii[124] as well as in the epigrams of Martial. Twice the poet writes of slave-boys appreciated for their ample members, calling them pueri mutuniati ("well-hung boys")[125] and another mischievous epigram concerns a man who outreaches Priapus himself in his phallic endowment:

> Drauci Natta sui vocat pipinnam,
> conlatus cui Gallus est Priapus. (Mart. 11.72)

> Natta calls it his stud's pee-pee, but compared to that guy, Priapus is a eunuch.

Although Natta bestows the affectionate diminutive pipinna on the penis of his draucus (a noun of unclear meaning),[126] the member in question puts even Priapus' to shame: in comparison to the draucus, Priapus is nothing but a Gallus, or castrated priest of the Asian Mother Goddess. Another of Martial's epigrams mocks a certain Hyllus, who would rather give his last cent to an amply endowed man than save his money to feed himself:

> Unus saepe tibi tota denarius arca
>   cum sit et hic culo tritior, Hylle, tuo,
> non tamen hunc pistor, non auferet hunc tibi copo,
>   sed si quis nimio pene superbus erit.
> infelix venter spectat convivia culi
>   et semper miser hic esurit, ille vorat. (Mart. 2.51)

> It often happens, Hyllus, that you have only a denarius in your entire money-chest, and it is more worn down than your own asshole. But it will go not to a baker, nor to an

innkeeper, but rather to someone glorying in his oversized penis. Your unhappy belly looks upon your asshole's banquets, and the one is always wretchedly hungry while the other devours.

The vividly incongruous phrase *convivia culi* ("your asshole's banquets") makes it quite clear that Hyllus does not intend to admire these men's gifts from afar: his anus has as much of an appetite as does his stomach, and he will see that it is satisfied. Another man, whom Martial teasingly refuses to name, seems interested in appreciating *drauci* in other ways:

> una lavamur: aspicit nihil sursum,
> sed spectat oculis devorantibus draucos
> nec otiosis mentulas videt labris. (Mart. 1.96.11–3)

> We go to the baths together: he looks at nothing higher up, but devours the studs with his eyes, staring at their dicks with lips hard at work.

The poet's mischievous comment that the man's lips twitch as he gazes upon their penises is usually interpreted, probably rightly, as hinting that he seeks to fellate them.[127] Elsewhere the poet teases his friend Cotta for his method of procuring dinner companions—like Hostius Quadra, he recruits in the baths:

> Invitas nullum nisi cum quo, Cotta, lavaris
>   et dant convivam balnea sola tibi.
> mirabar quare numquam me, Cotta, vocasses:
>   iam scio me nudum displicuisse tibi. (Mart. 1.23)

> Cotta, the only men you invite to dinner are those with whom you have bathed; the bathhouses alone provide your dinner partners. I was wondering, Cotta, why you had never invited me: now I know that you didn't like what you saw when I was nude.

The implication is that Martial has never received a dinner invitation from Cotta because he fails to measure up to Cotta's minimum requirements.[128] In another epigram Martial writes of a certain Phoebus whose obviously impressive penis had earned him two million sesterces (a great deal of money: perhaps, like Juvenal's Gillo, he was able to attract and impress a wealthy widow) with the result that he was able to afford an expensive slave-boy for his own pleasures.[129]

Encolpius, the protagonist and narrator of Petronius' *Satyricon*, afflicted with impotence due to the wrath of Priapus, is apparently himself quite well endowed. In a burlesque parody of the famous Homeric recognition of Odysseus by the nurse, Lichas recognizes him by handling his genitals (105.9), and later Encolpius laments to his boyfriend Giton that "the part of my body in which I was once an Achilles has been done away with."[130] We learn that Ascyltus is similarly gifted when we hear of an incident in the baths. After his clothes were stolen, Ascyltus wanders about naked, shouting for Giton, but his parts were of such impressive size that he had no trouble in finding assistance:

> habebat enim inguinum pondus tam grande, ut ipsum hominem laciniam fascini crederes. o iuvenem laboriosum: puto illum pridie incipere, postero die finire. itaque

statim invenit auxilium; nescio quis enim, eques Romanus ut aiebant infamis, sua veste
errantem circumdedit ac domum abduxit, credo, ut tam magna fortuna solus uteretur.

(Petr. *Sat.* 92.9–10)

You see, he had so ponderous a groin that you would think the guy himself was an
attachment to his penis. What a hard worker! I imagine he begins on the day before
and ends on the day after. So it was that he found assistance right away, in the form of
some member of the equestrian class who was said to be notorious. As Ascyltus was
wandering around this man covered him with his own clothes and took him home, I
suppose, so as to enjoy so sizeable a boon by himself.

This unnamed gentleman was far from unusual in his tastes. Priapus once notes
that "evidently even married ladies show good sense and like to look at a big dick."[131]
While the comment would no doubt have amused Roman readers with its inflated
sense of self-importance, it also contained an element of truth: sizeable penises
attracted attention.[132]

But attention is not necessarily identical with desire. Indeed, the scene from
Petronius reveals a further aspect of the Roman fascination for sizable penises. As
Ascyltus wanders around the baths naked, his ponderous appendage on open display, a large crowd gathers around him and applauds in timorous admiration
(*admiratione timidissima*),[133] and Eumolpus himself directs a similar admiration
to Encolpius' restored manhood in a passage cut off by one of the more suggestive
lacunae in the text of Petronius:

haec locutus sustuli tunicam Eumolpoque me totum approbavi. at ille primo exhorruit,
deinde ut plurimum crederet, utraque manu deorum beneficia tractat.

(Petr. *Sat.* 140.13)

After saying that I lifted up my tunic and displayed all of myself to Eumolpus. He was
stunned at first, but then, so as to solidify his belief, he stroked the gods' gifts with
both hands.

The kind of admiration proffered by Eumolpus and the anonymous crowd does
not seem to have an explicitly sexual charge. One has the impression that these
men's reactions to a penis of impressive size are motivated less by a desire to be
penetrated than by a deferential admiration (*admiratione timidissima*) of a manhood superior to their own. An interesting macho dynamic is at work as these men
admire one who is blessed with an impressive sign of the manliness that they themselves possess. These are hardly effeminate men who desire to subordinate themselves to another's phallic dominion; they are rather men who admire a magnified
image of their own masculinity in another. Such an impression is strengthened by
parallels from Martial, who imagines a scene in the baths almost identical to the
Petronian scene: "Flaccus, if you hear applause in a bathhouse, you will know that
Maro's dick is there."[134] The epigrammatist also makes two remarks on well-
endowed men that betray not so much a sexual interest as a frank curiosity blended
with admiration:

Mentula tam magna est quantus tibi, Papyle, nasus,
    ut possis, quotiens arrigis, olfacere. (Mart. 6.36)

Tanta est quae Titio columna pendet
quantam Lampsaciae colunt puellae.
hic nullo comitante nec molesto
thermis grandibus et suis lavatur.
anguste Titius tamen lavatur. (Mart. 11.51)

Papylus, your dick is as big as your nose, so that whenever you get a hard-on you can
smell it.

The column that hangs from Titius is as big as the one worshipped by the girls of
Lampsacus [viz., Priapus']. All by himself, bothered by no one else, he bathes in his
own oversized baths. Even so, Titius is cramped when he bathes!

In Juvenalian satire the baths constitute the backdrop before which another amply
endowed man is on display:

conspicuus longe cunctisque notabilis intrat
balnea nec dubie custodem vitis et horti
provocat a domina factus spado. (Juv. 6.374–6)

Visible from far off, conspicuous to everyone, a man who was made a eunuch by his
mistress enters the baths and issues a real challenge to the guardian of vine and garden.

This slave rivals Priapus himself, and the satirist's passing remark that his mistress
had him castrated reminds us of his central point in this passage: that she makes
sexual use of this slave. But these lines dwell on his considerable genital gifts, and
they reflect popular tastes and predilections.

These tastes clearly included a frank interest in conspicuous phallic endowment, whether out of sexual desire or out of an admiration for male potency.[135]
From our perspective, texts that evoke images of men and women expressing sexual
desire for well-endowed men serve a clear function within Roman ideological systems, as they reconfirm the supremacy of the phallus; here the interrelationship of
desire and power is undisguised. Even those texts suggesting admiration rather
than desire in the presence of an impressively large penis obviously bolster the
power of the phallus. And in both cases, we are in the presence of a specifically
Roman discourse, as the Greek sources, both textual and visual, offer little or no
hint of so widespread a phenomenon.

Visual Evidence

Indeed, the image of the penis, whether attached to Priapus or not, was clearly
popular among Romans. And just as the admiration of impressively sized penises
expressed in the literary sources cannot always be attributed to a desire to make
use of the penis for one's sexual pleasures, so visual representations of the phallus
frequently appear in contexts that we cannot accurately describe as "sexual."[136]
For one thing, the phallus often functions as a symbol of what we might call fertility, broadly speaking: fertility of crops, livestock, and humanity. Indeed, Romans
worshipped several phallic divinities connected with fertility. In addition to the

Greek import Priapus, who at least had a body, there were two gods who seem to have been represented merely by the phallus itself: Fascinus (*fascinum* is a word denoting the organ, especially in connection with its apotropaic and fertile functions)[137] and another, equally shadowy deity whose name is variously spelled Mutunus Titinus or Mutinus Titinus (compare *mut[t]o* or *mutunium*, other terms for the penis, and *mutuniatus*, an adjective describing a well-endowed male).[138] So too a phallus was carried about in procession on a festival held every year on March 17 in honor of the god Liber who, according to Augustine, presided over men's seed.[139]

In addition to being a symbol of fertility, the phallus could be a symbolic means of marking boundaries, its image simultaneously warding off unwelcome presences and asserting ownership or dominion; this practice finds parallels among other cultures (one thinks of the Greek practice of setting up herms, or pillars endowed with erect penises and bearded faces, at crossroads or at entrances to private homes) and indeed among other species.[140] In a Roman context, we find images of the penis at crossroads or at the threshold of private residences in Pompeii and Ostia. One such image distinctly reminds us of the conceptual connection with fertility and good luck: those entering a building in Pompeii beheld an image of the phallus accompanied by an inscription that announced "Here dwells happiness [*felicitas*]" (Plate 8), using a word that can also be translated as "fertility" or "prosperity."

The phallus could also be invoked to ward off evil influences, above all the evil eye: it had, in other words, an apotropaic function. Thus, Roman boys might wear phallic amulets as protective charms,[141] a phallic image of the god Fascinus was suspended underneath the chariot of a general celebrating a triumph,[142] and according to Augustine the cult of Liber, in whose honor a phallic image was carried in procession at a yearly festival, had as one of its objects the protection of fields from witchcraft or the evil eye (*fascinatio*).[143] It is probably in this light that we should interpret the phallic designs that appear on Roman jewelry[144] as well as on windchimes or *tintinnabula*, whose bells had the symbolic function of warding off evil influences. One such object from Pompeii represents Mercury seated on a ram, with a bell hanging from each of the ram's feet and from its pendulous penis,[145] and another chime from Trier in Germany is in the form of a winged penis boasting the hind legs of an animal and a phallic tail, as well as its very own scrotum and penis (Plate 9).[146] The conceit is taken to a delightful extreme in a first-century B.C. terracotta figurine which depicts two little phallus-men sawing an eyeball in half, thus visually evoking the power of the phallus over the evil eye.[147] The humorous touch is notable and recalls the earthy humor on the subject of penises, especially large ones, that pervades the textual tradition.

Another artifact that strikingly illustrates the comfortable sense of humor with which phallic imagery could be disseminated among Romans is a well-known fresco of Priapus weighing his enormous penis situated at the front door to the House of the Vettii in Pompeii (Plate 10).[148] Hardly an announcement of the erotic inclination of the house's inhabitants,[149] this painting represents a sophisticated confluence of several symbolic functions of the phallus: it evokes fertility (there is a basket of fruit at Priapus' feet), as well as a concern for marking boundaries (the painting is positioned at the front door of a private home, recalling the Greek herms), but it also makes a witty comment on the theme of phallic authority: Priapus balances his impossibly large member with a sack of coins, as if to signify that it is worth its weight in gold. Along similar lines, Clarke has argued that images of African men with unusually large penises in floor mosaics from Augustan baths do not primarily represent the men as "object[s] of sexual desire" but rather served apotropaic functions.[150]

Aside from the frequently occurring image of the phallus, explicit depictions of sexual practices appear on numerous objects surviving from Roman antiquity, from frescoes in brothels and bathhouses (and even a small chamber off the kitchen of the House of the Vettii), to pottery vessels known as Arretine ware, to clay lamps and silver cups.[151] Most surviving images depict male-female copulation, but, as we would have expected from the textual evidence, depictions of male couplings also circulated in antiquity, and a few of these have survived.[152] Neither should we be surprised to observe that this evidence displays some interesting differences from Greek representations of sexual practices between males. One of the most striking features of the sexual iconography of Attic vase painting from the sixth and fifth centuries B.C. is a convention whereby the anal penetration of a beardless youth by his older, bearded lover is not shown. This conventional visual silence can easily be understood as an ideological device that served to maintain and reinforce the distance between the beautiful young boys who would soon grow up to be Athenian citizens and the despised effeminates and *kinaidoi* of the invective tradition. To see their beloved boys publicly playing the receptive role that they wanted them to play in private (and which of course they did play—as ancient texts like Aristophanic comedy and epigrams from the *Palatine Anthology* remind us) would be for Athenian men too blunt a reminder of the thin line between golden boy and effeminate *kinaidos*.[153] (See chapter 5 for a discussion of the conceptual relationship between boys and *cinaedi* in Roman traditions.) In a Greek context, this anxiety is clearly connected with the freeborn status of the beloved boy; since Roman traditions, as we have seen, simultaneously discouraged romantic relations with freeborn boys as *stuprum* and encouraged men to make sexual use of their male slaves and of prostitutes, Roman artists interested in portraying sexual practices between males were not placed in the same kind of ideological bind as were Athenian vase painters.

So it is that Roman objects with depictions of sexual acts between males show a disregard for precisely the Athenian convention just described: on these Roman pieces, the anal penetration of beardless youths is portrayed openly and unabashedly. Two of them, fragments of an Arretine ware cup and of a mold for such a cup, also offer a visual counterpart to the equivalence between male-male and male-female sexual practices that we have detected throughout the textual tradition: on each of them there is a male-female couple on one side and a male-male couple on the other. In each case the penetration is distinctly indicated: the woman lowers herself onto her partner's erect penis, while the young man (whose genitals are visible) reaches back with one arm to pull his partner, who is penetrating him from behind, closer to himself (Plate 11).[154]

Perhaps the most remarkable piece of evidence is a silver cup thought to date from the Augustan period that shows many similarities to Arretine pottery in its design and conception and that offers two scenes of male-male copulation. Generally referred to as the Warren Cup (after Edward Perry Warren, its first known modern owner), this artifact is currently on display at the Metropolitan Museum of Art in New York as an anonymous loan (Plates 12A and 12B).[155] On one side (Plate 12B) we see a beardless but mature young man wearing a laurel wreath penetrating a boy whose long locks most probably indicate that he is a slave.[156] The other side of the cup (Plate 12A) shows precisely what Attic vase paintings avoid: a bearded man anally penetrating a beardless youth, who lowers himself onto his lover's penis while holding onto a strap conveniently suspended above the bed. This scene is suggestive for several reasons. First, it serves as a useful reminder of the limits of the language of "active" and "passive," since the receptive partner in this coupling takes an undeniably active role in the act. Next, the presence of the strap that he uses, along with the fact that a third young man looks in through a partially opened door (as Clarke suggests, either he is taking a voyeuristic peek or he is glancing back while discreetly exiting) may suggest that the act occurs in a brothel equipped with the appropriate amenities.[157] Equally interesting is the Hellenized feel of this scene: the insertive partner wears an elegant beard (Roman men of the Augustan period were generally beardless) as well as a laurel wreath in his hair—just as does the insertive partner on the other side of the cup—and there is a lyre resting on a ledge behind the couple.[158] Vermeule describes the insertive partner as "an elderly man" (an exaggeration to be sure) who has "the features of the Pheidian Zeus"; Clarke more plausibly sees in the lyre and laurel wreath an allusion to Apollo, whom Augustus claimed as his patron deity after his victory at Actium.[159] Clarke also notes that the presence of the third party looking in on a scene in which one male lowers himself onto another finds a close parallel in an Attic vase painting.[160]

Yet the cup seems clearly designed for a Roman audience. The two beardless males on the cup other than the slave-boy look thoroughly Roman, Augustan in particular, and Vermeule even sees faces of members of Augustus' own family.[161] I would add that the Roman quality of the imagery on this cup is further evident in the very fact that it blithely breaks a basic rule of Attic iconography by openly depicting the anal penetration of beardless youths and in the quintessentially Roman nature of the scene on side B, where a slave-boy is shown as the object of a man's sexual attentions. Side A, then, is portraying *l'amour à la grecque*—I use the phrase not, of course, because the cup displays male-male couplings, but rather because of the visual cues of the beard, laurel wreath, and lyre, all of them trappings of Greek culture[162]—but doing so for a Roman audience who did not share the qualms and preconceptions of sixth- and fifth-century Athenian audiences.

In sum, the tendencies of the surviving visual evidence noticeably parallel those of the textual evidence. Both groups of sources suggest a cultural environment that placed a high value on the phallus as symbol of male authority, whether construed as tool of penetrative domination, guarantor of fertility, or agent of apotropaic power; both reflect a certain fascination with impressively sized penises in general and the god Priapus in particular. And both the visual and the textual evidence suggests a willingness among Romans to imagine men wielding their phallic power with females and males alike, sometimes in configurations that were not constrained by Hellenic traditions. Thus, as we have seen, a Roman man could acceptably participate in hierarchically constructed sexual relations with his wife, his slaves, or prostitutes of either sex, and, as long as the man maintained the image of dominance, the slaves or prostitutes that he used could be of any age.

The Concept of *Stuprum*

The second of the protocols described at the beginning of chapter 1 is structured around the distinction between slave and free: according to this rule, a man's slaves were considered acceptable sexual objects, but freeborn Romans other than his wife were not. Thus, as we saw in chapter 2, Roman sexual ideologies discouraged pederastic relationships along the Greek model—publicly acknowledged romantic and sexual relationships between citizen men and freeborn youth—and Roman writers were able to distance pederasty as a Greek custom, but we also saw they did so far less frequently than one might have expected. The conceptual mechanisms giving rise to the condemnation of such relationships are explored in this chapter.

Roman writers often use the term *stuprum* to describe the offense consisting in the violation of the sexual integrity of freeborn Romans of either sex: pederasty was therefore a subset of *stuprum* and for that reason liable to condemnation.[1] Thus Cicero denounces Catiline's affairs with some of his young male followers as "disgraceful," and thus Quintilian wishes that Afranius, writer of *togatae* or comedies set in Rome, had not "defiled his plots with shameful love affairs with boys."[2] Here a basic point needs once again to be stressed: pederastic relationships were capable of being condemned in this way not because of their homosexual nature but because of the status of the younger partner. We will see that pederastic relationships seem to have been no more objectionable to Roman traditionalists than were relationships with freeborn girls or indeed with other men's wives. In fact, I will argue later in this chapter that adultery, another subset of *stuprum*, gave rise to a higher level of cultural anxiety than did pederasty. With regard both to adultery and to pederasty, another central point needs to be reemphasized here: a number of men obviously engaged in these traditionally frowned-upon practices, but these men were breaking rules, and by doing so they no doubt created a greater need in some people's minds for the kind of moralizing condemnation we find scattered throughout the sources.

A number of scholars, discussing *stuprum* as it relates to adultery and more generally to the regulation of women's sexual behavior, have defined the term primarily with reference to relations with freeborn women, implying that it had meaning with reference to relations with freeborn males only secondarily or by analogy.[3] But this is misleading, and in fact untrue to the language of the ancient texts. *Stuprum* was not defined with reference to the sex of a man's partner, and it is my argument in this chapter that pederasty is not normally represented in the ancient sources as being qualitatively distinct from other varieties of *stuprum*. I argue here that the ideology informing the language of *stuprum* was not concerned with enforcing a distinction between heterosexual or homosexual behavior, neither was its primary aim the management of women's sexual experience (though that was, of course, one of its effects in practice). Instead, the concept of *stuprum* served to idealize the inviolability of the Roman bloodline, to maintain the distinction between free and slave, and to support the proprietary claims of the *paterfamilias* or head of the household. I insist on the point because much of the scholarship on *stuprum* displays a certain confusion on the issue: Susan Treggiari's magisterial 1991 study of Roman marriage notes, for example, that traditional Roman morality condemned sexual relations with free persons of both sexes, but nonetheless invokes "homosexuality" as an apparently meaningful category.[4] Elaine Fantham's ground-breaking article on *stuprum* from the same year illustrates the problem well. On the one hand, Fantham observes that the language of *stuprum* applied to sexual relations with free persons of either sex entails "the notion of penetration as an assault damaging the woman/boy/man penetrated," and that slaves of both sexes were legitimate sexual objects for Roman men; on the other hand, she speaks of an ancient accusation of "homosexual promiscuity," of Augustus' "abstention from homosexual practice," of "heterosexual offenders" and a "homosexual rapist," of a man's potential need to establish "his own innocence of previous homosexual relations," and of men with "a homosexual lifestyle."[5] In short, whereas Fantham, describing Valerius Maximus' catalog of episodes illustrating traditional sexual morality, argues that "for our purposes it is useful to separate his heterosexual episodes from the homosexual and to take them out of order so as to illustrate common elements in the handling of both categories of sexuality,"[6] I wish to challenge the very notion of "both categories of sexuality" and to argue that such a dichotomy would have made little sense to Valerius Maximus and his readership.

The Language of *Stuprum* and *Pudicitia*

Illicit relations with freeborn Romans were described with a specific language, and that language was centered around the term *stuprum*. The word defies translation: English renditions have ranged from "debauchery," "immorality," "lewdness," and "fornication" to "illicit intercourse" and "sex crime,"[7] but no single term can capture the semantic and tonal range of *stuprum*, which displays a characteristically Roman tendency to blur the distinction between the legal and the moral. *Stuprum* falls somewhere in between "illicit intercourse" and "fornication."[8]

The word originally denoted any shameful behavior, without specific reference to sexual practices. Festus, writing in the late second century A.D., informs us that Romans of the republican period had used *stuprum* as a synonym for *turpitudo* ("disgrace" or "shame"), and he is even able to cite an adverb *stupre* ("shamefully"). Indeed, in the early texts that he quotes by way of illustration, the word has no apparent connection with sexual behavior:

> stuprum pro turpitudine antiquos dixisse apparet in Nelei carmine: "foede stupreque castigor cotidie." et in Appi sententiis: "qui animi conpotem esse, nequid fraudis stuprique ferocia pariat." Naevius: "seseque i perire mavolunt ibidem, quam cum stupro redire ad suos popularis." item: "sin illos deserant fortissimos viros, magnum stuprum populo fieri per gentis." (Festus 418.8–18)

> We can see that the ancients used the word *stuprum* for *turpitudo* in the *Song of Neleus*: "Every day I am foully and shamefully [*stupre*] chastened." And in the *Appi Sententiae*, " . . . to be sane, lest his ferocity give rise to any kind of deceit or disgrace [*stuprum*]." From Naevius: "They prefer to die there on the spot rather than returning to their people in disgrace [with *stuprum*]." Likewise: "But if they should abandon those bravest of men, there would be great *stuprum* among the peoples of the world."

But Festus' citations, taken from texts that date as early as the third century B.C., constitute the only attestations of the word with so broad a meaning, for the semantic field of *stuprum* soon contracted, and the term came to refer specifically to a sexual disgrace,[9] that is, to sexual behavior that violated traditional standards of propriety, and above all to the disgrace of engaging in sexual practices with freeborn Romans of either sex.

But the word's original meaning left its traces: a moral coloring is always in the background when a writer refers to *stuprum*. Thus the use of the language of *stuprum* invariably has the effect of representing a sexual experience as disgraceful or improper, even if it does not involve freeborn Romans. There are some texts in which sexual relations with slaves, prostitutes, or concubines are described with the language of *stuprum*,[10] and some orators describe the goings-on in brothels in terms of *stuprum*.[11] But the crucial factor in these cases is the tone of moral condemnation. Two of these texts, for example, pertain to men's use of *other men's* slaves, and others come from Tacitus' portrayal of the disgraceful sexual behavior of Nero and his crony Tigellinus, to which we will return in chapter 5. And we have already seen (chapter 1) that the entire enterprise of prostitution was always liable to being smeared as disgraceful. Thus in all of these cases, the sexual behavior at stake is being represented as somehow inappropriate or shocking, even though it involved such otherwise acceptable partners as male or female slaves, concubines, or prostitutes.

In most of their extant occurrences, however, *stuprum* and related words refer to the specific disgrace constituted by the violation of the sexual integrity of the

freeborn Roman, male or female. Obviously at stake here is the fundamental distinction between freeborn and slave, which in turn served to bolster the self-
identifying practices of the freeborn by promoting the ideal of the physical inviolability of the free Roman citizen.[12] This inviolability in a specifically sexual sense
could be referred to as the principle of *pudicitia*, and *stuprum* and *pudicitia* thus
stood in a complementary relationship: acts of *stuprum* violated the *pudicitia* of
Roman citizens.[13] Indeed, a Republican-period writer of mimes, Laberius, coined
the verb *depudicare* ("to remove the *pudicitia* of") that is glossed by Gellius as
stuprare ("to commit *stuprum* on," Gellius 16.7.2). The same complementarity
surfaces in a sonorous Ciceronian array of some of the most Roman of virtues and
their degraded opposites:

> ex hac enim parte pudor pugnat, illinc petulantia; hinc pudicitia, illinc stuprum; hinc
> fides, illinc fraudatio; hinc pietas, illinc scelus; hinc constantia, illinc furor; hinc honestas,
> illinc turpitudo; hinc continentia, illinc libido. (Cic. *Cat.* 2.25)

> For on our side there fights modesty, on theirs effrontery; on ours *pudicitia*, on theirs
> *stuprum*; on our side trustworthiness, on theirs cheating; on ours dutifulness, on theirs
> villainy; on ours steadfastness, on theirs frenzy; on ours decency, on theirs depravity;
> on ours self-control, on theirs lust.

So too Valerius Maximus' compilation of incidents from Roman history illustrating
the importance of *pudicitia* (6.1) implies a complementary relationship between
that ideal and the crime of *stuprum*. He begins with a hymnic invocation of the
personified concept of *pudicitia*:

> Unde te virorum pariter ac feminarum praecipuum firmamentum, Pudicitia, invocem?
> tu enim prisca religione consecratos Vestae focos incolis, tu Capitolinae Iunonis
> pulvinaribus incubas, tu Palatii columen augustos penates sanctissimumque Iuliae
> genialem torum adsidua statione celebras, tuo praesidio puerilis aetatis insignia munita
> sunt, tui numinis respectu sincerus iuventae flos permanet, te custode matronalis stola
> censetur. (Val. Max. 6.1.pr.)

> Where shall I begin my invocation to you, Pudicitia, the preeminent mainstay of men
> and women equally? For you inhabit the hearth of Vesta that is consecrated by ancient
> ritual; you recline upon the sacred couches of the Capitoline Juno; you honor with
> your constant watchful presence the summit of the Palatine, the imperial household
> gods, and the most sacred marriage-bed of Julia; by your protection the tokens of
> boyhood are safeguarded; out of consideration for your divinity the flower of youth
> remains intact; because of your guardianship the matron's *stola* has its value.

With its references to the imperial family and to the characteristic garb of both
freeborn boys and matrons, this stirring invocation leaves no doubt: *pudicitia* is
the province of the free. All of the incidents he proceeds to relate in fact concern
the rape or seduction of freeborn Romans, both male and female, and the language of *stuprum* peppers his narrative.[14]

Thus the concept of *stuprum* is intimately connected with the distinction between men's slaves (who have no real *pudicitia* to lose, and are thus fair game for
their sexual advances) and their fellow freeborn Romans (who are protected by

the concept of *pudicitia*). The position of freedmen and freedwomen in this scheme
is, not surprisingly, as ambivalent as was their position in Roman society generally:
as free Roman citizens (called *libertini*) they ideally enjoyed a protection from
stuprum, yet as former slaves they were traditionally held to be in a special position of subordination and dependence with regard to their former masters (called
their *patroni*), a dependence often described in terms of the concept of *officium*
or "moral duty."[15] The Augustan orator Haterius, defending a freedman who was
said to have been his patron's concubine, was able to argue that a freedman's duty
to his patron might well include sexual services: "A lack of *pudicitia* in a freeborn
man is matter of reproach, in a slave a matter of necessity, in a freedman a matter
of moral duty [*officium*]."[16] Haterius' use of *officium* in this sense became infamous: people jokingly used the noun to refer to sexual services ("You're not doing
your 'duty' by me"; "He is very much engaged in doing 'duties' for him"); the
adjective *officiosus* ("dutiful") was for some time a fashionable way of referring to
men who had been penetrated.[17] Both Haterius' argument and the jokes it inspired all derive from the generally unchallenged assumption that a Roman man's
sexual dominion over his slaves of both sexes might legitimately continue even
after he freed them.[18] Likewise, the jurist Ulpian offers the opinion that men can
safely keep as concubines only those "against whom *stuprum* is not committed"—
namely, their freedwomen and slaves—and Papinian refers to a professional con-
sensus that the concept of *stuprum* is not applicable to a freedwoman who has
refused to be the concubine of her patron.[19] In this connection, Ulpian raises an
obviously vexed question: Does a freedwoman filling the role of *concubina* have
the right to leave her patron and marry another man? The fact that this became a
legal problem suggests that many simply assumed a patron's will with regard to his
freedwomen to be, in this regard at least, incontrovertible.[20]

Haterius' formulation, blunt as it is, neatly summarizes for us the most salient
traditional distinctions, a triage of sexual propriety: relations with freeborn
Romans could arouse censure (*crimen*), but a Roman man could justify relations
with his former slaves as being one aspect of the duty (*officium*) they owed them,
whereas no one would question his right to use his current slaves, who had no
choice in the matter (*necessitas*).[21] The earliest clear enunciation of this code of
behavior, whereby slaves were designated as fair game and the freeborn as off-
limits, can be found in a scene from Plautine comedy. Having just learned to his
relief that his lovelorn young master pines for a prostitute rather than a freeborn
girl, a slave pompously reassures his master that his love is licit, delivering a miniature sermon on the subject of sexual propriety:

> nemo hinc prohibet nec vetat,
> quin quod palam est venale, si argentum est, emas.
> nemo ire quemquam publica prohibet via;
> dum ne per fundum saeptum facias semitam,
> dum ted abstineas nupta, vidua, virgine,
> iuventute et pueris liberis, ama quidlubet.(Plaut. *Curc.* 33–8)

No one keeps you from coming here or prohibits you from buying what is openly for
sale—if you have the money. No one keeps anyone from traveling on the public road;

as long as you do not make your way through a fenced-off farm, as long as you keep yourself from a married woman, an unmarried woman, a maiden, young men and free boys, love whatever you like!

The slave does not explicitly designate as *stuprum* the behavior that he proclaims as unacceptable (the specific nuance of the term had not yet become established, as can be seen from Festus' citations from Plautus' contemporary Naevius), yet he is distinctly announcing the Roman code of behavior that came to be associated with that term.[22] Indeed, the categories of sexual objects that he likens to a fenced-off farm (*saeptus fundus*) recur in a source of a widely different nature, dating from the end of the classical period, that explicitly refers to *stuprum*. The third-century A.D. jurist Modestinus makes this distinction between the legal concepts of *stuprum* and adultery:

> stuprum committit qui liberam mulierem consuetudinis causa non matrimonii continet, excepta videlicet concubina. adulterium in nupta admittitur: stuprum in vidua vel virgine vel puero committitur. (D. 48.5.35)

> He commits *stuprum* who keeps a free woman for the purpose of a relationship but not matrimony (with the exception, of course, of his concubine). Adultery is perpetrated with a married woman; *stuprum* is committed with an unmarried woman or a maiden or a boy.

The correspondence between the categories that he lists and those ticked off by the Plautine slave is obvious and striking.[23] The basic definitions clearly remained intact over the nearly four hundred years that elapsed between Plautus and Modestinus. Neither Plautus' slave nor the jurist places any weight on the distinction between homosexual and heterosexual behavior, and in this they are typical of Roman writers.

Homosexual versus Heterosexual *Stuprum*

Indeed, ancient representations of *stuprum* are characterized by an emphasis on the freeborn status of the man's partner that is combined with a striking indifference to his or her gender. In the eyes of traditional morality, *stuprum* was *stuprum* whether it was committed with a male or with a female. Thus Valerius Maximus apostrophizes *pudicitia* as the "preeminent mainstay of men and women equally," and in his catalog of incidents involving *stuprum* he intermingles narratives involving female victims with those involving male victims, offering no hint of any meaningful distinction between the two. Consequently, his narratives of those incidents involving male victims place little emphasis on the victims' sex, focusing instead on their freeborn status. In one passage we read that the tribunes refused to intervene in a proceeding against one of their number who had been accused of propositioning a freeborn young Roman; the tribunes took such a stand not because a young man had been accosted by an older man but rather because *pudicitia*—which, as we have seen, Valerius invokes as a principle that applies to free males and females alike—was at stake.[24] In another narrative we are informed that

M. Laetorius Mergus, who had served as tribune in the late fourth century B.C., was posthumously condemned for having made advances on his subordinate; but, as Valerius reports it, the problem was not the fact that his subordinate was a man but rather his status as a Roman soldier under Laetorius' authority:

> signa illum militaria, sacratae aquilae, et certissima Romani imperii custos, severa castrorum disciplina, ad inferos usque persecuta est, quoniam, cuius [virtutis] magister esse debuerat, sanctitatis corruptor temptabat exsistere. (Val. Max. 6.1.11)

> The army's standards, the consecrated eagles, and that surest guardian of the Roman empire, strict military discipline, followed him all the way to the grave, since he tried to become the corruptor of the integrity of one whose instructor he ought to have been.

Military discipline, not the suppression of homosexual *stuprum*, is the crucial issue here.[25]

Like Valerius Maximus, the historian Livy gives us an idea of the kinds of images of their revered past that traditionalizing Romans disseminated.[26] Both authors recount the incident that led to the passage, in the late fourth century B.C., of the law granting plebeians immunity from imprisonment for debt. According to Livy, a usurer named Lucius Papirius became enamored of his young debtor Gaius Publilius, but after being rejected by the youth he had him beaten, and the resulting scandal culminated in the passage of the law. Interestingly, Livy's narrative consistently directs the reader's focus away from the sexual dynamics of the incident. While condemning Papirius' lustfulness (*libido*), the narrative dwells not on the intended result of that desire (namely, the sexual violation of a young man) but rather on Papirius' beating of a Roman citizen. In Livy's terms, what kept the young Publilius from acceding to his creditor's wishes was not a horror of homosexuality, nor even the fact that his masculine integrity was being threatened, but a consideration of his status as freeborn.[27] Likewise what so greatly inflamed the crowd was not horror at an attempted homosexual seduction but pity for a freeborn youth who had been beaten: when the consuls convened an emergency meeting of the Senate, the people brought Publilius to the entrance of the Curia and there displayed the youth's lacerated back to the senators as they went in. They did not point fingers at Papirius as a pervert.[28] The principal issue for Livy is not Papirius' sexual desire for the youth but rather his arrogant disregard for the physical inviolability of the freeborn Roman citizen. Valerius Maximus relates the incident more briefly and with different names (according to his sources the debtor was T. Veturius and the cruel creditor P. Plotius), and he places more explicit emphasis on the issue of *pudicitia*:

> a quibus hac de re certior factus senatus Plotium in carcerem duci iussit: in qualicumque enim statu positam Romano sanguini pudicitiam tutam esse voluit. (Val. Max. 6.1.9)

> When informed by them of the situation, the Senate ordered Plotius to be imprisoned; for its desire was that the integrity [*pudicitia*] of the Roman bloodline should be kept safe in whatever status it might be found.

But of course Valerius has already defined the concept of *pudicitia* with reference both to men and women, and when he invokes the ideal in this particular narrative, the language is markedly unconcerned with Plotius' sex. It is worth noting that he writes of a concern for *pudicitia* "in whatever status" it might be found; these words could just as well have capped a narrative of the attempted violation of an impoverished freeborn girl.

Stuprum and Reputation

Tacitus records various rumors about well-known men who had illicit sexual relations with the freeborn, and he often uses the language of *stuprum*. He reports gossip to the effect that Tiberius' right-hand man Sejanus had in his youth sold his favors ("had sold *stuprum*") to a wealthy man named Apicius; that the same Tiberius had, at his island retreat on Capri, "polluted freeborn youth with *stupra* in the manner of tyrants"; and that Nero had raped the young Britannicus before killing him ("had polluted him with *stuprum* and then with poison").[29] Likewise, as we shall see below, the rhetoric of *stuprum* is often deployed in descriptions of wartime rape or of the forcible prostitution of the freeborn, two contexts that highlight the shaming nature of the violation of the *pudicitia* of the freeborn. In short, an accusation of having committed *stuprum* became a weapon gladly brandished by Roman men in their attacks on one another in the public arena:[30] Tacitus, describing the gradual alienation between Otho and Vitellius in A.D. 69, notes that at first they treated each other respectfully enough, but "soon, like men in a brawl, they accused each other of *stupra* and disgraceful acts, neither one of them falsely."[31] The historian's characteristically compressed expression betrays an important assumption: men engaging in a public quarrel were quite capable of hurling accusations of *stuprum* at each other, often without any basis in fact (though, Tacitus adds as an extra dig, in this case there actually was such a basis).

The incidents narrated by Valerius Maximus and Livy remind us of the potential seriousness of *stuprum*, and Tacitus' narratives illustrate the ways in which a charge of *stuprum* could damage a man's reputation. But the very dangers lurking behind sexual relations with the freeborn could also be a source of intrigue. Indeed, some ancient writers suggest that *stuprum* offered the allure of forbidden fruit. Ovid, as so often, provides a trenchant comment: "What is licit holds no appeal; the illicit burns us more fiercely. That man has a heart of steel who loves what another allows him."[32] An epigram by Martial toys more explicitly with the question of freeborn status:

> ingenuam malo, sed si tamen illa negetur,
>   libertina mihi proxima condicio est:
> extremo est ancilla loco: sed vincet utramque,
>   si facie nobis haec erit ingenua. (Mart. 3.33)

> I prefer a freeborn woman; but if she is denied me, a freedwoman is my second choice. Last of all comes a slave woman. But she will win out over the other two if she *looks* freeborn to me.

The epigram wittily combines an avowal of the appeal of the forbidden fruit ("I prefer a freeborn woman") with a more practical admission that the best option would be to eat fruit that, while *looking* dangerous, is actually the cheapest, most readily available, and safest of all varieties. A passing comment in Tacitus' description of Tiberius' decadent life on Capri reminds us that powerful men, the emperor above all, could dispense with such mental gymnastics and simply grab whatever fruit they wanted. The emperor's appetites for the freeborn youth whom he "polluted with *stupra*" were, the historian observes, sometimes whetted by their childlike modesty, sometimes by the very nobility of their ancestry.[33] But of course Tiberius was in a uniquely privileged position; Martial's hedonistic calculus and Ovid's wry comment on the allure of the illicit no doubt spoke more directly to the experience of most Roman men.

Wartime Rape and Prostitution

Roman writers often give voice to fears that victorious armies or generals will rape both males and females among the vanquished, and they consistently fail to make meaningful distinctions based on the sex of the victims, simultaneously emphasizing the victims' freeborn status. Not surprisingly, the language of *stuprum* sometimes appears, and such qualifiers as "freeborn" (*ingenuus*) or "noble" (*nobilis*) are practically *de rigueur*. Sallust has Julius Caesar speak of the insolent behavior of Catiline's troops in these words:

> rapi virgines, pueros; divelli liberos a parentum complexu; matres familiarum pati quae victoribus conlubuissent; fana atque domos spoliari; caedem, incendia fieri; postremo armis, cadaveribus, cruore atque luctu omnia compleri. (Sall. *Cat.* 51.9)

> Maidens and boys were raped; children were torn from their parents' embrace; married ladies were subjected to the conquerors' pleasure; temples and homes were looted; there was slaughter and arson. In short, everything was filled with weapons, bodies, blood, and lamentation.

Cicero writes of the corrupt military command exercised by Mark Antony's brother Lucius:

> epulantur milites; ipse autem se, ut fratrem imitetur, obruit vino; vastantur agri, diripiuntur villae, matres familiae, virgines, pueri ingenui abripiuntur, militibus traduntur. (Cic. *Phil.* 3.31)

> The soldiers partake in banquets; he himself, so as to imitate his brother, drowns himself in wine; fields are devastated; country estates are plundered; married ladies, maidens, and freeborn boys are carried off and handed over to the soldiers.

Elsewhere the outraged orator notes in a characteristic *praeteritio* that Verres' rule in Syracuse, though peaceful, was marked by a kind of abuse unparalleled even during the capture of that city by the Roman general Marcellus:

> mitto adhibitam vim ingenuis, matres familias violatas, quae tum in urbe capta commissa non sunt neque odio hostili neque licentia militari neque more belli neque iure victoriae. (Cic. *Verr.* 2.4.116)[34]

I will not even mention the violence committed against the freeborn and the violation of married ladies—things that were not done when the city was captured, neither out of the hatred that is felt for the enemy, nor out of the freedom that is allowed soldiers, nor in accordance with the custom of war or the privilege of victory.

Publius Vatinius, writing to Cicero from Dalmatia in 45 B.C., disparages a certain Catilius, "who killed, seized, and ruined so many of the freeborn, married ladies, and Roman citizens."[35] The anonymous early first-century B.C. rhetorical treatise known as the *Rhetorica ad Herennium* includes a model speech in the "grand style" that catalogs some traditional outrages against Roman morality. These include assault, murder, the enslavement of Roman citizens, the destruction of the city, and the rape of the freeborn of both sexes:

> o feros animos! o crudeles cogitationes! o derelictos homines ab humanitate! quid agere ausi sunt, aut cogitare possunt? . . . quo modo deum templis spoliatis, optimatibus trucidatis, aliis abreptis in servitutem, matribusfamilias et ingenuis sub hostilem libidinem subiectis, urbs acerbissimo concidat incendio conflagrata. (*Rhet. Herenn.* 4.12)[36]

> O savage hearts! O cruel plans! How devoid these people are of any human feeling! What have they dared to do, or what can they be planning? . . . [They are planning] how, the temples of the gods having been looted, the conservative faction slain and others carried off into slavery, and married ladies and the freeborn being subjected to the enemy's lust, our city may collapse in a conflagration of the harshest of flames.

Tacitus describes the mayhem that erupted when troops supporting Vespasian captured Cremona in A.D. 69:

> quadraginta armatorum milia inrupere, calonum lixarumque amplior numerus et in libidinem ac saevitiam corruptior. non dignitas, non aetas protegebat quo minus stupra caedibus, caedes stupris miscerentur. grandaevos senes, exacta aetate feminas, vilis ad praedam, in ludibrium trahebant: ubi adulta virgo aut quis forma conspicuus incidisset, vi manibusque rapientium divulsus ipsos postremo direptores in mutuam perniciem agebat. (Tac. *Hist.* 3.33)[37]

> Forty thousand armed men burst in, along with a greater number of servants and attendants even more corrupt when it came to lust and cruelty. Neither respectability nor age prevented an intermingling of *stuprum* and slaughter. Aged men and women of advanced years, worthless as booty, were dragged off for sport; and when a mature maiden or someone [masc.] of outstanding beauty appeared, they would be pulled in various directions by the violent hands of those who were seizing them; ultimately they would lead into mutual slaughter the very men who had seized them.

Livy presents the words of a leading citizen of Capua named Vibius Virrius, who is confronted with the prospect of an attack by the Romans in 211 B.C.:

> non videbo Ap. Claudium et Q. Fulvium victoria insolenti subnixos, neque vinctus per urbem Romanam triumphi spectaculum trahar, ut deinde in carcerem aut ad palum deligatus, lacerato virgis tergo, cervicem securi Romanae subiciam; nec dirui incendique patriam videbo, nec rapi ad stuprum matres Campanas virginesque et ingenuos pueros.
> (Livy 26.13.15)

I will not look upon Appius Claudius and Quintus Fulvius elated by their arrogant victory; I will not be dragged in chains through the city of Rome as a spectacle at a triumph, only to be taken to prison or bound to a stake, my back torn by the beatings of rods, and to offer my neck to a Roman axe; nor will I look upon my country being destroyed and burned, Campanian mothers, maidens, and freeborn boys being seized for *stuprum*.

Writing for a Roman readership, Livy transposes the Capuan's fears into the language of *stuprum*. So too Tacitus writes that Roman soldiers in what is today the Netherlands dragged off beautiful young men for the same purpose (the historian pointedly observes that many young Batavians are quite tall: apparently an exotically appealing trait); he, too, uses the language of *stuprum* to describe the fate of these freeborn Batavians, treated like slaves by the Romans.[38] Finally, the real possibility that freeborn Roman males themselves might be raped in time of war is reflected by a provision in the perpetual edict of the urban praetor, where it is specified that men who have been sexually penetrated are ineligible to appear in court on behalf of others; but an exception is made for those who have been raped by pirates or wartime enemies.[39]

Similarly, when Roman writers profess shock at the prostitution of the freeborn, they sometimes use the language of *stuprum* but never make any meaningful distinction between homosexual and heterosexual incidents. Valerius Maximus writes of a certain Gemellus, who in 52 B.C. set up a brothel in his own house, selling the services of two noble ladies and a noble boy; and Suetonius records that Caligula established a brothel on the Palatine in which both matrons and freeborn males were on display.[40] The prostitution of young men is neither more nor less shocking than that of women: the business is disgraceful as a whole, and Valerius' and Suetonius' language reminds us why. The women were matrons (*matronae*) and the young men were freeborn (*ingenui*), even noble (*nobilem*).

The trial of P. Clodius Pulcher in 61 B.C. for sacrilege following upon the Bona Dea scandal (see chapter 4) was notorious for many reasons, not least of which was the allegation that Clodius had bribed the jury by means of assignations with matrons and young noblemen. Both Valerius Maximus and Seneca, the latter writing more than a hundred years after the trial, speak of *stuprum* in duly horrified tones, but make no distinctions based on the sex of the pawns in this corrupt chess game:

> noctes matronarum et adulescentium nobilium magna summa emptae mercedis loco iudicibus erogatae sunt. quo in flagitio tam taetro tamque multiplici nescias primum quem detestere, qui istud corruptelae genus excogitavit, an qui pudicitiam suam sequestrem periurii fieri passi sunt, an qui religionem stupro permutarunt.
>
> (Val. Max. 9.1.7).

> atqui dati iudicibus nummi sunt et, quod hac etiamnunc pactione turpius est, stupra insuper matronarum et adulescentulorum nobilium stillari loco exacta sunt.
>
> (Sen. *Epist*. 97.2).

Nights with matrons and young noblemen, purchased for a great sum, were paid out to the jurors instead of a cash bribe. In so foul and so complicated a disgrace, one does not know whom to loathe first: the man who devised this variety of corruption, those who allowed their chastity [*pudicitia*] to become the go-between for perjury, or those who traded in their scruples for *stuprum*.

But cash was given to the jurors and, even more disgraceful than this arrangement, *stupra* with matrons and young noblemen were also exacted in payment in place of a bonus.

Closer to the event, Cicero had offered his assessment of the situation in a letter to his friend Atticus, and the manner in which he structures his comment is significant:

iam vero (o di boni, rem perditam!) etiam noctes certarum mulierum atque adulescentulorum nobilium introductiones nonnullis iudicibus pro mercedis cumulo fuerunt. (Cic. *Att.* 1.16.5)

What is more (ye gods, what a depraved affair!), nights with certain women and introductions to young noblemen served as additional pay for some of the jurors.[41]

His dismayed exclamation precedes the reference to the sexual use of both matrons and well-born young men, and it casts its shadow of disapproval over both of the categories equally.

Wives and Children

Such a disinclination to distinguish *stuprum* committed with males from *stuprum* committed with females is further reflected in a stereotypical phrase, "wives and children" (*coniuges liberique*), that appears in conjunction with the vocabulary of *stuprum*. The *pudicitia* of Roman men's wives and children is often invoked or *stuprum* committed against them condemned, and it is worth nothing that the phrase consistently refers to men's "wives and children" rather than their "wives and daughters, and even sons." If Roman writers had anticipated any meaningful bias against homosexual *stuprum* in their readership, they surely would have appealed to it in these evocations of the violation of *pudicitia*. This language also points to a further dimension of the ideology of *stuprum*. In addition to a concern for maintaining the purity of the Roman bloodline, *stuprum* was capable of being conceived as an offense against the proprietary claims of the *paterfamilias*. In other words, the phrase *coniuges liberique* appealed to Roman readers' commitment not only to the concept of the physical inviolability of the freeborn Roman but also to the notion of the protected dependent. Thus the rhetoric ultimately served to bolster the authoritative position of the father of the household: it is not coincidental that the phrase makes reference to *liberi* ("children"), a word that points to the division of the household or *familia* into the slave and free dependents of the *pater*, the *famuli* and *liberi*, respectively.[42] Some examples will illustrate these points.

Cicero boasts with characteristic persistence that he saved the Romans' wives and children from the aggression of Catiline and his followers, and he more or less explicitly describes this aggression in sexual terms:

nunc si hunc exitum consulatus mei di immortales esse voluerunt ut vos populumque Romanum ex caede miserrima, coniuges liberosque vestros virginesque Vestalis ex acerbissima vexatione, templa atque delubra, hanc pulcherrimam patriam omnium nostrum ex foedissima flamma, totam Italiam ex bello et vastitate eriperem, quaecumque mihi uni proponetur fortuna subeatur. (Cic. *Cat.* 4.2)[43]

Now if this was the outcome of my consulship willed by the immortal gods—that I should rescue you and the Roman people from a most wretched slaughter, your wives and children and the Vestal Virgins from an outrageous harassment, the temples and shrines and this our splendid country from the flames of disgrace, and all of Italy from war and destruction—I will submit to whatever fate lies in store for me and me alone.

The same orator elsewhere asserts even more bluntly that if Clodius had ever acquired magisterial authority (*imperium*), "he never would have kept those unbridled desires of his from your children and wives."[44] Elsewhere he professes outrage at L. Antonius' treatment of the inhabitants of Parma, simultaneously managing to make a swipe at his brother:

refugit animus, patres conscripti, eaque dicere reformidat quae L. Antonius in Parmensium liberis et coniugibus effecerit. quas enim turpitudines Antonii libenter cum dedecore subierunt, easdem per vim laetantur aliis se intulisse.

(Cic. *Phil.* 14.9)

Gentlemen of the Senate, my mind recoils and dreads to mention the things that Lucius Antonius did to the children and wives of the men of Parma. For whatever shameful things the two Antonii willingly underwent to their own disgrace, those same shameful things they rejoice to have perpetrated on others by force.

In Livy's narrative of the Bacchanalian scandal of 186 B.C. (to which we will return shortly), the consul Postumius imagines the possibility of placing men who have been sexually violated in the position of defending Roman citizens, posing a question that is pointedly structured around the complementary pair *stuprum* and *pudicitia*: "Will these men, covered with their own *stupra* and those of others, fight with the sword on behalf of the chastity [*pudicitia*] of your wives and children?"[45] And as Livy alludes to a Capuan man's fear of *stuprum* (26.13.15: see above), so Cicero represents the concern felt by non-Roman men for the sexual inviolability of their freeborn dependents in terms of *stuprum* and *pudicitia*. In one speech he alludes to the temptations that might greet a Roman general serving in the East:

nisi erit idem qui se a pecuniis sociorum, qui ab eorum coniugibus ac liberis, qui ab ornamentis fanorum atque oppidorum, qui ab auro gazaque regia manus, oculos, animum cohibere possit, non erit idoneus qui ad bellum Asiaticum regiumque mittatur.

(Cic. *Leg. Man.* 66)

Unless he is the kind of man who can keep himself from the allies' money and from their wives and children, and who can keep his hands, eyes, and mind off the decorations in the temples and towns, off the gold and the royal treasure, he will not be suitable to be sent to war with an Asian king.

Provincial governors were especially liable to succumbing to such temptations. The most infamous of these governors was Gaius Verres, propraetor of Sicily from 73 to 71 B.C.[46] In the course of his prosecution of Verres for extortion in 70 B.C., Cicero alludes to the corrupt governor's sexual exploitation of the inhabitants not only of Sicily but of other provinces in which Verres had served:

> in stupris vero et flagitiis nefarias eius libidines commemorare pudore deterreor; simul illorum calamitatem commemorando augere nolo quibus liberos coniugesque suas integras ab istius petulantia conservare non licitum est. (Cic. *Verr*. 1.14).

> quodsi hoc iure legati populi Romani in socios nationesque exteras uterentur, ut pudicitiam liberorum servare ab eorum libidine tutam non liceret, quidvis esse perpeti satius quam in tanta vi atque acerbitate versari. (Cic. *Verr*. 2.1.68)

Decency prevents me from mentioning his unspeakable lust in *stupra* and disgraceful acts; nor do I wish by mentioning them to increase the misfortune of those who were not allowed to keep their children and wives untouched by that man's outrageousness.

[The men of Lampsacus said that] if the legates of the Roman people were going to exercise their jurisdiction over allies and foreign nations in such a way that they would not be allowed to keep the chastity [*pudicitia*] of their children safe from them, then it would be better to suffer anything at all rather than to be subjected to such harsh violence.

Cicero's application of the language of *pudicitia* and *stuprum* to persons who were not Roman citizens, but who were freeborn citizens of their own cities, suggests that, at least for the purposes of his argument, the most fundamental distinction was not between Roman citizen and non-Roman citizen but between freeborn and slave. Moreover, the generalizing tenor of the phrases ("their children and wives," "the chastity of their children") is especially striking, for the most outstanding of Verres' sexual offenses while serving in Lampsacus was his attempted seduction of the daughter of a man named Philodamus (2.1.62–9). Instead of speaking of their "wives and daughters," even in the case of a man whose tastes were noticeably inclined to women,[47] Cicero's insistence on "wives and children" reflects the powerful appeal that the phrase had for his audience, and illustrates the pressure exerted by the conceptual systems giving rise to the phrase to elide the distinction between homosexual and heterosexual *stuprum*.

Stuprum and Masculinity

The prime directive of Roman masculinity rests, as we have seen, upon the fundamental distinction between the insertive and receptive role in penetrative acts. In view of this understanding, a sexual act between two males was normally understood to require the penetration of one of the two participants and thus an assimilation (whether forced or willing) of one of the men to the feminized receptive role. Consequently one might expect to find an emphasis on *stuprum* committed with males as being a more horrific outrage than *stuprum* with females, particularly when it was a question of rape. Yet this bias surfaces only rarely, and when Roman writers do appeal to it, their rhetorical strategy is not to distinguish between the homosexual and heterosexual desires of the active *stuprator* in the interests of condemning the former, but rather to focus on the plight of the passive victim, on the male who is forcibly feminized. In other words, although an opportunity existed to condemn those men who sought to penetrate freeborn males, Roman writers regularly failed to seize that opportunity, instead focusing either on the passive victim's violation and shame or on the active perpetrator's disregard for the integrity (*pudicitia*) of the freeborn Roman, whether male or female.

In the course of his treatise on the training of an orator, Quintilian considers various strategies that an advocate might deploy in difficult court cases, and at one point he turns to those particularly awkward cases that involve the sexual violation of the orator's client:

> illic maior aestus, ubi quis pudenda queritur, ut stuprum, praecipue in maribus, aut os profanatum. non dico, si loquatur ipse; nam quid aliud ei quam gemitus aut fletus et exsecratio vitae conveniat, ut iudex intellegat potius dolorem illum quam audiat? sed patrono quoque per similes adfectus eundum erit, quia hoc iniuriae genus verecundius est fateri passis quam ausis. (Quint. *I.O.* 11.1.84)

> There will be greater embarrassment when someone complains of shameful things, such as *stuprum*—particularly in the case of males—or the violation of a mouth. I do not even mention the possibility that the victim himself should speak, for what else suits him but groaning or weeping and cursing his existence, so that the juror may understand rather than hear of that grief? But his advocate will have to go through similar emotions, for with regard to this type of wrongdoing it is more embarrassing for those who have suffered it [*passis*] to acknowledge it than it is for those who have perpetrated it [*ausis*].

Quintilian explicitly notes that talk of *stuprum* is especially difficult when the victim is male, or when there has been oral rape. But the addition of the second instance, which is syntactically independent of the qualification "particularly in the case of males," demonstrates that Quintilian is not focusing on homosexual *stuprum* in and of itself but rather on sexual offenses that are especially embarrassing from the perspective of victim. If the victim is male, this means being the penetrated partner in an act of *stuprum*; and regardless of the sex of the victim, being subjected to oral penetration is perhaps the most degrading of sexual assaults (see chapter 5). Quintilian, in other words, is here adopting the perspective of the victim, and his explanation of why the victim could not possibly bring himself to speak of the incident himself draws out the assumption running just beneath the surface of nearly all of our sources: "With regard to this type of wrongdoing it is more embarrassing for those who have suffered it to acknowledge it than it is for those who have perpetrated it." The perpetrators of *stuprum* (Quintilian's *ausi*) are understood as acting out of an excessive masculine impulse, whereas male victims (*passi*) are, by being penetrated, robbed of their masculinity. There is a familiar double standard at work here: although these acts of *stuprum* were considered shameful in themselves, the brunt of the shame was borne by the victim.

The declamation offered by Calpurnius Flaccus on the subject of the *miles Marianus* or "Marian soldier" is also of interest. This soldier had been propositioned by his tribune, a relative of the commander Marius, during the war against the Cimbri in 104 B.C.; not only did he reject the tribune's advances, but he killed him in outrage, and despite the fact that the dead man was his relative, Marius ruled that it was a case of justifiable homicide.[48] Defending the soldier's action, the speaker in Calpurnius' declamation first poses a rhetorical question to the slain tribune: "Is he not yet a man to you, though he is already one of Marius' soldiers?"[49] That is, the speaker is arguing that, in trying to violate the soldier's sexual integrity, the tribune had disregarded his manhood. For a moment, then, the speaker, like Quintilian, considers the passive victim's perspective. But the declamation then shifts its focus to the active criminal, and ends on this note of condemnation: "He threatened *stuprum* against your soldier; it is a smaller matter that the Cimbri are threatening us."[50] With all the hyperbole of the courtroom (even an imaginary one), the speaker asserts that the potential sexual violation of a Roman soldier is a greater threat than the attack of the enemy. It deserves notice that the speaker fails to return to the fact of the soldier's maleness; instead of dwelling on that fact, he places the greatest part of the rhetorical weight on the consideration that the victim was one of Marius' soldiers. The emphasis has shifted from the soldier's sex to his status as a Roman soldier, and the implicit disparagement of the active *stuprator* is, in the end, not directed at his desires to feminize a Roman man but rather at his desires to disgrace a Roman soldier and to destroy the much-vaunted discipline of the Roman army.[51]

In fact, as we have seen, the great majority of Roman allusions to *stuprum* direct our focus precisely to the perpetrators (Quintilian's *ausi*); whether they commit *stuprum* with female or with male victims, the offense is the same. Livy's narrative of the Bacchanalian scandal of 186 B.C. is particularly illustrative, for here the issue of the forced feminization of young Roman citizens might have been exploited to a great degree. To be sure, an important factor in the scandal was the sexual excess thought to characterize the Bacchic rites, and this included the sexual initiation of young men under the age of twenty. Some scholars have emphasized this aspect of the scandal (one even detects an "anti-homosexual hysteria" among Romans),[52] but such a view hardly corresponds to Livy's perspective. While the sexual violation of young Roman men certainly provoked outrage, it is significant that, from beginning to end, Livy pitches both his own narrative voice and that of the participants in such a way as to highlight the concurrent presence of men and women in the rites. In his introductory narrative, the historian offers this overview:

> cum vinum animos incendisset, et nox et mixti feminis mares, aetatis tenerae maioribus, discrimen omne pudoris exstinxissent, corruptelae primum omnis generis fieri coeptae, cum ad id quisque, quo natura pronioris libidinis esset, paratam voluptatem haberet. nec unum genus noxae, stupra promiscua ingenuorum feminarumque erant, sed falsi testes, falsa signa testamentaque et indicia ex eadem officina exibant. (Livy 39.8.6–7)

> When wine had inflamed their minds, and night as well as the combination of men and women, those of tender age and their elders, had erased every scruple of decency, there first arose corruption of every kind, since everyone had ready at hand a source of pleasure for whatever his nature was inclined to desire. Nor was there only one variety of guilt, the indiscriminate *stupra* of freeborn [males] and women, but

falsified witnesses, falsified signatures, wills, and evidence came forth from the same workshop.

The keynote is loud and clear: this is not a tale primarily of homosexual vice or of the forced feminization of young Roman men. It is a tale of *stuprum* involving Romans of both sexes.[53] Livy's dramatization of the freedwoman Hispala's confession continues the theme. She suggests that the truly shocking aspects of the cult only arose as a consequence of the admission of men to rites that had originally been exclusively for women. To be sure, Hispala momentarily shifts her focus to those incidents of *stuprum* that occurred between men, noting that now there were "more incidents of *stuprum* of men amongst themselves than of women." But her next sentence is revealing: "If any of them resisted submitting to disgrace or were slow to commit crime, they were sacrificed instead of the animal victims."[54] In other words, Hispala concentrates on the homosexual incidents of *stuprum* to bring attention to the penetrated victims, the young male initiates who were sexually violated.[55] Livy later reports a speech delivered to an assembly of the Roman people by the consul Postumius, whose rhetorical strategies echo Hispala's. He too first cites the shocking blend of men and women, then darkly alludes to the sexual violation of young men:

> quales primum nocturnos coetus, deinde promiscuos mulierum ac virorum esse creditis? si quibus aetatibus initientur mares sciatis, non misereat vos eorum solum, sed etiam pudeat. hoc sacramento initiatos iuvenes milites faciendos censetis, Quirites? his ex obsceno sacrario eductis arma committenda? hi cooperti stupris suis alienisque pro pudicitia coniugum ac liberorum vestrorum ferro decernent? (Livy 39.15.12–4)
>
> What do you think those meetings were like, held at night, and moreover with women and men mingling indiscriminately? If you were to know at what ages the males are initiated, you would not only have pity on them but you would be ashamed as well. Citizens, is it your judgment that young men initiated with this oath should be made soldiers? That weapons should be entrusted to these men led forth from an obscene shrine? Will these men, covered with their own *stupra* and those of others, fight with the sword on behalf of the chastity [*pudicitia*] of your wives and children?

The phrasing of Postumius' final question is significant. True, these young men have been penetrated and their masculine integrity thereby damaged. Yet in describing them as "covered with their own *stupra* and those of others," the consul alludes to both the passive and the active role that they had played in acts of *stuprum*. Indeed, Postumius had earlier disparaged the participants in the rites by explicitly likening the men to women; yet their effeminacy is embodied in both the penetrated and the penetrating role in *stuprum* among other, nonsexual vices.[56] Throughout Livy's narrative, then, we see the same patterns detectable in Quintilian and Calpurnius Flaccus. When the homosexual incidents of *stuprum* become the object of scrutiny, the strategy is first to focus on the plight of the penetrated victims, but then to shift the emphasis to the penetrating perpetrators; and when this shift occurs, their crime is represented as being an instance of undifferentiated *stuprum* or a violation of traditional standards of military discipline.

Pederasty and Adultery

Roman traditions clearly discouraged the conceptualization of Greek-style pederasty, or indeed any sexual relations with freeborn males, as qualitatively distinct from other varieties of *stuprum*. Related to this fact is a tendency in the ancient sources that has gone unnoticed in contemporary scholarship. Not only was pederasty not treated as an unusually disgraceful type of *stuprum*, but also there is a good deal of evidence to suggest that, of all the varieties of *stuprum*, adultery was the most disturbing from the perspective of Roman masculine culture.[57]

Indications of a greater problematization of adultery than of pederasty surface in a variety of contexts. When Roman writers inveigh against contemporary decadence and corruption, the sexual offense that they regularly cite as an embodiment of moral decline is neither pederasty nor *stuprum* in general, but adultery; thus the so-called *locus de saeculo* or rhetorical commonplace bemoaning the corrupt state of contemporary morals normally focuses on adultery, not *stuprum* in general, and certainly not pederasty.[58] In Petronius' *Satyricon*, Trimalchio recites some verses of Publilius on the subject of *luxuria* that include a reference to adultery, but none to pederasty.[59] In the programmatic introduction to his *Histories*, Tacitus characterizes the period A.D. 69–96 as being marked by adultery in high places.[60] The speaker in Juvenal's third satire, in the course of his mordant description of life in the city, provides a list of activities one must indulge in if one is to succeed in Rome, all of which he professes himself unable to do: lying, praising bad books, learning astrology, plotting patricide, practicing divination from frogs' entrails, assisting thieves, accepting bribes, and acting as a go-between for adulterous couples.[61] In another Juvenalian satire we read of the Golden Age as being characterized by the absence of adultery specifically rather than all sexual offences,[62] and elsewhere we read that common folk (*mediocres*) consider gambling and adultery to be shameful (*turpe*), whereas the wealthy urban folk think them quite fashionable.[63] It is worth noting that pederasty, which in another cultural setting might have been a significant point of contention between rich and poor, city and country, is not cited as an issue at all. The same poet includes in a list of vices that parents impart to their children, in the company of gambling, cruelty to slaves, and extravagance, one sexual offense: neither *stuprum* generally nor pederasty in particular, but adultery.[64] In view of this preoccupation with adultery as a symptom of decline, it is not surprising that the champion of old-fashioned chastity (*pudicitia*) most frequently cited in ancient sources is Lucretia, the married woman whose rape by the son of the last king of Rome precipitated the downfall of the monarchy.[65]

Whenever Cicero catalogs instances of license or immorality in his philosophical works, adultery inevitably makes an appearance in the list, but pederasty never does.[66] In his *Odes*, Horace sometimes champions the Augustan party line regarding adultery (see, e.g., *Odes* 4.5); in one of his *Satires* (discussed in chapter 1) he observes the practical dangers of being caught in adultery;[67] but never does he or any other Roman writer spend such energy on attacking pederasty. The Stoic philosopher Musonius Rufus, in a discussion of sexual ethics marked by an extreme asceticism, argues that adulterous relations are "the most illicit" of all, apparently more than relations between males, even though he describes these as being "against nature."[68] Finally, this distinction is highlighted in Roman ethnographic texts. What Roman writers claim about other peoples' behavior often reveals a great deal about how Romans thought they themselves ought to behave, and here, too, it is adultery that is the issue, not *stuprum* in general, and certainly not pederasty.[69] In a similar vein, certain animal species are said to be blissfully ignorant of adultery; but at the same time there were bemused, even admiring stories about male dolphins and elephants who fell in love with human boys—just as humans do, notes Gellius.[70]

A similar pattern is noticeable in the *Controversiae* of the elder Seneca and the declamations attributed to Quintilian and Calpurnius Flaccus. Although the historicity of the legal provisions contained within them is doubtful, these texts do provide an indication of which topics held interest for Roman orators, and they reveal a greater preoccupation with adultery than with pederasty.[71] The actual provisions of Roman law seem to confirm the distinction. The Augustan legislation on adultery stipulated penalties that ranged from banishment with confiscation of property to death,[72] and Catharine Edwards has noted that "the law against adultery bore a disconcerting resemblance to that against treason—and adultery itself now took on a much more intimate association with political subversion."[73] None of this was true of other varieties of *stuprum*, and legal sanctions against pederastic relations appear to have been much less harsh. The notoriously elusive *lex Scantinia* probably penalized pederastic relationships as acts of *stuprum*, and the penalty was most likely a fine (see discussion later in this chapter). Certainty on this law has proven to be impossible, but that very fact is eloquent. There is a clear contrast between the amount of jurisprudential ink spilled in antiquity on the subject of the *lex Julia de adulteriis coercendis* (Digest 48.5) and the scattered and vague references to the *lex Scantinia*.

Some reasons for the greater Roman concerns with adultery readily suggest themselves. Most generally, the greater problematization of adulterous relationships than of pederastic relationships is surely related to an impulse on the part of Roman male culture to exercise control over women's sexual experience.[74] Specifically, too, adultery gave rise to questions over paternity: a crucial sticking point in so patriarchal a culture as Rome. The jurist Papinian explained that the offense was called *adulterium* "because of the offspring conceived from another [*ex altero*],"[75] and while his attempt at etymology might not satisfy modern linguists, his formulation suggests that ancient speakers of Latin readily perceived a close relationship between the concepts of adultery and illegitimacy.[76]

The inclination to represent adultery as being more problematic than *stuprum* with males highlights the gap between ancient and modern traditions quite vividly, and reminds us of the deeper logic involved in the concept of *stuprum*. Rather than drawing a line between homosexual and heterosexual behavior and condemning the former wholesale, these traditional Roman standards were concerned both with the distinction between free and slave (the notion of *stuprum* serving to bolster the self-defining practices of freeborn Romans by enforcing the principle of their inviolability and simultaneously disregarding that of slaves) and with the reinforcement of patriarchal authority of the Roman father and husband over his dependents. A man who committed *stuprum* was thought to have tampered with the idealized integrity of the Roman bloodline (Valerius Maximus' *Romanus sanguis*) and with the proprietary claims of other Roman men over their sons, daughters, and wives.

Adultery and Pederasty in the *Aeneid*

Rome's national epic displays a similar tendency to treat adultery as qualitatively distinct from, and ultimately more problematic than, other kinds of disapproved sexual practices. In the sixth book of the *Aeneid* we encounter a list of sinners subject to eternal punishment in the underworld:

> hic, quibus invisi fratres, dum vita manebat,
> pulsatusve parens et fraus innexa clienti,
> aut qui divitiis soli incubuere repertis
> nec partem posuere suis (quae maxima turba est),
> quique ob adulterium caesi, quique arma secuti
> impia nec veriti dominorum fallere dextras,
> inclusi poenam exspectant. (Vir. *Aen.* 6.608–14)

> Imprisoned here, awaiting their punishment, are those who hated their brothers while they were still alive; those who beat their father and devised deceit against their client; those who brooded in solitude over their new-found wealth and gave no share to those close to them (this is the greatest crowd); those who were slain for adultery; those who pursued an impious war and did not scruple to escape their masters' authority.

While the text surely reflects the specifically Augustan campaign against adultery, it remains a striking fact that in a morally weighty scene in the central book of the great Roman epic we find adulterers killed in the act—not everyone who commits any kind of *stuprum*, and certainly not pederasts in particular—singled out among those who will be punished in the underworld. Moreover, the tragedy of Dido's relationship with Aeneas is closely related to the Roman ideal of the *univira* or "one-man woman" who never remarries after her husband dies, an ideal that Dido has anachronistically vowed to uphold: "That man who was the first to join me to himself took away my love; may he have and hold my love with him in the grave." When she fails to live up to her vow—not only having a sexual relationship with Aeneas, but calling it a "marriage" (*coniugium*)—she commits a moral offence (*culpa*) and becomes involved in a relationship that is analogous to adultery.[77]

The deeply problematic status of adultery in the *Aeneid* stands in sharp contrast with the comfortable presence of pederastic relationships in the same poem. Among the Italian warriors slain in battle is a man named Cydon:

> tu quoque, flaventem prima lanugine malas
> dum sequeris Clytium infelix, nova gaudia, Cydon,
> Dardania stratus dextra, securus amorum
> qui iuvenum tibi semper erant. (Vir. *Aen.* 10.324–7)

You too, Cydon, unfortunate one, while pursuing your latest delight Clytius, his cheeks golden with their first down, were brought down by Trojan strength, now released from your constant love affairs with young men.

Cydon's flings with young men follow the Greek pederastic model and thus would be liable to the Roman label *stuprum*, for his boyfriends are surely freeborn, yet those affairs seem neither unusual nor liable to reproach. On the contrary, the narrative voice here appropriates them in order to heighten the pathetic contrast between Cydon's normally delightful experiences and his current pathetic situation.[78] Another Italian warrior, Cupavo, is said to be the son of Cycnus, who was transformed into a swan when his beloved Phaethon met his premature death.[79] The early fifth-century A.D. writer Macrobius noted that Virgil, unlike Homer, clearly indicates the sexual nature of Ganymede's relationship with Jupiter, thus adding a special piquancy to Juno's jealousy of the Trojans.[80] And an image of the rape of Ganymede decorates a cloak given by Aeneas as a prize at the funeral games of Anchises;[81] one might infer that the beautiful prince, carried off to be the servant and concubine of the king of the gods, was a part of their heritage in which Aeneas' Trojans, mythic ancestors of the Romans, took some pride.

In somewhat less direct language, the pair of Trojan warriors Nisus and Euryalus are cast in the roles of *erastes* and *eromenos*. Virgil's narrative of the two valorous young Trojans has, of course, various thematic functions and will have resonated in various ways for a Roman readership; here I focus on only one aspect of the narrative, namely the eroticization of their relationship, in the interests of exploring what this text might suggest about the preconceptions of its Roman readership.[82]

The two are first introduced in the funeral games in Book 5:

> Nisus et Euryalus primi,
> Euryalus forma insignis viridique iuventa,
> Nisus amore pio pueri. (Vir. *Aen*. 5.294–6)

First came Nisus and Euryalus: Euryalus outstanding for his beauty and fresh youthfulness, Nisus for his devoted love for the boy.

During the ensuing footrace, Nisus indulges in a questionable bit of gallantry: starting off in first place, he slips and falls in the blood of sacrificed heifers, then deliberately trips the man who was in second place, in order that Euryalus may come up from behind and win first place: "He was not forgetful of his love Euryalus, not he!"[83] The two Trojans reappear in a celebrated episode from Book 9, when they leave the camp at night in an effort to break through enemy lines and reach Aeneas. They succeed in killing a number of Italian warriors, but eventually are themselves both killed, Euryalus first and then his companion, who, after being mortally wounded, flings himself upon Euryalus' body. The episode begins with this description of the pair:

> Nisus erat portae custos, acerrimus armis,
> Hyrtacides, comitem Aeneae quem miserat Ida
> venatrix iaculo celerem levibusque sagittis;
> et iuxta comes Euryalus, quo pulchrior alter

non fuit Aeneadum Troiana neque induit arma,
ora puer prima signans intonsa iuventa.
his amor unus erat pariterque in bella ruebant. (Vir. *Aen*. 9.176–82)

> Nisus son of Hyrtacus was the guard at the gate, a most fierce warrior, swift with the
> javelin and with nimble arrows, sent by Ida the huntress to accompany Aeneas. And
> next to him was his companion Euryalus. None of Aeneas' followers, none who had
> shouldered Trojan weapons, was more beautiful: a boy at the beginning of youth,
> displaying a face unshaven. These two shared one love, and rushed into the fighting
> side by side.

Virgil's wording is decorous, but the emphasis on Euryalus' youthful beauty
and particularly the absence of a beard on his fresh young face, as well as the
comment that the two shared one love and fought side by side—imagery that is
repeated from the scene in Book 5 and is continued throughout the episode in
Book 9—is noteworthy.[84] Likewise the question that Nisus asks Euryalus when he
first proposes the plan to him has suggestive resonances: "Euryalus, is it the gods
who put this yearning [*ardor*] into our minds, or does each person's grim desire
[*dira cupido*] become a god for him?" In addition to its ostensible subject (a desire
to achieve a military exploit), Nisus' language of yearning and desire could also
evoke the dynamics of an erotic relationship.[85] So too the poet's depiction of Nisus'
reaction to seeing his young companion captured by the enemy is notable for its
emotional urgency and its portrayal of Nisus' intensely protective love for the youth:

tum vero exterritus, amens,
conclamat Nisus nec se celare tenebris
amplius aut tantum potuit perferre dolorem:
"me, me, adsum qui feci, in me convertite ferrum,
o Rutuli! mea fraus omnis, nihil iste nec ausus
nec potuit; caelum hoc et conscia sidera testor;
tantum infelicem nimium dilexit amicum." (Vir. *Aen*. 9.424–30)

> Then, terrified out of his mind, unable to hide himself any longer in the shadows or to
> endure such great pain, Nisus shouts out: "Me! I am the one who did it! Turn your
> weapons to me, Rutulians! The deceit was entirely mine; *he* was not so bold as to do it;
> he could not have done it. I swear by the sky above and the stars who know: the only
> thing he did was to love his unhappy friend too much."

There is, in short, good reason to believe that Virgil's Nisus and Euryalus, whose
relationship is described in the circumspect terms befitting epic poetry, would
have been understood by his Roman readers as sharing a sexual bond, much like
the soldiers in the so-called Sacred Band of Thebes constituted of *erastai* and their
eromenoi in fourth-century B.C. Greece.[86]

When Nisus, mortally wounded, flings himself upon his companion's lifeless
body to join him in death, the narrator breaks forth into a celebrated eulogy:

tum super exanimum sese proiecit amicum
confossus, placidaque ibi demum morte quievit.
fortunati ambo! si quid mea carmina possunt,
nulla dies umquam memori vos eximet aevo,

dum domus Aeneae Capitoli immobile saxum
accolet imperiumque pater Romanus habebit. (Vir. *Aen.* 9.444–9)

Then he hurled himself, pierced through and through, upon his lifeless friend, and
there at last rested in a peaceful death. Blessed pair! If my poetry has any power, no
day shall ever remove you from the remembering ages, as long as the house of Aeneas
dwells upon the immovable rock of the Capitol, as long as the Roman father holds
sway.

The praise of the two loving warriors joined in death could hardly be more
stirring,[87] and the language could not be more Roman. And Virgil's words obviously made an impression among those who wished to express feelings of intimacy
and devotion in public contexts, for we find his language echoed in funerary inscriptions for a husband and his wife as well as for a woman praised by her male
friend; the inscription on a joint tomb of a grandmother and granddaughter explicitly likens them to Nisus and Euryalus.[88] So too Seneca quotes the lines as an
illustration of the fact that great writers can immortalize people who otherwise
would have had no fame: just as Cicero did for Atticus, Epicurus for Idomeneus,
and Seneca himself can do for Lucilius (an immodest claim but one that was ultimately borne out), so "our Virgil promised and gave an everlasting memory to the
two," whom he does not even bother to name, so renowned had the poet's words
evidently become.[89]

The relationships between Cydon and Clytius, Cycnus and Phaethon, and
Jupiter and Ganymede all demonstrate that pederastic relationships enjoy a comfortable presence in the world of the *Aeneid*. Nisus and Euryalus are thus hardly
alone; some scholars have even detected an erotic element in Virgil's depiction of
the relationship between Aeneas and Evander's son Pallas.[90] But their relationship
is more complex than the rather straightforward attraction of Cydon for beautiful
boys, of Cycnus for the well-born young Phaethon, and even of Jupiter for
Ganymede. For while those couples conform unproblematically to the Greek
pederastic model (one partner is older and dominant, the other younger and subordinate), Nisus and Euryalus only do so at first glance. As the poem progresses
they are transformed from a Hellenic coupling of *erastes* and *eromenos* into a pair
of Roman men (*viri*). The valorizing distinctions inherent in the pederastic paradigm seem to fade with the Roman poet's remark that the two rushed into war side
by side (*pariter*); and they certainly disappear when the old man Aletes, praising
them for their bold plan, addresses the two as *viri*; when an enemy leader who
catches a glimpse of them shouts out "Halt, men!"; and, most poignantly, when the
sight of the two "men's" severed heads pierced on enemy spears stuns the Trojan
soldiers.[91] In other words, although Euryalus is the junior partner in this relationship, not yet endowed with a full beard and capable of being labeled the *puer*, his
actions prove him to be, in the end, as much of a *vir*—as capable of displaying
virtus—as his older lover Nisus.

There is a further complication in our interpretation of the pair, and indeed of
all the pederastic relationships in the *Aeneid*. Virgil's epic is of course set in the
mythic past and cannot be taken as direct evidence for the cultural setting of Virgil's

own day; moreover, the poem is suffused with the influence of Greek poetry. Thus one might argue that the rather elevated status of pederastic relationships in the *Aeneid* is a sign merely of the distances both cultural and temporal between Virgil's contemporaries and the characters of his epic. Yet, while the influence of Homer is especially strong in these passages of battle poetry (Virgil's passing reference to Cydon's erotic adventures echoes the Homeric technique of citing some touching detail about a warrior's past even as he is introduced to the reader and summarily killed off), it is a much-discussed fact that there are no unambiguous, direct references in the Homeric epics to pederastic relationships on the classical model.[92] Virgil might thus be said to "out-Greek" Homer in his description of Cydon.[93] And yet the pederastic relationships in the *Aeneid* occur not among Greeks but rather among Trojans and Italians, two peoples who are strictly distinguished in the epic from the Greeks and who, more importantly, together constitute the progenitors of the Roman race.[94] Virgil's readers found pederastic relationships in an epic on their people's origins, and temporal gap or no, this would have been unthinkable in a cultural context in which same-sex relationships were universally condemned or deeply problematized. One need only contemplate an epic poem on the mythic origins of the English people that featured male couples.

But is it still not the case that, since Nisus and Euryalus are freeborn Trojans, Virgil's poetry celebrates, even glamorizes, a relationship that in his own day would be labeled as instances of *stuprum*? Here the gap between Virgil's time and the mythic past of his poem has significance. While, due to their freeborn status, analogues to Nisus and Euryalus in Virgil's own day could not have found their relationship so openly celebrated, they did find heroized ancestors in Nisus and Euryalus, Cydon and Clytius, and perhaps also Aeneas and Pallas. Significantly, though, the aura of the mythic past does not extend so far as to conceal the moral problematization of a male-female relationship in the *Aeneid*, namely the doomed love affair of Aeneas with the would-be *univira* Dido. In other words, while a male-male relationship that corresponds to what would among Romans of Virgil's own day be considered *stuprum* is capable of being heroized in the epic, a male-female relationship that the text implicitly marks as a kind of *stuprum* is not.[95] This distinction reveals something about the relative degrees of problematization of the two types of relationships in the cultural environment of Virgil's readership. "Blessed pair! If my poetry has any power, no day shall ever remove you from the remembering ages, as long as the house of Aeneas dwells upon the immovable rock of the Capitol, as long as the Roman father holds sway." One can hardly imagine such grandiose praise of an adulterous couple in a Roman epic.

The Law on *Stuprum*

Scholars generally agree that during the Republic there was no fixed procedure for penalizing acts of *stuprum*, whether with males or females (one possible exception is the *lex Scantinia*, to which we will return). The offense was a private matter, and punishment was meted out at the discretion of the *paterfamilias*.[96] But with the *lex Julia de adulteriis coercendis*, passed at Augustus' urging in 18 B.C., things changed. Now at least one form of *stuprum*, and the most troublesome form at that—namely, *adulterium*, or sexual acts involving a married woman and someone other than her husband—became an actionable offense. If convicted, the guilty party faced banishment, loss of property, and permanent social disabilities: a woman could never again marry a freeborn citizen, and a man was deprived of certain basic legal rights, becoming *intestabilis* and *infamis*.[97]

But there was another law regulating sexual behavior already on the books, namely the *lex Scantinia*, first attested by Cicero.[98] What exactly this law penalized, what penalties it provided for, and when it was enacted are questions that no ancient source directly answers, and modern scholarly interpretations vary quite markedly. L. P. Wilkinson describes the law as "forbidding male homosexuality," while W. Thomas MacCary asserts that it "set the death penalty for convicted homosexuals,"[99] but such views cannot be correct. The existence of a law "forbidding male homosexuality" is unthinkable in such a cultural environment as the one described in chapters 1 and 2; in any case, as Cantarella and Lilja have observed, someone like Cicero would surely have made reference to such a law, if one had existed, in the course of his attacks on the likes of Catiline or Gabinius.[100] But if not male homosexuality, what *was* the law aimed against? Some have suggested castration,[101] and others pederasty—that is, *stuprum* committed with freeborn boys;[102] others argue that the law subjected men who played the receptive ("passive") role in intercourse to a legal penalty;[103] still others suggest that its provisions were directed both against such men and against pederasty.[104] Here I argue for another interpretation: that the *lex Scantinia* penalized *stuprum* as a whole, whether committed with females or with males.[105]

Such an interpretation seems the most likely for several reasons. Firstly, in view of the evidence gathered in this chapter, indicating a marked tendency to view *stuprum* as an undifferentiated offense, it is difficult to imagine why a law would have been passed that penalized only homosexual *stuprum* rather than the offense as a whole. The Augustan legislation on adultery did of course penalize one subset of *stuprum* rather than the offense as a whole, but adultery is a special case, qualitatively distinct in important ways from any other kind of *stuprum*, for the reasons outlined earlier: men's proprietary claims over their wives were significantly different from their claims over their sons and daughters.

Apart, then, from the specific issue of adultery, one would have expected that if the law were brought to bear on the issue of *stuprum*, all varieties of the offense would have been subject to scrutiny. In fact, there is evidence for the existence of a praetorian edict that did precisely this by protecting freeborn Romans from unwanted sexual advances. Although the exact words of the edict are lost to us, later sources make it clear that it was formulated to include both sexes. The Digest, for example, includes this provision:

> qui puero praetextato stuprum aliudve flagitium abducto ab eo vel corrupto comite persuaserit, mulierem puellamve interpellaverit, quidve pudicitiae corrumpendae gratia fecerit, donum praebuerit pretiumve quo id persuadeat dederit, perfecto flagitio capite

punitur, imperfecto in insulam deportatur: corrupti comites summo supplicio
adficiuntur. (D. 47.11.1.2)

> Whoever shall persuade a boy wearing the *toga praetexta* to commit *stuprum* or any
> other offense, after abducting or bribing his attendant; or who shall solicit a woman or
> girl or do anything for the purpose of corrupting her *pudicitia*; or who shall proffer a
> gift or give money in order to persuade her to do it: if the offense is actually perpe-
> trated he is punished capitally; if not, he is deported to an island. Attendants who have
> been bribed are subjected to the ultimate punishment.

The harsh punishments specified here probably reflect the increasingly punitive
stance taken by Roman law from the third century A.D. onward; but the interest in
protecting the freeborn of both sexes from sexual advances reflects Roman traditions of long standing. Indeed, it has been suggested that a republican praetorian
edict, perhaps dating from the second century B.C., designated as its purview the
following situation:

> si quis matrifamilias aut praetextato praetextataeve comitem abduxisse sive quis eum
> eamve adversus bonos mores appellasse adsectatusve esse dicetur.[106]

> If anyone shall be said to have abducted the attendant of a matron or of a boy or girl
> wearing the *praetexta*, or to have accosted or pursued him or her contrary to decent
> ways [he shall be liable to punishment].

It is my suggestion that the *lex Scantinia* took the provisions of the praetorian edict
one step further: that, whereas the edict penalized those who merely made sexual
advances against protected dependents, the Scantinian law punished those who
actually engaged in sexual relations with such persons.[107] Quintilian makes reference to a fine of 10,000 sesterces established for those who violate a freeborn
person:[108] perhaps this was the penalty stipulated by the *lex Scantinia*.

It is my argument, in other words, that the *lex Scantinia* represented the codi-
fication of traditional Roman sanctions against *stuprum*, just as the later *lex Julia*
codified those sanctions against the most troublesome variety of *stuprum*, namely
adultery. In this regard it is worth noting that in three out of the six surviving
ancient references to the *lex Scantinia* it is cited in conjunction with the *lex Julia*:
Suetonius reports that Domitian, as part of his *correctio morum* ("correction of
morals"), took action against a Roman knight who had remarried his wife after
having divorced her for adultery (thus violating the spirit if not the letter of the *lex
Julia*), and adds in the next clause that the emperor condemned several other men
under the *lex Scantinia*. In a passage to which we will return, Juvenal has a character respond to a spiteful invocation of the *lex Julia* with an equally malicious reference to the *lex Scantinia*, and the Christian writer Prudentius pointedly observes
that if Jupiter had been subject to the provisions of Roman law, he would have
been found guilty under both the Julian and the Scantinian laws.[109] This last is
particularly revealing, for if we recall that Jupiter was notorious for his affairs with
married women (such as Alcmene) on the one hand, and freeborn young men and
women (such as Ganymede and Danae) on the other, it seems clear that as far as
Prudentius at any rate was concerned, the *lex Scantinia* could be invoked against

perpetrators of *stuprum* in general and the *lex Julia* against perpetrators of *adulterium* in particular.

On the other hand, two out of the six surviving references to the law suggest something quite different, namely that the *lex Scantinia* could be invoked against men who had willingly been penetrated (in chapter 5 we consider other legal disabilities to which such men might be subject). An epigram by Ausonius describes a *semivir* ("half-man") who fears the Scantinian law,[110] and Juvenal's second satire depicts a squabble between a woman named Laronia[111] and an unnamed *cinaedus* who has been pontificating about the immoral behavior of women:

> non tulit ex illis torvum Laronia quendam
> clamantem totiens "ubi nunc, lex Iulia, dormis?"
> atque ita subridens: "felicia tempora, quae te
> moribus opponunt. habeat iam Roma pudorem:
> tertius e caelo cecidit Cato. sed tamen unde
> haec emis, hirsuto spirant opobalsama collo
> quae tibi? ne pudeat dominum monstrare tabernae.
> quod si vexantur leges ac iura, citari
> ante omnis debet Scantinia." (Juv. 2.36–44)

> Laronia could not bear one of these fierce men who was constantly crying out, "Where are you sleeping, *lex Julia?*" So she said with a smile, "What fortunate times we live in, that put *you* in charge of morals. Let Rome now have its modesty; a third Cato has come down from heaven. But come now, where do you buy the balms that your hairy neck exudes? Don't be ashamed to point out the owner of the shop. And if laws are being stirred up, above all the Scantinian ought to be cited."

Just as the man reproaches women in general (and, implicitly, Laronia in particular) for their adulterous behavior, asking in exasperation whether the *lex Julia* is dormant, so Laronia retorts by invoking the *lex Scantinia* against her interlocutor. This man is represented not as a lover of freeborn youth but rather as a *cinaedus*, or effeminate man who likes to be anally penetrated.[112]

Can we reconcile these two apparently distinct strands of evidence concerning the *lex Scantinia*, that it punished the penetrating perpetrators of *stuprum*, and that it penalized those who played the receptive role in acts of *stuprum*? I suggest that we can. Just as the *lex Julia* punished both the penetrating participant in an act of *adulterium* and the penetrated participant (that is, both the married woman and her partner), so the *lex Scantinia* might have contained provisions for the punishment not only of men who violated the sexual integrity of freeborn Romans, but also of those (male or female) who allowed their integrity to be compromised. Thus, on the one hand, Juvenal's Laronia is able to invoke the law against an effeminate *cinaedus*,[113] just as Ausonius writes of a *semivir* who fears the law; but on the other hand, Prudentius claims that Jupiter could be found guilty under the *lex Scantinia*.

If my interpretation is correct, and if the *lex Scantinia* penalized the general offense of *stuprum*, whereas the later *lex Julia* was directed against the specific variety of *stuprum* known as *adulterium*, another question arises: What was the relationship between the two laws? The question is complicated by the fact that several ancient sources describing the *lex Julia* make reference not just to adultery in particular but to *stuprum* in general, and occasionally to *stuprum* with males. This seems at first to suggest that the Julian law actually governed not just adultery but *stuprum* as a whole, and that it thus superseded the Scantinian law. But that was clearly not the case, at least originally, since both Suetonius' and Juvenal's references to the *lex Scantinia* imply that it had continued to exist and to be enforced (albeit sporadically) after the passage of the Augustan legislation. How can we resolve this difficulty?[114]

There can be no question that the *lex Julia* was primarily aimed at the specific offense of adultery; indeed, the overwhelming majority of the jurisprudential discussions of the law preserved in the Digest (48.5) concern relations with married women. Yet one ancient source reveals that the actual wording of the law included references to both *adulterium* and *stuprum*, and Suetonius describes Augustus' legislation as pertaining to *adulterium* and *pudicitia* (which, as we have seen, was a concept that stood in a complementary relationship with *stuprum*);[115] another source tells us that the law provided for the prosecution both of unmarried women (*viduae*) and of married women (*nuptae*);[116] and others observe that the law spoke indifferently of *stuprum* and *adulterium*, even though technically speaking the latter is committed only with married women and the former with unmarried women.[117] Modestinus, in his book of *Regulae* or *Rules*, even adds that *stuprum* can be committed with boys,[118] although he is giving a general definition of the term and is not necessarily addressing the *lex Julia* in particular.

It is thus possible that the *lex Julia*, whose wording included the broad term *stuprum*, was actually invoked only in cases of *stuprum* with females, and most often in cases of *stuprum* with married women (i.e., in cases of *adulterium*), while the *lex Scantinia*, itself worded so as to penalize undifferentiated *stuprum*, was now reserved for cases of *stuprum* with males. If this is true, the law now made a distinction between heterosexual and homosexual *stuprum*, but such a distinction is to be associated with a proprietary urge with regard to women in general and wives in particular rather than with an inclination to treat homosexual practices differently from heterosexual practices. For, whatever the provisions of the law may have been, all of the evidence reviewed in this chapter suggests that in popular conceptions of the central period, from about 200 B.C. to about A.D. 200, *stuprum* was viewed as a single offense, regardless of the sex of the Roman man's partner.

In later years, however, as an ascetic approach to sexual behavior became increasingly popular, there seems to have been a growing tendency to place restrictions upon sexual behavior outside of marriage, and consequently to problematize sexual practices between males (see the introduction); thus, at some point the *lex Julia* began to be invoked against acts of *stuprum* perpetrated with freeborn males. Writing in the third century A.D., Marcianus observes that someone who provides his house as a rendez-vous spot for someone to commit "*stuprum* or *adulterium* with a married woman or with a male" is liable to be punished as if he were an adulterer, that is, as if he had violated the *lex Julia*.[119] By the time of the Christian emperor Justinian (who reigned in the sixth century A.D.), the *lex Julia* was invoked in order to penalize not only adultery but also *stuprum* committed with males.[120] Of course this meant that the Julian law was now encroaching upon the territory of the *lex Scantinia*, and that is exactly what a fourth-century A.D. source suggests.[121] But it deserves to be emphasized that these developments reflect the preoccupations of later emperors and jurists, who became increasingly concerned with limiting sexual behavior outside of marriage, rather than the Augustan legislation itself.[122] After all, as late as the fourth century A.D., Prudentius was able to cite the Julian and the Scantinian laws in tandem, as if they were both still in effect and governed related but distinct offenses.

In sum, the punitive mechanisms of these laws directly reflected traditional Roman ideologies of masculine sexual behavior, penalizing those who infringed upon the sexual integrity of the freeborn, subjecting to especially rigorous treatment those who corrupted other men's wives, but not singling out instances of *stuprum* perpetrated between males for particular recrimination or penalization until the ascendancy of an ascetic tradition regarding sexual practices that encouraged the condemnation of all sexual acts outside of the context of marriage. In the end it is important to observe that, Domitian's loudly proclaimed revival of traditional standards aside, the Scantinian law was rarely enforced. We may well be skeptical of the degree to which any attempts to control sexual behavior by legal means—such as the praetorian edict protecting the *pudicitia* of matrons and boys, the *lex Scantinia*, or indeed the *lex Julia*—actually had an effect on men's sexual behavior. Despite traditional prohibitions against relations with the freeborn, Roman men must often have tried to live up to the model of Priapus by asserting their phallic dominion not only over their own slaves and prostitutes, but also over the freeborn of both sexes. Discussing the praetorian edict, and expressing a similar skepticism, Eva Cantarella offers some suggestive comments:

> These two supposedly respectable categories of people were defended in exactly the same way from a type of behaviour which is familiar to anyone who lives in a Mediterranean country. Actually, this behaviour is not exclusively motivated by a real desire to seduce the victim; it also stems from a need felt by the male of the species to give a theatrical display and proof of virility. A ritual game, in short, where each player performs a time-honoured part: the male plays the hunter, while the woman (or in Rome the boy) plays the prey.[123]

This impressionistic view certainly provides food for thought as we attempt a tentative reconstruction of the social and ideological landscapes of ancient Rome. The metaphor of theatricality and the suggestion that men feel the need to "prove" their virility are particularly apt: as we see in the next chapter, Roman ideologies of masculinity were predicated on the assumption that a real man must not only achieve but also constantly display and perform his status as a dominant male, in control of himself and others.

Plate 1. Marble statuary group
of Ganymede and the eagle;
2nd century A.D. (Naples,
Museo Nazionale 6355.)

Plate 2. Mosaic depicting Zeus' eagle carrying Ganymede aloft;
2nd or 3rd century A.D. (Rome, Museo Nazionale 1241.)

Plate 3. Marble statuary group of the eagle carrying Ganymede aloft; around A.D. 200. (Venice, Museo Archeologico 145.)

Plate 4. Marble statuary group depicting the eagle carrying Ganymede aloft; 2nd century A.D. Roman version of a famous original by the 4th-century B.C. Greek sculptor Leochares. (Vatican, Galleria dei Candelabri.)

Plate 5. Bust of Antinous, found at Patras in Greece.
(Athens, National Museum 418.)

Plate 6. Bust of Antinous, found at
Hadrian's Villa in Tivoli near Rome.
(Vatican, Sala Rotonda 540.)

Plate 7. Colossal marble statue of Antinous as the god Dionysus, found at Praeneste near Rome. (Vatican, Sala Rotonda 545.)

Plate 8. Travertine wall panel carved for good luck, with an image of the phallus and the inscription *hic habitat felicitas* ("here dwells happiness/prosperity"); from Pompeii, 1st century A.D. (Naples, Museo Nazionale, RP 27741.)

Plate 9. Bronze apotropaic wind-chime (*tintinnabulum*) with phallic design, from Trier in Germany; 1st century A.D. (Trier, Rheinisches Landesmuseum, G92.)

Plate 10. Wall painting of Priapus weighing his impressive member, with a basket of fruit at his feet; at the entrance to the House of the Vettii in Pompeii; 1st century A.D. (Photo Michael Larvey.)

Plate 11. Fragments of Arretine pottery depicting (top) male-female
and (bottom) male-male couplings.
(Boston, Museum of Fine Arts 13.109;
gift of Edward Perry Warren.)

Plate 12. The so-called Warren Cup, depicting two male-male couplings;
perhaps from the 1st century A.D.
(New York Metropolitan Museum of Art
L.1991.95; anonymous loan.)

4

Effeminacy and Masculinity

According to the prime directive of masculine sexual behavior, a Roman man who wished to retain his claim to full masculinity must always be thought to play the insertive role in penetrative acts, whether with males or females; if he was thought to have sought the receptive role in such acts he forfeited his claim to masculinity and was liable to being mocked as effeminate (see chapter 5 for further discussion of this protocol and of Roman representations of specific sexual acts and actors). In chapter 3 we saw that the second protocol of masculinity could be coordinated with the first, such that even if a man pursued freeborn persons, traditionally protected by the concept of *stuprum*, as long as he maintained an active, dominant (and penetrating) stance his own masculinity was not infringed upon. In this chapter, however, we see that masculinity was more complex than such a schematization suggests. Being penetrated was not the only practice that could brand a man as effeminate, and a man who was cast in the role of the insertive partner, whether of males or of females, could still be liable to an accusation of effeminacy. In other words, we see that playing the insertive role in penetrative acts, while being a necessary precondition for full masculinity, was not a sufficient one. Thus the writers and readers of Roman texts could easily imagine a notorious womanizer or adulterer as effeminate, and a Roman orator could curl his lip at a decadent young man who sashayed about more softly than a woman in order to please women.

These uses of the imagery of effeminacy form part of the larger discourses of masculinity which this book in general and this chapter in particular aim to interrogate. When I inquire into images of *effeminacy*, my ultimate goal is of course to attempt a reconstruction of the various possible meanings of *masculinity* for the writers and readers of ancient texts, since the concept of effeminacy in a man only has meaning with reference to the preexisting concepts of masculinity and femininity, and these two form part of a single discursive system. Effeminate men constitute a negative paradigm: in their failure to live up to standards of masculine comportment, they are what real men are not, and real men are what effeminate men are not.

Thus, in the interests of exploring the game of Roman masculinity—a serious game, to be sure—I focus on representations of those who broke its rules, first asking what precisely constituted a charge of effeminacy and then examining how effeminacy was thought to be embodied in men's behaviors, whether sexual or not. The most significant point to emerge is that a man labeled effeminate might be represented as playing the receptive role in penetrative acts, but he might just as well be thought to play the insertive role; or he could be playing both roles. Thus the landscape within which Roman discourses of masculinity and effeminacy were played out was one in which the distinction between insertive and receptive role did not stand in a nonproblematic, one-to-one relationship with the opposition between acceptably masculine and unacceptably effeminate behavior; in which the hetero-homosexual binarism did not appear as a meaningful opposition; and in which genital practices constituted only one among many problematized behaviors. In the end, a man's full masculinity was not guaranteed simply by asserting the penetrative power of his phallus at another's expense, and yielding his body to the power of another man's phallus was only one among many practices that could lay a man open to a charge of effeminacy.

Maud Gleason has likewise argued that in antiquity effeminacy involved more than the question of sexual role, and that men who desired to be penetrated were but a subset (albeit a significant one) of the larger set of effeminates.[1] Writing of various behaviors considered to be effeminate, she makes this point:

> These habits, while they might in some circumstances constitute a shorthand key to their practitioner's sexual preferences, might also bear a more generalized penumbra of meaning and indicate nothing more than his aspirations to elegance. After all, these mannerisms—from depilation to ingratiating inflections of the voice—were refinements aimed at translating the ideal of beardless ephebic beauty into adult life, and as such might appeal to women and boys, with whom one could not by definition play the pathic role, as well as to some adult men, with whom one could.[2]

Effeminacy was thus a disorder that was embodied in various symptoms, only one of which—and not a necessary one at that—was a predilection for being anally penetrated. But what is the nature of that fundamental disorder? Catharine Edwards, surveying the widely varying behaviors labeled effeminate by ancient writers, makes this comment:

> The apparent incoherence of accusations of effeminacy—the same people are accused of being both sexually passive and sexually insatiable—makes more sense if we look at effeminacy—"being like a woman"—as a wholly negative term when applied to men.

Whatever qualities were undesirable in a male member of the Roman elite were termed "feminine."[3]

This is certainly an accurate way of describing how accusations of effeminacy *function*, but it does not suggest much about the fundamental *nature* of effeminacy. Gleason is more specific, seeing the issue of pleasure, and a man's relation to it, as crucial. Discussing a passage from the Christian writer Clement of Alexandria, who disdainfully refers to *androgynoi* and *cinaedi* who engage in sexual relations with women, she observes:

> What is deviant in the behavior of these *androgynoi* and *cinaedi* is not the gender of their sexual object choice (a preoccupation of contemporary North Americans and Northern Europeans), but the style of their erotic pursuit. A man who actively penetrates and dominates others, whether male or female, is still a man. A man who aims to please—any one, male or female—in his erotic encounters is ipso facto effeminate.[4]

In the third volume of his *History of Sexuality*, Foucault discusses the ways in which philosophers and medical writers of the first centuries A.D. became increasingly preoccupied with the notion of "the care of the self" (*cura sui*).[5] Here I argue that these philosophers' and medical writers' impulse toward self-care, and even more the related concept of self-mastery, had deep roots in traditional Roman concepts of masculine identity. I suggest that the various manifestations of effeminacy are symptoms of an underlying failure to live up to the central imperative of masculinity: control and dominion, both of others and of oneself. As we will see, the language of masculinity often invokes such notions as *imperium* ("dominion") and *fortitudo* ("strength"), whereas the essence of a weak femininity, embodied in women and effeminate men, is *mollitia* ("softness").[6] Another crucial concept is that of *virtus*: etymologically nothing more than "manliness," this word came to refer to broad notions of valor and ultimately "virtue," but always in a strongly gendered sense. *Virtus* is the ideal of masculine behavior that all men ought to embody, that some women have the good fortune of attaining, and that men derided as effeminate conspicuously fail to achieve.

After considering the ways in which masculine *virtus* and *imperium* are represented and the various practices and behaviors, sexual and otherwise, associated with effeminacy, I close with a discussion of men who openly flaunted their failure to fully live up to the rules of the game, and I suggest that we should not succumb to the insistent rhetoric of the dominant voice in our sources, which maintained a strict opposition between a glorious Roman manliness and a despicable effeminacy. Intermediate positions, and even a degree of resistance, were possible.[7]

Signifiers of Effeminacy: Softness and Excessive Grooming

How precisely could a slur of effeminacy be effected by Roman writers? Often the language is direct: a man may be said not to be a "man" (*male vir, parum vir*, and the like) or he, his behavior, or his attributes can be described as *effeminatus* ("effeminate") or *muliebris* ("womanish"). Less direct, but equally meaningful, was metaphorical language depicting a man or his attributes as being the opposite of the tough man of action: *delicatus* ("delicate"), *enervis* ("enervated" or "sinewless"), and *fractus* ("broken"). But above all, to call a man *mollis* ("soft") or to associate him with *mollitia* ("softness") was a handy way of making the point that he was not fully masculine.[8] Eloquent testimony is provided by a passage from Ovid's *Metamorphoses* where we read of the transformation of Hermaphroditus, son of Hermes and Aphrodite, from a full male (*vir*) to an androgyne (*semivir*) when he is joined to the nymph Salmacis:

> ergo ubi se liquidas, quo vir descenderat, undas
> semimarem fecisse videt mollitaque in illis
> membra, manus tendens, sed iam non voce virili,
> Hermaphroditus ait: "nato date munera vestro,
> et pater et genetrix, amborum nomen habenti:
> quisquis in hos fontes vir venerit, exeat inde
> semivir et tactis subito mollescat in undis!" (Ov. *Met*. 4.380–6)[9]

So when he saw that the waters into which he had descended as a man (*vir*) had made him a half-male (*semimarem*), and as he saw his limbs made soft (*mollita*) in the water, Hermaphroditus stretched out his hands in prayer and, with a voice no longer manly (*virili*), said: "Father and mother, grant this gift to your son who takes his name from both of you: whoever shall enter this stream as a man (*vir*), let him step out a half-man (*semivir*) and let him grow soft (*mollescat*) just by touching the water!"

With characteristic rhetorical flourish, the poet makes explicit an assumption that is implied throughout the ancient sources: *softness is the antithesis of masculinity*. So it is that the language of softness appears in allusions to the most extreme type of unmanly men: eunuchs. Lucan describes the castrated as "unhappy youth, softened [*mollita*] by the blade, their manhood [*virum*] cut out," and Statius, in a poem of abject flattery celebrating Domitian's beloved eunuch Earinos, imagines the miraculous moment of his castration at the hands of none other than Asclepius, the god of healing and son of Apollo: "The authority to soften [*mollire*] the boy was entrusted to no one, but Apollo's young son with silent skill gently bade his body, struck by no wound, to take leave of its sex."[10] Perhaps the ultimate scare-figure of Roman masculinity was the *gallus* or castrated priest of Cybele, further discussed in the next chapter. Catullus' poem on the mythic figure Attis (63), a beautiful young man who was swept away by a band of *galli* and finally joined their ranks, castrating himself and dedicating his life to the goddess, exploits the relationship between these priests and masculinity. In his new state, Attis is of course represented as the antithesis of masculinity: he has in fact lost his "manhood" (*viro*, 6); he refers to the *galli* in the feminine, as *Gallae* (12), and uses feminine participles and adjectives to describe them, even as the narrator uses masculine forms to describe Attis before the castration and feminine forms afterwards, when he becomes a "fake woman" (*notha mulier*, 27). Attis himself follows the same practice, even after he comes to his senses and regrets what he has done: "Am I now to be called a servant-girl of the gods, a slave-girl of Cybele? Shall I be a Maenad, a part of myself, a sterile man?"[11] Of course, everything about Attis is now soft and womanish, as he holds the *tympanum* (itself called "smooth," *leve*) in his "snowy" hands and strikes it with his "delicate" (*teneris*) fingers.[12] Castration is an extreme instance of a conceptual all-or-nothing tendency that pervades Roman texts: softening a male constitutes a direct infringement upon his masculine identity.

Apart from these lexical means (above all, by using the language of *mollitia*), Roman writers could signify effeminacy by pointing to the ways in which a man was acting "like a woman." We frequently encounter descriptions of effeminate men walking delicately, talking in a womanish way, wearing loose, colorful, feminine clothing (including the *mitra* or Eastern-style turban), overindulging in perfume, curling their hair, and above all depilating themselves, particularly on the chest and legs.[13] If a man does these things, he is not only making himself look more like an idealized woman but he is also displaying an excessive concern for his appearance, a kind of self-absorption that was stereotypically associated with women.[14] And as a pseudo-woman he may well be thought to display a proclivity for what was held to be the woman's role in sexual acts. Thus Scipio Aemilianus' attack against P. Sulpicius Galus cited in chapter 1 includes an impressive list of effeminate traits: he wore perfume; he adorned himself in front of a mirror; he shaved his eyebrows and plucked out the hairs of his beard as well as his thighs; in his youth he wore a long-sleeved tunic when he accompanied his male lover (*amator*, a word whose active meaning would not have been lost on Scipio's audience) to parties; he was as fond of wine as he was of men. All of these signs combine to suggest, Scipio would have us believe, that Sulpicius has done "what *cinaedi* do."[15]

Suetonius relates the gossip spread by Lucius Antonius (brother of Augustus' enemy, the infamous Mark Antony) to the effect that Augustus had shared his favors not only with Julius Caesar (who, to translate Suetonius' phrase loosely, "took his virginity") but also (for a fee) with Aulus Hirtius, and that he was in the habit of singeing the hairs of his legs with hot nutshells so that the hairs might grow softer. Suetonius also reports that Julius Caesar himself was "quite exacting [*morosior*] about the care of his body," such that he not only trimmed and shaved himself, but even went to the extreme of plucking.[16] A century later Juvenal imagines the effeminate emperor Otho primping before a mirror, applying bread-poultices to soften his facial skin, and in general outdoing the legendary queens Semiramis and Cleopatra in his attention to his appearance.[17] Such was the gossip powerful men might find being spread by their enemies.

It is important to note that, while depilation of this kind was held to be a sure sign of effeminacy and was capable of being associated with a proclivity for being penetrated by men (as it was by Scipio in his attack on Sulpicius Galus, and by Lucius Antonius in his attack on Augustus), smoothness of leg, chest, and arm was also thought to be appealing to some women. An epigram of Martial directly reveals the assumption that an effeminate depilation—even of one's legs—might reveal a man's interest in attracting women:

> Quod pectus, quod crura tibi, quod bracchia vellis,
>   quod cincta est brevibus mentula tonsa pilis,
> hoc praestas, Labiene, tuae—quis nescit?—amicae.
>   cui praestas, culum quod, Labiene, pilas? (Mart. 2.62)

Labienus, that you pluck the hairs from your chest, your legs, and your arms, and that your shaven dick is surrounded by short bristles—you offer this to your girl-friend; who does not know that? But, Labienus, to whom do you offer your depilated asshole?

The joke is characteristic of Martial—a man who gives the appearance of engaging in acceptably masculine sexual practices in reality enjoys playing the "woman's" role as well—but his depilatory schematization must have made sense to his read-ership: that a man might pluck the hairs of his chest, legs, arms, and pubic region in order to please his girlfriend was clearly not an unthinkable possibility.[18] In an epigram discussed in chapter 5, the same poet writes of Gallus who is "softer than the shells of Venus" and who is pursuing a married lady.[19]

If effeminacy was embodied not only in attempts to make one's body softer and hairless but also in an excessive concern for one's appearance, masculinity was associated with a certain uncultivated roughness. The emperor Vespasian, inter-ested in reinforcing that ultimate bulwark of Roman masculinity, military disci-pline, revoked the appointment he had bestowed upon a young official because the young man came to him smelling of perfume: "I would have preferred that you had smelled of garlic," gruffly commented the emperor.[20] Juvenal imagines a young man desirous of promotion within the army being advised to affect neglect of his appearance, leaving his hair uncombed and the hairs of his nostrils and underarms untrimmed; the same poet describes *cinaedi* (effeminate men who sought to be sexually penetrated) attempting to conceal their true nature by presenting the ap-pearance of a fierce manliness in the form of "hairy limbs and bristly arms."[21] These men were participating in, and trying to manipulate, a traditional discourse that Gleason has astutely summed up with the phrase "hairier than thou."[22] Several epigrams of Martial toy with this discourse, trenchantly observing that while an unkempt hairiness would usually be taken as a sure sign of masculinity, in reality it might just be a smoke screen.[23]

Of course here, as everywhere, the concept of the golden mean came into play. Speaking of extremes in literary styles (for example, the use of only the aus-tere, harsh language of the ancients, or of only what is currently in vogue, or the exclusive use of high-flown, poetic language while shunning all everyday language), Seneca uses a physical metaphor to advocate the middle course:

> tam hunc dicam peccare quam illum: alter se plus iusto colit, alter plus iusto neglegit; ille et crura, hic ne alas quidem vellit. (Sen. *Epist.* 114.14)

> I would say that this man goes astray as much as that one; the one takes care of himself more than he ought to, while the other one neglects himself more than he ought to: the former removes the hair even from his legs, while the latter not even from his underarms.

Depilating one's underarms is an acceptable, even recommended, act of good grooming in a man, but doing it to one's legs is going too far.[24] An epigram of Martial's simultaneously points to some physical embodiments of the golden mean of masculinity and attacks a particular man for failing to attain it:

Flectere te nolim, sed nec turbare capillos;
　splendida sit nolo, sordida nolo cutis;
nec tibi mitrarum nec sit tibi barba reorum:
　nolo virum nimium, Pannyche, nolo parum.
nunc sunt crura pilis et sunt tibi pectora saetis
　horrida, sed mens est, Pannyche, volsa tibi. (Mart. 2.36)

I wouldn't want you to curl your hair, nor on the other hand to muss it up. I don't want your skin to be shiny, but I don't want it dirty. Nor should you have anything to do with bonnets, nor with a long, unkempt beard. Pannychos, I want neither too much of a man nor too little of a man. But as it is, Pannychos, your legs bristle with hair, and your chest likewise; but your mind is plucked.

Martial's images for what constitutes too much and too little of a man correspond to widespread assumptions: excessive masculinity is embodied in unkempt hair, skin, and beard as well as bristly legs and chest, while insufficient masculinity is shown by artificially curled hair, skin treated with the finest of cosmetics, feminine headgear, and depilated legs and chest. Somewhere in between, Martial implies, lies the happy medium.[25]

That men should avoid an entirely unkempt appearance, while steering clear of an excessive concern for their toilet that would mark them as effeminate, is precisely the advice offered by Ovid to a readership of Roman men interested in finding girlfriends:

sed tibi nec ferro placeat torquere capillos,
　nec tua mordaci pumice crura teras;
ista iube faciant, quorum Cybeleia mater
　concinitur Phrygiis exululata modis.
forma viros neglecta decet; Minoida Theseus
　abstulit, a nulla tempora comptus acu;
Hippolytum Phaedra, nec erat bene cultus, amavit;
　cura deae silvis aptus Adonis erat.
munditie placeant, fuscentur corpora Campo;
　sit bene conveniens et sine labe toga.
†lingua ne rigeat†; careant rubigine dentes;
　nec vagus in laxa pes tibi pelle natet;
nec male deformet rigidos tonsura capillos:
　sit coma, sit trita barba resecta manu.
et nihil emineant et sint sine sordibus ungues,
　inque cava nullus stet tibi nare pilus.
nec male odorati sit tristis anhelitus oris,
　nec laedat naris virque paterque gregis.
cetera lascivae faciant concede puellae
　et si quis male vir quaerit habere virum. (Ov. Ars 1.505–24)

But you, don't seek to curl your hair with an iron, nor rub your legs with the biting pumice stone: leave such things for those who sing hymns to the mother-goddess Cybele in their Phrygian modes. An unkempt beauty befits men: Theseus took the Minoan Ariadne, though his temples were adorned by no hair-pin; Phaedra loved

Hippolytus, and he was not particularly refined. The goddess [Venus] fell in love with Adonis, and he was suited to the woods. Your bodies should be pleasing in their cleanliness, and bronzed in the Campus Martius; your toga should fit you well and show no stains. . . . Your teeth should be free of tartar. Your feet should not swim around in shoes too big for them. Nor should your haircut make your hair ugly and standing on end: your hair and beard should be trimmed by an experienced hand. Your fingernails should be clean and not too long, and there should be no hairs showing in your nostrils. Your breath should not be offensive in its smell, nor should your underarms offend the nose by smelling like a he-goat. But as for the rest, leave that for wanton girls and for those—hardly men—who seek to have a man.

Beyond the bare necessities of trimming one's fingernails and nostril hairs and avoiding malodorous breath and underarms, he recommends that overdone grooming be restricted to girls and effeminate men—"hardly men"—who seek to play the receptive, "woman's" role in penetrative acts with men. But Ovid's advice in this didactic text seems to come as a reaction against relatively widespread practices, and if we add that consideration to the evidence provided by Martial's epigram on Labienus, it seems clear that in the urban landscape of first-century A.D. Rome there were men who, in hopes of attracting women (among other possible reasons), went to the extremes of beautification—for example, by depilating their arms, legs, and chest—even if doing so laid them open to charges of effeminacy.

Virtus and *Imperium*: **Masculinity and Dominion**

The Roman conceptualization of masculinity as being embodied in restraint and control, over others and oneself, informs two concepts basic to Roman masculinity: *virtus* and *imperium*. The first of these two words displays a significantly gendered quality. Derived from *vir* and thus etymologically meaning "manliness," *virtus* came to be used of a variety of moral traits considered admirable in men—concepts that might be translated as "valor" or "virtue."[26] Effeminate men, of course, failed to live up to this standard. Juvenal's eighth satire begins with an attack on a decadent, effeminate aristocrat that plays off the contrast between his unmanly, self-indulgent ways (he stays up all night gambling, he is greedy, vain, and soft [*mollis*], and he even depilates himself) and the *virtus* that he ought to have but does not, despite his noble ancestry:

> cur Allobrogicis et magna gaudeat ara
> natus in Herculeo Fabius lare, si cupidus, si
> vanus et Euganea quantumvis mollior agna,
> si tenerum attritus Catinensi pumice lumbum
> squalentis traducit avos emptorque veneni
> frangenda miseram funestat imagine gentem?
> tota licet veteres exornent undique cerae
> atria, nobilitas sola est atque unica virtus. (Juv. 8.13–20)

Why should Fabius, born in Hercules' home, exult in his [noble name of] Allobrogicus and the Great Altar, if he is greedy, empty, and so much softer than a Euganean lamb, and if he wears down his soft loins with pumice from Catania, exposing his hairy ancestors to scorn, and if by buying poison he pollutes the wretched family with his death-mask that ought to be smashed? Though ancient wax masks may adorn the whole atrium on every side, virtue [*virtus*] is the one and only nobility.

The *virtus* that this well-born man conspicuously fails to display is here clearly gendered as masculine. Indeed, a belief that *virtus* is fundamentally a man's rather than a woman's quality surfaces in a blessing issued by the poet Statius on his friend Julius Menecrates on the occasion of the birth of his third child, in which he observes that *virtus* is "more suited" to his sons, while his daughter will best serve him by providing grandsons.[27] In a philosophical essay addressed to his mother, Seneca suggests that *virtus* is antithetical to "women's vices" (*muliebria vitia*), and that women who display *virtus* rise to the level of "great men" (*magni viri*).[28] Women, indeed, may perpetrate acts of *virtus*, but in doing so they act like men: Valerius Maximus describes Cato the Younger's daughter Porcia, who committed suicide by swallowing live coals, as "having imitated the manly death of her father with a woman's spirit," while he prefaces his narrative of Lucretia's valorous suicide by noting that the poor woman had a "man's soul" trapped in a "woman's body."[29] As for Seneca's preachy remarks to his mother, it is revealing that the highest praise he can offer her is that she lacks all feminine vices. One could never praise a man by saying that he lacks all masculine vices—indeed, the very concept is oxymoronic. In short, *virtus* is an eminently praiseworthy quality, whether in a male (who should naturally have it) or a female (who may, exceptionally, attain to it); *mollitia*, while desirable in women and boys, is antithetical to full manliness.

Virtus could also be related to the concept of *imperium*, the rule or dominion that magistrates exercised over the Roman people, generals over their armies, the Roman people as a whole over their subjects, and Roman men over women and slaves. If a Roman writer wished to wax philosophical, he could even use the imagery of *imperium* to describe the dominion that reason ought to exercise over emotions. Cicero does precisely that in his *Tusculan Disputations*, and the manner in which he implicitly aligns reason with masculinity and domination, and emotion with effeminacy and softness, is telling:

est enim animus in partis tributus duas, quarum altera rationis est particeps, alter expers. cum igitur praecipitur, ut nobismet ipsis imperemus, hoc praecipitur, ut ratio coerceat temeritatem. est in animis omnium fere natura molle quiddam, demissum, humile, enervatum quodam modo et languidum. si nihil esset aliud, nihil esset homine deformius. sed praesto est domina omnium et regina ratio, quae conixa per se et progressa longius fit perfecta virtus. haec ut imperet illi parti animi, quae oboedire debet, id videndum est viro. "quonam modo?" inquies. vel ut dominus servo vel ut imperator militi vel ut parens filio. si turpissime se illa pars animi geret, quam dixi esse mollem, si se lamentis muliebriter lacrimisque dedet, vinciatur et constringatur amicorum propinquorumque custodiis; saepe enim videmus fractos pudore, qui ratione nulla vincerentur. (Cic. *Tusc.* 2.47–8)

Now, the soul is divided into two parts, of which one partakes of reason and the other does not. Thus, when we are told to control ourselves [*imperemus*], we are really being told to see to it that reason restrains impetuousness. In nearly every soul there is something naturally soft [*molle*], abject, abased, in some way or other spineless [*enervatum*] and listless. If that is all there were, nothing would be more repugnant than humanity; but reason stands ready as sovereign of all [*domina omnium et regina*]—reason, which, striving on its own and advancing far, finally becomes perfect virtue [*virtus*]. That reason should give orders to [*imperet*] the other part of the soul, the part that ought to be obedient—that is what a man [*viro*] must take care to do. "But how?" you will ask. The way a master gives orders to his slave, or a commander to his soldier, or a father to his son. If that part of the soul which I previously called soft [*mollem*] behaves disgracefully, if it gives itself over in womanish fashion [*muliebriter*] to tears and lamentation, let it be bound and constrained by friends and relatives. For we often see broken by shame those who would not be won over by any reasoning.

Reason is thus implicitly masculinized and contrasted with that which is soft and spineless (*molle* and *enervatum*) and which causes a man to weep like a woman (*muliebriter*). There is, though, a tension created by the fact that the noun *ratio* ("reason") is grammatically feminine: thus when he describes it as "sovereign over all," Cicero actually uses the grammatically feminine nouns *domina* and *regina* ("mistress" and "queen"). This is a fascinating moment, when we see an interference between ideological imperatives ("reason" is conceptually masculine) and the strictures of language (*ratio* is grammatically feminine). Grammatical gender yields, of course, to the overarching imperative of masculine ideology. Indeed, while *virtus* itself is grammatically feminine (soon after Cicero remarks on the derivation of the word *virtus* from *vir*, he personifies *Virtus* as a being, necessarily using feminine forms to describe it),[30] there is no doubt that *virtus* is a masculine virtue. Likewise in this case, even though the grammatical gender of the noun *ratio* induces Cicero to personify it as *domina* and *regina*, the tenor of the argument urges a masculinization of reason, which must control (*coerceat, imperet*) an emotional part of the soul that is soft and acts like a woman (*molle, muliebriter*) in just the way that a master controls his slave, a commander his soldier, and a father his son. We observe that all the images used are of men, not women, and all of them are in Roman terms men who by definition have authority and power over others: *dominus, imperator, parens*.

Further exploring the dominion of implicitly masculinized reason and *virtus* over the soft, womanish, emotions, Cicero later quotes from Pacuvius' *Niptrae*, in which a dying Odysseus has this to say:

> conqueri fortunam adversam, non lamentari decet:
> id viri est officium, fletus muliebri ingenio additus. (Cic. *Tusc*. 2.50)[31]

> It is fitting to complain about, but not lament, an adverse situation. This is a man's job; weeping is assigned to woman's nature.

The contrast between masculine and effeminate implicit throughout this discussion here comes to the surface, and it reappears shortly in Cicero's claim that a man who tries to fortify himself against indulgence in pain or grief will say some such thing to himself: "Beware of anything disgraceful, languid, unmanly."[32] Next, engaging in the favorite pasttime of Roman moralizers of every generation—drawing an unfavorable contrast between their contemporaries and the glorious Romans of old—Cicero claims that the men of his day are so ruled by an effeminate principle (*opinio effeminata ac levis*, 2.52), both in pleasure and in pain, that they cannot even endure a toothache or a beesting with fortitude. In sum, the guiding principle must be one of self-control or self-mastery, and to abandon this principle is to act like a slave or a woman:

> totum igitur in eo est, ut tibi imperes . . . sed hoc idem in dolore maxume est providendum, ne quid abiecte, ne quid timide, ne quid ignave, ne quid serviliter muliebriterve faciamus. (Cic. *Tusc.* 2.53, 55)[33]

> Thus everything comes down to this: that you rule yourself . . . But we must see to the same thing especially in pain: not to do anything in a base, timid, ignoble, slavelike, or womanish way.

We could hardly hope for a balder exposition of the theory. The status of being a Roman man is associated with dominion or *imperium* ("ut tibi imperes"), and the incarnations of the opposing principles are slaves and women.[34]

Masculine Dominion over Foreigners and Women

A common theme in the ancient sources is that true Roman men, who possess *virtus* by birthright, rightfully exercise their dominion or *imperium* not only over women (see below) but also over foreigners, themselves implicitly likened to women. An obvious implication is that non-Roman peoples were destined to submit to Rome's masculine *imperium*. It is interesting to observe that at two high points of the *Aeneid* we are given a superhuman glimpse at Rome's glorious destiny, and *imperium* is invoked as being central to Rome's position as ruler of the world: Jupiter grandly proclaims that he has granted the Romans "*imperium* without end," and Anchises' charge to Aeneas in the Underworld is structured around the notion that Rome's greatness will lie in "ruling the peoples of the world with *imperium*."[35] Several other texts explicitly praise Roman greatness in terms of Roman men's special claim to *virtus*. According to Nepos, for example, "no one doubts" that the Romans have surpassed all others in *virtus*, while Pliny confidently states that "without a doubt" the Roman race ranks first in the world in terms of *virtus*.[36] The opposition between Rome, endowed with *virtus*, and the rest of the world, over which it by rights exercises *imperium*, is clearly given a gendered quality. Icons or characteristics of traditional Roman culture were occasionally given an explicitly masculine identity: Horace writes of the "masculine Curii and Camilli" while Persius praises the "manly" sound of the Latin lyre.[37] The corresponding implication that foreigners were inherently effeminate in their tastes for luxury was a commonplace, especially with regard to Easterners.[38] Thus we sometimes encounter the rhetoric of effeminacy being employed in the countless skirmishes of the cultural conflict between Rome and Greece, as when Silius Italicus has the Roman commander Marcellus encourage his troops in Greek Sicily with these words:

> ite, gregem metite imbellem ac succidite ferro . . .
> pigro luctandi studio certamen in umbra

molle pati docta et gaudens splendescere olivo
stat, mediocre decus vincentum, ignava iuventus. (Sil. Ital. *Punic.* 14.134–8)

Go now, mow down the warless flock, cut them down with the sword . . . They stand
there, a middling glory for those who conquer them: idle youth, taught to endure a
soft [*molle*] contest in the shade in the lazy pursuit of wrestling, and rejoicing to gleam
with olive oil.

He represents the Greek soldiers as soft and lazy, more interested in being slathered
with olive oil in their shaded exercise grounds than in fighting a real man's war;
with the description of their exercises in the gymnasia and palaestrae as *certamen
molle*, the designation of effeminacy is made explicit.[39] In one of his *Satires* Horace
constructs a contrast between traditional Roman training in hunting and riding
and Greek athletic pursuits that similarly deploys the language of softness.[40] Even
more than Greece, though, the cities of Asia Minor seem to have represented to
Romans the ultimate in decadence and luxury and consequently softness and effeminacy. Sallust points to the entry of Sulla's army into Asia as a watershed, marking the beginning of a decline in Roman manly discipline:

huc accedebat quod L. Sulla exercitum quem in Asia ductaverat, quo sibi fidum faceret,
contra morem maiorum luxuriose nimisque liberaliter habuerat. loca amoena voluptaria
facile in otio ferocis militum animos molliverant. ibi primum insuevit exercitus populi
Romani amare, potare; signa, tabulas pictas, vasa caelata mirari; ea privatim et publice
rapere, delubra spoliare, sacra profanaque omnia polluere. (Sall. *Cat.* 11.5–6)

Moreover, in order to ensure the loyalty of the army that he had brought with him in
Asia, Lucius Sulla treated them luxuriously and too freely, violating the standards of
our ancestors. The lovely, pleasant regions had easily softened [*molliverant*] the soldiers' fierce minds in an environment of leisure. There for the first time the army of
the Roman people became accustomed to love and drink; to admire statues, paintings,
engraved vessels; to steal such things both in private and in public; to loot temples; to
desecrate everything, both sacred and profane.

The notion of effeminacy latent in Sallust's language of "softening" (*molliverant*)
becomes explicit in Valerius Maximus' report of a lapse in Spartan austerity in the
person of Pausanias: "As soon as he adopted Asian ways, he was not ashamed to
soften [*mollire*] his own fortitude with the effeminate [*effeminato*] Asian style."[41]
With equal bluntness, Virgil, in passages to which we will return, has the African
king Iarbas and the Italian warriors Remulus Numentanus and Turnus swaggeringly
deride Aeneas and his fellow Trojans as soft and effeminate, even *semiviri* ("half-
men"), and in a piece of real-life bravado, Cato the Younger claims that in their
war against the Asian king Mithridates the Romans had fought with "mere women."[42]

Masculine *imperium* was also thought to be rightfully exercised over women.
Livy, commenting on the public protest by Roman matrons organized in 195 B.C.
against the *lex Oppia*, which curtailed their public displays of luxury, observes with
a tone of faint disapproval that "they could not be contained within the threshold
by any sense of authority or modesty, or by the *imperium* of men."[43] He then reports a speech given by Lucius Valerius, who supported the repeal of the law, and

his comments on the ways in which Roman men traditionally exercised over their women a dominion much like that with which they ruled their slaves are revealing. Sympathetically describing the women's plight, he notes: "Women's slavery is never removed as long as their men are alive and well, but the women themselves hate the liberation that is brought by being widowed or childless." He suggests a more moderate approach, namely that men should keep their women only in the legal forms of guardianship (*manus* or *tutela*), and not in a slavelike state (*servitium*): "You ought to prefer that they call you fathers and husbands rather than masters."[44] He is obviously arguing against a common tendency to liken women and slaves with regard to their position vis-à-vis men, at least. The elder Seneca, for example, preserves an orator's comment to the effect that if a praetor performs his official duties in the clothing of either a slave or a woman, he will be insulting the dignity of his office.[45]

A reversal of this ideal dominion of Roman men over women was held to be especially shocking. Cato the Elder, ever the pessimist, complained that "all men rule over their women, and we rule over all men, but our women rule over us;"[46] two centuries later we find Juvenal satirizing wives who dominate their husbands, and he ironically uses the language of *imperium*.[47] According to Tacitus, Tiberius tried to stir up feeling against Agrippina by representing her as manlike in her thirst for power and dominion.[48] Antony was ridiculed for being enslaved to the foreign queen Cleopatra, and even to her eunuchs,[49] and Valerius Maximus provides a scandalized description of the shockingly submissive men of Cyprus:

> sed tamen effeminatior multitudo Cypriorum, qui reginas suas mulierum corporibus velut gradibus constructis, quo mollius vestigia pedum ponerent, currus conscendere aequo animo sustinebant: viris enim, si modo viri erant, vita carere quam tam delicato imperio optemperare satius fuit. (Val. Max. 9.1.ext.7)

> But even more effeminate was the male population of Cyprus, who patiently allowed their queens to climb into their chariots on top of their women's bodies, which were arranged as steps so that they might tread more softly. It would have been better for those men—if they were in fact men—to die than to submit to such a delicate dominion.

Not only is the implicit alignment of "foreign" and particularly "Eastern" with "effeminate" notable, but we also see a reversal of Cicero's recommendation that a man should "rule himself" (*ut tibi imperes*). The men of Cyprus not only submit to *imperium*, but it is *imperium* wielded by women (hence *delicatum*), and they thus fail what is arguably the most basic test of manhood. We can rely on Valerius Maximus to make the rhetorical underpinnings perfectly obvious. The conceptual anomaly inherent in this situation (men submitting to women's dominion) is directly embodied in Valerius' language, through the oxymoronic *delicato imperio*: if *imperium* is masculine it is normally anything but *delicatum*. Thus a *delicatum imperium* is a self-contradictory impossibility, and these men are depicted as gender deviants: an *effeminatior multitudo* whose claim to the title *viri* is disputed. Masculinity meant being in control, both of oneself and of others, and femininity meant ceding control.

Masculinity and Self-Control

The belief that a man who cedes control over his own desires and fears is less than
fully masculine surfaces in many contexts. Excessive displays of pain or grief, for
example, are often dismissed as womanish. Thus Cicero opines that "there exist
certain precepts, even laws, that prohibit a man from being effeminate in pain"
and various other texts describe excessive mourning (and, synecdochically, tears)
as being womanish.[50] Similarly, giving in to sickness by failing to endure it stead-
fastly was liable to being branded as effeminate: Seneca, for one, asserts that "if I
must suffer illness, it will be my wish to do nothing out of control, nothing effeminately."[51] So too yielding to the fear of death was held to be a sure sign of effeminacy. Valerius Maximus, in fact, devotes a chapter to the topic of "The Desire for
Life" ("De Cupiditate Vitae"), and his introduction exploits the contrast between
masculine and effeminate behavior in the face of death:

> verum quia excessus e vita et fortuitos et viriles, quosdam etiam temerarios oratione
> attigimus, subiciamus nunc aestimationi enerves et effeminatos. (Val. Max. 9.13.pr.)
>
> But since my treatise has touched upon departures from life both accidental and manly,
> and some that were even reckless, let me now present for your consideration those
> that were spineless and effeminate.

The same author, in his chapter on military discipline ("De Disciplina Militari"),
tells the fate of Gaius Titius, who had disgraced the Roman army by surrendering
his troops' weapons to a band of fugitive slaves, and was harshly punished by the
consul L. Calpurnius Piso as a lesson:

> . . . ut qui cupiditate vitae adducti cruce dignissimis fugitivis tropaea de se statuere
> concesserant libertatique suae servili manu flagitiosum imponi iugum non erubuerant,
> amarum lucis usum experirentur mortemque, quam effeminate timuerant, viriliter
> optarent. (Val. Max. 2.7.9)
>
> . . . so that those who, motivated by a desire to live, had allowed fugitive slaves worthy
> of being crucified to set up trophies from spoils taken from them, and who had not
> been ashamed to see the disgraceful yoke of conquest placed upon their freedom by
> slaves, might find the light of day to be bitter and might manfully wish for the death
> that they had effeminately feared.

By contrast, Cleopatra is portrayed in a famous Horatian ode as manfully taking
her own life.[52] And Tacitus, writing of the conspiracy against Nero led by Piso in
A.D. 65, describes one of the participants, the senator Afranius Quintianus, as
"notorious for his bodily softness," but records approvingly that when the conspiracy failed he met his death "not in accordance with the previous softness of
his life."[53]

Military discipline, pertinacity, endurance, and bravery in the face of death
are all coded as masculine, and their absence as effeminate, in a speech attributed
by Livy to Appius Claudius, grandson of the *decemvir*, encouraging the Roman
people in their campaign against Veii in 403 B.C.:

adeone effeminata corpora militum nostrorum esse putamus, adeo molles animos, ut hiemem unam durare in castris, abesse ab domo non possint? ut tamquam navale bellum tempestatibus captandis et observando tempore anni gerant, non aestus, non frigora pati possint? erubescant profecto si quis eis haec obiciat, contendantque et animis et corporibus suis virilem patientiam inesse, et se iuxta hieme atque aestate bella gerere posse nec se patrocinium mollitiae inertiaeque mandasse tribunis, et meminisse hanc ipsam potestatem non in umbra nec in tectis maiores suos creasse. (Livy 5.6.4–5)

Do we think our soldiers' bodies to be so effeminate and their minds so soft, that they cannot last one winter in their camps, away from their homes? That, as if they were waging a war at sea, considering the season and looking for the right weather conditions, they are unable to endure either heat or cold? They would certainly be ashamed if someone should reproach them with these things, and they would argue that they have a manly endurance [*virilem patientiam*] in both mind and body; that they can wage wars in winter as well as in summer; that they had not entrusted the tribunes with the protection of softness [*mollitia*] and idleness; and that their ancestors created this very power [sc., of the tribunes] neither in the shade nor indoors.

His rhetoric insistently plays off the contrast between manliness, associated with endurance and power (*durare, ausi, virilem, potestatem*) and effeminacy, associated with softness and idleness (*effeminata, molles, pati, mollitia, inertia*).[54] The soldiers' physical effeminacy (*effeminata corpora*) and mental softness (*molles animos*) have nothing to do with sexual behavior and everything to do with vigor, endurance, and discipline.

Roman writers also apply the language of effeminacy to individuals and behaviors considered luxurious, hedonistic, self-indulgent, or avaricious; here too masculinity is by implication a matter of dominion or control: control of one's desires. Sallust opines that avarice "makes the manly body and soul effeminate," and Seneca has much the same to say about excessive delightfulness: it "makes the soul effeminate."[55] The same philosopher, attacking Epicurean beliefs, ironically refers to pleasure (*voluptas*) as "that effeminate good," contrasting it with the "manly discomforts" of hard work and pain, and elsewhere avers that pleasures "make men effeminate."[56] Julius Caesar, introducing his commentary on the peoples of Gaul, claims that one of the reasons that the Belgae are the strongest of the Gauls is that they have largely avoided contact with the refinements of Mediterranean civilization which "make souls effeminate."[57]

One form of civilized luxury at Rome that seems to have drawn especially vigorous accusations of effeminacy was the performing arts. Actors, singers, and dancers—especially those who played women's roles—were liable to slurs of effeminacy, and indeed the entire enterprise could be described as enervated, weak, soft, and unmanly.[58] Columella, writing a treatise on the virtues of agriculture, makes this sad observation:

intellego luxuriae et deliciis nostris pristinum morem virilemque vitam displicuisse . . . attonitique miramur gestus effeminatorum, quod a natura sexum viris denegatum muliebri motu mentiantur decipiantque oculos spectantium. (Colum. *R.R.* 1.pr.14–5)

> I understand that the old-fashioned way of life and manly existence [sc., the agricultural life] is not agreeable to today's luxury and delicacies. . . . We watch in amazement the gestures of effeminates, because with a womanish movement they imitate the sex denied men by nature, thereby deceiving the audience's eyes.

He focuses on those actors who play women's roles, but there is a subtler and more telling contrast at work between the hard, manly life of agriculture and the soft, womanish life of entertainment. Indeed, the speech put in the mouth of the British queen Boudicca by Dio Cassius (see chapter 2) is structured around a contrast between the hard, disciplined, manly Britons and the decadent, soft, effeminate Romans ruled by Nero, who himself is unworthy of the label "man" precisely because of his penchant for singing and performing: "While he may have the name of 'man'," Boudicca sneers, "he is in fact a woman, and the evidence for this is that he sings and plays the lyre and prettifies himself."[59] In his fulsome panegyric to the emperor Trajan, Pliny the Younger points to the Roman populace's condemnation of the "effeminate arts" of the pantomime as an effect of Trajan's benign influence over them. This, he notes, was the same populace that had once applauded Nero's own efforts:

> idem ergo populus ille, aliquando scaenici imperatoris spectator et plausor, nunc in pantomimis quoque aversatur et damnat effeminatas artes et indecora saeculo studia. ex quo manifestum est principum disciplinam capere etiam vulgus . . .
>
> (Plin. *Panegyr.* 46.4–5)

> Therefore that same populace, having at one time watched and applauded an emperor who was an actor, is now opposed even to the pantomime, condemning effeminate arts and pursuits not befitting our era. And so it is quite clear that the discipline of emperors can take hold of the entire people as well . . .

In his moralizing depiction of pantomime and related arts as not only "not befitting our era" but also effeminate Pliny is appealing to some very traditional conceptualizations.

Indeed, the gendered prejudice against entertaining the public was so ingrained that even being a gladiator, a profession which one might have thought to be the paragon of a brutish masculinity, could be represented as a disgrace of the worst kind. Both Seneca and Juvenal culminate their discussions of a decadence that they clearly mark as effeminate with the image of Roman men hiring themselves out to be gladiators. In Juvenal's second satire, after describing in scandalized tones a nobleman named Gracchus who is married to a low-class musician in a wedding ceremony in which he plays the role of bride (*nova nupta*, 120: see appendix 2), and concluding with the image of male brides like him who bitterly regret their inability to bear children (137–42), the speaker caps his tirade off with these lines:

> vicit et hoc monstrum tunicati fuscina Gracchi,
> lustravitque fuga mediam gladiator harenam
> et Capitolinis generosior et Marcellis . . . (Juv. 2.143–5)

> This monstrosity has been surpassed by Gracchus, wearing only his tunic and holding a harpoon; a gladiator more noble than the Capitolini and the Marcelli has traversed the midst of the arena . . .

And Seneca offers two illustrations of the ways in which his contemporaries do damage to their manhood (*virilitas*): one castrates himself, another hires himself out as a gladiator, thereby displaying a "disease" (*morbus*).[60] Seneca's juxtaposition of self-castration with the act of hiring oneself out as a gladiator, as well as his use of the imagery of disease (which, as we will see in the next chapter, could also be applied to men who displayed an effeminate desire to be sexually penetrated), like Juvenal's association of male brides with noblemen who become gladiators in a poem that likewise uses the imagery of disease (2.17, 50), suggests that Roman readers were likely to conceive of effeminacy as a disorder or disease that manifested itself not only in the desire to be sexually penetrated but also in a desire to put oneself on display, even to sell oneself, for the purpose of entertaining others.[61] It is worth noting that each writer uses the image of the gladiator to form a climax: Juvenal's speaker explicitly notes that Gracchus' appearance in the arena "surpassed even this monstrosity" (of a male bride: *vicit et hoc monstrum*), while Seneca spends more time on the gladiators who culminate his description than on those who castrate themselves, who receive only passing notice.

I have suggested that control and dominion constituted the prime directive of masculinity. A man must exercise dominion over his own body and his own desires as well as the bodies and desires of those under his jurisdiction—his wife, children, and slaves—just as the Roman citizenry as a whole ideally dominates most of the rest of the world. A man might lose his grip on masculine control, and thus be labeled *effeminate*, in various ways: by indulging in an excessive focus on his appearance or making himself look like a woman, by seeking to be dominated or even penetrated by his sexual partners, by subjugating himself to others for the sake of pleasuring or entertaining them, or by yielding to his own passions, desires, and fears. Masculinity was not fundamentally a matter of sexual practice; it was a matter of control.

Why was masculine status so dependent upon notions of dominion? Anthropological studies point to a widespread phenomenon: the conviction that masculinity is an achieved status, and a tenuous accomplishment at that. Boys must be *made* men, while girls just *become* women.[62] There are constant struggles involved not only in attaining masculinity—one thinks of the often painful and always challenging rites of passage by means of which boys are made men—but also in maintaining one's masculine status. Threats lurk everywhere, and a man can all too easily slip and fall. And if he does, according to the relentlessly binary logic of this system he is *ipso facto* behaving like a woman. Indeed an insinuation or, worse, outright declaration that a man is "not acting like a man" or is "acting like a woman" is one of the most devastating weapons that can be used by masculine cultures around the world in their campaign to mold "real men" and keep them that way. To describe a woman as "not acting like a woman" or as "acting like a man" is another matter entirely, and, in fact, is often a compliment.[63] Along these lines Maud Gleason argues that "masculinity in the ancient world was an achieved state, radically underdetermined by anatomical sex," and that it "remained fluid and incomplete until firmly anchored by the discipline of an acculturative process."[64]

The difficulties in achieving and maintaining masculine status may well account for the tremendous importance placed on the notion of control in Roman ideologies of masculinity, just as the intensity of Roman men's assertions of masculinity or of its absence may reflect the tenuousness and artificiality of a constructed identity in need of policing and control. Vigilance was crucial. The house of cards might collapse with the removal of just one card. The tenuous nature of achieved masculinity also offers an explanation for the easy interchangeability among the various traits that Roman traditions identified as effeminate. If a man loses control in just one aspect of his life—if he displays any one of the effeminate traits or any combination of them—he is susceptible to being called effeminate, and can be suspected of any other effeminate traits.

The oppositional pair masculine/effeminate can be aligned with various other binarisms: moderation/excess; hardness/softness; courage/timidity; strength/weakness; activity/passivity; sexual penetration/being sexually penetrated; and, encompassing all of these, domination/submission. If a man is associated with the second term in any one of these antitheses, he is *ipso facto* effeminate. Thus a man who is found guilty of excessive grooming, yet is aggressively active in seeking penetrative sexual relations with women, is effeminate; a man who plays the receptive role in anal intercourse is automatically effeminate, no matter how bold and courageous he might be in the arena of public life; equally effeminate is a man who leads a luxurious, self-indulgent life, surrounding himself with loose women. In other words, if a man breaks just one rule, he loses the game; in the balancing act of masculinity, one stumble can ruin the entire performance.[65]

Masculinity, Effeminacy, and Sexual Practices

It should be clear by now that a Roman accusation of effeminacy did not automatically entail an imputation that the man in question had been penetrated or was likely to play that role. Indeed, the Roman concept of *effeminacy* must be kept distinct from concepts of sexual role—whether homosexual or heterosexual, insertive or receptive—and I explore that insight in this section. Surveying a variety of sources that describe men who play the insertive role (with male or female partners indifferently), the receptive role with male partners,[66] or both, as effeminate, I will be arguing that we must abandon the attempt to describe Roman concepts of effeminacy in terms of sexual roles. It is just as fruitless to link effeminacy with a predilection for what is sometimes called "passive homosexuality" as it is to connect it with adultery: Roman effeminacy is a deep disorder that may or may not be embodied in sexual practices of practically any kind.[67]

Men who sought to play the receptive role in penetrative acts (often called *impudici*, *pathici*, or *cinaedi*: see chapter 5) are generally represented in Roman texts as effeminate. This should not be surprising, since they displayed a predilection for a sexual role deemed to be "feminine" by definition: they were imagined wilfully to abrogate their own masculinity, and in the inexorably oppositional logic of Roman masculinity, if one is not manly, one is womanly. So it is that the textual references to such men that are surveyed in chapter 5 are fairly insistent in their representation of them as unmanly: Martial contrasts *cinaedi* with "real men" (*veri viri*), they are said to "suffer womanly things" (*muliebria pati*), and they are frequently described with the language of "softness" (*mollitia*). Phaedrus' fable of the drunken Prometheus, further discussed in chapter 5, has him mistakenly attaching female genitals to males who are called soft.[68] The effeminate status of men who have been penetrated is concisely illustrated by the verb *mulierare* ("to woman-ize"), apparently coined by Varro in his *Menippean Satire* as a euphemism for penetration: a tantalizingly pithy fragment of that work reads, "he womanized the lad."[69] In a similar vein, the historian Curtius Rufus records an incident in which a concubine of Alexander the Great, a eunuch named Bagoas, was insulted as a "whore" made "effeminate" by *stuprum*, and in a stinging piece of courtroom in-vective, Apuleius speaks of his opponent Herennius' lovers in his youth as his *emasculatores*.[70] So too Juvenal, cynically describing the fates that may await a beautiful boy—being raped or even castrated by men—comments that in either case such a youth "is not allowed to be a man."[71]

Thus effeminacy sometimes functions as a metonymy for the receptive role in intercourse. But a man labeled as effeminate might just as well be represented as pursuing sexual relations with women, either in a generally unrestrained way or specifically by pursuing such inappropriate women as other men's wives. The fact that these insults are hurled with never a hint of surprise at the combination of effeminacy and heterosexual behavior is of crucial significance. Equally significant is the impressive range of contexts in which the figure of the effeminate woman-izer appears: from a throwaway line in Plautine comedy to the bitter attacks of oratorical invective, to a public speech given by a consul as recorded by Livy, to the philosophical speculations of Seneca, to Virgil's epic narrative of Rome's origins. One thing is clear: Roman audiences were not predisposed to find anything anoma-lous in the figure of a womanish man sexually pursuing women.[72]

Perhaps the earliest illustration of this conceptualization is found in Plautine comedy. In a scene from the *Truculentus,* the soldier Stratophanes, out to insult Diniarchus, his rival for the affections of the courtesan Phronesium, poses this incredulous question to his beloved:

> tun tantilli doni caussa,
> holerum atque escarum et poscarum, moechum malacum, cincinnatum,
> umbraticulum, tympanotribam amas, hominem non nauci? (Plaut. *Truc.* 608–11)

> What?! For the sake of such a piddling little gift (some vegetables, some things to nibble on, some cheap vinegar) you're giving your love to a soft womanizer who has his hair in ringlets, who lives in the shade, who plays a tambourine—a worthless guy?

The lines give a glimpse at Roman machismo at work: a blustering soldier angrily attacks his rival in love, a dandified city youth.[73] Stratophanes dismisses Diniarchus as a "man of no worth" (*hominem non nauci*), using a scornful diminutive to de-scribe his gift (*tantilli doni*), which he then dismisses in earthy, commonplace terms. As part of his program of diminishment, he endows his rival with the effeminate attributes of softness (*malacum*) and artificially curled hair (*cincinnatum*), further-more associating him with a life of shady relaxation (*umbraticulum*), and placing in his hand a *tympanum*, the tambourine-like instrument associated with effeminate Eastern dancers and *cinaedi*.[74]

A soft, romantic disposition in men could be taken as a sign of effeminacy, regardless of the sex of their beloved. Propertius refers to his love poetry, which is dominated by his mistress Cynthia, as his "soft book," and Catullus takes the insinuations about the "soft" verses on kisses that he composed for both Lesbia and Juventius to be a direct assault on his masculinity.[75] Indeed, there was a long tradition of viewing with suspicion men who had become enslaved to their passions; they could even be thought to have lost their *virtus* by falling in love.[76] Tacitus reports the disgraceful behavior of the military commander Fabius Valens who marched with a "soft marching-column of female concubines and eunuchs."[77] Cicero, too, found the image of a soft, effeminate man surrounded by loose women to be a useful weapon in his attack on Gaius Verres, the provincial governor of Sicily whom he prosecuted for extortion in 70 B.C. Following the traditions of oratorical invective, Cicero pulls no punches in his speeches against Verres, gleefully assailing the man's personal life on a number of counts. Chief among these was his evident fondness for the company of women, especially the two most unsuitable kinds of women: prostitutes and entertainers on the one hand and married ladies on the other.[78] At one climactic moment, Cicero speaks in scandalized tones of Verres shirking his duties both as a Roman official and as a man:

> hic dies aestivos praetor populi Romani, custos defensorque provinciae, sic vixit ut muliebria cotidie convivia essent, vir accumberet nemo praeter ipsum et praetextatum filium—etsi recte sine exceptione dixeram virum, cum isti essent, neminem fuisse. nonnumquam etiam libertus Timarchides adhibebatur, mulieres autem nuptae nobiles praeter unam mimi Isidori filiam, quam ipse propter amorem ab Rhodio tibicine abduxerat. erat Pipa quaedam, uxor Aeschrionis Syracusani, de qua muliere plurimi versus qui in istius cupiditatem facti sunt tota Sicilia percelebrantur; erat Nice, facie eximia, ut praedicatur, uxor Cleomeni Syracusani. hanc vir amabat, verum tamen huius libidini adversari nec poterat nec audebat, et simul ab isto donis beneficiisque multis devinciebatur. (Cic. *Verr.* 2.5.81–2)

> Here he—praetor of the Roman people, guardian and protector of the province!— spent his summer days in such a way that there were women's parties daily, and there was no man present except for himself and his young son—although, since it was they who were there, I really could have said without qualification that there was no man present. Sometimes his freedman Timarchides was there too, and women who were both married and noble, the one exception being the daughter of Isidorus the mime-actor, whom Verres himself had fallen in love with and taken from a Rhodian flute-player. There was a certain Pipa, wife of the Syracusan Aeschrion; a large number of verses attacking Verres' desire for this woman are quite popular all through Sicily. There was Nice, renowned for her stunning appearance and married to the Syracusan Cleomenes. Although her husband loved her, he possessed neither the ability nor the daring to stand up to Verres' lust, and he was in any case bound to him by numerous gifts and kindnesses that had been bestowed upon him.

Even as Verres and his son are surrounded by the women they love, their claim to the title "man" is challenged: "Since it was they who were there, I really could have said without qualification that there was no man present." It is worth noting the flow of his description, from the women's parties (*muliebria convivia*) to the lack of men (*virum neminem fuisse*) and back again to the women (*mulieres nuptae*): the structure reinforces the image of Verres the non-man and his equally effeminate son surrounded by women. Cicero's implication is that these men are no men precisely because of their unchecked womanizing and their fondness for exclusively female gatherings.

Cicero could hardly have hoped for a clearer embodiment of the stereotype of the effeminate womanizer than his archenemy P. Clodius Pulcher. Allegedly dressing himself up as a slave-woman and appearing at an exclusively female religious rite in honor of the Bona Dea in December of 62 B.C., all for a tryst with Julius Caesar's wife Pompeia, Clodius made himself an easy target for Cicero's scorn.[79] Peppering the orator's attacks on Clodius are more or less direct allusions to the incident, ranging from a wickedly detailed description of Clodius' outfit (complete with dress, snood, and women's shoes)[80] to blunt attributions of effeminacy[81] to the simple assertion that in his fatal encounter with Milo ten years later, Clodius was a woman who had come upon a group of men.[82] Throughout his career Cicero accused Clodius of a wide variety of sexual misdeeds, including not only the Bona Dea affair but also having been penetrated in his youth as well as an incestuous relationship with his sister, the infamous Clodia.[83] But it is the arresting image of Clodius dressed as a woman in order to meet his female lover that seems to have piqued the orator's imagination most; certainly he seems to have expected that it would have the same effect on his audience. It is likely that this incident in particular lurks behind every description of Clodius as effeminate: certainly Juvenal, nearly 150 years later, invokes Clodius as the paradigmatic womanizer, just as Verres is the prime example of a thief and Milo of a murderer,[84] and the fact that his three examples are all Ciceronian suggests that the image of Clodius qua adulterer was inspired by Cicero's own descriptions of the man.

It is amusing to read in Dio that when Q. Fufius Calenus attacked Cicero before the Senate in 43 B.C. following Cicero's own nasty assaults on Antony, he used some very Ciceronian techniques. He attributes effeminacy to Cicero both indirectly and directly,[85] and he links the orator's lack of manliness first to vanity (he wears a flowing tunic to hide his ugly legs, and he perfumes his hair) and then to sexual misdeeds, all of them with women: Fufius mocks Cicero's affair with an older woman named Caerellia and bluntly accuses the orator of having prostituted his own wife and having had incestuous relations with his beloved daughter Tullia.[86] Once again we see a man who is marked as effeminate engaging in inappropriate sexual practices with women.

One could hardly find a context more alien to the poisoned invective of Roman oratory than Virgil's epic on the origins of Rome. But the stereotype of the womanish womanizer makes several appearances in the *Aeneid*. In the epic's fourth book we meet Iarbas, a North African king who had failed in his attempt to win the hand of Dido in marriage. Upon hearing that she has taken the Trojan Aeneas as her lover, he pours out his bitter disappointment in a prayer to Jupiter:

> et nunc ille Paris cum semiviro comitatu,
> Maeonia mentum mitra crinemque madentem
> subnexus, rapto potitur. (Vir. *Aen*. 4.215–7)

And now he—that Paris!—together with his half-male companions, takes possession of the booty, a Maeonian snood tied around his chin and oiled hair.

Here two images are tightly interwoven: Aeneas as a woman-stealer on the level of the infamous Paris, whose affair with the married Helen set off the Trojan War (*ille Paris . . . rapto potitur*); and Aeneas as an Asian effeminate, sporting perfumed locks and an eastern *mitra*, accompanied by a band of half-men (*semiviro comitatu*). Later in the epic, a charge of effeminacy is leveled at the Trojans as a whole by the Italian warrior Remulus Numanus:

> en qui nostra sibi bello conubia poscunt!
> . . . .
> vobis picta croco et fulgenti murice vestis,
> desidiae cordi, iuvat indulgere choreis,
> et tunicae manicas et habent redimicula mitrae.
> o vere Phrygiae, neque enim Phryges, ite per alta
> Dindyma, ubi adsuetis biforem dat tibia cantum.
> tympana vos buxusque vocat Berecyntia Matris
> Idaeae; sinite arma viris et cedite ferro. (Vir. *Aen*. 9.600, 614–20)

> Behold, these are the ones who seek marriage with our women through warfare! . . . Your delight is in idleness, in clothing dyed with saffron and gleaming purple; you love to indulge in the dance; your tunics have sleeves while your snoods are tied on with bands. You—truly Phrygian women rather than Phrygian men—go to the heights of Dindymon where you are used to hearing the song of the double-piped flute. The tambourines and the Idaean Mother's Berecynthian box-wood flute call you; leave warfare for men [*viris*] and give way to our sword.

Again, the ethnic contrast would have been familiar to Roman readers: decadent and effeminate Easterners (such details as the *tympanum* and the reference to Cybele suggest the goddess' castrated priests or *galli*) as opposed to strong, manly Italians (*viris*).[87] And this stereotype is here blended with that of the effeminate womanizer. Remulus represents these effeminate Trojans as a threat—though here, in a show of macho bravado, they are dismissed as no real threat—precisely because they are seeking to steal Italian men's wives: "These are the ones who seek marriage with our women through warfare!" Immediately after Remulus delivers his taunting speech, Aeneas' son Ascanius demonstrates that he, for one, is no weak, womanish warrior as Remulus becomes his first victim. When Apollo then congratulates Ascanius for his *nova virtus* ("new-found manly valor") the rhetorical circle is complete, for *virtus* is, as we have seen, both etymologically and conceptually the preeminent embodiment of manliness.[88]

Most outstanding among these Trojan wife-stealers is Aeneas, who claims the lovely young Lavinia as his own. But Lavinia is already betrothed to the Rutulian prince Turnus, and when Turnus lashes out at Aeneas we hear a variation on the theme sounded by Iarbas. As Turnus takes his sword up, he addresses it in language whose gendered quality is striking. Indeed, one could hardly conceive of a more masculine moment, as the outraged warrior brandishes his weapon, poised to vanquish his feminized enemy:

> da sternere corpus
> loricamque manu valida lacerare revulsam

semiviri Phrygis et foedare in pulvere crinis
vibratos calido ferro murraque madentis. (Vir. *Aen*. 12.97–100)

Grant that I may lay low the body of the half-male Phrygian, mangle his corselet, torn off by my strong hand, and befoul his hair in the dust—that hair curled with the iron and damp with perfume.

Both Iarbas and Turnus swaggeringly dismiss Aeneas and his companions as less than men—the disdainful *semivir* appears in each passage, and each speaks of the Trojan's damp, perfumed hair (*crinem madentem, crinis . . . madentis*)—and each of them not coincidentally assails Aeneas for infringing upon their proprietary claims on a woman.[89]

The stereotype that Virgil is appropriating in each of these passages was said to have found a real-life embodiment, ironically enough, in the person of Virgil's own patron Maecenas, a long-time friend of Augustus and patron of such other renowned poets as Horace and Propertius. Maecenas' effeminate traits seem to have been fairly widely discussed: the historian Velleius Paterculus describes him as at times "practically surpassing a woman in his leisurely softness;"[90] Porphyrio reports that some readers of Horace's *Satires* understood the character Malthinus, who walks around with flowing tunics, to be a pseudonym for Maecenas;[91] and Macrobius preserves a teasing letter addressed to Maecenas by Augustus himself that fairly drips with images of softness and delicacy, at the same time insinuating a penchant for erotic entanglements with women.[92] The younger Seneca makes the point in a less friendly way. Citing Maecenas as an illustration of how literary style and lifestyle can reflect each other,[93] he simultaneously portrays Maecenas as a man who flaunted his lack of manliness and tweaks him for his frequent fallings-out with his wife:

> quodomo Maecenas vixerit notius est quam ut narrari nunc debeat quomodo ambulaverit, quam delicatus fuerit, quam cupierit videri, quam vitia sua latere noluerit. quid ergo? non oratio eius aeque soluta est quam ipse discinctus? . . . non statim, cum haec legeris, hoc tibi occurret, hunc esse qui solutis tunicis in urbe semper incesserit? . . . hunc esse, qui in tribunali, in rostris, in omni publico coetu sic apparuerit, ut pallio velaretur caput exclusis utrimque auribus, non aliter quam in mimo fugitivi divitis solent? hunc esse, cui tunc maxime civilibus bellis strepentibus et sollicita urbe et armata comitatus hic fuerit in publico, spadones duo, magis tamen viri quam ipse? hunc esse, qui uxorem milliens duxit, cum unam habuerit? (Sen. *Epist*. 114.4–6)

Maecenas' lifestyle is so well known that there is no need to tell of the way he walked, how delicate he was, how he desired to be seen, how he refused to keep his vices secret. Consequently, isn't it true that his style is just as loose as his tunic was? . . . When you read these words of his, will you not instantly realize that he is the man who always walked around the city with his tunic unbelted? . . . That he is the man who appeared on the tribunal, on the rostra, in every public assembly with his head veiled by a *pallium* and his ears sticking out on either side, just like the rich man's runaway slaves in a mime? That he is the man who—of all times, with a civil war raging and the city up in arms and in great turmoil—was accompanied in public by two eunuchs who were, though, more manly than he himself was? That he is the man who, while only having one wife, married her a thousand times?

The comment that Maecenas' eunuchs were more manly than he himself was, devastating as it is meant to be, relies on the kinds of conceptualizations of effeminacy that we have seen elsewhere. For Seneca, Maecenas' effeminacy is manifested in a variety of behaviors: in his deportment and manner of self-presentation (*quomodo ambulaverit; discinctus; solutis tunicis*), in his use of eunuchs, and in his irregular relations with a woman—in this case, his own wife.[94] Indeed, Maecenas became a byword for a dissolute, luxurious, and effeminate lifestyle (Juvenal pictures a shipwreck at which everything is thrown overboard, even the "purple clothing suitable for a delicate Maecenas"), but throughout the ancient tradition his sexual experiences were most often imagined to be with women.[95]

Seneca's own father offers us the stereotypical picture of the effeminate womanizer with stunning crispness in the words of an orator pleading the case of a man who is disgusted with the excesses of his decadent young son:

> madentem unguentis externis, convulneratum libidinibus, incedentem ut feminis placeat femina mollius, et cetera quae morbi non iudici sunt . . . (Sen. *Contr.* 2.1.6)

> Dripping with foreign perfumes, crippled by his lusts, walking more softly than a woman in order to please women—and all the other things that show not judgment but disorder.

Here we find the intersection of several themes: foreign luxuries and inappropriate deportment (wearing imported perfumes and walking delicately),[96] softness, and uncontrolled desires ("crippled by his lusts"). But above all, the image of a luxurious young man sashaying about precisely to attract women is a familiar one: this young man would have fit in perfectly at one of Verres' banquets. The stereotype of the effeminate womanizer seems to have thrived among ancient Romans.[97]

The same author who gives us the image of the effeminate young Don Juan just cited also provides the *locus classicus* for another important stereotype, that of the effeminate man indulging his uncontrolled lust with both male and female partners. Despairing of the new generation of orators, the elder Seneca moralizes in explicitly gendered terms:

> torpent ecce ingenia desidiosae iuventutis nec in unius honestae rei labore vigilatur; somnus languorque ac somno et languore turpior malarum rerum industria invasit animos; cantandi saltandique obscena studia effeminatos tenent, [et] capillum frangere et ad muliebres blanditias extenuare vocem, mollitia corporis certare cum feminis et immundissimis se excolere munditiis nostrorum adulescentium specimen est. quis aequalium vestrorum quid dicam satis ingeniosus, satis studiosus, immo quis satis vir est? emolliti enervesque quod nati sunt in vita manent, expugnatores alienae pudicitiae, neglegentes suae. in hos ne dii tantum mali ut cadat eloquentia: quam non mirarer nisi animos in quos se conferret eligeret. (Sen. *Contr.* 1.pr.8–9)

> Consider today's lazy young men: their minds are sluggish, and they are vigilant in working on not a single honorable thing. Sleep and languor and, more disgraceful than sleep and languor, hard work (but at bad things) has taken hold of their minds. The revolting pursuits of singing and dancing have taken hold of these effeminates; braiding their hair and thinning their voices to a feminine lilt, competing with women in bodily softness, beautifying themselves with disgusting finery—this is the pattern of our young men. Why should I ask who among your peers is sufficiently gifted or suf-

ficiently studious? Rather, who is sufficiently a man? Born softened and spineless, they stay that way: taking others' *pudicitia* by storm, careless of their own. God forbid that eloquence—which I would hardly esteem if it failed to choose those on whom it conferred itself—should befall *them*.

This text, like the younger Seneca's discussion of Maecenas cited earlier, betrays an assumption that there is an intimate relationship between a man's lifestyle and his literary style, and the specific image that Seneca offers is especially interesting for our purposes.[98] The young orators of today, he laments, are weak and languorous (*torpent*; *somnus languorque*), soft (*mollitia corporis*), and outright effeminate (*effeminatos*; *muliebres blanditias*; *certare cum feminis*; *quis satis vir est?*). With regard to the specifics of sexual behavior, how does their lack of manliness manifest itself? The answer comes in a trenchant *sententia*: "taking others' *pudicitia* by storm, careless of their own." This phrase, which finds parallels in other Roman authors,[99] appeals to the notion of *pudicitia* discussed in chapters 3 and 5: to say that these men seize the *pudicitia* of others means that they violate the sexual integrity of freeborn Romans of either sex by actively perpetrating *stuprum* with them; to say that they disregard their own *pudicitia* means that they allow their own sexual integrity to be violated by being penetrated. It is precisely this free-ranging disregard for standards of sexual comportment, among other characteristics, that contributes to their being branded as *effeminati, emolliti,* and *enerves.*

In Seneca's tirade, the distinction between insertive and receptive role, while rhetorically useful for bringing home the point that their sexual misdeeds are many and varied, has no specific bearing on their being defined as effeminate. They are not effeminate because they are penetrated by others, or because they penetrate others, or because they do both; they are effeminate because of their active disregard for standards of behavior. This very point lies behind another, slightly more knotted, *sententia*:

> ite nunc et in istis vulsis atque expolitis et nusquam nisi in libidine viris quaerite oratores. (Sen. *Contr.* 1.pr.10)

> So go, look for orators among *them*: plucked and pumiced, in no way men except in their lust.

There is a deliberate paradox here: the only way these soft and decadent creatures behave like active, dominant men is in asserting their lusts, but since they do so in inappropriate and uncontrolled ways, they show themselves to be, in the end, not men at all. The rhetorical question posed earlier, "Who is sufficiently a man?", now finds its answer: none of them, since they are "in no way men except in their lust."

A similar combination of sexual practices, both insertive and receptive, is attributed to men derided as effeminate in Cicero's second oration against Catiline, delivered to an assembly of the Roman people in 63 B.C. Cicero dismisses Catiline's followers en masse as luxurious and effeminate, flitting about the forum in their perfumes and expensive purple clothing, yet in fact quite dangerous:

> hos quos video volitare in foro, quos stare ad curiam, quos etiam in senatum venire, qui nitent unguentis, qui fulgent purpura, mallem secum suos milites eduxisset: qui si

hic permanent, mementote non tam exercitum illum esse nobis quam hos qui exercitum deseruerunt pertimescendos. (Cic. *Cat.* 2.5)

These men whom I see flitting about the forum, standing before the Senate House, even going into meetings of the Senate, glistening in their perfumed oils, gleaming in their purple clothing—I would rather Catiline had led them out of Rome as his fellow-soldiers. For if they remain here, bear in mind that we will not have to fear that army of his as much as these men who have deserted his army.

Later in this cutting speech, breaking down Catiline's associates into various groups and enumerating their respective vices, he arrives at the last, most disgraceful, most degenerate group:

in his gregibus omnes aleatores, omnes adulteri, omnes impuri impudicique versantur. hi pueri tam lepidi ac delicati non solum amare et amari neque saltare et cantare sed etiam sicas vibrare et spargere venena didicerunt. . . . verum tamen quid sibi isti miseri volunt? num suas secum mulierculas sunt in castra ducturi? quem ad modum autem illis carere poterunt, his praesertim iam noctibus? quo autem pacto illi Appenninum atque illas pruinas ac nivis perferent? nisi idcirco se facilius hiemem toleraturos putant, quod nudi in conviviis saltare didicerunt. (Cic. *Cat.* 2.23)

All gamblers, all adulterers, all impure and unchaste [*impudici*] men spend their time in these groups. These boys, so charming and lovely, have learned not only to love and be loved, to dance and sing, but also to brandish daggers and infuse poison. . . . But what do these wretches want? Surely they do not intend to take their little women with them on the campaign? And yet how on earth will they be able to do without them, especially during these nights? How, too, will they be able to endure the Appennines, their frost and snow? Unless perhaps they think that they will be able to make it through the winter more easily because they have learned how to dance nude at parties!

The rhetoric deprives them of full manliness, dismissing them as "boys" (*pueri*), attaching the epithet *delicati* to them, and citing their abilities at singing and dancing. And, like Seneca, Cicero paints a picture of effeminates perpetrating sexual misdeeds both active and passive: they are both *adulteri* and *impudici*, and they have learned "to love and be loved" (*amare et amari*), a phrase which displays on the level of morphology the contrast between active and passive. In fact, the brunt of the attack is directed at the weak dependency on women displayed by Catiline's men: such is the point of the mordantly sarcastic questions concerning their plans to take their women with them on campaign. These "soft and delicate boys" depend on the kindness of their women, a reversal that highlights the distance between their behavior and that of real men.

A similar invective is found in Livy's narrative of the Bacchanalian scandal, in which, as with Cicero and the Catilinarian conspiracy, we hear the vigorous language of a consul addressing the citizenry at a time of crisis. Postumius, having summoned the people in order to inform them of the breaking scandal, offers this opinion on the participants in the cult:

primum igitur mulierum magna pars est, et is fons mali huiusce fuit; deinde simillimi feminis mares, stuprati et constupratores, fanatici, vigiliis, vino, strepitibus clamoribusque nocturnis attoniti. (Livy 39.15.9)

First, then, the majority of them are women, and that was the source of this evil; next come men very much like the women, debauched and debauchers, frenzied, dazed by their all-night vigils, by wine, by nocturnal hue and cry.

The syntactic structure of the comment suggests that the effeminacy of the men who participate (*simillimi feminis*) is embodied in the entire range of illicit and uncontrolled behaviors subsequently listed in a series of phrases describing these men (*mares*): sexual misdeeds both passive (*stuprati*, morphologically passive) and active (*constupratores*, morphologically active), and an indulgence in wild, drunken, noisy, nocturnal celebrations.[100] The image of effeminacy ("men very much like the women") constitutes an umbrella for all that follows, and it is not linked to any one particular behavior, sexual or otherwise.

A poem included in the *Appendix Vergiliana* well illustrates the dynamics of gendered invective. The poet opens on a tone of outraged masculine pride:

> Iacere me, quod alta non possim, putas,
> ut ante, vectari freta,
> nec ferre durum frigus aut aestum pati
> neque arma victoris sequi?
> valent, valent mihi ira et antiquus furor
> et lingua, qua mas sim tibi,
> et prostitutae turpe contubernium
> sororis. o quid me incitas? ([Vir.] *Cat.* 13.1–8)

> Do you think that I am lying low, unable to travel on the open seas as before? That I cannot bear the harsh cold, or endure the stifling heat, or follow the victor's army? They are alive and well: my wrath, my furor of old, my tongue with which I can be a man with you, and your disgraceful intimacy with your prostituted sister. Why are you provoking me?

There follows a torrent of invective. Apart from his incestuous relations with his sister, the addressee—whom the poet calls a woman (*femina*) and a *cinaedus*—has wasted his inheritance, was sexually penetrated by men in his youth, and now has a wife, with whom (according to one reading of the text) he is engaging in cunnilinctus.[101] There may thus be a striking contrast between what this man does with his tongue and the poet's own aggressive, staunchly masculine tongue (*lingua, qua mas sim tibi*). To be sure, both the allusion to cunnilinctus and the explicit gendering of the speaker's tongue as masculine depend upon specific readings of the text,[102] but even if those readings are incorrect, there still remains a meaningful opposition between the feminized addressee (*femina*) who "licks" his wife with kisses (*lambis saviis*) and the masculine speaker who assails the addressee with his own angry tongue (*valent, valent mihi ira et antiquus furor / et lingua*).

The traditions of invective were long-lasting. On trial in A.D. 158 for having exercised magical powers to convince a rich widow to marry him, Apuleius indulged in the time-honored tradition of attacking one of his accusers as being less than a man. In his defense speech, Apuleius ticks off Herennius Rufinus' sexual misdeeds: in his youth he had freely given his favors to men (whom Apuleius dubs with the elsewhere unattested noun *emasculatores*, cited earlier), and he is now married to a woman whose adulteries he not only condones but derives profit from. As we saw in Cicero's invective against Catiline's followers, it is the notion of a man being submissive to or dependent upon women that especially fuels the fire of Apuleius' outrage; indeed, when he describes Herennius as "obliging" (*morigerus*) to his *emasculatores*, he uses a word that invokes the traditionally dutiful stance of a Roman wife to her husband.[103]

Next, having insulted Herennius' wife as a whore (*uxor lupa*, 75) and Herennius himself as her slave (*aquariolus iste uxoris suae*, 78), Apuleius reports that Herennius had threatened to kill him (78). Here, swelling with manly indignation, Apuleius reaches a rhetorical climax:

> vix hercule possum irae moderari, ingens indignatio animo oboritur. tene, effeminatissime, tua manu cuiquam viro mortem minitari? at qua tandem manu? Philomelae an Medeae an Clytemestrae? quas tamen cum saltas—tanta mollitia animi, tanta formido ferri est—sine cludine saltas. (Apul. *Apol*. 78).

> Good gods, I can barely restrain my anger! My mind is seized by tremendous outrage. That you, most effeminate one, should threaten any man with death at *your* hand! With which hand, pray tell? Philomela's? Medea's? Clytemnestra's? Even when you dance their roles, you go without a sword, so soft is your mind, so fearful of weaponry are you.

Herennius is beneath contempt, a soft, effeminate dancer who yielded to men in his youth and now submits to his own wife.

The differently gendered reputations of Galba and Otho, two of the four men who held imperial power in the chaotic year A.D. 69, nicely illustrate the point that the concept of effeminacy, far from being linked to sexual practices between members of the same sex, was associated with general notions of excess, self-indulgence, and lack of self-control, whether embodied in one's sexual practices or in other ways. Galba's sexual tastes, according to Suetonius, ran to mature men, one of whom was with him on the day he was hailed emperor.[104] Yet Galba managed to keep his masculine reputation unsullied: clearly he was thought to have played the insertive role with his male sexual partners. Indeed, far from being accused of an effeminate softness, Galba acquired a reputation for harshness and severity, to such an extent that, again according to Suetonius, he came to be hated by many, his own soldiers above all.[105] By contrast, Otho, reputed to have been overly fond of pampering himself, acquired a distinct reputation for effeminacy: Juvenal pillories him for a womanish primping that surpassed that of Semiramis or Cleopatra; Suetonius reports that on the day he was hailed as emperor he was traveling in a woman's sedan, and that he was fond of adorning himself in an effeminate manner, even depilating his body; and Plutarch speaks of his "softness and effeminacy of body."[106] What was his reputation in terms of sexual practices? Juvenal calls him *pathicus*, but it is interesting to note that, apart from the rumor that he had in his youth bestowed his favors upon Nero (and we see in chapter 5 that this kind of rumor was practically *de rigueur* for public figures), Otho was most notorious for his relationship with Nero's mistress Poppaea Sabina: he was said to have married her so that Nero might have easier access to her, but Otho's own desires for Poppaea led him to become, in the words of a couplet that circulated among Romans, "the [adulterous] lover of his own wife."[107] Tacitus' references to Otho fall squarely in line with traditional stereotypes: an enemy described him as effeminate in his manner of dressing, walking, and adorning himself and pointedly associated him with *stuprum*, adultery, and "gatherings of women;"[108] Otho himself wrote letters to Vitellius that Tacitus describes as being "infected with womanish flattery;"[109] but Tacitus notes that, ultimately, Otho's spirit was not as soft (*mollis*) as his body was—a backhanded compliment if ever there was one.[110] While Otho's own soldiers were said to have hailed him as a brave man (*fortissimus vir*),[111] the fact remains that his masculine reputation seems to have suffered quite seriously, while Galba's did not.

What do all of these images of effeminate men suggest about the deeper logic of masculinity and femininity as they relate to sexual practices? Catharine Edwards, drawing on the insights of Michel Foucault and Aline Rousselle, points to traditional beliefs that excessive sexual activity is weakening and enervating,[112] and such beliefs surely contribute to these representations of men who excessively indulge in sexual behavior as unmanly. Also relevant are ancient beliefs that women craved or even needed sex more than men;[113] sex-crazed men were thus acting like women. On the other hand, the elder Seneca's paradoxical description of the dissolute and effeminate young men of his day as men in no way except in their lust (*nusquam nisi in libidine viris* [*Contr.* 1.pr.10]) points to a certain tension inherent in the Priapic model of masculine identity. According to that paradigm, the male is by definition lustful, rightly driven by a desire to plant his penis in others' bodies, thereby asserting his masculine dominion. The men whom Seneca describes do just that, and to that extent they are "real men" (*viri*). But Seneca's decadent young men fail to acknowledge that even these masculine impulses need to be kept in check, both indulging their desires to be penetrated and wantonly disregarding the *pudicitia* or sexual integrity of others.[114] In short, all of these men, from Cicero's Verres to Iarbas' Aeneas and Seneca's *effeminati*, display their unmanliness not only in their effeminate appearance but also in their overall self-indulgence and inability to control themselves and their desires, even those usually thought of as masculine. According to the conceptualizations of masculinity prevalent in the Roman textual tradition, a real man is in control of his own desires, fears, and passions, and he exercises dominion over others and their bodies. An effeminate man cedes control and is dominated, whether by his own desires and fears or by others' bodies—and those bodies may be male or female.

Other Voices

There is an interesting implication lurking within all of these ancient images of effeminacy. In their struggle to maintain their masculine image, men must have been fighting urges that dwelt within them: to adorn themselves, to pamper themselves, to surrender themselves to pleasures sexual and sensual, to be possessed, to be dominated. And no doubt the recognition, whether conscious or not, of the presence and power of these desires merely confirmed the supposed need for policing and vigilance. Thus the urges destructive of masculinity and the measures designed to combat them were caught in an endless, vicious cycle. Once the dangers were conceived as such, defensive measures were put in place and constantly justified by the very existence of those dangers, and every defensive response served to reinforce the notion that there really was a danger. The struggle—the show— must go on.

Or must it? Up to this point my formulations have been deliberately replicating the rigid black-and-white rhetoric of Roman masculinity: either one is a man, in control, or else one is a despised effeminate. Indeed, it is a notable characteristic of hegemonic ideologies that they make themselves seem absolute and unquestionable, and thus deal in extremes. But this kind of unbending rhetoric cannot always have spoken to the ways in which real Roman men performed in the arena of public interactions, and we may well ask just how absolute the theoretical demands of masculinity were in practice.[115] The images that we have seen of men who failed to maintain a reputation for unimpeachable masculinity have so far been overwhelmingly negative: they are laughable losers. But the surviving textual record also gives us some glimpses of a certain flexibility: the ability of some men in certain contexts to bend the rules of the game and even to flaunt their failure to perform their masculinity with perfection. As Gleason trenchantly observes, "not every Greco-Roman gentleman could be expected to transact civic business—much less attend a dinner party—in the shaggy garb of a cynic philosopher."[116]

It has been recognized for some time that Roman love poetry plays with traditional notions of gender. Judith Hallett has written of a "countercultural" persona in Roman love poetry;[117] Jasper Griffin has discussed the ways in which Propertius' persona resembles that of the effeminate Antony;[118] Eva Cantarella has observed that the romantic outlook of love poetry is antithetical to traditional Roman notions of masculinity;[119] and Barbara Gold has offered this overview of the nontraditional stances taken by the persona of Propertius' poetry:

> Propertius removes from Cynthia traits that would have been traditionally ascribed to females, such as devotion, submissiveness, loyalty, subservience, passivity, and procreativity, and he appropriates them for himself. He becomes the loyal and devoted slave (Prop. 1.1; 1.6.25–30; 3.11.1–8; 3.25.1–4), the passive husband waiting at home (1.15; 2.8; 2.9), the faithful lover even after death (3.15.46), the one who gives birth to poetry (1.7; 2.1.1–4; 3.17; 3.24). Cynthia, on the other hand, has attributes that are a mimesis of the values recognized in the classical tradition by and for the male: she is demanding, faithless, hard-hearted, domineering, self-absorbed, and interested in competition and rivalry (Prop. 1.1; 1.7; 1.10.21–30; 3.8).[120]

Indeed, Propertius' poetry, which calls itself "soft" (*mollis liber*, 2.1.2), rather insistently celebrates the pleasures and pains of being dominated by a "mistress" (*domina*). And if she is the mistress, then the poet is of course the slave:

Quid mihi tam multas laudando, Basse, puellas
     mutatum domina cogis abire mea?

quid me non pateris vitae quodcumque sequetur
   hoc magis assueto ducere servitio? (Prop. 1.4.1–4)[121]

Bassus, why do you praise so many girls to me, trying to make me change and leave my mistress? Why do you not instead allow me to lead whatever life awaits me in this slavery to which I have grown accustomed?

In fact, the phrase *servitium amoris* ("the slavery of love") has become a standard way of describing this imagery in Roman love poetry.[122] Yet we need hardly be reminded that to be enslaved to a woman was a distinctly unmasculine fate. Valerius Maximus' dismissal of the Cypriots as unworthy of being called *viri* because they submitted to the *imperium* of their queens comes to mind.

Catullus sometimes toys with his own masculine image in surprising ways. In one poem he calls the praetor Memmius an *irrumator*, using the term that literally describes a man who orally penetrates others to invoke his arrogant misuse of his authority over others; in another poem he strains the metaphor to stunning effect, picturing the man stuffing his "long pole" into his subordinates, Catullus himself among them.[123] Elsewhere this poet compares his suffering at the hands of his mistress to a flower that has been nicked by a passing plow, and since plowing is a traditional metaphor for penetration there is a fairly clear gender-reversal at work.[124] In yet another poem, meditating on his mistress' infidelities, Catullus cites the example of Juno, queen of the gods:

quae tamen etsi uno non est contenta Catullo,
   rara verecundae furta feremus erae,
ne nimium simus stultorum more molesti.
   saepe etiam Iuno, maxima caelicolum,
coniugis in culpa flagrantem concoquit iram,
   noscens omnivoli plurima furta Iovis.
atqui nec divis homines componier aequum est. (Catull. 68.135–41)

Nevertheless, although she is not content with Catullus alone, I will put up with the rare cheatings of my modest mistress, so as not to be too annoying, the way fools are. Even Juno, greatest of the goddesses in heaven, often burns off her wrath at her husband's wrongdoing when she learns of the numerous cheatings of the all-desiring Jupiter. And yet it is not right for humans to be compared to gods.

The tone is ironic, but the gendered dynamics are striking nonetheless. He refers to his beloved as his *era* ("mistress," the word used by slaves to refer to the lady of the household) and, even though he immediately drops the comparison out of alleged piety, for a moment he places himself in Juno's celestial shoes. Just as she puts up with Jupiter's affairs, so should he learn to accept the fact that his mistress will stray.

In the context of love poetry, then, we find Roman men toying with the implications of not being entirely masculine in their comportment. These poets flirt with effeminacy.[125] Likewise, an anecdote regarding the celebrated orator Hortensius, a contemporary and occasional rival of Cicero, gives us an idea of what the voice of an orator who flaunted his bending of the rules of masculinity might have sounded like:

ad eundem modum Q. Hortensius omnibus ferme oratoribus aetatis suae, nisi
M. Tullio, clarior, quod multa munditia et circumspecte compositeque indutus et
amictus esset manusque eius inter agendum forent argutae admodum et gestuosae,
maledictis compellationibusque probris iactatus est, multaque in eum, quasi in
histrionem, in ipsis causis atque iudiciis dicta sunt. sed cum L. Torquatus, subagresti
homo ingenio et infestivo, gravius acerbiusque apud consilium iudicum, cum de causa
Sullae quaereretur, non iam histrionem eum esse diceret sed gesticularium
Dionysiamque eum notissimae saltatriculae nomine appellaret, tum voce molli atque
demissa Hortensius, "Dionysia," inquit, "Dionysia malo equidem esse quam quod tu,
Torquate, ἄμουσος ἀναφρόδιτος ἀπροσδιόνυσος." (Gell. 1.5.2–3)

In the same way, Quintus Hortensius, who was more renowned than nearly any other
orator in his day except for Cicero, was bombarded with insults, reproofs, and reproaches, and many things were said against him—even in the courtroom—as if he
were an actor, because he dressed himself and arranged his toga with a good deal of
refinement, thought, and care, and because in pleading his cases his hands were quite
eloquent and expressive in their gestures. Once, when Sulla's case was being tried,
Lucius Torquatus, a man of a rather boorish and inelegant nature, said in the presence
of the jury that Hortensius was not an actor but rather a mime-actress, and he called
him Dionysia, using the name of a celebrated female dancer. At that point Hortensius
replied in a soft, subdued voice: "Let me tell you, I would rather be Dionysia—yes,
Dionysia—than what you are, Torquatus: artless, loveless, pointless."

His masculinity having been attacked in a very public setting indeed (the trial of
P. Cornelius Sulla in 62 B.C.), Hortensius proudly contrasts his own effeminacy
with the uneducated, unrefined, boorish manliness of the one who has insulted
him. The dynamics are familiar: his manner of dress, deportment, and speech provoke a slander of effeminacy together with an assimilation to actors and female
dancers.[126] But the story, whether apocryphal or not, also demonstrates that some
men felt free to suggest by their behavior or speech that the game of masculinity
was not always worth playing. Torquatus' insulting *Dionysia* provokes from
Hortensius (who casts the name back at Torquatus not once but twice) the equally
insulting *aprosdionusos*, but the differences between the two words are significant. Torquatus' *Dionysia* is a blustering and not particularly clever insult, whereas
Hortensius' *aprosdionusos* is an artfully sharp pun: the sequence Muses-Aphrodite-
Dionysus evokes the related pleasures of art, love, and wine, but while *aprosdionusos*
literally means "without reference to Dionysus," it also has the metaphorical meaning "not to the point, mal à propos."[127] In his sharp retort to Hortensius' blunt
insult, Hortensius simultaneously shows off his refined cleverness and reveals just
how little he cares what Torquatus and his ilk might think. It is also worth noting
that Hortensius caps his retort in Greek (as if to highlight the contrast between
rough Roman and refined philhellene) and delivers the whole in a noticeably effeminate way (*voce molli atque demissa*). But the content of his response is anything but meek and mild—it is in fact a manfully aggressive assertion, effected by
means of an anaphora of privatives in crescendo that serve to hammer the point in
and that reach their climax in a masterful pun.

      By maintaining that Torquatus' affectedly rough and implicitly masculine style
is incompatible with the pleasures of love, wine, and poetry, Hortensius constructs

two extremes (a boorish masculinity divorced from the exquisite pleasures of civilized life, and a soft, refined, effeminacy deeply implicated in those pleasures) and leaves no doubt as to which extreme he would embrace if forced to make a choice. Thus this text suggests a perspective rather different from the otherwise universal belief that masculinity is an unquestionable *desideratum* and effeminacy an unqualified disgrace. Hortensius' response—both what he says and how artfully he says it—creates space for an alternative viewpoint: that in the game of masculinity, those who are deemed its losers can sometimes claim their own voice and suggest that the game of masculinity might not always be worth playing in its entirety. His teasing response reminds us that, despite the black-and-white rhetoric of Roman masculinity that almost entirely dominates the textual record left to us, real life is often a gray zone.[128] And Hortensius was surely not alone.

Indeed, we have seen that Augustus' associate Maecenas acquired a distinct reputation for effeminacy, above all in his manner of dress and his luxurious lifestyle. There are no surviving texts by Maecenas himself in which he responds to charges of luxury and effeminacy, but we do have two poems known as the *Elegiae in Maecenatem*. Neither the author nor the date of composition of this text has been established (although it is generally agreed that it comes from the classical period),[129] but for our purposes its significance lies in the fact that it sets out to be a eulogy for Maecenas, and thus establishes for itself the related goals of praising and of defending him on the charges leveled against him. How, indeed, could a supporter of Maecenas respond to the devastating accusations of the likes of Seneca, who sneered that Maecenas' eunuchs were more manly than himself?

The poet of the *Elegiae* begins in the traditional fashion of a Roman funeral oration, by stressing Maecenas' noble origins and public achievements: he was descended from Etruscan kings and was Augustus' right-hand man (*Caesaris dextra*), serving as guardian of the city of Rome in his powerful friend's absence and exercising his power with gentleness.[130] He was also a gifted scholar and poet, blessed by Athena and Apollo and surpassing his peers as much as a beryl surpasses grains of sand.[131] Since a fondness for jewelry was a traditionally effeminate trait, this imagery is bold, even defiant, and it signals the beginning of the poet's impassioned defense of Maecenas on the charge of luxury and effeminacy. In the next lines the poet turns directly to Maecenas' reputation for an effeminate lifestyle in general and his predilection for loose, flowing tunics in particular:

> quod discinctus eras, animo quoque, carpitur unum:
> > diluitur nimia simplicitate tua.
> sic illi vixere, quibus fuit aurea Virgo,
> > quae bene praecinctos postmodo pulsa fugit.
> livide, quid tandem tunicae nocuere solutae
> > aut tibi ventosi quid nocuere sinus?
> num minus urbis erat custos et Caesaris opses?
> > num tibi non tutas fecit in urbe vias?
> nocte sub obscura quis te spoliavit amantem,
> > quis tetigit ferro, durior ipse, latus?
> maius erat potuisse tamen nec velle triumphos,
> > maior res magnis abstinuisse fuit. (*Eleg. Maec.* 1.21–32)

The one thing held up against you is that you were loosely-girt, in your mind too. This is refuted by your extreme simplicity. That is the way that people lived when the golden maiden [Justice] was among them; afterwards she was driven away and fled people who were well-girt. You spiteful man, what harm did his flowing tunics do to you, or what harm did his billowing garments do? Surely he was no less the guardian of the city and the stand-in for Caesar? Surely he did not make the city streets unsafe for you? In the dark nighttime, who robbed you while you were in love, who touched your flank with a steel blade than which he himself was harder? It was greater for him [Maecenas] to have been able to have triumphs yet to have refused them; it was a greater matter for him to have abstained from great things.

The libertarian stance is reminiscent of an epigram by Martial (7.10) discussed in chapter 5: both texts ask why we should be bothered by a man's private life if it does not interfere with our own pursuit of happiness. But this poet adds a further defense: Maecenas' noteworthy public achievements and his laudable decision not to pursue further glory when he could easily have done so should outweigh any qualms one might have about how he dressed or how luxuriously he led his life in private. There are two points implicated in this argument, and the poet takes them up in turn. First he stresses that Maecenas had shown himself to be a brave man (*fortis*) where it really counts: the battlefield.[132] Next the poet advances the arguments that there is a time and place for everything and that among the perquisites of victory one may include a certain relaxed leisure.[133] He proceeds to offer divine parallels: after the victory at Actium, Apollo played the lyre; after his conquest of India, Bacchus partied—in flowing tunics, no less; his labors completed, Hercules became the feminized slave of the foreign queen Omphale, also wearing loose gowns; even Jupiter, after defeating the Giants, relaxed in the company of his beloved Ganymede.[134] Then, having recapitulated the arguments that there is a proper time for everything, and that a victorious commander may legitimately indulge in the soft life of parties and love affairs after his work is done, the poet once again emphasizes Maecenas' powerful connections:

> Caesar amicus erat: poterat vixisse solute,
>   cum iam Caesar idem quod cupiebat erat.
> indulsit merito: non est temerarius ille.
>   vicimus: Augusto iudice dignus erat. (*Eleg. Maec.* 1.103–6)

> Caesar was his friend; he was able to live loosely, now that Caesar was exactly what he wanted to be. He indulged him [Maecenas] deservedly; he is not rash. We have won: in the judgment of Augustus, he was worthy.

The second of the elegies, in the voice of Maecenas himself, expands upon the notion that, because of their intimate friendship, Augustus *allowed* Maecenas to live his luxurious lifestyle:

> exemplum vixi te propter molle beati,
>   unus Maecenas teque ego propter eram.
> arbiter ipse fui; volui, quod contigit esse;
>   pectus eram vere pectoris ipse tui. (*Eleg. Maec.* 2.23–6)

> Because of you I lived as the soft [*molle*] example of a blessed man; and because of you I was the only Maecenas. I myself was my arbiter. I wanted what it befell me to be. I was truly the breast of your breast.

The emphasis is clear and is in fact a mainstay of the defense. Maecenas indulged in his "soft" lifestyle, flowing tunics and all, with Augustus' approval.

But that approval was actually an indulgence (*indulsit; te propter*), a special favor given in recognition of Maecenas' public service to Rome and private intimacy with Augustus. That his behavior is intrinsically something *needing* indulgence is never questioned. Moreover, not everyone was a Maecenas or a Hortensius, safely ensconced in positions of privilege and power. Maecenas' reputation certainly suffered, but as the poet imagines him to say, he remained *beatus*: wealthy, comfortable, successful. And Hortensius hardly abandoned his masculine image wholesale: his reputation among posterity was one of an eloquent, patriotic Roman (Valerius Maximus tellingly contrasts Hortensius, who worked for the "safety of the citizens," with his degenerate grandson who indulged in the degrading sexual practice of cunnilinctus).[135] And as for the love poets, one could argue that their poetic flirtations with effeminacy were precisely that—flirtations, poetic experiments, literary games; in the end, their image is solidly masculine, albeit a bit soft around the edges. It is true that men like Hortensius, Maecenas, and the love poets bent the rules, but for them, as Gleason puts it, "there was something manly, after all, about taking risks—even the risk of being called effeminate."[136] And I have suggested that Hortensius' reply can itself be seen as possessing a certain masculine aggression.

What, though, of those who ignored the rules altogether, who considered the game of masculinity simply not worth playing *at all*? In the performance of masculinity, actors like Hortensius, Maecenas, and Propertius had their fun peeking out from behind the mask or wilfully changing some of their lines, even at the risk of some jeers from the audience. But there must have been others who never put on the mask, who never set foot on the stage. All that remains of these people are men's impersonations of them. Their own voices have been silenced, and it is up to us to imagine what they might have sounded like.

5

Sexual Roles and Identities

What sorts of identities were possible for Roman men as sexual subjects, and how were those identities related to specific sexual practices? An obvious but crucial point needs perhaps to be stressed once more: the Priapic paradigm, centered around the man as penetrator and noticeably unconcerned with the sex of his partner, necessarily implies that the fundamental antithesis informing Roman representations of men as sexual subjects was the opposition between the insertive role in penetrative acts, which was normative for men, and the receptive role in penetrative acts, which was not, rather than the opposition between heterosexual and homosexual behavior. A. E. Housman suggested as much in an article published in 1931 in the decent obscurity of Latin, and more recently scholars have reiterated and refined the point in plain English, French, and Italian.[1] But while the importance of the insertive/receptive dichotomy has been recognized, I wish to insist on its utter centrality. The question "Who penetrated whom?" lies behind practically every surviving ancient allusion to a sexual encounter, even between women.[2]

This chapter thus argues that, rather than being endowed with a deeply entrenched sexual identity as heterosexual, homosexual, or bisexual, based on the sex of the sexual partners to which he was oriented, a Roman man was normally assigned to one of two identities, "man" (*vir*) or "non-man"; and that when these identities were embodied in specific sexual practices, the sex of the man's partner was irrelevant to his own status. In this chapter I first discuss the ancient evidence to the effect that, with regard to their sexual practices, *men* were defined by playing the insertive role in penetrative acts (we saw in the previous chapter that this is a necessary but not sufficient condition for masculine status); I then suggest that the various linguistic labels available to describe these men referred to the specific acts that they performed rather than the sex of their partners. Next, I argue that a particular class of adult *non-men* who were marked as deviant—whom I, following other scholars, will refer to with the ancient word *cinaedi*—were certainly endowed with an identity, but that this identity was based on the notion of gender deviance rather than on an orientation toward sexual partners of the same sex or even toward an exclusive performance of the receptive role in anal intercourse.

This chapter then turns to ancient descriptions of men who engaged in oral sexual practices, where we see that a man's observable predilection for fellatio was not held to be incompatible with a predilection for cunnilinctus. On the contrary, it appears that if a man displayed a desire to perform the one act, he was considered likely to want to perform the other as well. Thus a man's desire to perform fellatio, and even a desire to be anally penetrated, was not held to signify an identity that we could call homosexual. Finally, I argue that while *cinaedi* were certainly conceived of as being deviant, they were not ultimately outcast, and that while they were imagined by outsiders as gathering together in groups, and may well have partaken of some kind of cohesive group identity, it would be misleading to speak of a "homosexual subculture" in ancient Rome. In the end, my object in this chapter is to probe the discontinuity between ancient and modern modes of categorizing male sexual agents: the ancient as observably inclined to engage in certain sexual practices, the modern as erotically oriented toward persons of one or the other sex, or both.

Differences from Greek Traditions

In their emphasis on the distinction between insertive and receptive roles, Roman ideologies of masculine behavior resembled those of the Greeks. But the Roman textual tradition often displays a uniquely macho style that is especially evident in its tendency to focus on specific penetrative acts, and the very words available to Romans as they described sexual acts display a degree of phallic specificity not found in the Greek sexual vocabulary. The set of Latin verbs referring to penetrative acts can in fact be arranged in a chart, with the mode of penetration (vaginal, anal, or oral) on one axis and the distinction between insertive and receptive role on the other:

	INSERTIVE	RECEPTIVE
VAGINAL	*futuere*	*crisare*
ANAL	*pedicare*	*cevere*
ORAL	*irrumare*	*fellare*

As *futuere* denotes the act of vaginally penetrating and *crisare* describes the motions of a woman who is vaginally penetrated, so *pedicare* means "to penetrate anally" and *cevere* describes the movements of one who is anally penetrated. Similarly *irrumare* means "to penetrate orally" while *fellare* describes the action of the receptive partner in such an act, namely "to suck the penis."[3] We will return to the implications of this vocabulary for our reconstruction of the conceptual system that informs it, but for now it is worth noting that this collection of verbs stands in striking contrast with both ancient Greek and more recent terminology: in particular, the verbs *irrumare*, *crisare*, and *cevere* display a specificity not seen in other languages' sexual vocabularies.[4]

The existence of the verb *irrumare*, "to penetrate orally," is particularly suggestive. Roman men were encouraged to conceptualize sexual acts in terms of penetration to such an extent that they could describe fellatio as an act of oral penetration in which the fellating partner, often an active participant indeed, could not only be the subject of an active verb (*fellat*) but could also be the subject of a passive verb (*irrumatur*) and thus be represented as having something done to him or her; while the fellated partner, today often conceived of as the one "receiving" a service, could be the subject of an active verb (*irrumat*) and thus represented as "doing" something to someone else. In other words, an act of fellatio could be represented either as one person "fellating" (*fellare*) a man or as a man "irrumating" (*irrumare*) another. Thus, while Roman men were, as we will see, prompt to condemn men and women who performed fellatio, they were also disposed to represent fellatio as an aggressive act of penetration that embodied the assertion of a man's masculinity at another's expense.[5] Indeed, *irrumare* is used in contexts that emphasize the passivity or degradation of the person fellating, and the agent noun *irrumator* is sometimes put to a nonliteral use, denoting a man who has his own way with others or treats them with contempt or disrespect.[6]

Beyond the bluntly phallic focus of these verbs (which all describe actions relating to the insertion of a penis into an orifice), Roman representations of sexual practices often display a striking candor that constitutes a further point of contrast between Greek and Roman traditions. While Greek epigram and Aristophanic comedy certainly had a license for open obscenity, Roman writers managed to tell highly detailed and often quite lurid stories of a sexual nature even when working in genres whose traditions prohibited open obscenity. The rhetorician Murredius speculates as to whether a young woman has been anally penetrated; Cicero wickedly insinuates that various enemies have a penchant for oral sex; Ovid's poetic letter from Paris to Helen includes an indirect but fairly clear allusion to anal intercourse; and the Stoic moralist Seneca inserts into his discussion of mirrors (though duly peppering his narrative with expressions of outrage and disgust) the tale of one Hostius Quadra, who involved himself in a complicated, even athletic, *ménage à quatre* complete with anal intercourse, fellatio, and cunnilinctus.[7] Perhaps the gap between Greek and Roman traditions opens most widely when we juxtapose Suetonius' biographies and those of Plutarch. Whereas the Roman writer frequently informs his readership of surprisingly specific details regarding his subjects' sexual habits (such as Q. Remmius Palaemon's well-known penchant for cunnilinctus and Tiberius' fondness for that act as well as for being fellated),[8] such information is nowhere to be found in Plutarch's Lives. Roman men were, it seems, inclined to discuss earthy details of sexual experience in a variety of public contexts. Here one might well detect a fixation on the penetrative power of the phallus: as Amy Richlin puts it, "these texts manifest a Rabelaisian interest in the physical body, with the male genitalia serving as a source of bellicose pride, and the female genitalia as a source of (male) disgust."[9] And Roman male audiences were, it seems, endlessly fascinated to know precisely how, where, and when the phallus was being put to use. To the question "Who penetrated whom?" we might add "How did he do it?"

Viri: **Real Men**

Normative sexual experience is regularly portrayed in Roman texts less as loving intercourse between two partners and more as a series of penetrative encounters in which one party (a *man*) acts upon another (a *non-man*, whether a female, a boy, an effeminate man or *cinaedus*, or a slave). According to the Priapic prime directive, a *real man* must always and only play the insertive role in hierarchically constructed encounters of this sort.[10] Indeed, one cannot read far in the Roman sources without perceiving the consistent understanding that the penetrating role is quintessentially and definitively masculine. Just as Seneca wrote that women were "born to be submissive,"[11] so the prevailing belief was that men were born to penetrate: we recall the image of the hypermasculine god Priapus, who eagerly seeks to wield his manhood with boys and girls, men and women alike. Paul Veyne's incisive phrase accurately summarizes the outlook regularly offered by Roman texts: "To be active is to be a male, whatever the sex of the passive partner."[12]

Since men who played the insertive role were performing precisely the action that was understood to be masculine by definition, the noun *vir* ("man") and its derivative adjectives and adverbs often have a specific nuance, referring not simply to a biological male but to a fully gendered "real man," that is, one who penetrates.[13] Tacitus provides an illustration of this usage that offers a suggestive glimpse into the workings of Roman sexual polemic. In his narrative of the attempt in A.D. 47 by the emperor Claudius' wife Messalina to destroy her rival Poppaea Sabina, along with the distinguished nobleman Decimus Valerius Asiaticus, we read that, having arrested Valerius in Baiae and having brought him to Rome in chains, Messalina's crony Publius Suillius Rufus quickly arranged a private hearing before the emperor:[14]

> neque data senatus copia: intra cubiculum auditur, Messalina coram et Suillio corruptionem militum, quos pecunia et stupro in omne flagitium obstrictos arguebat, exim adulterium Poppaeae, postremum mollitiam corporis obiectante. ad quod victo silentio prorupit reus et "interroga" inquit "Suilli, filios tuos: virum esse me fatebuntur."
>
> (Tac. *Ann.* 11.2)

Nor was he granted the privilege of a hearing before the Senate. The case was heard in the emperor's bedroom, in the presence of Messalina. Suillius accused Valerius of corrupting the soldiers, asserting that with money and *stuprum* he had bound them to himself for the purpose of committing every crime; of adultery with Poppaea; and finally of softness of body. At this the defendant broke his silence and burst out: "Suillius, cross-examine your sons: they will confess that I am a man."

Patiently enduring the first two accusations, Valerius cannot bear this final imputation of effeminacy (*mollitia corporis*: for the language, see chapter 4) and retorts
by suggesting that Suillius' sons know perfectly well how much of a man he is.[15]
Unfortunately for Valerius, neither this insulting allegation nor his subsequent
defense had any effect: he was quickly found guilty on the trumped-up charges,
although at the recommendation of Claudius' associate Vitellius he was allowed to
commit suicide rather than being subjected to the humiliation of execution.[16] Yet
Valerius remained intransigent to the end, and in his last moments issued another
sexual insult against one of Claudius' friends, declaring as he cut open his veins
that he would rather have died under Tiberius or Caligula than "by a woman's
deceit or the unchaste mouth of a Vitellius"; as we will see later in this chapter, the
latter remark implies that Vitellius had defiled his mouth and degraded his masculinity by engaging in oral sexual practices.[17]

Valerius' gestures of macho defiance—simultaneously asserting his masculinity and feminizing the sons of the man who dared question it, then directly im-
pugning the masculinity of another of his enemies—are strikingly reminiscent of
the sexual rhetoric of Catullus' sixteenth poem:

> Pedicabo ego vos et irrumabo,
> Aureli pathice et cinaede Furi,
> qui me ex versiculis meis putastis,
> quod sunt molliculi, parum pudicum.
> nam castum esse decet pium poetam
> ipsum, versiculos nihil necesse est;
> qui tum denique habent salem ac leporem,
> si sunt molliculi ac parum pudici,
> et quod pruriat incitare possunt,
> non dico pueris, sed his pilosis
> qui duros nequeunt movere lumbos.
> vos, quod milia multa basiorum
> legistis, male me marem putatis?
> pedicabo ego vos et irrumabo. (Catull. 16)

I will fuck you and make you suck me, *pathicus* Aurelius and *cinaedus* Furius. Because my poems are soft little things you have thought me not very chaste. Now, while
the dutiful poet ought himself to be pure, there is no need for his poems to be so; they
only have wit and charm if they are soft little things and not very chaste, and if they
can arouse what itches—not among boys, but among these hairy men who are unable
to stir up their toughened groins. So then, because you have read my many thousands
of kisses, you think me hardly a man? I will fuck you and make you suck me.

As in Tacitus' narrative, the language of softness appears, this time accompanied
by an explicit assault on Catullus' masculinity (*male marem*, "hardly a man") as well
as the even more specific implication that he has played the receptive role in intercourse (*parum pudicum*, "not very chaste": for the language of male *pudicitia*, see
discussion later in this chapter): all because he has written "soft" (*molliculi*) love
poetry.[18] Catullus' response, like Valerius Asiaticus', is swift and vigorous: hurling
the epithets *pathicus* and *cinaedus* at Aurelius and Furius, he frames the poem

with a famously obscene line in which he threatens (or promises) to penetrate his accusers anally and orally. Just as Valerius had responded to a slur on his masculinity effected by means of the language of softness by insinuating that he had sexually subjugated his accuser's sons, so Catullus' poetic persona deflects a similar slur deploying the imagery of softness directly back onto its originators, declaring himself ready, willing, and able to subject them to his phallic power.[19] In these two very different contexts—a historian's narrative of an event from the reign of Claudius and a poetic scenario from the late Republic—we perceive the dynamics of Roman masculine identity in full force. These texts offer blunt testimony to a central assumption of Roman ideologies of manhood: a man's status as a fully gendered *vir* is not only not compromised but in fact bolstered by his penetration of other males.

It deserves emphasis that in Tacitus' narrative Valerius silently withstands the accusations of corrupting soldiers and adultery, but can no longer restrain himself when accused of "softness of body" (*mollitia corporis*), only then bursting out with his own counterattack. Although vigorously rejecting the imputation of effeminacy, Valerius is willing to be thought guilty not only of adultery but also, since Suillius' sons were freeborn Roman citizens, of *stuprum*. Likewise, the Furius and Aurelius whom Catullus swaggeringly threatens to penetrate were freeborn, and elsewhere in his poetry Catullus presents a persona that unabashedly engages in acts of *stuprum* and adultery (with Juventius and Lesbia, respectively). Ancient historians' comments about Julius Caesar's sexual experiences provide a further parallel. Suetonius tells us that at his Gallic triumph Caesar's own soldiers chanted ribald jokes concerning his adulteries as well as his affair with King Nicomedes of Bithynia in which he was alleged to have played the subordinated receptive role.[20] Neither were Caesar's soldiers the only ones to tease him about the Nicomedes affair. Suetonius reports that Bibulus, his colleague in the consulship, referred to Caesar in his public edicts as "the queen of Bithynia" who was previously in love with a king and now with a kingship, and that in another public context a man named Octavius referred to Caesar as a queen just as Pompey was a king.[21] The gendered insults, and no doubt especially the contrast with his rival Pompey, must have galled in a way that the accusations of adultery did not. To acquire the reputation of being an adulterer was one thing; to be called "queen of Bithynia" was quite another.[22] Indeed, Dio Cassius adds a crucial detail: while Caesar generally welcomed his soldiers' jokes, taking their openness as a sign of their trust in him, he did not extend this tolerance to their allusions to Nicomedes. These he attempted vigorously to deny, only to fan the flames of suspicion by the very alacrity of his response.[23]

Catullus, Tacitus, Suetonius, and Dio offer a glimpse at what appears to have been a normally unspoken understanding: it was less damaging for one's reputation as a man to be thought guilty of adultery or more generally *stuprum* (provided that one was thought to have played the insertive, "man's" role) than of having been sexually penetrated. Neither is this surprising. While the former could be conceived as a fault deriving from an excess of masculinity, the latter represented nothing less than the abandonment of masculine identity. In terms of the protocols of masculine behavior outlined in chapter 1, the first protocol—that a man should be the penetrator—takes precedence over the second—that the freeborn are off-limits.

Labels and Categories for "Men"

The perquisites of Roman manliness thus included the freedom to engage in a vigorous, open pursuit of penetrative sexual relations with either male or female partners. Not surprisingly, this conceptual turn surfaced in linguistic habits. We often find the language of manhood employed in such a way as to establish an equivalence between manhood and penetration, whether of males or of females. In a Priapic poem included in the *Appendix Vergiliana*, the first-person narrator, afflicted with impotence, laments his penis' inability to act like a man (*viriliter*) and penetrate a boy:

> silente nocte candidus mihi puer
> tepente cum iaceret abditus sinu,
> Venus fuit quieta, nec viriliter
> iners senile penis extulit caput. ("Quid hoc novi est?" 2–5)

> In the still of the night, as a fair boy lay enfolded in my warm embrace, my sex was dormant, nor did my inert penis manfully rear its aged head.[24]

In one of Ovid's *Amores*, the poet imagines himself to be a ring that he has sent to his mistress, and he fantasizes that, coming in contact with her body, his "limbs will swell with desire" and he will "play the man's role."[25] Seneca, with a remarkably prurient profession of outrage, writes of a slave-boy put to sexual use by his master, climaxing with a malicious *sententia*: "He is a man [*vir*] in the bedroom, a boy in the dining room."[26] Seneca's keen point is aimed at the slave's master (if the slave is a man in the bedroom, what is the master?), and its thrust is conveyed precisely by the word *vir*.[27]

This specifically phallic nuance of the language of manhood is also evident in a synecdoche through which the noun *virilitas* ("manhood" or "virility") can signify the penis,[28] and also informs descriptions of men who have lost the use of their manhood either by castration or by some other kind of injury as *semiviri* ("half-men").[29] As eunuchs had been deprived of their *virilitas*, so women were imagined to lack it naturally, but one of Martial's more scandalized epigrams describes a woman who manages to remedy that situation. Bassa engages in sexual relations with other women and "her monstrous Venus falsely plays the man." The import of the poet's words is that Bassa usurps the male role (*vir*) with her genitalia (*Venus*) by penetrating her partners.[30]

Moreover, just as women and eunuchs lacked what it took truly to be a *vir*, those males who assumed the receptive role in intercourse were understood to have forfeited their masculinity and thus could be explicitly contrasted with *viri*. In Suetonius' biography of Vespasian, we read of the emperor's gentle reproach of his friend Licinius Mucianus who, although well known for his predilection for the receptive role ("of well-known *impudicitia*"), had been so bold as to criticize his powerful friend. Vespasian was content to voice his complaints to a mutual acquaintance, though adding the pungent observation, "Well, but *I* am a man" ("ego tamen vir sum"). Unlike Mucianus, in other words, he lived up to the definition of *vir* as penetrator.[31] Equally pointed but considerably less indulgent is Cicero's contrast between Tongilius, who had been Catiline's beloved even before coming of age and who fled Rome with Catiline during the chaotic events of 63 B.C., and the "real men" (*viros*) who have stayed behind in Rome.[32] Ovid describes a male who seeks a man as sexual partner (with the implication that he desires to be penetrated by him) as comparable to a woman, indeed "hardly a *vir*," and a Plautine character makes the contrast even sharper by tossing as a throwaway insult the comment, "I think you are a *cinaedus* rather than a *vir*," only to retract it hastily when confronted with a threat of violence.[33] In short, in Roman terms a man is fully a *vir* when he penetrates, regardless of the sex of his penetrated partner.[34]

Moreover, the labels other than *vir* that were available to Romans seeking to describe men as penetrative sexual agents were markedly unconcerned with the sex of their partners, and instead bore a direct relationship to specific practices. There existed a set of obscene agent nouns derived from the verbs surveyed at the beginning of this chapter, that thus described men who performed certain sexual acts: *fututor* (one who vaginally penetrates), *pedico/pedicator* (one who anally penetrates),[35] and *irrumator* (one who orally penetrates). The conceptual framework that gives these words their meaning is characteristically Roman in its blunt phallocentrism: the nouns, like the verbs from which they are derived, relate to various actions connected with the insertion of a penis into an orifice. Consequently, a male sexual agent who played the insertive role could be described not as heterosexual, homosexual, or bisexual, but rather as one who inserts his penis into any or all of three orifices (vagina, anus, mouth). It was, in short, a question of preferred role rather than immutable object-choice.

It might be objected that *fututor* served as a functional equivalent of the term *heterosexual male*, since the only possible partner of such a man is female.[36] But in terms of the conceptual apparatus informing the Latin sexual vocabulary, the sex of a *fututor*'s partner is coincidental.[37] The noun means not "a man who has sexual relations with women" but specifically "a man who penetrates vaginally," and Martial, for one, imagines some men as having sexual relations with women that do not include vaginal penetration: such a man engages in heterosexual practices yet cannot be called a *fututor*. The following epigram illustrates the point well:

> Lingis, non futuis meam puellam
> et garris quasi moechus et fututor.
> si te prendero, Gargili, tacebis. (Mart. 3.96)
>
> You are licking, not fucking, my girl and you babble as if a seducer and *fututor*. If I catch you, Gargilius, you will be silent.

Gargilius is gratifying the poet's girlfriend orally without penetrating her vaginally, and Martial ends with a traditional threat: he will avenge himself by means of *irrumatio*, that is, by compelling Gargilius to fellate him.[38] But the second line is telling. Gargilius brags as if he were a womanizer or seducer (*moechus*) and a *fututor*, and the implication of Martial's *quasi*, together with the emphatic opening, "You are licking, not fucking" (*lingis, non futuis*), is that the second label does not in fact apply to him. While he is a *moechus* to the extent that he is involved with another man's woman, he is not a *fututor*.[39] Indeed, several other epigrams present the image of a man who, like Gargilius, could be called a *cunnilingus* but not a *fututor*.[40] To understand *fututor* as a functional equivalent of "heterosexual man" is to distort its sense.

Likewise one might argue that *pedico* and *pedicator* were used to describe men who today would be labeled "homosexuals," or more specifically men who play the insertive role in penetrative acts with other males. But the literal meaning of the words, denoting "a man who anally penetrates," deserves emphasis.[41] The anal penetration of women was one among several options for Roman men, sometimes indeed being represented as a rather exquisite pleasure for men, and this fact was reflected in linguistic usage: the verb *pedicare* ("to penetrate anally") can have female objects.[42] Thus when a man wrote "I want to butt-fuck" (*pedicare volo*) on the wall of the famous brothel of the Vico del Lupanare in Pompeii, those who read his unabashed phrase would have been inclined to understand it not as expressing a yearning for male sexual partners but rather as proclaiming a desire to perform a certain pleasurable activity, whether with females or males.[43] Other graffiti scratched on the walls of this same brothel seem to demonstrate precisely this point. On at least three occasions someone (perhaps the man himself) was inspired to scribble a few words about a certain Phoebus, the first two messages being found in the same cubicle:

> Phoebus unguentarius optume futuet. (*CIL* 4.2184)
>
> Phoebus pedico. (4.2194)
>
> Phoebus bonus fut(ut)or. (4.2248)[44]

> Phoebus the perfume-dealer fucks really well.
>
> Phoebus is a *pedico*.
>
> Phoebus is a good *fututor*.

Phoebus is both *fututor* and *pedico*, indulging in vaginal and anal penetration alike; whether he does the latter with female or with male partners is not specified, neither is that information contained within the epithet *pedico*. In view of the tradition embodied in the sexual personae of such poets as Catullus, Horace, Tibullus, and Martial (all of whom exercise their masculinity with women and boys indiscriminately),[45] it is most likely that the graffiti concerning Phoebus were neither intended nor perceived as describing an anomaly. On the contrary, Phoebus acts like a real man.[46]

Phoebus of Pompeii finds a parallel in one of the men described in Martial's epigrams, a certain Cantharus who pays a visit to a brothel, buying time with either a boy or a girl:

> Intrasti quotiens inscriptae limina cellae,
>   seu puer adrisit sive puella tibi,
> contentus non es foribus veloque seraque
>   secretumque iubes grandius esse tibi:
> oblinitur minimae si qua est suspicio rimae
>   punctaque lasciva quae terebrantur acu.

nemo est tam teneri tam sollicitique pudoris
   qui vel pedicat, Canthare, vel futuit. (Mart. 11.45)

> Whenever you cross the threshold of an inscribed cubicle, whether it is a boy or a girl who smiles at you, you are not satisfied with the door, the curtain, and the lock, and you require greater secrecy. If there is the slightest hint of a crack in the wall, or if there are any holes poked by a naughty needle, they are patched up. No one, Cantharus, is of such delicate and anxious modesty who fucks either butts or cunts.

Cantharus is strikingly (though of course only coincidentally) reminiscent of Phoebus, proclaimed as both *pedico* and *fututor* on the walls of a brothel cubicle, and the gist of Martial's poem is that if Cantharus were a *pedico* or a *fututor* he would have no need of the extreme measures he takes to ensure privacy, and that he must therefore be engaging in other, shameful activities (namely, fellatio or cunnilinctus). Clearly either anal or vaginal penetration (*pedicatio* or *fututio*), or a combination of both, constituted the activities a man might be expected to perform in such a setting. In any case, Martial's generalizing statement ("qui vel pedicat . . . vel futuit") implies what the Pompeiian graffiti make explicit: it was possible for a single man to be called both *pedico* and *fututor*.[47]

This emphasis on specific practices as opposed to the sex of a man's partners reappears in an epigram addressed to a certain Gallus:

Subdola famosae moneo fuge retia moechae,
   levior o conchis, Galle, Cytheriacis.
confidis natibus? non est pedico maritus.
   quae faciat duo sunt: irrumat aut futuit. (Mart. 2.47)

> Gallus, smoother than Venus' conch shells, I'm warning you: flee the treacherous net of the infamous adulteress. Are you relying on your buttocks? Her husband is not a *pedico*. There are two things that he does: he fucks mouths or he fucks cunts.

The question here is not one of orientational identity ("Is the husband homosexual or heterosexual?") but of observably preferred activities ("What does he like to do?"), and the answer is that he likes to penetrate orally and vaginally, but not anally: in the coarse language of epigram, he is an *irrumator* and a *fututor*, but not a *pedico*. He can of course engage in the first activity with either a male or a female partner, and this lack of specificity constitutes the hinge on which the joke turns. The point is not that the husband is not an "active homosexual" and thus will avoid sexual contact with Gallus, but rather that the man does not enjoy anally penetrating partners of either sex and, consequently, that instead of exacting a traditional punishment for adultery on Gallus by anally penetrating him, he will inflict the more humiliating punishment of compelled fellatio.[48] Furthermore, Martial's specification that the husband is not in fact a *pedico* necessarily implies that he might very well have been one. In other words, this man could indulge in anal intercourse (whether with his wife or with other partners, female or male) and also engage in vaginal intercourse with his wife, and thus be called a *pedico* as well as a *fututor* and *irrumator*. Again we see that *pedico* and *fututor*, unlike "homosexual" and "heterosexual," are not mutually exclusive terms and can easily be applied to one and the same man.

Thus, on the few occasions when they faced the prospect of describing men who happened to have observable predilections for persons of one sex or the other, ancient writers, not having a linguistic or conceptual framework enabling them succinctly to label a man as exclusively homosexual or heterosexual in his behavior, resorted to periphrasis.[49] Suetonius has this to say of the emperor Claudius: "He was possessed of an extravagant desire for women, having no experience with males whatsoever."[50] The qualification "having no experience with males whatsoever" would be otiose in modern discourse (if he is heterosexual, why note that he never had any homosexual experiences?) and signals the absence of concepts like modern notions of sexual orientation in the ideological systems shared by Suetonius and his readership. We find a similar qualification in Martial's description of a man whom he calls Charidemus: "But then you were a *pedico* and for a long time no woman was known to you."[51] The fact that the speaker apparently feels the need to tack on an emphatic observation that Charidemus never had sexual relations with women again suggests that *pedico* did not function as a metonymic substitute for "homosexual." Other references to men with apparently exclusive tastes for male sexual partners similarly speak in extremes. The elder Pliny reports a folk belief that the genitals of a female hyena will stimulate desire for women even among "men who hate intercourse with women," while the fourth-century A.D. astrological writer Firmicus Maternus speaks on several occasions of "lovers of boys" as an apparently observable type of man, sometimes emphasizing their aversion to sexual relations with women.[52]

Paul Schalow, describing similarly extreme language in seventeenth-century Japanese literature, makes this observation:

> In early modern Japanese sexuality, both the love of women (*joshoku*, or "female love") and the love of men (*nanshoku*, or "male love") were considered normal components of sexual love and represented the two varieties of sexual activity open to adult males. . . . Those who pursued sexual relations exclusively with women or exclusively with youths were in a minority and were considered mildly eccentric for limiting their pleasurable options. Because homosexual relations were not marked as aberrant, men with an exclusive preference for youths were identified not in terms of their preference for youths but as *onnagirai*, or "woman-haters."[53]

Such men, both Japanese and Roman, would be called homosexuals if they lived in the contemporary United States, just as Claudius would be called a heterosexual. But the qualifications made by Roman writers ("having no experience with males whatsoever"; "for a long time no woman was known to you") and the extreme language used by both Roman and Japanese writers (they "hate intercourse with women" or are "women-haters") underscore the exceptional quality of these men's exclusive tastes in their own cultural setting, at the same time pointing to the absence in that setting of the identities "homosexual" and "heterosexual" as universally applicable means of categorizing and evaluating male sexual subjects.

The case of Firmicus Maternus' astrological treatise is particularly interesting. Written in the fourth century A.D., a period that witnessed the triumph of an ascetic approach to sexuality and of Christianity (Firmicus himself converted at some point after writing this treatise), this work displays a markedly moralizing approach to sexual practices that surpasses even the asceticism of Cato the Censor (consider, for example, Firmicus' reference to "lustful lovers of boys" who can become implicated in various crimes including homicide "on account of these vices").[54] But even in this ideological context, encouraging as it did the pigeonholing and marginalization of same-sex practices as luxurious and nonprocreative, we do not find the modern concept of "sexual orientation" at work. To be sure, Firmicus acknowledges that there were men who displayed an open predilection for certain kinds of sexual partners (he speaks of "lovers of women" and "lovers of boys"),[55] but we have seen that Suetonius and Martial do something similar. Firmicus goes a step further when he describes such men's predilections as innate, yet, like earlier writers, he clearly does not assume that *all* men are innately either "lovers of women" or "lovers of boys," neither does he consider these propensities to be fundamentally opposed in nature. In one revealing passage, he argues that one and the same conjunction of stars will produce men who are sterile, lovers of boys, lovers of actresses, or those who will manage brothels.[56] Whether or not Firmicus imagined that an individual man might display more than one of these propensities, the important point is that he clearly considered those propensities to be fundamentally similar character traits that are conditioned by the same astrological environment. Moreover, Firmicus is responding to a variety of observable tendencies among men: he gives astrological aetiologies for (and thus considers as innate) the inclination of some men to marry early in life, to become innkeepers, to engage in incestuous relations, to become involved with female slaves or prostitutes, and so on.[57] We can call these "orientations" if we wish, but they are not the same as the "sexual orientation" of today; Firmicus is not working within a conceptual framework that pigeonholes *all* human beings as innately and permanently homosexual, heterosexual, or bisexual. To assimilate his discourse to modern discourses of "sexual" or "erotic orientation," as Brooten seems to do, would be more misleading than helpful.[58]

Even though no universally applicable system of categorization in terms of sexual object-choice was in use, the evidence offered by Firmicus, Pliny, Suetonius, and Martial shows that some Roman men displayed a proclivity toward or even an exclusive interest in sexual partners of one sex or the other, while other men displayed a proclivity toward married women, slave women, or prostitutes. There were also those who were observably inclined toward either male or female partners but who did not strictly limit their sexual experience to one sex or the other. In ancient descriptions of these men, instead of awkwardly emphatic periphrases signifying exclusivity, we find comparative phrases. Suetonius observes that the emperor Galba was "more inclined" (*pronior*) to men, but that he also married and produced children.[59] Virgil's desires are reported to have been "more inclined" (*pronioris*) to boys, but in the same source we are told that he was reputed to have had an affair with a woman. Obviously his reputation for a fondness for boys was not thought to be incompatible with a dalliance with a woman.[60] And Ovid, who presents the persona of a dedicated womanizer, notes that he is "less" (*minus*) interested in sexual encounters with boys because they receive no pleasure from the act.[61]

Thus, as against the implications of John Boswell's suggestion that "homosexual or heterosexual 'orientation' . . . were common and familiar concepts" in antiquity,[62] I would argue that an ancient allusion to a man's observable inclination toward sexual partners of one or the other sex is comparable to a contemporary American (or even ancient Roman) description of a man as being inclined toward women of a certain physical type or particular hair color.[63] Such preferences really do exist and no doubt have always existed, and they can be noticed. But the cultural heritage of twentieth-century Americans does not include a system of analysis that pigeonholes all men as either blonde-lovers or redhead-lovers or brunette-lovers or, for intractable cases, all-hair-color-lovers. The evidence strongly suggests that the cultural heritage of ancient Romans treated what is today called "sexual orientation" in the same way. In their native cultural context, Suetonius' descriptions of Galba and Claudius function more like contemporary American descriptions of one man as "liking redheads" and another as "liking blondes, with no experience of brunettes" than like contemporary acts of labeling one man "homosexual" and another "heterosexual." David Halperin makes a similar point with regard to Greek traditions:

> It is not immediately evident that differences in sexual preference are by their very nature more revealing about the temperament of individual human beings, more significant determinants of personal identity, than, for example, differences in dietary preference. And yet, it would never occur to us to refer a person's dietary object-choice to some innate characterological disposition or to see in his or her strongly expressed and even unvarying preference for the white meat of chicken the symptom of a profound psychophysical orientation, leading us to identify him or her in contexts quite removed from that of the eating of food as, say (to continue the practice of combining Greek and Latin roots), a "pectoriphage" or a "stethovore."[64]

Likewise Arno Schmitt, discussing the concepts of homosexuality and heterosexuality in some contemporary Islamic cultures, notes the following:

> In the societies of Muslim North Africa and Southwest Asia male-male sexuality plays an important role. But in these societies there are no "homosexuals"—there is no word for "homosexuality"—the concept is completely unfamiliar. There are no heterosexuals either . . . As the male-male act . . . happens between a man and a non-man, it would be absurd to group both under one category, to label them with one word—as absurd as calling both the robber and the robbed one "criminals" and implying they are basically the same.[65]

These analogies can also be applied to Roman concepts of male sexual agents. It is not mere hair-splitting to argue that males who are gendered as "real men" with regard to their sexual practices are described in the Roman textual tradition as inclined to *do* various things rather than as *being* heterosexual, homosexual, or bisexual. The only thing they can be said to *be* is "men."

Labels for the Penetrated Man: *Impudicus*, *Pathicus*, and *Cinaedus*

How are men who played the receptive role in penetrative acts represented in Roman texts? First we need to ask how a Roman might make an imputation that a man had been penetrated, or desired to be. Apart from calling him a *cinaedus* (a word to which I shall return), one could use indirect, even euphemistic language. Above all, one could claim that a man's *pudicitia* ("sexual integrity" or "chastity") had been taken from him, or that he was *impudicus* ("unchaste"). As we saw in chapter 3, the concept of *pudicitia* could represent the ideal sexual integrity of the freeborn Roman citizen that was violated by acts of *stuprum*. Indeed, in its broadest sense, *pudicitia* is a virtue that is violated by sexual misconduct in general, with the result that its opposite *impudicitia* ("unchastity") can insinuate a general lewdness or indecency with no specific reference to the receptive role.[66] But most often an accusation of *impudicitia* leveled against a man has an even nastier thrust and a more precise effect, namely to signify that he has been penetrated. In this sense *pudicitia* represents no vague notion of chastity or purity but rather the specific ideal of masculine bodily integrity understood as impenetrability. In other words, a claim that a man was *impudicus* usually functioned as a coded way of signifying that his masculine inviolability had been compromised, and ancient discussions of a man's *pudicitia* can almost always be reduced to this question: Has he been penetrated or not?

Suetonius, writing of Julius Caesar's sexual misdeeds, sums up by citing the elder Curio:

> at ne cui dubium omnino sit et impudicitiae et adulteriorum flagrasse infamia, Curio pater quadam eum oratione omnium mulierum virum et omnium virorum mulierem appellat. (Suet. *Jul.* 52.3)

> Lest there be any doubt in anyone's mind that he was notorious indeed both for his *impudicitia* and for his adulteries, the elder Curio called him in one of his speeches "every woman's man and every man's woman."

The distribution of Caesar's vices is neatly effected. As the adulteries are covered by "every woman's man" (*omnium mulierum virum*) so *impudicitia* corresponds to "every man's woman" (*omnium virorum mulierem*). The latter phrase has particular reference to Caesar's relationship with King Nicomedes discussed earlier, an affair to which Suetonius himself elsewhere alludes in terms of Caesar's damaged *pudicitia*.[67] Cicero's notoriously malicious attacks on Mark Antony in the *Philippics* include various sexual slurs, among them the accusation that in his adolescence Antony acted as "wife" to the younger Curio:

> sumpsisti virilem, quam statim muliebrem togam reddidisti. primo volgare scortum; certa flagiti merces nec ea parva; sed cito Curio intervenit qui te a meretricio quaestu abduxit et, tamquam stolam dedisset, in matrimonio stabili et certo conlocavit. nemo umquam puer emptus libidinis causa tam fuit in domini potestate quam tu in Curionis. (Cic. *Phil.* 2.44–5)

> You put on the man's toga and instantly turned it into a [loose] woman's toga. At first you were a common whore: there was a fixed price on your shame, and not a small one at that. But Curio soon came to your rescue, taking you away from your career as a prostitute and, as if he had given you a matron's *stola*, settling you in a fixed and stable marriage. No slave-boy bought for the sake of lust was ever so much under his master's control as you were under Curio's.

Cicero's point could not be plainer. Upon assuming the *toga virilis* (a step usually taken between one's fifteenth and seventeenth years), Antony began a promising career—in prostitution—and soon settled down in a comfortable marriage—as Curio's bride. But the stately *matrona* is too flattering an image for Antony: rather, he was like a slave-boy whom a man buys to satisfy his lusts. The wicked invective fills in the background to an earlier passage in the speech that deploys the rhetoric of *pudicitia*. Denying that Antony had been his student, Cicero adds the barbed comment that if he had been, it would have been far better both for Antony's reputation and for his *pudicitia*; but even if Antony had wanted to study with Cicero, Curio would not have allowed him to do so.[68] The reference to Curio and his dominance over the young Antony is calculated, for the *pudicitia* that Antony disregarded was violated precisely by his being Curio's "wife."[69] This physical connotation of male *pudicitia* can also be found in a passage from Seneca comparing the school of Epicurus to an anomalous figure indeed:

> hoc tale est quale vir fortis stolam indutus: constat tibi pudicitia, virilitas salva est, nulli corpus tuum turpi patientiae vacat, sed in manu tympanum est. (Sen. *Dial.* 7.13.3)

> This is comparable to a strong man wearing a matron's *stola*: your *pudicitia* is intact, your manhood is safe, your body is open to no shameful submissiveness. Yet there is a tambourine [*tympanum*] in your hand.[70]

The three successive clauses (*constat tibi pudicitia*; *virilitas salva est*; *nulli corpus tuum turpi patientiae vacat*) stand in a tight relationship, for the man's *pudicitia* is intact and his manhood safe precisely because his body is not available for "shameful submissiveness" (*turpis patientia*). An especially blunt illustration of this sense of *pudicitia* is found in one of the *Priapea*, where the god issues this warning to those who would enter his garden: "If you come in as a thief, you'll leave *impudicus*."[71] As we have seen, other poems in the collection make it brutally clear that Priapus' punishment for thieves is to put his prodigious member to use by raping them, whether vaginally, anally, or orally.[72]

In addition to claiming that his *pudicitia* was no longer intact, Romans had rather more direct means of signifying that a man had been penetrated. In euphemistic but blunt language, for example, a man could be said to have played "the woman's role."[73] There seems also to have been a rather well developed system of slang vocabulary that is mostly lost to us; ancient lexicographers preserve a few precious scraps such as *intercutitus* and *scultimidonus*, the former being glossed as "one who is vigorously skinned, that is, thoroughly disgraced by *stuprum*,"[74] and the latter being explained as meaning "those who bestow for free their *scultima*, that is, their anal orifice, which is called the *scultima* as if from the inner parts of whores [*scortorum intima*]."[75]

A more common and equally blunt term was *pathicus*. The noun is derived from a Greek adjective *pathikos*, and although the Greek word is in fact unattested, the meaning it would have had is clear.[76] The Greek verb *paskhein* and related words are used in sexual contexts in precisely the same way that Romans used the cognate *pati* ("to undergo; to submit to; to endure; to suffer") and such related words as the noun *patientia*, namely to refer to the receptive role in a penetrative sexual act.[77] Thus *pathicus* denotes a male who is anally penetrated.[78] In his forceful assertion of his masculinity at the expense of Aurelius and Furius, Catullus insults the men as *pathicus* and *cinaedus*, respectively (16.2), and, in a poem to which we will return, he uses the same two nouns of Mamurra and Caesar.[79] Juvenal's ninth satire, on the woes of Naevolus, who has made a living by sexually servicing married women and their husbands, includes the wry remark that Naevolus will never want for a patron (*pathicus amicus*) as long as Rome's hills stand.[80]

The word most often used to describe man who had been anally penetrated was the noun *cinaedus*. But unlike the blunt *pathicus* or the florid *scultimidonus*, which (as their etymologies show) primarily signify a man who is anally penetrated, *cinaedus* is not actually anchored in that specific sexual practice. As I shall argue later in this chapter, it refers instead to a man who has an identity as gender deviant. In other words, a *cinaedus* is a man who fails to live up to traditional standards of masculine comportment, and one way in which he may do so is by seeking to be penetrated; but that is merely a symptom of the deeper disorder, his gender deviance. Indeed, the word's etymology suggests no direct connection to any sexual practice. Rather, borrowed from Greek *kinaidos* (which may itself have been a borrowing from a language of Asia Minor), it primarily signifies an effeminate dancer who entertained his audiences with a *tympanum* or tambourine in his hand, and adopted a lascivious style, often suggestively wiggling his buttocks in such a way as to suggest anal intercourse.[81] (That a salient characteristic of the dancer called *kinaidos* was his tendency to shake his buttocks is clear from the fact that Greeks referred to a certain kind of bird as *kinaidion* or *seisopugis* ["butt-shaker"], and Pliny the Elder mentions a fish called the *cinaedus*: these animals were obviously notable for the way they moved their hindquarters.)[82] Nonius informs us that "among the men of old, dancers or pantomime performers were called *cinaedi* from their 'moving their body' (*kinein to sôma*)," and an anonymous lexicographer defines *cinaedi* as "those who publicly shake their buttocks, that is to say, dancers or pantomime performers." Firmicus Maternus describes *cinaedi* who have soft, effeminate bodies and who dance on stage, imitating the finales of plays from the old days.[83]

As was true of most performers and actors, *cinaedi* were liable to being described by Romans as effeminate and lascivious.[84] In particular, since these dancers were given to wiggling their buttocks in suggestive ways, they were assumed to be interested in being penetrated, thus embodying their effeminate identity in their sexual practices. Plautus uses the word *cinaedus* several times to refer to dancers in such a way as to stress their softness and unmanliness, and one joke directly invokes their predilection for being anally penetrated.[85] In one of his speeches, Scipio Aemilianus professes outrage at the thought of freeborn boys and girls going to a dancing-school filled with *cinaedi*, and in another he insinuates that P. Sulpicius Galus, who when an adolescent had displayed signs of effeminacy, reclining at banquets with an older male lover, has done "what *cinaedi* do."[86] This phrase, with its euphemistic but direct tone, demonstrates the kind of reputation that *cinaedi* had acquired for themselves: soft, effeminate, decadent, and, when it came to sexual practices, liable to play the receptive role.

Thus the word *cinaedus* came also to be used to refer to any man, professional dancer or not, who displayed an effeminacy that was most noticeably embodied in a penchant for being anally penetrated. Catullus lampoons Vibennius *père et fils*:

> o furum optime balneariorum
> Vibenni pater et cinaede fili
> (nam dextra pater inquinatiore,
> culo filius est voraciore),
> cur non exilium malasque in oras
> itis, quandoquidem patris rapinae
> notae sunt populo, et nates pilosas,
> fili, non potes asse venditare? (Catull. 33)

> Vibennius senior, best of bathhouse thieves, and you *cinaedus* his son (the father has a filthier right hand, the son a greedier asshole): Why don't you go into exile in a dreadful region, since everyone knows of the father's thefts and you, son, can't sell your hairy butt for a dime?

The father is slandered as a thief and the son as a *cinaedus*, and the accusations are anchored in the appropriate body parts: as the father's right hand is befouled, so the son's anus is rapacious.[87] Martial writes of a certain Charinus who has indulged in the receptive role in anal intercourse to such an extent that, in the poet's hyperbolic phrase, his anus has been split all the way to his navel; yet his craving to be penetrated has lost nothing of its intensity. "How great an itch the poor man suffers from!" Martial exclaims. "He has no asshole, yet is a *cinaedus*."[88] Likewise Juvenal disparagingly describes a hypocritical philosopher as "the best-known ditch among Socratic *cinaedi*": this *cinaedus* is someone to be dug or plowed.[89] Martial also uses the term to refer to slaves who provide their masters with sexual services, twice irreverently calling Ganymede, Jupiter's beautiful young concubine (whose services to the god are not usually said to include dancing), "the Trojan *cinaedus*."[90]

In each of these texts the word *cinaedus* is used in its transferred sense: none of these people are dancers. Yet the primary meaning of *cinaedus* never died out; the term never became a dead metaphor. Pliny the Younger, for example, refers to *cinaedi* who appear at extravagant banquets as hired entertainers in the company of jesters and buffoons. The parallel with the two other types of performers suggests that Pliny is using *cinaedus* as a technical term referring to dancers; in any case, one can hardly imagine the eminently proper Pliny using the word in its transferred sense.[91] There are times, too, when the term *cinaedus* is used in such a way as to draw on the entire range of its possible meanings, from Eastern dancer to effeminate man who is likely to want to be penetrated. A comedy staged during the time of Augustus included a line referring to a *gallus*, or castrated priest of the Asian Mother Goddess, as a *cinaedus*. But the term *cinaedus* was invested with a double meaning by the audience, who took it as a gendered slur against Augustus, hardly an Eastern dancer but indeed rumored to have been penetrated in his youth.[92] A similar flexibility can be seen in a detail from Encolpius' narrative of a decadent night at Quartilla's home in Petronius' *Satyricon*. At one point a *cinaedus* comes in, claps his hands, and sings this song:

huc huc <cito> convenite nunc, spatalocinaedi,
pede tendite, cursum addite, convolate planta,
femore <o> facili, clune agili, [et] manu procaces,
molles, veteres, Deliaci manu recisi. (Petr. *Sat.* 23.3)

Come here now—quick!—bejeweled *cinaedi*; hasten on foot, come running, fly hither
with the soles of your feet: O ye of easy thigh and nimble buttock, naughty with your
hands, soft, old, hand-gelded Delian capons.

Both the lively meter and the content suggest that the *cinaedus* is a dancer, as are
the *spatalocinaedi* to whom he appeals.[93] But Encolpius' subsequent narrative leaves
no doubt that this *cinaedus* is both willing and able to assume the receptive role in
anal intercourse, a role he takes on with gusto.[94] Indeed, the *cinaedus'* allusion to
the nimble and agile thighs, buttocks, and hands of his colleagues can be understood simultaneously in sexual terms and in terms of dancing.[95]

This *cinaedus* describes his colleagues as castrated, a detail which invokes the
image of the *gallus* or castrated priest of the Mother Goddess who appeared in the
comedy staged during Augustus' principate just mentioned.[96] I would suggest that
the image of an effeminate Eastern dancer lurked behind every description of a
man as a *cinaedus* in the transferred sense, and that behind the Eastern dancer in
turn lurked the image of the *gallus*. Thus a man who showed himself to be effeminate, most notably by seeking to play "the woman's role" sexually, could be insulted
as a type of dancer (*cinaedus*), who in turn could be compared to the ultimate in
unmanliness: the *gallus*. Several ancient texts testify to this conceptual continuum.
In the dramatic line quoted by Suetonius, the *gallus* on stage is called a *cinaedus*;[97]
in Juvenal's second satire the narrator, disgusted at the hypocritical Socratic *cinaedi*
he sees everywhere in Rome, wonders what keeps them from going all the way and
becoming *galli*, "cutting off their useless piece of meat in the Phrygian manner;"[98]
and the narrator of Apuleius' *Metamorphoses*, transformed into an ass, is sold to an
effeminate old man whom he calls a *cinaedus*, who is one of a gang of devotees of
the Syrian Mother Goddess who, while not explicitly said to be eunuchs, are certainly effeminate and make a living by going from town to town and putting on
feverish displays of dancing and self-mutilation.[99]

We might say, in other words, that the *cinaedus* and above all the *gallus* were
ideological scare-figures for Roman men:[100] a man who flaunted his breaking of
the rules of masculinity could be said to have taken the first step on the dangerous
road toward becoming a castrated priest of the Mother Goddess. Thus *cinaedus*
was a multifaceted insult. To call a Roman man a *cinaedus* was to associate him
with the East (and, as seen in chapter 4, there was already a tendency to create a
gendered contrast between decadent, effeminate Easterners and virtuous, masculine Romans), with dancing (a disgraceful profession that was often gendered as
effeminate anyway), and with the effeminate sexual role of being penetrated.[101]

Finally, both *pathicus* and *cinaedus* were capable of being used in contexts
other than those referring to penetrated males. Martial describes sexually explicit
poetry as *pathicissimi libelli* and uses the term *cinaedus* to refer to the poet Sotades,
who specialized in verses that yielded obscenities when read backward, while Varro

seems to have referred to writers of lewd comedies as *cinaedici* and one author in particular as a *cinaedologos*.[102] This usage may reflect a belief that men called *pathici* or *cinaedi* displayed a desire that was both objectionable and excessive; thus the terms could be applied to lewd poems and poets.[103] The terms could also be applied to women: in the *Priapea* the adjective *pathica* describes women who are avid devotees of the god and particularly of his distinctive member, while Catullus describes a woman whom he calls a *scortillum* ("little whore") as *cinaedior*.[104] How are we to interpret these labels? As its etymology shows, *pathicus* has fundamentally to do with sexual behavior designated as "passive," namely the receptive role in an act of penetration. But since women could be said to be "born" to that role (cf. Sen. *Epist.* 95.21: *pati natae*), there seems no need to understand a specific allusion to anal penetration in the feminine form *pathica*.[105] Instead, I would argue that Priapus' *pathicae puellae* are those who take a special delight in playing the role assigned to them.[106] As for Catullus' whore, we have already seen that the word *cinaedus* itself has no clear etymological connection with any specific sexual practice, instead designating a lascivious, effeminate male dancer; when applied to a female prostitute, it might simply suggest that she is especially lustful.[107]

In sum, the word *cinaedus* originally referred to men who were professional dancers of a type associated with the East, dancing with a *tympanum* and seductively wiggling their buttocks in such a way as to suggest anal intercourse. In a transferred sense it came to describe a man who was not a dancer but who displayed the salient characteristics of a *cinaedus* in the strict sense: he was a gender-deviant, a "non-man" who broke the rules of masculine comportment and whose effeminate disorder might be embodied in the particular symptom of seeking to be penetrated. This usage is the more common of the two in the extant sources, and it is in this sense that I use the word here, with two important caveats. First, *cinaedus* was a term used as an insult by men who were at pains to distance themselves from those they called *cinaedi*,[108] and thus whenever I use the term the reader should imagine it surrounded by quotation marks so as to mark a certain ironic distance: I am speaking of that type of man whom others disparagingly called *cinaedi*. Second, it must always be kept in mind that when a Roman called a man a *cinaedus* he was not ruling out the possibility that the man might play sexual roles other than that of the receptive partner in anal intercourse.[109] I will argue later that the *cinaedus* was not the same thing as a "passive homosexual," since it was neither his expression of sexual desire for other males nor his proclivity for playing the receptive role in anal intercourse that gave him his identity or uniquely defined him as a *cinaedus*: he might engage in sexual practices with women and still be a *cinaedus*, and a man did not automatically become a *cinaedus* simply by being penetrated (victims of rape, for example, would not normally be described as such). A *cinaedus* was, rather, a man who failed to be fully masculine, whose effeminacy showed itself in such symptoms as feminine clothing and mannerisms and a lascivious and oversexed demeanor that was likely to be embodied in a proclivity for playing the receptive role in anal intercourse. *Cinaedi* were, in other words, a prominent subset of the class of effeminate men (*molles*) discussed in chapter 4, but hardly identical to that whole class.

Stereotypes of the *Cinaedus*: Effeminacy and "Disease"

To imply or state outright that a man had played the receptive role in a penetrative act was a distinct assault on his masculinity, and was clearly meant to be a stinging blow. Jokes at the expense of men who liked to be penetrated pervade Roman satire and epigram,[110] and even in the idyllic world of pastoral poetry, one character nastily implies to another that he knows not only that he has been penetrated but also who his partner was.[111] When a passage from Juvenal describes a man as being "more shameless than a *cinaedus* who writes satire," we are clearly in the realm of paradox, and the *cinaedus* represents an inherently passive object of scorn, the designated victim.[112] The degradation of such men, along with the notion that they have abrogated their masculinity, is a prominent theme in Persius' first satire, where the receptive role in anal penetration becomes an image for the degraded, subservient role embraced by decadent Roman aristocrats.[113] Martial refers to a man's desire to be penetrated as an "obscene itch" (*obscena prurigo*) and to some wealthy *cinaedi* themselves as "obscene."[114] Men who lived and worked in the public arena laid themselves open to gossip to an even greater degree than others, and an insinuation or outright assertion that a public figure had at some point in his life played the receptive role in intercourse was a stock element in the repertoire of Roman orators;[115] Suetonius' lives of the emperors are peppered with reports of such rumors.[116] Nonliterary sources that attest to insults of this kind include graffiti[117] as well as a corpus of ivory or bone tiles (*tesserae*) found in Rome, Pompeii, and Perugia, that are inscribed with epithets such as "thief" (*fur*), "adulterer" (*moice*), "drunkard" (*ebriose*), "glutton" (*gulo*), "idiot" (*fatue*), cinaidus [*sic*], and *pathicus*.[118]

In Juvenal's second satire, a woman named Laronia attacks hypocritical *cinaedi*, painting a vivid picture that gives us some idea of the stereotypes circulating among the satirist's readership. These *cinaedi* stick together, finding protection in numbers (she ironically likens them to a phalanx of soldiers protected by their interlocking shields);[119] they act like women, for example by spinning wool (54–7); some of them have wives but enjoy the sexual services of their freedmen (58–61). Juvenal's own persona then continues the attack, imagining these hypocrites dressed in womanish see-through clothing (65–78) and complaining that these practices are spreading like a contagion, infecting more and more Romans (78–81). He then paints a vivid picture of these hypocritical *cinaedi* gathering to conduct their sacred rites in honor of the Good Goddess (rites normally observed only by women—but these *cinaedi* resolutely exclude all females), replete with makeup, mirrors, women's clothing, and phallically shaped drinking vessels (83–114); all that remains is for them to castrate themselves like the *galli* do (115–6). Finally, the speaker observes that some of these men are taking husbands and that before long they will celebrate their weddings openly (117–42; see Appendix 2).

In his ninth satire, Juvenal presents a man named Naevolus, who has the reputation of a womanizer (*moechus*, 25) but who is also known to penetrate his female partners' husbands (26: see chapters 1 and 2 for earlier discussions of Naevolus). Naevolus proceeds to paint a picture of the wealthy man who enjoys his services, whom he pejoratively calls a *cinaedus* (37): he displays a noticeable appreciation for well-endowed studs (33–7); he fancies himself soft, pretty, and boyish (46–7; cf. 95); he has a wife but never has sexual relations with her, instead relying on Naevolus to impregnate her (70–90); and he desperately wants to keep this arrangement secret (93–101), although his secrets, like those of all rich men, will not be kept for long (102–23). Finally, we hear from Naevolus' interlocutor that Rome is filled with men like this, and always will be:

> ne trepida, numquam pathicus tibi derit amicus
> stantibus et salvis his collibus; undique ad illos
> convenient et carpentis et navibus omnes
> qui digito scalpunt uno caput. (Juv. 9.130–3)[120]

> Fear not, you will never lack a *pathicus* friend as long as these seven hills stand and are safe; from every direction they will flock to those hills in carts and ships, scratching their head with one finger.

The fear that throngs of *pathici* will pile into Rome by land and sea is surely exaggerated; still, Juvenal may well be playing off a perception in his readership that more than a few *pathici* already lived in the seven hills. The comment, in other words, tells us not so much about historical realities as about popular prejudices ("they're everywhere"),[121] but those prejudices are precisely my interest here.

In a scene from Petronius' *Satyricon* discussed earlier in this chapter, a *cinaedus* makes an appearance at a decadent party, and he bears a striking resemblance to the *cinaedi* in Juvenal, wearing makeup and singing a rousing song to his fellow *cinaedi* in which he appeals to their tastes for jewelry and dancing, lovingly cites their softness as well as their old age (one thinks of Juvenal's *cinaedus* who wants to be known as a *puer*), and finally describes them as castrated (Petr. *Sat*. 23). Finally, Apuleius describes an old *cinaedus* with carefully arranged hair who campily addresses his friends as *puellae*. These "girls" embody the extreme scenario imagined in Juvenal's second satire: although not explicitly said to have been castrated,[122] they are devotees of an Eastern goddess who make the rounds of villages, providing a spectacle of frenzied dance and self-mutilation, and making a pretty penny. And Apuleius makes no bones about their sexual tastes: they keep a young stud as their *concubinus* and at one point he complains of being worn out; they pick up and take home with them a well-hung country boy and orally stimulate him.[123]

These stereotypes were hardly meant to be flattering. Indeed, effeminate men who sought to be penetrated were said to be characterized by a *morbus* ("disease," "disorder," or "affliction"). In one of the *Priapea*, the god bluntly insults a woman: she is darker than a Moor, shorter than a pygmy, rougher and hairier than a bear, her vagina is looser than Persian or Indian breeches, and she is "more diseased [*morbosior*] than any *cinaedus*."[124] The medical writer Caelius Aurelianus offers a lengthy discussion of why it is that some men enjoy being penetrated in a treatise on chronic diseases.[125] A comment from Seneca's *Epistles* and some remarks from Juvenal likewise invoke the imagery of "disease" or "affliction" with reference to men who sought to be penetrated.[126] Pliny the Elder reports the practice of using an ointment containing the burnt hairs from a hyena's anal region to cause men "of disgraceful softness" (*probrosae mollitiae*) to act "chastely" and even "austerely."[127] Richlin suggests that this was as a homeopathic cure for the disease of "pathic homosexuality,"[128] but, as seen in chapter 4, the attribution of softness to a man simply meant that he was effeminate and did not necessarily impute a desire to be penetrated. Thus the folk practice reported by Pliny might well have been directed not at "pathic homosexuality" but rather at a soft, licentious, effeminate tendency to overindulge in sexual practices of various kinds. Indeed, the animal's orifice was thought to have an important connection with sexual desire in general: in the same passage we read that if a man straps a hyena's anus onto his left arm, it will act as a potent love charm, attracting any woman whom he sees.[129]

In any case, the disease or affliction of men who sought to be penetrated was certainly not homosexuality as such[130]—no one seems to have called a man's desire to penetrate a lovely boy a *morbus*—but rather a gender inversion that might be manifested, among other ways, in a desire to be penetrated. Moreover, it is worth noting that a predilection for various kinds of excessive or disgraceful behavior was capable of being called a disease. Lysidamus, the oversexed old man in Plautus' *Casina* (see chapters 1 and 2), describes what he wants to do with his lovely young slave-girl as a *morbus* that he wishes were afflicting him.[131] Neither was he alone: other Plautine characters speak of a man's sexual desire for a woman or a woman's for a man as a *morbus*.[132] In one of his philosophical works, Cicero describes an excessive lust for women as a *morbus*, while in his prosecution of Verres he notes that the defendant's fondness for expensive *objets d'art* is described by his own friends as a *morbus* and *insania*.[133] Seneca the Elder refers to a man who had a "sick" desire (*morbus*) for big things (slaves, drinking vessels, shoes, figs, and female concubines); Horace draws on philosophical notions of "disease" and "unhealthiness" (*morbus* and *insania*) when referring to a lust for collecting art, avarice in general, and a man's love for a female prostitute; the younger Seneca uses the term *morbus* to describe the impulse that leads a man to hire himself out as a gladiator.[134] And there was a long tradition in both Greek and Roman literature of representing erotic passion in general as a disease.[135] In short, the evidence suggests that *cinaedi* were not said to be *morbosi* in the way that twentieth-century homosexuals have been pitied or scorned as "sick."[136]

The Double Standard

Although the imagery of disease or affliction was hardly flattering, nonetheless *cinaedi* (the lucky ones, at least) had their desires satisfied by someone, and that arrangement must have been mutually agreeable. Who were their sexual partners? As Amy Richlin reminds us, they cannot only have been prostitutes paid by *cinaedi* to satisfy their desires[137] (or, we might add, slaves bought by them for that purpose). In other words, *cinaedi* must have found some of their sexual partners among the "real men" (*viri*) whose voices dominate the surviving textual tradition. Thus, among the very men who wrote and read epigrams, satires, and graffiti at the expense of *cinaedi* were men who privately shared sexual pleasures with them. There is a distinct double perspective, indeed double standard, at work here: the "passivity" of women and *cinaedi* was embodied in encounters with the very men who mocked them. Men's sexual partners were thus liable *ipso facto* to being disparaged—women for being "naturally" passive and inferior, *cinaedi* for deliberately seeking to act like women—and a single sexual encounter was capable of two intertwined meanings. With reference to the man on top, it was an act of domination or even aggression in which the masculine penetrative identity triumphed, while with reference to the person on bottom, it was a forfeiture, an invasion, a loss.

Of course, when they had sexual relations with *cinaedi*—and indeed with women—Roman men who considered themselves real men could not always have been acting out an aggressive desire to subjugate and to stigmatize a despised "other," closing their eyes and thinking of Priapus. Apuleius' troop of *cinaedi* is suggestive. On one occasion they bring home a well-endowed country lad (*rusticanus iuvenis*) to have dinner with them, but before they get to the main course they have another kind of feast, providing him with oral stimulation. The young peasant is hardly an unwilling captive and apparently has no complaints. On another occasion the *cinaedi* buy themselves a stud to service them (he is called their *partiarius concubinus* ["joint concubine"]): when the narrator (in the form of an ass) arrives, the concubine imagines that he has received a colleague, and while he does end up complaining, it is only of exhaustion and not of disgust at the perversions he was forced to participate in.[138] We might recall Juvenal's Naevolus as well. He disparages his patron for his desires to be penetrated, but he has obviously been content to do his job as long as he was getting something out of it. Only when it becomes clear that his patron will not be giving him satisfactory compensation does he turn on him and bitterly denounce his desires and describe his own job as disgusting—behind his back.[139] This insidiously aggressive stance may well be an exaggerated version of common attitudes toward men who were ridiculed as *cinaedi*: they were handy, even pleasurable, outlets for men's sexual pleasures, but also convenient butts for ridicule. This ugly paradox is not coincidentally reminiscent of ancient images of female prostitutes and indeed of women in general—useful and even desirable, but at the same time liable to being mocked and scorned.[140] In their public posturing at least, those Romans who prided themselves on being real men showed themselves capable of quietly suppressing the fact that it takes two to tango, or even of imagining that it did not really take two at all.[141]

What were the reasons for this double standard, especially with regard to *cinaedi*? One way to approach the question is to return to the listing of obscene verbs relating to penetrative acts offered earlier. We saw there that the verbs *futuere*, *pedicare*, and *irrumare* (referring to the actions of penetrating vaginally, anally, and orally respectively) are both morphologically and conceptually active in Roman terms: they describe the actions of a man who *does* something, who asserts his manhood by penetrating another. By contrast, the corresponding verbs *crisare*, *cevere*, and *fellare*, which describe the actions of the person who plays the receptive role, conceived of as passive, are nonetheless morphologically active, and that disjuncture highlights the problem.[142] Men who seek to be penetrated are anomalies in this system because their subjectivity is embodied in actively being passive. Women who lasciviously shimmy (*crisare*) and men who wiggle their buttocks (*cevere*) display an active delight in being penetrated; men and women who "suck" (*fellare*) take an active role indeed in an act that not only marks them as penetrated but befouls their mouths and degrades their being (see the discussion of oral sex later in this chapter).

The behavior of adult males who actively sought to play the receptive role in intercourse obviously did not align itself with traditional antithetical notions of what men and women were. These were men who, in the unforgiving logic of binary conceptualizations of masculinity and femininity, ceded their masculinity; who, as Winkler, following Halperin, puts it, actually wanted to lose in the zero-sum game of masculinity.

> Since sexual activity is symbolic of (or constructed as) zero-sum competition and the relentless conjunction of winners with losers, the *kinaidos* is a man who desires to lose. . . . Women too, in this ideology, are turned on by losing, a perception which is at the core of Greek misogyny.[143]

Thus one might say that the very existence of *cinaedi* constituted an implicit challenge to the game; and that it was because they were a threat that they were subject to hostility and scorn. And yet one can argue that the ridicule directed at them had the effect of keeping the threat contained, of keeping *cinaedi* safely in their place as the subordinated other, and thus that this mockery—and the double standard that went along with it—maintained the sacrosanctity of masculinity and kept gender categories intact. In other words, the figure of the *cinaedus*, rather than posing a threat to Roman concepts of masculinity, ultimately supported the ideological system by constituting a necessary negative. The *cinaedus* was what a real man must not be.[144]

Boys versus *Cinaedi*

Whereas the adult *cinaedus* was an anomalous figure, deviant in his womanish being and effeminate desires, the beautiful boy (*puer*) was, as we saw in chapters 1 and 2, an acceptable, even idealized object of Roman men's penetrative desires. While the effeminacy of *cinaedi* was a serious failing, we will see that beautiful boys might be charmingly butch or delightfully soft and girlish. In other words, boys could get away with things that *cinaedi* could not.[145] Indeed, one might say that the image of the *cinaedus* served as a reminder of what could happen if the normative transition from passive, penetrated *puer* to active, penetrating *vir* did not take place as expected.[146]

Some ancient sources remind us that *cinaedi* were precisely mature men and not boys, however much they might wish it were otherwise. Seneca, for instance, while refraining from using the word *cinaedus*, condemns those men who try to maintain a boyish appearance in order to attract male lovers:

> non vivunt contra naturam qui spectant ut pueritia splendeat tempore alieno? quid fieri crudelius vel miserius potest? numquam vir erit, ut diu virum pati possit? et cum illum contumeliae sexus eripuisse debuerat, non ne aetas quidem eripiet?
>
> (Sen. *Epist.* 122.7)

Is it not the case that those who see to it that their boyishness shines forth at the inappropriate time live contrary to nature? How could anything be crueler or more miserable? Will he never be a man so that he can take on a man for a long time? And although his sex ought to have rescued him from indignity, will he not even be rescued by his age?

Seneca's argument comes in response to an obviously common assumption that boys, at least, could justifiably be penetrated, but mature men never;[147] his rhetoric also assumes that, justifiably or not, some mature men sought to play the role thought to be more appropriate for boys. Juvenal's Naevolus, speaking of a man who seeks well-endowed male sexual partners to "plow" him, observes that he wishes to be called a "boy" comparable to Ganymede, thereby making it clear that he is in reality hardly a boy. Elsewhere in Juvenal we read of a perverse celebration of the rites in honor of the Good Goddess by effeminate men who are compared to *galli*, and their chief priest is described as a gray-haired old man.[148] And Martial makes passing reference to an "aged *cinaedus*" as one of the less-than-reputable characters who populate the urban landscape of his day.[149]

In boys, by contrast, effeminacy could be charming. In Tibullus' poem presenting Priapus' advice on how to catch a boy (discussed in chapter 1), desirable *pueri* are described as either athletically masculine or possessed of a "maidenly modesty":

o fuge te tenerae puerorum credere turbae:
    nam causam iusti semper amoris habent.
hic placet, angustis quod equum compescit habenis;
    hic placidam niveo pectore pellit aquam;
hic, quia fortis adest audacia, cepit: at illi
    virgineus teneras stat pudor ante genas. (Tibull. 1.4.9–14)

Ah! Avoid entrusting yourself to the tender crowd of boys; they always give a reason for a justified love. This one is pleasing because he restrains a horse with tightened reins; this one strikes the calm water with his snow-white breast; this one has captivated you because he shows brave daring; while that one's tender cheeks are marked with a maidenly modesty.

Horace complains of his painful passion for Lyciscus, who "boasts of surpassing any woman in softness,"[150] while Martial professes delight in a panoply of boys, most of whom display undeniably effeminate traits:

Festinat Polytimus ad puellas;
invitus puerum fatetur Hypnus;
pastas glande natis habet Secundus;
mollis Dindymus est sed esse non vult;
Amphion potuit puella nasci.
horum delicias superbiamque
et fastus querulos, Avite, malo
quam dotis mihi quinquies ducena. (Mart. 12.75)

Polytimus chases after girls; Hypnus unwillingly admits he is a boy; Secundus has buttocks fed on acorn; Dindymus is soft but doesn't want to be; Amphion could have been born a girl. These boys' affectations, their haughtiness and arrogant complaints, I prefer, Avitus, to a million in dowry.

The naughty comment regarding Secundus ("acorn" [*glans*] is a metaphor for the *glans penis* specifically or the penis as a whole generally)[151] illustrates an interesting point. Even boys' desires to be penetrated, so scandalous in *cinaedi*, could occasionally be noted with a certain frank playfulness. As seen in chapter 2, there were some linguistic associations between boys and anal intercourse: the verb *pedicare* ("to penetrate anally") seems to be based on the Greek word *paidika* ("boyfriend"); Martial refers to anal intercourse with a woman as *illud puerile* ("that boyish thing") and elsewhere describes the traditional punishment that a husband might exact from a man who cuckolded him—anal rape—as *supplicium puerile* ("the boys' punishment"); the narrator in Apuleius' *Metamorphoses* describes anal intercourse with a woman as *puerile corollarium* ("a boyish bonus"); and Priapus seeks to punish women with vaginal, men with oral, and boys with anal penetration.[152] Boys and anal intercourse, it seems, went hand in hand.

Thus not only was a certain degree of softness, even effeminacy, allowed boys, but the potentially troublesome facts that they might be sexually penetrated by men, and that they might derive some pleasure from the act, were occasionally acknowledged. In Livy's narrative of the Bacchanalian scandal of 186 B.C., the freedwoman Hispala observes that it had become the practice among the cult's members not to initiate anyone older than twenty years of age, since youths under twenty are "susceptible to [lit., "submitting to," *patientes*] being led astray and to *stuprum*."[153] The implications of this decorous language are brought out in the ribald tale from Petronius' *Satyricon* of Eumolpus' adventures with a boy in Pergamum who not only enjoys the sexual act (the text clearly implies anal penetration) but, in the end, wears his lover out by constantly asking for more:

> ego vero deposita omni offensa cum puero in gratiam redii ususque beneficio eius in somnum delapsus sum. sed non fuit contentus iteratione ephebus plenae maturitatis et annis ad patiendum gestientibus. itaque excitavit me sopitum et "numquid vis?" inquit. et non plane iam molestum erat munus. utcumque igitur inter anhelitus sudoresque tritus, quod voluerat accepit, rursusque in somnum decidi gaudio lassus; interposita minus hora pungere me manu coepit et dicere: "quare non facimus?" tum ego totiens excitatus plane vehementer excandui et reddidi illi voces suas: "aut dormi, aut ego iam patri dicam." (Petr. *Sat*. 87.6–10)

> [After having made up once] we laid aside all ill will and I returned to the boy's favor, and having enjoyed his kindness [for a second time] I fell asleep. But the youth, fully ripe and of an age that was eager to be submissive [*patiendum*], was not content with the repeat performance, so he woke me up from my sleep and said, "Don't you want something?" The task was hardly unpleasant, so somehow he got what he wanted as I ground away at him gasping and sweating. I fell asleep again worn out with joy. But after less than an hour had gone by he began to poke at me with his hand and to say, "Why don't we do it?" Having been awakened so many times, I really got very upset and told him exactly what he had told me earlier: "Either you go to sleep, or I'll tell your father!"

This hilarious scene seriously undercuts the ideal of the coolly disinterested boy who derives no pleasure from being penetrated. Eumolpus' wry phrase *annis ad patiendum gestientibus* echoes Livy's more somber *aetates stupri patientes*; in two quite different contexts we find what amounts to an acknowledgment that young men are susceptible to the pleasures of being pursued and even penetrated by men. Indeed Tibullus' Priapus offers this advice:

> tunc tibi mitis erit, rapias tum cara licebit
>   oscula: pugnabit, sed tibi rapta dabit.
> rapta dabit primo, post adferet ipse roganti,
>   post etiam collo se implicuisse velit. (Tibull. 1.4.53–6)

> Then the boy will be gentle with you—then you will be able to seize some lovely kisses. He will fight back, but he will give them to you when you seize them. At first he will give them to you when you seize them, but then he will on his own offer them to you when you ask, and finally he might even want to cling to your neck.

Priapus speaks of the boy's pleasure in kisses, but in view of the passages from Livy and Petronius, we might read this as a euphemistic synecdoche: kisses are not the only things that boys enjoy getting from their lovers.[154] Finally, in a medical treatise that aims to explain why some men experience pleasure in being penetrated, Caelius Aurelianus observes in passing that "many people suppose boys to be afflicted by this passion, for just like old men they lack the masculine function, which does not yet exist in them just as it has deserted old men."[155] Not only does this text admit that some boys derive pleasure from being penetrated, but it also implies an understanding among "many people" (*plurimi*) that boys' desires can be understood, and perhaps even forgiven, by virtue of the fact that they do not yet fully possess "the masculine function" (*virile officium*).[156]

But of course Caelius is describing a pathology (*morbus*), and when he speaks of boys being afflicted by a "passion" (*passio*) for being penetrated, he reveals a certain problematization of that desire. We recall, too, such invective as Scipio Aemilianus' attack on the young Sulpicius Galus who was accompanied at banquets by his older male lover (fr. 17; see chapter 1). Likewise, to the remark from Livy about young men's susceptibility to *stuprum* should be compared a comment attributed by the same historian to the man who was consul during the Bacchanalian crisis, to the effect that the young men who had been initiated were not worthy of fighting for the fatherland.[157] In short, Eumolpus' story is outrageous, Livy's narrative is scandalized, and Caelius' aetiology is aimed at explaining a problem. These texts reflect a cultural tradition according to which normal males should not derive pleasure from being penetrated, and thus any boy or man who seemed actively to pursue that pleasure could be viewed with suspicion, although in the case of boys there was room for forgiveness.[158]

There was therefore a delicate balancing-act for boys to perform: they could be delightfully soft, but they must not seem *too* effeminate; they might enjoy being penetrated, but that enjoyment could also be held up against them. If a boy played his part discreetly, subscribing to the convenient fiction that he did not actually desire to play the "woman's role" and not displaying an outrageous effeminacy, all was well: an arrangement especially convenient for the men, and no doubt for some boys, too. Yet if a boy broke these unwritten rules, for example by seeming too eager to fill the sexual role destined for him, he became a ready target for abuse, and the weapon ready at hand was to claim that in the end the boy was no different from a *cinaedus* or a woman. Thus Martial irreverently refers to Ganymede, the stereotypical image of the beautiful slave-boy, as a *cinaedus*.[159] Far less indulgent than this witticism is Scipio's verbal assault on Sulpicius Galus for having been in his youth both effeminate and "fond of men" (*virosus*): can we not assume, Scipio asks, that he has done what *cinaedi* do?[160] Such dynamics also characterize some of the relationships in Petronius' *Satyricon*. The narrator Encolpius usually describes his erotic relationship with the sixteen-year-old Giton in terms that sidestep the issue of penetrative role. Each, for example, is the "brother" (*frater*) of the other,[161] and Encolpius recalls the lovemaking that they enjoyed upon their return home from Trimalchio's banquet in lyrical language:

> qualis nox fuit illa, di deaeque,
> quam mollis torus. haesimus calentes
> et transfudimus hinc et hinc labellis
> errantes animas. (Petr. *Sat.* 79.8)

> Ye gods and goddesses, what a night that was! How soft the bed! We clung together, hot, and on this side and that we exchanged our wandering souls by our lips.

These lovers engage in a passionate intercourse whose reciprocal quality is stressed by Encolpius' proclamation that they effected a transfer of their souls by way of their lips; the phrase *hinc et hinc* conveys the notion of mutuality with particular clarity. But later, when Encolpius recalls the time when he was abandoned by Giton, he drops the language of brotherly love and reciprocity, and invokes instead the discourse of penetration, of macho domination and effeminate subordination, and he likens Giton to a female whore.

> quid ille alter? qui die togae virilis stolam sumpsit, qui ne vir esset a matre persuasus est, qui opus muliebre in ergastulo fecit, qui postquam conturbavit et libidinis suae solum vertit, reliquit veteris amicitiae nomen et, pro pudor, tamquam mulier secutuleia unius noctis tactu omnia vendidit. (Petr. *Sat.* 81.5)

> And what about that other one? On the day he should have assumed the man's toga he put on the matron's gown; he was persuaded by his mother not to be a man; he did woman's work among the chain-gangs; after he went bankrupt and became an emigrant in lust, he abandoned the name of an old friendship and (the shame of it!) sold everything for one night of groping, like some loose woman.

At a moment of crisis, then, we see a man appealing to the penetrative, differential model for sexual relations in order to debase and insult his younger partner. To judge by Petronius and Scipio, when a boy was felt to have behaved badly (or when it suited the rhetorical or emotional needs of the men who talked about him), he became liable to assimilation to the scare figure of the *cinaedus*, mocked for his sexual role by the very men who had enjoyed him as he played that role.

Finally, it is worth considering the status of these desirable boys. The Greek names of most of the boys mentioned in Martial's poetry (in the epigram quoted above, Secundus is the only one with a Latin name) suggest that they are slaves, and in their case it could be argued that their sexual role was simply part of their job description, regardless of the fact that they had never actually applied for the job. The remark of the Augustan orator Haterius cited in chapters 1 and 3 demonstrates that in fact this argument could be made quite unabashedly: "Unchastity [*impudicitia*] is a matter of reproach in the freeborn, a matter of necessity in the slave, a matter of duty in the freedman."[162] And yet not all of the lovely boys who appear in Roman poetry were slaves. Catullus is characteristically candid in using the name of a freeborn Roman (Juventius) to represent his boyfriend. While other poets such as Horace and Tibullus, like Martial, generally use Greek names to describe their boyfriends, these could easily be pseudonyms for Roman boys, just as Apuleius tells us that Catullus, Propertius, and Tibullus used the Greek pseudonyms Lesbia, Cynthia, and Delia for the Roman ladies Clodia, Hostia, and Plania, respectively.[163] Indeed, the boys whom Tibullus' Priapus describes as so easily arousing men's desires act like aristocratic young Romans, engaging in the traditional exercises of horsemanship and swimming in the Tiber (11–12), eager to travel on both land and sea (41–46) or to amuse themselves by hunting or fencing (49–52).[164] These are not the pastimes of slaves.

In short, it is far from unlikely that what Catullus' poetry openly invokes (affairs with a married woman and with a freeborn youth) the works of other Roman poets describe more obliquely. After all, the anxious protectiveness toward young Roman boys who were in the vulnerable "flower of youth," as discussed in chapter 2, must have derived from an awareness that those boys were likely to be pursued by Roman men. In any case, it is worth noting that the word *puer* could be used not only of a freeborn "boy" but also of a male slave of any age.[165] In either sense a *puer* was automatically subordinate to the mature, freeborn Roman man, whereas an adult Roman man who had acquired the reputation of being a *cinaedus* was engaging in a serious transgression of his identity as a man.

Appearances and Reputation

As *pueri* who failed to make the normative transition to *viri*, *cinaedi* constituted a reminder not only of the dangers inherent in not becoming a man but perhaps also of the tenuousness of the distinctions whose importance was usually asserted with such insistence. If boys normally became men by, among other things, ceasing to play the receptive role in penetrative acts, but if boys who were unwilling to give that up turned into *cinaedi*, and if all men were once boys, the gap between men and *cinaedi* was, in the end, uncomfortably narrow. After all, one could tell who the boys were just by looking at them, but what of *cinaedi*? A number of Martial's epigrams, and Juvenal's second satire, raise the possibility that some *cinaedi* were able to conceal their identity, presenting to the world the appearance, for example, of an ascetic bearded philosopher.[166] Among the different kinds of *cinaedi* for whom Firmicus Maternus suggests astrological etiologies are those he calls "hidden" (*latentes*).[167] Likewise an anonymous physiognomical writer explicitly notes that some *cinaedi* try to conceal their identity by putting on a virile appearance.[168]

The fact that people who looked and acted for all the world like men might actually want to play the role of the subordinate non-man must have been disturbing to some, and it was no doubt partially in response to this worrisome problem that men often reassured themselves that they could spot a *cinaedus* a mile away, by the way he talked, walked, and dressed. Amy Richlin and Maud Gleason have surveyed the ways in which Romans went about supplying answers to the pressing question of how one could recognize a man who was not fully manly.[169] One ancient discussion of just that problem is worth examining closely. Quintilian observes that someone might claim that stereotypical traits associated with effeminacy, such as the way a man walks or the fact that he wears women's clothes, are signs of the fact that he is "soft and insufficiently a man" (*mollis et parum viri signa*), and in fact characterized by an underlying *impudicitia*. To be sure, Quintilian himself considers this an unjustifiable conclusion, arguing that such traits are not really *signa* but instead what he calls *eikota*, signs that do not suffice to prove anything by themselves, but that require further substantiating evidence. He offers some revealing analogies: some might consider the fact that the mythical virgin Atalanta was often in the company of young men to be a *signum* of her having in fact lost her virginity, but not Quintilian. Others might claim that a woman's familiarity with young men is a *signum* of her being an adulteress, but not Quintilian. Some might say that the outward signs of effeminacy cited above flow from a man's *impudicitia* just as blood flows from a fatal wound, thus proving that a murder has occurred; but not Quintilian, who observes that blood can come from a nosebleed as well. For Quintilian, proof that a man has played the role of *cinaedus*, that he is *impudicus*, requires more than the outward signs of effeminacy. Just as bloodstained clothing is insufficient to prove murder unless accompanied by other evidence (such as a previous enmity, threats, and opportunity), so the fact that a man carries himself and dresses himself like a woman does not suffice, in Quintilian's opinion, to prove his *impudicitia* (one can only imagine what kind of confirming evidence would satisfy him).[170] Ultimately, however, this entire discussion, in all its insistence, reveals that Quintilian was fighting against a tendency that he saw all around him, and one has the impression that it was a losing battle. For most people, the telltale *signa* probably sufficed to establish guilt.

Here a fable by Phaedrus is relevant, and while it is set in Athens, it is told in Latin to a Roman audience and surely appeals to that audience's conceptual habits. We read of Demetrius of Phaleron, who, seeing a man drenched in perfume, draped in flowing clothes, and walking delicately and languidly, growls, "Who is that *cinaedus* who dares come into my presence?" Informed that the man was none other than the celebrated comic poet Menander, he changed his tune, exclaiming that "there couldn't be a more beautiful person."[171] Phaedrus tells the story in order to illustrate for his Roman audience how the names of great artists of former times carry a distinct cachet,[172] but the fable also shows how a man might be identified as a *cinaedus* solely from his appearance, and it even offers a suggestive hint at the ways in which Roman men of power and status could work around a reputation (whether deserved or not) for being a *cinaedus*. We remember Julius Caesar, who, contending with rumors regarding his affair with King Nicomedes, managed to lead a successful public life despite them, and is even said by Suetonius to have teasingly compared himself to Semiramis and the Amazons.[173]

In any case, men's sexual practices were clearly liable to being the subject of speculation, and equally clearly many men were interested in keeping gossip about themselves to a minimum. According to Tacitus, even the emperor Nero, confronted with Petronius' detailed reports of his sexual adventures with male prostitutes as well as with women, exiled the woman whom he suspected of having revealed his secrets;[174] such was the wrath of the powerful, and such was even their discomfort at having certain things made public. Men's sexual reputation is also an important theme in Juvenal's ninth satire, where Naevolus has come to his patron's rescue by sexually servicing not only him but his wife as well: if it were not for Naevolus, she would never have had a child, and her husband would have been the subject of nasty rumors. Consequently this man will do anything to conceal the truth—to no avail, as Naevolus sardonically observes, since people will always gossip about the rich and powerful anyway.[175]

Martial's epigrams are peppered with comments that reveal the extent to which Romans of his day speculated and gossiped about each other's sexual practices.[176] "Rumor has it that you are not a *cinaedus*," he writes in one epigram that wickedly ends up insinuating something even worse, namely that the man performs fellatio.[177] In another he puts on a show of concern for a friend's reputation, evoking the persona of the gossip-monger: "I didn't call you a *cinaedus*—I am not so bold, so outrageous; nor am I the kind of person who likes to tell lies."[178] (This epigram, too, as we will see, ends by nastily accusing the man of an even more shocking sexual practice: cunnilinctus.) Another character in Martial's poems presents a resolutely masculine appearance, complete with hairy legs and chest. He does so in order to counter rumors (*fama*), but Martial advises him that since "many people are saying many things" about him, he should be content with the reputation of being anally penetrated; again the poet's mischievous implication is that the truth is worse, namely that he engages in oral practices.[179]

Another epigram illustrates the fact that some men tried to control their reputation:

> Reclusis foribus grandes percidis, Amille,
>   et te deprendi, cum facis ista, cupis,
> ne quid liberti narrent servique paterni
>   et niger obliqua garrulitate cliens.
> non pedicari qui se testatur, Amille,
>   illud saepe facit quod sine teste facit. (Mart. 7.62)

> Amillus, you screw big boys with the doors wide open, and you want to be caught when you do it, in order to prevent your freedmen and your father's slaves from gossiping, or your malicious client with his indirect garrulousness. Amillus, the man who summons witnesses to show that he is not being butt-fucked, often does what he does without a witness.

This man is obviously contending with rumors that he was playing the receptive role in intercourse with the "big boys" (*grandes*) in whose company he was seen:

he seems to take it for granted that his slaves, freedmen, and clients will gossip about his sexual proclivities. But he decides to fight fire with fire: since they will inevitably talk, he gives them something to talk about. Martial's wry closing comment exposes the limitations of this kind of response and at the same time suggests the inescapable power of the gossip machine: people will always speculate about what goes on behind closed doors.[180]

Another of Martial's poems offers a panorama of the sorts of things that Romans apparently delighted in whispering about each other, at the same time proclaiming the poet's own laissez-faire approach:

> Pedicatur Eros, fellat Linus: Ole, quid ad te
>   de cute quid faciant ille vel ille sua?
> centenis futuit Matho milibus: Ole, quid ad te?
>   non tu propterea sed Matho pauper erit.
> in lucem cenat Sertorius: Ole, quid ad te,
>   cum liceat tota stertere nocte tibi?
> septingenta Tito debet Lupus: Ole, quid ad te?
>   assem ne dederis crediderisve Lupo.
> illud dissimulas ad te quod pertinet, Ole,
>   quodque magis curae convenit esse tuae.
> pro togula debes: hoc ad te pertinet, Ole.
>   quadrantem nemo iam tibi credit: et hoc.
> uxor moecha tibi est: hoc ad te pertinet, Ole.
>   poscit iam dotem filia grandis: et hoc.
> dicere quindecies poteram quod pertinet ad te:
>   sed quid agas ad me pertinet, Ole, nihil. (Mart. 7.10)

Eros takes it up the butt; Linus sucks dick. But Olus, what is it to you, what this man or that one does with his own hide? Matho pays hundreds of thousands to fuck. What is it to you, Olus? You won't be a poor man because of it: Matho will. Sertorius parties until dawn. What is it to you, Olus? You can snore all night long. Lupus owes Titus seven hundred. What is it to you, Olus? Neither give nor lend an *as* to Lupus. But Olus, you are ignoring what really does have to do with you, and what you ought to be more concerned about. You are in debt for your little toga: this has to do with you, Olus. No one lends you even a quarter of an *as* any more: this, too. Your wife sleeps around: this has to do with you, Olus. Your grownup daughter is now asking for her dowry: this, too. I could say fifteen times what has to do with you; but Olus, what you do has nothing to do with me.

Olus represents a type that must have been instantly recognizable to Martial's readers: someone who maliciously gossips about other people's lives (especially their sexual and financial situations), while himself hardly being unimpeachable in either area. Martial claims to be annoyed by Olus' tendency to gossip about things that do not affect him personally, and the poem naughtily gives Olus a taste of his own medicine.[181] But the irony is worth noting. In the end, even this alleged protest against a gossip-monger ends up fanning the flames of rumor. This poem fits into a cultural landscape dominated by a large, unavoidable monument: the gossip mill.

The crucial importance of shame and reputation in ancient and modern Mediterranean cultures, both in general and with regard to sexual practices in particular, has been much discussed. One study of sexuality in contemporary Islamic societies, for example, notes that "as long as nobody draws public attention to something everybody knows, one ignores what might disrupt important social relations."[182] Ovid voices analogous Roman beliefs with regard to women's sexual practices:

> non peccat, quaecumque potest peccasse negare,
>   solaque famosam culpa professa facit. (Ov. *Am.* 3.14.5–6)

> Whoever is able to deny that she has done wrong does no wrong; openly confessed guilt alone makes a woman disreputable.

Of course, the poem from which this quotation is taken is hardly a manifesto on the workings of shame-culture; it is a plea by the poet to his girlfriend that she keep him in the dark about her affairs with others. Still, in trying to convince her that it is best for him not to know of her misdeeds, he draws on a belief obviously shared by Romans as a group: that in the absence of open signs of guilt, one can live the life of the innocent regardless of what one has actually done.

Thus if, on the basis of how he walked, talked, and looked, a man's peers believed and—more importantly—said that he had played "the woman's role" in sexual acts, the man labored under a social disability by virtue of his reputation alone. Even if in fact he staunchly lived up to the ideal of masculine impenetrability, his reputation was "fucked" even if he himself had not been. On the other hand, if no one ever raised the possibility that he might enjoy being penetrated, his masculine reputation was intact at least in that regard, even if in reality he eagerly sought to play "the woman's role" behind closed doors. Of course, this returns us to the interesting (and to some Romans uncomfortable) possibility that the manliest man sitting next to one in the theater or at the circus had been sexually penetrated the night before, and it is no doubt this anxiety that surfaces in various jokes at the expense of men who give every appearance of an unimpeachable masculinity, but who are actually *cinaedi*.

An anecdote related by Phaedrus regarding a soldier in the army of Pompey the Great illustrates the ways in which a Roman man might live with the reputation for being a *cinaedus*:

> Magni Pompeii miles vasti corporis
> fracte loquendo et ambulando molliter
> famam cinaedi traxerat certissimi. (Phdr. *App.* 10.1–3)

> A soldier of Pompey the Great, a huge man, had acquired the reputation of being a notorious *cinaedus* by his effeminate speech and his delicate way of walking.

One night this soldier stole some clothing, gold, silver, and mules belonging to Pompey. After rumor spread his deed abroad, he was brought before his leader, but vigorously denied the deed, and Pompey accepted his defense, thinking it unlikely that such a man—"a disgrace to the camp"—could commit so daring a crime.[183] Some time later, an enemy warrior issued a challenge to the Romans: let one of them come forth and engage in single combat with him. The soldier reputed to be a *cinaedus* volunteered, but Pompey was disinclined to accept his offer until one of his advisors recommended sending that soldier, since his death would be less of a loss, and less damaging to Pompey's reputation as leader, than would be the death of a strong, brave man *(fortis vir)*.[184] Pompey agreed and sent the soldier, who to everyone's surprise immediately decapitated the enemy. As a result, Pompey publicly honored him with a wreath and praised him for his deed, teasingly adding that he was now certain that the soldier had stolen his supplies.[185]

Even if this anecdote is a total fabrication, it reveals a great deal about the kinds of things that a Roman readership could imagine happening within an army camp. On the one hand, the soldier suffered noticeable social disabilities because of his reputation for being a *cinaedus*: he is called a "disgrace," and Pompey is willing to see him die rather than lose a "strong man." On the other hand, despite his reputation he is still a part of the military community. And, to return to the question of the double standard raised above, it is hardly unthinkable that some of Pompey's soldiers who publicly called the reputed *cinaedus* in their midst "the camp's disgrace" also took their pleasure with him in the privacy of their tents. Most importantly, the reputed *cinaedus* is publicly honored by Pompey after killing the enemy. To be sure, the honor is combined with a jab, yet this is directed not at his being a *cinaedus* but rather at his audacious theft of his leader's supplies. In the end, his reputation as *cinaedus* is outweighed by other factors, above all his meritorious service to the army and thus to the Roman *imperium*. The reputation with which he lived was certainly a stigma, but it does not seem to have been a disabling one.[186] It is instructive to contrast the scene imagined by Phaedrus with the witch-hunts against "sodomites" in the armies and navies of seventeenth- and eighteenth-century Europe, when not only was the presence of such men not tolerated in the military community, but they were in fact liable to being executed.[187]

Phaedrus' anecdote certainly does not give us the unmediated voice of the *cinaedus*, but it does suggest possible ways that a man known as a *cinaedus* might live with his reputation in the charged environment of an army on campaign. We may speculate that the dynamics were similar, although perhaps less exaggerated, in everyday situations where it was not a question of military discipline or of life and death. The story, like Suetonius' and Dio's tales of the fate of Julius Calvaster in Saturninus' army (discussed later in this chapter), suggests that while the *cinaedus* was liable to mockery and ridicule, he was still a tolerated member of the larger community. Maud Gleason has observed that ancient astrological literature on the *cinaedus*, by arguing that such men's identity was innate, may have contributed to "a limited form of social acceptance for them."[188] The possibility should not be discounted. Certainly the texts reviewed here suggest a similar outlook among Romans: the *cinaedus* was a deviant, to be sure, but not an outcast.[189]

The Law

In addition to the stereotypes and prejudicial beliefs with which men who enjoyed playing the receptive role in anal intercourse—or at least those who acquired a reputation for it—had to contend, there were also some potential legal disabilities. Some scholars have argued that the *lex Scantinia* penalized Roman citizens who had been sexually penetrated; in the previous chapter I suggested that although this was not the principal aim of the law, which was instead formulated to penalize *stuprum* or the violation of the sexual integrity of the freeborn Roman male or female, nonetheless the *lex Scantinia* could at least in theory be invoked against the receptive partner in such an act. But certainty regarding this law (which was in any case little enforced in antiquity) is ultimately impossible.

We do know, however, that one of the provisions of the praetorian edict specified certain classes of people who were excluded from appearing before a magistrate to make an application on behalf of someone else (*postulare pro aliis*): all women; any man who was blind in both eyes, who had been convicted of a capital offense (*capitali crimine damnatus*) or of calumny in a criminal court (*calumniae publici iudicii damnatus*), who had hired himself out to fight against beasts, or who had "submitted to womanly things with his body" (*qui corpore suo muliebria passus est*)—although the praetors made an exception in this last case for men who had been raped by pirates or by the enemy in time of war.[190] The exception shows that it was not the mere fact of having been penetrated that disqualified men from this legal privilege: only those who actually *sought* to play "the woman's role" were subject to this restriction.[191] Interestingly, too, the qualification shows that Roman lawmakers were aware of what actually happened in wartime conditions (namely, that victorious soldiers raped their victims of both sexes: see chapter 3). But perhaps the most striking thing about this legal sanction placed on men who sought to be penetrated is its limited scope. It is hardly a sweeping punishment. Such men were denied the ability to appear before a magistrate on behalf of someone else, but they could still appear before a magistrate on their own behalf (the only classes of people forbidden to do that, according to Ulpian, were persons under seventeen years of age and the deaf; and he tells us that the praetor would assign an advocate even for those persons).[192] In fact, by being subject to this restriction, men who had "played the woman's role" in a sexual act were being treated like women, although of course they retained all the other rights and privileges that citizen males had that women did not, such as the right to vote in the assemblies.[193] To be sure, the exclusion from performing *postulatio* on behalf of others must have constituted a social handicap, most noticeably for the elite; but even for them it would not have been debilitating.[194] It is also instructive to contrast this relatively mild legal restriction placed on men who had been penetrated with the harsher and more sweeping concept of *infamia* that, according to the Digest, applied to various categories of disgraceful persons. Julian quotes from the praetorian edict a listing of those who are marked by *infamia*: soldiers who had been dishonorably discharged; actors; brothel-keepers; those convicted of theft, robbery with violence, *iniuria*, or fraud; and those who had entered upon agreements of betrothal or marriage with two different people other than at the order of their legal guardian.[195] There is no mention of those who "played the woman's role" in this or any comparable lists.[196]

The one legal restriction that we know to have been placed on men who "played the woman's role"—the prohibition from appearing before a magistrate to make an application on someone else's behalf—raises another interesting question. How could a man be *proven* to have been penetrated unless there were eye-witnesses to the act, or the man himself confessed it? Such men were, after all, in a fundamentally different category from women, the blind, and those who had been found guilty of capital offenses, in that the alleged disability was not easily verifiable. If it was sufficient for another to claim that he had penetrated the man in question, then it would be one man's word against another's, and in that case no one—or anyone—could have been found "guilty." On the other hand, there is the sobering possibility that a praetor might have accepted as "proof" that a man had been sexually penetrated the "signs" (*signa*) considered by Quintilian (see discussion earlier in this chapter). If the approach advocated by Quintilian himself was followed, it would have been difficult to prove that any man had "played the woman's part" in the absence of supporting evidence (again, one can only imagine what kind of evidence that might be). But Quintilian was a teacher of rhetoric and not a praetor sitting on a tribunal, and he was obviously arguing against a tendency that he saw around him. We may infer that at least some Roman officials did in fact take a man's effeminate appearance (the way he walked, talked, and dressed, for example) to be sufficient proof of his *impudicitia*. Thus certain men might have been quite vulnerable, depending on the disposition of the praetor sitting in judgment.[197]

And yet, to judge by our evidence, there never were any witch-hunts. Neither should we be surprised. In the absence of a tradition condemning homosexual practices as unnatural, abnormal, or sinful, Roman antipathy against *cinaedi* and the legal disabilities to which they could be subjected must have been far removed in both tone and intensity from the fulminations against and persecutions (not to mention executions) of "sodomites" and "homosexuals" that marred later European and American history.[198] The trial of Oscar Wilde could not have occurred in ancient Rome.

Alternative Strategies

Still, as Richlin has reminded us, life for a *cinaedus* in Rome certainly had its difficulties, and it is not surprising that many men strenuously avoided acquiring the reputation of being a *cinaedus*; nor do we have to look far to discover the reason why in the surviving texts the voice of men who desire to be penetrated, like the voice of women, is almost entirely absent from the surviving source material.[199] Yet two incidents recorded by ancient writers suggest that the imperative of penetrative masculinity was not always triumphant, and that sometimes saving one's life could be more important than saving one's reputation. We do not directly hear the voice of these men, but we do have outsiders' descriptions of what they said and did, and those descriptions suggest that in critical situations some men were able to manipulate traditional biases against men who had been penetrated.

First, Suetonius informs us that two men implicated in the military uprising against Domitian led by Saturninus avoided the torture and death that almost certainly awaited them by claiming that they had played the receptive role in intercourse ("that they were *impudici*," as Suetonius decorously puts it) and that in

view of that fact neither Saturninus nor any of the soldiers would have paid them
any attention.[200] Dio gives a more detailed report, noting that one of the two, Julius
Calvaster, claimed that he had been sexually involved with Saturninus himself.[201]
The fact that Domitian was convinced by the argument made by Calvaster and the
other, nameless man concretely illustrates the contempt in which men who openly
professed to have played the receptive role in intercourse were generally held. But
it also reminds us, like Phaedrus' tale of the soldier in Pompey's army, that such
men did form a part, albeit marginalized, of a larger community (in this case
Saturninus' army), and that having an unimpeachable reputation for an impenetrable masculinity was not always the ultimate desideratum. We are also once
again reminded of the double standard: Calvaster's sexual partners may have included the very ringleader who, he alleged, considered him to be of no account
and thus excluded him from his plans.

Tacitus tells us of another man who made a similar ploy in the bloodbath that
ensued upon the emperor Claudius' discovery that his wife Messalina had not only
participated in countless orgies but had even taken part in a wedding ceremony
with another man, Gaius Silius. Terrified that Silius was plotting to overthrow him,
Claudius had Silius and a number of his associates killed, and Messalina herself
was also put to death. But Tacitus gives the names of two men who managed to
escape execution: Plautius Lateranus and Suillius Caesoninus. The former was
spared because of the merits of his uncle,[202] while the latter was, as Tacitus puts it,
"protected by his vices, on the grounds that he had submitted to the woman's role
[passus muliebria] in that most disgraceful of gatherings."[203] How did it come to be
known that Caesoninus had played "the woman's role" at Messalina's lively gathering? Tacitus' wording ("vitiis protectus est") implies that Caesoninus had confessed
it himself. Why might he have revealed this disgraceful fact? Of course we cannot
know what was going on in Caesoninus' mind at this critical moment, but the possibilities are suggestive of the ways in which Roman men could manipulate sexual
rhetoric. Perhaps Caesoninus made the revelation in a desperate attempt to clear
himself of the suspicion of adultery with the emperor's wife: he was otherwise
occupied. Or he might have been relying on the kinds of prejudices that the two
men in Saturninus' army counted on: Claudius would reckon that if Caesoninus
had been so shameless as to play "the woman's role" openly, he surely would not
have been admitted to the inner circle of conspirators. Or Caesoninus' defense
could have combined both of these consideration: in the first place, he had not
committed adultery with Messalina since his own desires took him elsewhere, and,
secondly, in view of the dishonorable role that he played, the big players in the
conspiracy surely would not have included him in their plot.

Equally fascinating is Caesoninus' family name: Suillius. He was almost certainly one of the sons of the P. Suillius Rufus who, attacking Valerius Asiaticus'
masculinity one year earlier, had elicited the stinging retort that Suillius' own sons
could attest to Valerius' masculinity.[204] This coincidence suggests that Valerius'
implication that he had penetrated Suillius' sons was something more than a piece
of empty bravado.[205] Indeed, desperately fighting to save his life, Valerius probably
would not have made such an allegation if it were manifestly untrue, since Suillius'
sons were available to deny it. And the gossip (or revelation) concerning the role

played by one of those sons at Messalina's orgy a year later certainly might suggest that he had earlier played a similar role with Valerius Asiaticus. This is a rare moment in the midst of the innuendoes and accusations that pervade our sources, a moment when we come temptingly close to being able to ascertain what actually happened.

But apart from speculations about what these men may actually have done, these texts give us a valuable glimpse at the complex ways in which sexual discourses among Roman men worked. An alleged sexual act, namely the anal penetration of Suillius Caesoninus first by Valerius Asiaticus and later by an unnamed man or men at Messalina's gathering, is appropriated for rhetorical purposes in two different but equally critical situations, and its significance is negotiated in two rather different ways. In the first instance, Caesoninus' partner, Valerius Asiaticus, aggressively invokes the act as proof of his own masculine honor and as badge of shame both for Caesoninus and for his father. One notes that Caesoninus himself has no say in the matter, and silently looks on as his body and its experiences are coopted in a struggle between his father and his sexual partner. In the second instance, a year later, Caesoninus' sexual experience is once again invoked in a desperate life-or-death struggle, but this time the struggle is his own and the public revelation of his sexual experience is his choice.[206] This time he himself gives public meaning to his private experience, and this time, in an important sense, he comes out on top. While his reputation was surely damaged by the revelation, his life was spared.[207] The figure of Suillius Caesoninus suggests one way in which an individual might manipulate the system to his own advantage, even when he had placed himself in the role that the system itself branded as dishonorable and unmasculine.[208]

Fellatores and *Cunnilingi*: The Problem of Oral Sex

I argue in more detail below that *cinaedi* were not endowed with an identity analogous to that of the modern "homosexual," and that the derision directed against them cannot be said to be "homophobic." Instead, the basic issue was one of gender deviance: men called *cinaedi* engaged in behaviors that were considered unmanly. Roman images of men who perform fellatio, a sexual practice likewise deemed unmanly and "passive" and thus capable of being associated with *cinaedi*, support this argument. We will see that fellators are the target of abuse, sometimes even more than those who are anally receptive, but we will also see that men who practice cunnilinctus are the target of similar abuse, sometimes even more intensely than fellators, and, crucially, that men accused of performing one oral practice could readily be assumed to perform the other. A fellator could also be thought to engage in other disgraceful sexual practices, whether with male or female partners. If these men possess an identity in ancient texts, it is neither as homosexual nor as heterosexual; rather, they are pigeonholed as men given to certain degrading and unmanly practices.

The ancient sources display a noticeable bias against both women and men who sought to perform fellatio that is clearly related to a conviction that oral-genital contact befouls the mouth.[209] This notion surfaces in various jokes revolving around the dirtiness of the mouths of those who perform fellatio. Martial, for example, observes that Lesbia does well to drink water after fellating (2.50) and that kissing a fellator is comparable to submerging one's head in dirty bathwater (11.95). The same bias lies behind various statements by the poet to the effect that certain women and men ought not to be kissed or that one should not share drinking vessels with them, and is evident in a general tendency both in Martial and in other writers to apply the language of "purity" (*purus/impurus*) and the imagery of uncleanness to oral sex.[210]

It is also worth recalling that one who performed fellatio could be conceived as being the "receptive," even passive, partner. The existence of the verb *irrumare*, denoting the act of penetrating someone's mouth, meant that a person who actively performed fellatio (*fellat*) could also be said to be passively irrumated (*irrumatur*).[211] And if the fellator was male, by being orally penetrated he could also be said to have violated his sexual integrity, his impenetrability (*pudicitia*).[212] In view of this understanding of fellatio as an activity that doubly degrades those who perform it—for they are simultaneously penetrated and made unclean—it comes as no surprise that insinuations or outright accusations of fellatio are tossed about with malicious abandon throughout our sources, and the range of genres represented is remarkable. As Martial constructs epigrams whose points derive their sharpness from the conviction that fellators' mouths are filthy, so Catullus offers a coarse claim that Gellius has a penchant for performing fellatio (Catull. 80). In another of his attacks on Gellius, Catullus uses the image of self-fellatio to represent neither an impressive gymnastic feat nor an exquisite pleasure, but a supremely filthy and degrading act:

> nam nihil est quicquam sceleris, quo prodeat ultra,
> non si demisso se ipse voret capite. (Catull. 88.7–8)

> For there is no villainy to which he could descend further, not even if he were to lower his head and devour himself.

In the course of a speech delivered to the Senate upon his return from exile in 57 B.C., Cicero manages to specify quite unmistakably—yet in the indirect language befitting his surroundings—that Gabinius, whom he held at least partially responsible for his exile, pleasured men orally in his youth. The orator's scandalized description contains a phrase that exposes an important assumption informing the condemnation of fellators: Gabinius allowed his mouth, "the most sacred part of his body" (*sanctissima pars corporis*), to be defiled.[213] In a letter to Atticus, Cicero snidely attributes a similar predilection to L. Afranius, a supporter of Pompey and consul in 60 B.C.,[214] and the presence of such an accusation in his private correspondence suggests that his public invective was hardly empty. It drew on some real attitudes.

These attitudes appear in nonliterary sources as well. Numerous graffiti scratched on Pompeiian walls make reference to both men and women who fellate, sometimes for money[215] but often without financial incentive, and in most of these cases the goal is clearly to denigrate. One graffito states the obvious: "Sabina, you give head; you don't act nicely!"[216] A bias against those who perform fellatio plays into at least two graffiti of the type that insults the reader:

> amat qui scribet, pedicatur qui leget,
> qui opscultat prurit, paticus est qui praeterit.
> ursi me comedant, et ego verpa(m) qui lego. (*CIL* 4.2360)
>
> qui lego felo; sugat qui legit. (Diehl 582 - *CIL* 4.2360)[217]

> He who writes this is in love; he who reads it is butt-fucked; he who listens is horny, he who passes it by is a *pathicus*. May bears eat me, and may I who read this eat dick.

> I who read this suck dick; may he who reads this suck.

The effect of these insulting graffiti must have been particularly piquant if, as seems to have been the usual practice, a passerby were to read the words aloud.[218] And finally, among the *glandes Perusinae* discussed in chapter 1 is one inscribed "Greetings, Octavius, you suck dick" and another bearing the message "You're hungry and you suck me".[219]

This attitude toward oral-genital contact also makes itself felt in the equally severe stigma placed on men who performed cunnilinctus.[220] The implication that a man was a *cunnilingus* was as much—or, as we will see, possibly more—of a slur as an implication that he was a *fellator*. Martial, in an epigram characterized by a level of graphic coarseness rarely attained in the poet's work, writes of a certain Nanneius who is given to cunnilinctus to such an extent that even the prostitute Leda is disgusted by him, actually choosing to fellate him rather than kiss his filthy mouth (11.61). Of Martial's other epigrams on cunnilinctus, one associates the practice with a sickly pallor and another draws an implicit parallel between the performance of cunnilinctus and vomiting.[221] Elsewhere the poet recalls an evening with an especially lascivious girlfriend who readily agreed to be anally penetrated and even to fellate him, but only if the poet returned the favor and gratified her orally: a condition he firmly rejected.[222]

Just as those who wrote in contexts that prohibited open obscenity nonetheless succeeded in referring quite unmistakably to fellatio, so these writers did not hesitate to attribute a penchant for cunnilinctus to various men. Cicero maliciously insinuates as much of Antony[223] and of other enemies.[224] In his chapter on people who failed to live up to the legacy of their famous ancestors, Valerius Maximus includes the grandson of the celebrated orator Hortensius, observing that his "tongue serviced the lust of everyone in the whorehouses just as his grandfather's tongue had been vigilant for the safety of the citizenry in the forum,"[225] while in his life of the famed grammarian Q. Remmius Palaemon, Suetonius observes that his subject was notorious for his passion for cunnilinctus, adding a revealing anecdote. A certain man whom Remmius was eager to greet with a kiss unsuccessfully tried to avoid him, exclaiming, "Professor, must you lick up everyone you see hurrying?"[226] Whether apocryphal or not, this story implies that a man might have a fairly widespread reputation for performing cunnilinctus, and the biographer gives further evidence on this point in his life of Tiberius, whose liking for the practice was evidently a matter of public knowledge.[227] Tacitus writes of another powerful personage, Nero's crony Tigellinus, whose predilection for the same sexual practice was used against him as the basis of an insult.[228] Finally, the writers of the Pompeiian graffiti refer to cunnilinctus with the same tone that characterizes their allusions to fellatio,[229] and among the *tesserae* earlier discussed, which bear such unflattering messages as *fatue* ("fool"), *ebriose* ("drunkard"), *patice*, and *cinaidus*, are two inscribed *cunulinge* and *cunilinge*; another, reading *cunnio*, probably has the same meaning.[230]

It is a significant fact that a variety of sources attribute to certain men a predilection both for cunnilinctus and for fellatio, the assumption evidently being that a man whose tastes are debased enough to induce him to perform one of these disgusting acts will readily perform the other. Martial has much to say of a *parvenu* whom he calls Zoilus, and among his less than reputable traits are a penchant both for fellatio (3.82, 11.30) and for cunnilinctus (6.91, 11.85). Thus when the poet notes that if Zoilus really wants to befoul bathwater, instead of washing his anus he should wash his head in it (2.42), the reference to oral sex is clear, but whether fellatio or cunnilinctus is at stake is left unspoken. Neither is any such specificity needed, for both practices are said to make men's mouths dirty. The same bias against those who perform oral sexual acts underlies an epigram earlier cited. Cantharus insists on the strictest of privacy when visiting a brothel, whether he is paying for the favors of a boy or of a girl. Curtains and locked doors are not enough; he even patches over any cracks or holes in the wall.[231] The final point comes resolutely home: no one who penetrates either anally or vaginally ("qui vel pedicat . . . vel futuit") is so modest. Cantharus must be doing something else, something he wants to keep hidden, and this can only be an act that dirties his mouth, whether he is with a boy or a girl.[232] The writer of the *Historia Augusta* notes that the emperor Commodus was "polluted with regard to each sex in every part of his body, including his mouth" and that he kept certain slaves, called by the names of the genitals of each sex, whom he delighted to kiss.[233] The fourth-century A.D. poet Ausonius is clearly reflecting classical notions when he writes of a man named Castor who desires to fellate but, for lack of men, turns to his wife and satisfies his oral desires with her.[234] Finally, some of those who scratched messages on the walls of Pompeii envisioned one and the same man engaging both in fellatio and in cunnilinctus. One somewhat mysterious graffito found on the interior wall of a house reads as follows:

> Satur, noli cunnum lingere extra porta(m) set intra porta(m). rogat te Artocra ut sebi lingeas mentulam. at, fellator, quid[. . . (*CIL* 4.2400)[235]
>
> Satur, don't lick cunt outside of the opening but inside the opening. Artocra asks you to lick his cock. But, fellator, what . . .

Another presents two drawings of a phallus with two messages: "Onesimus, the *curicilla* is a wedding present for [your] lip," and "Onesimus, lick cunt." The word *curicilla* is otherwise unattested, but if (as the drawings suggest) it refers to the penis, Onesimus is being enjoined both to fellate and to perform cunnilinctus.[236]

Fellatio and cunnilinctus were thus understood as two aspects of a single, repellent phenomenon: two sides of one repulsive coin. Both acts dirty the mouth, and a man who performed one could easily be thought guilty of the other.[237] Here the distinction between heterosexual and homosexual behavior fades in the presence of other, more pressing concerns—the cleanliness and purity of the mouth—and an important gap between ancient and modern sexual ideologies opens up. On the one hand, the extreme bias against *cunnilingi*, together with the very existence of *cunnilingus* as a common insult, finds no parallels in twentieth-century American sexual discourses. On the other hand, whereas the contemporary insult "cocksucker" stands metonymically for "homosexual man" and consequently functions as an equivalent of "faggot," a Roman man slandered as a *fellator* might receive the epithet *cunnilingus* in the next breath. *Fellatores*, in short, were fundamentally categorized not as homosexuals but as men who were inclined to befoul their mouths by oral-genital contact, while *cunnilingi* were not necessarily exclusively heterosexual in their desires and practices.

There are several indications that the prejudice against men who befouled their mouths with genital contact may have been stronger even than the bias against being anally penetrated. In the *Carmina Priapea*, Priapus threatens a first-time offender with anal penetration but a repeat offender with the evidently more disgraceful penalty of compelled fellatio, and an epigram of Martial's discussed earlier revolves around the notion that *irrumatio* would be a more degrading punishment for an adulterer than anal rape.[238] In another poem, Martial addresses his friend Callistratus, who wants the poet to think that he is completely honest with him—so candid, in fact, as to admit that he has often been anally penetrated. But Martial responds with the mischievous charge that his friend is not telling all, "for whoever talks about things like that keeps quiet about more." His unmistakable insinuation is that Callistratus indulges in oral practices, in this particular case probably fellatio.[239]

Martial similarly draws on the idea that fellating is more disgraceful for a man than being anally penetrated in an epigram about Charidemus, to whom the poet makes the unexpected recommendation that he pluck his entire body and even make it known that he depilates his buttocks, so that people will think he seeks to be anally penetrated. Martial obviously advises him to steer people's suspicions in this direction because the truth is something worse, namely that he practices fellatio.[240]

Elsewhere he writes that the mythical character Philoctetes was "soft" and "easy for men" as a result of his having killed Paris: such was Venus' revenge for the death of her favorite. Why, asks the poet, does the Sicilian Sertorius seek to perform cunnilinctus? Obviously he must have killed Venus' son Eryx.[241] The poem's logical movement (if we can speak of logic here) is clear: Sertorius' preferences are worse than Philoctetes' to the precise extent that Venus was more outraged by the death of her own son than by that of her protégé. Elsewhere Martial mischievously slanders Coracinus as a *cunnilingus*, first swearing that he never called him a *cinaedus* and concluding thus:

> quid dixi tamen? hoc leve et pusillum,
> quod notum est, quod et ipse non negabis,
> dixi te, Coracine, cunnilingum. (Mart. 4.43.9–11)[242]

Well then, what did I say? Only this trivial little thing, that is well known anyway, and you yourself won't deny it: Coracinus, I called you a *cunnilingus*.

The joke only works if Martial's readership understood *cunnilingus* to be a harsher insult than *cinaedus*, and the qualification "this trivial little thing" (*hoc leve et pusillum*) is obviously laden with considerable irony. One might also observe the parenthetical comment "that is well known anyway and you yourself won't deny it" (*quod notum est, quod et ipse non negabis*): again we see that a predilection for cunnilinctus could give rise to gossip. In an especially revealing epigram, Martial addresses Sextillus:

> Rideto multum qui te, Sextille, cinaedum
>   dixerit et digitum porrigito medium.
> sed nec pedico es nec tu, Sextille, fututor,
>   calda Vetustinae nec tibi bucca placet.
> ex istis nihil es, fateor, Sextille: quid ergo es?
>   nescio, sed tu scis res superesse duas. (Mart. 2.28)

Sextillus, laugh heartily at the man who calls you a *cinaedus* and give him the finger. But, Sextillus, you are neither *pedico* nor *fututor*, nor does the warm cheek of Vetustina please you. I admit it, Sextillus, you are none of these things. What then are you? I don't know, but *you* know that there are two things left.

Here we get a strikingly clear glimpse of the conceptual apparatus common to poet and audience as Martial runs down the list of possible labels that might be applied to Sextillus: he is not a *cinaedus*, not a *pedico*, not a *fututor*, not an *irrumator*. What, indeed, is left? The final line is characteristically pointed, for the two things remaining can only be *cunnilingus* and *fellator*.[243] The epigram derives its pungency from the notion, obviously not a startling one for Martial's readership, that being either a *cunnilingus* or a *fellator* is more degrading even than being a *cinaedus*.

Why could a man's performance of cunnilinctus be represented in this way? In the broadest terms, *cunnilingi* befouled their mouths and subjugated themselves to another just as did those who performed fellatio, but whereas in an act of fellatio there was at least one man doing what he ought to do (dominating another with his phallus, which was being given the respect and adoration it deserved), in an act of cunnilingus the phallus was extraneous, and it was the woman's sexual organs that were the focus of attention. As we saw in chapter 4, for a man to subordinate himself to a woman constituted a direct violation of fundamental concepts of masculinity; thus a man who served a woman or subjugated himself to her was considered effeminate. Another factor in the bias against cunnilinctus must have been a misogynistic aversion to the female genitalia and menstrual blood.[244] Furthermore, the structure of the Latin vocabulary for sexual acts (see discussion earlier in this chapter) sheds light on the problem of cunnilinctus in conceptual terms. While there were verbs denoting the act of orally penetrating another or describing the movements of one who is penetrated anally or vaginally, there was no single verb denoting the performance of cunnilinctus.[245] This suggestive hole in the system is obviously related to the phallocentric nature of the vocabulary: cunnilinctus is an act that does not require the intervention of a penis, thus offering no place for the phallus to assert its power. In Roman terms, cunnilinctus is not *virile* because there is no place for the *vir*.[246]

The image of cunnilinctus as unmanly governs an epigram of Martial's that may provide a glimpse at a normally unspoken understanding: that of the two repulsive oral acts, cunnilinctus was the more unmanly. Here we read of a woman named Philaenis who is endowed with noticeably masculine traits. She plays the penetrative role in sexual relations with boys and girls; she exercises in the wrestling school; she eats and drinks to excess. Finally, she refuses to fellate since that is not manly enough (*parum virile*) for her, yet she does perform cunnilinctus, and this practice provokes Martial's concluding jab: "May the gods give you your own mind, Philaenis: you think it manly to lick cunt."[247] Clearly cunnilinctus is held to be no more manly than is fellatio, but the final point is especially sharp for readers predisposed to view cunnilinctus as being an even less manly act. Philaenis is thus truly perverse: penetrating when she should be penetrated; in the gymnasia when she should be at home spinning and weaving; thinking fellatio unmanly and cunnilinctus manly, when the truth is that while fellatio is indeed unmanly, cunnilinctus is even more so.[248]

Crossing Boundaries

The ease with which the barrier between homosexual and heterosexual practices is crossed in ancient texts is suggested by the frequency with which Roman writers present the image of a man who manages to combine all three practices considered inappropriate for a man: performing fellatio and cunnilinctus as well as being anally penetrated. One of the most crisply vivid pictures of such a man appears in an unexpected setting, Seneca's discussion of mirrors in the first book of his *Naturales Quaestiones* (1.16). Indulging in a moralizing digression on how anything, even a mirror, can be put to a disreputable use, Seneca tells the sordid tale of one Hostius Quadra.[249] This disreputable man, who lived during the reign of Augustus, was characterized by such *obscenitas* that the emperor judged him unworthy of vindication when he was killed by his slaves, and furthermore that his story was enacted on the stage (*obscenitatis in scaenam usque productae*)—a telling hint at the fascination with the specifics of sexual behavior that seems to have characterized Roman culture. It is Hostius' penchant for oral sex that at first provides the fuel for Seneca's indignation, as we see in a series of increasingly explicit accusations: from the euphemistic ("he was impure not with one sex only, but was eager for men as well as for women") to the disgusted ("the things done and said by that freak who ought to be torn apart by his own mouth are revolting even to mention") to the stylized (". . . that he might take in not only with his mouth but with his eyes as well") to the breathtakingly direct (he "buried his head, clinging to other people's groins").[250] Thus Hostius, like Martial's Zoilus and Ausonius' Castor, like Satur and Onesimus of Pompeii, engaged in oral practices with partners of both sexes. But this is only the beginning. Seneca's loudly professed disgust modulates into a thinly veiled prurience, as he provides a tableau that illustrates all of Hostius' deviant practices at once. Hostius puts mirrors to a special use:

spectabat illam libidinem oris sui; spectabat admissos sibi pariter in omnia viros; nonnumquam inter marem et feminam distributus et toto corpore patientiae expositus spectabat nefanda. (Sen. *N.Q.* 1.16.5)

He would look at that lustfulness of his mouth; he would look at men whom he took into himself all over; sometimes he would look at unspeakable horrors as he was divided between a male and a female partner, open to submissiveness [*patientia*] with his whole body.

Each of the three clauses makes a pointed accusation. First on the list, not surprisingly, is a reference to oral practices. The second clause informs us that Hostius also derived pleasure from being penetrated.[251] The third item on Seneca's list ("divided between a male and a female partner, open to submissiveness with his whole body") is clarified by a subsequent passage in which Seneca imagines Hostius' perverse boast:

"simul," inquit, "et virum et feminam patior. nihilominus illa quoque supervacua mihi parte alicuius contumelia marem exerceo; omnia membra stupris occupata sunt." (Sen. *N.Q.* 1.16.7)

He said, "I simultaneously submit both to a man and to a woman. Yet I also play the man's role to someone else's disgrace, using that redundant part of mine. My entire body is engaged in *stupra*."

In more clinical terms, Seneca creates a scenario in which Hostius, while being anally penetrated from behind, performs cunnilinctus on a woman in front of him, simultaneously himself being fellated by a fourth person, exercising his manhood (*marem exerceo*) by putting his penis to use.[252] Here we see the performance of cunnilinctus being represented as a "passive" act. Hostius boasts of submitting to (*patior*) a man and a woman simultaneously, and earlier Seneca had darkly hinted that Hostius "submitted to unprecedented and unheard-of things" (4: *inaudita et incognita pati*); as we have seen, Hostius looks at himself in a mirror when he is "divided between a male and a female partner, open to submissiveness [*patientia*] with his whole body." We are, moreover, given to understand that, since the performance of cunnilinctus is an embodiment of passivity (*patientia*), it is also unmanly: Hostius' boast that he only acts like a man (*marem exerceo*) when orally penetrating another contains the implication that his other activities do not constitute manly behavior.

Suetonius offers a sampling of Nero's sexual exploits that represents cunnilinctus in similar ways, and that likewise attributes a variety of sexual practices to one man. The emperor, we read, enacted debased imitations of animal shows in which he was released from a cage dressed in animal skins and proceeded to devour the groins of both men and women who were tied to a stake; afterwards he was "finished off" by his freedman Doryphorus, to whom, moreover, he was married, playing the part of the bride and going so far as to imitate the cries of a maiden being deflowered.[253] Apart from the stunning specificity of the information that Suetonius conveys to his readership, all the while refraining from obscenity, the biographer's treatment of Nero's oral proclivities is revealing. He introduces these scenes as examples of how Nero "prostituted his *pudicitia*" ("suam quidem pudicitiam usque adeo prostituit . . ."), and given the usual resonance of the term *pudicitia* when it is predicated of an individual man (namely, impenetrability), cunnilinctus is being implicitly represented as a "passive" act that is somehow on a par with performing fellatio and being anally penetrated. All three acts violate Nero's sexual integrity.

Perhaps the most celebrated villain in Cicero's speeches is Catiline. On several occasions Cicero accuses him of adultery and *stuprum* either directly or by association,[254] but in the course of his second speech against Catiline, delivered before an assembly of citizens, the outraged consul hints at other vices: "He himself loved some of them disgracefully, and was a slave to the love of others most shamefully."[255] Likewise in his first speech against Catiline, delivered to the Senate, the consul poses this stylized but pointed question: "What lust has ever been absent from your eyes, what crime from your hands, what disgrace from your entire body?"[256] The phrase "from your entire body" is reminiscent of Seneca's horrified description of Hostius Quadra and constitutes a claim that he has been defiled in every available organ or orifice.[257] Catiline is thus thoroughly depraved, both exercising his manhood inappropriately (with the freeborn in general and other men's wives in particular) and disregarding it entirely (by being penetrated anally and even orally). In a passage discussed in chapter 4, Cicero similarly uses language that confounds the distinctions between insertive and receptive, homosexual and heterosexual, when he considers the most depraved group of Catiline's followers:

> in his gregibus omnes aleatores, omnes adulteri, omnes impuri impudicique versantur. hi pueri tam lepidi ac delicati non solum amare et amari neque saltare et cantare sed etiam sicas vibrare et spargere venena didicerunt. . . . verum tamen quid sibi isti miseri volunt? num suas secum mulierculas sunt in castra ducturi? quem ad modum autem illis carere poterunt, his praesertim iam noctibus? (Cic. *Cat.* 2.23)

> All gamblers, all adulterers, all impure and unchaste [*impudici*] men spend their time in these groups. These boys, so charming and lovely, have learned not only to love and to be loved, to dance and to sing, but also to brandish daggers and to infuse poison. . . . But what do these wretches want? Surely they do not intend to take their little women with them on the campaign? And yet how on earth will they be able to do without them, especially during these nights?

These decadent "boys" have learned "to love and be loved" (*amare et amari*): the phrase reflects at the morphological level the antithesis between active and passive. But, interestingly, the combination is not marked as particularly unusual. The orator could have signaled an anomaly, for example by exclaiming, "they have learned not only to love but also to be loved"; but, while he does make use of the "not only/but also" structure, the pair *amare et amari* is included within the first element rather than being distributed between the two. Thus the surprising combination of traits that Cicero emphasizes is not the blend of insertive and receptive sexual practices, but rather the combination of skill at the pleasures of love (both active and passive), song, and dance on the one hand (*non solum*), and murder on the other (*sed etiam*).

In his second Philippic, Cicero recounts with mordant sarcasm the emotional reunion of Antony with his estranged wife Fulvia. In twentieth-century terms, the scene is thoroughly heterosexual (a husband who has been spending time with an actress swears to his wife that he is ending that relationship and will love only her from now on, and the wife tearfully accepts his apology), but as he brings his disdainful narrative to a close, Cicero feels no compunction about calling Antony *catamitus*, the Romanized form of Ganymede's name and here being used as an insult: "So then, was it for this that you rocked the city with night-time terror, and all of Italy with many days' worth of fear: that the woman might lay her eyes on you, a *catamitus*, when you unexpectedly appeared before her?"[258] By slandering Antony as a *catamitus*, Cicero may be recalling his earlier reference to his enemy's alleged relationship with Curio, in which the young Antony played the role of bride or even slave-boy (Cic. *Phil.* 2.44–5). But even though Antony's relationship with Curio was a thing of the past, it is interesting that Cicero fails to mark it as such here. Rather than offering a temporally distancing qualification (for example, "you who were a *catamitus* in your youth") the orator unobtrusively applies the label as a dismissive epithet for Antony even as his wife sees him again (*ut te catamitum . . . praeter spem mulier aspiceret*).[259] Cicero obviously does not expect his readership to be surprised that a man whom he insults as a *catamitus*, and to whom he elsewhere attributes a predilection for cunnilinctus,[260] should be married and at the same time involved in an affair with an actress.

In another passage from the same speech Cicero wickedly hints that Antony had begun his relationship with Fulvia while she was still married to Cicero's other great enemy Clodius, and shortly thereafter he makes a passing reference to Curio as Antony's "husband" (*vir*), again with no distancing between these two relationships.[261] The temporal gap is simply elided, as it also is in one of the orator's more spectacular attacks on Clodius, where he alludes in rapid succession to the man's various vices, slandering him as "the whore of rich idlers, the adulterer of his own sister, the priest of debauchery."[262] Although elsewhere Cicero specifically associates Clodius' performance of the receptive role in anal intercourse with his youth (*Har. Resp.* 42), it is revealing that the orator here casts his rhetoric in such a way as to issue the attacks simultaneously, in phrases whose parallelism is marked by anaphora of *cum* as well as alliteration of *s*.

Not only is the unmarked juxtaposition of slurs implying the insertive and receptive role in these passages interesting, but the combination of insults against Antony as both adulterer (with Fulvia) and "wife" (with Curio) brings us to a fascinating figure that makes several appearances in Roman texts: the womanizing *cinaedus*. While it was possible to imagine *cinaedi* as being so effeminate as to be incapable of engaging in sexual relations with women (as if they were indeed eunuchs, like the *galli* or castrated priests to whom they were sometimes likened),[263] it was also possible to conceive of *cinaedi* engaging in sexual practices with women, especially other men's wives, without viewing the scenario as bizarre or anomalous.

The cultural landscape imagined by the writers of Roman love elegy certainly included erotic entanglements in which a man was simultaneously involved with a woman (presumably playing the insertive role with her) and with a man (with whom he played the receptive role). Ovid imagines a madam telling his mistress (in this case pictured as a prostitute) that if a nobleman should ask for a night with her free of charge, she should tell him to get some money from his male lover (*amator*); elsewhere he imagines a woman who has a male lover smoother than she is and who might possess even more male lovers (*viri*) than she does.[264] These are poetic constructs, of course, but they could not have seemed inherently outrageous or unrealistic to Ovid's readership. This poet styled himself an "instructor in love" (*praeceptor amoris, Ars Amatoria* 1.17), and as such needed to appeal to the experiences of his potential students.

Ovid's speaker refrains from insulting these men who have male lovers as *cinaedi*, but surely they would have been liable to being slandered as such. In any case, the image of a man explicitly identified as both *cinaedus* and womanizer first appears in a characteristically blunt line from Lucilius whose original context is unfortunately lost to us: "beardless *androgyni*, bearded *moechocinaedi*."[265] The two compounds correspond to real Roman stereotypes: men who combine both masculine (*andro-*) and feminine (*-gyni*) traits, and men who both pursue women (*moecho-*) and are themselves womanish (*-cinaedi*).[266] We have already considered an incident reported by Suetonius in his biography of Augustus that can be interpreted in light of this stereotype. A line delivered at a dramatic performance by an actor referring to a *gallus* as a *cinaedus* was taken by the audience to be a double entendre referring to Augustus himself. But immediately after relating this incident, Suetonius observes that Augustus was known for his affairs with married women, and that not even his friends tried to deny his adulterous dalliances.[267] In other words, Augustus could be thought of as a *cinaedus* by the same Roman audiences who gossiped about his weakness for married ladies.

A poem by Catullus provides further illustration not only of the ways in which sexual rhetoric could be applied to public figures, but also of the apparent ease with which a Roman readership might accept the imputation of womanizing to men who were insulted as *cinaedi*:

> Pulchre convenit improbis cinaedis,
> Mamurrae pathicoque Caesarique.
> nec mirum: maculae pares utrisque,
> urbana altera et illa Formiana,
> impressae resident nec eluentur:
> morbosi pariter, gemelli utrique,
> uno in lecticulo erudituli ambo,
> non hic quam ille magis vorax adulter,
> rivales socii puellularum.
> pulchre convenit improbis cinaedis. (Catull. 57)

The shameless *cinaedi* are getting along really well: Mamurra the *pathicus* and Caesar. No wonder. Their equal stains, one from the city and one from Formiae, are deeply ingrained and cannot be removed. They are equally afflicted, this pair of twins—two little scholars together on one couch, the one as greedy an adulterer as the other, allied rivals for girls. The shameless *cinaedi* are getting along really well.

While Caesar and Mamurra, slandered as *cinaedi* and *pathici*, are said to be afflicted or diseased (*morbosi*), the disease that characterizes them is obviously not homosexuality,[268] nor even their desire to be penetrated, for without further comment Catullus describes them as being equally voracious adulterers. Their disease is an unmanly submission to their own uncontrolled desires (see chapter 4). The closing repetition of the opening line serves, as it does in poem 16, to bring home the invective, and the resulting juxtaposition in the poem's last two lines ensures that there can be no mistake. These men are simultaneously rivals for girls' attention (*rivales socii puellularum*) and *cinaedi* (*pulchre convenit improbis cinaedis*).[269]

Martial teases a man named Cinna, claiming that none of his seven children are actually his: one of them, fathered by his African cook Santra, has curly hair; another, the son of his wrestling-trainer Pannychos, has a pug nose and thick lips; yet another, sired by his *concubinus* Lygdus, inherited his father's *cinaedus*-like appearance. Trying to make the best of a bad situation, the poet adds cavalierly, "Screw your son if you feel like it; it's not wrong."[270] The joke reminds us of what Lygdus' own function is vis-à-vis Cinna: like father like son. But while Lygdus was his master's *concubinus* and *cinaedus*, and was penetrated by him, that fact did not prevent Martial from imagining him having an intrigue with his master's wife, or from wryly commenting on this development, without suggesting that such a combination of behaviors in one man is at all striking or in need of explanation. Although he does not use the word *cinaedus*, Martial attributes the same combination of sexual practices to a young man whom he calls Hyllus. Like Gallus in another poem from the same book (2.47, discussed earlier in this chapter), Hyllus is involved with a married woman and, like Gallus, he is prepared to pay the price by being anally penetrated by the husband should he discover them (2.60). But in yet another epigram published in the same book, Hyllus is said to have an anal orifice with a voracious appetite: he spends his last dime on procuring well-endowed men.[271]

Writing of the emperor Caligula, Suetonius uses the coded phrase "pudicitiae neque suae neque alienae pepercit" ("he spared neither his own nor others' *pudicitia*," signifying that he played the receptive and insertive roles in penetrative acts respectively),[272] and then reports some examples in rapid succession: two relationships with men that seem to have involved an exchange of role; an affair with a young nobleman named Valerius Catullus in which Caligula was obviously playing the receptive role (Valerius claimed to have been worn out by his exertions); his incestuous relationships with his sisters; a notorious affair with a female prostitute; and his habit of recruiting married ladies at banquets.[273] Although Suetonius himself does not refer to any occasions on which someone insulted Caligula as *cinaedus*, we can be fairly certain that his enemies must have thrown the epithet at him. Caligula, like Martial's Hyllus and Lygdus and Catullus' Caesar and Mamurra, could be called a *cinaedus* as well as a womanizer or adulterer.

A startlingly obscene poem of the *Appendix Vergiliana* that was discussed in chapter 4 ([Vir.] *Catalepton* 13) presents an unflinching assault on a man, perhaps named Luccius, who is accused of a combination of sexual behaviors:[274] vividly portrayed as having been anally receptive in his youth (while asleep at drunken banquets his "buttocks were damp" and "Thalassio! Thalassio," the ritual cry at Roman weddings, was uttered above him), and bluntly called a *cinaedus* and even a woman (*femina*), this object of the speaker's considerable wrath is imagined dancing at a disgraceful festival on the banks of the Tiber in honor of the foreign goddess Cocyto. We think not only of the primary meaning of *cinaedus* (an effeminate dancer from Asia) but also of the ever-lurking image of the castrated priests of the

Asian Mother Goddess, the *galli*: it is worth noting that in this poem's description of the festival in honor of Cocyto, just as in Juvenal's scandalized description of rites in honor of the Bona Dea or Good Goddess conducted by Roman *cinaedi* whom he likens to the devotees of Cocyto herself and who only need to castrate themselves in order to complete their transformation, phallic objects play a role in the rites, and Luccius seems to be wearing women's clothes.[275] In addition to all this, Luccius is said to have had incestuous relations with his sister and is imagined returning home from his effeminate revels by the Tiber to his repulsive wife, perhaps in order to give her oral pleasure.[276] One scholar has recently noted that the man's wife "seems nothing more than a lugubrious concession to the dominant culture,"[277] but I would argue instead that the image of an effeminate *cinaedus* who has sexual relations with women is hardly unusual in the Roman sources.[278]

The *Cinaedus*: Passive Homosexual or Gender Deviant?

What was the nature of the identity signified by the word *cinaedus* in its transferred sense? Was he, as is fairly often asserted, fundamentally defined as a "passive homosexual"?[279] That, indeed, is one of the central arguments of Amy Richlin's 1993 article "Not Before Homosexuality."[280] Similarly, Elaine Fantham's 1991 study of *stuprum* describes the object of the invective in Juvenal's second satires as "homosexuals,"[281] and speaks of an accusation of "homosexual promiscuity" leveled against a son who was described as being "of doubtful chastity" (*dubiae castitatis*, a phrase which she interprets, probably rightly, to be equivalent to saying he was *impudicus*).[282] Bernadette Brooten's 1996 analysis of Caelius Aurelianus' discussion of men who desire to be sexually penetrated and women who desire to penetrate, while noting that both Caelius and his model Soranos assumed that healthy men will be attracted to boys as well as women, nonetheless occasionally uses the word "homoeroticism" when referring to the desire of certain men to be penetrated: she observes, for example, that "Soranos views homoeroticism as a disease of the mind."[283] Most recently, a 1997 article by Rabun Taylor argues for the existence of a "homosexual subculture" in Rome; Taylor uses the words "homosexual" and "homosexuality" with reference to "men who found primary fulfillment in same-sex unions that at times involved the assumption of the passive role."[284] Here Taylor makes explicit an assumption implied by the other scholars' formulations, that the receptive partner in a penetrative act between males is in some sense more "homosexual" than his insertive partner.[285]

These scholars clearly believe that ancient *cinaedi* (but apparently not the men who penetrated them) were conceived as displaying "homoeroticism," as being themselves "passive homosexuals" or simply "homosexuals." A much-discussed formulation of Michel Foucault's, contrasting ancient images of men who engaged in homosexual acts with the nineteenth-century figure of "the homosexual," suggests the opposite:

> As defined by the ancient civil or canonical codes, sodomy was a category of forbidden acts; their perpetrator was nothing more than the juridical subject of them. The

nineteenth-century homosexual became a personage, a past, a case history, and a childhood, in addition to being a type of life, a life form, and a morphology, with an indis-
creet anatomy and possibly a mysterious physiology. Nothing that went into his total
composition was unaffected by his sexuality. . . . The sodomite had been a temporary
aberration; the homosexual was now a species.[286]

I will argue that the truth lies between these two extremes. The Roman *cinaedus*
could in fact justifiably be said to be a species or a personage, but his identity was
hardly the same as that of the modern homosexual. Winkler has made similar points
regarding the Greek *kinaidos*:

> The *kinaidos*, to be sure, is not a "homosexual" but neither is he just an ordinary guy
> who now and then decided to commit a kinaidic act. The conception of a *kinaidos* was
> of a man socially deviant in his entire being, principally observable in behavior that
> flagrantly violated or contravened the dominant social definition of masculinity. To
> this extent, *kinaidos* was a category of person, not just of acts.[287]

Maud Gleason offers similar arguments:

> The *cinaedus* was a "life-form" all to himself, and his condition was written all over
> him in signs that could be decoded by those practiced in the art. What made him
> different from normal folk, however, was not simply the fact that his sexual partners
> included people of the same sex as himself (that, after all, was nothing out of the
> ordinary), nor was it any kind of psychosexual orientation—a "sexuality" in the
> nineteenth-century sense—but rather an inversion or reversal of his gender identity:
> his abandonment of a "masculine" role in favor of a "feminine" one.[288]

In a forthcoming article that takes Foucault's formulation and scholarly interpretations of it as a starting point, David Halperin suggests the following:

> The *kinaidos*, on this view, is not someone who has a different sexual orientation from
> other men, or who belongs to some autonomous sexual species. Rather, he is someone
> who represents what *every* man would be like if he were so shameless as to sacrifice
> his dignity and masculine gender-status for the sake of gratifying the most odious and
> disgraceful, though no doubt voluptuous, bodily appetites. . . . The catastrophic fail-
> ure of male self-fashioning which the *kinaidos* represents is so complete, in other
> words, that it cannot be imagined as merely confined within the sphere of erotic life or
> restricted to the occasional performance of disreputable sexual acts: it defines and
> determines a man's social identity in its totality, and it generates a recognizable social
> *type*—namely, the "scare-image" and phobic stereotype of the *kinaidos*, which Winkler
> so eloquently described.[289]

Likewise I am suggesting that the Roman *cinaedus* was in fact a category of person
who was considered "socially deviant," but that his social identity was crucially
different from that of the "homosexual," since his desire for persons of his own sex
was not a defining or even problematic feature of his makeup as a deviant: his
desire to be penetrated was indeed one of his characteristics, but, as we have seen,
men called *cinaedi* were also thought capable of being interested in penetrative
sexual relations with women. Thus the deviance of the *cinaedus* is ultimately a

matter of gender identity rather than sexual identity, in the sense that his predilection for playing the receptive role in penetrative acts was not the single defining
feature of his identity but rather a sign of a more fundamental transgression of
gender categories.[290]

As opposed to the rather absolute implications of Gleason's "inversion or reversal," however, I will suggest that *cinaedi* were conceptualized as transgressing
gender norms without necessarily "inverting" or "reversing" their gender identity
irrevocably and always. They crossed the line, and did it often; but they were still
capable of a certain degree of masculine behavior. We might use the term adopted
by an anthropologist of Polynesian societies and describe the *cinaedus* as a "gender-
liminal"[291] or even "gender-transgressive" person. Thus, as was noted in the introduction, sexual relations between men and *cinaedi* fit into a worldwide pattern
that historians and sociologists have called transgenderal: according to this paradigm, males who are fully gendered as "real men" may acceptably engage in sexual
practices with males who are not so gendered.

One of Phaedrus' fables offers a strikingly lucid exposure of the conceptual
apparatus that informs the ancient textual tradition, shedding a good deal of light
on the fundamental categorization of the *cinaedus* as gender-deviant rather than
homosexual:

> Rogavit alter, tribadas et molles mares
> quae ratio procreasset. exposuit senex:
> "idem Prometheus, auctor vulgi fictilis
> qui simul offendit ad fortunam frangitur,
> naturae partis veste quas celat pudor,
> cum separatim toto finxisset die,
> aptare mox ut posset corporibus suis,
> ad cenam est invitatus subito a Libero.
> ubi irrigatus multo venas nectare,
> sero domum est reversus titubanti pede.
> tum semisomno corde et errore ebrio
> applicuit virginale generi masculo
> et masculina membra applicuit feminis.
> ita nunc libido pravo fruitur gaudio." (Phdr. 4.16)

> The other man asked what principle it was that had brought tribads and soft men into
> being. The old man explained: "That same Prometheus, the creator of the pottery race
> that is broken as soon as it comes up against its fate, had spent a whole day fashioning
> the private parts that modesty hides under clothes, making them separately so that he
> could later attach them to the appropriate bodies. After receiving an unexpected invi-
> tation to dinner from the wine-god Liber, and having flooded his veins with a good
> deal of nectar, he stumbled home late at night and in a drunken stupor attached the
> maiden's organ to the male sex and male organs to women. And so it is that lust now
> enjoys its depraved pleasure."

This unforgettable story, with its characteristically Roman physicality, shows what
it was that needed explanation to its Roman audience: that some men ("soft men,"
molles mares) enjoy being penetrated and some women ("tribads," *tribades*) enjoy
penetrating.[292] Phaedrus' story of a drunken Prometheus sloppily attaching a va-

gina to some male bodies and a penis to some female bodies draws a clear picture. *Molles mares* and *tribades* are problematic not because they are men who seek sexual contact with other men and women who seek sexual contact with other women, but because they are people whose desires fail to align themselves with a set of fundamental rules: the male is to penetrate, the female to be penetrated. The "depraved pleasure" of these people is not homoerotic pleasure but pleasure taken in performing activities inappropriate to their gender: men who might penetrate these *molles*, or women who might be penetrated by the *tribades* are implicitly normal, need no pseudo-mythic aetiology, and do not seek a "depraved pleasure." This is a point with important implications: while the desire of some men to be penetrated and the desire of some women to penetrate are here explained as resulting from a primordial slip-up, the desire of some men to penetrate adolescent males, for example, seems to need no explanation or justification either here or elsewhere. By contrast, we have seen that Martial offers an equally humorous pseudo-mythical explanation for why a certain man enjoys performing cunnilinctus (2.84), and while his answer—that the man must have killed Venus' son and received his taste for cunnilinctus as punishment—may be whimsical, the fact remains that the question seemed worth asking: Why would a man want to do *that*?

Phaedrus' problematization of the *mollis* or "soft" man together with the *tribas* is echoed in a text of a very different nature, Caelius Aurelianus' fifth-century A.D. treatise on chronic diseases. Caelius' work is in large part a translation of the work of Soranos, who published treatises in Greek in the second century A.D. that are no longer extant, but Caelius' text is still relevant to an inquiry into Roman ideologies. On the one hand, the very fact that Caelius writes in Latin signifies that he is appealing to a Roman audience (indeed, Soranos himself had worked in Rome); on the other hand, scholars have recognized for some time that Caelius is not offering a word-for-word translation of Soranos and that his own perspective is often evident in the text.[293] Caelius' discussion of the fact that some men derive pleasure from being penetrated—he calls them *molles* ("soft") or *subacti* ("subjugated," i.e., penetrated)— is aimed at a Roman readership whose preconceptions it both draws on and replicates. The similarities between this technical treatise of the fifth century and Phaedrus' poetic fable of the first century suggest how lasting these assumptions were; indeed, one might say that Caelius' explanatory paradigm represents a medicalization of precisely the conceptualizations informing Phaedrus' mythic fable.

In Caelius' opinion, men who enjoy being penetrated are afflicted not with a physical ailment but rather with a mental disorder. But this disorder does not consist in an abnormal attraction to members of their own sex, but rather in an excessive lustfulness that may well lead them to engage in traditionally masculine (i.e., insertive) sexual practices as well:

> tum denique volentes <alliciunt> veste atque gressu et aliis femininis rebus quae sint a passionibus corporis aliena sed potius corruptae mentis vitia. nam saepe timentes, vel quod est difficile, verentes quosdam, quibus forte deferunt, repente mutati parvo tempore virilitatis quaerunt indicia demonstrare, cuius quia modum nesciunt, rursum nimietate sublati plus quoque quam virtuti convenit faciunt et maioribus se peccatis involvunt. (Cael. Aurel. *Morb. Chron.* 4.9.131–2)[294]

Then, by their clothing and way of walking and other feminine practices, they attract things that are not related to physical ailments but are rather vices of a corrupt mind. For often, fearing or (something difficult for them) respecting those to whom they happen to defer, they suddenly seek to display signs of a virility [*virilitas*] that has changed in a brief time; and since they do not know moderation in that area, once again carried away by excess they do more than befits manly virtue [*virtus*], and they involve themselves in greater misdeeds.

Caelius' language is dense, but it seems clear that when he says that such effeminate men display signs of "virility" and involve themselves in "greater misdeeds," he means that they penetrate others whose integrity they ought to respect. He does not specify whether these are males or females, but in view of the stereotype of the womanizing *cinaedus* discussed above, it is quite likely that a Roman reader could imagine these *molles* engaging in penetrative relations both with male partners and with such inappropriate female partners as married women.[295]

Caelius goes on to liken these men, carried away by their excessive lustfulness first to seek to be penetrated and then to penetrate others (implicitly of either sex), to "the women who are called *tribades*":

> nam sicut feminae tribades appellatae, quod utramque venerem exerceant, mulieribus magis quam viris misceri festinant et easdem invidentia paene virili sectantur . . .
>
> (4.9.132)

> For just like the women who are called *tribades* because they engage in both kinds of sexual practice, are eager to join with women more than with men and pursue women with something like a manly jealousy . . .

Commentators interpret Caelius' reference to "both kinds of sexual practice" (*utramque venerem*) to mean that these women engage in sexual relations with both male and female partners,[296] and indeed, it is worth noting that he says they are eager for sexual relations with women "more than" (*magis quam*) with men, not "rather than" (*potius quam*). In other words, the disorder that afflicts both *tribades* and *molles mares* is hardly homosexuality: indeed, Caelius himself elsewhere assumes that healthy men will be sexually aroused by both women and boys.[297] Thus, as Brooten herself observes, in this text the "diseased" ones are males who desire to be penetrated, but not those who penetrate them, and females who desire to penetrate others, but not their receptive partners.[298]

Caelius ends his discussion by reaffirming his conviction that such "diseased" men may play both the receptive and the insertive role in their youth, but as they grow older any masculine vigor that they might have disappears and they seek only to be penetrated:

> in aliis enim aetatibus, adhuc valido corpore et naturalia veneris officia celebrante, gemina luxuriae libido dividitur, animo eorum nunc faciendo nunc patiendo iactato; in his vero qui senectute defecti virili veneris officio caruerint, omnis animi libido in contrariam ducitur appetentiam et propterea femineam validius venerem poscit. hinc denique coniciunt plurimi etiam pueros hac passione iactari; similiter enim senibus virili indigent officio, quod in ipsis nondum <est> et illos deseruit. (4.9.137)[299]

For at other periods in their life, when their body is still strong and observing the natural sexual functions, their lust for luxury is divided into two: their mind is tossed about, now being active, now being passive. But in those who, worn out by old age, have lost the masculine sexual function, the mind's entire desire is led to the opposite appetite and as a result it more strongly demands the female sexual role. It is from this that very many people suppose boys to be afflicted by this passion, for just like old men they lack the masculine function, which does not yet exist in them just as it has deserted old men.

When in the prime of their life, these "soft men" exercise both the "active" and the "passive" role (*nunc faciendo nunc patiendo*), and the fact that Caelius does not specify that they do the former exclusively with male partners once again suggests that the sex of their receptive partners is beside the point; again we think of the stereotype of the womanizing *cinaedus*. Moreover, the common beliefs that Caelius here reports (*coniciunt plurimi*) are implied in many another Roman text, as we have seen. Boys, not yet being men, may indeed derive pleasure from being penetrated. But when normal boys turn into men, they lose interest in that practice, now feeling the urge to fill their "masculine function" (*virile veneris officium*) of penetrating others. On the other hand, those who are afflicted by the disorder that Caelius discusses experience a desire to perform both the masculine and the feminine function, at least when in the prime of their life; but as they grow older and their masculine function wanes, they are increasingly drawn toward the feminine role. For this stereotype concerning old men, we might compare Martial's obviously pejorative reference to an aged *cinaedus* (*vetulus cinaedus*) as one of the characters on display on the streets of Rome, as well as Apuleius' equally unflattering description of the old *cinaedus* (*senex cinaedus*)—"you know the type," remarks the narrator—and his gang of "girlfriends" (*puellae*) who are themselves *cinaedi*.[300]

Caelius' aetiology and Phaedrus' fable raise an interesting question. One might at first imagine that the "soft" men they describe sought to be penetrated only by males and tribads to penetrate only females, but what was to keep a phallically endowed *tribas* from penetrating a receptive *mollis*? Might not the two share a "depraved pleasure" (Phaedrus' *pravum gaudium*) with each other, thus enacting a true perversion of gender roles? Seneca reports this very thing happening in one of his epistles to Lucilius, discussing with obvious distaste the existence of women afflicted with such masculine medical problems as gout and baldness. His description of these women—who must have really existed in the world of his readers, or else his argument would collapse—is reminiscent both of Phaedrus' *tribades* and of Martial's Philaenis (7.67, discussed earlier in this chapter). As Philaenis eats and drinks to excess, so Seneca refers to women who "drink no less than men and, challenging them in the amount of oil and wine that they consume, bring up what they have stuffed into bellies that are just as unwilling [as men's], and vomit all the wine." And as Philaenis penetrates both boys and girls, so these women, Seneca notes with dismay, "although born to be submissive (may the gods and goddesses damn them!), devise so perverse a variety of unchastity that they enter men."[301] It is telling indeed that Seneca makes no mention of sexual relations between women. What arouses his indignation is that these women penetrate, and the fact that they penetrate men is especially shocking as it upends the normative distribution of sexual role. So too Martial's Philaenis is anomalous not because she is a lesbian but because she penetrates, and the poet is careful to specify that she penetrates both female and male partners.[302]

What about this figure of the woman who penetrates? The ancient texts focus on their deviant desires, but we might well ask who their male partners were.[303] How would *they* be categorized in Roman terms? Surely it would not have seemed outrageous to include them among Phaedrus' soft males (*molles mares*) who were mistakenly given a pseudo-vagina by Prometheus, or among Caelius' soft, penetrated males (*molles sive subacti*); in the end they were just as surely open to a charge of *impudicitia* as were men penetrated by men.[304] Seneca's remark reminds us that males who sought to be penetrated did not necessarily or exclusively seek sexual encounters with members of their own sex; and that some Romans at least were aware of the fact that a man's desire to be penetrated and a man's desire for other men—which we might take to be tautologous—are not necessarily the same thing. These "soft men" are anomalous not because they desire other men but because they break a primary rule of masculinity by wanting to be penetrated. They are gender deviants, not homosexuals.[305]

The issue of gender deviance surfaces in an anecdote first reported by Plutarch and then translated for a Roman audience by Aulus Gellius.[306] There once was a rich man of a markedly effeminate appearance (he is dainty, has curled hair, and speaks with a mincing voice); but he was said to be free from sexual disgrace (*stuprum*). This leads the philosopher Arcesilaus to retort wittily that it makes no difference to him "with which parts you people are *cinaedi*, the ones in back or the ones in front."[307] This rich man and men like him (Arcesilaus generalizes, speaking in the plural) are *cinaedi* by virtue of their gender deviance, regardless of whether they are penetrated or penetrate others. Indeed, Plutarch elsewhere indicates that Arcesilaus' words were aimed at "womanizers" and "wanton men."[308]

A common understanding unites the wide range of texts surveyed in this chapter. The class of human beings is not divisible into the two distinct groups *homosexual* and *heterosexual*, each with the subgroups *male* and *female*. Rather, the class of human beings is divided into the groups *male* and *female*, and each of these has the subgroups *insertive* and *receptive*, with *insertive male* and *receptive female* being the normative types, *receptive male* and *insertive female* being considered deviant. It is precisely these two deviant types—and only these two—that are explained by Caelius Aurelianus as suffering from a chronic mental disorder, and by Phaedrus' tale of the drunken Prometheus as anomalies that are as old as humanity itself.

Cinaedi Desiring Men

Although I am arguing that these deviant males were not defined as homosexual, they were nevertheless usually imagined to desire to be penetrated not by women but by men. In the conclusions to this book I will return to the necessarily speculative issue of how such men understood themselves; no doubt many of these men not only sought the physical and psychological pleasures of being penetrated but also consciously desired sexual contact with men. Yet if we wish to understand how they were represented *by others* in the public discourse of their cultural environment—my main interest in this book—we must still describe them as gender deviants rather than as homosexuals. For even as they displayed a desire for men (*viri*)— and we note that these effeminate males are always said to desire men (*viri*) in particular, not male partners (*mares*) in general and certainly not boys (*pueri*: a choice of erotic object that would never have raised an eyebrow)—they were acting as women were expected to act. A review of the texts in which their desire for men is held up against them will illustrate my point.

In a speech delivered in 142 B.C. (and cited several times previously), Scipio Aemilianus indirectly but unambiguously portrays P. Sulpicius Galus as an effeminate *cinaedus*, and he describes him as "fond not only of wine but of men too" (*non modo vinosus sed virosus quoque*).[309] According to Plutarch, on the occasion of the celebrated trial of Milo in 52 B.C., Clodius heckled Pompey with a series of taunting questions insinuating effeminacy; one of them asked, "Who is the man who is looking for a man?" (τίς ἀνὴρ ἄνδρα ζητεῖ;).[310] A similar jibe against Pompey was penned by Calvus: "He scratches his head with one finger. What would you think he wants? A man [*virum*]."[311] In a passage discussed in chapter 4, Ovid recommends that excessive grooming be reserved for girls and for "anyone, hardly a man, who seeks to have a man [*virum*]."[312] And Juvenal's second satire includes the outraged remark that "a man of outstanding background and wealth is being handed over in marriage to a man [*viro*]."[313]

Richlin has argued that these texts testify to a condemnation of men as being desirous of men and thus as "homosexual" and that consequently these and other texts display "homophobic" reactions.[314] But it is difficult to attribute homophobia to a cultural tradition that simply assumed as part of human nature the fact that men desire and engage in penetrative acts with boys; it is significant that none of the texts just quoted issues a condemnation of the insertive partner of the man under attack as effeminate. Scipio, Clodius, Calvus, and Ovid all aim their jab at the one who seeks a man (*virosus*; ἄνδρα ζητεῖ; *sibi velle virum*; *quaerit virum*), and Juvenal mocks the one who is given in marriage to a man (*traditur viro*). The emphatic presence of the term "man" in these texts is also worth noting. Given the specific coloring of *vir* discussed earlier, these remarks are equivalent to saying that the men in question, although themselves men (*viri*), paradoxically desire a penis.[315] In view of the normative configuration of man desiring and penetrating non-man (girl or boy, woman or *cinaedus*), to say that someone who is biologically male desires a man is precisely to make him a non-man.[316] So Scipio predicates *virosus* of a man marked as effeminate, while Ovid denies full manhood to the one who desires a *vir*, dismissing him as "hardly a man" (*male vir*).[317]

In short, the language of men desiring men may make the modern reader think of homosexuality, as if the sameness of the gender of the parties involved were the issue. But for ancient writers and their readers, to desire a man was not principally a sexual object choice: it was a sexual role choice. Since a fully gendered *vir* was not just a male, but a male defined as penetrator, to desire a *vir* was to make a male not a man.[318] It is certainly true, as Richlin reminds us, that there were real hardships involved in living the role of the *cinaedus* in Rome, and that ancient antipathy against *cinaedi* bears some similarities to contemporary homophobia; certainly both phenomena concern sexual practices between males. But we must not allow that point of similarity to lead us to fully identify the two. While one might argue that gay men in contemporary American culture are subject to antipathy and oppression both because they violate the heterosexual norm and because of their putative effeminacy, ancient *cinaedi* were not marginalized qua homosexual any more than were their insertive partners in sexual acts; they violated not a norm of heterosexuality but a norm of masculinity. Consequently, modern homophobia and ancient antipathy to *cinaedi* share not a suspicion of sexual practices between males but rather a fear of effeminacy. To describe ancient bias against *cinaedi* as "homophobic" or as constituting a problematization of male homosexuality is, I suggest, comparable to suggesting that Roman biases against female prostitutes or adulteresses were "heterophobic" or in some way problematized heterosexuality.[319]

Likewise, to translate *cinaedus* as "fag," "faggot," "fairy," or "queen" is to skew the word's meaning. Even the more clinical sounding "passive homosexual," practically standard in the scholarship, will not do: in addition to the problem of "homosexuality," the phrase reveals itself upon closer inspection to be quite peculiar. Does it refer to a man who is *really* homosexual but fails to *enact* his desires? A man who sits at home waiting for the telephone to ring? Might we call a woman who is fond of being penetrated by men a "passive heterosexual"? Moreover, we have seen that, unlike a "faggot," a *cinaedus* might well engage in sexual relations with women without causing eyebrows to rise at such heterosexual behavior. It was earlier seen, too, that men inclined to play the penetrative role in sexual acts were categorized as real men (*viri*) regardless of whether they were thought to penetrate males or females or both. But when such a man was observed to have a predominant or exclusive taste for male partners (and would thus be classified as a "homosexual" or insulted as a "faggot" if he lived today), there is no indication that he was understood as belonging to a discrete class of individuals differentiated as homosexual and thus including his male partners,[320] just as there is no indication that men like Claudius were conceptually grouped together with their female partners as members of a discrete class of individuals differentiated as heterosexuals. Neither did Romans conceive of men who sexually penetrated *cinaedi* as a distinct or coherent group; there is certainly no word meaning "*cinaedus*-fucker."[321]

In sum, there obviously existed in antiquity individuals who desired sexual contact with persons of one sex or the other, or both, and if they were alive today they would be pigeonholed as heterosexual, homosexual, or bisexual. But my interest lies in exploring them in their native cultural setting, considering how their sexual practices and the inclinations thought to underlie those practices were publicly labeled by their peers. I have suggested that the labels given them operated quite differently from contemporary labels, which are universally applicable to every human being: on this model, everyone is fundamentally, and always will be, heterosexual, homosexual, or bisexual. By contrast, a Roman man could be pegged as a *fellator*, but this would strongly suggest that he also was a *cunnilingus*; or he might be labeled a *fututor*, but no one would be surprised if he also seized an occasional opportunity to anally penetrate a male slave, thus playing the role of *pedico*; a man called a *cinaedus* might also be an *adulter* or a *moechus*. None of these labels refers to an absolute, all-encompassing, unchangeable identity. Rather, each of them describes a man's observable behavior, and thus of course entails an assumption of some kind of underlying predilection. But one predilection need not exclude all others, and the combinations of predilections that Roman writers attributed to men conspicuously fail to align themselves with the concepts of heterosexuality and homosexuality.[322]

The Question of "Subculture"

Amy Richlin has argued that "the possibility of a male homosexual subculture at Rome should not be set aside."[323] John Clarke, in his discussion of the Warren Cup and other images of sexual relations between males in Roman art, suggests that these artifacts, together with "the relatively large number of poems addressed by poets to their male lovers," are "positive signs of a homosexual culture in Roman society."[324] And Rabun Taylor has recently presented an extensive argument for the "development of homosexual subcultures in the face of adversity" in ancient Rome.[325]

But to speak of "homosexual subcultures" in antiquity creates more problems than it solves. The difficulties are clearly illustrated when we compare the putative subcultures of ancient Rome with those of later times. George Chauncey's study *Gay New York* provides extensive documentation of clubs and saloons in late-nineteenth- and early-twentieth-century New York City, where effeminate men who engaged in sexual practices with men and who were often called "fairies" congregated, and he argues that these establishments "fostered and sustained a distinctive gay culture in a variety of ways."[326] Randolph Trumbach describes a similar situation in early-eighteenth-century London, where establishments known as "molly houses" formed part of "a subculture of the like-minded where men who could be both active and passive sought each other."[327] In other words, in more recent times "homosexual subcultures" have arisen from the need of the "like-minded" (that is, persons defined by their desire for persons of their own sex) to meet in a protected environment that offers them a safe haven from an outside world hostile to homosexuality. Indeed, sociologists and historians studying contemporary gay subcultures are united in their conviction that the pressures exerted by living within a cultural environment hostile to same-sex desires are a crucial factor in the establishment of gay subcultures.[328] Thus some historians argue that one cannot speak of a "homosexual subculture" in the West until the eighteenth century or later, when the identity of "the homosexual" in the modern sense was established, and when the hostility to homosexual desire and practices became increasingly virulent.[329] We return to Trumbach's summary of the situation in eighteenth-century London:

It was dangerous to attempt to seduce men who did not share such tastes. Such relations could be more safely pursued in a subculture of the like-minded where men who could be both active and passive sought each other.[330]

This formulation raises an important point: "homosexual" or "sodomitical subcultures" also served as environments in which men could meet potential sexual partners, a difficult and dangerous thing to do in the outside world. Writing of male prostitutes in late-nineteenth- and early-twentieth-century England, Jeffrey Weeks makes these observations:

> A sexual subculture can fulfill a number of complementary functions: alleviating isolation and guilt, schooling members in manners and mores, teaching and affirming identities. The most basic purpose of the homosexual subculture in the nineteenth and early twentieth centuries, however, was to provide ways to meet sexual partners.[331]

Likewise George Chauncey has suggested that the bars and clubs in early twentieth-century New York where fairies gathered served a dual purpose: not only did they provide a safe haven and a site for group cohesion and identity, but they also provided an environment where fairies and their potential sexual partners might meet, since the "normal" men with whom fairies sought sexual contact also came to these establishments.[332]

But the cultural landscape of ancient Rome was significantly different from eighteenth-century London or twentieth-century New York. If we were to apply later models, the "like-minded" in ancient Rome would include both *viri* and *cinaedi*. But the textual tradition strongly discourages us from imagining these two types of men as belonging to one group, just as it discourages us from conceiving of men and the female prostitutes whom they visited, or men and the male slaves whom they used, as belonging to a cohesive group. The young studs picked up by Apuleius' *cinaedi* certainly did not form a part of any subculture that they shared with the *cinaedi*; Petronius' characters Encolpius and Ascyltos, who have been sexually involved with each other as well as with the boy Giton, do not share a subculture with the repulsive *cinaedus* who jumps on them at Quartilla's house. Men who were interested in sexual experience with other males (whether boys, slaves, prostitutes, or *cinaedi*) in which they would play the insertive role did not have to contend with cultural traditions that condemned their desires or restricted their behavior; they did not have to go underground to a subculture. A fully gendered man (*vir*) interested in a sexual encounter with a male could make use of his slaves if he owned any, or, if he had the financial means, he could pay for the services of a male prostitute. If he was interested in the forbidden fruit of freeborn youth, he had plenty of opportunity for contact, since freeborn men and boys constantly intermingled. And, to judge by the evidence of Juvenal, Petronius, Martial, and Phaedrus, if a man was interested in finding a *cinaedus*, he could meet one practically anywhere: on the streets, in the baths, at private dinner parties and orgies (with or without the additional presence of women), even in an army camp.[333] Plutarch, relating the downfall of the Roman general Sertorius, reports that the conspiracy against him led by Perpenna was prompted to take action by a breach in security: a new member of the conspiracy, Manlius, tried to win over a young man with whom he was in love (ἐρῶν τινος τῶν ἐν ὥρᾳ μειρακίου) by telling the youth of the plot, saying that he should forget his other lovers (τῶν ἄλλων ἐραστῶν) since within a few days Manlius would be in a powerful position. Unfortunately for Manlius, the boy reported this to another one of his lovers, Aufidius, who happened also to be a conspirator. Aufidius, alarmed at the breach of security, went straight to Perpenna; it was decided to take action forthwith.[334] Plutarch is of course a Greek writing for Greeks, but he must have had some sources for this story, and it is interesting to observe the evidently unremarkable presence of this clearly desirable young man (perhaps a local Spaniard) among the men in Sertorius' army. This anecdote is perfectly in line with the evidence reviewed in this book in its implication that men interested in penetrative sexual contact with males had no need for a subculture because they constituted the dominant culture.

In this regard the comments of Michael Rocke, who has described evidence for extensive participation in homosexual practices ("sodomy") among men and boys in fifteenth-century Florence, are worth quoting:

> The links between homosexual activity and broader male social relations were so dense and intertwined that there was no truly autonomous and distinctive "sodomitical subculture," much less one based on a modern sense of essential diversity or "deviance." There was only a single male sexual culture with a prominent homoerotic character. . . . Sodomy was an integral facet of male homosocial culture.[335]

Likewise for ancient Rome, if one is to use the language of sexual cultures or subcultures, it is best to speak of one dominant masculine sexual culture, composed of men interested in penetrating various kinds of partners: women, prostitutes of both sexes, boys, or *cinaedi*. And while each of those groups in turn might have shaped their own identities and their own internal cohesions in response to the dominant masculine culture and its demands on them, to call each of these groups subcultures (for example, a *boy subculture*, an *adulteress subculture*, or a *pathic subculture*) is to misrepresent the kinds of internal cohesion or group identity these collections of individuals may have had.[336]

Some formulations of the argument that there was a "homosexual subculture" do not withstand scrutiny. Clarke, as we have seen, suggests that artifacts depicting sexual practices between males, together with "the relatively large number of poems addressed by poets to their male lovers" are "positive signs of a homosexual culture in Roman society." But one can just as well say that artifacts depicting sexual practices between men and women, together with poems addressed by Roman men to girls or women, are "positive signs of a heterosexual culture in Roman society." Taylor offers the following remarks:

> We know little about how or where the men of this subculture congregated. Urban baths seem to have served as cruising grounds. . . . The evidence of Petronius and other sources further suggests that brothels and wharves were fairly comfortable environments for homosexual fraternizing and soliciting. The Roman theater was reputed to be a hotbed of pathic activity and seems to have been a favorite hangout for prostitutes, both male and female.[337]

But Taylor's subsequent description of what went on at the baths includes an acknowledgment that they were, albeit "less frequently," a locus for male-female contacts.[338] And as he himself notes, the theater was a hangout for prostitutes of both sexes; it was also a notoriously convenient place for men and women to meet each other in noncommercial ways—Ovid's how-to manual for men interested in picking up women makes that perfectly clear.[339]

As for brothels, one might reasonably suppose that there existed some staffed only by males, just as there were others staffed only by females. The only direct textual reference to brothels staffed exclusively by males comes from the fourth century A.D., in a punitive decree from the Christian emperor Theodosius I that mentions *virorum lupanaria*.[340] But of course this comes from a period that witnessed an increasing antipathy toward homosexual practices, and we cannot automatically project either the term or the concept back to earlier times. Indeed, the textual tradition of the classical period consistently discourages us from imagining a distinct world of "gay brothels" as opposed to "straight" ones. The landscape of Petronius' *Satyricon*, for example, includes a brothel that the narrator Encolpius calls a "brothel" and a "whorehouse" (*fornix, lupanar*) to which an old woman mischievously takes him, and where he unexpectedly runs into his friend Ascyltus. The latter reports that he was brought there by a gentleman who had met him on the street and who wanted to become more intimately acquainted with him on short notice. This was obviously the kind of place where one could rent a room by the hour, and indeed the unnamed man shells out some money for a room, but, interestingly, he pays a female prostitute (*meretrix*). Although at the moment she is fulfilling merely an administrative function, she clearly also discharged her usual professional obligations in the same seedy establishment: Encolpius sees nude female whores wandering furtively through the brothel holding placards that presumably advertised the services they offered along with the prices they charged.[341] Likewise, in an epigram we have already seen, Martial imagines a man he calls Cantharus entering a brothel to find either a boy or a girl:

Intrasti quotiens inscriptae limina cellae,
   seu puer adrisit sive puella tibi,
contentus non es foribus veloque seraque
   secretumque iubes grandius esse tibi . . . (Mart. 11.45.1–4)

Whenever you cross the threshold of an inscribed cubicle, whether it is a boy or a girl who smiles at you, you are not satisfied with the door, the curtain, and the lock, and you require greater secrecy for yourself.

Even though the cubicle with the boy is not necessarily in the same establishment as the one with the girl, nonetheless Martial's casual alternatives ("whether it is a boy or a girl," *seu . . . sive . . .*) suggest that his readership would not have been startled by the notion of a single brothel containing a male prostitute in one cubicle and a female in another. In any case, both Petronius and Martial suggest a milieu in which a man might walk into a brothel where prostitutes of both sexes were available just as easily as he might visit an establishment staffed with only one sex and walk down the street to find one staffed with the other sex. Certainly there

are no hints that same-sex and mixed-sex brothels belonged to different neighbor-
hoods, let alone to different subcultures.[342]

We cannot, in short, speak of a "homosexual subculture" in ancient Rome any
more than we can speak of a "heterosexual subculture." Recognizing the difficulties in doing so, some scholars have spoken instead of a "passive homosexual" or
"pathic" subculture among those effeminate men who were pejoratively called
cinaedi or *pathici*.[343] And indeed one might well imagine that such men, faced as
they were with widespread prejudice and united in their status as deviants, would
have banded together. Several ancient authors that give us some insight into the
ways in which outsiders, at least, thought about *cinaedi* imagine them in groups.
As we have seen, in Juvenal's second satire, Laronia imagines "soft men" sticking
together, finding protection in numbers (she ironically likens them to a phalanx of
soldiers protected by their interlocking shields), and the satirist's own persona continues the attack, complaining that these practices are spreading like a contagion
that infects more and more Romans, and painting a vivid picture of hypocritical
cinaedi gathering to conduct their sacred rites in honor of the Good Goddess.[344]
The *cinaedus* at Quartilla's house in Petronius obviously conceives of himself as
part of a larger group, singing a song (quoted earlier in this chapter) in which he
invites his fellow *cinaedi* to come and join in on the fun; and, as we have also seen,
Apuleius' *Metamorphoses* presents a band of *cinaedi* who make the rounds of the
villages, putting on spectacular shows of dancing and self-mutilation, and recruiting sexual partners as they went along.

But if, as I have argued, these men were fundamentally identified as effeminate rather than as "passive homosexuals" or even as penetrated men, any group
identity they might have shared was based first and foremost on their effeminacy,
their flouting of the rules of masculinity in general, and not on the specific sexual
practice of being penetrated. After all, a *cinaedus* might be a womanizer without
losing his identity as *cinaedus* both on an individual level and as a member of the
group. Thus the glue that held them together—to the extent that they were held
together—was not a sexual practice but a gendered identity. In fact the various
signs and norms that some scholars have taken to be indications of a "passive homosexual subculture" are precisely signs of a gender deviance rather than of a
sexual orientation: wearing flowing or brightly colored clothes, speaking mincingly,
sashaying about, depilating oneself, wearing makeup and perfume. As we saw in
chapter 4, and as Richlin herself notes, these traits are associated with men who
are effeminate but who might be associated with sexual practices with women as
well as with men.[345] Thus, in a passage quoted in chapter 4, Cicero disparages
Catiline's followers as effeminate, with carefully groomed hair and flowing clothes,
but they include both adulterers and *impudici*, and Cicero tweaks them for their
dependence on their girlfriends.[346]

One of the most peculiar of these putative signs of a "passive homosexual
subculture" illustrates the point well: the practice of scratching the head with one
finger.[347] Taylor's discussion reveals the difficulties inherent in describing this as
belonging to members of a subculture defined as "homosexual," whether "passive"
or not:

Because of the nature of the literature, we have little surviving evidence of an argot among the Roman subculture, but the various physical mannerisms served as a sort of rudimentary sign language misunderstood by outsiders. The curious habit of scratching one's head with a single finger, attested in several sources, appears to have been a code gesture among homosexual or bisexual men, perhaps for soliciting sex.[348]

Here the term "homosexual" seems to refer to men who engage in such practices exclusively with male partners, and "bisexual" to men who engage in such practices with both male and female partners. Yet the implication of describing this subculture as including "homosexual or bisexual men" is that it included men who engaged in sexual practices with females; but how can we call it a "homosexual subculture" if "homosexual" refers to men who engage in sexual practices exclusively with males? It would seem that we need to speak of a "bisexual subculture." But, if we are to use this language, was not the dominant culture itself the purview of men who were "bisexual"? The vocabulary will not work.

More specifically, it is difficult to imagine how the act of scratching the head with one finger could function as a signal "for soliciting sex," or more precisely as a gesture that sends the message "I want to be penetrated." Of course, given the sometimes arbitrary nature of such signals, such a signification is not impossible; but in view of what we know about Roman notions of effeminacy, it is much easier to see the gesture as a sign proclaiming one's effeminacy. I would argue that the gesture was associated with a desire to avoid disturbing one's carefully coiffed, and perhaps artificially curled, hair.[349] According to Plutarch, Cicero mocked Julius Caesar for his carefully arranged hair (a sure sign of effeminacy), observing that he could not find it within himself to be afraid of a man who scratches his head with one finger.[350] In other words, the gesture is a sign of an effeminate concern for one's coiffure, a marker of a soft womanishness (*mollitia*), not of a desire to be penetrated. As we saw above, Calvus' ditty on Pompey assumes that a man who makes this gesture, being a pseudo-woman, might "want a man," like any "woman" ought to. But that is merely an effect of the underlying cause, which is not homosexuality but effeminacy.

Beyond such physical signs, there is also the question of linguistic signals characterizing a putative subculture: a specialized jargon, as it were. Taylor, citing my own analysis of some of the relationships between male characters in Petronius' *Satyricon* as departures from the usual phallocentric patterns, reaches a conclusion with which I must disagree: "In the Roman world, this kind of relationship could only have existed in a subculture."[351] I hope to explore the dynamics of the seemingly nonhierarchical relationships in the *Satyricon* in another context; as a preliminary comment, I would note that instead of saying that Petronius' characters and their relationships belong to a subculture, we can take them as evidence for the fact that even within the reigning paradigms—the so-called dominant culture—there existed the possibility of sidestepping the issue of who penetrated whom.[352] Furthermore, pointing to the fact that certain sexual partners in the *Satyricon* refer to each other as *frater* ("brother"), Taylor notes that "just as 'brother' and 'sister' are common terms of affection within the American homosexual subculture, so *frater* and *soror* are the terms in which the members of the *Satyricon's* subculture identify their current love interest."[353] But the use of *frater* and *soror* to refer to one's boyfriend or girlfriend is hardly limited to Petronius or indeed to same-sex couples: both Martial and the writer of an elegiac poem in the Tibullan corpus attest to the usage of this language between partners of the opposite sex,[354] and indeed *soror* is used in the *Satyricon* not by a member of a "homosexual subculture" but rather by a woman who wishes to become the sister (that is, girlfriend) of the male narrator Encolpius, just as Giton is his brother:

> "si non fastidis" inquit "feminam ornatam et hoc primum anno virum expertam, concilio tibi, o iuvenis, sororem. habes tu quidem fratrem, neque enim me piguit inquirere, sed quid prohibet et sororem adoptare?" (Petr. *Sat.* 127.1–2)

> "Young man," she said, "if you don't think it beneath you to have a distinguished woman who had her first man this year, I can give you a sister. To be sure, you have a brother (I wasn't embarrassed to ask), but what prevents you from adopting a sister, too?"

Arguments that words like *frater* characterized a "homosexual subculture" rest on tenuous foundations.

The problems created by speaking of "pathic subcultures" in antiquity are well illustrated by Taylor's suggestion, in the course of an interesting discussion of the *galli*, that some Roman men who desired to play the "woman's role" might have found a home among the castrated priests of the Mother Goddess:

> Within a society that condemns the pathic, the cults just described have their attractions as an environment where men can exercise their minority sexual preference—if not with outright approval, at least with less ostracism than in the lonelier and more dangerous context of society at large. That they sacrifice their genitals is remarkable evidence of the lengths to which some homosexually oriented men will go to seek acceptance of an outlet for their sexuality.[355]

Perhaps some "homosexually oriented men" in some other cultural contexts might go to such lengths, but there is no reason to imagine that a Roman man who experienced a desire to be penetrated would feel himself compelled to run from the "lonelier and more dangerous context of society at large" into the arms (and knives) of the castrated priests of the Mother Goddess. Roman society was not that "lonely" or that "dangerous" for such men. As we have seen, the antipathy directed against them by the dominant culture, while considerable, did not make *cinaedi* outcasts, terrified of being "discovered." Neither was this hostility comparable in its intensity and likely effects to the later persecutions of sodomites and homosexuals, who risked not only ostracism but imprisonment and even death at the hands of the law. Among Romans, *cinaedi* were liable to ridicule for their violation of the rules of masculine comportment, but they were not despised or feared as homosexuals.

Conclusions

While I hesitate to offer a "conclusion" to a study that aims to open up further discussion, it may be helpful for precisely that reason to look back over the reconstructions of Roman discourses on masculinity that I have offered and to point to the kinds of questions raised by my study. In particular, since this book has for the most part necessarily dealt with representations and conceptual paradigms more than with the actual behaviors of Roman men, it may be useful to offer a positive model—tentative as it must be—for the range of sexual practices that an adult freeborn man living in Rome between roughly 200 B.C. and A.D. 200, and belonging to the leisured classes toward which our sources are biased, could admit to having engaged in without damaging his image as a "real man."

Above all, these men were not encouraged to make any meaningful distinctions between homosexual and heterosexual practices as such. What was most important for a man's reputation was that he be thought to play the insertive and not the receptive role in penetrative acts. If he played the insertive role, he might do so with either male or female partners, or both, as he pleased; the sex of his partner had no bearing on his own status as a man. This view of what it means to be a man with regard to sexual practices has characterized many cultural traditions over the course of human history, but for a Roman man there was a further consideration: Were his sexual partners slaves or free? Freeborn Romans of both sexes (apart from his wife) were officially considered off-limits, and any sexual relations with such persons would constitute acts of *stuprum* and could be described as disgraceful behavior. Thus if a Roman man was known to have engaged in sexual relations with another freeborn Roman, whether it was the son, daughter, wife, or widow of one of his peers (or indeed one of his peers themselves, although the sources overwhelmingly concern themselves with other men's dependents), he was liable to the censure of moralists, to legal penalties, and in general to being portrayed as one who was unable to control his desires to such an extent that he tampered with the integrity of a freeborn Roman, not to mention the proprietary claims of other Roman men.[1] In the end, though, despite the potentially troublesome consequences, a man who engaged in sexual relations with free Romans other than his wife could still keep his title to masculinity as long as he maintained the image of the active, insertive partner.

If he wished absolutely to avoid raising any eyebrows, there were two categories of persons among whom a Roman man could freely seek sexual partners: prostitutes (who might be free persons or slaves of either sex) and his own slaves of either sex. No one except for philosophers like Seneca and Musonius Rufus questioned a man's right to do what he pleased with his own slaves, and as for prostitutes, while there was always the possibility of being tainted by association with those who sold themselves for others' pleasure, still, if it was done discreetly and in moderation, no one would talk. Indeed, Romans were able to imagine the arch-conservative Cato the Elder actually commending a young man for visiting a prostitute rather than going after other men's wives.

My discussion has rather relentlessly concerned sexual acts. What about affairs, like those imagined in the poetry of Catullus, Tibullus, Ovid, and others, that go beyond a one-time encounter—"relationships" as opposed to "relations"? In general, it seems that traditional codes of behavior were not concerned with any such distinction. The off-limits categories were off-limits whether it was a question of a single sexual act or of a life-long bond. As a result, among the options officially unavailable to a Roman man was a lasting, reciprocal relationship with another freeborn man, or indeed with a freeborn woman other than his wife.[2] But here in particular we must recall the potentially significant gaps between representational systems and lived reality. The silencing of such couples in the surviving sources cannot be interpreted to mean that they did not exist. (See Appendix 2, for example, for a discussion of the question of marriages between Roman men.)

I have also argued that the protocols outlined here applied to Roman men regardless of whether or not they were married. To be sure, if a man was married, his wife might well complain about his dalliances with slaves or prostitutes, and her complaints might find some support from sympathetic outsiders who paid at least lip service to an ideal of mutual fidelity between spouses, or from philosophers generally suspicious of physical pleasure. But if the husband chose to ignore her claims and quietly disregard the ideal, his peers were generally prepared to go along with him; he was, after all, acting like a man.

What exactly did it mean to act like a man? In chapter 4 I argue that being associated with the insertive role in penetrative practices was a necessary but not a sufficient condition for full masculinity. In other words, in addition to playing the insertive role and scrupulously avoiding the receptive "woman's role," a man must also not seem womanish in his clothing, in his manner of walking or talking, in his care for his body (he must not, for example, use too much perfume or depilate himself inappropriately), or by displaying an unbridled lust or descending into a life of uncontrolled self-indulgence and pleasure, whether he sought the company of male or female sexual partners. We have seen that a man walking delicately, dripping with perfume, and surrounding himself with the women he loved was a prime target for an accusation of effeminacy. In short, when a man made choices (to the extent that he could) as to which practices he would allow others to know he engaged in, the distinction between homosexual and heterosexual acts, conceived as such, would not have been a factor in his decisions. What mattered for his reputation was not whether he sought sexual pleasure with males or females, but rather which practices he sought to engage in (to be penetrated was bad, as was pleasuring others, male or female, with his mouth) and the extent to which he lived an acceptably "masculine" lifestyle, one that was self-controlled and not excessively self-indulgent.

How exactly could men be categorized as sexual subjects? We have seen that several ancient texts describe in passing various men as being noticeably or even exclusively inclined to sexual partners of one sex or the other: Suetonius says that Claudius had no experience of males, while Martial writes of men who knew only that (11.78, 11.87). While Suetonius' claim might be inaccurate, and Martial's characters entirely fictional, nonetheless these writers and their readers clearly recognized that men with such exclusive experiences actually existed, and these men are represented as being significantly inclined or even oriented toward persons of one sex. If they were alive today, they would no doubt be called, and would likely call themselves, *straight* or *gay*. But of course they are not alive today, and if we consider them in their native cultural context, making reference to the conceptual categories in which their peers would have placed them, we cannot speak of them as *heterosexuals*, *homosexuals*, and *bisexuals*, as beings defined in terms of the sex of their preferred sexual partners within the context of a universally applicable system of categorizing human beings on that basis. In Roman terms they were either men (*viri*), who might seek to penetrate females vaginally (*fututores*, to use the coarse Roman vocabulary), to penetrate either males or females anally (*pedicones*), or to penetrate either males or females orally (*irrumatores*), or any combination of these three; or they were ridiculed as *non-men*, who might befoul their mouths by giving others pleasure (*fellatores* or *cunnilingi*), or who might abrogate their masculinity by being anally penetrated (*pathici* or *cinaedi*).

But these labels only reflect the ways in which Roman men pigeonholed *each other* in the public utterances that have survived. Here a difficult question arises: To what extent do these labels correspond to the ways in which a Roman man might have conceived of himself as a sexual subject? Would he really be disinclined to define himself in terms of the sex of his partners, as a homosexual, heterosexual, or bisexual? It is after all one thing to claim, as I have, that his peers were not encouraged by their cultural heritage to describe him in any such terms; it is another thing to make claims about the subjective experiences of individual Roman men. Such questions cannot, of course, be answered with certainty. There are unbridgeable distances between those men and us; we cannot interview a native subject. But we can speculate.

I would hardly claim that all Roman men defined themselves only in terms of which actions they sought to perform, the sex of their partners being an irrelevant detail. Such a claim is contradicted by ancient allusions to men like Suetonius' Claudius and Martial's Victor, described as seeking to play the insertive, penetrative role with persons of one sex only. Since Roman men were not encouraged by their cultural traditions to restrict their sexual practices in that way, it seems that the observable practices of these men (whether those particular individuals or others like them) reflect a subjectively experienced desire for *persons* of one sex, and not merely for certain *practices*. Nor can Claudius and Victor have been alone.

And yet they were hardly the norm. One has the distinct impression that men who sought sexual pleasure with partners of one sex only were in the minority, eccentric in the literal sense of the word. Today, by contrast (Kinsey's theories aside), people who label themselves bisexuals constitute a sexual minority whose political and cultural struggles are often connected with those of other sexual minorities, above all gay men, lesbians, and the transgendered. It is tempting to relate this significant point of divergence between antiquity and modernity to differences in cultural traditions. The power of culture to shape individual experience should not be underestimated. Men raised in a culture that has a strong tradition of ridiculing and verbally abusing men who sought to be penetrated may well be more likely to participate in the oppression of such people and to avoid assimilating themselves to them. Men raised in a culture that ignores or problematizes the possibility of long-term sexual and emotional bonds between socially equal men may well be less open to exploring such possibilities in practice. Likewise, men raised in a culture that discourages them from pigeonholing each other as heterosexual, homosexual, or bisexual, and instead encourages them to label each other in terms of the sexual practices they seek to engage in, may well be more likely to avoid restricting their sexual experiences to partners of one sex only, and less likely to perceive any significant differences between their own practices on the basis of whether their partners happen to be male or female.

I end with some questions that are posed but not answered by my work; I hope that the material reviewed here will help pave the way for future discussions of these and related issues. First, there is need for more broadly based discussion of the differences between Roman traditions and those of neighboring Mediterranean cultures with regard to gender and sexual practices. For example, why is the pederastic paradigm of relations between men and freeborn youth so prominent in Greek traditions, and why do Roman traditions instead emphasize the sexual integrity of the freeborn? How might this distinction be related to differences in the social frameworks of the two cultures: their family structures, educational traditions, and the like?[3] On another note, why do we find a widely attested fascination with unusually large penises in the Roman sources but not in the Greek? Next, while this book has largely focused on those aspects of masculine gender identity that relate to sexual practices (although in chapter 4 I took the first step in widening the scope), we need also to ask how prominent a role sexual practices actually played in the construction and maintenance of masculine image. I have argued that a man could be considered effeminate if he was thought to have been penetrated, to have been dominated by women, to have indulged in a life of luxury, or to have lost his self-control in the face of death; but which of these reputations ultimately did the most damage to his masculinity? Or can we even ask the question so absolutely?

There are even larger questions posed by the masculine self-defining practices of Greek, Roman, and other cultures both preceding and following classical antiquity. Why has it been so important that a man be thought to be the penetrator? Why have these cultures propagated degrading images of those who are penetrated, whether male or female? Why has the penetrated role been so resolutely feminized, so consistently viewed as a source of shame for a mature male, but not always for boys, who seem sometimes to fall between the cracks? The hierarchical nature of these ideologies is clearly related to the huge problem of male domination and the oppression of women and indeed of effeminate men in Western and other cultures. What contributions to ongoing attempts to wrestle with that problem can a study of Roman masculinity make?

And finally there is the equally large question of how, when, and above all why various shifts in conceptualizations of masculinity occurred between antiquity and modernity, such that in contemporary Western cultures men are practically compelled to be heterosexual and the very concept of a discrete homosexuality is deeply entrenched indeed. Scholars have offered various suggestions as to when and how this shift occurred, and some have tackled the biggest and hardest question of why it occurred. But no single explanation has been entirely satisfying, and I hope that my own account of Roman ideologies will contribute to that debate as well.

APPENDIX *1*

The Rhetoric of Nature and Same-Sex Practices

An assumption generally shared by those who wrote and read the texts surveyed in this book is that men's desires could normally and normatively be directed at either male or female objects, or both. If this configuration was held to be normal and normative, we might expect that it would also be represented as *natural*, and it is thus worthwhile to consider the role played by the discourse of *nature* in ancient representations of sexual behavior. The question is both huge and complex,[1] but one thing is clear: the ancient rhetoric of nature as it relates to sexual practices displays significant differences from more recent discourses. John Boswell, for example, observes that while "what is supposed to have been the major contribution of Stoicism to Christian sexual morality—the idea that the sole 'natural' (and hence moral) use of sexuality was procreation—was in fact a common belief of many philosophies of the day," at the same time "the term 'unnatural' was applied to everything from postnatal child support to legal contracts between friends."[2] Thus, as John Winkler writes, the contrast between nature and culture, when deployed in ancient writings, simply "did not possess the same valence that it does today."[3] Moreover, nearly all of the texts that offer opinions on whether or not specific sexual practices are in accordance with nature are works of philosophy; the question does not seem to have seriously engaged the writers of texts that more directly spoke to and reflected popular moral conceptions (e.g., graffiti, comedies, epigram, love poetry, oratory).[4] In short, as Amy Richlin warns us, the question is "something of a red herring, since the concept of naturalness takes a larger and more ominous form in our post-Christian culture than it did in antiquity, where it was a matter for philosophers."[5] But it may nonetheless be worthwhile to attempt a preliminary exploration of how the rhetoric of nature was applied by some Roman philosophers to sexual practices, particularly those between males,[6] always bearing in mind, however, that to the extent that it was mostly taken up by philosophers, the question of "natural" sexual practices seems not to have played a significant role in most public discourse among Romans.

Animal Behavior

Nonphilosophical texts sometimes do deploy the rhetoric of nature in conjunction with sexual practices, at least insofar as they offer representations of animal behavior, one possible component in arguments about what is natural.[7] It will come as no surprise that Roman writers' images of animals' sexual practices are transparently influenced by their own cultural traditions. Thus in no Roman text do we find an explicit appeal to animal behavior in order to condemn sexual practices between males as unnatural.[8] A Juvenalian satire does make reference to animal behavior in order to condemn cannibalism (claiming that no animals eat members of their own species [Juvenal 15.159–68]), and, in a passage discussed later in this appendix, Ovid has a character argue that no female animals experience sexual desire for other females. These claims are as unsupportable as the claim that sexual practices between males do not occur among nonhuman animals.[9] But the fact that we find animal behavior cited by Roman authors to condemn such phenomena as cannibalism and same-sex desire among females, but not same-sex desire among males, merely proves the point: these rhetorical strategies reveal more about Roman cultural concerns than about actual animal behavior.

A poem in the *Appendix Vergiliana* introduces us to a lover unhappily separated from his beloved Lydia. In the throes of his grief he cries out that this miserable fate never befalls animals: a bull is never without his cow, nor a he-goat without his mate. In fact, sighs the lover:

> et mas quacumque est, illa sua femina iuncta
> interpellatos numquam ploravit amores.
> cur non et nobis facilis, natura, fuisti?
> cur ego crudelem patior tam saepe dolorem? (*Lydia* 35–8)

> Wherever the male is, there his female is joined to him and has never wept for her separated love. Why, Nature, have you not been easy on us too? Why must I suffer such cruel pain so often?

The lover is melodramatically weepy, and that consideration partially accounts for his ridiculous claim that male animals are never to be seen without their mates. Still, amatory hyperbole aside, the verses nicely illustrate the tendency to shape both *natura* and animal behavior into whatever form is convenient for the argument at hand. Thus Ovid, suggesting that the best way to appease one's angry mistress is in bed, portrays sexual behavior among early human beings and animals as the primary force that effects reconciliation (*Ars* 2.461–92). The poet offers a lovely panorama in which animal behavior is invoked as a positive paradigm for specific human practices: uniting otherwise scattered groups (2.473–80) and mollifying an angry lover (2.481–90). Less than two hundred lines later, the same poet invokes animals as a negative paradigm, again in support of a characteristically human concern, discretion in sexual matters:

> in medio passimque coit pecus: hoc quoque viso
>   avertit vultus nempe puella suos.
> conveniunt thalami furtis et ianua nostris
>   parsque sub iniecta veste pudenda latet,
> et, si non tenebras, at quiddam nubis opacae
>   quaerimus atque aliquid luce patente minus. (Ovid, *Ars* 2.615–20)

> Livestock copulate here and there out in the open: when she sees this, a girl averts her gaze. Bedrooms and a door are what befit our secret love; our private parts lie hidden under the clothing we put over them; and we look, if not for total darkness, at least for a dark shadow or something less than full daylight.

Drawing his object lesson to a close, Ovid holds up his own behavior as a pattern to follow: "I confess even my true loves only sparingly, and my secret love affairs are hidden by a solid trustworthiness" (*nos etiam veros parce profitemur amores, / tectaque sunt solida mystica furta fide*, 639–40), and we are reminded of the strategies of this passage's broader context. If you want to keep your girlfriend happy, do not kiss and tell: that is the argument in service of which animal behavior is invoked as negative paradigm. These two Ovidian passages illustrate the utility of arguments from the animal world. Just look at the animals and see how much we resemble them; just look at the animals and see how far we have come.[10] It all depends on the eye—and rhetorical needs—of the beholder.

So it is that Roman writers show how Roman they are through the picture they paint of sexual practices among animals of the same sex. Ovid himself, in his *Metamorphoses*, imagines the plight of young girl named Iphis who has fallen in love with another girl: in a torrent of self-pity and self-abuse, she expostulates on her passion, making a simultaneous appeal to *natura* and to the animals that is reminiscent of Ovid's sweeping review of animal behavior in the *Ars Amatoria* just cited. But this time the paradigm is an emphatically negative one:

> si di mihi parcere vellent,
> parcere debuerant, si non, et perdere vellent,
> naturale malum saltem et de more dedissent.
> nec vaccam vaccae, nec equas amor urit equarum:
> urit oves aries, sequitur sua femina cervum.
> sic et aves coeunt, interque animalia cuncta
> femina femineo conrepta cupidine nulla est. (Ov. *Met.* 9.728–34)

> If the gods wanted to spare me, they should have spared me; if not—if they wanted to destroy me—then at least they should have given me a natural, customary evil. A cow is not burned by love for a cow, nor a mare by love for a mare: a ram is what burns

ewes, and it is his female mate that pursues a stag. That is the way that birds, too, join. Among all the animals no female is seized by desire for a female.

As with Lydia's lover, so here we have the melodramatic expostulations of an unhappy lover, and similarly her view of animal behavior does not correspond to the realities of that behavior. Still, these arguments are pitched in such a way as to invite a Roman reader's agreement, and the sexual practices invoked as natural and occurring among the animals demonstrate a suspicious similarity to the sexual practices and desires deemed acceptable by Roman culture (the female never leaves the male, heterosexual intercourse is a convenient and pleasurable way of uniting different social groups, and females never lust after females), or to specifically human erotic strategies: we do not copulate in public, and we should not kiss and tell if we want to keep our partners happy. It cannot be coincidental that, whereas Ovid invokes animal behavior in the context of a girl's tortured rejection of her own passionate yearnings for another girl, the mythic compendium in which this narrative is found is peppered with stories involving passion and sexual relations between males: both Orpheus (after losing his wife Eurydice) and the gods themselves (whether married or not) are represented as "giving over their love to tender males, harvesting the brief springtime and its first flowers before maturity sets in."[11] None of Ovid's characters ever questions the "natural" status of that kind of erotic experience or invokes the animals in order to reject it.

Aulus Gellius preserves for us some anecdotes that further demonstrate the manner in which animal behavior could be made to conform to human paradigms. Writing of (implicitly male) dolphins who fell in love with beautiful boys—one of them even died of a broken heart after losing his beloved—Gellius exclaims that they were acting "in amazing, human ways."[12] Once again, the comment tells us more about "human ways" than about dolphins. The elder Pliny, who also relates this story regarding the dolphin, introduces his encyclopedic discussion of elephants by observing that they are not only the largest land animals but the ones closest to human beings in their intelligence and sense of morality. In particular, they take pleasure in love and pride (*amoris et gloriae voluptas*), and by way of illustration of the "power of love" (*amoris vis*) among elephants he cites two examples: one male fell in love with a female flower-seller, another with a young Syracusan man named Menander who was in Ptolemy's army. Likewise he tells of a male goose who fell in love with a beautiful young Greek man, and of another who loved a female musician whose beauty was such that she also attracted the attentions of a ram.[13]

Contra Naturam

Turning to the concept of *natura* as it is applied to sexual practices by ancient writers, we begin with a basic problem. The very term *natura* has various referents in those texts: sometimes it seems simply to refer to the way things are or to the inherent nature *of* something, sometimes to the way things *should* be according to the intention or dictates of some transcendent imperative. Thus Foucault speaks of the "three axes of nature" in philosophical discourse: "the general order of the world"; "the original state of mankind"; and "a behavior that is reasonably adapted to natural ends."[14]

The first two of these axes are evident in a wide variety of Roman texts. Departures from what is observably the usual physical constitution of various beings could be called unnatural even by nonphilosophical authors: the Minotaur, centaurs, a snake with feet, a bird with four wings, and a sexual union between a woman (the mythic Pasiphae) and a bull.[15] The elder Pliny claims that breech births are "against nature," since it is "nature's way" that we should be born head first.[16] Quintilian argues that to push one's hair back from the forehead in order to achieve some dramatic effect is to act "against nature,"[17] and Seneca himself opines that being carried about in a litter is *contra naturam*, since nature has given us feet and we should use them.[18] Finally, the belief that physical disabilities and disease are unnatural—and thus, implicitly, that a healthy body displaying no marked deviations from the norm illustrates what nature designed or intended—surfaces in a number of texts, ranging from Celsus' medical treatise to Cicero's philosophical works to declamations attributed to Quintilian, to a moral epistle of Seneca, to the *Digest*.[19] Along the same lines, some ancient writers also suggest that to harm a healthy body with poisons and the like is unnatural.[20]

As for the third of the axes described by Foucault, anthropologists and others have long observed that proclamations concerning practices that are in accordance with nature often turn out to reflect specific cultural traditions; as John Winkler puts it, for nature we may often read culture.[21] Roman sources of various types certainly support that contention. Thus, for example, violations of traditional principles of language and rhetoric—which are surely among the most intensely cultural of human phenomena—are sometimes said to be unnatural;[22] one legal writer invokes the rhetoric of *natura* to justify the principle of individual ownership (joint possession of a single object is said to be *contra naturam*);[23] Sallust describes the violation of the cultural and more specifically philosophical tradition privileging the soul over the body as unnatural.[24]

Likewise practices violating Roman ideologies of masculinity are represented as infractions not of cultural traditions but of the natural order. Cicero's philosophical treatise *De Finibus* includes a discussion of the parts and functions of the body that illustrates the relationship between nature and masculinity with some clarity. Our bodily parts, he argues, are perfectly designed to fulfill their functions, and in doing so they are in conformance with nature. But there are certain bodily movements not in accord with nature (*naturae congruentes*): if a man were to walk on his hands or to walk backwards, he would manifestly be rejecting his identity as a human and would thus be displaying a "hatred of nature" (*naturam odisse*).[25] (The claim that walking on one's hands is unnatural nicely illustrates the gap between ancient and more recent uses of the rhetoric of nature.) The next illustration Cicero offers of bodily movements not in accord with *natura* concerns correctly masculine ways of deporting oneself:

quamobrem etiam sessiones quaedam et flexi fractique motus, quales protervorum hominum aut mollium esse solent, contra naturam sunt, ut etiamsi animi vitio id eveniat tamen in corpore mutari hominis natura videatur. itaque e contrario moderati

aequabilesque habitus, affectiones ususque corporis apti esse ad naturam videntur.
(Cic. *Fin.* 5.35–6)

Therefore certain ways of sitting down as well as the kinds of bent and broken movements that wanton or soft [*mollium*] men usually display are against nature, so that
although this arises from a mental flaw nonetheless human nature seems to undergo a
bodily transformation. So it is that, on the contrary, moderate and regulated bodily
postures, dispositions, and practices seem in agreement with nature.

Deemed "against nature" are certain ways of carrying oneself that are "wanton"
and "soft," movements that, like walking on one's hands or stepping backwards,
clash with the evident purpose of the body's various parts. Implicitly, then, nature
wills men's bodies to move and to function in certain ways; men who violate these
principles of masculine comportment are acting both effeminately (as we saw in
chapter 4, *mollitia* is a standard metaphor for effeminacy) and unnaturally. Cultural traditions regarding masculinity—here, appropriate bodily gestures—are identified with the natural order.[26]

How, then, is the rhetoric of nature applied to same-sex practices? One scholar
has recently suggested that the elder Pliny describes men's desires to be anally
penetrated as occurring "by crime against nature."[27] But that is probably a misin-
terpretation of Pliny's language:

in hominum genere maribus deverticula veneris excogitata omnia, scelera [*or* scelere]
naturae, feminis vero abortus. (Plin. *N.H.* 10.172)

In the race of human beings, the males have come up with all manner of sexual deviations by a crime of nature [*or* "have come up with all manner of sexual deviations that
are crimes of nature"], while the females have come up with abortion.

The phrase *deverticula veneris*, which one might translate "by-ways of sex" or "sexual
deviations," is vague; there is no reason to think it refers specifically, let alone
exclusively, to the practice of being anally penetrated. Moreover, the phrase *scelera
naturae* or *scelere naturae*, rather than "crime against nature," is most obviously
translated as "crime *of* nature," that is, a crime perpetrated by nature.[28] In any case
Pliny is not implying that all sexual desires or practices between males are unnatural: in this same treatise (significantly called the *Historia Naturalis* or "Natural
Investigations") he reports the story of a male elephant who fell passionately in
love with a young man from Syracuse as an illustration of the obviously natural
power of love (*amoris vis*) among elephants; likewise he reports the story of a
goose who loved a beautiful young man.[29]

More explicitly referring to those men who take pleasure in being penetrated,
the speaker in Juvenal's second satire ridicules men who have wilfully abandoned
their claim on masculine status by wearing makeup, participating in women's religious festivals, and even taking husbands, and notes with gratitude that nature
does not allow them to give birth.[30] The orator Labienus decries wealthy men who
castrate their male prostitutes (*exoleti*: see chapter 2) in order to render them
more suitable for playing the receptive role in intercourse: these men use their
riches in unnatural ways (*contra naturam*), and the natural standard that they vio-

late is apparently the principle that mature males both should make use of their penises and should be impenetrable.[31] Firmicus Maternus refers to men's desires to be penetrated as *contra naturam* (5.2.11), and Caelius Aurelianus' medical writings also reveal the assumption that men's "natural" sexual function is to penetrate and not to be penetrated.[32] In short, nature's dictates conveniently accorded with cultural traditions, such as those discouraging men from seeking to be penetrated, or those deterring them from engaging in sexual relations with other men's wives: in a poem that urges on its male readers the principle that *natura* places a limit on their desires, Horace recommends, as implicitly being in line with the requirements of nature, that men avoid potentially dangerous affairs with married women and stick to their own slaves, both male and female.[33]

In one of his *Epistles* (122), Seneca provides a lengthy and revealing discussion of "unnatural" behaviors that includes a reference to sexual practices among males. He begins, however, by despairing of "those who have perverted the roles of daytime and nighttime, not opening their eyes, weighed down by the preceding day's hangover, until night begins its approach."[34] These people are objectionable not simply because of their overindulgence in food and drink but because they do not respect the proper functions of night and day,[35] and this perversion of night and day is, in the end, "unnatural":

> interrogas quomodo haec animo pravitas fiat aversandi diem et totam vitam in noctem transferendi? omnia vitia contra naturam pugnant, omnia debitum ordinem deserunt.
> (Sen. *Epist.* 122.5)

> You ask how this mental depravity comes about—the practice of turning the day upside-down and of transferring one's entire life to the night? All vices fight against nature, all of them abandon the proper order.

He then proceeds to tick off a series of behaviors that are similarly *contra naturam*. First, people who drink on an empty stomach "live contrary to nature."[36] Young men nowadays, Seneca continues, go to the baths before a meal and work up a sweat by drinking heavily; according to them, only hopelessly philistine hicks (*patres familiae rustici . . . et verae voluptatis ignari*) save their drinking for after the meal.[37] The latter comment, with its contrast between urban and rustic life, austerity and luxury, is a valuable reminder for us: the standard violated by those who drank before eating was what we would call a cultural norm, but for Seneca they were violating the dictates of *natura*, abandoning the proper order (*debitum ordinem*) of things.

This important point must be borne in mind as we turn to the next practices that come under Seneca's fire:

> non videntur tibi contra naturam vivere qui commutant cum feminis vestem? non vivunt contra naturam qui spectant ut pueritia splendeat tempore alieno? quid fieri crudelius vel miserius potest? numquam vir erit, ut diu virum pati possit? et cum illum contumeliae sexus eripuisse debuerat, non ne aetas quidem eripiet? (Sen. *Epist.* 122.7)

> Do you not think that those who exchange their clothing with women live against nature? Do not those who aim to have their boyhood shine in an inappropriate time of

life live against nature? What could be more cruel or more wretched? Will he never be a man [*vir*], so that he may submit to a man [*virum pati*] for a long time? And when his sex ought to have rescued him from indignity, will not even his age rescue him?

The concept of the *proper order* is very much in evidence here, and here again that order shows unmistakable signs of cultural influence. Just as those who turn night into day or drink wine before they eat a meal are engaging in unnatural activities, so men who wear women's clothes live contrary to nature—yet what could be more cultural than the designation of certain kinds of clothing as appropriate only for men and others as appropriate only for women? Moving on to his next point, Seneca continues to focus on external appearance: men who attempt to give the appearance of the boyhood that is in fact no longer theirs also "live contrary to nature." Again the order of things has been disrupted; boys should be boys, men should be men. But these particular men want to *look* like boys in order to find older male sexual partners to penetrate them: such is the tenor of Seneca's decorous but blunt phrase "so that he may submit to a man for a long time" ("ut diu virum pati possit"). If we filter out Seneca's moralizing overlay, this detail gives us a fascinating glimpse at Roman realities. These men scorned by Seneca acted upon the awareness that men would be more likely to find them desirable if their bodies seemed like those of boys: young, smooth, hairless. Moreover, the very fact that these men made the effort suggests that the actual age of the beautiful "boys" we always hear of may not have mattered to their lovers so much as their youthful *appearance*.[38] All of this is very much a matter of convention, of cultural traditions concerning the "proper order" of things, but Seneca insistently pays homage to *natura*.[39]

The importance of this order is especially clear in the climactic illustrations of those who live "contrary to nature." These are people who wish to see roses in winter and employ artificial means to grow lilies in the cold season; who grow orchards at the tops of towers and trees under the roofs of their homes (this latter provoking Seneca to a veritable outburst of moral indignation); and those who construct their bathhouses over the waters of the sea.[40] Finally Seneca returns to the example of unnatural practices that sparked the whole discussion: those who pervert the functions of night and day engage in the ultimate form of unnatural behavior.[41] That the practices of growing trees indoors, of building bathhouses over the sea, and of sleeping by day and partying by night should be considered unnatural makes some sense in relation to notions of the "proper order" of things: plants should be outdoors, buildings should be on dry land, and people should sleep at night. But that these practices should be cited as the most egregious examples of unnatural behavior—they constitute the climax of Seneca's argument—demonstrates just how wide the gap is between ancient moralists and their modern counterparts on the question of what is natural.

With regard to mature men who seek to be penetrated by men, the third of Seneca's examples of unnatural behavior, Seneca makes in passing a surprising remark: "When his sex ought to have rescued him from indignity will not even his age rescue him?" (*cum illum contumeliae sexus eripuisse debuerat, non ne aetas quidem eripiet?* 122.7). The clear implication is that a mature man certainly ought to be safe from "indignity" (here a moralizing euphemism for penetration), but ultimately the very fact that he is male, *regardless of his age*, ought to protect him. With this one pointed sentence, then, Seneca is suggesting that maleness in itself is ideally incompatible with being penetrated, and since sexual acts were almost without exception conceptualized as requiring penetration, this amounts to positing the exclusion of sexual practices between males from the "proper order." This is a fairly radical suggestion for a Roman man to make, and Seneca was no doubt aware of that fact: he slips the comment quietly into his discussion, makes the point rather subtly (it might take a second reading even to realize it is there), and then instantly moves on to other, less controversial arguments. For as opposed to Seneca's suggestion that all males, even boys, should somehow be "rescued" from "indignity," the usual Roman system of protocols governing men's sexual behavior required the understanding that boys were different from men precisely because they could be penetrated without necessarily forfeiting all claim to masculine status (see especially chapter 5 on this last point).

But Seneca, waxing Stoic, here voices a dissenting opinion, as does the first-century A.D. Stoic philosopher Musonius Rufus, in one of whose treatises we find the remark that sexual practices between males are "against nature" (*para phusin*, Muson. Ruf. 86.10 Lutz). The remark needs to be put in the context of Musonius' philosophy of nature. According to Musonius, every creature has its own *telos* beyond the goal of simply being alive. Even horses would not be fully living up to their *telos* if all they did were to eat, drink, and copulate (106.25–7 Lutz), while the *telos* or goal of human beings is to live the life of *aretê* or virtue; thus "each one's nature [*phusis*] leads him to his particular virtuous quality [*aretê*], so that it is a reasonable conclusion that a human being is living in accordance with nature not when he lives in pleasure, but rather when he lives in virtue" (108.1–3 Lutz). Elsewhere he opines that human nature (*phusis*) is not aimed at pleasure (*hêdonê*: 106.21–3 Lutz). Consequently "luxury [*truphê*] is to be avoided in every way, as being the cause of injustice" (126.30–1 Lutz). By implication then, eating, drinking, and copulating are not in themselves evil, but they can easily become signs of a life of luxury, and if those activities constitute the goals of our existence, we are failing to fulfill our potential as human beings (namely, the practice of virtue), and consequently not living in accordance with nature. Thus, as part of a regime of self-control, Musonius argues that men should engage in sexual practices only within the context of marriage for the purpose of begetting children; any other sexual relations, *even within marriage*, should be avoided:

> Those who do not live licentiously, or who are not evil, must think that only those sexual practices are justified which are consummated within marriage and for the creation of children, since these practices are licit [*nomima*]. But [such people must think that] those [sexual practices] which hunt for mere pleasure are unjust and illicit, even if they take place within marriage. Of other forms of intercourse, those committed in *moikheia* [i.e., sexual relations with freeborn women under another man's control] are the most illicit; no more moderate than this is intercourse of males with males, since it is a daring act contrary to nature. As for those forms of intercourse with females apart from *moikheia* which are not licit [*kata nomon*], all of these too are shameful, because done on account of a lack of self-control. If one is to behave tem-

perately, one would not dare to have relations with a courtesan, nor with a free woman outside of marriage, nor, by Zeus, with one's own slave-woman. (Musonius Rufus 86.4–14 Lutz)

As I argued in chapter 1, Musonius' final remark reveals the extent to which the sexual morality that he is preaching is at odds with mainstream Roman traditions. Nor is his suggestion that men should keep their hands off prostitutes and even their own slaves the only surprising statement to be found in the treatises attributed to Musonius. He elsewhere argues against the obviously widespread practices of giving up for adoption or even exposing unwanted children (96–97 Lutz), of eating meat (here he explicitly contrasts himself with *hoi polloi*, who live to eat rather than the other way around [118.18–20 Lutz]), of shaving the beard (128.4–6 Lutz), of using wet nurses (42.5–9 Lutz), and, most appositely, of allowing husbands sexual freedoms not granted to wives (86–8 Lutz).

Thus his condemnation of sexual practices between males is issued in the context of a condemnation of all sexual practices other than those between husband and wife aimed at procreation (strictly speaking, vaginal intercourse when the wife is ovulating), and also in the context of a suspicion of all luxury and of pleasures beyond those relating to the bare necessities of life. Thus he condemns sexual relations between males as contrary to nature (the implication being that the two sexes are designed to unite with each other in the context of marriage), while sexual relations between males and females outside of marriage are criticized as "illicit" (*paranoma*) and as signs of a lack of self-control.

Here Musonius is obviously manipulating the ancient contrast between "law" or "convention" (*nomos*) and "nature" (*phusis*), and, interestingly, procreative relations within marriage are ultimately given his seal of approval not because they are more "natural" than other sexual practices, but because they are "licit" or "conventional" (*nomima*), just as adulterous relations are most "illicit" or "unconventional" (*paranomôtatai*). In other words, Musonius invokes the rhetoric of nature only by way of secondary support: male-male relations are no more "moderate" than adulterous relations and anyway, he adds, they are "unnatural." But relations between a man and another man's wife, while implicitly "natural," are in the end more "illicit" than male-male relations. Even for the Stoic Musonius, nature may not be the ultimate arbiter.

Interestingly, when he describes sexual practices between males as being against nature, Musonius does not appeal to animal behavior, as does Plato in his *Laws* (836c). Indeed, such an argument would have ill suited Musonius' arguments elsewhere that humans are different from other animals and should not take them as a model for behavior. Thus he argues that wise men will not attack in return if attacked—such revenge is the province of mere animals (78.26–7 Lutz)—and that, while among animals an act of copulation suffices to produce offspring, human beings should aim for the lifelong union that is marriage (88.16–17 Lutz).

Finally, there is an important distinction to observe between Musonius' remark concerning sexual practices between males and later Christian fulminations against "the unnatural vice," which came to be a code term for "sodomy." On the one hand, Musonius did not go so far as to condemn such relations as *the* unnatural vice; indeed, if we think about the implications of his words, relations between males do not even constitute the ultimate sexual crime. He declares that adulterous relations are "the most illicit of all" (*paranomôtatai*) and thus clearly more "illicit" than relations between males, which are, however, "equally immoderate." Furthermore, Musonius' approach to the problem of sexual behavior differs from later Christian moralists in a fundamental respect. As Foucault puts it, according to Musonius, "to withdraw pleasure from this form [sc., of marriage], to detach pleasure from the conjugal relation in order to propose other ends for it, is in fact to debase the essential composition of the human being. The defilement is not in the sexual act itself, but in the 'debauchery' that would dissociate it from marriage, where it has its natural form and its rational purpose."[42]

Cicero, in a passage from one of his major philosophical works, the *Tusculan Disputations*, approaches the ascetic stance advocated by Seneca and Musonius Rufus, although he nowhere makes an explicit commitment to the extreme suggested by Seneca and preached by Musonius. Speaking in the *Tusculan Disuptations* of the detrimental effects of erotic passion, he observes that the works of Greek poets are filled with images of love. Focusing on those who describe love for boys (he mentions Alcaeus, Anacreon, and Ibycus), Cicero notes in an aside that "nature has granted a greater permissiveness [*maiorem licentiam*]" to men's affairs with women.[43] The comparative is noteworthy. Nature has granted "greater"—not "exclusive"—license to affairs with women than to affairs with boys. The latter are evidently not forbidden by nature; discouraged perhaps, but not outlawed. A further implication of Cicero's phrase is worth noting. Nature grants men greater "license" to have sexual relations with women: this is a begrudging admission, in perfect agreement with the tenor of the whole discussion of sexual passion, which had opened thus:

> et ut turpes sunt, qui ecferunt se laetitia tum cum fruuntur veneriis voluptatibus, sic flagitiosi qui eas inflammato animo concupiscunt. totus vero iste, qui volgo appellatur amor—nec hercule invenio, quo nomine alio possit appellari—tantae levitatis est ut nihil videam quod putem conferendum. (Cic. *Tusc.* 4.68)

> And just as those who are carried away with delight when they are enjoying sexual pleasures are base, so also those who desire those pleasures with an inflamed mind are disgraceful. That entire thing which is commonly called "love" (for, by God, I cannot come up with any other name for it) is of such great inconstancy that I see nothing else that I consider comparable.

These words disparage sexual passion as a whole—particularly a hot, inflamed desire (*qui eas inflammato animo concupiscunt*)—whether indulged in with women or with boys. Nature, according to Cicero, makes it easier to indulge in this passion with women, so that when men do indulge in it with boys, they show just how deeply they have fallen victim to love, that treacherous and destructive power, "the originator of disgraceful behavior and inconstancy (*flagitii et levitatis auctorem*, 4.68).[44] In fact, remarkably enough, Cicero later claims that love itself is not natural.[45]

Cicero's remark on *natura* and sexual relations with women is in fact little more than a passing comment. Still, its implications deserve some consideration.

In what way does nature grant "greater permissiveness" to relations with women than with boys? Why does Seneca suggest that men's maleness ought to preclude them from being penetrated, and why does Musonius Rufus condemn all sexual practices between males as unnatural? These philosophers' comments seem to rest on certain assumptions about the function of sexual organs; certainly Seneca emphasizes the notion of the proper order or *debitus ordo*, according to which men should not drink wine before eating, grow roses in the winter, build buildings over the sea, or penetrate males. In short, some kind of argument from "design" seems to lurk in the background of Cicero's, Seneca's, and Musonius' claims: the penis is "designed" to penetrate a vagina, the vagina is "designed" to be penetrated by a penis.[46]

But on the whole very few Roman writers seem to have taken this kind of argument to heart. In general, Roman men's behavioral codes reflect an awareness that the penis is suited for purposes other than penetrating a vagina, and that the vagina is not the only organ suited for being penetrated. Such is the implication of a witty comment in an epigram of Martial's addressed to a man who, instead of doing the usual thing with his boy and anally penetrating him, has been stimulating his genitals; this is objectionable because it will speed up the process of his maturation and thus hasten the advent of his beard (11.22.1–8). Martial tries to talk some sense into his friend, and the epigram ends with this appeal to nature:

> divisit natura marem: pars una puellis,
>   una viris genita est. utere parte tua. (Mart. 11.22.9–10)

> Nature has divided the male into two parts: one was made for girls, the other for men. Use *your* part.

The comment is of course a witticism,[47] but if the humor was to succeed, the notion that boys' anuses were designed by nature for men to penetrate cannot have seemed outrageous to Martial's readership. After all, the rhetorical goal of the epigram is to steer the man onto the path of right behavior, the path which Martial's own persona dutifully, even proudly, followed.

This sort of comment—rather than the passing remarks of such thinkers as Cicero, Seneca, and Musonius Rufus—reflects the mainstream Roman understanding of what constitutes normative and natural sexual behavior for boys and men. It is significant, moreover, that neither Cicero nor Seneca nor Musonius Rufus nor any other surviving Roman text, philosophical or not, argues that men's *desires* to penetrate boys is "contrary to nature"; Musonius, for one, speaks only of sexual acts (συμπλοκαί). We return to the Epicurean perspective offered by Lucretius, cited in chapter 1:

> sic igitur Veneris qui telis accipit ictus,
> sive puer membris muliebribus hunc iaculatur
> seu mulier toto iactans e corpore amorem,
> unde feritur, eo tendit gestitque coire
> et iacere umorem in corpus de corpore ductum. (Lucr. 4.1052–6)

> Thus he who is struck by the weapons of Venus—whether it is a boy with feminine limbs who takes aim at him, or a woman casting forth love from her entire body—

heads for the origin of his wound and is eager to mingle with it and to cast into a body
the liquid derived from a body.

These are lines from a poem dedicated to teaching its Roman readers about "the
nature of things" (*de rerum natura*, 1.25).[48] Obviously the susceptibility of men to
the allure of boys and women is a part of that natural order for Lucretius: the
beams of atomic particles that emanate from the bodies of boys and women and
attract men to them are an integral part of the nature of things.

It is the mentality evident in such diverse texts as Lucretius' poetic treatise *On
the Nature of Things*, Martial's epigrams, and graffiti scrawled on ancient walls that
we need to keep in mind when we evaluate the comments of Musonius Rufus,
Seneca, and Cicero. These are the words of philosophers, Cicero expounding on
the dangers of love, Seneca inveighing against the corruptions of the world around
him, and Musonius arguing that men should engage only in certain kinds of sexual
relations and only with their wives, the goal being the production of legitimate
offspring and not the pursuit of pleasure. These pronouncements tell us something about the world in which the philosophers who made them lived, and about
what men and women in that world were actually doing (Seneca, for example, is
hardly fulminating about imaginary vices), but they tell us even more about Cicero,
Seneca, and Musonius, and their own philosophical allegiances. We have every
reason to believe that comments like theirs represented a minority opinion.

Indeed, the men against whom Musonius argues, who believed that a master
had absolute power to do anything he wanted with his slaves, are precisely those
whose voices dominated the public discourse on sexual practices. Moreover, as
John Winkler trenchantly observes, Seneca's condemnation of such "unnatural"
behavior as growing hothouse flowers or throwing nighttime parties, "though ar-
ticulated as universal, is obviously directed at a very small and wealthy elite—those
who can afford the sort of luxuries Seneca wants 'all mankind' to do without."[49] It
is telling, too, that Cicero himself never made this kind of appeal to nature in the
sexual invective scattered throughout the speeches he delivered in the public are-
nas of the courtroom, Senate, or popular assembly (see chapter 5), and that the
argument appears nowhere else in the considerable corpus of Seneca's moral treatises. Likewise it is worth noting that Musonius Rufus, who makes the most extreme case, not only wrote his treatise in Greek rather than Latin, as if to underscore its distance from the everyday beliefs and practices of Romans, but was a
professional philosopher committed to Stoicism in a way that Cicero and Seneca
were not.[50]

Finally, it is worth noting that both Seneca and Cicero were thought not to
have practiced what they preached: in a discussion of how Seneca's behavior often
stood in contradiction to his own teachings, the historian Dio Cassius observes
that although he married well, Seneca also "took pleasure in older lads, and taught
Nero to do the same thing too,"[51] and the younger Pliny informs us that Cicero
addressed a love poem to his faithful slave and companion Tiro.[52] Of course, neither of these pieces of information tells us anything about Cicero's or Seneca's
actual experiences; Cicero's poem could have been a literary game and the stories
about Seneca that constituted Dio's source may well have been unfounded gos-

sip.[53] On the other hand, it is not impossible that Cicero actually did experience desire for Tiro and that Seneca did enjoy the company of mature male sexual partners; and above all it is important to recognize that later generations of Romans were willing to imagine those things happening. Dio's gossipy remarks and Pliny's comments on Cicero remind us of the cultural context in which Roman philosophers' allusions to *natura* must be placed.

Marriage between Males

Scattered throughout the Roman sources we find allusions to marriages between males. The earliest relevant source is a scathing remark by Cicero to the effect that in his youth Mark Antony, having started out by living the life of a whore, was taken in by Curio, who "established you in a fixed and stable marriage [*matrimonium*], as if he had given you a *stola*" ("sed cito Curio intervenit qui te a meretricio quaestu abduxit et, tamquam stolam dedisset, in matrimonio stabili et certo conlocavit," Cic. *Phil.* 2.44).[1] This remark can, however, hardly be taken as serious evidence for social practices; it is rather a typically hyperbolic piece of Ciceronian invective. These are fighting words, and the rhetoric makes the point that Curio and Antony were involved in a sexual relationship in which Antony, the younger partner, played the receptive role; the language of marriage is invoked so as to heap further scorn on Antony. Not only had he played the "woman's role" in the sexual relationship, but he was as much under Curio's control as a wife is under her husband's authority. Indeed, the centrality of the issue of subjugation is brought resolutely home in the sentence that immediately follows: "No boy purchased for lust's sake was ever as much under his master's control as you were under Curio's" ("nemo umquam puer emptus libidinis causa tam fuit in domini potestate quam tu in Curionis," 2.45). With *tam . . . quam* ("as much . . . as") we can compare the clause *tamquam stolam dedisset* ("as if he had given you a *stola*") in the preceding sentence; Cicero's description, in other words, does not imply that Curio and Antony were joined in *matrimonium* as legitimate spouses any more than it signifies that Curio purchased Antony as a slave.[2]

There are, however, later sources that explicitly speak of men who are married to other men and that cannot be so easily discounted. I begin with a survey; more detailed discussion will follow. Two of Martial's epigrams sardonically allude to such marriages (1.24, 12.42), and Juvenal's second satire includes a diatribe against effeminate aristocrats who celebrate their weddings to men (2.117–142). Suetonius, Tacitus, Dio Cassius, and Aurelius Victor tell us that the emperor Nero publicly celebrated at least two wedding ceremonies with males, one in which he was the groom and one or perhaps two in which he was the bride, and they provide stunning details: dowry was given, a bridal veil worn.[3] Both Dio Cassius and Lampridius (to whom the biography in the *Historia Augusta* is attributed) relate that the early third-century A.D. emperor Elagabalus was married as bride to a male partner, and the latter biographer also relates that the emperor's courtiers included old men with philosophical pretensions who boasted of having husbands (although the biographer reports that some people say that these courtiers did not actually have husbands, but only pretended to be married in order to imitate their emperor).[4] Finally, a legal text from the fourth century A.D. takes a firm stand against men who "marry in the manner of a woman," subjecting them to the death penalty.[5] Some scholars have argued that the verb "to marry" (*nubere*, regularly used of the bride's role in a wedding) is being used metaphorically here, and that this text addresses not men who were formally married to other men but rather men who played the bride's or woman's role in a sexual relationship with men.[6] This possibility cannot be excluded. But in view of the earlier references just reviewed, we also cannot exclude the possibility that the fourth-century emperors were setting out to curtail the specific practice of formal marriages between males. Indeed, such a coy metaphor (*nubere* signifying the receptive role in a sexual act) does not seem in keeping with the style of these legal texts, which elsewhere speak more directly, if euphemistically, of "men's bodies" being used in "feminine" ways.[7]

In short, the evidence certainly suggests that some Roman men participated in wedding ceremonies with other men and considered themselves to be married to those men. While we might be tempted to dismiss the stories regarding Nero and Elagabalus as unfounded gossip concerning unpopular emperors, the fact remains that the ancient sources speak of Nero's weddings, at least, as being publicly celebrated: this was not a case of malicious speculation regarding what went on behind the closed doors of the palace. Writing several decades after Nero's death, neither Martial nor, for all the acerbic bombast of his language, Juvenal seems to expect his readership to react to the existence of marriages between males with a start of unfamiliarity: disapproval perhaps, but not shock. The speaker in Juvenal's satire, while expressing a fear that the participants in such ceremonies will eventually want their weddings entered into the official registry (*acta diurna*), nonetheless imagines that, among those whose friends participate in them at any rate, such weddings are not particularly unusual;[8] of course the comment that these men will some day want their weddings entered into the public record shows that they were not so entered in Juvenal's day. Still, as a rule Martial and Juvenal appropriate actual practices in their satiric commentary on Roman society, and it seems that weddings between males, though certainly not officially sanctioned, were a feature of the social landscape, like (although perhaps less widespread than) such other practices as legacy-hunting, adultery, and oral sex, practices that these poets similarly used as fodder for satire. There is, in short, no compelling reason to doubt that Nero or Elagabalus actually engaged in the wedding ceremonies described in such evocative detail by ancient historians.[9]

But if these marriages were a feature of the social landscape, how acceptable were they? What cultural and legal status did they enjoy? Was marriage to another man a feasible option for a Roman man concerned with publicly maintaining his masculine image? There are a number of considerations that point to a negative answer to the last question. Firstly, Susan Treggiari's magisterial study of Roman marriage demonstrates that a (perhaps *the*) fundamental purpose of formal marriage between freeborn Romans was the production of legitimate children; the traditional phrase *liberorum quaerundorum causa*, "for the sake of begetting [freeborn] children" illustrates the ideology well.[10] It is also worth considering the very term *matrimonium*: derived from *mater* ("mother"), it illustrates the extent to which the institution was identified with the creation of a mother, simultaneously suggesting that the basic function of a wife was as mother. Note, too, the complementary concept of *patrimonium*: derived from *pater* ("father"), it signifies the property that is passed down from father to son. In other words, one could say that a basic function of Roman marriage was to make a *mater*, *pater*, and *liberi* ("freeborn children"), the *mater* serving the function of creating the *liberi* or legitimate offspring to whom the property of the *pater* could be handed down. Thus, *matrimonium* by definition required the presence of a woman. Moreover, despite the idealizing language of *concordia*, Roman marriage was an inherently hierarchical institution structured around the pervasive power-differential between freeborn Roman men and everyone else, in this case women. Spouses were *coniuges* (and thus "joined together"), to be sure, but no one had any illusions as to which of the two *coniuges* had the ultimate authority.[11]

In sum, *matrimonium* can be described as a private contract between a man and a woman (and their families) that had specific legal ramifications. A marriage between two men, while it might have had the same meaning in private as a traditional marriage between husband and wife—and might thus have permitted private understandings or renegotiations of the strictures that publicly constrained *viri*—could not have had the same public and, above all, legal status.[12] In this sense, "matrimony" (*matrimonium*) between two men was an anomaly in the conceptual and linguistic terms of traditional Roman belief systems. It was impossible for both men to keep their gendered identity as *viri* intact: one of them had to be the "wife." Indeed, in the uniformly hostile reports from outside observers that survive, the assumption is never challenged that one partner in a marriage must be the husband and the other the wife: there is a notable insistence upon the gendered model, and particularly the trappings of a traditional ceremony joining husband and wife (dowry, torches, veil, and the like) that were represented by those hostile sources as being grotesquely inappropriate. It may be worth pointing out the obvious fact that from the perspective of those men who actually participated in these weddings, things may well have been quite different. It may be equally worthwhile to insist on an important distinction: marriages between men were represented as anomalous not because of homophobic anxieties regarding intimacy between males, but rather because of hierarchical, androcentric assumptions regarding the nature of marriage. The fundamental problem was not that two men joined themselves to each other, but that one man was thought necessarily to play the role of the bride.

It is in fact precisely the figure of the male bride, rather than the concept of a male couple, that provokes the sometimes anxious reactions to these marriages found in the ancient sources. Even in Cicero's rhetorical application of the image of matrimony to Curio and Antony, we note that the object of the attack is the bride, Antony, and not the groom, Curio. The same dynamics are evident in Martial's two epigrams alluding to marriages between males. In one, we read that Callistratus (described as "bearded," probably suggesting that he had philosophical pretensions) was wedded to a man named Afer (described as "rigid": perhaps a double entendre) in a ceremony that included such traditional components as a dowry, the bridal veil, and the ritual cry "Talassio":

> Barbatus rigido nupsit Callistratus Afro,
>   hac qua lege viro nubere virgo solet.
> praeluxere faces, velarunt flammea vultus,
>   nec tua defuerunt verba, Talasse, tibi.
> dos etiam dicta est. nondum tibi, Roma, videtur
>   hoc satis? expectas numquid ut et pariat? (Mart. 12.42)[13]

> The bearded Callistratus became a bride to the rigid Afer, on the same terms with which a maiden is usually wedded to her husband. Torches led the way and a veil concealed his face; nor did you lack your invocation, Talassus. Even a dowry was provided. O Rome, don't you think this is enough already? Or are you waiting for him to give birth?

The apostrophe to Rome may suggest that what Callistratus has done is hardly unique and represents something that should be of concern to the entire city; in any case, it is the male bride Callistratus rather than his husband Afer who bears the brunt of the ridicule.

Martial's other reference to male marriages conjures up the same stock figure, the outwardly austere (even philosophical) man who in reality enjoys playing the receptive role in sexual relations with men:

> Aspicis incomptis illum, Deciane, capillis,
>   cuius et ipse times triste supercilium,
> qui loquitur Curios adsertoresque Camillos?
>   nolito fronti credere: nupsit heri. (Mart. 1.24)

> Decianus, do you see that man with unkempt hair, whose stern brow you yourself fear, who talks of the Curii and of the Camilli as his champions? Put no credence in his appearance: yesterday he became a bride.

The epigram's point comes with the single word *nupsit*, since the verb is regularly used of the bride and not of the groom.[14] The brevity of the remark may reflect the fact that the practice to which it refers was not entirely unheard of: there was no need to belabor the point. In any event it is once again the male bride, rather than the unnamed groom, who is singled out.

In Juvenal's second satire, the speaker portrays an aristocrat named Gracchus as a newly wedded bride reclining in the lap of her husband who is, in fact, a trumpeter (*cornicen*) and thus probably a slave:

> quadringenta dedit Gracchus sestertia dotem
> cornicini, sive hic recto cantaverat aere;
> signatae tabulae, dictum 'feliciter,' ingens
> cena sedet, gremio iacuit nova nupta mariti. (Juv. 2.117–20)

Gracchus has given a dowry of four hundred [thousand] sesterces to a trumpeter—or maybe he blew on a straight horn. The documents were signed and sealed; people shouted "Best wishes!"; they sat down to an enormous dinner; the newly wed bride lay in her husband's lap.[15]

Later in the same poem we read of male brides who are tormented by the realization that they cannot give birth to heirs and thereby keep a hold on their husbands—a fact for which the satiric speaker is glad:

> interea tormentum ingens nubentibus haeret
> quod nequeant parere et partu retinere maritos.
> sed melius, quod nil animis in corpora iuris
> natura indulget: steriles moriuntur . . . (Juv. 2.137–140)

Meanwhile these brides are afflicted by a great torment: they cannot bear children and hold on to their husbands by childbirth. So much the better, though, that nature grants their minds no jurisdiction over their bodies: they are sterile until the day they die . . .

It is notable that the brunt of the speaker's vitriolic disapproval falls upon these male brides and would-be mothers rather than on their husbands:

> scilicet horreres maioraque monstra putares,
> si mulier vitulum vel si bos ederet agnum?
> segmenta et longos habitus et flammea sumit
> arcano qui sacra ferens nutantia loro
> sudavit clipeis ancilibus. o pater urbis,
> unde nefas tantum Latiis pastoribus? unde
> haec tetigit, Gradive, tuos urtica nepotes?
> traditur ecce viro clarus genere atque opibus vir,
> nec galeam quassas, nec terram cuspide pulsas,
> nec quereris patri? (Juv. 2.122–31)

Surely you would shudder and think it a greater monstrosity if a woman gave birth to a calf or a cow to a lamb? Flounces, a long dress, and a veil: this is what is worn by one who [as a Salian priest] carried the sacred objects that swayed from the mystic strap, sweating under the figure-of-eight shields. O father of the city, where did so great a crime, now among your Latin shepherds, come from? Gradivus [Mars], where did this stinging nettle come from that has now struck your grandsons? Look! A man renowned for his family background and his wealth is handed over [in marriage] to a man, and you do not shake your helmet, or strike the ground with your spear-point, or complain to your father?

The "great crime" (*nefas tantum*) so loudly decried is not homosexual marriage but the fact that a man, and a noble one at that, is playing the woman's role, wearing the veil and being given to a husband, and a man of lower status at that, as his bride. Juvenal's speaker is apparently not interested in heaping abuse on the husbands of these pseudo-women.[16]

Much as Juvenal's satire inveighs against Gracchus and other male brides and avoids attacking their husbands, it is the male brides and not the bridegrooms who are singled out for scorn by Elagabalus' biographer:

> nupsit et coit cum illo ita ut et pronubam haberet clamaretque 'concide Magire,' et eo quidem tempore quo Zoticus aegrotabat. (SHA *Elagab*. 10.5)

> erant amici inprobi et senes quidam et specie philosophi, qui caput reticulo componerent, qui inproba quaedam pati se dicerent, qui maritos se habere iactarent. (ibid. 11.7)

> He was wedded and joined to him [Zoticus, nicknamed Magirus or "Cook"] as a bride in such a way that he had a matron of honor and shouted "Butcher me, Cook!"—even though Zoticus happened to be sick at the time.[17]

> He had shameless friends, certain old men who gave the appearance of being philosophers but who arranged their hair in nets, who would say that they had submitted to [*pati*, implying the receptive role in penetrative acts] some shameless things, and who bragged that they had husbands.

Dio is straightforward enough in his disparaging references to Elagabalus' own practices, noting that the emperor was called "wife," "mistress," and "queen," referring to the emperor's spouse (according to him, Hierocles rather than Zoticus) as "her husband," and reporting that when Elagabalus met Zoticus, who had been recommended to him for his impressive genital endowment, to Zoticus' formal greetings "sir" and "emperor," Elagabalus replied, "Don't call me 'sir'—I'm a lady."[18]

In the same way, Nero was attacked for having played the role of bride in weddings with male partners. According to Tacitus, in A.D. 64 Nero was formally married to his slave Pythagoras:

> inditum imperatori flammeum, missi auspices, dos et genialis torus et faces nuptiales, cuncta denique spectata quae etiam in femina nox operit. (Tac. *Ann*. 15.37)

> A veil was placed over the emperor, the interpreters of the auspices were sent; a dowry, a wedding bed and marriage torches—in the end, everything that is concealed by night even in the case of a woman was on display.

Suetonius mentions a wedding in which Nero was the bride to his freedman Doryphoros:

> . . . conficeretur a Doryphoro liberto; cui etiam, sicut ipsi Sporus, ita ipse denupsit, voces quoque et heiulatus vim patientium virginum imitatus. (Suet. *Nero* 29)

> He was finished off by his freedman Doryphoros, to whom he was wedded as a bride, just as Sporos had been wedded to Nero himself; Nero even imitated the words and cries of maidens being deflowered.

Since, as we will see, Suetonius also reports that Nero made Sporos his bride in a traditional ceremony, the implication is that Nero played the role of the bride to Doryphoros in a formal ceremony: dowry, veil, and all. Aurelius Victor repeats the story of Nero the bride, omitting the name of the bridegroom:

> ad extremum amictus nubentium virginum specie, palam senatu, dote data, cunctis festa more celebrantibus in manum conveniret lecto ex omnibus prodigiosis.
> (Aurel. Vict. *Caes.* 5.5)

> And finally, clothed in the manner of maidens who were being married, he was given in marriage to a man chosen from among his freaks, in the presence of the Senate, with a dowry given, and everyone celebrated it as if it were a holiday.

But in addition to being the bride to Doryphoros and Pythagoras,[19] Nero was also said to have played the role of bridegroom to a male, namely his former slave Sporos, to whom (according to Dio Cassius) Nero was first attracted because he physically resembled his dead wife Poppaea Sabina; Dio notes that the emperor had previously found a woman who reminded him of Poppaea. Both Dio (who places this among the events of A.D. 67) and Suetonius record that Nero had Sporos castrated and then took him as his wife in a formal public ceremony (Suetonius speaks of a dowry and bridal veil); thereafter Sporos was called "Sabina," "mistress," "queen," and "lady," the wedding was celebrated by both Greeks and Romans, and Sporos appeared in public with Nero on numerous occasions, adorned as an empress. This marriage prompted one daring man, when asked his opinion, to quip that he wished Nero's father had had a bride like Sporos. (Dio dutifully explains the joke for his slower-minded readers: "If that had happened, Nero would not have been born and the state would be free from its great evils.")[20] With regard to this Sporos, Plutarch and Dio report two fascinating details that have generally escaped scholarly notice. Plutarch relates that immediately after Nero's death (his corpse was still burning on the pyre, says Dio), Nymphidius Sabinus, Galba's principal rival in his claim to the succession, sent for Sporos, took him as his own wife and called him Poppaea. Although not using the language of marriage, Dio notes that Galba's successor Otho alienated many people by having relations with Sporos and generally associating with Nero's follow-ers.[21] It is intriguing indeed that these historians or their sources were able to imagine Nero's eunuch bride playing a role in the vicissitudes of the imperial succession.

It is also noteworthy that, according to Dio at least, the unnamed man was asked his opinion about Nero's marriage. Obviously it was a matter of some controversy, and indeed Dio reports (we cannot tell how accurately) that when a certain Gaius Julius Vindex was stirring up a rebellion against Nero in Britain he made good rhetorical use of Nero's marriages. In a speech reported by Dio, Vindex first cites the emperor's shameless plundering of the empire and murder of senators, along with his incestuous relations with and eventual murder of his mother. But such outrages, he continues, have been perpetrated by others before Nero. This emperor has gone further:

σφαγαὶ μὲν γὰρ καὶ ἁρπαγαὶ καὶ ὕβρεις καὶ ὑπ᾽ ἄλλων πολλαὶ πολλάκις ἐγένοντο – τὰ
δὲ δὴ λοιπὰ πῶς ἄν τις κατ᾽ ἀξίαν εἰπεῖν δυνηθείη; εἶδον, ὦ ἄνδρες φίλοι καὶ σύμμαχοι,
πιστεύσατέ μοι, εἶδον τὸν ἄνδρα ἐκεῖνον, εἴγε ἀνὴρ ὁ Σπόρον γεγαμηκώς, ὁ Πυθαγόρᾳ
γεγαμημένος, ἐν τῷ θεάτρου κύκλῳ καὶ ἐν τῇ ὀρχήστρᾳ ποτὲ μὲν κιθάραν ἔχοντα καὶ
ὀρθοστάδιον καὶ κοθόρνους, ποτὲ δὲ ἐμβάτας καὶ προσωπεῖον. (Dio 63.22.4)

Murder and plunder and outrageous abuse have often been perpetrated by others.
But as for the rest, how could one speak of it as it deserves? I have seen—trust me, my
friends and allies—I have seen that man (if the one who has been husband to Sporos
and bride to Pythagoras is in fact a man) in the midst of the theater and in the orches-
tra, sometimes holding a lyre and wearing a loose tunic and tragic actor's boots, at
other times wearing half-boots and a mask.

Clearly the ultimate disgrace is that the emperor has appeared on the public stage
as an actor.[22] Vindex cites Nero's two marriages parenthetically, by way of firing up
his audience's outrage, but the pressure of his rhetoric is clear: Nero's taking a
male bride and being one himself were bad enough, but his appearance on stage
was absolutely beyond the pale.[23] Here it is worth noting that when Aurelius Victor
records Nero's marriage to Pythagoras, in which the emperor played the role of
bride, he explicitly states his opinion that this offence was overshadowed by his
other crimes: his penchant for engaging in oral sexual practices, his practice of
castrating males, and his incest with his mother.[24]

Still, Dio has Vindex disparagingly deny Nero's masculinity in his snarling pa-
renthesis "if the one who has been husband to Sporos and bride to Pythagoras is in
fact a man." Acting as a bride was by Roman standards a clear enough abrogation of
masculinity, but why should Vindex assail Nero's masculinity for having acted as a
bridegroom to Sporos? It cannot be simply because Nero engaged in sexual relations with a male. Rather, I think it crucial that Nero had *castrated* Sporos, a fact that
both Suetonius and Dio emphasize. Moreover, Suetonius notes vaguely and omi-
nously that Nero had tried to transform Sporos into a woman in other ways as well,[25]
while Dio relates that Nero called him Sabina and appeared with him in public
(Suetonius adds that he gave him the *ornamenta* of empresses), and that others
referred to him as "mistress," "lady," and "queen." In other words, Nero feminized
Sporos to an extreme, even shocking degree.[26] This public flaunting of Sporos'
demasculinization may well have been perceived as a significant threat to masculine
privilege, and it may not be coincidental that among the male couples to which the
extant sources allude, Nero and Sporos constitute the only example in which the
"husband" rather than the "wife" is the specific object of criticism from outsiders.[27]

In sum, it seems clear that some Romans did participate in formal wedding
ceremonies in which one male was married to another (hostile outsiders imagined
the full ceremony, complete with dowry, bridal veil, and ritual acclamations) and that
these men considered themselves joined as spouses. But it is equally clear that such
marriages were, by traditional Roman standards, anomalous in view of the fundamental nature of *matrimonium*, a hierarchical institution that was aimed at creating
legitimate offspring as well as a route for the transmission of property (*patrimonium*)
and that required the participation of a woman as subordinate partner. In traditional
Roman terms, a marriage between two fully gendered "men" was inconceivable; if
two males were joined together, one of them had to be "the woman."[28]

A Note on the Sources

The great majority of the sources used in this study are literary texts of various genres; I here offer a brief overview of the most commonly cited texts, grouped by genre. This survey does not pretend to do justice to the various literary issues involved in the interpretation of these texts, but is merely intended both as an introductory guide for those unfamiliar with the Roman literary tradition and as an indication of how various types of ancient texts are useful to a study such as mine.

Dramatic texts are especially helpful in an attempt to reconstruct popular conceptions of gender and sexual behavior. This is above all true of the scripts of Roman comedies. For their humor to be successful, the playwrights must have been responding to beliefs and prejudices found among their audiences. Thus we can ask: What was funny to Romans in the area of sexual behavior, and what was not? The characters in comedy may well represent extremes, and the jokes may be outrageous, but in order for them to have raised a laugh, they must in the end have been an exaggeration of real phenomena. In other words, there must have been a difference in quantity rather than in quality between what Roman audiences saw and heard on stage and what they saw and heard around them in everyday life.

The interpretation of the earliest surviving plays, those of **Plautus** (d. ca. 184 B.C.) and **Terence** (ca. 190 B.C.–159 B.C.), is complicated by the fact that their comedies are adaptations of Greek originals. But, as we saw in chapter 1, in the case of Plautus in particular the plays are securely anchored in the Roman realities of their audiences and we can, with care, use the plays as evidence for Roman attitudes and mores. The comedies of such writers as **Afranius** (b. ca. 150 B.C.), **Pomponius** (fl. ca. 100–85 B.C.), and **Novius** (fl. ca. 95–80 B.C.) do not present that difficulty, as they were not directly inspired by Greek originals. Their principal difficulty arises from the fact that no single play is preserved in its entirety, and we have to rely on fragments, mostly in the form of brief quotations by later lexicographers and grammarians (such as **Festus** [late second century A.D.] and **Nonius Marcellus** [early fourth century A.D.]).

Humorous exaggeration also characterizes Roman satire, a genre that Quintilian claims to be entirely Roman,[1] and whose most outstanding authors are **Lucilius** (d. 102/1 B.C.), **Horace** (65–8 B.C.), **Persius** (A.D. 34–62), and **Juvenal** (d. after A.D. 127). These four poets wrote in very different times, but as satirists they share certain basic features. The narrative voice of the satiric poem attacks the foibles and vices of contemporaries, in a tone ranging from the bemused to the savage. But, as with comedy, the poetic persona must have been perceived by a Roman readership as responding to something real, however exaggerated.[2] Thus, satire opens a window on to the social realities of its time. Moreover, the satirist's persona sets itself up as normative: we hear the voice of a Roman man who would have his masculine identity seem unimpeachable, and who addresses an audience of men likewise interested in projecting a traditionally masculine image. With that consideration in mind, we can look at the sorts of assumptions regarding men's sexual experiences that are made in the texts of satire.

The writers of epigrams, including **Catullus** (? 84–54 B.C.), **Martial** (ca. A.D. 40–104), and the anonymous author or authors of the **Priapea** (late first century B.C. or early first century A.D.), likewise offer extensive commentary on the practices and attitudes of the Romans among whom they lived, at the same time maintaining staunchly masculine personae themselves.[3] Like satire, epigrams open windows onto various types of people who were obviously familiar to their Roman readers. To be sure, Martial claims that his poetry satirizes vices rather than specific individuals (10.33.9–10). Thus, we cannot know anything about the individuals behind his characters (whether, for example, Martial's Zoilus is simply a disguised version of a real man whom Martial knew, or a composite of various individuals). Neither is that unanswerable question particularly significant for our purposes: the important question is what is represented in these texts as normal or deviant. Similar principles can guide our reading of ancient prose narratives: often called *novels*, the **Satyricon** of **Petronius** (d. A.D. 65) and the **Metamorphoses** of **Apuleius** (b. ca. A.D. 123) share with epigrams and satire a tendency to portray a world that their readers would recognize as an exaggerated version of their own world.[4] In the end, the characters and humorous situations of satire, epigrams, and the novel (like those of comedy) must have responded to and thus reflected the conceptual predispositions of Roman readers.

The same is true of a very different genre, the eminently serious epic poetry of which the most celebrated example is the *Aeneid* of **Virgil** (70–19 B.C.). This poem (like such others as **Valerius Flaccus' Argonautica** [completed before A.D. 93] or **Statius' Thebaid** [published ca. A.D. 91]) is set in a mythic past before Rome existed, and thus has a less obvious relationship to the realities of living in the

Rome of the first centuries B.C. and A.D. Still, these epics, and above all the *Aeneid*—which evokes the mythic origins of the Roman people and has some fairly clear resonances for the political situation of its time—must ultimately have appealed to their Roman readership's sense of morality and propriety, of the overall order of things. Indeed, sometimes this relevance is undisguised, as in Virgil's evocation of the Roman ideal of the *univira* (or *one-man woman*) in his narrative of the fate of the mythic Carthaginian queen Dido (see chapter 3).

Roman love poetry, often called "elegy" after its characteristic meter, and represented by the works of **Catullus** (? 84–54 B.C.), **Tibullus** (d. 19 B.C.), and **Propertius** (d. before 2 B.C.), as well as the *Amores* of **Ovid** (43 B.C.–A.D. 17), who also wrote an extensive didactic treatise called the *Ars Amatoria* or *Art of Love*, represents a blend of the seriousness of epic with the comic elements of epigram in its evocation of the ecstatic pleasures and depressing heartache of being in love. Here, too, if the poetry was to communicate, the persona of the lover must have seemed basically realistic, albeit exaggerated, to the Roman readership. Since this persona is that of a man, the poetry appeals to common notions of masculinity, although we saw in chapter 4 that in this particular genre there is an interesting tendency to play with and even to subvert traditional concepts of masculinity. In any case, the beloved in this poetry can be either male or female.

Quite different are various prose texts of a historical or biographical nature that set out to describe to their readers the events of the Roman past or the lives of great men. Authors of such texts include **Nepos** (ca. 99–24 B.C.), who wrote biographies of foreign leaders for a Roman readership; **Livy** (? 59 B.C.–A.D. 17), who wrote a monumental history of Rome from its foundation to his own times that survives only in portions; **Tacitus** (b. ca. A.D. 56), whose partially surviving *Annals* stretched from the death of Augustus in A.D. 14 to A.D. 69, and whose *Histories*, also partially preserved, covered the period from A.D. 69 to A.D. 96; **Suetonius** (b. ca. A.D. 69), who wrote biographies of the "twelve Caesars" from Julius Caesar (d. 44 B.C.) to Domitian (d. A.D. 96); and the various contributors to the so-called *Historia Augusta* (from the third century A.D. or later), which includes biographies of the emperors who ruled from A.D. 117 to A.D. 284. Greek writers whose discussions of Roman history are especially useful include **Polybius** (ca. 200–after 118 B.C.), **Plutarch** (after A.D. 50–after A.D. 120), and **Dio Cassius** (late second and early third centuries A.D.). With all of these texts I am less interested in assessing the historical veracity of what the writers report than I am concerned with the attitudes, beliefs, and practices that they attribute to Romans, as well as the assumptions regarding Rome's past that the writers themselves display. Given the tendency of ancient historians to be explicitly moralistic, this often turns out to be less difficult than one might have thought.

A text that is particularly helpful is **Valerius Maximus'** first-century A.D. compilation of *Memorable Deeds and Sayings* (*Facta et Dicta Memorabilia*). This work, designed for Roman orators seeking material on such diverse topics as omens and prodigies (1.5, 1.6), military discipline (2.7), old age (8.13), avarice (9.4), lustfulness and luxury (9.1), and sexual morality (6.1), is useful to us not only for its content (it preserves sometimes priceless anecdotes) but also for the profoundly traditional morality that informs its narratives. Valerius Maximus is a self-conscious conduit of Roman traditionalism, and his work simultaneously reinforces and re-produces quintessentially Roman ideals.

An equally self-conscious traditionalist is **Cicero** (106–43 B.C.), whose exten-sive corpus of speeches written for delivery in courtrooms, in the meeting places of the Senate, or at assemblies of citizens constitutes an extremely valuable source for our inquiry. As K. J. Dover notes in his 1974 study *Greek Popular Morality*, a speaker in such situations wants above all to persuade his audience—whether it is a political body or a jury—and consequently will not risk offending commonly held beliefs.[5] Indeed, Cicero and other Roman orators often explicitly appeal to the exalted *mos maiorum* or "custom of the ancestors," adopting the persona of an ordinary Roman with whose eminently traditional set of beliefs no one could pos-sibly disagree. Another characteristic of Ciceronian oratory is its penchant for in-vective, a notorious feature of ancient oratory in general. Here too, I am less inter-ested in whether the often outrageous slurs that Cicero makes of his opponents had any basis in fact than I am concerned with determining what kinds of behav-iors could be subjected to Cicero's eloquent scorn.

Finally, there are some specialized classes of ancient writing: letters; declama-tion and works of rhetorical theory; scientific and medical texts; philosophical writ-ings; and legal texts. For letters of varying degrees of formality, we have the writ-ings of **Cicero**, **Seneca the Younger** (d. A.D. 65), and **Pliny the Younger** (ca. A.D. 61–112). Surviving rhetorical works include the anonymous *Rhetorica ad Herennium* (ca. 86–82 B.C.) and those written by **Cicero**, **Seneca the Elder** (ca. 55 B.C.–A.D. 40), and **Quintilian** (b. A.D. 30–5): these texts provided explicit theo-rizing and practical guidance for would-be orators, and thus offer us glimpses into how Roman speakers might have gone about the business of persuading their au-diences and manipulating their sense of morality. Collections of declamations, or set speeches on various legal and moral topics, include those attributed to **Quintilian** and **Calpurnius Flaccus** (second century A.D.). Writings of a scien-tific nature include the encyclopedic *Natural History* of **Pliny the Elder** (A.D. 23/4–79), the medical treatises of **Caelius Aurelianus** (fifth century A.D.) based on the work of the Greek medical writer Soranos (first century A.D.), and the astro-logical treatise of **Firmicus Maternus** (fourth century A.D.). Such texts attempt to explain to their Roman readership various aspects of the world around them, often recording popular preconceptions and generally expressing a more or less tradi-tional moral outlook. Pliny's compendium of natural phenomena, for example, clearly participates in the moralizing tradition pervading Roman literature, and as a result it has been suggested that "Pliny provides the student of cultural history with an invaluable balance to more overtly intellectual writers."[6] Indeed, philo-sophical texts like those of Cicero (such as his *Tusculan Disputations*), Seneca the Younger (such as his *Epistulae Morales*), and **Musonius Rufus** (first century A.D.) present a special challenge for inquiries into cultural traditions, as the voice of these texts is pitched for a particular audience, one interested in the pursuit of philosophy: indeed, philosophical writers sometimes explicitly contrast their own beliefs with those of Romans as a group. Still, although the *conclusions* that Cicero and Seneca may draw cannot be used as evidence for Roman popular morality or traditional ideologies,[7] their arguments very often play off of precisely those ideologies and thus can be helpful in our attempt to reconstruct those ideologies, if used with care. In the end, Cicero and Seneca wrote even their philosophical works with the goal of convincing an audience of Roman men, and to that extent they would have sought to appeal to commonly inherited habits of speech and conceptualization just as would an orator in the courtroom.

Finally there are texts relating to Roman law, most notably the **Digest**, a collection of more than three centuries' worth of jurisprudential writings assembled in the sixth century A.D. This and similar texts are useful not only because they preserve some of the actual provisions of Roman law but also because they record the perspectives of a range of ancient legal thinkers.

In addition to these literary sources, we also have the evidence of formal inscriptions (epitaphs, in particular) and of informal messages (graffiti) scrawled on walls all over the Roman world. Such graffiti have been found in Rome itself, its port city of Ostia, and above all on the walls of Pompeii, the small city on the Bay of Naples that was buried in the cataclysmic eruption of Mount Vesuvius in August of A.D. 79. Of course, these messages were produced by and for the literate only, and the literacy rate in antiquity was nowhere near as high as it is today.[8] Still, we can be confident that these graffiti were written by and for a broader cross-section of society than the literary texts, and that they thus constitute a kind of control evidence.[9] Many of these usually anonymous messages have to do with sexual behavior (for example, a man boasting of his conquests or insulting someone else in sexual terms), and the preconceptions and prejudices detectable in these graffiti fall squarely in line with the evidence of the literary texts.

NOTES

Introduction

1. There is an obvious but significant limitation on our source material: the ideologies of masculinity that we are considering turn out to be the province of men who are usually upper class and always free. Although the graffiti scratched on the walls of Rome and Pompeii and the rude messages incised on sling bullets at Perugia do help correct the bias of the literary sources (in fact, they generally confirm the literary evidence), we are almost entirely denied the ability of hearing the voices of women, lower-class men, slaves, or, indeed, upper-class men who chose to live in ways that countered the prevalent codes (cf. Richlin 1993). But I am seeking to make a virtue of this necessity by aiming to expose the workings of a code of sexual behavior precisely as the dominant ideology.

2. See Gilmore 1990 for a cross-cultural study of masculinity from an anthropological perspective, and Cornwall and Lindisfarne 1994 and Berger, Wallis, and Watson 1995 for further, more theoretically oriented, discussion. The questions that I ask obviously stem from a quintessentially feminist problematization of gender, but since claiming the label *feminist* could be interpreted as an act of appropriation, I will simply say that this work owes an enormous debt to its feminist predecessors. See Tong 1989 for a helpful overview of feminist theory, and Rabinowitz and Richlin 1993 for illustrations of a feminist approach to classical scholarship. Like feminist scholarship, the growing tradition in which my study is placed aims to historicize certain oppressive paradigms and thus to challenge them.

3. What constitutes the "sexual" (and how it might differ from the "erotic") is, of course, a problem; genital stimulation, for example, is not necessarily a decisive criterion.

4. See, for example, Hallett 1993. In particular, scholars point to the varieties of cultural traditions contributing to the fabric of the Roman Empire.

5. I will sometimes also use texts written in Greek for a Greek audience: descriptions of social realities among Romans from an outsider's perspective can be very useful. See appendix 3 for an overview of my sources and their utility.

6. A book-length study of this nature has not previously been published. Among articles, Veyne 1978 and Veyne 1985 have many helpful insights, but they are brief sketches with little documentation or close reading of ancient texts. Fantham 1991 anticipates some of the conclusions of chapter 3, but differs from my analysis in its assumption that the analytical category of homosexuality can be applied to the ancient material. Richlin 1993 offers a thought-provoking discussion of the figure of the *cinaedus*, but see chapter 5 for my theoretical disagreements with some of its premises. See the same chapter for my responses to the central argument of Taylor 1997, that there were "homosexual subcultures" in ancient Rome. Among monographs, Lilja 1983 is a review of the Republican and Augustan sources that begins from the premise that "though Greek and Latin had no terms corresponding to 'homosexual' and 'heterosexual,' these modern terms, of course, can be applied to the Greeks and Romans as naturally as so many other terms which have no equivalents in the ancient languages" (p. 9, n. 17); it thus dismisses in a footnote an issue central to my study. Another major point of divergence between Lilja's study and mine stems from her belief in significant diachronic change. Richlin 1992a is an indispensable and groundbreaking study of the workings of Roman sexual humor that is rich in insights into ancient representations of sexual practices, but it does not attempt the kind of survey with regard to such practices between males that I am aiming for. Cantarella 1992 paints a picture in some ways similar to mine, but her strokes are often quite broad and her interpretation of specific details is sometimes problematic. Moreover, see below for my disagreement with her arguments for diachronic change.

7. I thank David Halperin for helping me to formulate this point. Much the same could be said about the very concept of the "sexual" and its relationship to such other concepts as the "social" or the "political."

8. Cf. Halperin 1990: 40: "To the extent, in fact, that histories of 'sexuality' succeed in concentrating their focus on *sexuality*, to just that extent are they doomed to fail as *histories* (Foucault himself taught us that much), unless they also include as an integral part of their proper enterprise the the task of demonstrating the historicity, conditions of emergence, modes of construction, and ideological contingencies of the very categories of analysis that undergird their own practice." See Halperin's article "Homosexuality" in the third edition of the *Oxford Classical Dictionary* for further discussion and Katz 1995 on modern concepts of heterosexuality.

9. Fantham 1991: 279, 285, and 286, respectively.

10. Richlin 1993 (e.g., 526, 530).

11. Taylor 1997: 322, 326, 327, 348–9. Taylor uses the words "homosexual" and "homosexuality" with reference to "men who found primary fulfillment in same-sex unions that at times involved the assumption of the passive role" (322), but the qualifications ("primary" and "at times") reveal the inherent difficulty of trying to fit ancient sexual stereotypes into the modern category of the homosexual. See chapter 5 for further discussion.

12. Cantarella 1992: vii.

13. Cantarella 1992: 100; cf. 120 ("homosexuality was undergoing a sea-change" over the course of the second century B.C.; yet on the next page she observes that some Roman love poems addressed to boys from the late second century B.C. are cited by their ancient source "side by side with ones on heterosexual love. No distinction is drawn"); 126 ("what the Romans thought permissible in the line of homosexuality" for a man meant "relationships with slaves" before marriage but not afterwards); 128 ("a new model of homosexual relationships"); 137 (a transformation within "Roman homosexual culture"); 145 ("we must

try to understand the effective social and moral evaluation of homosexuality"); and elsewhere. Each one of these statements gets at a certain truth, but the truths in each case have to do with sexual practices in general, not an artificially delimited homosexuality. We could replace "homosexual(ity)" with "heterosexual(ity)" in every one of the above sentences without altering its truth. Like Cantarella, Robert 1997: 52 is careful to note that "l'homosexualité est un terme récent et qui n'a, à Rome, aucune signification (nous ne l'utiliserons que par commodité)," but his occasional uses of the concept "par commodité" are revealing, as when his language implies that men who are anally penetrated are somehow more "homosexual" than the men who penetrate them. Nero, he writes, "était persuadé que nul homme ne s'abstenait de relations homosexuelles (comprenons: ne se privait de jouer le rôle passif dans ces relations)" (258).

14. Lilja 1983: 122.

15. Matters are complicated here by hierarchical notions of gender: sexual relations between Roman *women* and their male slaves are not directly comparable to those between Roman men and their male slaves (see chapter 1).

16. Or is it XY? In any case, it has meaning only in relation to the logically prior concepts of homosexuality and heterosexuality.

17. Boswell 1990: 69–70 argues that the absence of such terms in Latin is not necessarily significant, pointing to certain linguistic anomalies in English (e.g., the lack of an abstraction for "aunts" and "uncles" comparable to "siblings," or the lack of gender distinction between male and female cousins as opposed to the French *cousin/cousine*) that prove little or nothing with regard to conceptual systems. But those linguistic data can be described (as Boswell indeed implies) as exceptions that prove a rule, or alternatively as ultimately insignificant gaps within a larger discursive system of kinship relations. With regard to orientational labels, however, the triad homosexual/heterosexual/bisexual *constitutes* the system. The absence of corresponding terms in Latin and Greek cannot be represented as an exception or fluke. Rather, the entire system is lacking.

18. Because I avoid speaking of homosexuality and homosexuals in antiquity, it follows that I cannot predicate homophobia of ancient Romans. Here I part ways from Richlin, who argues that "'homosexual' in fact describes, in Roman terms, the male penetrated by choice" (1993: 526), and that the existence of passive men identified as homosexual was "marked both by homophobia within the culture and by social and civil restrictions" (1993: 530). See chapter 5 for my arguments against these views.

19. Thus at Juvenal 2.47–50 Laronia draws a parallel between male-male and female-female sexual behavior, claiming that no women perform cunnilinctus, whereas countless men fellate and are penetrated by other men. But I would note the typical Roman emphasis in that passage on physical practices and the accompanying problematization of receptive males only, and not their insertive partners. As I will argue in chapter 5, this kind of statement is significantly different from a late twentieth-century claim that "There are many gay men, but no gay women."

20. Here I refer to popular conceptions of human sexuality; the rather specialized circle of sexologists has sometimes seen things differently. In popular American discourse, however, the question "Is he gay or straight?" has real meaning and expects a definite answer, while people who cannot easily be described as either gay or straight produce noticeable consternation and confusion. A man who is married with children but fond of an occasional encounter with another man, and who may describe himself as bisexual, might be declared, for example, to be "*actually* gay."

21. McIntosh 1968 (quote taken from p. 183).

22. Weeks 1977: 2–3.

23. Greenberg 1988: 14.

24. For Greece, see Dover 1978, Foucault 1985 and 1986, Halperin 1990, Winkler 1990; for Renaissance Florence, Rocke 1996; for Japan, Schalow 1989; for Native American cultures, Whitehead 1981, Walter L. Williams 1986, and Roscoe 1991; for Melanesia, Herdt 1981 and 1993; for New York City, Chauncey 1994.

25. In this regard I follow Veyne 1978 and 1985, Foucault 1986, Cantarella 1992, and Edwards 1993 (e.g., p. 66). Richlin 1993, arguing that the *cinaedi* were identified as homosexual and subject to homophobia, resists the trend, as does Taylor 1997, positing a homosexual subculture in Rome.

26. See n. 24 for some basic bibliography; Greenberg 1988 offers an encyclopedic overview.

27. Cf. Greenberg 1988: 25; Halperin 1990; Duberman et al. 1989: 8–11.

28. For ancient images of sexual practices between women, see Kroll 1924, Hallett 1989, Cantarella 1992: 164–71, and Brooten 1996. It should be noted that the English translation of Cantarella's work contains a significant error on this point: her remark that in Artemidorus' book on the interpretation of dreams "i rapporti fra donne, a differenza di quelli fra uomini, sono collocati fra quelli 'contro natura'" (1988: 217) is rendered thus: "Relations between women, like those between men, are grouped among dreams 'contrary to nature'" (1992: 169). Of course, as the Italian original makes clear and indeed as Cantarella 1992: 204–6 demonstrates, the truth is precisely the opposite of what the English translation claims: dreams of sexual activity between males are included among those that are "according to nature." In general, as Cantarella observes, "female homosexuality was evaluated by a Roman male in a very different way from his view of the homosexual aspect of his own virile bisexuality" (164).

29. Ov. *Met.* 10.162–219, 3.339–510. Note too the passing reference to Narcissus as an object of attention from both men and women (3.353: "multi illum iuvenes, multae cupiere puellae"), an erotic configuration that the text portrays as entirely normal.

30. See Kennedy 1993 for a complex problematization of the representation/reality antithesis as it applies to Roman literature.

31. Paul Veyne's comments on the word *discourse*, often associated with the work of Michel Foucault, are worth bearing in mind: "Je rapelle que, chez Foucault, ce mot trompeur de discours n'a *justement* rien à voir avec ce qui est 'dit' et avec les tartes à la crème de la sémiologie et la linguistique, mais qu'il désigne au contraire ce qui est préconceptuel et non-dit" (Veyne 1978: 52).

32. Françoise Gonfroy made the point well in an early and groundbreaking article: "Ce n'est bien sûr pas l'authenticité historique des 'délits' concernés qui importe, mais l'idéologie que les accusations et moqueries mettent en lumière" (Gonfroy 1978: 221). See also Richlin 1993: 538–9 and Edwards 1993: 12: "We cannot get any closer to the ancient Romans than to the texts we read; we need to recognise that, for us, these highly rhetorical texts are Roman reality. Rather than trying to see through them, we can choose to look at them—an enterprise which can prove entertaining as well as enlightening."

33. At Catullus 16.5–6, for example, we read that whereas a poet ought himself to be chaste, his verses need not be: "nam castum esse decet pium poetam / ipsum, versiculos nihil necesse est." But this assertion of a gap between poetry and poet describes itself as a response to an accusation of effeminacy; the verses could thus be said to support the contention that Roman readers were predisposed to make conclusions about poets from their poetry. See chapter 5 for further discussion of this text, and see especially Selden 1992 for the slipperiness of the stance adopted here by the poetic speaker. For the ancient tendency to identify narrative voice and author, see, e.g., Skinner 1997: 132 and David Konstan, "The Death of Argus, or What Stories Do: Audience Response in Ancient Fiction and Theory," *Helios* 18 (1991): 15–30.

34. All translations of ancient texts in this book are my own. My aim has been to convey the sense and, to some extent, the tone of the original; I make no claim of literary artistry.

35. Cf. Winkler 1990: 20: "We are not simply trying to 'map' a culture and find its system or complex of competing systems. . . . Rather we would like to make some statements about that social conglomerate which manage both to characterize the fundamental conventions or protocols and to show the limits of their application to real lives."

36. I do not aspire to a comprehensive survey of all relevant texts, but rather to an overview that is simultaneously broad and deep.

37. Dover 1974 constitutes a paradigm for this methodology (see especially his introductory chapter, pp. 1–45), and Dover 1978 represents one application of this approach to the question of sexual behavior. See Richlin 1992a: xxvii and Edwards 1993: 9–19, 24–8. It should be noted that the interpretations of ancient texts I will be offering here make no claim to being a "full appreciation" (a chimerical notion anyway). Instead, like any reader, I approach texts with specific interests and agendas, and my readings reflect those interests and agendas. If my readings contribute to an understanding of some of the ways in which words on a page or on a wall became a "text" for a Roman readership, I will be content.

38. Lilja 1983: 12.

39. So too Wiseman 1985: 3, and Richlin 1993: 531. See also Boswell 1980: 71–2. In general, as John Crook (*Law and Life of Rome* [Ithaca, 1967], p. 9) puts it, "the 'Roman Revolution' was a revolution of government, not of social structure; and in the age of the Principate the ground-bass of both society and law remained the same, however subtle and remote the variations played above it."

40. Robert 1997, for example, schematizes the history of Roman sexual morality in terms of a progression from early Republican *vertu* to late Republican *jouissance* to *passion* under the first centuries of the Roman Empire and finally to *tempérance* in late antiquity. While his schematization is balder than most, something like this pattern is either implicitly or explicitly proposed by a number of other scholars, such as Cantarella 1992.

41. Cantarella 1992: 148–64 (the quotation is from p. 154). Cf. Robert 1997: 258: "Si l'on juge par la force de la charge lancée contre ces *pathici*, non seulement leur nombre s'est accru sous l'Empire, mais surtout ils ne se cachent même plus."

42. Similarly weak is the argument of Robert 1997: 261 that certain inscriptions from first-century A.D. Pompeii reveal a previously unattested (because traditionally disapproved) celebration of a romantic sort of love: "Il faut noter une évolution que transmet la poésie de certaines inscriptions. L'amour n'est plus un tabou, comme au temps de Caton. Il s'affiche, se célèbre, et se vit dans la joie." This, too, rests on an argument from silence: we simply have no comparable graffiti from earlier periods.

43. Compare the sensible remarks at Boswell 1980: 71: "The only historical basis for these notions [of an increased tolerance of homosexuality in the Empire] is the relatively greater occurrence of references to homosexual behavior in imperial than in republican literature. Information about almost every single aspect of Roman life survives in greater abundance from the Empire than from the Republic. It cannot be shown that *proportionally* more evidence survives from imperial than republican Rome regarding gay people and acts." On the other hand, I am uncomfortable with the reference to "gay people and acts" in antiquity, and Boswell goes on, anticipating Cantarella, to claim that prejudice against men who played the receptive role "declined considerably" in the early Empire, "possibly because some emperors were known as or admitted to being passive" (75). To support his thesis, he claims that Juvenal 9 suggests that "there is no hint . . . that it is scandalous for an adult citizen to be employing an *active* prostitute," but one of the points of the poem is precisely that such behavior is scandalous in the extreme.

44. Cantarella 1992: 154.

45. Taylor 1997 advances a hypothesis similar to Cantarella's, but, taking Pomponius into account, he pushes the date back, arguing that by the first century B.C. "habitual sexual behavior among adult males seemed a dangerous new development to the moralists" (346). This, too, is based on the same argument from silence that weakens Cantarella's hypothesis: he notes elsewhere, for example, that the word *cinaedus* "like so many words . . . is not attested earlier than Plautus" (351), and that "aristocratic and domestic effeminates in the Greek style begin appearing in Rome during or shortly after Plautus's time, as we know from various fragments attributed to the elder Cato" (345). But the corpus of Plautus's plays constitutes the earliest extensive, nonfragmentary literary source that survives. As Taylor himself notes, Plautus provides the earliest attestation of a great many words; we cannot conclude that, simply because a word first appears in Plautus, the practices or beliefs to which it refers had only recently arisen. Who knows what kinds of sexual stereotypes were exploited in the subliterary farces and mimes staged at Rome well before Plautus' time and now lost?

46. Between the second and fourth centuries A.D. there did, however, occur a gradual but decisive transformation in the realm of Roman morality, as witnessed by an increasingly ascetic approach to the body in general and sexual practices in particular. This process culminated in the problematization of all sexual activity not considered strictly necessary, i.e., not leading to procreation. This paradigm, which eventually triumphed under the reinforcing influence of Christianity, necessarily entailed the condemnation of homosexual practices per se. (See Veyne 1978; Boswell 1980: 119–36; Rousselle 1988; Foucault 1986; Boswell 1990: 73–5; Cantarella 1992: 187–210.) But this mode of conceptualizing sexual practices stands in marked and illustrative contrast with the traditional ethic inherited by the audiences and readerships of Plautus, Catullus, Cicero, and Martial that is the subject of the present study.

47. See especially Richlin's essay "The Ethnographer's Dilemma and the Dream of a Lost Golden Age" in Rabinowitz and Richlin 1993: 272–303.

48. I take it to be a sign of the phallocentric nature of Roman traditions that, apart from cunnilinctus (which is itself distinctly problematized), nonpenetrative acts such as mutual masturbation among males are very rarely mentioned (see chapter 5).

49. For the notion of gender as performance, see especially Judith P. Butler, *Gender Trouble: Feminism and the Subversion of Identity* (New York, 1990).

Chapter 1

1. Hor. *Epist.* 2.1.156: "Graecia capta ferum victorem cepit."

2. More recent work (with references to earlier scholarship) includes Petrochilos 1974; Balsdon 1979; Ferrary 1988; Gruen 1990; MacMullen 1991; Gruen 1992; see Edwards 1993: 22–4 for a concise overview. Important studies of the literary problems include Fraenkel 1960, Williams 1968, and Griffin 1985.

3. By "pederasty" I mean *paiderastia*, or publicly celebrated romantic and sexual relationships between mature, bearded citizen males and freeborn adolescent males who were conventionally called *paides* ("boys": see discussion later in this chapter). See further, chapter 2.

4. Wilkinson 1978: 136.

5. MacMullen 1982: 488, 491.

6. Cf. Richlin 1992a: 223 (originally published in 1982): "While it cannot be denied that erotic epigram has a Hellenistic form, the Greek and Asiatic influence on Roman pederasty must be seen as an augmentation, not as the basis." More than sixty-five years

ago, Wilhelm Kroll expressed a similar view in an insightful article that is often unjustly ignored: "Bei einer Sitte, die sich so leicht von selbst einstellt, auf fremden Einfluß zu schließen, ist mißlich" (Kroll 1988: 93; the article was originally published in *Zeitschrift für Sexualwissenschaft und Sexualpolitik* 17 [1930], 145–78).

7. Veyne 1978: 50: "Il est faux que l'amour 'grec' soit, à Rome, d'origine grecque: comme plus d'une société méditerranéenne de nos jours encore, Rome n'a jamais opposé l'amour des femmes à celui des garçons: elle a opposé l'activité à la passivité; être actif, c'est être un mâle, quel que soit le sexe du partenaire passif."

8. Veyne 1985: 28–9. I quote from the English translation published in the 1985 collection *Western Sexuality*. The original article, "L'homosexualité à Rome," appeared in *Communications* 35 (1982): 26–33.

9. Cantarella 1992: 104.

10. According to J. P. V. D. Balsdon (*Romans and Aliens* [London, 1979], p. 225), Cicero believed that "homosexuality . . . could not have originated spontaneously in Rome; it must have been caught like an infection from abroad, from Greece"; Verstraete 1980: 227 argues that "the pervasive Hellenization of Roman society in the second and first centuries B.C. mitigated the traditional hostility towards homosexuality and homosexual relations"; Jocelyn 1985: 13–4 claims that "for the average upper-class Roman the reality [of "pederasty"] was something Greek and rather distasteful, even when the love object was a slave or a foreigner" (although Jocelyn uses the term *pederasty*, he clearly means male homosexual behavior as a whole); Dalla 1987: 10 concludes that "il *mos Graecorum* diviene così sinonimo di omoerotismo e pederastia"; Hallett 1988: 1274 states that "Roman society of the second century B.C. thought of male homosexuality as a Greek custom"; Hallett 1989: 223 speaks of "republican Roman references to male same-sex love as a Greek import"; Edwards 1993: 94 writes of "Roman claims that homosexuality was a Greek practice which was adopted in the later republic by some Romans"; and Taylor 1997: 348 argues that "the Romans blamed 'unnatural' homosexual acts on Greece or the barbarians."

11. Greenberg 1988 offers an encyclopedic overview, with extensive bibliography. Subsequent studies include: for ancient Greece Halperin 1990, Winkler 1990, and Cohen 1991; for seventeenth-century Japan, Schalow 1989 together with his 1990 translation of Ihara Saikaku's *Great Mirror of Male Love*, and Gary P. Leupp, *Male Colors: The Construction of Homosexuality in Tokugawa Japan (1603–1868)* (Berkeley, 1995); for seventeenth-century China, Vivien W. Ng, "Homosexuality and the State in Late Imperial China," Duberman et al. 1989: 76–89, and Charlotte Furth, "Androgynous Males and Deficient Females: Biology and Gender Boundaries in Sixteenth- and Seventeenth-Century China," Abelove et al. 1993: 479–97; for Native American cultures, Walter L. Williams 1986 and Roscoe 1991; for Polynesian societies, Besnier 1994; for contemporary Islamic cultures, Schmitt and Sofer 1991 and Murray and Roscoe 1997; for Melanesian cultures, Herdt 1993.

12. Thus a passage from the so-called *Sibylline Oracles* (*Or. Sib.* 3.596–600), speaking from a Jewish perspective, contrasts the sexual practices of the Jews, whose men do not engage in "impure" relations with "male children," with those of the rest of the known world, including the Egyptians, Greeks, Persians, Asians, and Romans: κοὐδὲ πρὸς ἀρσενικοὺς παῖδας μίγνυνται ἀνάγνως, / ὅσσα τε Φοίνικες Αἰγύπτιοι ἠδὲ Λατῖνοι / Ἑλλάς τ' εὐρύχορος καὶ ἄλλων ἔθνεα πολλά / Περσῶν καὶ Γαλατῶν πάσης τ᾽ Ἀσίης παραβάντες / ἀθανάτοιο θεοῦ ἁγνὸν νόμον . . .

13. Livy 34.4.1–2 reconstructs a speech that Cato gave in the year 195 B.C. in opposition to a proposal to repeal a law restricting women's extravagances (possession of gold, wearing colored clothing, riding in carriages within the city), and he has Cato make this proud observation to an assembly of citizens: "You have often heard me complaining about

the money spent by women and by men (not only private citizens but also magistrates), and that our country is suffering from those two divergent vices, avarice and luxury—plagues that have destroyed all great empires" ("saepe me querentem de feminarum, saepe de virorum nec de privatorum modo sed etiam magistratuum sumptibus audistis, diversisque duobus vitiis, avaritia et luxuria, civitatem laborare, quae pestes omnia magna imperia everterunt"). Scholarly discussions of the man and his image include D. Kienast, *Cato der Zensor* (Heidelberg, 1967); F. Della Corte, *Catone Censore* (2nd ed., Florence, 1969); A. E. Astin, *Cato the Censor* (Oxford, 1978); Gruen 1992: 52–83.

14. Plut. *Cato Maior* 17.7. Segal 1968: 98 discusses this incident in conjunction with a passage from Plautus' comedy *Bacchides* (115–124), where we meet a "barbarian" (i.e., a Roman from a Greek perspective) who does not believe in the divinity Suavisaviatio ("Kissy-kissy"). This incident provides a useful background for Suetonius' report of gossip to the effect that the emperor Galba, upon hearing the news of Nero's death, publicly smothered one of his male concubines with kisses, telling him to get ready for more (Suet. *Galba* 22: "ferebant in Hispania Icelum e veteribus concubinis de Neronis exitu nuntiantem non modo artissimis osculis palam exceptum ab eo, sed ut sine mora velleretur oratum atque seductum"). It is worth noting that Cato issues a moralizing disapproval of an act—a kiss between husband and wife—itself considered normal; as we will see in chapter 5, there were also sexual practices between males and females (cunnilinctus above all) that were in themselves considered abnormal.

15. I follow Winkler 1990 in using this term.

16. While the distinction between active and passive is also found in the ancient sources, it is of course untrue to the psychological and physiological complexities of penetrative acts that the receptive partner is merely passive and the insertive partner active. Hesitant to contribute to the continued survival of this invidious distinction, I avoid using the terms in this sense.

17. See n. 11.

18. I follow Richlin 1992a in using the metaphor.

19. Thus we might say that Priapus is fertility figure *cum* scarecrow. For Priapus, see Kytzler 1978, Parker 1988, O'Connor 1989, Richlin 1992a. See Fehling 1974 for a discussion of parallels between this function of Priapus and animal behavior (e.g., he discusses the aggressive display of the erect phallus by male baboons making territorial claims). It is interesting that surviving Greek texts fail to exploit the sexual dimensions of the god's nature to the extent that Roman texts do, and that Priapic poetry is attributed to nearly all of the most famous Roman poets (Catullus, Tibullus, Virgil, Horace, Ovid, Petronius, and Martial); neither is there anything resembling the *Carmina Priapea* in extant Greek literature (cf. Kytzler 1978: 13). Parker 1988: 4 observes that one tradition in Greek poetry endows Priapus with feminine traits (e.g., *A.P.* 5.200, where he has "girlish eyes"), something hardly seen in Roman images of the god. I have not yet been able to consult Christiane Goldberg, *Carmina Priapea: Einleitung, Übersetzung, Interpretation und Kommentar* (Heidelberg, 1992).

20. Cf. Parker 1988: 50, Richlin 1992a: 57–63, and Edwards 1993: 94. Kroll 1988: 112 claims that in the *Priapea* "Priapus erscheint . . . als der Schutzgott der Päderasten," but the god's desire to penetrate is emphatically nonspecific with regard to the sex of his victims.

21. Discussion in this chapter will focus on slaves and prostitutes. On the question of noncitizens who were not slaves, the textual tradition is notably and interestingly silent. While Martial sometimes uses Greek names to refer to his sexual partners of both sexes, we know that earlier poets had used Greek names as pseudonyms for freeborn Romans (e.g., Catullus' "Lesbia" stood for a woman named Clodia, Tibullus' "Delia" for a woman named Plania, and so on: Apul. *Apol.* 10). Thus Martial's Greek names may refer either to slaves or to disguised Romans (cf. Richlin 1993: 537 n. 34)—whether we are meant to

think of particular individuals or generic types. But they might possibly represent real Greeks who were not slaves, and if so, it is significant that Martial seems to feel no compunctions about describing his sexual experiences with them.

22. See especially Richlin 1984 and 1992a. The evidence from fifteenth-century Florence surveyed in Rocke 1996 suggests that this pattern was long-lived in Italy.

23. For ancient ideas concerning boyhood and adolescence, see Eyben 1972 and Kleijwegt 1991.

24. For discussion of ancient concepts of *natural* and *unnatural* sexual behavior, see Appendix 1.

25. Diehl 1091 = *CLE* 1899: "hoc qui scripsit Surianus pedicavit Maev[iu]m."

26. *CIL* 13.10047.41: "dec(ies) pedic(avi) Nis(um)"; or possibly "Dec(imus) pedic(avi) Nis(um)" ("I, Decimus, butt-fucked Nisus").

27. *CIL* 4.4523: "pedicavi VI"; cf. 13.10017.42 and *Année Epigr.* 1983 n. 684 ("III vices pidico qui legeret"), cited at *TLL* s.v. *pedico*.

28. Diehl 689: "accensum qui pedicat, urit mentulam"; literally, "he who butt-fucks an *accensus* burns his dick." *Accensus* either can mean "enflamed" (with desire? with a disease?) or can be the title of an official or attendant (see *OLD* s.v.). Diehl, citing Buecheler, notes "'accensum' ambiguum significans ardorem velut irae et officium civile" and adds the possibility that Accensus might be a proper name. Lilja 1983: 99 n. 53 understands the word simply to mean "enflamed with desire, aroused." Varone 1994: 120 notes the pun, citing the graffito in his section on venereal diseases.

29. Diehl 691: "futuitur cunnus pilossus multo melius [qu]am glaber: e[ad]em continet vaporem et eadem v[ell]it mentulam."

30. Diehl 1085a: "hic ad Callinicum futui orem, anum, amicom o[. .]re. nolite, [c]inaedi [. . .]"

31. See Solin 1981, Lilja 1983: 101. I am suggesting a pun on *sacculus* as both "money bag" and "scrotum": love affairs with both boys and girls can be a drain on one's resources, both financial and physical. Adams 1982: 74–6 provides no parallels for such a meaning of *sacculus*, but does cite *fiscus*, "money bag" (Isid. *Etym.* 11.1.105: "fiscus est pellis in qua testiculi sunt") and *suffiscus* (Festus 403.11–2: "suffiscus folliculus testium arietinorum, quo utebantur pro marsuppio, a fisci similitudine dictus").

32. Diehl 1078a = *CLE* 2153: "quisquis amat pueros sene finem puellas, rationem saccli no refert." The writer of the graffito in Germany seems to have dispensed with the niceties of meter, although the *CLE* editor makes a desperate attempt to salvage it ("voluit fere hexametrum 'quisquis amat pueros, quisquis sine fine puellas,' cui adhaeret dimeter iambicus"). Perhaps coincidentally, the same phrase "quisquis amat pueros" ("whoever loves boys") that opens the graffito appears in a pastoral poem by the third-century A.D. poet Nemesianus (*Ecl.* 4.56: Lycidas, suffering in his love for the boy Iollas, laments: "quisquis amat pueros, ferro praecordia duret").

33. *CIL* 11.6721.7: "pet[o] Octavia[ni] culum"; 11: "laxe Octavi, sede"; 9: "[s]alv[e] Octavi felas"; 14: "L. A(ntoni) calve, Fulvia: culum pand(ite)"; 5: "peto [la]ndicam Fulviae." See also C. Zangemeister, ed., *Ephemeris epigraphica*, vol. 6 (Rome and Berlin, 1885), nos. 52–80; A. Degrassi, ed., *Inscriptiones latinae liberae rei publicae*, vol. 2 (Florence, 1963), nos. 1106–1118; and, for fuller discussion, Hallett 1977.

34. See *OLD* s.v. *glans* 3, Klaus Rosen, "Ad glandes Perusinas," *Hermes* 104 (1976): 123–4, and Adams 1982: 72.

35. See Buchheit 1962, Kytzler 1978, Parker 1988, O'Connor 1989, Richlin 1992a: 141–3.

36. The "third" penalty awaiting bearded thieves is *irrumatio* or oral penetration: the god will force the man to fellate him. An inscription found near Padua (*CIL* 5.2803 = *CLE*

861, vv. 5–6) gives a sanitized version of the threat: "improbus ut si quis nostrum violabit agellum, / hunc tu—sed teneo, scis puto quod sequitur."

37. Cf. Herter 1932: 232–9; Buchheit 1962: 69–72 (arguing that the inscription predates Martial); Kytzler 1978: 98–101, 208–9. Parker 1988 considers the possibility that the inscription was not intended as a serious prayer, but even if it is in some sense a joke, the text relies on certain conceptions of Priapus' personality.

38. Tibull. 1.4 (for further discussion, see chapter 5). The distinctly Roman environment that the poem invokes is noteworthy, as is the element of wish-fulfillment: Priapus is neither beautiful nor rich, but he gets boys to come to him by his patience, cleverness, and (so the implication runs) overall irresistibility.

39. The Romans' children in Sardinia were only their sons; daughters would not have been brought along with them. Tac. *Ann.* 3.33 makes reference to the traditional practice of not taking women to the provinces: "haud enim frustra placitum olim ne feminae in socios aut gentis externas traherentur."

40. For *cinaedus*, see chapter 5. For the adjective *virosa* used of women (always in a negative way), see Lucilius 282 Marx, Afranius 62 Ribbeck, Apul. *Met.* 9.14. [Vir.] *Cat.* 13.13–6 evokes a scene similar to the one described by Scipio, but dispenses with the indirection: "vel acta puero cum viris convivia / udaeque per somnum nates / et inscio repente clamatum insuper / 'Thalassio, Thalassio'" (see chapter 5 for further discussion).

41. Plaut. *Truc.* 105: "fit pol hoc, et pars spectatorum scitis pol haec vos me haud mentiri."

42. Lucil. 1186 Marx: "haec inbubinat, at contra te inbulbitat <ille>." The meaning is made clear by Festus' observation that *bubinare* means "to befoul with women's menstrual blood" and *inbulbitare* means "to befoul with boys' excrement" (Festus 29.2–5: "menstruo mulierum sanguine inquinari" [*inquinare* O. Mueller]; "puerili stercore inquinare"). The sound-play (*inbubinat/inbulbitat*) is conveyed by the translation offered by Rudd 1986: 166 n. 17: "She bloodies you, but the youngster on the other hand muddies you."

43. It is worth recalling Quintilian's celebrated declaration that, unlike so many other literary genres that were inspired by Greek precedents and suffused with Greek influence, "satire is totally ours," that is, Roman (Quint. *I.O.* 10.1.93: "satura quidem tota nostra est"). At *Sat.* 1.10.66 Horace might be describing Lucilius as "Graecis intacti carminis auctor"; Lucilius' poetry is certainly full of Greek words and references to Greek culture, but the genre that he was creating was something unique to Rome, and it obviously spoke to a Roman audience, drawing on Roman morality and traditions.

44. Lucil. 296–7 Marx: "quod gracila est, pernix, quod pectore puro, / quod puero similis."

45. Ov. *Met.* 8.322–3: "facies quam dicere vere / virgineam in puero, puerilem in virgine possis."

46. Cf. F. Charpin, ed., *Lucilius: Satires* (Paris, 1978), *ad loc.*: "Le fragment s'insère dans une comparaison entre les mérites des femmes et ceux des garçons comme le révèle la particule *tam.*" Marx notes that "comparantur mulieres cum pueris" and later makes the insightful comment that because of the subjunctives *maneat* and *sidat*, these must be the words not of the Lucilian persona himself but of someone else.

47. Lucil. 173 Marx: "cumque hic tam formosus homo ac te dignus puellus." Marx, clearly thinking of Horace, *Satires* 1.2 (discussed later in this chapter) reasonably suggests that the gist of the Lucilian passage was as follows: "You are pursuing a filthy and disgraceful prostitute, or a married lady, risking your body and your reputation, when you could instead make use of a licit sexual pleasure and when this slave boy, so beautiful and worthy of you, is here at hand for you to pounce on!" ("De puerorum amore intellegi debet versus quem ita fere in ordinem sententiae componas: 'meretricem fetidam et turpem consectaris aut matronam cum periculo corporis et famae, concessa venere uti cum possis cumque hic

tam formonsus homo . . . ac te dignus . . . puellus sit praesto, impetus in quem fiat.'") For Lucil. 174–6 Marx, see Nonius 458.2–6M, and for Lucil. 173 Marx, see Nonius 158.17-8M. Krenkel 1970: I.67 links the two Lucilian fragments in a similar fashion: "Thema: Vorzüge und Nachteile der Frauen- und Knabenliebe werden gegeneinander abgewogen. Ein Gesprächspartner (Lucilius?) schwärmt von einem Knaben [173 Marx], wobei die Frage des Alters eine Rolle gespielt zu haben scheint, doch sein Gegenüber preist die Vorzüge und Reize einer Frau [174–6 Marx]."

48. Lucil. 866–7 Marx: "qui et poscent minus et praebebunt rectius multo / et sine flagitio"; Nonius 313.18–9M: "vitium quod virgini infertur." Cf. Marx: "Ipsum verbum flagitium demonstrat non fieri comparationem meretricum cum pueris qualem Plaut. Truc. 153 seqq., sed matronarum vel virginum." The text *qui et poscent* represents an emendation of the obviously erroneous manuscript reading *quiete poscente*; the LCL editor (Warmington) adopts Schmitt's emendation *quae et poscent*, and if that is correct, the speaker of this line is talking about female prostitutes. But the manuscript reading *quiete* is much more likely to represent a corruption of *qui et* than of *quae et*, and in view of the other Lucilian passages reviewed here, a comparison between boys and women would be more apt.

49. Krenkel 1970: I.70.

50. Novius fr. 20–1: "puerum mulieri praestare nemo nescit, quanto melior / sit cuius vox gallulascit, cuius iam ramus roborascit." Atellan farce (*fabula Atellana*) was a genre of native Italian comedy (Atella was a town of Campania) characterized by stock figures such as Bucco ("Fool") and Dossennus ("Hunch-back") and a rambunctious, coarse humor. It became a literary form for a brief period in the early first century B.C., Novius and Pomponius being the best known writers. (The text of Novius given above is that of Frassinetti: see his apparatus for the textual difficulties.)

51. If Novius fr. 19 ("pati dum poterunt, antequam pugae pilant") comes from the same context, the speaker adds the qualification that they are desirable from this point until the appearance of hair. Lilja 1983: 44 finds in fr. 20–1 a hint "at a slightly more mature age than was usual." But the reference is to a boy whose voice is just breaking and whose penis is just growing, that is, to a boy who is going through the initial stages of puberty, perhaps in his thirteenth or fourteenth year (see Eyben 1972). That would hardly be more mature than usual.

52. See Richlin 1992a: 36–7, 42–3 for discussion of other ancient representations of boys' penises. Mart. 11.22 humorously chides a man for masturbating his boy too much: the concluding advice is that the boy's penis ought to be left to girls, and the man ought instead to enjoy the boy's anus—designed by "nature" for men's use. (See Appendix 1 for further discussion.) I have not yet been able to consult the most recent relevant study of Martial: Hans Peter Obermayer, *Martial und der Diskurs über männliche 'Homosexualität' in der Literatur der frühen Kaiserzeit* (Tübingen, 1998).

53. See, e.g., Prop. 2.4.17–22, Ov. *Ars* 2.683–4, Juv. 6.33–7.

54. Novius fr. 19 Ribbeck: "pati dum poterunt, antequam pugae pilant."

55. Quint. *I.O.* 10.1.100: "utinam non inquinasset argumenta puerorum foedis amoribus." As Lilja 1983: 45–6 argues, these boys must have been freeborn, for Quintilian would hardly have expressed so severe a disapproval of representations of sexual advances upon male slaves (indeed, he makes no allusion to Plautine jokes on that very theme). In other words, Quintilian is concerned about *stuprum* (see chapter 3).

56. Afranius fr. 32 Ribbeck: "praeterea nunc corpus meum pilare primum coepit."

57. Plin. *N.H.* 30.41: "ne sint alae hirsutae formicarum ova pueris infricata praestant, item mangonibus, ut lanugo tardior sit pubescentium, sanguis e testiculis agnorum, cum castrantur." Another perspective is offered by the former slave Trimalchio, who says that he tried to hasten the arrival of his beard (Petr. *Sat.* 75.10).

58. Plin. *N.H.* 30.132: "vespertilionum sanguis psilotri vim habet, sed alis puerorum inlitus non satis proficit nisi aerugo vel cicutae semen postea inducatur. . . ."

59. Festus 245.13–7: "pullus Iovis dicebatur Q. Fabius, cui Eburno cognomen erat propter candorem, quod eius natis fulmine icta erat. antiqui autem puerum, quem quis amabat, pullum eius dicebant" (cf. *CGL* 7.159, and see *RE* 111 for this Fabius). Richlin 1992a: 289 suggests that he was not literally struck by lightning but instead possessed some sort of birthmark on his buttocks.

60. Auson. *Epigr.* 77.8, pp. 340–1 Peiper: "Lucili vatis 'subpilo pullipremo' (such is Peiper's reading; Lucil. 967–76 Marx reads "subpilo, pullo, premo").

61. Festus 279.5: "pullariam Plautus dixit manum dextram." For the interpretation I am tentatively suggesting, compare Martial's rueful admission of having to resort to masturbation when unable to get hold of a lovely slave-boy (2.43.14: "at mihi succurrit pro Ganymede manus"). Krenkel 1979a: 161 suggests that Plautus called the right hand *pullaria* because men used it to masturbate their boyfriends (*pulli*), but this seems much less likely (consider the apparently common notion, alluded to at Mart. 11.22, that boys should be anally penetrated, not manually stimulated). A late Greek-Latin word list gives as the Latin equivalent of the Greek *paiderastes* both *puerarius* (based on *puer*, "boy") and *pullarius* (*CGL* 7.602), and if we accept an emendation of the manuscript reading, at Petr. *Sat.* 43.8 a character is called *pullarius*.

62. See, for example, Richlin 1992a: 144–56 on Catullus' Priapic persona (where she points out that this poet at times strikes an "anti-Priapic stance," too) and Sullivan 1991: 185–210 on Martial's sexual persona.

63. On Martial's "wife" see especially Kay *ad* Mart. 11.104 and Sullivan 1991: 25–6. In reality Martial himself was most likely unmarried during the period when his epigrams were being published, but his poetic persona is sometimes married, sometimes a bachelor.

64. Mart. 11.43.11–2: "parce tuis igitur dare mascula nomina rebus / teque puta cunnos, uxor, habere duos." See Richlin 1992a: 34–56 for other comparisons between women's genitalia and anuses on the one hand and boys' anuses on the other, always in favor of the latter.

65. For *dare* ("give," here roughly the equivalent of "put out"), cf. Mart. 2.9, 4.7.1, 4.71.6; *Priap.* 38.4; Ov. *Ars* 1.345; Catull. 110.4; and Cicero's scathing remark to Caesar that, as for his relationship with Nicomedes, "everyone knows what he gave you and what you gave him" (Suet. *Jul.* 49.3: "notum est et quid ille tibi et quid illi tute dederis").

66. For the special association of anal intercourse with boys evident in the phrase *supplicium puerile*, see chapters 2 and 5.

67. The scenario that Martial here fondly imagines is played out in Apuleius' *Metamorphoses* (9.28: "solus ipse cum puero cubans gratissima corruptarum nuptiarum vindicta perfruebatur"). For other Roman references to this punishment, see Hor. *Sat.* 1.2.44, 133 with Porphyrio *ad* 44 ("perminxerunt pro stupraverunt positum est"). Richlin 1992a: 176, 251 n. 8, argues that *perminxerunt* is to be taken literally ("urinated all over") but line 133's reference to *pugae* and the striking parallel with Valerius Maximus 6.1.13 ("Cn. etiam Furium Brocchum qui deprehenderat familiae stuprandum obiecit") strongly argue for Porphyrio's interpretation.

68. Mart. 1.46: "cum dicis 'propero! fac si facis!' Hedyle, languet / protinus et cessat debilitata Venus. / expectare iube: velocius ibo retentus. / Hedyle, si properas, dic mihi ne properem." For *properare* and *facere*, see Adams 1982: 144–5, 204. Howell ad loc. offers an intriguing quotation from J. Atkins: "In successful buggery, the boy ejaculates at the same moment as the pederast." Although the mode of intercourse is not explicitly designated in Martial's epigram, anal penetration is strongly suggested by the two other references to a Hedylos in Martial's corpus (4.52 and 9.57), which imply his predilection for being anally penetrated. Bentley emended *Hedyle* to *Hedyli*, by a stroke of the pen chang-

ing the poet's partner from male to female, but this emendation (adopted by Shackleton-Bailey in his 1990 Teubner and 1993 LCL editions) has no manuscript support and seems unnecessary at best.

69. See chapter 3; often they record incidents in which men pursued freeborn (hence off-limits) Romans of either sex, and were punished for it.

70. For example, in an explicitly autobiographical passage (he speaks of his temper, his short stature, and his tendency to live beyond his means), Horace confesses to an endless series of infatuations with boys and girls (*Sat.* 2.3.325: "mille puellarum, puerorum mille furores"; cf. *Epod.* 11.4, *C.* 4.1.29–32). The body of scholarly literature on the Roman love poets and their personae is massive: for overviews, see Griffin 1985, Veyne 1988, Richlin 1992a, Kennedy 1993; for a specific study of sexuality in Catullus, see Arkins 1982.

71. Prop. 2.4.17–22; Ovid *Ars* 2.684: "hoc est cur pueri tangar amore minus." Cantarella 1992: 139 offers an interesting comment on the latter: "One can hardly overlook the fact that in the *Ars amatoria*, where Ovid translates this notion into a statement of personal preference, he feels obliged to justify it, almost as though it was an unusual, surprising choice (as indeed it was), which his fellow citizens would otherwise not have understood."

72. Propertius in his overview of Virgil's *Eclogues* (Prop. 2.34.67–76) refers to both girls and the boy Alexis. Indeed, in Virgil's second *Eclogue*, Corydon burns for Alexis (1), having earlier desired the boy Menalcas and the girl Amaryllis (14–6); in the third *Eclogue*, Menalcas sings of his love for the boy Amyntas who has replaced the girl Delia (66–7), while Damoetas sings of the girl Galatea (64–5), and both Menalcas and Amyntas call upon the lovely Phyllis (76–9). In the eighth *Eclogue*, Alphesiboeus sings an incantation to cause the boy Daphnis to fall in love with him (64–109); and in the tenth, Gallus (a real Roman man poetically transported to the world of the pastoral) laments the loss of his girlfriend Lycoris but imagines other loves as well, in the form of the girl Phyllis and the boy Amyntas (37–41). The conceit lasted: in a late third-century imitation of Virgil, Nemesianus imagines Lycidas singing of the boy Iollas, and Mopsus of the girl Meroe; "and a comparable furor for opposed sexes was forcing them to run through the whole forest in a frenzy" (Nemes. *Ecl.* 4.5–6: "parilisque furor de dispare sexu / cogebat trepidos totis discurrere silvis").

73. *Priap.* 23.3: "defectus pueroque feminaque"; Hor. *C.* 4.1.29–32: "me nec femina nec puer / iam nec spes animi credula mutui / nec certare iuvat mero / nec vincire novis tempora floribus"; Petr. *Sat.* 134.8: "nam neque puero neque puellae bona sua vendere potest."

74. Ov. *Am.* 1.1.20: "aut puer aut longas compta puella comas."

75. Lucretius' ensuing advice, while again influenced by Epicurean thought, must likewise have appealed to many among his Roman readership: it is better to discharge one's seed into any available body and be done with it ("et iacere umorem collectum in corpora quaeque," 1065) than to become entangled in the painful passion of love (1058–72).

76. Marx ad loc.: "Meretrices dicit ita avaras esse, ut ne aegrotantes quidem menstruo sanguinis profluvio et sibi parcant et amatori, item pueros ne in alvi quidem morbo parcere venere."

77. Mart. 11.88: "multis iam, Lupe, posse se diebus / pedicare negat Charisianus. / causam cum modo quaererent sodales, / ventrem dixit habere se solutum."

78. Mart. 13.26: "sorba sumus, molles nimium tendentia ventres: / aptius haec puero quam tibi poma dabis." For this effect of sorb-apples cf. Plin. *N.H.* 23.141.

79. Other Roman texts allude to this aspect of anal intercourse (Mart. 9.69; Juv. 9.43–4; *Priap.* 68.8 ["et pediconum mentula merdalea est"]; *CIL* 10.4483). Consequently, in Lucilius' line, just as a male partner might dirty the penis even if he is not suffering from diarrhea, a female could be said to befoul her partner's penis with the "dirty" substance in her vagina,

which could readily be understood as menstrual blood, even if she is not actually menstruating at the time of intercourse. For ancient medical writers' views of women, and the notion that their bodies are generally bloodier than men's, see Ann Ellis Hanson, "The Medical Writers' Woman," in Halperin, Winkler, and Zeitlin 1990: 309–37; for some Roman views of menstrual blood see Pliny, *N.H.* 7.63–4, 19.176 and Amy Richlin, "Pliny's Brassiere," Hallett and Skinner 1997: 197–220.

80. Rudd 1986: 167 n. 17 comments, "One wonders how many readers would have thought the word-play worth while." I suspect quite a few.

81. Lucil. 72 Marx: "si natibus natricem inpressit crassam et capitatam." The line comes from a description of the prosecution in 120 or 119 B.C. of Q. Mucius Scaevola by L. Albucius on a charge of embezzlement. Some have conjectured that Scaevola was being attacked for pederastic proclivities (so Krenkel 1970: I.64 and Lilja 1983: 49), and F. Charpin, in his 1978 Budé edition, appears to understand the line as directed against the insertive partner in an act of anal penetration, translating "s'il lui plante dans les fesses une anguille charnue à grosse tête." But, like Richlin 1992a: 168, I think the line makes more sense as an attack on a man (perhaps Scaevola) for *having been penetrated*: *natibus*, in other words, is not "his butt" but "your butt," and the subject of *inpressit* is not Scaevola but some other man. This is more consistent with the traditions of Roman invective (why would a man be attacked simply for anally penetrating someone?), and the line more naturally reads as a malicious comment directed at the person whose buttocks have received the "water-snake" than at the man who has pressed the snake into someone else's buttocks: Mart. 9.47.6 ("in molli rigidam clune libenter habes") comes to mind. Adams 1982: 31 raises the possibility that the "water-snake" might not be a penis but a whip, and claims that "there is no certain example" of the metaphorical use of "snake" for "penis," but Tacitus reports a rude joke by Nero that, while there were rumors that serpents had protected him in his infancy, only one "snake" had ever appeared in his bedroom ("unam omnino anguem in cubiculo visam," Tac. *Ann.* 11.11). Moreover, as Lilja 1983: 49 n. 146 observes, the fact that in Lucilius' line the snake is *pressed into* the buttocks should be decisive.

82. Lucil. 73 Marx: "in bulgam penetrare pilosam." Actually, the line might not have referred to anal penetration: *bulga* is used as a coarse image for the uterus or vagina at 623 Marx ("ita uti quisque nostrum e bulga est matris in lucem editus"). On the other hand, since Nonius attributes both line 73 Marx and line 72 Marx to Lucilius' second book, it is probable that the two lines come from the same context and refer to the same act. If so, the adjective *pilosam* is striking: the line could hardly come from a description of Scaevola's pederastic inclinations, since boys' anuses were famously smooth. As is the case with line 72 Marx, I think it more likely that this came from an insulting depiction of Scaevola himself, a mature man, being penetrated.

83. Lucil. 1267 Marx: "podicis, Hortensi, est ad eam rem nata palaestra" (*podicis* is a universally accepted emendation of the manuscripts' *pudicis*). Rudd 1986: 167 n. 17 explains: "*Palaestra* 'wrestling-place' or 'wrestling" had become naturalised by Lucilius' time. Here it perhaps means 'adroitness' as it does later in Cicero. So the sense would be 'the adroitness of the anus, Hortensius, is suited to that purpose.'" See Adams 1982: 157–8 for the imagery of "wrestling." The Lucilian fragment does not specify that the anus belongs to a male (see chapter 5 for references to anal intercourse with women); Marx in fact thinks it more likely that the line refers to a woman. There is simply no way to know.

84. Novius 75–6: "dum istos invitabis suffragatores, pater, / prius in capulo quam in curuli sella suspendes natis." For this fragment, see Adams 1982: 19–21, Cody 1976: 475, and Lilja 1983: 44.

85. Pomponius fr. 124–5 Frassinetti = 125–6 Ribbeck: "nisi nunc aliquis subito obviam

occurrit mihi qui ocquiniscat / quo conpingam terminum in tutum locum." See Lilja 1983: 42 on the vocabulary; the metaphors are unmistakable.

86. Pomponius fr. 154–5 Frassinetti = 148–9 Ribbeck: "ut nullum civem pedicavi per dolum / nisi ipsus orans ultro qui ocquinisceret."

87. Pomponius fr. 149 Frassinetti = 153 Ribbeck: "continuo ad te centuriatim current qui penem petent." The adverb *centuriatim* introduces the humorously incongruous image of the Roman citizenry assembled in the *comitia centuriata* to enact laws or elect magistrates. It should be noted that the manuscripts read *panem* ("bread"), but Frassinetti insightfully emended this to *penem* ("correxi, his verbis Bucconem ad turpe sui commercium invitari ratus") and his emendation has won wide acceptance. Line 158 Frassinetti (= 150 Ribbeck) has been interpreted as describing an act of fellatio (see Frassinetti), though, if so, it is impossible to know who is fellating whom.

88. Pomponius fr. 150 Frassinetti = 151 Ribbeck: "ego quaero quod comedim, has quaerunt quod cacent: contrariumst." Although some have tried to emend the manuscript reading *has* (Ribbeck suggests *his*, Buecheler *hi si*), Frassinetti rightly argues that *has* is "quasi contemptim de pathicis dictum."

89. For this prostitute's desperate straits, compare fr. 148 Frassinetti (= 152 Ribbeck): "ego rumorem parvi facio, dum sit, rumen qui inpleam." Frassinetti suggests that this man was forced by poverty to take a job working in a brothel (*ad* 154–5: "in fornice, dum ventris causa prostat, Bucco deprehensus crimen libidinis lepide propulsare conatur").

90. Novius fr. 7 Frassinetti = 6 Ribbeck: "quod editis nihil est; si vultus quod cacetis, copia est"; *Priap.* 69.4: "quot pondo est tibi mentulam cacandum." As so often in this article, Housman offers an illuminating explanation of the imagery: the receptive partner "shits out, in other words pushes out like a turd, a dick as the fucker is pulling it out of him when the act is completed" ("cacat, hoc est merdae modo emittit, mentulam cui eam finito opere extrahit pedicator," Housman 1931: 404–5). Housman also cites *CIL* 10.8145 ("hanc [sc., mentulam] ego cacavi"), for which see chapter 5. Adams 1982: 171–2 calls Housman's interpretation "far-fetched," arguing that the receptive partner is said not to "shit out" the penis but to "shit on" it or to defile with shit; it is certainly true, as we have seen, that some ancient texts allude to the possibility that the penis may be dirtied in an act of anal penetration. Yet Housman's interpretation of the passages from Pomponius, Novius, and the *Priapea* not only nicely evokes the sensation but also seems preferable on philological grounds: the simplex verb *cacare*, used in these three passages but not in those passages that refer to the notion of dirtying the penis with shit, normally means "to shit out" ("to void as excrement," *OLD*), whereas it is the compound *concacare* that means "to shit on" ("to make foul with ordure," *OLD*). In any case, commentators all agree that the jokes from Pomponius and Nonius refer to anal intercourse.

91. On the other hand, the language of "shitting (out) a dick" might simply refer to the observable physiology of the process: that is, it might only represent the perspective of the insertive partner. Yet from that perspective the focus on the *removal* rather than the insertion of the penis seems odd, even anticlimactic; *cacare* seems to represent more directly the perspective of the receptive partner.

92. Cato *Agr.* 2.7; compare Plutarch's shocked reaction to this at *Cato Maior* 5, and see also Varro *R.R.* 1.17.1 (*instrumenti genus vocale*).

93. See Segal 1968: 102–3, 137–40; Gonfroy 1978; Martin 1978; Morabito 1981; Dalla 1987: 39–49; Cantarella 1992: 101–4; and for more general discussion of master-slave relations, see Balsdon 1979: 77–81 and Joshel 1992 (both with bibliographies).

94. It is theoretically possible that writers like Livy or Valerius Maximus imposed later perspectives onto earlier times. But even if these later writers did rewrite the history

of Roman sexuality to match their own expectations—even if Valerius Maximus was guilty of describing the fourth century B.C. as it appeared to him through a first-century A.D. lens—that would say a great deal about how ingrained such a perspective had become, and that very consideration supports the contention that there were no significant ruptures in ideologies of gender and sexuality caused by (for example) Greek influence.

95. Sen. *Epist*. 47.7: "in cubiculo vir, in convivio puer"; Mart. 3.71: "mentula cum doleat puero, tibi, Naevole, culus, / non sum divinus, sed scio quid facias."

96. Columella *R.R.* 1.8.1: "praemoneo ne vilicum ex eo genere servorum qui corpore placuerunt instituamus." Gurlitt 1921: 167–8 cites a piece of advice proffered by the fourth-century A.D. writer Palladius as a parallel: "Do not rashly put one of your beloved slaves in charge of the field, since, relying on a past love, he expects impunity for any present failing" (*Agr*. 1.6.18: "agri praesulem ne ex dilectis temere servulis ponas, quia fiducia praeteriti amoris impunitatem culpae praesentis exspectat").

97. Catull. 61.119–43 and especially 139–40 ("scimus haec tibi quae licent / sola cognita"). As Fedeli 1983: 97 observes, "there is no reason to believe that the reference to the *concubinus* is a literary τόπος." The poet goes on to recommend that Manlius keep his hands off his *glabri* once he marries ("marito / ista non eadem licent," 140–1): this comment (*pace* Cantarella 1992: 126 and Thomsen 1992: 70) cannot be interpreted as a general recommendation that all men, once married, should renounce homosexual affairs in the interests of conjugal bliss. The comment is generically conditioned, coming as it does in the course of a marriage hymn whose very purpose is to celebrate a certain ideal, namely the mutual and exclusive love between husband and wife. Catullus' advice to Manlius surely also pertains to his potential use of female slaves or other sexual partners (cf. reference to a *mala adultera* in 97–8; and for Roman wives' jealousy of their husbands' use of female slaves, see, e.g., Mart. 11.23, Val. Max. 6.7.1, D. 45.1.121), and thus constitutes not a recommendation to renounce homosexuality per se (as Cantarella 1992: 151 observes, seemingly inconsistently with her earlier interpretation) but a recommendation to practice marital fidelity. See further discussion later in this chapter.

98. Mart. 8.44.16–7: "tuoque tristis filius, velis nolis, / cum concubino nocte dormiet prima."

99. Petr. *Sat*. 75.11: "ad delicias ipsimi annos quattuordecim fui; nec turpe est quod dominus iubet. ego tamen et ipsimae [dominae] satis faciebam. scitis, quid dicam: taceo, quia non sum de gloriosis."

100. Sen. *Contr*. 4.pr.10: "impudicitia in ingenuo crimen est, in servo necessitas, in liberto officium." For the resonance of the term *impudicitia*, see chapter 5.

101. Val. Max. 8.1.damn.8: "innocens, nisi tam prisco saeculo natus esset."

102. Colum. *R.R.* 6.pr.7: "cuius tanta fuit apud antiquos veneratio, ut tam capital esset bovem necuisse quam civem"; Plin. *N.H.* 8.180: "tantae apud priores curae ut sit inter exempla damnatus a populo Romano die dicta qui concubino procaci rure omassum edisse se negante occiderat bovem, actusque in exilium tamquam colono suo interempto." See also Varro *R.R.* 2.5.3–5.

103. Val. Max. 8.1.abs.12. Valerius notes that despite the strongly suspicious nature of the circumstances, "his confession of a lack of self-control caused the charge of lust to be dropped" ("crimen libidinis confessio intemperantiae liberavit"). As Valerius represents it, Calidius' affair with the slave boy is merely an instance of *intemperantia*, an inability to control one's desires, whereas the alleged adultery is a far more serious matter, a matter of *libido* and *infamia*. The implication is that Calidius has given free rein to desires that anyone might have, but that ought to be subject to a certain amount of control—like all desires for such things as food, money, and sex.

104. Sen. *Contr*. 2.1.34–6. Although the general sense is clear, the exact meaning of

the word *paparium* in the phrase "ut dominicae libidini paparium faceret" (35) is elusive: the LCL editor Winterbottom translates "to give a 'sop' to his master's lust," and the *OLD* s.v. notes "perhaps having the sense of 'food' or 'fuel.'"

105. Cf. Hor. *Sat.* 1.4.113–5: "ne sequerer moechas concessa cum venere uti / possem, 'deprensi non bella est fama Treboni'/aiebat." For detailed discussion of Hor. *Sat.* 1.2, see Marcello Gigante, *Orazio: Una misura per l'amore* (Venosa, 1993).

106. Used, that is, by their own masters: elsewhere Horace, offering advice to Lollius on how to cultivate and maintain the friendship of a powerful man, warns him not to become involved with the man's slaves, male or female (Hor. *Epist.* 1.18.72–5: "non ancilla tuum iecur ulceret ulla puerve / intra marmoreum venerandi limen amici; / ne dominus pueri pulchri caraeve puellae / munere te parvo beet aut incommodus angat"). Porphyrio thinks this is an allusion to Pollio's gift of the beautiful slave-boy Alexandrus to Virgil (see n. 110).

107. Pliny the Elder tells us (*N.H.* 7.129) that a certain Clutorius Priscus paid an astronomical price (50 million sesterces) for a beautiful eunuch named Paezon, who belonged to Tiberius' crony Sejanus. Pliny observes that this was the price more of Clutorius' lust than of Paezon's beauty ("sed hoc pretium . . . libidinis, non formae"), and that no one challenged Clutorius only because Rome was preoccupied by the grim state of affairs under Sejanus ("in luctu civitatis").

108. For the bawdiness of epigram see, for example, Martial's prefaces to his first and second books, and the discussion at Sullivan 1991: 56–77. Other poems on slave-boys include 3.65, 4.7, 4.42, 5.46, 6.34, 12.75; see further Richlin 1992a: 39–44, 135–6 and Sullivan 1991: 207–10. For an interpretation of 11.58 see Housman 1930: 411.

109. Suet. *Verg.* 9: "libidinis in pueros pronioris"; ibid.: "vulgatum est consuesse eum et cum Plotia Hieria"; 11: "cetera sane vitae et ore et animo tam probum constat, ut Neapoli Parthenias vulgo appellatus sit."

110. Suet. *Verg.* 9: "quorum maxime dilexit Cebetem et Alexandrum, quem secunda Bucolicorum ecloga Alexim appellat, donatum sibi ab Asinio Pollione"; cf. Porph. *ad* Hor. *Epist.* 1.18.75: "adludit ad Vergilium, cui Alexandrum puerum Pollio dominus dono dedit."

111. Mart. 5.16, 6.68, 7.29, 8.55 (where Maecenas, rather than Pollio, is said to have given Alexis to Virgil).

112. Mart. 8.73.10: "si qua Corinna mihi, si quis Alexis erit." Juvenal 7.69–71 sarcastically notes that if Virgil had had to do without a slave-boy or decent lodgings, he would never have written the *Aeneid* (writing poetry won't pay the rent): "nam si Vergilio puer et tolerabile desset / hospitium, caderent omnes a crinibus hydri, / surda nihil gemeret grave bucina." Courtney *ad loc.* notes that the reference need not be specifically to Alexis, but I think it likely that a Roman reader seeing a reference to a slave-boy of Virgil's would immediately think of Alexandrus/Alexis.

113. Mart. 8.pr.: "ego tamen illis non permisi tam lascive loqui quam solent."

114. Suet. *Aug.* 69: "adulteria quidem exercuisse ne amici quidem negant."

115. Plut. *Ant.* 59.4: ὁ δὲ Σάρμεντος ἦν τῶν Καίσαρος παιγνίων παιδάριον, ἃ δηλίκια Ῥωμαῖοι καλοῦσιν; compare the more gossipy remark at Ps.-Aurel. Vict. *Epit.* 1.22 to the effect that Augustus was in the habit of sleeping in the company of twelve catamites and an equal number of girls ("inter duodecim catamitos totidemque puellas accubare solitus erat"). Sarmentus is mentioned by Antony's friend Dellius in order to underscore the shocking disparity between the way in which Antony's friends were being mistreated by Cleopatra: sour wine was served them at dinner in Egypt, whereas even Octavian's slave Sarmentus was being served expensive Falernian wine in Rome. (Richlin 1992a, 93, by contrast, takes this passage to mean that Antony's followers "taunted Caesar for his indulgence in pederasty.") Horace (*Sat.* 1.5.52) and Juvenal (5.3) associate a Sarmentus with Maecenas.

Courtney (*ad* Juvenal 5.3) and C. B. R. Pelling (*Plutarch: Life of Antony* [Cambridge, 1988], pp. 263–4) suggest that this is the same person: if so, Octavian may have given Sarmentus as a gift to Maecenas (much as Pollio or Maecenas himself gave Alexandrus to Virgil), who subsequently freed him. See Treggiari 1969: 271–2 for more discussion.

116. *CIL* 6.8817: Liarus, *glaber ab cyatho*; 6.8956: Dipantius, *ornator glabrorum*; 6.33099: Chloe, *puerorum ornatrix*; cf. 6.33426 ("Apollonius Antoni paed[. .] glabrorum"). See Griffin 1985: 29–31.

117. Suet. *Vit.* 12: "hunc adulescentulum mutua libidine constupratum . . . primo imperii die aureis donavit anulis super cenam . . ."

118. SHA *Hadrian* 4.5. Rumor had it that one way in which Hadrian established his influence with Trajan was by corrupting his freedmen and cultivating his *delicati*, with whom he had sexual relations once he became a frequent visitor to the palace ("corrupisse eum Traiani libertos, curasse delicatos eosdemque saepe inisse per ea tempora quibus in aula familiarior fuit, opinio multa firmavit"). The same biographer earlier notes that Hadrian himself had been loved by Trajan and refers to the guardians of the "boys whom Trajan loved quite intensely" (*Hadr.* 2.7: "fuitque in amore Traiani, nec tamen ei per paedagogos puerorum quos Traianus impensius diligebat Gallo fovente defuit"). Dio reports that Trajan's taste for boys was pursued with a tasteful moderation and never "bothered" anyone (Dio 68.7.4: καὶ οἶδα μὲν ὅτι καὶ περὶ μειράκια καὶ περὶ οἶνον ἐσπουδάκει . . . νῦν δὲ τοῦ τε οἴνου διακόρως ἔπινε καὶ νήφων ἦν, ἔν τε τοῖς παιδικοῖς οὐδένα ἐλύπησεν; cf. 68.21.2: ὑπὸ τοῦ υἱέος Ἀρβάνδου καλοῦ καὶ ὡραίου ὄντος καὶ διὰ τοῦτο τῷ Τραϊάνῳ ᾠκειωμένου πεισθείς . . .).

119. Mart. 9.11–3, 16, 17, 36; Stat. *Silv.* 3.4. For the poetry on Earinos, see Garthwaite 1984 and Richlin 1992a: 40–1. Dio 67.2.3 also mentions Domitian's affair with Earinos, adding that the emperor's brother and predecessor Titus had shared his tastes for eunuchs. For discussion of eunuchs in Greek and Roman culture, see Stevenson 1995.

120. Stat. *Silv.* 3.4.12–20. Less prepared to accept Statius' abject flattery as *pro forma* hyperbole, Garthwaite 1984: 113–4 suggests that, as neither Statius' general readership nor the emperor himself would have been prepared to believe that Domitia "happily accepts the presence of Earinus," Statius' words are dripping with irony: "he is enjoying a gibe at the emperor—all in the guise of utterly ingenuous sincerity." Garthwaite's reading of the poem as a whole (see n. 121 for a further example) argues that its flattery is so excessively fulsome as to be ironic; he even raises the possibility that this poem, and Domitian's reaction to it, was a factor in Statius' decision to leave Rome (*Silv.* 3.5: Garthwaite 1984: 124).

121. Stat. *Silv.* 3.4.65–77. On this point, too, Garthwaite is more cynical, noting that whereas Martial nowhere alludes to the castration, Statius' elaborate account is savagely ironic: "There is a vicious, mocking cruelty in the suggestion that Earinus' castration is clear evidence of heaven's favor" (Garthwaite 1984: 118). In any case, Statius reassuringly adds (73–7) that Earinos was made a eunuch before the prohibition against castration of boy slaves issued by none other than Domitian himself. (For this prohibition, see Suet. *Dom.* 7.1, Mart. 6.2. Dio 67.2.3 suggests that Domitian's prohibition stemmed from an ongoing rivalry with his brother and predecessor Titus, who had also been fond of eunuchs! As the same historian later notes [68.2.4], Domitian's successor Nerva again forbade castration within the Roman Empire; it would seem that Domitian's original decree had not been especially effective.)

122. See Suet. *Dom.* 22, Plin. *Epist.* 4.11.6, Dio 67.3.

123. Such is the argument of MacMullen 1982.

124. See in general Fraenkel 1960; Williams 1968; Segal 1968; Konstan 1983; Anderson 1993.

125. It deserves note that even Zwierlein, who sets out to argue that the text of Plautus as we have it contains many later interpolations and that Plautus himself was a closer imitator of his Greek originals than is usually thought, considers this speech to be genuinely Plautine, including only line 475 in his "Liste der unechten Verse" (Zwierlein 1990: 269).

126. This is precisely the premise of Gurlitt 1921 (e.g., 15: "In dieser Welt lebte Plautus, für diese Welt schuf er"). Kroll 1988: 111 n. 108 is quite critical of Gurlitt's work, calling his translations "amateurish" ("in seiner dilettantischen Übersetzung") and dismissing his attempts to uncover numerous obscene double-entendres in Plautus' plays as both unsuccessful and frivolous. But, joined as they are with an admission that he has not actually seen Gurlitt's monograph, Kroll's comments pique one's curiosity. Thanks to Ralph Hexter I have been able to consult it, and have read it with Kroll's criticisms in mind. It is true that Gurlitt is given to unscholarly expostulations (14: "In sexueller Hinsicht haben sich die heißblütigen Südländer zu allen Zeiten die Zügel locker gelassen"; 25: "Abgestoßen von all den Kümmerlichkeiten unserer kranken Gesellschaft flüchte ich mich in die gesunde Luft der plautinischen Welt und kehre stets erfrischt und neu gestärkt aus ihr zurück"), and that he feels the need to explain that, when it comes to pederasty, he has as much personal experience and understanding of the matter as he has of cannibalism (119: "Ich stehe, um das hier ein für allemal auszusprechen, diesen Dingen vollständig verständnislos gegenüber. Sie haben in meinem Leben niemals auch nur die geringste Bedeutung gewonnen, und ich kann über sie sprechen etwa wie über den Kannibalismus: Sie gehen mich nichts an"). But his attempt to find double-meanings does not strike me as entirely outlandish. He rightly points (32–7) to discussions in Quintilian (*I.O.* 8.3.44–7) and Cicero (*Fam.* 9.22) that suggest that Romans were sensitive to obscene puns (*cum nos* ["when we . . ."] might be perceived as *cunnos* ["cunts"], *illam dicam* ["shall I call that one . . ."] might be taken as containing *landicam* ["clitoris"], and so on). If, as scholars are ready to concede, Plautine references to *testes* pun on the word's two meanings ("witnesses" and "testicles"), the possibility is also worth considering that, as Gurlitt argues, *anus* ("old woman") might have evoked *anus* ("anus") for a Roman audience, or that words such as *oculus* ("eye") might have been interpreted as punning on *culus* ("anus"). See Richlin 1992a: 1–31 for discussion of Roman concepts of the obscene, especially in language.

127. A good example of this kind of textual trace can be found in a scene to be discussed in chapter 3 (*Curc.* 23–39), in the course of which a slave proclaims a strictly Roman code of behavior, there is a purely Latin pun on *testes* (30–1), and Phaedromus twice says that the house they are standing in front of belongs to a pimp (33: "quin leno hic habitat"; 39: "lenonis hae sunt aedes"). There is the distinct possibility that in the Greek original the dialogue moved directly from Phaedromus' denial of an affair with a married woman (26–7) to his assertion that this is a pimp's house (39); the intervening material, with its Latin pun, its enunciation of Roman sexual morality, and its textual seams, was inserted by Plautus to get a laugh out of his Roman audience.

128. Cf. Lilja 1983: 31, 47.

129. Plaut. *Pseud.* 1180–1: "noctu in vigiliam quando ibat miles, quom tu ibas simul, / conveniebatne in vaginam tuam machaera militis?" Ballio and Simo are in fact convinced that Harpax is an impostor since Pseudolus has already gotten Simia to pass himself off as Harpax in order to acquire the lovely *meretrix* Phoenicium, but this typical twist in the plot does not affect my point. Zwierlein 1991: 223–6 argues that these lines and others in the scene (1177–82, 1188–9, 1196, 1205–7, 1214, 1232–7) are not the work of Plautus himself but rather of a later interpolator, yet—crucially—he observes that "die päderastischen Anspielungen als solche könnten natürlich auch von Plautus selbst stammen" (224). What troubles Zwierlein here is not the content but rather the "sprachlichen und metrischen Anstöße, verbunden mit der unbeholfenen Dialogführung in 1177f. und der Vorausnahme

des Wahnsinnsmotivs in 1179," along with certain aspects of the "Gedankenentwicklung" (225).

130. Plaut. *Asin.* 703: "asta igitur, ut consuetus es puer olim. scin ut dicam?" The joke might possibly be empty of sexual content, but cf. *Pseud.* 1177–8 ("quid ais? tune etiam cubitare solitu's in cunis puer? / . . . etiamne—facere solitun es—scin quid loquar?") and especially *Capt.* 867 ("tuo arbitratu, facile patior.—credo, consuetu's puer"), where the sexual charge of *patior* is unmistakable. See Segal 1968: 104–9 for discussion of the *Asinaria* scene as an example of the Plautine inversion of the master-slave relationship.

131. Plaut. *Cas.* 455: "credo hercle ecfodere hic volt vesicam vilico" (Adams 1982: 91–2, on *vesica*, fails to cite the passage); cf. 465: "hodie hercle, opinor, hi conturbabunt pedes"; 461–2: "et idem me pridem, quom ei advorsum veneram, / facere atriensem voluerat sub ianua." There is no reason to believe that a Roman audience would have thought Lysidamus' expressions of lust to be anything but genuinely felt: see further, chapter 2.

132. Plaut. *Rud.* 1073–5: "comprime hunc sis, si tuost. /—quid? tu idem mihi vis fieri quod erus consuevit tibi? / si ille te comprimere solitust, hic noster nos non solet."

133. Plaut. *Most.* 890: "ferocem facis, quia te erus amat"; 894–5: "novit erus me.— suam quidem [pol] culcitulam oportet."

134. Shortly thereafter, Sagaristio utters a veiled sexual threat against Paegnium, who then insults his potency (291–2: "itane? specta / quid dedero.—nihil, nam nihil habes"); cf. Lilja 1983: 17.

135. Adams 1982: 182 notes that this use of *comprimere* "does not seem to have been determined by any term in Greek New Comedy." For this usage of *dare* see n. 65, on Mart. 2.49.

136. See Adams 1982: 150. This material is one piece of evidence that might be cited against the argument that Greek borrowings such as *cinaedus* and *pathicus* suggest a Roman distancing of homosexuality as foreign (e.g., Adams 1982: 123, 228); see Williams 1995 for further discussion.

137. So too Verstraete 1980: 232; Veyne 1985: 28; Kroll 1988: 112–113; and Cantarella 1992: 99–100. (MacMullen 1982: 488 argues for precisely the opposite view.) Gurlitt 1921: 18 places Plautine jokes about the sexual use of slaves in the context of a more general critique of the morality of slave economies: "Auch die Vorstellung ist falsch, als hätte die Zeit des Plautus auf dem Gebiete der sexuellen Sittlichkeit wesentlich höher gestanden, als die der folgenden Jahrhunderte. Wo Sklavenwirtschaft besteht, sind der Willkür der Männer keine Grenzen gezogen."

138. Plut. *Rom. Ques.* 101.288A: τοῖς μὲν παλαιοῖς οἰκετῶν μὲν ἐρᾶν ὥραν ἐχόντων οὐκ ἦν ἄδοξον οὐδ᾽ αἰσχρόν, ὡς ἔτι νῦν αἱ κωμῳδίαι μαρτυροῦσιν. These comedies surely include the *palliatae* of Plautus, given the prominence of jokes on the subject in those plays. Plutarch notes that the "men of old" strictly refrained from freeborn boys, who were protected (as seen in chapter 3) by the concept of *stuprum*.

139. See, for example, Cic. *Verr.* 2.1.91–3, *Fin.* 2.23, *Tusc.* 5.61, *Amic.* 55, *Q.Fr.* 1.1.8; Tac. *Ann.* 3.53.

140. Juv. 7.132–3: "perque forum iuvenes longo premit assere Maedos / empturus pueros argentum murrina villas"; Juv. 7.141–3: "an tibi servi / octo, decem comites, an post te sella, togati / ante pedes."

141. Nep. *Att.* 13.4: "neque tamen horum quemquam nisi domi natum domique factum habuit; quod est signum non solum continentiae sed etiam diligentiae."

142. Gracchus *apud* Gell. 15.12.2: "nulla apud me fuit popina, neque pueri eximia facie stabant"; 3: "si ulla meretrix domum meam introivit aut cuiusquam servulus propter me sollicitatus est . . ."

143. Cato, *Agr.* 2.7; Plut. *Cato Maior* 4.5: ὡς ἂν οὐ τρυφερῶν οὐδ᾽ ὡραίων, ἀλλ᾽

ἐργατικῶν καὶ στερεῶν, οἷον ἱπποκόμων καὶ βοηλατῶν, δεόμενος – καὶ τούτους δὲ πρεσβυτέρους γενομένους ᾤετο δεῖν ἀποδίδοσθαι καὶ μὴ βόσκειν ἀχρήστους.

144. Cf. Hor. *C.* 2.4.1: "ne sit ancillae tibi amor pudori"; in Valerius Maximus' narrative of the man who killed an ox for his slave boy (Val. Max. 8.1.damn.8), it is worth noting that the man is described as being head-over-heels in love with his slave (*nimio amore correptus*).

145. General discussions of prostitution in antiquity include Herter 1960, Krenkel 1988, and McGinn 1989. For male prostitution, see Krenkel 1978 and 1979b, Edwards 1997, and (in Athens) Halperin 1990: 88–112. I have not yet been able to consult Thomas A. J. McGinn, *Prostitution, Sexuality, and the Law in Ancient Rome* (New York, 1998).

146. Plautine comedy is filled with lovely young women in just that position, and the *Fasti Praenestini* (see discussion later in this section) refer to *pueri lenonii* ("pimps' boys").

147. D. 3.2.4.2 (having stated that whoever practices *lenocinium* will be *infamis*, Ulpian proceeds to a definition): "lenocinium facit qui quaestuaria mancipia habuerit: sed et qui in liberis hunc quaestum exercet, in eadem causa est." He then gives a fascinating glimpse at life in the provinces, where the owners of bathhouses sometimes acted as *lenones* with slaves (presumably of both sexes) that they had rented to guard the clothes of bathers: "velut in quibusdam provinciis fit, in balineis ad custodienda vestimenta conducta habens mancipia hoc genus observantia in officina."

148. Suet. *Tib.* 58.1: "ut haec quoque capitalia essent: . . . nummo vel anulo effigiem [sc., Augusti] impressam latrinae aut lupanari intulisse"; Sen. *Contr.* 1.2.8: "omnis sordida iniuriosaque turba huc influit"; ibid. 1.2.20: "fuit in loco turpi, probroso."

149. Hor. *Epist.* 1.14.21–6.

150. Nepos *Dion* 4.3–4: ". . . ut indulgendo turpissimis imbueretur cupiditatibus. nam puero, priusquam pubes esset, scorta adducebantur, vino epulisque obruebatur . . ."

151. Cic. *Quinct.* 95 and Ov. *Pont.* 2.3.19–20 respectively.

152. Servius, for one, observes that the Romans of old freely enjoyed the services of boy prostitutes (*ad V. Ecl.* 8.29: "meritorii pueri, id est catamiti, quibus licenter utebantur antiqui, recedentes a turpi servitio nuces spargebant"). The evidence suggests that male prostitutes (often explicitly designated as boys) were, like their female counterparts, usually hired by men and not by women. To be sure, that women might pay for male prostitutes is implied by Petr. *Sat.* 126.4, and we read on a Pompeiian wall that a man named Maritimus charged four *asses* to perform cunnilinctus (*CIL* 4.8939: "Maritimus cunnu(m) linget a(ssibus) IIII"), although Varone 1994: 138 rightly cautions that such graffiti might merely be jokes at the expense of the men named in them.

153. The noun seems originally to have denoted a pelt or hide; thus a whore is piece of skin to be used. Such is one explanation offered by Donatus (*ad* Ter. *Eun.* 424: "abdomen in corpore feminarum patiens iniuriae coitus scortum dicitur, ideo quia scorta sunt dura coria. a parte ergo sui meretrices scorta dicuntur") and, with a different nuance, by Walde-Hofmann (s.v.: "von der weichen abgezogenen Haut benannt; es handelt sich um eine affektische Erweiterung vom Körperteil auf die ganze Person"). A late Greek-Latin word list testifies to the existence of a specifically masculine form *scortus* (*CGL* 2.413.63 *pornos: scortus*), but this is the only attestation of the word.

154. *CIL* 1², p. 236: "festus est puerorum lenoniorum quia proximus superior meretricum est." Cantarella 1992: 102 interprets *proximus superior* to mean not April 24 but April 26, but see *OLD* s.v. *superior* 4.

155. *CIL* 4.1969 add. p. 213, 4.5408. It is just possible that these are not actual advertisements but malicious slurs against Lais, Felix, and others (I thank Daniel Selden for reminding me of that possibility). But even if that is the case, the pungency of these and related graffiti derives its strength precisely from the fact that there really were prostitutes of both sexes in Pompeii and elsewhere.

156. *CIL* 4.4024, 4592: "bellis moribus."

157. *CIL* 1².593: "queive corpore quaestum fecit fecerit; queive lanistaturam artemve ludicram fecit fecerit; queive lenocinium faciet." The text is conveniently printed, with brief discussion and bibliography, in S. Riccobono, *Fontes iuris Romani anteiustiniani* (Florence, 1941), I.140–52; the text cited above constitutes Riccobono's lines 122–3. See now M. Crawford, ed., *Roman Statutes* (London, 1996), I.355–91.

158. Plaut. *Curc.* 470–84 (473: "ibidem erunt scorta exoleta quique stipulari solent"; 482: "in Tusco vico, ibi sunt homines qui ipsi sese venditant"). Since *exoletus* later became a technical term for a male prostitute (see chapter 2), it is likely that Plautus' *scorta exoleta* are male. Likewise, the manner in which the prostitutes of the Vicus Tuscus are described strongly suggests that they include males: the word *homines* refers to human beings of both sexes, and in any case if it were a question of exclusively female prostitutes, the speaker would no doubt have used feminine pronouns and perhaps the word *meretrices*. Lilja 1983: 30 observes that the use of the pronoun *ipsi* in line 482 implies that these "were freedmen or even free, forced by necessity to earn their livelihood by offering their services for money."

159. Cf. Hor. *Sat.* 2.3.228 ("Tusci turba impia vici") with Porphyrio *ad loc.* ("lenones dicit, ibi enim commanent").

160. Fraenkel 1920 argues that the speech is a later interpolation, but his logic seems circular: he believes that no text as early as Plautus could contain such a direct reference to homosexual behavior, and prostitution above all, and therefore the scene must be an interpolation. Gurlitt 1921: 122 argues with characteristic force that this scene is not only genuinely Plautine ("ein Stück des echten Plautus!") but in fact added by Plautus to his Greek original in order to raise a laugh from his Roman audience. Lilja 1983: 19 also accepts the scene as genuinely Plautine. Zwierlein 1990: 65 detects an interpolation, arguing that the scene presents us with "ein befremdliches Abweichen von der sonst beobachteten Dezenz." He suggests that as Plautus originally wrote the scene, the *puer* was a "harmlos" slave (71) who complained only about "der *servitus* bei einem Kuppler allgemein," not about "die speziellen Nöte eines *puer delicatus*" (67), and that it was a later interpolator, misinterpreting a Plautine pun, who added lines 768, 773–4, and 783–7 (which he labels "obszönen"). The objections seem strained: I am not convinced that the boy's words are significantly less decent or more obscene than those of many another Plautine character. Also, Zwierlein argues that there is an important distinction between scenes in which adult men are insulted "durch homoerotische Anspielungen" and a scene in which a boy prostitute himself actually comes on stage and complains about his job; but such a distinction is not self-evidently significant.

161. Plaut. *Truc.* 105: "pars spectatorum scitis pol haec vos me hau'mentiri"; 149–57 (152: "utrosque pergnovi probe").

162. Plaut. *Truc.* 87: "ut cum solo pergraecetur militi." See chapter 2 for further discussion of Greek luxury, particularly in sexual contexts.

163. Lucil. 273–4 Marx, with Marx ad loc. (This might explain why Apuleius [*Apol.* 10]) complains that Lucilius prostituted [*prostituit*] the boys in his poetry by not concealing their names.) That slave-boys might try to earn some money by selling their favors to men other than their masters is a reality lying behind poems of Catullus and Horace: Catull. 106 and Hor. *Epist.* 1.20 (cf. Acro ad loc.: "ad librum suum loquitur, tamquam ad puerum prostaturum").

164. Val. Max. 6.1.10: "palam atque aperte corpore quaestum factitasset." Cantarella 1992: 105 dates the incident to about 280 B.C. For the phrase *corpore quaestum facere* cf. Val. Max. 6.1.6, Tac. *Ann.* 2.85, and the *Tabula Heracleensis* (n. 157).

165. See Val. Max. 6.1.6 for a reference to a slave-boy forced by his master to prostitute himself ("in pueritia corpore quaestum a domino facere coactum").

166. Cato fr. 212 Malcovati (from the speech *De Re Floria*): "sed nisi qui palam corpore pecuniam quaereret aut se lenoni locavisset, etsi famosus et suspiciosus fuisset, vim in corpus liberum non aequum censuere afferri." The circumstances and date of this speech are not known, but one point is clear. Cato refers to a Roman tradition, expressed in a decree of the Senate (so much is suggested by his use of the verb *censuere*) that, whatever his reputation might be, a free man's body was inviolate, with the sole exception of those who publicly prostituted themselves or hired themselves out to pimps. The same speech also contained this sentence: "ibi pro scorto fuit, in cubiculum subrectitavit e convivio, cum partim illorum iam saepe ad eundem modum erat" (213). The surviving words do not specify who the subject is, or even whether the subject is male or female, but one possible interpretation is that the case concerned a free man who had been the victim of some kind of violence, and that his attackers had claimed that they were immune from prosecution since the man had acted like a prostitute, shuttling back and forth between dining room and bedroom. (The argument would be reminiscent of ps.-Dem. 59, *Against Neaera*.)

167. Val. Max. 9.1.8: "lupanari enim domi suae instituto Muniam et Flaviam, cum a patre tum a viro utramque inclitam, et nobilem puerum Saturninum in eo prostituit." See chapter 3 for further examples of the forced prostitution of the freeborn.

168. Tac. *Ann*. 2.85: "cautumque ne quaestum corpore faceret cui avus aut pater aut maritus eques Romanus fuisset" (cf. Suet. *Tib*. 35.1–2, D. 48.5.11.2). The incident (which, according to Tacitus, came in response to the case of a noble woman named Vistilia who registered herself as a prostitute with the proper authorities in order to avoid being prosecuted as an adulteress under Augustus' *lex Julia*) is discussed at Richlin 1981a: 386–7 and Treggiari 1991: 297. See Gardner 1986: 132–4 for discussion of the legal situation of freeborn women who worked as prostitutes.

169. Calp. Flacc. 20; Sen. *Ben*. 2.21 ("quid faciendum sit captivo, cui redemptionis pretium homo prostituti corporis et infamis ore promittit. patiar me ab impuro servari? servatus deinde quam illi gratiam referam? vivam cum obsceno? non vivam cum redemptore?"). Seneca's solution is to accept the ransom, repay the man as soon as possible, and be ready to save him if he falls into similar danger—but not to enter into a friendship with him, since friendship can only exist between similar people (*similes iungit*).

170. Juv. 1.46–7: "hic spoliator / pupilli prostantis" (for the figure of the cheating guardian, see also Juv. 10.222–3 and 15.135–6 and contrast 8.79).

171. Cic. *Cat*. 2.10: "quod si in vino et alea comissationes solum et scorta quaererent, essent illis quidem desperandi, sed tamen essent ferendi." For the associations of gambling with an immoral lifestyle that often includes sexual excess, see also Naev. *pall*. 118: "pessimorum pessime, audax, ganeo, lustro, aleo"; Sextus Turpilius 201–2: "coronam, mensam, talos, vinus, haec huius modi, / quibus rebus vita amantum invitari solet"; Cic. *Cat*. 2.23: "omnes aleatores, omnes adulteri, omnes impuri impudicique"; Cic. *Verr*. 2.1.32–4, 2.5.33–4; *Phil*. 2.56, 2.67, and especially 3.35: "libidinosis, petulantibus, impuris, impudicis, aleatoribus, ebriis servire, ea summa miseria est summo dedecore coniuncta"; Suet. *Aug*. 71.

172. [Sall.] *Oratio ad Caesarem* 1.8.2: "ei quibus bis die ventrem onerare, nullam noctem sine scorto quiescere mos est."

173. Hor. *Epist*. 1.18.34–5: "dormiet in lucem, scorto postponet honestum / officium, nummos alienos pascet"; Hor. *Sat*. 1.2.58–9: "verum est cum mimis, est cum meretricibus, unde / fama malum gravius quam res trahit." It is interesting to compare Hor. *Sat*. 2.2.95–6 ("grandes rhombi patinaeque / grande ferunt una cum damno dedecus"), suggesting a parallel between food and sex, and *Sat*. 1.4.48–50 ("at pater ardens / saevit, quod meretrice nepos insanus amica / filius uxorem grandi cum dote recuset"). See also Titinius 43–4 Ribbeck: "si rus cum scorto constituit ire, clavis ilico / abstrudi iubeo, rusticae togai ne sit copia" (surely the words of an angry father); Sen. *Contr*. 2.1.14–5, 2.3.5; Calp. Flacc. 30 (a

father disinherits his luxurious son "ob amorem meretricis"); Quint. *Decl. Min.* 260.8, 356. See generally Kroll 1988: 97–103 and Treggiari 1991: 300–2.

174. Lucil. 398–9 Marx: "praetor noster adhuc, quam spurc<os> ore quod omnis / extra castra ut stercus foras eiecit ad unum"; Val. Max. 2.7.1: "nam constat tum maximum inde institorum et lixarum numerum cum duobus milibus scortorum abisse"; Liv. *Perioch.* 57: "duo milia scortorum a castris eiecit"; [Plut.] *Apophth. Scip. Min.* 201B. Valerius Maximus and the summary of Livy use the neuter *scorta* to refer to the prostitutes, but Lucilius (if Marx's reading, printed above, is correct) uses the masculine plural *spurcos*, which directly implies that the prostitutes included males as well as females.

175. Cic. *Mil.* 55 (*scorta, exoleti, lupae*).

176. Val. Max. 3.5.3: "perdito etiam amore vulgatissimae meretricis infamis fuit."

177. SHA *Elagab.* 27.7 (*meretrices, lenones, exoleti*).

178. See Edwards 1997.

179. For Sulla see Plut. *Sull.* 2, 36; for Maecenas, Tac. *Ann.* 1.54, and perhaps Dio 54.17.5 and Hor. *Epod.* 14 (cf. Griffin 1985: 12–3, 25); for Antony, Cic. *Phil.* 2.20, 8.26 (*mimorum et mimarum greges*).

180. Plin. *N.H.* 7.180 ("mortes repentinae, hoc est summa vitae felicitas") and 7.184: "Cornelius Gallus praetorius et T. Hetereius eques Romanus in venere obiere et, quos nostra adnotavit aetas, duo equestris ordinis in eodem pantomimo Mystico tum forma praecellente."

181. Publ. Syr. *Sent.* M45: "meretrix est instrumentum contumeliae"; M50: "muneribus est, non lacrimis, meretrix misericors."

182. Cic. *Verr.* 2.1.138: "respondit illa ut meretrix non inhumaniter." At 2.1.137 he smugly notes that Junius' decent guardians and relatives would never have visited a whore's house except under the most exceptional of pressures, and at 2.1.139–40 he claims that L. Domitius, an exemplary character, was induced only with great difficulty to mention Chelidon's name in public.

183. 133–4: "neve quis, quei ibei mag(istratum) potestatemve habebit, eum cum senatu decurionibus conscripteis ludos spectare neive in convivio publico esse sinito sc(iens) d(olo) m(alo)." MacMullen 1982: 495 misinterprets this to mean that Romans "protected decent citizens . . . against finding a known homosexual sitting next to them in public gatherings."

184. The man whom Cicero assails, in a fragment of an unidentified speech, as a prostitute who has been penetrated ("o te, scelerate, qui subactus et prostitutus es," *Orat. Incert.* 14 Schoell) may or may not be Clodius.

185. For his language of matrimony, see Appendix 2.

186. Another kind of double standard appears from a comparison of two different declamations of Calpurnius Flaccus: in one, a father disinherits a son "ob amorem meretricis" (30), but in another, a father and a son each love a *meretrix*, and the father actually gives money to his son so that he can buy the father's companion for him (37).

187. It deserves reemphasis that even if this anecdote is entirely apocryphal, it opens a window onto what Romans of Horace's day were willing to accept as a traditionalist, Catonian perspective on the question of men's sexual behavior.

188. For the combination of financial and moral restraint in these matters, compare Livy's comment on the relationship between the young Aebutius and the *nobile scortum* Hispala: unusually, it was damaging neither to the young man's financial resources nor to his reputation ("minime adulescentis aut rei aut famae damnosa"), but this was because *she* had sought him out rather than the other way around, and he was not paying for her favors (39.9.6).

189. Polyb. 31.25.5 (see chapter 2 for further discussion, where it will be argued that "homosexuality" was not the issue for Cato). The remark seems to have become famous: cf.

Diod. 31.24, 37.3.6, Athen. 6.274F–275A, Plut. *Quaest. Conv.* 668B–C, and *Cato Maior* 8.2 (where Cato's motives are explained: κατηγορῶν τῆς πολυτελείας).

190. Cat. *Agr.* pr. 4: "ex agricolis et viri fortissimi et milites strenuissimi gignuntur." For some other invocations of the agricultural/military ideal, cf. Cic. *Off.* 2.89 (also in the mouth of Cato), *Verr.* 2.2.149, *Rosc. Amer.* 42–5, 50, 75; Hor. *Epist.* 2.1.139 ("agricolae prisci, fortes parvoque beati"); Juv. 2.72–4.

191. Livy 39.42–3; cf. Plutarch, *Cato Maior* 17, *Titus Flamininus* 18 (and consider also Lucilius 273–4 Marx on Gentius and the praetor for a possible parallel). Livy calls Philippus "an expensive and well-known whore" ("carum ac nobile scortum," 39.42.8): *carum* can be trans-lated as either "expensive" or "dear," but Livy's emphasis on the price Flamininus had to pay for him ("spe ingentium donorum perductum," ibid.) suggests the former. On the other hand, Plutarch (*Cato Maior* 17) speaks of a relationship of long standing, so that Philippus might in fact have been "dear" to Flamininus in both senses. *Nobile*, however, here surely means "well-known" rather than "noble" (*pace* Boswell 1980: 68 with n. 33 and Richlin 1992a: 222). Writing of the Bacchanalian scandal of two years earlier, Livy describes the freedwoman Hispala Fecenia, who played so crucial a role in the sequence of events, as *scortum nobile* (which Kroll 1988: 100 oddly translates "vornehme Dirne"); cf. Lucilius 263 Marx, "Phryne nobilis illa." Sage's LCL translation, "a notorious degenerate whom he loved," approaches the correct sense of *nobile*, and possibly of *carum*, but misrepresents the tone of *scortum*.

192. Livy 39.42.8–12.

193. Livy 39.43.5: "ignominiane sua quemquam doliturum censeret, cum ipse vino et Venere amens sanguine hominis in convivio lusisset?"

194. Cf. Cantarella 1992: 101–2: "Lucius Flaminius [*sic*: "Lucio Flaminino" in the Italian original] was not punished for his homosexuality: his crime was killing a man with-out respecting the rules governing capital punishment." Referring to Roman reactions to this incident, Richlin 1992a: 87 speaks of "sadism and pederasty (a great scandal)," but there is no support here or elsewhere in the ancient sources for the supposition that a man's sexual use of one of his own youthful male slaves or of a male prostitute could give rise to scandal in and of itself. MacMullen 1982: 490 n. 21 asserts on the basis of the passage from Livy that Cato "often reprobate[s] L. Cornelius Scipio for (the mere posses-sion of) a hired catamite"—a surprisingly skewed reading, for the incident had nothing to do with Scipio, and Cato reproached Flamininus neither "often" nor for "the mere posses-sion of" Philippus.

195. Livy 39.43.2: "Placentiae famosam mulierem"; Val. Max. 2.9.3: "mulierculae cuius amore tenebatur"; Sen. *Contr.* 9.2 (*meretrix*); Cic. *Sen.* 42: "notandam putavi libidinem" (the neuter noun *scortum* is used to refer to the prostitute).

196. So too Boswell 1980: 68–69, Lilja 1983: 31 n. 71, and Cantarella 1992: 101–2.

197. *De Vir. Illustr.* 47.4: "quod ille in Gallia ad cuiusdam scorti spectaculum eiectum quendam e carcere in convivio iugulari iussisset."

198. Balsdon 1979: 170 cites Flamininus in a discussion of abuses by provincial gover-nors of their power and compares the story of John the Baptist's death. Cicero draws a similar picture of Verres, provincial governor of Sicily, who seems to have flaunted his relationship with a female prostitute named Chelidon; Cicero would have us believe that she had a significant influence on Verres' decisions as governor (see, e.g., Cic. *Verr.* 2.1.137–40, with Kroll 1988: 101 and Lyne 1980: 12). Suetonius reports that the emperor Vitellius made many of his decisions based on the advice of "the basest sort of people, actors and chariot-drivers, and especially his freedman Asiaticus," with whom he had had an on-again-off-again sexual relationship (Suet. *Vit.* 12: "talibus principiis magnam imperii partem non nisi consilio et arbitrio vilissimi cuiusque histrionum et aurigarum administravit et maxime Asiatici liberti").

199. Sen. *Contr.* 9.2.1–11.

200. It is revealing that according to the ancient biographer, the third-century A.D. emperor Severus Alexander contemplated outlawing male prostitutes (*exoleti*: for the term, see chapter 2) in a climate of gradually increasing asceticism, but realizing that this would not stop them from finding customers (and might in fact increase their desirability, given the lure of the illicit), he decided in the end merely to dedicate the funds raised by the tax on all prostitutes, male and female, to public works (SHA *Sev. Alex.* 24.3–4: "lenonum vectigal et meretricum et exoletorum in sacrum aerarium inferri vetuit, sed sumptibus publicis ad instaurationem theatri, circi, amphitheatri, stadii deputavit. habuit in animo ut exoletos vetaret, quod postea Philippus fecit, sed veritus est ne prohibens publicum dedecus in privatas cupiditates converteret, cum homines inlicita magis prohibita poscant furore iactati"). As the biographer notes, the later emperor Philippus (also in the third century) actually did outlaw male prostitutes—Aurelius Victor tells us he took this step after having seen a young male prostitute who resembled his own son—but, just as Severus Alexander had feared, even that prohibition turned out to be ineffectual. (Aurel. Vict. *Caes.* 28.6: "tum quia forte praeteriens filii similem pro meritorio ephebum conspexerat, usum virilis scorti removendum honestissime consultavit. verumtamen manet: quippe condicione loci mutata peioribus flagitiis agitatur, dum avidius periculosa quibusque prohibentur mortales petunt.") See Cantarella 1992: 173–86 for a survey of the ups and downs of the suppression of male prostitution in the late Empire.

201. This rhetorical commonplace is often called the *locus de indulgentia* (see Treggiari 1991: 300–1, where she cites some central texts: Plaut. *Bacch.* 409–10, 1079–80; Ter. *Ad.* 100–10; Sen. *Contr.* 2.4.10, 2.6.11; Juv. 8.163–6).

202. Cic. *Cael.* 42: "parcat iuventus pudicitiae suae, ne spoliet alienam, ne effundat patrimonium, ne faenore trucidetur, ne incurrat in alterius domum atque familiam, ne probrum castis, labem integris, infamiam bonis inferat, ne quem vi terreat, ne intersit insidiis, scelere careat."

203. Given the particulars of the case, Cicero is focusing on female prostitutes (*meretrices*), but the evidence on boy prostitutes reviewed earlier suggests that his audience could easily have applied Cicero's arguments about *meretricii amores* to the use of boy prostitutes (*pueri meritorii*) as well.

204. Edwards 1993: 92.

205. See, e.g., Plaut. *Cas.* 459, 591, 969; Lucil. 416 Marx.

206. For the cultural pressure to marry and beget legitimate children exerted on Roman men, consider Augustus' legislation which discouraged men from remaining unmarried and childless (discussed in Treggiari 1991: 60–80 and Edwards 1993: 41–2); for earlier periods, see Treggiari 1991: 57–60 and cf. Val. Max. 2.9.1, as well as the sources on Q. Caecilius Metellicus Macedonicus' speech in 131 B.C. urging Roman men to marry and produce children (Gell. 1.6: see Treggiari 1991: 205–6); Lucil. 678–9 Marx seems to represent a response to this speech (see also 686 Marx). For legitimate children as the goal of marriage, consider Catull. 61.204–5 ("ludite ut lubet, et brevi / liberos date") and Juv. 9.70–91 (Naevolus' patron should be grateful for the fact that he gave him a child), and see Treggiari 1991: 5–13.

207. Martial offers the persona *both* of married man *and* of bachelor; it is probable that in reality he was unmarried. See Sullivan 1991: 25–6 and Kay *ad* Martial 11.104.

208. Petr. *Sat.* 74–5. After the "not unattractive" slave (*puer non inspeciosus*) walks in and Trimalchio pounces on him (*invasit . . . et osculari diutius coepit*), Fortunata assails him for not being able to control his desires, in order, as the narrator puts it, to assert her rights over her husband: "itaque Fortunata, ut ex aequo ius firmum approbaret, male dicere Trimalchioni coepit et purgamentum dedecusque praedicare, qui non contineret libidinem

suam" (74.9). Trimalchio himself later claims that Fortunata has misunderstood him: he kissed the boy not because of his beauty but because of his thriftiness and skill at arithmetic and reading: "puerum basiavi frugalissimum, non propter formam, sed quia frugi est: decem partes dicit, librum ab oculo legit . . ." (75.4). Trimalchio is surely bluffing, but Schievenin 1976, perhaps uniquely among scholars, takes him at his word, arguing that "il furibundo litigio tra marito e moglie è il risultato di una incomprensione, di un malinteso che ha assunto tinte drammatiche perché in Fortunata è scoppiata violenta, come è naturale, la gelosia" (299). In any case, what is worth noting is the assumption shared by Trimalchio, Fortunata, the narrator, and the readership: that a man might be attracted to his male slaves. Note that in this same scene Trimalchio, himself born in slavery, claims to have offered sexual services to both his master and mistress (Petr. *Sat.* 75.11: see earlier in this chapter).

209. Mart. 11.23.5–10: "nec futuam quamvis prima te nocte maritus, / communis tecum nec mihi lectus erit; / complectarque meam, nec tu prohibebis, amicam, / ancillam mittes et mihi iussa tuam. / te spectante dabit nobis lasciva minister / basia, sive meus sive erit ille tuus."

210. The dismissive statement that his wife has "two cunts" (11.43.12, cited earlier in this chapter) is an obvious parallel; cf. also 12.75 (discussed in chapter 5), where the poet claims that any number of willful boys are preferable to a rich but demanding wife.

211. On the other hand, Martial elsewhere cautions against going to extremes: addressing a man who has used his wife's dowry to buy male slaves for his sexual pleasure and has then proceeded to expend all his sexual energy on them, leaving nothing for his wife, the poet sardonically observes that he is acting unjustly, since he has in fact "sold" his penis to his wife (12.97.11: "non est haec tua, Basse: vendidisti"). Behind Martial's hyperbolic humor lies the notion that, after all, men's wives do deserve some attention.

212. Suet. *Aug.* 69.2: "an refert, ubi et in qua arrigas?" Boswell 1990: 72 removes the specificity of the gender, translating "where or in whom you stick it," noting (n. 15) that "*qua* may be feminine because Antony is thinking primarily of females, but it could also refer to parts of the body, male or female," but that seems highly unlikely to me. The Latin phrase is most naturally construed as referring to women, as Antony's scandalous relationship with Cleopatra is precisely the issue here.

213. SHA *Aelius* 5.11: "idem uxori conquerenti de extraneis voluptatibus dixisse fertur: 'patere me per alias exercere cupiditates meas; uxor enim dignitatis nomen est, non voluptatis.'"

214. In her discussion of legal and moral concepts regarding sexual relations within marriage, Treggiari 1991: 301 comes to a similar conclusion: "Fewer problems are caused by purely physical encounters with slaves of either sex. There is no need here to ask whether the man is married or not."

215. Mart. 3.92 creates a scenario in which his wife asks him to accept the fact that she has a lover on the side, and while he harshly rejects the proposal, the pungency of the epigram must derive from the fact that it reflects a certain reality.

216. See the general discussion in Treggiari 1991: 299–319.

217. For a husband who has a male lover who penetrates him, cf. Mart. 2.54 (a wife has taken the precaution of hiring a eunuch as a guardian for her husband). Cato's use of the unnecessary pronoun with the passive form of the verb may reflect the rather more shocking nature of this possibility; as for the form itself, *adulterare* is used in the passive voice elsewhere only regarding women (e.g., Quint. *Decl. Min.* 325.pr., D. 48.5.30.4; cf. Hor. *Epod.* 16.32). Kroll 1988: 73 translates the two clauses, "wenn du aber eine Ehe brachest oder dich verführen ließest"; Grimal 1963: 119 omits *sive tu adulterarere* in his translation without comment ("si c'était toi qui commettais l'adultère . . ."). Richlin 1981a:

383 simply paraphrases, "if she catches him in adultery." Hallett 1988: 1269 is somewhat ambiguous ("if you were to take the active or the passive role in an extramarital affair"), while Treggiari 1991: 270 n. 35 notes that *adulterari* seems to refer to passive homosexuality."

218. D. 48.5.25.pr. Cf. Richlin 1981a: 382, 384. There is a double standard also in the rule that the children of unions other than *iustae nuptiae* inherited the status of their mother: consequently sexual relations between a free woman and a male slave would produce free but illegitimate children, whereas relations between a free man and his slave woman would produce more slaves for the household. See P. R. C. Weaver, "The Status of Children in Mixed Marriages," in Rawson 1986: 145–69, especially pp. 147–50 and pp. 150–4, on the *Senatusconsultum Claudianum* restricting cohabitation between free women and male slaves.

219. Quint. *I.O.* 5.11.34–5: "si turpis dominae consuetudo cum servo, turpis domino cum ancilla; si mutis animalibus finis voluptas, idem homini. cui rei facillime occurrit ex dissimilibus argumentatio: non idem est dominum cum ancilla coisse, quod dominam cum servo; nec, si mutis finis voluptas, rationalibus quoque."

220. For a different approach to Catullus' poems on marriage (less cynical and, I would argue, less critical) see Arkins 1982: 117–56, and see Fedeli 1983 for a detailed study of Catullus 61. Cantarella 1992: 171 observes that "it hardly needs to be said that Roman men, exactly like their Greek counterparts, very often continued to have homosexual liaisons even after getting married. Manlius Torquatus is certainly not the only one to be suspected (as Catullus says) of showing reluctance to accept the rule whereby he must forget *pueri* after his wedding-day." I would question whether we can speak of a "rule" here: it would be better to speak of a "convention" in poetic and other contexts celebrating the ideals of marriage. Similarly, Robert 1997: 264 notes the belief that, once married, a man should give up his slave-boys—"du moins partiellement, et en théorie; car la femme a toutes les raisons de craindre la rivalité de ces éphèbes sur qui le mari prend plaisir à exercer sa virilité."

221. Plin. *N.H.* 10.104: "inest pudicitia illis plurima et neutri nota adulteria. coniugi fidem non violant communemque servant domum." (His invocation of the concepts of *pudicitia* and *adulterium* illustrates a tendency to describe animals' sexual behavior in human terms: see appendix 1.)

222. D. 48.5.14.5: "periniquum enim videtur esse, ut pudicitiam vir ab uxore exigat quam ipse non exhibeat."

223. Married to Mark Antony's daughter Antonia, Drusus Germanicus was stepson of Augustus, brother of the emperor Tiberius, and father of the emperor Claudius. Cf. Plin. *N.H.* 7.84, Dio Cassius 55.1.

224. Writing of the late second-century A.D. emperor Pescennius Niger, the biographer Aelius Spartianus observes that he only engaged in sexual relations for the procreation of legitimate children (SHA *Pescennius Niger* 6.6: "rei veneriae nisi ad creandos liberos prorsus ignarus"). But the author goes on to note that the same emperor performed certain Gallic rites limited to "the most chaste": "denique etiam sacra quaedam in Gallia, quae semper castissimis decernunt consensu publico celebranda, suscepit." In other words, Niger, even more than Drusus (for Valerius Maximus does not specify that he engaged only in *procreative* relations with his wife), represents an extreme of chastity and purity. Like Drusus, he is an exception that proves the rule.

225. Treggiari 1991: 511–3 provides a handy list of philosophical texts espousing such views on sexual behavior.

226. For Musonius' life and teachings, see Lutz 1947. For the role of philosophical texts in Greek cultural history see Dover 1974 and Winkler 1990. Winkler 1990: 21 makes the point especially eloquently: "Athens was a society in which philosophers were often

ignored and when noticed were easily represented not as authority figures but as cranks and buffoons. If we focus our attention not on that eccentric côterie but on the citizen body (in its own way an elite in the population of Athens), we get quite a different picture, one in which the debates of philosophers have no discernible impact." For Roman biases against philosophers, see Petrochilos 1974: 163–96.

227. Compare Musonius' comment on sexual relations between males (ὅτι παρὰ φύσιν τὸ τόλμημα) with Plato, *Laws* 636c: ἀρρένων δὲ πρὸς ἄρρενας ἢ θηλειῶν πρὸς θηλείας παρὰ φύσιν καὶ τῶν πρώτων τὸ τόλμημα εἶναι δι' ἀκράτειαν ἡδονῆς. For Stoic and other philosophical beliefs on sexual behavior, see Boswell 1980: 128–32, 145–56. The second-century A.D. emperor Marcus Aurelius, whose *Meditations* are suffused with Stoic philosophy, claims that he learned from his father to suppress sexual involvement with boys (καὶ τὸ παῦσαι τὰ περὶ τοὺς ἔρωτας τῶν μειρακίων, *Medit.* 1.16), but he is speaking about a matter of personal discipline rather than public morality, as he certainly made no attempts to force his own ascetic regimen on Roman society as a whole. The fact that he, like Musonius Rufus, wrote in Greek rather than Latin at least partially signals the status of the *Meditations* as philosophical text and its distance from everyday Roman discourse.

228. Muson. Ruf. 86.30–2 Lutz: ὅπερ νομίζουσί τινες μάλιστά πως εἶναι ἀναίτιον, ἐπεὶ καὶ δεσπότης πᾶς αὐτεξούσιος εἶναι δοκεῖ ὅ τι βούλεται χρῆσθαι δούλῳ τῷ ἑαυτοῦ.

229. For Apollo and Hyacinth, see (e.g.) Lucil. 276–7 Marx and perhaps also 895–6 Marx; Stat. *Silv.* 2.1.112; Mart. 11.43, 14.173; for Hercules and Hylas, see Stat. *Silv.* 1.5.22, 2.1.106–36, Mart. 6.68, 7.15, 7.50, 9.25, 9.65, 11.43. Prop. 3.7.21–4 refers to Argynnus, Agamemnon's boyfriend, who drowned in Boeotia.

230. Comprehensive overviews of Ganymede in Greek and Roman myth and art include Friedländer 1912, Sichtermann 1953, Kempter 1980, and Sichtermann 1988.

231. See Festus 38.22: "Catamitum pro Ganymede dixerunt, qui fuit Iovis concubinus"; 7.8–9: "alcedo dicebatur ab antiquis pro alcyone, ut pro Ganymede Catamitus, pro Nilo Melo" (cf. 16.29–30); Serv. *ad* Virg. *Aen.* 1.28: "hic Ganymedes Latine Catamitus dicitur"; Accius, *tr. fr.* 653a–b: "Iouis Dardanum progenuit, Troum Dardanus, / Trousque Assaracum et Ilum et Catamitum [creat]"; and the other sources cited at *TLL* s.v. For the Etruscan form *Catmite*, see *LIMC* s.v.

232. Plaut. *Men.* 143–4: "tabulam pictam in pariete, / ubi aquila Catameitum raperet aut ubi Venus Adoneum."

233. Vir. *Aen.* 1.28 ("rapti Ganymedis honores") with Servius *ad loc.* Cf. also Ov. *Fast.* 6.43 ("rapto Ganymede dolebam") and Macr. *Sat.* 5.16.11 (contrasting Homer, who portrays Ganymede only as Zeus' cup-bearer and not as his concubine, and Virgil, who "propter Catamiti paelicatum totam gentem eius vexasse commemorat"). Ganymede appears later in the *Aeneid* as the subject of an ecphrasis (5.252–7), for which see Putnam 1995.

234. Prop. 2.30.27–32. Cf. *Eleg. Maec.* 1.87–92, where Zeus' abduction of Ganymede is cited as an example of how even the king of the gods indulged himself after his military victories.

235. See Hor. *C.* 3.20.15–6; Petr. *Sat.* 92.3; Stat. *Silv.* 1.6.28–34, 3.1.25–7, 4.2.10–2; Juv. 5.59, 9.46–7, 13.42–5; Mart. 1.6, 3.39, 5.55, 9.11, 9.22, 9.36, 9.73, 9.103, 10.66, 10.98, 12.15, 13.108.

236. *CIL* 6.19519: "Q. Hordionius Q. l. Catamitu(s)"; Mart. 11.28: "invasit medici Nasica phreneticus Eucti / et percidit Hylan. hic, puto, sanus erat."

237. Cic. *Tusc.* 4.71: "quis aut de Ganymedi raptu dubitat, quid poetae velint, aut non intellegit quid apud Euripidem et loquatur et cupiat Laius?"

238. Festus 18.44: "Catamitum pro Ganymede dixerunt, qui fuit Iovis concubinus."

239. Mart. 2.43.14: "at mihi succurrit pro Ganymede manus"; 8.46.5: "tu Ganymedeo poteras succedere lecto"; 11.26.6: "esse negem melius cum Ganymede Iovi"; 11.43.3–4:

"dixit idem quotiens lascivo Iuno Tonanti! / ille tamen grandi cum Ganymede iacet";
11.104.17–20: "pedicare negas: dabat hoc Cornelia Graccho, / Iulia Pompeio, Porcia, Brute,
tibi; / dulcia Dardanio nondum miscente ministro / pocula Iuno fuit pro Ganymede Iovi."
Martial elsewhere refers to a mythic tradition according to which Mercury enjoyed
Ganymede's favors as well (7.74, 9.25).

240. *Priap.* 3.5–6: "quodque Iovi dederat, qui raptus ab alite sacra, / miscet amatori
pocula grata suo."

241. See *TLL* s.v.; Servius also reports the transferred meaning, though he uses it to
refer to boy prostitutes ("nam meritorii pueri, id est catamiti, quibus licenter utebantur
antiqui, recedentes a turpi servitio nuces spargebant . . ." *ad Ecl.* 8.29).

242. Ps.-Aurel. Vict. *Epit.* 1.22: "inter duodecim catamitos totidemque puellas accubare
solitus erat."

243. Cic. *Phil.* 2.77: "te catamitum" (discussed in chapter 5); *Orat. Incert.* fr. 29:
"quasi vero ego de facie tua, catamite, dixerim."

244. Ov. *Met.* 10.300–10. The words are put in Orpheus' mouth, but they have clear
resonances for Ovid's Roman readers.

245. Hor. *C.* 4.4.1–4: "qualem ministrum fulminis alitem, / cui rex deorum regnum in
avis vagas / permisit expertus fidelem / Iuppiter in Ganymede flavo . . ."; *Laus Pisonis* 152–4:
"ignea quin etiam superum pater arma recondit / et Ganymedeae repetens convivia mensae
/ pocula sumit ea, qua gessit fulmina, dextra."

246. Juv. 9.22–3 (note that this statue is said to serve as a place of assignation between
men and women); Lactant. *Inst.* 1.11.29: "quod aliud argumentum habet imago Catamiti
et effigies aquilae, cum ante pedes Iovis ponuntur in templis et cum ipso pariter adorantur,
nisi ut nefandi sceleris ac stupri memoria maneat in aeternum?"

247. Sichtermann 1953: 73–98 provides a comprehensive catalogue of images of
Ganymede in Greek and Roman art; see Sichtermann 1988 for a condensed version.

248. Here I rely on the selective catalogue offered by Sichtermann 1988, and I
refer to his numeration. Wall painting: 76 (Ostia), 95–100 (Pompeii), 139 (Pompeii), 140
(Stabiae), 206–8 (Pompeii), 209 (Palmyra), 257 (the Domus Aurea in Rome). Mosaics:
101 (Nîmes), 102 (Lower Egypt), 107 (Antioch), 108 (Spain), 173 (Baccano), 174 (Tarsos),
175 (Ostia), 176–9 (original location not indicated), 210 (Cyprus), 211 (Switzerland),
212 (Cyprus), 213 (Thysdrus), 214–5 (Spain), 216 (Vienne), 217 (Sussex, England); 259
(Hadrian's Villa in Tivoli [?]). Jewelry: 111–4, 144–64, 218–23, 261–6. Coins: 223 (all
from Asia Minor). Sarcophagi: 105, 109–10, 181–4, 260. Statuary groups: 115–137,
188–91, 250–6.

249. Likewise, Mart. 5.55 is inspired by an image of the eagle carrying Jupiter himself, and the poet imagines the bird speaking to the god about the beautiful Ganymede.

250. Hyg. *Astron.* 2.16.1: "Aquila. haec est quae dicitur Ganymedem rapuisse et amanti
Iovi tradidisse . . . itaque supra Aquarium volare videtur; hunc enim complures Ganymedem
esse finxerunt"; cf. ibid. 2.29.1: "Aquarius. hunc complures Ganymedem esse dixerunt,
quem Iuppiter propter pulchritudinem corporis ereptum parentibus, deorum ministrum
fecisse existimatur"; Serv. *ad Georg.* 3.304: "aquarium autem multi Ganymedem volunt";
Ampel. *Lib. Mem.* 2.11.1: "Aquarius, qui putatur esse Ganymedes"; Hyg. *Fab.* 224.4:
"Ganymedes Assaraci filius in Aquario duodecim signorum."

251. See, for example, Sichtermann 1988, nos. 138–65.

252. For further examples see Sichtermann 1988, nos. 122–131.

253. Sichtermann 1988, no. 173; Rome, Museo Nazionale 1241. In Sichtermann 1988,
no. 180 (a marble relief from the early imperial period) Ganymede's resistance is even
clearer.

254. Sichtermann 1988, no. 226.

255. Sichtermann 1988, no. 253; Venice, Museo Archeologico 145.

256. Sichtermann 1988, no. 251 ("noch immer als die treueste Nachbildung des Werkes von Leochares anzusehen"). For the Leochares group see Plin. *N.H.* 34.79.

257. Cf. Sichtermann 1988, no. 190.

258. Mart. 3.39 (*Iliaco ministro*), 2.43.13 (*Iliaco cinaedo*); for Ganymede as Jupiter's servant or slave, see also 9.22.11–2, 10.66.7–8, 11.104.19–20 (*Dardanio ministro*), 13.108.2. In 7.74, Martial imagines that Mercury might be interested in a *furtum* with either Paphie or Ganymede (cf. 9.25), thereby stealing the favorite slave of the head of the household. Other references to Ganymede as Jupiter's servant include Cic. *Tusc.* 1.65, *DND* 1.112; Hyg. *Astron.* 2.29.1; *Laus Pisonis* 152–4; Stat. *Silv.* 1.6.28–34, 3.1.25–7, 3.4.12–5, 4.2.10–2; Juv. 13.42–5; Ov. *Met.* 10.155–61.

259. V. *Aen.* 1.28: "rapti Ganymedis honores"; Ov. *Met.* 10.161: "invitaque Iovi nectar Iunone ministrat." In his fulsome poem on Domitian's eunuch Earinos (see earlier in text), Statius observes that whereas Juno petulantly refuses to be served by Ganymede (*Silv.* 3.4.14–5: "quem turbida semper / Iuno videt refugitque manum nectarque recusat"), the Roman Juno on earth, Domitian's wife Domitia, happily accepts Earinos' presence (*Silv.* 3.4.17–9: "placida quem fronte ministrum / Iuppiter Ausonius pariter Romanaque Iuno / aspiciunt et uterque probant"). One might read this, too, as a bit of fantasy; Garthwaite 1984: 113–4 argues by contrast that no one would be fooled into thinking that Domitia actually welcomed Earinos' presence, and that Statius is thus being bitterly ironic.

260. Apul. *Met.* 1.12: "hic est, soror Panthia, carus Endymion, hic Catamitus meus."

261. Hyg. *Fab.* 271 ("qui ephebi formosissimi fuerunt"): Adonis (loved by Venus), Endymion (loved by Luna), Ganymede (loved by Jupiter), Hyacinth (loved by Apollo), Narcissus (loved by himself [!]), Atlantius (who became known as Hermaphroditus), Hylas (loved by Hercules), and Chrysippus (raped by Theseus [*sic*; the usual tradition is that Laius raped him]).

262. Juv. 6.110: "sed gladiator erat. facit hoc illos Hyacinthos." In chapter 5 it will be noted that some modern translations obscure this point.

263. The parallel between Ganymede and Antinous seems to have suggested itself to at least one hostile Christian writer: see Tertull. *Apol.* 13.1, 13.12, *Ad Nat.* 2.10, *De Corona Milit.* 13 (discussed in Lambert 1984: 7, 95). Lambert 1984, while containing a number of errors in detail and some questionable speculations, conveniently brings together all the ancient evidence, textual and visual, on Antinous. See Waters 1995 for a more recent discussion, primarily focusing on images of Antinous in the nineteenth century.

264. Indeed, Aelius Spartiatus reports malicious gossip concerning Hadrian's tendency to pry into his friend's affairs, as well as his weakness for mature males and married ladies (SHA *Hadr.* 11.7: "et hoc quidem vitiosissimum putant atque huic adiungunt quae de adultorum amore ac nuptarum adulteriis, quibus Hadrianus laborasse dicitur, adserunt"). Given the parallel with *nuptarum adulteria*, *adultorum amor* must refer to an interest in freeborn Roman males (the explicit qualifier *ingenuorum* is omitted because it is understood, as it sometimes is in phrases such as *puerorum amor* and *iuvenum amor*: see chapter 3). In other words, the subject of this gossip was Hadrian's penchant for *stuprum* with the freeborn; since Antinous was not a freeborn Roman, that was not a problem in his case.

265. Lambert 1984: 7–12 gives a sketch of Antinous' *Nachleben* from Christian moralists to twentieth-century scholars; see 94–5 for an overview of ancient Christian condemnations of the relationship.

266. The third- or fourth-century A.D. author of the biography of Hadrian in the *Historia Augusta* notes that among his contemporaries there are different stories about Antinous' death, some claiming that he gave his life for Hadrian as part of a religious vow, and others pointing to Antinous' beauty and Hadrian's "excessive desire" (Did they think it

was a lovers' quarrel gone terribly wrong?): "de quo varia fama est, aliis eum devotum pro Hadriano adserentibus, aliis quod et forma eius ostentat et nimia voluptas Hadriani" (SHA *Hadr*. 14.6). Likewise Aurelius Victor (*Caes*. 14.6–9), writing in the same period, observes that, because of Hadrian's luxurious ways (*luxus lasciviaeque*), there were rumors that he engaged in relations with young men (*stupra puberibus*) and, above all, that he "burned with Antinous' infamous service to him" (*Antinoi flagravisse famoso ministerio*). While some think, Aurelius continues, that Hadrian's decision to name a city after Antinous and to set up statues of him were pious, reverent actions (*pia religiosaque*), he himself considers the matter to be "suspicious" (*suspectam*) in view of Hadrian's "loose morals" (*remissum ingenium*) and the difference in age between himself and Antinous (*aestimantes societatem aevi longe imparilis*). Both writers' comments reveal an assumption perfectly in line with beliefs studied in this book—that a beautiful young man under the age of twenty might well stir up the passions of a hedonistic older man given to sensuality (see chapter 2); neither of them, of course, offers evidence for the response by Hadrian's own contemporaries to his relationship with Antinous.

267. See, e.g., Suet. *Jul*. 2, 49–52, *Aug*. 68 (rumors about having been anally penetrated); *Tib*. 45 (rumors about his fondness for cunnilinctus).

268. SHA *Comm*. 10–1, *Elag*. 8–12. See further discussion in chapter 2.

269. See Appendix 2.

270. Consider the cases of Claudius and Agrippina (e.g., Tac. *Ann*. 11.25, *nuptiae incestae*) and Domitian and Julia (e.g., Suet. *Dom*. 22, Plin. *Ep*. 4.11.6, Juv. 2.29–33).

271. Consider the ancient gossip concerning Caligula and his sisters (Suet. *Cal*. 24) and Nero and his mother (Suet. *Nero* 28.2, Tac. *Ann*. 14.2, Dio 61.11.3–4).

272. SHA *Hadr*. 14.5: "Antinoum suum, dum per Nilum navigat, perdidit, quem muliebriter flevit." See chapter 4 for discussion of the standards of masculine self-control implicit in this comment.

273. Paus. 8.9.7, Dio 69.11.1–4, Amm. Marc. 22.16.2, Just. *Apol*. 29.4.

274. Dio 69.11.4.

275. See Aurel. Vict. *Caes*. 14.8: "quae quidem alii pia volunt religiosaque: quippe Hadriano cupiente fatum producere, cum voluntarium ad vicem magi poposcissent, cunctis retractantibus Antinoum obiecisse se referunt, hincque in eum officia supra dicta." This story is presumably what lies behind Dio's phrase ἐθελόντης ἐθανατώθη ("was put to death willingly" 69.11.3).

276. Lambert 1984 provides a representative sample of illustrations, along with a catalog of surviving sculptures of Antinous. For Antinous as Vertumnus, see Lambert 1984, no. 86; as Silvanus or Aristaios, Lambert 1984, no. 9; as Osiris, Lambert 1984, no. 76.

277. We are told that a certain Numenius wrote a consolation to Hadrian (Suda 3.481.22 Adler) and that Pancrates and Mesomedes addressed poems to Antinous himself (see Athen. 15.677D and Pap. Oxy. 8.1085 for the former and Suda 3.367.9 Adler for the latter). Inscriptions in honor of Antinous include *CIL* 6.1851 (from Rome) and *ILS* 7212 (from Lanuvium).

278. *CLE* 879 = *CIL* 14.3535: "Antinoo et Beleno par aetas formaque si par, / cur non Antinous sit quoque qui Belenus?" (the suggestion that it accompanied a statue is made by the *CLE* editor).

279. SHA *Hadr*. 11.3: "Septicio Claro praefecto praetorii et Suetonio Tranquillo epistularum magistro multisque aliis, quod apud Sabinam uxorem iniussu eius familiarius se tunc egerant quam reverentia domus aulicae postulabat, successores dedit, uxorem etiam ut morosam et asperam dimissurus, ut ipse dicebat, si privatus fuisset." In a room at the Museo della Civiltà Romana in Rome, one finds copies of ancient busts of Hadrian, Sabina, and Antinous displayed together, as if they were one happy family. This was hardly the

reputation they had in antiquity: when Sabina eventually died, there was a rumor that Hadrian himself had poisoned her (SHA *Hadr.* 23.9).

Chapter 2

1. And yet, as David Halperin has reminded me, since the statuary group largely survives through Roman copies, it would seem that the pair were hardly banned from public representation in Roman contexts. For Harmodios and Aristogeiton, see Thuc. 6.54–59, Pl. *Symp.* 182c, Aeschin. 1.132–3, 140; for the statuary group see (e.g.) Andrew Stewart, *Greek Sculpture: An Exploration* (New Haven, 1990), I:135–6.

2. Such is the implication of MacMullen 1982: 493 (see further chapter 3, n. 1).

3. For discussions of Greek pederastic traditions, see especially Dover 1978, Halperin 1990, Winkler 1990, and Cohen 1991. Both Veyne (1978 and 1985) and Cantarella 1992 have argued that it was specifically the question of *pederasty* and not *homosexuality* that distinguished Roman from Greek traditions; in the first section of this chapter I seek to substantiate that point further by means of a more thorough survey of the evidence than they offer, and in its remaining sections I consider related questions not treated by either Veyne or Cantarella.

4. Nepos pr. 4: "laudi in Graecia ducitur adulescentulis quam plurimos habuisse amatores." The LCL translator, J. C. Rolfe, obscures the specific reference to pederasty: "In Crete it is thought praiseworthy for young men to have had the greatest possible number of love affairs." Rolfe accepts Valkenaer's emendation of the MS reading *Graecia* to *Creta*, as do Nipperdey (Berlin, 1879), Malcovati (Turin, 1944), and Marshall (Leipzig, 1977). In favor of the MS reading, Nepos' statement is applicable not just to Crete but to classical Athens, Sparta, Thebes, and many other Greek city-states. On the other hand, the reading *Creta* establishes a sequence in Nepos' examples: Athens, Crete, Sparta, and most of the Greek world. On pederasty and Crete, see Dover 1978: 185–96; Bremmer 1980: 287; Sergent 1986: 7–15, 26–39; Koehl 1986 and 1997.

5. Nepos, *Alc.* 2.2: "ineunte adulescentia amatus est a multis more Graecorum."

6. Cic. *Tusc.* 5.58: "haberet etiam more Graeciae quosdam adulescentis amore coniunctos." The tone with which Cicero writes of Dionysius and his love affairs is illuminating. He takes this kind of sexual behavior for granted, appropriating the "Greek custom" for his own purposes with no hint of disapproval. The fact that Dionysius was involved in erotic affairs with these young men functions merely as a further support for Cicero's argument: even though he loved them, he did not trust them. A telling parallel is to be found at *Off.* 2.25. Here Cicero illustrates Dionysius' suspicious nature by means of a different example (due to his fear of knives, he had his hair singed rather than cut), and he adds the further instance of Alexander of Pherae, who did not trust his wife. Cicero treats Dionysius' love for his *adulescentes* no differently from Alexander's love for his wife, apart from the observation that the former is in conformance with *mos Graeciae*.

7. Cic. *Rep.* 4.3.fr.3: "opprobrio fuisse adulescentibus, si amatores non haberent." The line is preserved by Servius *ad Aen.* 10.325. Servius understands the words to apply to Greece in general, but the LCL editor of Cicero (Clinton Walker Keyes, 1928) suggests that this pertains specifically to Sparta, given what follows.

8. Cic. *Rep.* 4.4: "iuventutis vero exercitatio quam absurda in gymnasiis! quam levis epheborum illa militia! quam contrectationes et amores soluti et liberi! mitto Eleos et Thebanos, apud quos in amore ingenuorum libido etiam permissam habet et solutam licentiam."

9. Cic. *Tusc.* 4.70: "mihi quidem haec in Graecorum gymnasiis nata consuetudo videtur, in quibus isti liberi ac concessi sunt amores." *Amor amicitiae* refers to male friendships

with philosophical airs, but clearly they can include a sexual element, for Cicero later dryly asks why no one ever loves an ugly youth (*deformem adulescentem*) or a beautiful old man, and points out that everyone knows what the poets mean when they speak of Jupiter and Ganymede or of Laius and Chrysippus (4.71). Another Roman writer who possibly alludes to the pederastic associations of the gymnasia is Silius Italicus, although the allusion, if even present, is muted (Sil. Ital. *Pun.* 14.136–8: "pigro luctandi studio certamen in umbra / molle pati docta et gaudens splendescere olivo / stat, mediocre decus vincentum, ignava iuventus").

10. Nepos, pr. 5: "quae omnia apud nos partim infamia, partim humilia atque ab honestate remota ponuntur."

11. Cic. *Rep.* 4.4: "mitto Eleos et Thebanos, apud quos in amore ingenuorum libido etiam permissam habet et solutam licentiam."

12. Cic. *Tusc.* 4.70 (quoting Ennius): "flagiti principium est nudare inter civis corpora." On the Roman resistance to nudity among male citizens, see also Crassus fr. 45; Cic. *Off.* 1.129; Plut. *Cato Maior* 20.7–8, *Rom. Ques.* 274A.

13. Cf. Aeschin. 1.138–9; Plut. *Amatorius* 751B, *Solon* 1.6.

14. Nearly all of the scholars cited above conflate homosexuality with pederasty; only Veyne 1978 and 1985 and Cantarella 1992 clearly and consistently make the distinction. Lilja 1983: 112 at first appears to do so, but then writes that Cicero's discussion in the *Tusculans* represents his "opinions on the origin of and different traits in homosexuality" (p. 123; cf. also pp. 50, 107). So too Edwards 1993: 94 n. 99, citing Lilja, asserts that Cic. *Tusc.* 4.70 is "on homosexual relations as a peculiarly Greek practice" and elsewhere argues that "a taste for homosexual relations might be associated with the 'Greek' literary life" (Edwards 1993: 96). I would argue that only a taste for pederastic relations might be so associated.

15. Some scholars (e.g., Adams 1982: 123, 228; MacMullen 1982: 486; Hallett 1989: 223; and Edwards 1993: 94) have pointed to the presence in Latin of such loan-words from Greek as *cinaedus* (signifying a penetrated male) and *pedicare* ("to anally penetrate") as a sign of an association made by Romans themselves between male homosexual behavior and Greece. See Williams 1995 for arguments against making such an inference.

16. For overviews, see MacMullen 1982 and 1991, Gruen 1990 and 1992.

17. *Pace* Boswell 1980: 77, there is no reason to doubt that Juventius is freeborn: cf. Chester Louis Neudling, *A Prosopography to Catullus* (Oxford, 1955), pp. 94–6.

18. Val. Max. 8.1.abs.8. Valentinus had brought Gaius Cosconius on charges under the Servilian law, but after a poem by Valentinus, in which he spoke of his having seduced a freeborn boy and girl ("carmen quo puerum praetextatum et ingenuam virginem a se corruptam poetico ioco significaverat"), was recited in the courtroom, Cosconius was acquitted; as Valerius Maximus notes, "Valerius was condemned in Cosconius' acquittal more than Cosconius was absolved in his own case" ("magis vero Valerius in Cosconii absolutione damnatus quam Cosconius in sua causa liberatus est"). Cf. *RE* 372, where the incident is dated to ca. 111 B.C.

19. To repeat a point made earlier: while Catullus' sixteenth poem contains a celebrated statement of the separability of poet and poetry (for which see especially Selden 1992), and positively prevents us from speaking of Catullus' actual experiences, the very existence of the poem suggests that he knew the risks involved in writing such seemingly personal poetry; what is interesting for our purposes is that he was willing to take the risk of writing about affairs with a freeborn boy and a married woman.

20. That the ἐρώμενοι are prostitutes is suggested not only by the parallelism with ἑταίρας but also by Cato's disparaging remark (quoted in the next citation from Polybius) to the effect that Romans were "buying" boyfriends for great sums of money.

21. Plut. *Cato Maior* 8.2: κατηγορῶν δὲ τῆς πολυτελείας; Diod. 37.3.6: κατηγορῶν τῆς ἐπιπολαζούσης ἐν τῇ Ῥώμῃ τρυφῆς; Athen. 6.109 (274F–275A): ἐδυσχέραινε καὶ ἐκεκράγει, ὅτι τινὲς τὰς ξενικὰς τρυφὰς εἰσήγαγον εἰς τὴν Ῥώμην.

22. Diod. 37.3.5 adds costly wine and skilled chefs to the list. See also Diod. 31.24 and Plut. *Quaest. conv.* 668B-C. Cantarella 1992: 102 interprets Cato's reaction as I do, whereas Hallett 1989: 223 and Edwards 1993: 95 n. 104 see homosexuality as the issue (although Edwards 1993: 176–8 casts her discussion in terms of luxury). MacMullen 1982: 486 selectively quotes Polybius, thereby misrepresenting him: "Some gave themselves up to love affairs with youths . . . having quickly adopted Greek laxity in this regard, during the war with Perseus."

23. Gruen 1992: 261 points out that the reference to "Greek permissiveness" is in Polybius' voice rather than Cato's, and thus that "the only unequivocal association of moral decline with the effects of Hellenism in this period was made by a Greek!"

24. Livy 34.4.3: "haec ego, quo melior laetiorque in dies fortuna rei publicae est, quo magis imperium crescit—et iam in Graeciam Asiamque transcendimus omnibus libidinum inlecebris repletas et regias etiam adtrectamus gazas—eo plus horreo, ne illae magis res nos ceperint quam nos illas."

25. See, e.g., Livy 39.6.7–9, Pliny, *N.H.* 34.14.

26. Sall. *Cat.* 13.3: "sed lubido stupri ganeae ceterique cultus non minor incesserat; viri muliebria pati, mulieres pudicitiam in propatulo habere . . ."

27. The consul Postumius opens his address to the assembled citizenry on a note of fearful warning with regard to foreign gods (39.15.2–3; he returns to the theme at 39.16.8). For other indications of Roman feeling against foreign religious practices, consider the incidents summarized in Val. Max. 1.3 ("De Superstitionibus"); Propertius' claim that in primitive Rome, "nulli cura fuit externos quaerere divos" (Prop. 4.1.17); and one of the laws proposed by Cicero in his *De Legibus*: "separatim nemo habessit deos neve novos neve advenas nisi publice adscitos" (2.19; cf. 2.25–6). According to the ancient biography of Hadrian, even that emperor (called *Graeculus* by some because of his love of Greek studies [1.5]) was suspicious of non-Roman cult practices and cherished traditional Roman practices (SHA *Hadr.* 22.10: "sacra Romana diligentissime curavit, peregrina contempsit"). This may or may not be an accurate reflection of Hadrian's actual beliefs and practices, but it reveals something about the biases of the biographer and his readership.

28. MacMullen 1991: 429–30.

29. Consider the phrase "stupra promiscua ingenuorum feminarumque" (39.8.7), and compare 39.8.5 ("per viros mulieresque"), 39.13.10 ("permixti viri feminis"), 39.15.12 ("promiscuos [sc., coetus] mulierum ac virorum"), and 39.18.5 ("virorum mulierumque"). It is suggestive that Livy writes of "stupra . . . ingenuorum feminarumque" rather than, for example, "stupra adulescentium feminarumque." This underscores what is particularly disgraceful in the entire affair: not the initiates' gender but their freeborn status. See chapter 3 for further discussion of *stuprum*.

30. Cf. Tac. *Hist.* 2.68: "apud Vitellium omnia indisposita, temulenta, pervigiliis ac Bacchanalibus quam disciplinae et castris propiora"; ibid. 2.69: "vires luxu corrumpebantur, contra veterem disciplinam et instituta maiorum apud quos virtute quam pecunia res Romana melius stetit." Note that in his narrative of the scandal of 186 B.C., Valerius Maximus (6.3.7) speaks only of the sexual misdeeds of women ("quae sacris Bacchanalium inceste usae fuerant"). At Juv. 2.3, the austere Curii are opposed to the licentious Bacchanalia in a poem attacking hypocritical *cinaedi*, but there is no suggestion that either the Bacchanalia or the Curii are themselves connected with any specific sexual practices.

31. Tac. *Ann.* 5.3: "sed non arma, non rerum novarum studium, amores iuvenum et impudicitiam nepoti obiectabat." This was hardly a concerted effort by Tiberius to curtail

pederastic pursuits, for in another letter from the same period he criticized "friendships with women"—a comment which was, according to Tacitus, a barely concealed attack on the consul Fufius, who had a talent for attracting women (Tac. *Ann.* 5.2: "quin et parte eiusdem epistulae increpuit amicitias muliebris, Fufium consulem oblique perstringens. is gratia Augustae floruerat, aptus adliciendis feminarum animis . . .").

32. Tac. *Ann.* 3.59: "nominatim arguens insolentiam sententiae aureasque litteras contra patrium morem."

33. See, for example, Petrochilos 1974; Griffin 1985: 4–31; Rudd 1986: 162–92; Balsdon 1979; Gruen 1992: 52–83 (on Cato), 223–71. Florus 7 offers a concise illustration of Roman attitudes toward other cultural traditions and particularly those of the Greeks: "sperne mores transmarinos, mille habent officia. / cive Romano per orbem nemo vivit rectius: / quippe malim unum Catonem quam trecentos Socratas."

34. Plaut. *Bacch.* 742–3, *Most.* 22–4, 64–5, 959–61, *Poen.* 602–3, *Truc.* 86–7; Hor. *Sat.* 2.2.9–13 with Porphyrio. Cf. Festus 235.22: "pergraecari est epulis et potationibus inservire." Segal 1968: 71 argues that "the implicit theme of all Plautine comedy" is precisely "Roman austerity versus *pergraecari*."

35. For *levitas*, see, e.g., the sources cited in Petrochilos 1974: 40–5 (a striking example is Cicero's defence of Flaccus, throughout which the orator draws on the prejudicial sentiment that Greeks are characterized by *levitas*). For Greek frivolity, hedonism, and self-indulgence, see also Cic. *Pis.* 22, 42, 67, *Prov. Cons.* 14, *Verr.* 2.2.7; Plut. *Cic.* 5.2. For luxury, see, e.g., Hor. *Epist.* 2.1.93–102, and Edwards 1993: 92–7. In sum, cf. Griffin 1985: 6: ". . . a life of *amours*, parties, drinking, jealousy, and (for some) poetry and music. And this is the life, one of sloth and debauchery, *inertia* and *nequitia*, which the Augustan elegists proclaim as their own. And of course from an early date such a life was felt to be Greek."

36. For more or less disparaging references to *Graeculi*, none of which contain any allusion to pederasty, see, e.g., Cic. *Verr.* 2.2.72, 2.4.127, *Red. Sen.* 14, *Sest.* 110, *Pis.* 70, *Scaur.* 4, *Mil.* 55, *Phil.* 5.14, 13.33, *De Orat.* 1.47, 1.102, 1.221, *Tusc.* 1.86; Sen. Rhet. *Suas.* 1.6.16; Sen. *Apocol.* 5.4; Petr. *Sat.* 88.10; Plin. *Epist.* 10.40.2, *Pan.* 13.5; Suet. *Tib.* 11.1, 56.1, *Claud.* 15.4; Tac. *Dial.* 3.4, 29.1.

37. SHA *Hadrian* 1.5: "imbutusque impensius Graecis studiis, ingenio eius sic ad ea declinante ut a nonnullis Graeculus diceretur."

38. Juv. 3.109–112: "praeterea sanctum nihil †aut† ab inguine tutum, / non matrona laris, non filia virgo, nec ipse / sponsus levis adhuc, non filius ante pudicus. / horum si nihil est, aviam resupinat amici."

39. Juv. 6.195 (ζωὴ καὶ ψυχή); cf. Mart. 10.68.5 (κύριέ μου, μέλι μου, ψυχή μου).

40. Cf. Balsdon 1979: 34–6, Ferrary 1988: 517–26. For Roman exercises, see, e.g., Hor. *Sat.* 2.1.7–8, *C.* 1.8, 3.7.25–8; Plut. *Cato Maior* 20.4.

41. Courtney *ad* Juv. 3.114–8; he gives fuller references *ad* 3.67.

42. Plut. *Cato Maior* 20.7–8. For mixed baths, see Plin. *N.H.* 33.153, Quint. *I.O.* 5.9.14, Mart. 3.51, 3.72, 3.87, 11.47. In a period of growing austerity, the third-century A.D. emperor Severus Alexander outlawed mixed public baths; the ancient biographer notes that they had previously been outlawed, but that his predecessor Elagabalus had permitted them to return (SHA *Sev. Alex.* 24.2: "balnea mixta Romae exhiberi prohibuit, quod quidem iam ante prohibitum Heliogabalus fieri permiserat").

43. Such was my assumption in Williams 1995. Michael Grant's Penguin translation appears to make the same assumption, although perhaps overdoing the moralizing tone: "foreign influences demoralize our young men into shirkers, gymnasts, and perverts."

44. And yet the objections reported by Tacitus also include a reference to a "mixed gathering" (*coetus promiscuus*) at night, when anything goes. This kind of anxiety is remi-

niscent of the fears that Livy portrays as surrounding the worship of Bacchus by groups of men and women who likewise met in "mixed gatherings" (*coetus promiscui*) at night, and indeed, according to Livy at least, the mixture of men and women was a hallmark of these rites, a sure sign of their degeneracy. In an impassioned speech to the assembled people, the consul Postumius asks (Livy 39.15.12): "quales primum nocturnos coetus, deinde promiscuos mulierum ac virorum esse creditis?" (cf. also 39.8.7, 39.13.10, 39.18.5). It is just possible, then, that the "disgraceful love-affairs" to which Tacitus refers took place both in the all-male gymnasia and in the mixed nocturnal gatherings associated with the contest. These affairs (*turpes amores*) need not be exclusively linked with the gymnasia any more than is the idleness (*otia*) criticized in the same clause.

45. Itching to appear on stage, the emperor decided to have his premiere in Naples, a Greek city, not having the audacity to appear in Rome first (15.33; cf. 14.14); Tacitus himself condemns Nero's eventual performances at Rome as a "public disgrace" (*publicum flagitium*, 16.4). Juvenal repeats the theme, describing Nero as "gladly prostituting himself with a foul song on a foreign stage" (8.225–6: "gaudentis foedo peregrina ad pulpita cantu / prostitui"). For other references to this bias, see Nepos, pr.5, and cf. Balsdon 1979: 35 (who cites Plin. *Pan.* 33.1 and Plin. *Epist.* 4.22.1–3).

46. *Turpis amor* refers to a man's relationship with a female prostitute (Hor. *Sat.* 1.4.111–2), the passion that might induce a woman to poison a man (*Rhet. Herenn.* 4.23), and Antony's love for Cleopatra (Prop. 2.16.36; cf. 3.21.33). See also Catull. 61.99 (*probra turpia*, of a man's adulterous passion).

47. Note, too, that when he lists Roman customs at odds with Greek traditions, he does not explicitly remind his readers that Romans disapprove of courting freeborn boys. Instead he focuses on differences between Greek and Roman traditions regarding the role of women. (Nepos also refers to his uneducated Roman readers at *Pelop.* 1: "ne rudibus Graecarum litterarum minus dilucide appareat quantus fuerit ille vir.")

48. Nepos, *Paus.* 4.1: "Argilius quidam adulescentulus, quem puerum Pausanias amore venerio dilexerat"; *Alc.* 2.2: "ineunte adulescentia amatus est a multis more Graecorum." At *Alc.* 2.3 we read the following: "posteaquam robustior est factus, non minus multos amavit, in quorum amore, quoad licitum est odiosa, multa delicate iocoseque fecit; quae referremus, nisi maiora potiora haberemus." There is a textual problem here: I give John C. Rolfe's 1929 LCL text; Nipperdey, for example, reads *otioso*. But even if Nepos did use the adjective *odiosus* in a discussion of pederasty, the word would here signify not so much "hateful" (as Rolfe translates) as "disagreeable." Talk of Alcibiades' erotic exploits is contrasted with "more important matters" (*maiora potiora*), and one is reminded of Nepos' inclusion of pederasty among those Greek customs that are by Roman standards "partim infamia, partim humilia atque ab honestate remota" (pr. 5). At *Hamilcar* 3.2, Nepos records rumors to the effect that Hamilcar loved the beautiful young Hasdrubal "turpius quam par erat" (*turpius* because both were freeborn, indeed noble Carthaginians and thus by Roman standards the relationship would be an instance of *stuprum*); but note that Nepos makes no mention of "Greek custom" here.

49. Other Greek customs identified as such by Nepos include the role of the Eleven as public executioners at Athens (*Phocion* 4.2); the two kings at Sparta (*Agesilaus* 1.2; cf. *Hannibal* 7.4, where we read that the Carthaginians had two kings a year, as Rome had two consuls); the Spartan practice of hiring unmarried women to provide entertainment at dinner parties (pr. 4); and the value placed on being proclaimed an Olympic victor or on appearing on stage (pr. 5).

50. Cantarella 1992: 97. When Cantarella places "the Greek vice" ("il vizio greco") in quotation marks, one receives the impression that she is translating a Latin phrase. But a search of the PHI disk for *viti-* in conjunction with *Graec-* turns up no such phrase.

51. Cic. *De Orat*. 2.18: "hoc vitio cumulata est eruditissima illa Graecorum natio"; Sen. Rhet. *Contr*. 1.2.22: "hoc autem vitium aiebat Scaurus a Graecis declamatoribus tractum, qui nihil non et permiserint sibi et impetraverint"; Plin. *N.H.* 15.19 (on olive oil): "usum eius ad luxuriam vertere Graeci, vitiorum omnium genitores, in gymnasiis publicando."

52. The only possible exception consists of a variant manuscript reading at Nepos, *Alc*. 2.2 (instead of *more Graecorum* some manuscripts read *amore Graecorum*), but see Williams 1995 for arguments against accepting the variant. Even if Nepos actually did write *amore Graecorum*, the phrase would refer only to the specific Greek tradition of pederasty and not to male homosexuality in general.

53. Cic. *Verr*. 2.1.66: "fit sermo inter eos et invitatio ut Graeco more biberetur"; ibid.: "negavit moris esse Graecorum ut in convivio virorum accumberent mulieres" (cf. Nepos, pr. 6–7); Livy 32.20.1: "sicut Graecis mos est"; Livy 10.47.3: "translato e Graeco more"; Livy 29.16.6: "ut Graecis mos est" (cf. Pliny, *N.H.* 11.251, "antiquis Graeciae in supplicando mentum attingere mos erat" and Livy 36.28.4–5, also on suppliants: "quae moris Graecorum non sint"); Front. *Strat*. 3.2.6: "in theatro, ubi ex more Graecorum locus consultationi praebebatur" (cf. Tac. *Hist*. 2.80); Petr. *Sat*. 111.2: "positum in hypogaeo Graeco more corpus"; Apul. *Met*. 10.10: "nec rota vel eculeus more Graecorum tormentis eius apparata iam deerant"; Suet. *Nero* 12.3: "instituit et quinquennale certamen primus omnium Romae more Graeco triplex" (cf. Tac. *Ann*. 14.20, "quinquennale ludicrum Romae institutum est ad morem Graeci certaminis" and Stat. *Theb*. 6.5–7, "Graium ex more decus"); Serv. *ad Aen*. 2.247: "licet Terentius Graeco more dixerit 'agrum in his regionibus meliorem neque pretii maioris nemo habet'"; ibid. 3.691: "epitheton ad inplendum versum positum more Graeco"; ibid. 11.213: "more Graeco epitheton incongruum loco posuit"; Festus 293.33: "quam consuetudinem Ennius mutavisse fertur, utpote Graecus Graeco more usus, quod illi aeque scribentes ac legentes duplicabant mutas . . ." See Williams 1995 for further examples.

54. For παῖδες and γυναῖκες as the standard objects of Greek men's erotic attention, see, among many examples, Mimnermus 1; Arist. *Clouds* 1071–4; Achilles Tatius 2.35–8; Plutarch, *Amatorius*; and Ps.-Lucian, *Amores*.

55. See especially Dover 1978: 6, 111–24.

56. Novius 19 Ribbeck: "pati dum poterunt, antequam pugae pilant."

57. Catull. 61.134–6: "diceris male te a tuis / unguentate glabris marite / abstinere."

58. Sen. *Epist*. 47.7: "alius vini minister in muliebrem modum ornatus cum aetate luctatur: non potest effugere pueritiam, retrahitur, iamque militari habitu glaber retritis pilis aut penitus evulsis tota nocte pervigilat, quam inter ebrietatem domini ac libidinem dividit et in cubiculo vir, in convivio puer est." For other references to *glabri*, see Sen. *Dial*. 10.12.5, Varro, *R.R.* 1.2.26. Boswell 1980: 79 n. 87 inexplicably asserts that *glabri* were male prostitutes who played the *active* role.

59. Mart. 1.31: Encolpos has vowed to dedicate a lock of his hair to Apollo if his lover receives the privilege of the *primus pilus*, and the poet expresses the wish that this may come about, but with the proviso that Encolpos' face and neck remain smooth and hairless, so that the couple may continue to remain together (7–8: "utque tuis [sc., of Apollo] longum dominusque puerque fruantur / muneribus, tonsum fac cito, sero virum"). The pair are again mentioned in 5.48, where we read that Pudens has tearfully allowed Encolpos to cut his long hair; the poet again expresses the wish that Encolpos' beard may come late.

60. For phrases like *flos aetatis*, see, for example, Cic. *Cael*. 9, *Phil*. 2.3, *Top*. 32.9, *Sen*. 20; Virg. *Ecl*. 7.4; Livy 8.28.3, 21.3.4, 29.1.2, 42.11.6; Val. Max. 6.1.pr.; Curt. *Alex*. 4.8.7, 7.2.4, 7.9.19, 10.5.10; Sen. *N.Q.* 1.17.4; Suet. *Poet*. 11, *Jul*. 49.3; Apul. *Apol*. 9.38, *Met*. 9.28.

61. On the *depositio barbae* (which is attested to have occurred as late as the twenty-fourth year), see Marquardt 1886: 599–600 and Blümner 1911: 269–70. Tacitus (*Ann.* 14.15) tells us that in A.D. 59 Nero instituted the games called Iuvenalia, and Dio (61.19.1) adds that he did so in honor of the arrival of his beard; Nero was twenty-one years old at the time. Elsewhere we read of a young man approaching his twentieth year whose cheeks are just beginning to darken (*Laus Pisonis* 259–61). A funerary inscription found near Rome (*CLE* 1948) marks the grave of a man "living out his twenty-third year having dedicated his beard" ("barba deposita peragens tertium et vicensimum annum"). By contrast, Statius notes that the young Crispinus, now in his seventeenth year, still does not show the tell-tale signs on his cheeks (Stat. *Silv.* 5.2.12–3, 62–3); and the pastoral poet Nemesianus imagines two fifteen-year-old boys, both in love with a girl, and both blessed with smooth cheeks (Nemes. *Ecl.* 2.16–7).

62. *CLE* 465.16–7: "bis denos vixi depletis mensibus annos / et virtute potens et pulcher flore iuventae"; 1116: "cum mihi prima novos spargebat flore iuentus [*sic*]" (of a man who lived twenty years); 1119: "quintum annum et decimum Narcissus flore iuventae / hoc iacet abreptus conditus in tumulo"; 1149: "invida florentem rapuerunt fata iuenta [*sic*]" (of a man who lived twenty-one years); 1240: "quem mors erip[u]it prima florente iuve[nta]" (of a man who lived twenty-three years). In one epitaph (*CLE* 1170.3–4) the beard itself is called "the new flower" on a young man's face: "non potui parvus puerilem implere iuventam / nec vestire meam flore novo faciem."

63. Livy 39.13.14: "captari aetates et erroris et stupri patientes" (cf. 39.10.6).

64. Some wish to delete this remark (see R. G. Nisbet, ed., *M. Tulli Ciceronis De Domo Sua ad Pontifices Oratio* [Oxford, 1939]), but Nisbet observes that "it alludes to immoral relations and is absolutely in harmony with the spirit of the speech."

65. Suet. *Poet.* 11: "quibus etiam corporis gratia conciliatus existimatur, quod et ipsum Fenestella arguit, contendens utroque maiorem natu fuisse." Suetonius adds that Nepos claimed that all three were about the same age, but Porcius wrote some verses including a line referring to Terence's having been often taken to the Alban villa "on account of the flower of his youth" ("dum in Albanum crebro rapitur ob florem aetatis suae").

66. Cf. Gonfroy 1978; Richlin 1992a: 98 with n. 30, 101; Lilja 1983: 95–6; Richlin 1993: 537–9, 545–8 (citing Livy 2.13.10, "opportuna [sc., aetas] iniuriae"), where she helpfully refers to this invective tradition as *locus de aetate*. Examples from Cicero include *Verr.* 2.1.32 (on Verres): "nihil a me de pueritiae suae flagitiis audiet, nihil ex illa impura adulescentia sua; quae qualis fuerit aut meministis, aut ex eo quem sui simillimum produxit recognoscere potestis" (cf. 2.1.33, "damna, dedecora, quae res patris eius, aetas ipsius pertulit, praetereantur"); *Har. Resp.* 42 (on Clodius): "qui post patris mortem primam illam aetatulam suam ad scurrarum locupletium libidines detulit, quorum intemperantia expleta in domesticis est germanitatis stupris volutatus . . ."); *Phil.* 13.17 (on Antony): "si eius pueritia pertulerat libidines eorum qui erant in eum tyranni, etiamne in nostros liberos dominum et tyrannum comparabat?" (cf. 13.19); and *De Orat.* 2.277 (on Opimius): "adulescentulus male audisset."

67. Cic. *Cael.* 6–9; on Caelius' age, see R. G. Austin, ed., *M. Tulli Ciceronis Pro M. Caelio Oratio* (3rd ed., Oxford, 1960), pp. 144–6. Cicero's response to such charges is merely to note that the young Caelius had spent those years in a *tirocinium fori* under the tutelage of himself: a more chaste teacher could not be imagined.

68. Cf. Richlin 1992a: 223–4. Horace (*Sat.* 1.6.81–4) makes this boast concerning his father's careful handling of his education: "ipse mihi custos incorruptissimus omnis / circum doctores aderat. quid multa? pudicum, / qui primus virtutis honos, servavit ab omni / non solum facto, verum opprobrio quoque turpi . . ." The poet's pride clearly relates to some concerns about what Pliny calls *hoc lubricum aetatis* (for the phrase, Cic. *Verr.* 2.5.137: "ut aetati maxime lubricae atque incertae exempla nequitiae parentis vita praeberet").

69. Juv. 10.224: "quot discipulos inclinet Hamillus"; Martial refers to an Amillus, or perhaps Hamillus, who "screws big boys" ("grandes percidis," 7.62.1). For anxieties concerning the morality of teachers (more or less explicitly related to their sexual behavior) see also Quint. *I.O.* 1.2.4, 1.3.17.

70. Juv. 7.238–41 (of teachers): "exigite ut sit / et pater ipsius coetus, ne turpia ludant, / ne faciant vicibus. non est leve tot puerorum / observare manus oculosque in fine trementis." The last sentence seems to refer to masturbation, whether solitary or mutual (for the latter, cf. Sen. *Contr.* 4.pr.11: "inter pueriles condiscipulorum sinus lasciva manu obscena iussisti").

71. Pompon. 75–6: "praeteriens vidit Dossenum in ludo reverecunditer / non docentem condiscipulum, verum scalpentem natis"; see Adams 1982: 149 for a brief discussion, where *scalpere* is taken to be a metaphor for penetration.

72. See Adams 1982: 123–5. As seen in chapter 5, however, the verb is also used of the anal penetration of women—one among many ways in which the boundary between homosexual and heterosexual behaviors is seen to be permeable.

73. *Priap.* 13, 22, 74. Such an understanding of what "boys" do may underlie a Plautine joke: "I must do a boy's duty: I'll squat down in front of the box" ("faciundum est puerile officium: conquiniscam ad cistulam," Plaut. *Cist.* 657; for *conquiniscere*, see Adams 1982: 193).

74. See *OLD* s.vv., and compare the discussions at Maurin 1975, Boswell 1980: 81 and Boswell 1990: 70.

75. Tibull. 1.8.31–2: "carior est auro iuvenis, cui levia fulgent / ora nec amplexus aspera barba terit"; Juv. 6.356: "levibus athletis"; Calp. Sic. *Ecl.* 2.84–7. Indeed, even Greek sources do not restrict the appeal of beardlessness to pederastic contexts. At Theocritus 15.129–30, a priestess sings of Adonis' kisses that do not chafe: ὀκτωκαιδεκετὴς ἢ ἐννεακαίδεχ' ὁ γαμβρός – / οὐ κεντεῖ τὸ φίλημ' – ἔτι οἱ περὶ χείλεα πυρρά. See Halperin 1990: 90 with n. 21 for further evidence from the Greek sources for the appeal of youthful male beauty to women.

76. Mart. 4.28.7. Friedlaender's explanation of the term in his 1886 Leipzig commentary is reasonable: "Liebhaberin von glabri, glatten jungen Leuten" (cf. *TLL* s.v. *glabraria*: "amatrix glabrorum i. homunculorum levatorum et comptorum"). The *OLD* provides a surprising gloss: "(perh.) a shorn sheep (. . . fig.)."

77. Stat. *Silv.* 3.4.40–3.

78. Hyginus, *Fab.* 271 ("qui ephebi formosissimi fuerunt"): Adonis (Venus); Endymion (Luna); Ganymede (Jupiter); Hyacinth (Apollo); Narcissus (himself); Atlantius, son of Venus and Mercury (= Hermaphroditus); Hylas (Heracles); Chrysippus (Theseus).

79. Juv. 6.110: "facit hoc illos Hyacinthos"; Apul. *Met.* 1.12: "hic est. . . carus Endymion, hic Catamitus meus." Interestingly, in his 1991 Oxford translation of Juvenal, Niall Rudd substitutes "Adonis"—who was loved by Venus—for "Hyacinth," using a "better-known name," as William Barr puts it in the accompanying notes, and thereby creating an image more in line with contemporary paradigms for sexual experience. Edwards 1997: 78 similarly replaces Hyacinth with Adonis.

80. *Priap.* 13.2 (*barbatum*); 22.1 (*vir*); 74.2 (*barbatis*).

81. Cf. Fraenkel 1960: 105–34 in general, and Cody 1976: 472 on this scene in particular.

82. Lilja 1983: 21 reads Chalinus' comment on Lysidamus' tastes in precisely the opposite way: "Chalinus' amazed comment . . . shows that it was out of the ordinary to have a bearded man, i.e. an adult male, as a minion." W. T. MacCary and M. M. Willcock, in their commentary *ad* 449–70 (*Plautus: Casina* [Cambridge, 1976]) claim that Lysidamus makes "what seem to be amorous advances" upon Olympio and that Chalinus "comes for a time to the wrong conclusion." I would say that Chalinus comes to precisely the right conclusion:

Otherwise, what do we make of his allusion to the time when he was the object of the master's lusts (461–2)?

83. The young man Pleusicles later disguises himself as this ship captain (1175ff.), and is addressed while in disguise as *adulescens* (1297); but Roman men were quite capable of using the term *adulescens* to describe men well into their twenties (see discussion earlier in this chapter).

84. Fraenkel 1960: 249 suggests that both the character of the sister and the slave's joke are Plautine creations: "se ... è un' aggiunta da lui liberamente apportata all'originale, egli pensava che appunto la doppia esemplificazione basata sul genus femininum e masculinum avrebbe suscitato la particolare ilarità del suo pubblico." Cf. Lothar Schaaf, *Der Miles Gloriosus des Plautus* (Munich, 1977), p. 314: "Die Verse 1104ff. sind also auf jeden Fall für das Original in Anspruch zu nehmen, lediglich die Derbheit 1111ff. wird man mit einigem Recht auf Plautus zurückführen dürfen, vor allem, weil sie nicht recht zu dem typischen Frauenjäger passen will und nur eine platte Wiederholung des charakteristischen und sicher aus dem Vorbild stammender Scherzes 1106f. darstellt; ferner scheint das *hoc age nunc* in 1114a die von Plautus eingesetzte Formel zur Rückleitung ins Original zu sein."

85. Suet. *Galba* 22: "libidinis in mares pronior et eos non nisi praeduros exoletosque."

86. Ibid.: "ferebant in Hispania Icelum e veteribus concubinis de Neronis exitu nuntiantem non modo artissimis osculis palam exceptum ab eo, sed ut sine mora velleretur oratum atque seductum."

87. Suet. *Aug.* 68: "videsne, ut cinaedus orbem digito temperat?"; *Tib.* 45: "hircum vetulum capreis naturam ligurire."

88. Suet. *Galba* 13: "quare adventus eius non perinde gratus fuit, idque proximo spectaculo apparuit, siquidem Atellanis notissimum canticum exorsis: 'venit Onesimus a villa' cuncti simul spectatores consentiente voce reliquam partem rettulerunt ac saepius versu repetito egerunt."

89. Suet. *Tib.* 44: "maiore adhuc ac turpiore infamia flagravit, vix ut referri audirive, nedum credi fas sit, quasi pueros primae teneritudinis, quos pisciculos vocabat, institueret, ut natanti sibi inter femina versarentur ac luderent lingua morsuque sensim adpetentes"; *Claud.* 33.2: "libidinis in feminas profusissimae, marum omnino expers"; *Virg.* 9: "libidinis in pueros pronioris."

90. Plut. *Sulla* 36.1 (οὐκ ἀρνούμενος); cf. 2.3–4.

91. Dio 61.10.4: καὶ μειρακίοις ἐξώροις ἔχαιρε, καὶ τοῦτο καὶ τὸν Νέρωνα ποιεῖν ἐδίδαξε. This comment comes as part of the historian's discussion of how Seneca failed to practice what he preached as a philosopher. He also puzzles over the fact that Seneca had previously asked Nero not to kiss him: "The only thing one might have suspected, namely that he [Seneca] did not wish to kiss such a mouth, is shown to be untrue by his boyfriends" (61.10.5: ὁ γάρ τοι καὶ μόνον ἄν τις ὑποπτεύσειεν, ὅτι οὐκ ἤθελε τοιοῦτο στόμα φιλεῖν, ἐλέγχεται ἐκ τῶν παιδικῶν αὐτοῦ ψεῦδος ὄν). In other words, Dio is assuming (merely, it seems, on the basis of their age) that Seneca fellated his male partners and thus had already befouled his own mouth: Why would he refuse to kiss Nero's equally foul mouth? See chapter 5 for discussion of the language of "purity" and oral sex, as well as for ancient gossip about Nero's sexual practices.

92. Dio 62.6.4: εἴ γε καὶ ἄνδρας χρὴ καλεῖν ἀνθρώπους ὕδατι θερμῷ λουμένους, ὄψα σκευαστὰ ἐσθίοντας, οἶνον ἄκρατον πίνοντας, μύρῳ ἀλειφομένους, μαλθακῶς κοιμωμένους, μετὰ μειρακίων, καὶ τούτων ἐξώρων, καθεύδοντας, κιθαρῳδῷ, καὶ τούτῳ κακῷ, δουλεύοντας.

93. Cf. Halperin 1990: 88–90. Boswell 1980: 28 rightly reminds us of the gap between cultural ideals and individual experience, noting that "it does not seem likely that,

with a few exceptions, the apparent prevalence of erotic relationships between adults and boys in the past corresponded to reality." Still, there are only a very few hints among the Greek sources at pederastic relationships that continued once the younger partner had passed adolescence, and in the case of the best-known such couple—Pausanias and Agathon—the younger partner, Agathon, habitually shaved his beard, with the result that the couple still conformed, at least visually, to the model of older, bearded *erastês* and younger, beardless *erômenos* (cf. Dover 1978: 144).

94. See Krenkel 1978 and Halperin 1990: 88–112.

95. Pomponius fr. 153 Ribbeck: "continuo ad te centuriatim current qui penem petent" (the text is that of Frassinetti 149); 148–9: "ut nullum civem pedicavi per dolum / nisi ipsus orans ultro qui ocquinisceret."

96. Although most commentators assume that this man is the Virro who is mentioned earlier in the satire (9.35), Braund 1988: 242 n. 32 points out that this is not necessarily true.

97. See Braund 1988: 130–77 for a detailed discussion of Naevolus. At n. 234 Braund points out that it is misleading to describe Naevolus as a "male prostitute," as nearly all commentators have done; rather, she suggests, "Naevolus should be regarded as client first and foremost." As for the breathtakingly coarse imagery that Naevolus uses to describe his anal penetration of his patron, Martin Winkler, *The Persona in Three Satires of Juvenal* (Hildesheim, 1983), p. 144 n. 137, suggests a comparable innuendo at Petr. *Sat*. 76.11 ("intestinas meas noverat").

98. Braund 1988: 174 speaks of a "sustained allusion" to Pomponius' play in Juvenal 9; in particular she compares Juvenal's "et mea Clotho / et Lachesis gaudent, si pascitur inguine venter" (9.135–6) with Pomponius' "ego quaero quod comedim, has quaerunt quod cacent" (150 Frassinetti = 151 Ribbeck) and "ego rumorem parvi facio, dum sit, dum rumen qui impleam" (148 Frassinetti = 152 Ribbeck); and Juvenal's "numquam pathicus tibi derit amicus / stantibus et salvis his collibus; undique ad illos / convenient . . ." (9.130–2) with Pomponius' "continuo ad te centuriatim current qui penem petent" (149 Frassinetti = 153 Ribbeck).

99. Cantarella 1992: 154, ignoring Pomponius, takes Juvenal's satire as evidence for a change in Roman practices, in particular the introduction of male prostitutes paid to penetrate their male customers (see the introduction for arguments against this view).

100. Festus implicitly contrasts *exoletus* with *adolescens*: "exoletus, qui adolescere, id est crescere desiit" (70.17); "adolescit a Graeco ἀλδήσκω id est adcresco, venit. unde fiunt adultus, adulescens . . .et exoletus, qui excessit olescendi, id est crescendi, modum" (5.10–3). Festus' derivation of *adolesco* from the Greek ἀλδήσκω, like many ancient etymologies, does not meet the standards of modern linguistics.

101. Plaut. fr. 103 Lindsay: "domi reliqui exoletam virginem" (*apud* Priscian, *GLK* 2.489).

102. Firm. *Math*. 1.7.28: "senex exoletus."

103. Sen. *Epist*. 114.10: "antiqua verba atque exoleta"; Quint. *I.O*. 8.2.12: "exoletos scrutatus auctores." The verb *exolescere* has attestations that extend to the time of Apuleius (*Met*. 9.32: "lactucae veteres et insuaves illae quae . . .in amaram caenosi sucus cariem exolescunt") and the jurist Sextus Pomponius (D. 1.2.2.3: "exactis deinde regibus lege tribunicia omnes leges hae exoleverunt").

104. Plaut. *Curc*. 473: "ibidem erunt scorta exoleta quique stipulari solent"; *Poen*. 17–8: "scortum exoletum ne quis in proscaenio / sedeat."

105. Lewis and Short offer an enticingly vague gloss for this meaning of *exoletus*: "abandoned youth of ripe age." Servius observes that the ancients referred (perhaps euphemistically) to *exoleti* as *pulchri* ("lovely ones"); this is how he explains a passage in Lucilius where Apollo shuns the label *pulcher* (Serv. *Aen*. 3.119: "et quidam 'pulcher Apollo'

epitheton datum Apollini reprehendunt; pulchros enim a veteribus exoletos dictos; nam et apud Lucilium Apollo pulcher dici non vult.")

106. Cic. *Mil.* 55: "ille qui semper secum scorta, semper exoletos, semper lupas duceret . . ."; Mart. 12.91.1–2: "communis tibi cum viro, Magulla, / cum sit lectulus et sit exoletus . . ."; SHA *Elagab.* 31.6: "causa vehiculorum erat lenonum, lenarum, meretricum, exoletorum, subactorum etiam bene vas<a>torum multitudo" (cf. 27.7). *Exoletus* was at all times able to function either as an adjective meaning simply "grown up, past adolescence," as in Suetonius' comment on Galba quoted earlier (*Galba* 22: "et eos non nisi praeduros exoletosque"), or as a noun signifying a type of male prostitute.

107. Boswell 1980: 79 n. 87. On the other hand, Dalla 1987: 15 n. 24 and Cantarella 1992: 156 assert without further discussion that the term was used to denote men who were penetrated.

108. At Suet. *Tib.* 43 we read that Tiberius stimulated himself by watching people copulating in triple rows consisting of *puellae, exoleti,* and *spintriae*: "in quam undique conquisiti puellarum et exoletorum greges monstrosique concubitus repertores, quos spintrias appellabat, triplici serie conexi, in vicem incestarent coram ipso." I interpret this to mean that each group consisted of an *exoletus* penetrating a *spintria* penetrating a *puella.*

109. Sen. *Contr.* 10.4.17: "exoletos suos ut ad longiorem patientiam impudicitiae idonei sint amputant"; cf. Sen. *Dial.* 1.3.13: "quanto magis huic [sc., Socrati] invidendum est quam illis quibus gemma ministratur, quibus exoletus omnia pati doctus exsectae virilitatis aut dubiae suspensam auro nivem diluit"; Sen. *Epist.* 66.53: "an potius optem ut malaxandos articulos exoletis meis porrigam? ut muliercula aut aliquis in mulierculam ex viro versus digitulos meos ducat?" Likewise a surviving line from a mime of Laberius (70) seems to speak of an *exoletus patiens*: "scinde una exoleto <huic> patienti <hanc> catulientem lupam," although the textual difficulties are notable. On the text, see especially the critical apparatus *ad loc.* in Mario Bonaria, *I Mimi Romani* (Rome, 1965). For *patior*, see Adams 1982: 149–51.

110. Tac. *Ann.* 15.37: "naves auro et ebore distinctae, remigesque exoleti per aetates et scientiam libidinum componebantur."

111. Sen. *Epist.* 95.24: "transeo puerorum infelicium greges quos post transacta convivia aliae cubiculi contumeliae exspectant; transeo agmina exoletorum per nationes coloresque discripta ut eadem omnibus levitas sit, eadem primae mensura lanuginis, eadem species capillorum, ne quis cui rectior est coma crispulis misceatur . . ." Note, too, the phrase *puberibus exoletis* ("mature *exoleti*") at SHA *Commodus* 5.4.

112. Aeschin. 1.95: ἐπειδὴ δὲ ταῦτα μὲν ἀπωλώλει καὶ κατεκεκύβευτο καὶ κατωψοφάγητο, οὑτοσὶ δ' ἔξωρος ἐγένετο, ἐδίδου δ' εἰκότως οὐδεὶς ἔτι οὐδέν, ἡ δὲ βδελυρὰ φύσις καὶ ἀνόσιος ἡ τούτου ἀεὶ τῶν αὐτῶν ἐπεθύμει, καὶ καθ' ὑπερβολὴν ἀκρασίας ἕτερον ἐφ' ἑτέρῳ ἐπίταγμα ἐπέταττε, καὶ ἀπεφέρετο εἰς τὸ καθ' ἡμέραν ἔθος, ἐνταῦθα ἤδη ἐτράπετο ἐπὶ τὸ καταφαγεῖν τὴν πατρῴαν οὐσίαν. Aeschines' opponent Demosthenes had earlier argued that Timarchus' sexual misdeeds would normally be characteristic only of "boys" (1.94): τὸ μὲν γὰρ ἡμαρτηκέναι τι περὶ τὸ σῶμα παιδὸς εἶναί φησι. This remark implies anal penetration.

113. Ach. Tat. 8.9.1: παρελθὼν δὲ ὁ ἱερεὺς (ἦν δὲ εἰπεῖν οὐκ ἀδύνατος, μάλιστα δὲ τὴν Ἀριστοφάνους ἐζηλωκὼς κωμῳδίαν) ἤρξατο αὐτὸς λέγειν πάνυ ἀστείως καὶ κωμῳδικῶς εἰς πορνείαν αὐτοῦ καθαπτόμενος . . .

114. Note, for example, that ancient criticisms of men's use of *exoleti* seem no different in nature from those of their use of prostitutes in general.

115. See especially Dover 1978: 124–35.

116. I thank Gregory Pflugfelder and David Halperin for helping me to formulate this distinction.

117. This question has not adequately been addressed in the scholarship (Halperin 1990: 183 n. 31 briefly alludes to it). Clarke 1993: 195 claims that "Roman art and literature corroborate and continue the Greek aesthetic distaste for men with large penises," but my discussion here, I hope, demonstrates that such a claim is contradicted by the textual evidence.

118. While nothing in this poem itself indicates that Priapus' member is particularly large, the iconographic and textual tradition regarding the god is unanimous on the point: Priapus is the iconic figure of the well-endowed male (see, e.g., Mart. 11.51 and Juv. 6.374–6, quoted in the chapter text), and consequently when the god imagines inserting his member all the way up to his pubic hair, a Roman reader would certainly be put in mind of the size of that member.

119. SHA *Comm.* 10.9: "habuit et hominem pene prominentem ultra modum animalium, quem onon appellabat, sibi carissimum. quem et ditavit et sacerdotio Herculis rustici praeposuit."

120. SHA *Elag.* 12.2: "ad honores reliquos promovit commendatos sibi pudibilium enormitate membrorum"; ibid. 8.7: "ut ex tota penitus urbe atque ex nauticis onobeli quaererentur; sic eos appellabant qui viriliores videbantur." The word used to designate these men was either *monobiles* (*monobeleis*, "with one weapon") or *onobeli* (derived from *onos*, reflecting the usage just seen in the case of Commodus). See Adams 1982: 21 on this passage and the textual difficulty. According to Dio Cassius, Elagabalus assigned to certain people the task of seeking out such gifted men (79.16.2).

121. Cf. Adams 1982: 78: "These stories were no doubt fabrications, but they at least indicate the obsessions of Roman voyeurs."

122. Juv. 9.92: "neglegit atque alium bipedem sibi quaerit asellum."

123. Sen. *N.Q.* 1.16.2–3: "haec autem ita disponebat ut, cum virum ipse pateretur, aversus omnes admissarii sui motus in speculo videret ac deinde falsa magnitudine ipsius membri tamquam vera gaudebat. in omnibus quidem balneis agebat ille dilectum et aperta mensura legebat viros, sed nihilominus mendaciis quoque insatiabile malum oblectabat." For this usage of *admissarius* ("stud"), see Adams 1982: 206–7. The poet Horace is also said to have fitted out his bedroom with mirrors (Suet. *Hor.*: "ad res Venerias intemperantior traditur; nam speculato cubiculo scorta dicitur habuisse disposita, ut quocumque respexisset ibi ei imago coitus referretur").

124. *CIL* 4.2268: "Myrtale vassatos fellas"; *CIL* 4.7240: "masculus cum codatis ubiq(ue)" (Krenkel 1980a: 87 understands *Masculus* as a personal name); and perhaps *CIL* 4.8666: "Lucilius Viriliori." (For this last graffito, Krenkel 1980a: 87 compares SHA *Elag.* 8.7, "sic eos appellabant qui viriliores videbantur," and translates, "Lucilius sends greetings to Mr. More-than-man.") See further Krenkel 1980a: 85–7. For *vasati*, see Adams 1982: 41–3 and for *codati* see Adams 1982: 36–7.

125. Mart. 3.73, 11.63. The adjective *mutuniatus* is derived from the noun *muto*, denoting "penis," evidently related to the name of the phallic deity Mutunus Tutunus (or Mutinus Tutinus); see Ernout-Meillet and Walde-Hofmann s.v. *muto*.

126. See Kay 1985 ad loc. and Housman 1930 on this word. Boswell 1980: 79 n. 87 suggests that both *draucus* and *exoletus* denote male prostitutes paid to penetrate their customers (see discussion earlier in chapter 2 for my arguments against such an interpretation of *exoletus*). "Stud" is the tentative translation offered by Richlin 1992a: 43.

127. Cf. Howell ad loc. and Juv. 9.33–7.

128. At Mart. 7.55.6 the poet describes his own penis as *proba et pusilla*, and in 3.51 he toys with the notion that the woman Galla, like Cotta, will be disappointed by his genital endowment.

129. Mart. 1.58. That the boy was bought for sexual purposes is clear from the poet's

lament: "hoc dolet et queritur de me mea mentula secum / laudaturque meam Phoebus in invidiam" (3–4). The epigram concludes on a note of wry irony: apostrophizing his own penis, the poet exclaims, "If you give me as much money, I will pay even more for the boy!" ("hoc da tu mihi, pluris emam," 6; for the motif of addressing one's penis, see Howell and Citroni ad loc.). Elsewhere, punning on the meaning of *pascere*, Martial observes that Phoebus lives off the kindness (and the meals) of *cinaedi*: "ad cenam invitant omnes te, Phoebe, cinaedi. / mentula quem pascit, non, puto, purus homo est" (9.63). In other words, his penis guarantees him invitations to dinner, and since "his dick feeds him" (as it also does Naevolus [Juv. 9.136: "si pascitur inguine venter"]), he must in some sense not be *purus* (that is, he, as it were, practices fellatio: for *purus*, see chapter 5). In another poem (3.73) Martial seems to hint that Phoebus actually does perform fellatio (with his *pueri mutuniati*); if so, Phoebus crosses the boundary between insertive and receptive practices (see chapter 5).

130. Petr. *Sat.* 105.9: "sed continuo ad inguina mea luminibus deflexis movit officiosam manum et 'salve' inquit 'Encolpi'" 129.1: "funerata est illa pars corporis, qua quondam Achilles eram." By itself, of course, the latter phrase does not necessarily refer to the size of Encolpius' genital endowment (it might only be a nonspecific image for endurance or accomplishment), but Lichas' recognition and Eumolpus' later admiration (140.13, discussed later in this section) suggest that at the very least there was something visually distinctive about Encolpius' penis.

131. *Priap.* 8.4–5: "nimirum sapiunt videntque magnam / matronae quoque mentulam libenter." Cf. Mart. 3.68: a *matrona* is interested in his obscene verses, especially when she realizes that he writes openly of penises (11–2: "si bene te novi, longum iam lassa libellum / ponebas, totum nunc studiosa leges").

132. Also of interest is a scene from Trimalchio's banquet in Petronius' *Satyricon* (60.4–6), where a figure of Priapus made of pastries, supporting with its penis a plenitude of apples and grapes, is brought in. The dinner guests reach out to partake of the god's bounty with a noticeable eagerness: "quod medium Priapus a pistore factus tenebat, gremioque satis amplo omnis generis poma et uvas sustinebat more vulgato. avidius ad pompam manus porreximus . . ."

133. Petr. *Sat.* 92.8: "illum autem frequentia ingens circumvenit cum plausu et admiratione timidissima."

134. Mart. 9.33: "audieris in quo, Flacce, balneo plausum / Maronis illic esse mentulam scito."

135. It may not be inappropriate here to make mention of a fragment from Lucilius' satires (534–6 Marx) in which the speaker rather loudly professes his awe at a ram's enormous, dangling testicles: "ibat forte aries, inquit, iam quod genus! quantis / testibus! vix uno filo ho<sc>e haerere putares, / pellicula extrema exaptum pendere onus ingens."

136. See Johns 1982 and Clarke 1998 for extended discussions of this and related points.

137. See Adams 1982: 63 and *OLD* s.v. *fascinum*. For Fascinus, see Plin. *N.H.* 28.39.

138. For *mutuniatus*, see *Priap.* 52.10; Mart. 3.73, 11.63 (discussed earlier in this chapter); for *mut(t)o, mutunium*, and Mutunus Tutunus/Mutinus Titinus, see Adams 1982: 62–3 and Robert 1997: 80–3, as well as Ernout-Meillet and Walde-Hofmann s.v. *muto*.

139. Aug. *Civ. D.* 4.11.6, 6.9, 7.21 (*virorum seminibus*). The textual tradition also attests to the existence of drinking vessels in the shape of penises, which are probably to be connected with fertility rites: Juv. 2.95–8 associates them with effeminate men observing rites in honor of the Good Goddess that were traditionally observed by women only (see Courtney ad loc.).

140. See Fehling 1974 for a discussion of the practice among male baboons of displaying the erect penis as a warning against intruders or enemies.

141. Varro, *L.L.* 7.97: "quod pueri[li]s turpicula res in collo quaedam suspenditur, ne quid obsit."

142. Plin. *N.H.* 28.39: "quamquam religione eum tutatur et Fascinus, imperatorum quoque, non solum infantium, custos, qui deus inter sacra Romana a Vestalibus colitur, et currus triumphantium, sub his pendens, defendit medicus invidiae . . ."

143. See n. 139, and cf. Porph. *ad* Hor. *Epod.* 8.18 (*fascinum*): "aeque pro virili parte posuit, quoniam praefascinandis rebus haec membri deformitas adponi solet."

144. Johns 1982, pl. 10.

145. Johns 1982, fig. 54.

146. A less fine example is illustrated at Johns 1982, pl. 13 (cf. Johns 1982, pl. 14, for a windchime in the form of a gladiator attacking his own penis, which has taken the shape of a wild animal).

147. Johns 1982, fig. 51.

148. See discussion in Clarke 1998: 169–77.

149. Cf. Kroll 1988: 98 n. 83: "Daß aber auch die Mentalität der höheren [sc., Schichten der Bevölkerung] sehr erotisch eingestellt war, beweist die Vorliebe für pikante und teilweise sogar obszöne Bilder. So finden sich in dem eleganten Vettierhause unflätige Priapusbilder, die man unter Heranziehung einiger Wandkritzeleien zu dem Schluße mißbraucht hat, einige Räume seien als Bordell benutzt worden." While he rightly rejects the theories that some rooms of the House of the Vettii served as brothels, he considers the painting of Priapus weighing his penis as "obscene" and a sign of the "erotic mentality" of the house's inhabitants.

150. Clarke 1996.

151. See especially Clarke 1998. Other discussions of sexual themes in the Roman visual tradition include Marcadé 1965, Brendel 1970, Johns 1982, Myerowitz 1992, Clarke 1991, 1993, and 1996, and relevant essays in Kampen 1996.

152. It is an interesting, perhaps surprising, fact that the great majority of published artifacts depict male-female acts. In view of the ancient literary evidence, we cannot imagine among Romans any kind of prudery or censorship with regard to the representation of male-male acts; it is thus tempting to speculate that a number of artifacts depicting male-male practices remain unpublished. John Clarke suggests an even more sobering possibility: "One wonders if the excavators who uncovered erotic wall paintings in the past might have destroyed—through prudery—other evidence of male-male lovemaking" (Clarke 1993: 286). Along the same lines, Ralph Hexter has suggested to me that, in view of the prejudices of the intervening centuries, there might also have been differential destruction of such items even before the period of modern excavation and publication.

153. See, in general, Dover 1978: 94–100, H.A. Shapiro, "Eros in Love: Pederasty and Pornography in Greece," Richlin 1992b: 53–72, and DeVries 1997. Sometimes the anal penetration of an *eromenos* by his *erastes* is hinted at (see, e.g., Dover 1978, fig. B53), and it is more than hinted at in scenes between beardless agemates (see, e.g., Dover 1978, fig. R223, R954). But when it comes to age-differentiated pederastic couples, there is plenty of kissing, fondling, and the notorious intercrural copulation (the bearded lover thrusting his penis between the thighs of his beardless beloved), but painters noticeably shied away from directly representing the anal penetration of the idolized Athenian youth.

154. See Clarke 1998: 72–8 for a concise overview of Arretine ware in general and these two pieces in particular. Clarke sees in the male-male scenes a certain tenderness, even mutuality: "Whereas representations of rear-entry penetration of boys and women by males on Greek vases emphasize male domination and power over his (unwilling) and often unattractive partner, these Roman depictions make *both* males as attractive as possible and show them mutually attracted to each other" (78). There are, though, some problems

with the contrast formulated here: the only depictions on Greek vases of "rear-entry penetration of boys" by males show other boys as the penetrators (we never see bearded men penetrating boys), and do not seem to represent the boy as unwilling or unattractive. As for depictions of male-female acts on Greek artifacts, there were some contexts apart from Attic vase painting in which a greater sense of mutuality was depicted (see, e.g., Keuls 1985, figs. 156–60, 162, and Andrew Stewart, "Reflections," in Kampen 1996: 136–54), and even within Attic painting the question is not so clear-cut: see Martin F. Kilmer, *Greek Erotica on Attic Red-Figure Vases* (London, 1993).

155. Metropolitan Museum of Art, L.1991.95. See Clarke 1998: 61–72, 86–90 for detailed discussion. For Warren, see David Sox, *Bachelors of Art: Edward Perry Warren and the Lewes House Brotherhood* (London, 1991). Sullivan 1968: 244 n. 2 cites the cup as an illustration of voyeurism in antiquity; Wiseman 1985: 131 n. 4 refers to it in his discussion of Juventius as an example of how some young aristocrats were "prepared to make [themselves] sexually available." It should be noted that some scholars have expressed doubts—none so far in print—as to the cup's authenticity. But the cup's imagery certainly reflects the trends, both literary and artistic, that have been outlined here.

156. Clarke 1993: 292, with nn. 82–3, and 1998: 86.

157. Clarke 1993: 275, 293; Clarke 1991: 92–3.

158. For variations in Roman treatments of the beard over time, see Blümner 1911: 269.

159. Vermeule 1963: 39; Clarke 1991: 93.

160. Clarke 1991: 92–3, with figs. 4–2 and 4–3.

161. Vermeule 1963: 39. Cf. Taylor 1997: 326: "The Apollonian features of the scene, the elder partner's laurel crown and a lyre resting nearby, suggest a satirization of the family of Augustus, which often adopted this imagery in its official art." Clarke 1998: 87 suggests that rather than being specific members of Augustus' family, "these are generic Augustan males." Clarke 1998: 86 argues that on side A "the artist strove to make the two [partners] as equal as possible in age, size, and activity," suggesting that this scene may constitute a departure from the differential model of same-sex relationships usual in the textual tradition. But the insertive partner's beard is a crucial marker: even if the bearded man does not seem significantly older than his partner in other regards, his beard signifies the traditional hierarchical distinction between the two partners. This couple conforms to the differential model as much as does the couple on the other side (a beardless but mature young man penetrating a noticeably younger boy). Taylor's interpretation of this scene is confused: first he speaks of the two partners as being "apparently of equal age," but then on the same page mentions "the elder partner" (Taylor 1997: 326).

162. Brendel 1970: 56–7 describes the Hellenizing tone of the sexual scenes—almost all of them involving male-female couplings—on Arretine ware, to which the Warren Cup is deeply indebted. See further Clarke 1998: 88–9.

Chapter 3

1. MacMullen 1982: 493 pointedly refers to a "total silence about any pair of lovers in some casual episode, case at law, oration, essay, letter, or history of any period (as opposed to what is easily found in Greek literature)," but Nisus and Euryalus (see discussion later in chapter 3) and Hadrian and Antinous (see chapter 1) constitute arguable counterexamples, and in any case the explanation for this silence lies not, as MacMullen suggests, in a Roman antipathy to homosexuality but in the strictures imposed by the concept of *stuprum*. (Indeed, throughout his article MacMullen pays insufficient attention to the distinctions drawn by the ancient sources between freeborn and slave, penetrating and penetrated, instead

imposing the modern distinction between heterosexual and homosexual, and occasionally confusing the latter with effeminacy.)

2. Cic. *Cat.* 2.8 (*turpissime*); Quint. *I.O.* 10.1.100 ("utinam non inquinasset argumenta puerorum foedis amoribus"). For Quintilian's comment, see chapter 1, n. 55.

3. E.g. Gardner 1986: 121: "'Adultery', we are told, should be used specifically of relations with a married woman, and *stuprum* of those with unmarried or widowed women (or indeed with boys)." Despite his clear understanding of the applicability of *stuprum* to relations with males and females alike, Veyne 1988: 223 n. 65 argues that in the case of pederastic relationships, "there is no crime unless the adolescent in question is freeborn, and then his case his [*sic*] assimilated to that of a freeborn virgin."

4. She notes that "the Augustan law defined all sexual intercourse with people of either sex who fell under the law as *stuprum*," but proceeds to claim that the word was "in general use for any irregular or promiscuous sexual acts, especially rape or homosexuality" (Treggiari 1991: 263). Similarly the *RE* article on *stuprum* (*RE* 2.7 [1931]: 423) suggests that the term denotes relations with free women on the one hand and all sexual acts between males on the other: "S[tuprum] ist demnach der unzüchtige Geschlechtsverkehr mit einer freien, anständigen unverheirateten Frau oder von Personen männlichen Geschlechts untereinander . . ."

5. Fantham 1991: 270, 279 with n. 31, 285, 287 with n. 50. Fantham also implies (277) that it was a worse fate for a man to be anally penetrated than to be castrated or perhaps even killed: "The list [of punishments meted out to adulterers] includes one thrashing, possibly fatal, one beating up, two castrations, and the extreme misfortune of Furius Brocchus, surrendered to the domestic staff to be buggered."

6. Fantham 1991: 277.

7. "Debauchery," Lewis and Short *s.v.*; "immorality," LCL translation of Livy 39.14.8; "lewdness," LCL translation of Sall. *Cat.* 13.3; "fornication," Fantham 1991: 277; "illicit intercourse," *OLD s.v.* and Treggiari 1991: 263; "sex crime," Richlin 1992a: 30.

8. Recent discussions of *stuprum* include Gardner 1986: 121-5, Dalla 1987: 71-99, Fantham 1991, and Richlin 1992a: 224-5. For the Roman tendency to create overlaps between the moral, the legal, and the political see, in general, Donald Earl, *The Moral and Political Tradition of Rome* (Ithaca, 1967) and Edwards 1993.

9. Similarly, in contemporary English the adjective "perverse" and especially the noun "pervert" have come to be used almost exclusively with reference to sexual practices or agents.

10. See, for example, Tac. *Ann.* 16.19 (Petronius' description of Nero's sexual excesses): "flagitia principis sub nominibus exoletorum feminarumque et novitatem cuiusque stupri perscripsit"; Tac. *Hist.* 1.72: Tigellinus died a shameful death "inter stupra concubinarum"; D. 1.18.21: "de servo corrupto vel ancilla devirginata vel servo stuprato"; D. 47.10.25: "si stuprum serva passa sit." Fantham 1991: 270 notes that "we find no instances of *stuprum* that do not involve intercourse with male or female citizens," but on the next page states that "sexually promiscuous men are described as debauched with *stupra* even when their partners are likely to have been slaves or prostitutes."

11. E.g., Sen. *Contr.* 1.2.7: "pretia stupri accepisti"; 1.2.11: "stuprum videas."

12. Cato the Elder appealed to this very ideal in a speech *De Re Floria*, fragments of which are discussed in chapter 1 (fr. 212–3 Malcovati).

13. Cf. Fantham 1991: 271; see chapter 5 for a discussion of other meanings of *pudicitia*.

14. Val. Max. 6.1.1 (Lucretia was forced to submit to *stuprum*), 6.1.2 (Appius Claudius sought *stuprum* from Verginia), 6.1.6 (P. Atilius Philiscus killed his daughter because she was thought guilty of *stuprum*), 6.1.7 (C. Scantinius Capitolinus was accused of having

sought *stuprum* from the son of M. Claudius Marcellus), 6.1.9 (P. Plotius beat the young T. Veturius because he refused to submit to *stuprum*), 6.1.10 (C. Cornelius was punished for having had relations of *stuprum* with a freeborn boy), 6.1.11 (M. Laetorius Mergus was accused of having propositioned his assistant for *stuprum*), 6.1.12 (C. Plotius killed C. Lusius after he propositioned him for *stuprum*), 6.1.13 (Cn. Furius Brocchus, having been caught with a married woman, was punished by the outraged husband by being forced to submit to *stuprum* by the husband's slaves).

15. In a famous comment, Cicero observed that "our ancestors exercised control over them [sc., their freedmen] not much differently from the way they did over their slaves" (Cic. *Q. Frat.* 1.1.13: "maiores nostri . . . non multo secus ac servis imperabant"). For discussions of the position of *libertini*, see Treggiari 1969: 37–86 (especially 68–86), Fabre 1981, and Gardner 1993: 7-51.

16. Sen. *Contr.* 4.pr.10: "impudicitia in ingenuo crimen est, in servo necessitas, in liberto officium." It is significant that Haterius uses the word *libertus*, which designates the freedman of a specific citizen, rather than *libertinus*, which designates a freedman as a member of the entire class of the freed.

17. Sen. *Contr.* 4.pr.10: "res in iocos abiit: 'non facis mihi officium' et 'multum ille huic in officiis versatur.' ex eo impudici et obsceni aliquamdiu officiosi vocitati sunt."

18. Cf. Kroll 1988: 75, on the delicate situation of the *liberta*: "Diese ist zwar Bürgerin, steht aber unter dem Patronat ihres früheren Herrn und hat zu ihm ein gewisses Pietätsverhältnis; das verpflichtet sie natürlich nicht, sich ihm hinzugeben, macht es ihr aber unter Umständen schwer, seinem Drängen Widerstand zu leisten."

19. Ulpian: "cum Atilicino sentio et puto solas eas in concubinatu habere posse sine metu criminis, in quas stuprum non committitur" (D. 25.7.1); Papinian: "quoniam stuprum in ea contrahi non placuit, quae se non patroni concubinam esse patitur" (D. 34.9.16.1). For a discussion of Roman *concubinae*, see Rawson 1974, Susan Treggiari, "*Concubinae*," *PBSR* 49 (1981): 59-81, and the brief overview at Treggiari 1991: 51–2.

20. D. 25.7.1: "quae in concubinatu est, ab invito patrono poterit discedere et alteri se aut in matrimonium aut in concubinatum dare?" Another jurist opines (D. 38.1.38) that those services which cannot be offered to a patron without disgrace (*turpitudo*) or risk of death need not be imposed upon the freed. His example of the latter is a *harenarius* who, once manumitted, need no longer perform the same duties for his patron, and his example of the former is a *meretrix* ("nec enim si meretrix manumissa fuerit, easdem operas patrono praestare debet, quamvis adhuc corpore quaestum faciat"). This, however, is a specialized case of a prostitute who, once freed by her pimp, need no longer work for him, and does not speak to the broader issue of a Roman man's sexual claims over his freed slaves.

21. Seneca, in fact, cites Haterius' formulation as an example of his unfortunate tendency to come up with expressions that were liable to ridicule: "sed dum nihil vult nisi culte, nisi splendide dicere, saepe incidebat in ea quae derisum effugere non possent" (*Contr.* 4.pr.10). Cantarella 1992: 112 misleadingly notes that "Seneca thus affirms without hesitation that the same behaviour, in a free citizen, would be a crime," attributing the argument to Seneca himself rather than to Haterius, and taking *crimen* to mean a legally actionable offense ("crime"); but the word does not have so specific a reference to the provisions of the law, broadly denoting instead an accusation or reproach, or something worthy of accusation or reproach (see *OLD* s.v.).

22. While the adjective *liberis* ("free") strictly modifies *pueris* ("boys") only, the qualifier obviously applies to all of the categories listed. Jocelyn 1985: 14–5 objects that we cannot adduce this passage as evidence for Roman attitudes since the play, like all of Plautus' and Terence's work, is based on a Greek original. But this speech is clearly a Plautine expansion upon that original. Not only is the morality to which the slave appeals a quintessentially

Roman one (it is hard to imagine a slave in a Greek comedy issuing a prohibition against pederasty, especially since, in Athens at least, slaves were explicitly forbidden from participating in *paiderastia*, which was held to be the privilege of the freeborn citizen: Aeschin. 1.139; Plut. *Solon* 1.6, *Amatorius* 751B), but the passage bears all the textual hallmarks of a Plautine creation. An earlier pun on *testes* (30–1) is purely Latin, and we can detect at lines 27 and 39 seams in the structure of the dialogue that are characteristic of Plautus' additions to his Greek originals (cf. Fraenkel 1960: 105–34): the dialogue's flow is interrupted by the insertion of the slave's pompous enunciation of a Roman code of behavior. For further discussion, see chapters 1 and 2.

23. The only difference between them is insignificant: Plautus' "young men and free boys" have been collapsed into "a boy" in Modestinus. The law on *stuprum* clearly applied to free persons only (cf. Papinian at D. 48.5.6.pr.: "inter liberas tantum personas adulterium stuprumve passas lex Iulia locum habet"). For the meaning of *adulterium*, see discussion later in this chapter.

24. Val. Max. 6.1.7: "M. Claudius Marcellus aedilis curulis C. Scantinio Capitolino tribuno plebis diem ad populum dixit, quod filium suum de stupro appellasset, eoque asseverante se cogi non posse ut adesset, quia sacrosanctam potestatem haberet, et ob id tribunicium auxilium implorante, totum collegium tribunorum negavit se intercedere quo minus pudicitiae quaestio perageretur." The incident (for which see also Plut. *Marc*. 2) is usually dated to around 226 B.C.

25. This incident (for which see also Dion. Hal. 16.4) is dated by Cantarella 1992: 105 to 317 B.C., by Lilja 1983: 107 to 291–0 B.C.

26. The historian's expression of profound respect for Roman moral traditions in his preface should not be forgotten: "ceterum aut me amor negotii suscepti fallit, aut nulla umquam res publica nec maior nec sanctior nec bonis exemplis ditior fuit, nec in quam [civitatem] tam serae avaritia luxuriaque immigraverint, nec ubi tantus ac tam diu paupertati ac parsimoniae honos fuerit" (pr. 11).

27. Livy 8.28.4: "cum ingenuitatis magis quam praesentis condicionis memorem videret, nudari iubet verberaque adferri."

28. Livy 8.28.6–7: "ingens vis hominum cum aetatis miseratione atque indignitate iniuriae accensa, tum suae condicionis liberumque suorum respectu, in forum atque inde agmine facto ad curiam concurrit; et cum consules tumultu repentino coacti senatum vocarent, introeuntibus in curiam patribus laceratum iuvenis tergum procumbentes ad singulorum pedes ostentabant."

29. Tac. *Ann*. 4.1: "non sine rumore Apicio diviti et prodigo stuprum veno dedisse"; 6.1: "ut more regio pubem ingenuam stupris pollueret"; 13.17: "stupro prius quam veneno pollutum."

30. As Fantham 1991: 271 aptly puts it, "in post-Augustan authors it becomes a stick to beat with." Opelt 1965: 202–3 offers a survey of the uses of an accusation of *stuprum* in declamation and comedy.

31. Tac. *Hist*. 1.74: "mox quasi rixantes stupra ac flagitia in vicem obiectavere, neuter falso."

32. Ov. *Am*. 2.19.3–4: "quod licet, ingratum est; quod non licet, acrius urit: / ferreus est, si quis, quod sinit alter, amat"; cf. *Am*. 3.4.

33. Tac. *Ann*. 6.1: "nec formam tantum et decora corpora sed in his modestiam pueritiam, in aliis imagines maiorum incitamentum cupidinis habebat."

34. He makes a similar point, again with *praeteritio*, in another of the speeches against Verres (*Verr*. 2.1.62): "quam multis istum ingenuis, quam multis matribus familias in illa taetra atque impura legatione vim attulisse existimatis? ecquo in oppido pedem posuit ubi non plura stuprorum flagitiorumque suorum quam adventus sui vestigia reliquerit? sed

ego omnia quae negari poterunt praetermittam." In both cases, Cicero uses the adjective *ingenuus* as a substantive in a generalizing masculine plural, which his readers would have understood to include both male and female victims. (The usage is in itself significant: their freeborn status is the crucial factor, and their sex is irrelevant).

35. Cic. *Fam*. 5.10a.1: "qui tot ingenuos, matresfamilias, cives Romanos occidit, arripuit, disperdidit." As Shackleton Bailey suggests in his 1977 commentary, Vatinius may be indulging in an extended chiasmus, his point being that Catilius killed (*occidit*) Roman citizens, seized (*arripuit*) Roman matrons, and ruined (*disperdidit*) the free-born.

36. Cf. *Rhet. Herenn*. 4.12: "in iis qui violassent ingenuum, matremfamilias constuprassent, vulnerassent aliquem aut postremo necassent."

37. Cf. Tac. *Hist*. 2.56: "dispersi per municipia et colonias Vitelliani spoliare, rapere, vi et stupris polluere: in omne fas nefasque avidi aut venales non sacro, non profano abstinebant"; 2.73: "tum ipse [sc., Vitellius] exercitusque, ut nullo aemulo, saevitia libidine raptu in externos mores proruperant."

38. Tac. *Hist*. 4.14: "rursus impubes et forma conspicui (et est plerisque procera pueritia) ad stuprum trahebantur"; the Batavian leader Civilis complained that they were being treated no longer as Roman allies but as slaves ("neque enim societatem, ut olim, sed tamquam mancipia haberi").

39. D. 3.1.1.6: "removet autem a postulando pro aliis et eum, qui corpore suo muliebria passus est. si quis tamen vi praedonum vel hostium stupratus est, non debet notari, ut et Pomponius ait." See chapter 5 for further discussion of this provision. For another reference to the practice of wartime rape, see Tac. *Ann*. 6.1: Tiberius' slaves on Capri would grab free youths for him, and if their relatives tried to resist their capture, the slaves would rape the youths, treating them like wartime captives ("et si retinerent propinquus aut parens, vim raptus suaque ipsi libita velut in captos exercebant").

40. Val. Max. 9.1.8: "lupanari enim domi suae instituto Muniam et Flaviam, cum a patre tum a viro utramque inclitam, et nobilem puerum Saturninum in eo prostituit"; Suet. *Cal*. 41.1: "lupanar in Palatio constituit, districtisque et instructis pro loci dignitate compluribus cellis, in quibus matronae ingenuique starent, misit circum fora et basilicas nomenculatores ad invitandos ad libidinem iuvenes senesque." Cf. Suet. *Nero* 28.1: "ingenuorum paedagogia et nuptarum concubinatus," where the phrase "ingenuorum paedagogia" suggests an establishment at which freeborn youth were treated like slaves, perhaps a brothel.

41. Cf. Cic. *Att*. 1.18.3: "adflicta res publica est empto constupratoque iudicio." Other references to this trial include Cic. *Mil*. 87 and Dio 37.45–6.

42. In the case of marriage *sine manu*, the wife was not technically under her husband's control, remaining under her father's, but *de facto* she was subject to her husband, living under his roof and bearing his children. (Consider, for example, Cic. *Off*. 1.12: it is nature's will that a man "studeat parare ea quae suppeditent ad cultum et ad victum, nec sibi soli sed coniugi liberis ceterisque quos caros habeat tuerique debeat.") Cf. Treggiari 1991: 309–10.

43. Cf. also *Cat*. 4.12 ("tum lamentationem matrum familias, tum fugam virginum atque puerorum ac vexationem virginum Vestalium perhorresco") and 3.1, 3.23, 4.3, 4.18, 4.24; at *Flacc*. 1 he claims to have saved them from death.

44. Cic. *Mil*. 76: "a liberis . . . et a coniugibus vestris numquam ille effrenatas suas libidines cohibuisset."

45. Livy 39.15.14: "hi cooperti stupris suis alienisque pro pudicitia coniugum ac liberorum vestrorum ferro decernent?"

46. See Balsdon 1979: 170–6 for discussion of Verres as prime example of the corrupt provincial official.

47. Cf., e.g., Cicero's snide comments about Verres' relationship with the prostitute Chelidon (*Verr*. 2.1.104, 106, 120, 136–40; 2.2.24, 39; 2.3.30; 2.5.38), his penchant for adultery (2.2.115–6; 2.4.144; 2.5.31), and his excessive womanizing in general (2.3.31, 56; 2.5.27–38, 100). One trenchant summary speaks of "istius cotidiana adulteria, meretriciam disciplinam, domesticum lenocinium" (2.3.6) and another describes "domum suam plenam stupri, plenam flagiti, plenam dedecoris . . . in qua semper meretricum lenonumque flagitia versantur" (2.4.83). It is true that Cicero makes a charge, almost *de rigueur* in Roman invective, that Verres had been sexually penetrated by men, but he conspicuously directs those allegations only at Verres' youth (2.1.32, 2.3.148, 2.5.33–4). On this commonplace in rhetorical invective, see Gonfroy 1978 (for Cicero) and Richlin 1993: 538–9.

48. Calp. Flacc. 3. Other references to the incident include Val. Max. 6.1.12; Cic. *Mil*. 9, *Inv*. 2.124; Quint. *I.O.* 3.11.14; [Quint.] *Decl. Maior.* 3; Plut. *Marius* 14. See the discussion in Walters 1997.

49. Calp. Flacc. 3: "tibi nondum vir est, qui Mario iam miles est?"

50. Ibid.: "stuprum minatus est militi tuo: minus est quod nobis Cimbri minantur."

51. [Quint.] *Decl. Maior.* 3 does in fact expatiate on the tribune's disregard for the soldier's manhood, but this text is most likely quite late, even postclassical.

52. Verstraete 1980: 229; cf. MacCary 1975: 462 ("The most frightening aspect of the whole business was the inversion of the sexual instincts of Roman men"); Gruen 1990: 35 (Hispala "ascribed to them every form of wickedness and crime, nocturnal orgies, homosexual excess, frenzied rituals, the initiation of young boys, and the murder and sacrifice of objectors"); and MacMullen 1991: 429 ("What is offered as the principle [*sic*] charge, somewhat muffled for decency's sake, was aimed against male homosexuality which characterized the meetings and had become their main purpose of recent years. Outlandish abomination!").

53. Cf. Livy 39.8.5 ("initia erant quae primo paucis tradita sunt deinde vulgari coepta sunt per viros mulieresque") and Val. Max. 1.3.1 ("Bacchanalium mysteria fuere Romae. sed cum temporibus nocturnis viri ac feminae pariter essent furerentque, multo colentium sanguine †se et peregrina sacra abolita sunt").

54. Livy 39.13.10–1: "ex quo in promiscuo sacra sint et permixti viri feminis, et noctis licentia accesserit, nihil ibi facinoris, nihil flagitii praetermissum. plura virorum inter sese quam feminarum esse stupra. si qui minus patientes dedecoris sint et pigriores ad facinus, pro victimis immolari." The language is decorous, but the use of *patientes* directly implies penetration (see chapter 5), as does Hispala's phrase *stuprum pati* at 39.13.13.

55. It should be noted, too, that Hispala is far from being an objective observer and has good reasons to emphasize the horrors of initiation. Indeed, trying to dissuade her lover Aebutius from becoming initiated, she had earlier spoken in quite lurid terms: "They lead the initiates into a place that resounds with wailings and the song of musicians as well as the beatings of cymbals and tambourines, so as to drown out the voice of the one crying out as he is forcibly subjected to *stuprum*." (Livy 39.10.7: "eos deducere in locum, qui circumsonet ululatibus cantuque symphoniae et cymbalorum et tympanorum pulsu, ne vox quiritantis, cum per vim stuprum inferatur, exaudiri possit.")

56. Livy 39.15.9: "primum igitur mulierum magna pars est, et is fons mali huiusce fuit; deinde simillimi feminis mares, stuprati et constupratores, fanatici, vigiliis vino strepitibus clamoribusque nocturnis attoniti." The implications of this passage for Roman meanings of effeminacy are discussed in chapter 4.

57. I use "adultery" to translate *adulterium*, referring to sexual relations between a married woman and someone other than her husband. A married man's relations with his own female slaves were not generally considered to be *adulterium*, whereas, for example, a married woman's relations with her male slaves were. See Treggiari 1991: 262–4 for an overview of the Roman language of adultery.

58. See, e.g., Sen. *Contr.* 2.7.1: "quamquam eo prolapsi iam mores civitatis sunt ut nemo ad suspicanda adulteria nimium credulus possit videri"; Sen. *Ben.* 1.9.4, 3.16.3. Edwards 1993: 34–62 provides a useful discussion of the prevalence of adultery as an image for decline and social disruption.

59. Petr. *Sat.* 55.6.10–1: "an ut matrona ornata phaleris pelagiis / tollat pedes indomita in strato extraneo?"

60. Tac. *Hist.* 1.2: "pollutae caerimoniae, magna adulteria."

61. Juv. 3.45–6: "ferre ad nuptam quae mittit adulter, / quae mandat, norunt alii." Cf. Mart. 4.5.

62. Juv. 6.1–24; note that the speaker imagines adultery to have first appeared in the Silver Age, followed by other offenses in the Iron Age (23–4: "omne aliud crimen mox ferrea protulit aetas: / viderunt primos argentea saecula moechos"). Cf. Hor. *Sat.* 1.3.99-110, *C.* 3.6.

63. Juv. 11.176–7: "alea turpis, / turpe et adulterium mediocribus."

64. Juv. 14.25–30.

65. Valerius Maximus begins his chapter on *pudicitia* with Lucretia, bestowing on her the not insignificant praise "dux Romanae pudicitiae" (6.1.1). In Hyginus' list of "quae castissimae fuerunt" (256), Penelope is the first of several Greek examples, Lucretia the one and only Roman example. Martial uses Lucretia as a figure for the extreme of sexual purity on three occasions (1.90, 11.16, 11.104). Both Calpurnius Flaccus and the author of the *Declamationes Maiores* attributed to Quintilian have the *miles Marianus* defend his action by citing Lucretia—rather than, for example, the young Marcellus, who was propositioned by Scantinius (Val. Max. 6.1.7)—as an example of the value placed by his Roman ancestors on chastity ([Quint.] *Decl. Maior.* 3.11; cf. Calp. Flacc. 3). While both speakers indicate the oddity of citing the example of a woman, the fact remains that they nonetheless draw a meaningful parallel between Lucretia and the man whose *pudicitia* had been threatened. Petronius provides a boisterously humorous invocation of Lucretia that is likewise found in an exclusively male context. Coming at night to make a sexual advance on Giton, Encolpius' boyfriend, Ascyltus draws his sword with the words, "If you are Lucretia, you've found your Tarquinius!" (Petr. *Sat.* 9.5: "si Lucretia es, Tarquinium invenisti").

66. See, e.g., Cic. *Fin.* 2.27, *Leg.* 1.43, *Off.* 1.128.

67. Hor. *Sat.* 1.2; the same theme appears in Hor. *Sat.* 2.7 and Juv. 10.311–7.

68. Muson. Ruf. 86.8–10 Lutz: συμπλοκαὶ δ' ἄλλαι αἱ μὲν κατὰ μοιχείαν παρανομώταται, καὶ μετριώτεραι τούτων οὐδὲν αἱ πρὸς ἄρρενας τοῖς ἄρρεσιν, ὅτι παρὰ φύσιν τὸ τόλμημα. For further discussion of this passage, see Appendix 1.

69. See, e.g., Hor. *C.* 3.24.17–20 (there is no adultery among the Getae) and Tac. *Germ.* 19 (a wistful contrast between the pristine Germans and decadent Romans). At *Germ.* 12 ("ignavos et imbelles et corpore infames caeno ac palude, iniecta insuper crate, mergunt"), Tacitus notes that men who are *corpore infames* are subject to capital punishment, but if this phrase has a sexual reference (as is likely but not certain), it must refer to men who seek to be sexually penetrated.

70. On adultery, Plin. *N.H.* 8.13 (elephants): "nec adulteria novere"; 10.104 (pigeons): "inest pudicitia illis plurima, et neutri nota adulteria"; for a male elephant in love with a human youth, see Plin. *N.H.* 8.14: "alius Menandrum Syracusanum incipientis iuventae in exercitu Ptolemaei, desiderium eius, quotiens non videret, inedia testatus" (the incident is related in the context of a discussion of "the power of love" [*amoris vis*] among elephants); for dolphins and boys, see Gell. 6.8.3: "neque hi amaverunt quod sunt ipsi genus, sed pueros forma liberali in naviculis forte aut in vadis litorum conspectos miris et humanis modis arserunt" (cf. Plin. *N.H.* 9.25–8). See Appendix 1 for further discussion of paradigms of animal behavior (and, implicitly, "nature") as they relate to human sexual practices.

71. Cases involving adultery: Sen. *Contr.* 1.4, 1.7, 2.7, 6.6, 7.5, 8.3, 9.1; Calp. Flacc. 2, 31, 40, 48, 49; Quint. *Declam. Minor.* 244, 249, 273, 275, 277, 279, 284, 286, 291, 300, 310, 319, 330, 335, 347, 355, 357. Cases involving *stuprum* with young men: Sen. *Contr.* 3.8, 5.6; Calp. Flacc. 3, 20; Quint. *Declam. Minor.* 279, 292.

72. Discussions include Richlin 1981a; Gardner 1986: 127–32; Richlin 1992a: 215–9; Cantarella 1992: 142–5; and Edwards 1993: 37–42.

73. Edwards 1993: 61.

74. For discussions of this immense question see, for example, Richlin 1992a and Edwards 1993: 47–58.

75. D. 48.5.6.1: "sed proprie adulterium in nupta committitur, propter partum ex altero conceptum composito nomine."

76. See Treggiari 1991: 262–4 for discussion of Festus' rather different etymology of *adulterium* (Festus 20L: "adulter et adultera dicuntur, quia et ille ad alteram et haec ad alterum se conferunt"). In the end, she concludes, "the juristic usage [of the term] is closer to the norm in making *adulterium* an extra-marital sexual relationship of a married woman." Edwards 1993: 49 cites the passage from the Digest, but argues that otherwise "there are few examples in classical Roman texts of directly expressed concern with illegitimate births as a consequence of adultery." But see Catull. 61.214–23, where Junia's bearing a child that is not her husband's would be the most egregious violation of her *pudicitia*, and her best possible fate is to be likened to Penelope, the archetypal opposite of the adulteress. See also Mart. 6.39, Juv. 6.597–601.

77. Vir. *Aen.* 4.28–9: "ille meos, primus qui me sibi iunxit, amores / abstulit; ille habeat secum servetque sepulchro"; for *culpa*, see 4.19 ("huic uni forsan potui succumbere culpae") and 4.172 ("coniugium vocat, hoc praetexit nomine culpam"). It is clear from Cicero's defense of Caelius (see chapter 1) that the prosecution capitalized on similar feelings concerning Caelius' affair with the widowed Clodia. On the *univira*, see Williams 1958.

78. We might recall Cicero's treatment of Dionysius' love affairs, *more Graeciae*, with *adulescentes* (*Tusc.* 5.58: see chapter 2), where the implication is that these affairs ought to have given Dionysius happiness, but his suspicious nature prevented him from trusting those close to him. For Virgil's treatment of Cydon, see Williams 1983: 193 (the apostrophe and especially the surprising adjective *infelix* add a "special touch of pathos and pity," 195) and Alessandro Fo, "Cidone," *Enciclopedia Virgiliana* (Rome, 1985) 1: 780 ("E' una di quelle tenere figure, cariche di umanità, che V. si compiace di abbozzare rapidamente nel quadro delle azioni belliche, sottolineando così per contrasto quanto queste ultime siano assurde e crudeli"). Servius ad loc. suggests that Cydon's name reflects the tradition that the Cretans, also called Cydones, "in amores puerorum intemperantes fuerunt." (For Crete and pederasty, see the discussion of Nepos in chapter 2.)

79. Vir. *Aen.* 10.188–9: "crimen, Amor, vestrum formaeque insigne paternae. / namque ferunt luctu Cycnum Phaethontis amati . . ."

80. Macr. *Sat.* 5.16.10–1: "nullam commemorationem de iudicio Paridis Homerus admittit. idem vates Ganymedem non ut Iunonis paelicem a Iove raptum sed Iovalium poculorum ministrum in caelum a dis ascitum refert velut θεοπροπῶς. Vergilius tantam deam, quod cuivis de honestis feminae deforme est, velut specie victam Paride iudicante doluisse, et propter Catamiti paelicatum totam gentem eius vexasse commemorat." See Putnam 1985 for a subtle interpretation of the *Aeneid* that discerns a relationship between Juno's anger over Ganymede at the epic's opening and Aeneas' anger over Pallas at its close.

81. Vir. *Aen.* 5.250–7; see Putnam 1995 for a detailed analysis.

82. See Makowski 1989 for an overview of ancient and modern views of the pair, along with arguments for describing them as *erastes* and *eromenos* on the Greek model (he finds particular parallels with Plato's *Symposium*). For literary discussions of Nisus and

Euryalus that take as their starting point the erotic nature of their relationship, see Gordon Williams 1983: 205–7, 226–31; Lyne 1987: 228–9, 235–6; and Hardie 1994: 23–34. Maria Bellincioni, "Eurialo," *Enciclopedia Virgiliana* (Rome, 1985) 2: 426, observing that Virgil has added the motif of their friendship to his Homeric models, summarizes thus: "L'amore che unisce E. e Niso è un sentimento intermedio fra l'amicizia e la passione . . . pur nella sua purezza, tende all'eros. Comunque è passione che si pone fine a se stessa e non si subordina a principi morali, come la slealtà sportiva di Niso nel 5o chiaramente dimostra." She cites C. Colmant, "L'épisode de Nisus et Euryale ou le poème de l'amitié," *LEC* 19 (1951): 89–100.

83. Vir. *Aen*. 5.334: "non tamen Euryali, non ille oblitus amorum." The plural *amores* is ordinarily used of one's sexual partner, one's "love" in that sense (see *OLD* s.v. 1c; Virgil himself uses the word in the plural to refer to a bull's mate at *Georgics* 3.227). Indeed, Servius (*ad Aen*. 5.334), writing in a different cultural climate, was worried by precisely that fact, observing that Virgil's phrase *oblitus amorum* contradicts his earlier *amore pio pueri* because *amores* in the plural "can only signify something disgraceful" whereas the description of Nisus' love for the boy as *pius* apparently precludes, for Servius, physicality: "'oblitus amorum' amare nec supra dictis congrue: ait enim 'amore pio pueri,' nunc 'amorum,' qui pluraliter non nisi turpitudinem significant.'"

84. For Euryalus' youth, cf. 217, 276 (*puer*) and especially the evocation of his beauty even in death (433–7, language which recalls the erotic imagery of Catullus and Sappho: Lyne 1987: 229). For their inseparability, cf. 203 ("tecum talia gessi") and 244–5 ("vidimus . . . venatu adsiduo"); note how Nisus gallantly presents his plan to the assembled troops not as his own but as his and Euryalus' (235–6: "neve haec nostris spectentur ab annis / quae ferimus"; 237: "conspeximus").

85. Vir. *Aen*. 9.184–5: "dine hunc ardorem mentibus addunt, / Euryale, an sua cuique deus fit dira cupido?" Cf. Makowski 1989: 8 and Hardie 1994: 109. For the phrase *dira cupido*, compare *dira libido* at Lucretius 4.1046 (concerning men's desire to ejaculate) and *muta cupido* at 4.1057.

86. Note, also, that 9.199-200 ("mene . . . fugis?") seems to echo Dido's words to Aeneas at 4.314 ("mene fugis?": so too Makowski 1989: 9–10), and 9.390-3 ("'Euryale infelix, qua te regione reliqui? / quave sequar?' rursus perplexum iter omne revolvens / fallacis silvae simul et vestigia retro / observata legit dumisque silentibus errat") might recall the scene where Aeneas loses Creusa at the end of Book 2. (Hardie 1994: 26 points to parallels with the story of Orpheus and Eurydice in the *Georgics*, as well as to that of Aeneas and Creusa in *Aeneid* 2.) For the Sacred Band of Thebes, see Plut. *Amat*. 761B, *Pelop*. 18–9, Athen. 13.561F and 602A, and the probable allusion at Pl. *Smp*. 178e–179a.

87. Cf. Williams 1983: 205–7, Lyne 1987: 235 (for their "elegiac union as *lovers in death*" he adduces Prop. 2.20.18 ["ambos una fides auferet, una dies"] and Tibull. 1.1.59–62 as parallels).

88. *CLE* 1142 = *CIL* 6.25427, lines 25–6 (husband and wife): "fortunati ambo —si qua est, ea gloria mortis— / quos iungit tumulus, iunxerat ut thalamus"; *CLE* 491 = *CIL* 11.654 (a woman praised by her male friend): "unus amor mansit, par quoque vita fidelis" (cf. *Aen*. 9.182, "his amor unus erat pariterque in bella ruebant"); *CLE* 1848.5-6 (grandmother and granddaughter): "sic lumine vero / tunc iacuere simul Nisus et Eurialus."

89. Sen. *Epist*. 21.5: "Vergilius noster duobus memoriam aeternam promisit et praestat: 'fortunati ambo! si quid mea carmina possunt . . .'" It is revealing of the sometimes porous boundary in Roman texts between what we might call "friendship" and "eroticism" among males—an overlap I hope to discuss in another context—that Ovid cites Nisus and Euryalus as the ultimate embodiment of male friendship, putting them in the company of Theseus and Pirithous, Orestes and Pylades, Achilles and Patroclus (*Tristia* 1.5.19–24, 1.9.27–34);

but the relationship between Achilles and Patroclus, at least, was openly described as including a sexual element by classical Greek writers (see n. 92) and, with characteristic bluntness, by Martial (11.43), who cites the pair as an illustration of the special pleasures of anal intercourse.

90. See, e.g., Gillis 1983, Putnam 1985, and Moorton 1990. In unpublished papers, Mario Erasmo and Charles Lloyd have independently described erotic elements in the relationship between the young Evander and Anchises, a relationship that, they argue, is then replicated in the next generation, with Pallas and Aeneas.

91. Vir. *Aen.* 9.182: "pariterque in bella ruebant"; 252–3: "quae vobis, quae digna, viri, pro laudibus istis / praemia posse rear solvi?"; 376: "state viri"; 471–2: "simul ora virum praefixa movebant / nota nimis miseris atroque fluentia tabo."

92. The relationship between Achilles and Patroclus was understood by later Greek writers to have a sexual component: see, e.g., Aesch. fr. 135–7 Nauck (from the *Myrmidons*); Pl. *Smp.* 180a-b; Aeschin. 1.133, 141–50 (Lyne 1987: 235 n. 49, crediting Jasper Griffin, adds Bion 12 Gow). But the text of the *Iliad* itself, while certainly suggesting a passionate and deeply intense bond between the two, does not represent them in terms of the classical pederastic model. See further W. M. Clarke, "Achilles and Patroclus in Love," *Hermes* 106 (1978): 381–96, Sergent 1986: 250-8, and Halperin 1990: 75–87.

93. G. Knauer, *Die Aeneis und Homer* (Göttingen, 1964), p. 415, cites no Homeric parallel for these lines.

94. Cf. Turnus' rhetoric at 9.128–58, based on sharp distinctions among the Trojans, Greeks, and Italians; and the weighty dialogue between Jupiter and Juno at 12.808–40, where it is agreed that Trojans and Italians will become one race.

95. The issue is complex: Dido is of course neither Roman nor Trojan, and thus at first glance Aeneas' relationship with her does not constitute *stuprum*. But since Dido's experiences are, in important ways, seen through a Roman filter—above all, the commitment to her first husband that makes her a prototypical *univira*— her involvement with Aeneas (a *culpa*: 4.19, 172) constitutes an offense within the moral framework proposed by the text in a way that the relationship between Nisus and Euryalus does not.

96. See Gardner 1986: 121–5 and Treggiari 1991: 264–77.

97. For discussions of the law and its punishments, see Raditsa 1980, Richlin 1981a, Gardner 1986: 121–32, Treggiari 1991: 277–98, Cantarella 1992: 142–5, Edwards 1993: 37–42.

98. For the evidence on this frustratingly shadowy law, and a variety of interpretations as to what it covered, see Boswell 1980: 65–9, Lilja 1983: 112–21, Dalla 1987: 71–99, Fantham 1991: 285–7, Cantarella 1992: 106–19 (who follows the less usual spelling *Scatinia*), and Richlin 1993: 569–71. There exists no clear proof of when exactly the law was passed, but the earliest unambiguous reference to it dates from 50 B.C. (Cic. *Fam.* 8.12, 14: the suggestion of Lilja 1983: 120, that perhaps we should emend *Scantinia* to *Atinia* [cf. Cic. *Phil.* 3.16], if correct, would mean that the earliest attestation of the law is Suetonius). Some, arguing on the basis of a papyrus fragment, have suggested 149 B.C. (so Treggiari 1991: 277), but Cantarella 1992: 110–1 is rightly skeptical.

99. Wilkinson 1978: 136; MacCary 1975: 464 n. 11.

100. Cantarella 1992: 108; Lilja 1983: 118; cf. Boswell 1980: 69. Sextus Empiricus (*Pyrrhon. hypotyp.* 1.152) claims that Roman law prohibits ἀρρενομιξίαις χρῆσθαι; this cannot refer to all sexual acts between males, but must instead refer to sexual acts with freeborn males, in other words, to certain acts of *stuprum*.

101. E.g., Lilja 1983: 112-21.

102. Kroll 1988: 91.

103. Richlin 1993.

104. Dalla 1987, Cantarella 1992.

105. Krenkel 1979b: 185 and Veyne 1985: 29 make this suggestion, too, but only in passing.

106. The wording is the reconstruction offered by Otto Lenel, *Das Edictum Perpetuum: Ein Versuch zu seiner Wiederherstellung* (3rd ed., Leipzig, 1927), p. 400. Cf. Gaius 3.220; Justin. *Inst.* 4.4.1; D. 47.10.9.4 ("si quis tam feminam quam masculum, sive ingenuos sive libertinos, impudicos facere adtemptavit, iniuriarum tenebitur"); and see Dalla 1987: 124-5 and Cantarella 1992: 115-9 (where a date from the early second century B.C. is suggested).

107. Cantarella 1992: 117 argues that the *lex Scantinia* must have predated the edict, suggesting that the edict came in response to the fact that the law had been ineffective in deterring men from seducing the freeborn.

108. Quint. *I.O.* 4.2.69 (a hypothetical defense of a client in which it is strategically advantageous to admit guilt of one crime so as to emphasize innocence of another: "ingenuum stupravit et stupratus se suspendit, non tamen ideo stuprator capite ut causa mortis punietur, sed decem milia, quae poena stupratori constituta est, dabit"); cf. 4.2.71, 7.4.42.

109. Suet. *Dom.* 8.3; Juv. 2.36–44; Prud. *Peristeph.* 10.201–5.

110. Auson. *Epigr.* 91 Peiper: "Iuris consulto, cui vivit adultera coniunx, / Papia lex placuit, Iulia displicuit. / quaeritis, unde haec sit distantia? semivir ipse / Scantiniam metuens non metuit Titiam."

111. See Braund 1995 for a general discussion of Laronia's role in the poem.

112. Cf. Juv. 2.10: "inter Socraticos notissima fossa cinaedos." For *fossa* as a metaphor for *cunnus*, see *Priap.* 83.31–2 (and perhaps Catull. 17.19: cf. Justin Glenn, "*Fossa* in Catullus' Simile of the Cut Tree [17.18–19]," *CPh* 65 [1970]: 256–7, and Arkins 1982: 5). Both Glenn and Arkins, however, inappropriately cite *Priap.* 78.5–6 ("nunc misella landicae / vix posse iurat ambulare prae fossis"), where the *fossae* are grooves on a woman's clitoris that Priapus, indulging in a horrific hyperbole, imagines to have been created by an over-zealous *cunnilingus.*

113. Or, as Gordon Williams has suggested to me, it is possible that Laronia cites the *lex Scantinia* to spite her interlocutor in a slightly different way: if the law penalizing those who commit *stuprum* with the freeborn were to be enforced, his potential lovers might be deterred from becoming involved with him, just as enforcement of the *lex Julia* would limit a married woman's choices. In support of this interpretation, it should be noted that just before mentioning the *lex Scantinia*, Laronia cattily asks the *cinaedus* where he bought his perfume (42–4). Perhaps Laronia is maliciously hinting that the shop owner is her interlocutor's lover (the connective *quod* may suggest some close relation between the references to the *dominus tabernae* and the law), and that enforcement of the law might well result in his condemnation and thus in the *cinaedus'* loss of a sexual partner. So too Ausonius' *semivir* could be said to fear the Scantinian law because it might discourage potential partners.

114. Treggiari 1991: 277 suggests caution: "The Scantinian Law of 149 B.C. on homosexual behaviour might have been among those abrogated [by the Julian Law], but we have evidence of its survival alongside the adultery law. We must conclude that it is not clear whether Augustus abolished actual statutes."

115. D. 48.5.13 (Ulpian): "haec verba legis, 'ne quis posthac stuprum adulterium facito sciens dolo malo' et ad eum qui suasit et ad eum qui stuprum vel adulterium intulit pertinent"; Suet. *Aug.* 34: "leges retractavit et quasdam ex integro sanxit, ut sumptuariam et de adulteriis et de pudicitia, de ambitu, de maritandis ordinibus"; cf. also *CJ* 9.9 ("de adulteriis et de stupro") and 9.9.8 ("de pudicitia").

116. D. 48.5.5 (Julian): ". . . cum aperte lege Iulia de adulteriis coercendis caveatur, si

quidem vidua sit, de cuius adulterio agetur, ut accusator liberum arbitrium habeat, adulterum an adulteram prius accusare malit; si vero nupta sit, ut prius adulterum peragat, tunc mulierem."

117. D. 48.5.6 (Papinian): "lex stuprum et adulterium promiscue et καταχρ-ηστικώτερον appellat. sed proprie adulterium in nupta committitur . . . stuprum vero in virginem viduamve committitur"; D. 50.16.101.pr (Modestinus): "inter stuprum et adulterium hoc interesse quidam putant, quod adulterium in nuptam, stuprum in viduam committitur. sed lex Iulia de adulteriis hoc verbo indifferenter utitur." Gardner 1986: 127 observes that it is not surprising that the *lex Julia* should be primarily invoked against adultery, since in that offense, above all, "there would usually be at least one other person with a motive for bringing a prosecution."

118. D. 48.5.35: "adulterium in nupta admittitur: stuprum in vidua vel virgine vel puero committitur."

119. D. 48.5.9: "qui domum suam, ut stuprum adulteriumve cum aliena matre familias vel cum masculo fieret, sciens praebuerit vel quaestum ex adulterio uxoris suae fecerit: cuiuscumque sit condicionis, quasi adulter punitur."

120. Just. *Inst*. 4.18.4: "item lex Iulia de adulteriis coercendis, quae non solum temeratores alienarum nuptiarum gladio punit, sed etiam eos qui cum masculis infandam libidinem exercere audent."

121. *Collatio legum Mosaicarum et Romanarum* 4.2.2: "et quidem primum caput legis prioribus legibus pluribus obrogat"; cf. Dalla 1987: 104.

122. So too Lilja 1983: 121, Dalla 1987: 102–3, and Cantarella 1992: 142–5.

123. Cantarella 1992: 117.

Chapter 4

1. Gleason 1995: 55-130, especially 62–7 and 74–7.

2. Gleason 1995: 74.

3. Edwards 1993: 81.

4. Gleason 1995: 65.

5. Foucault 1986.

6. Edwards 1993: 5 similarly observes in her introductory discussion that "all the vices discussed here can be seen as manifestations of what Roman moralists sometimes termed *incontinentia*, 'self-indulgence,' 'lack of self-control' (although they by no means exhaust this category)." But her subsequent discussion does not seem to use the notions of "control" or "dominion" as a central analytical category.

7. That this is true within every system of masculine ideology (and indeed any ideological system at all) is the initial premise of Cornwall and Lindisfarne 1994, whose "explicit focus is on the negotiation and plurality of masculinities" (10). Another preliminary comment of theirs is worth keeping mind: "One reason the rhetoric of hegemonic versions of masculinity is so compelling is that it rests on an apparent certainty: that 'a man is a man' everywhere, and everywhere this means the same thing" (3).

8. See *TLL* s.v. *mollis* (8.1378.13–1379.52) and *mollitia* (8.1384.22–76).

9. The story explains why the spring Salmacis in southwestern Asia Minor softens (*remolliat*) and enervates (*enervet*) men (Ov. *Met*. 4.285–7). See further Georgia Nugent, "This Sex Which Is Not One: De-Constructing Ovid's Hermaphrodite," *Differences* 2 (1990): 160–85.

10. Lucan 10.133–4: "infelix ferro mollita iuventus / atque exsecta virum"; Stat. *Silv*. 3.4.68–71: "haud ulli puerum mollire potestas / credita, sed tacita iuvenis Phoebeius arte / leniter haud ullo concussum vulnere corpus / de sexu transire iubet."

11. Catullus 63.68–9: "ego nunc deum ministra et Cybeles famula ferar? / ego Maenas, ego mei pars, ego vir sterilis ero?" The priests: *quae* (14), *exsecutae* (15), *rapidae* (34), *lassulae* (35); Attis: *vectus* (1), *stimulatus* and *vagus* (4), but then *citata* (8), *adorta* and *tremebunda* (11), *furibunda* (31), *comitata* (32), *excitam* (42), *ipsa* (45), *allocuta* and *maesta* (49), *teneram* (88), *illa* (89), *famula* (90); Attis of himself: *ipsa pupula* (56), *remota* (58; although this might be modifying *nemora* instead of *ego*), *ministra* and *famula* (68). Interestingly, Cybele, angered at Attis' resistance, uses masculine forms to describe him: *hunc* (78), *qui* (80).

12. Catull. 63.8-10: "niveis citata cepit manibus leve typanum, / typanum tuum, Cybebe, tua, mater, initia, / quatiensque terga tauri teneris cava digitis . . ." See Skinner 1997 for discussion of this poem.

13. Herter 1959 provides a neatly schematized overview of such traits, with copious documentation. For a useful discussion of the meanings of depilation, see Gleason 1995: 67–70 ("Stoic cosmetology"), 74–6. In this regard it is interesting to observe that in his moralizing discussion of the effeminate Maecenas (see discussion later in this chapter), Seneca makes the point that when success brings on luxury, the first symptom of the consequent corruption is precisely an excessive care for bodily appearance (Sen. *Epist.* 114.9: "ubi luxuriam late felicitas fudit, cultus primum corporum esse diligentior incipit").

14. Cf. Livy 34.7.9, where L. Valerius is speaking in favor of repealing the *lex Oppia*, which had limited women's display of jewelry and other fineries: "munditiae et ornatus et cultus, haec feminarum insignia sunt, his gaudent ut gloriantur, hunc mundum muliebrem appellarunt maiores nostri." His grand language, complete with a tricolon crescendo, underscores what is obviously meant to be a serious point, that women take (and have always taken) special pride in their appearance.

15. Scipio fr. 17 (Gell. 6.12.5): "nam qui cotidie unguentatus adversus speculum ornetur, cuius supercilia radantur, qui barba vulsa feminibusque subvulsis ambulet, qui in conviviis adulescentulus cum amatore cum chiridota tunica inferior accubuerit, qui non modo vinosus sed virosus quoque sit, eumne quisquam dubitet quin idem fecerit quod cinaedi facere solent?"

16. Suet. *Jul.* 45.2: "circa corporis curam morosior, ut non solum tonderetur diligenter ac raderetur, sed velleretur etiam"; *Aug.* 68.1: "item L. Marci frater, quasi pudicitiam delibatam a Caesare Aulo etiam Hirtio in Hispania trecentis milibus nummum substraverit solitusque sit crura suburere nuce ardenti, quo mollior pilus surgeret."

17. Juv. 2.99–109.

18. Alternatively, the question "quis nescit?" ("who does not know?") may well be sardonic, even patronizing: we are willing to go along with your claim that you depilate your body for your girlfriend, but we cannot pretend that your depilated buttocks are meant for a girlfriend, too. Still, even if people suspected that he had depilated his chest, legs, and pubic region for a male lover, the fact remains that Labienus thought his explanation might be accepted by some.

19. Martial 2.47. For effeminate adulterers, see also Juvenal 6.O and Martial 5.61 (and perhaps 12.38).

20. Suet. *Vesp.* 8.3: "maluissem alium oboluisses."

21. Juv. 14.194–5: "sed captu intactum buxo narisque pilosas / adnotet et grandes miretur Laelius alas" (cf. Persius 3.77, "aliquis de gente hircosa centurionum"); Juv. 2.11–2: "hispida membra quidem et durae per bracchia saetae / promittunt atrocem animum."

22. Gleason 1995: 74.

23. Martial 2.36, 6.56. For the associations of hairiness with traditional masculine austerity, cf. Mart. 9.27.6–9 ("Curios, Camillos, Quintios, Numas, Ancos, / et quidquid umquam legimus pilosorum / loqueris sonasque grandibus minax verbis, / et cum theatris

saeculoque rixaris") and 9.47.1–2 ("Democritos, Zenonas inexplicitosque Platonas / quidquid et hirsutis squalet imaginibus").

24. Seneca returns to the image of depilation later in this text, comparing the self-conscious and pretentious literary style of Maecenas and others like him to those who pluck out their beard either entirely or partially, who closely shave around their lips while leaving the rest of the beard full, who wear cloaks of a disgraceful color or translucent togas ("qui aut vellunt barbam aut intervellunt, qui labra pressius tondent et adradunt servata et summissa cetera parte, qui lacernas coloris improbi sumunt, qui perlucentem togam . . ." *Epist.* 114.21). For depilation of the underarms, cf. Sen. *Epist.* 56.2 and Juv. 11.157 (with Courtney ad loc.). For the legs, cf. Juv. 8.16 (where a decadent aristocrat is said to depilate his "loins" [*lumbi*]: see discussion later in this chapter), 8.114–5 (with Courtney), and 9.12–5, where Naevolus has given up depilating his legs along with everything else characteristic of his previously dandified, urbane existence.

25. While not endowing his language with a specifically gendered quality, Seneca elsewhere recommends a similar moderation in one's appearance for those who wish to pursue philosophy (*Epist.* 5.2–3): "asperum cultum et intonsum caput et neglegentiorem barbam . . . evita . . . non splendeat toga: ne sordeat quidem."

26. See Varro, *L.L.* 5.73 ("virtus ut viritus, a virilitate") and Cic. *Tusc.* 2.43 ("appellata est enim ex viro virtus"). For discussions of *virtus*, see Hamblenne 1984 (with bibliographical references) as well as Werner Eisenhut, *Virtus Romana: Ihre Stellung im römischen Wertsystem* (Munich, 1973).

27. Stat. *Silv.* 4.8.27: "aptior his virtus, citius dabit illa nepotes"; cf. 59–62, where he wishes that the daughter may marry a patrician, and the sons become senators.

28. Sen. *Dial.* 12.16.2, 5: "non potest muliebris excusatio contingere ei a qua omnia muliebria vitia afuerunt"; "non potes itaque ad optinendum dolorem muliebre nomen praetendere, ex quo te virtutes tuae seduxerunt"; "si modo illas intueri voles feminas quas conspecta virtus inter magnos viros posuit." The *muliebria vitia* that Seneca details constitute a helpful overview of "feminine" vices: *impudicitia* (a sexual term, for which see chapter 5); weakness for jewels and riches; excessive pride in appearance (seen in their desire to conceal a pregnancy or even to have an abortion, and in their fondness for makeup and skimpy clothing).

29. Val. Max. 4.6.5 (on Porcia): "muliebri spiritu virilem patris exitum imitata"; 6.1.1 (on Lucretia): "cuius virilis animus maligno errore fortunae muliebre corpus sortitus est."

30. Cic. *Tusc.* 2.43: "appellata est enim ex viro virtus"; 2.46: "loquetur enim eorum voce Virtus ipsa tecum."

31. Interestingly, Cicero earlier notes that Pacuvius does "better" than his Greek original, Sophocles, because, unlike the Greek playwright, he does not have Odysseus indulge in excessive lamentation (2.49: "Pacuvius hoc melius quam Sophocles; apud illum enim perquam flebiliter Ulixes lamentatur in volnere"). Here Cicero is perhaps aligning the opposition between masculine reason and effeminate emotion with the opposition between Romans and Greeks (see the discussion later in this chapter on Greeks and effeminacy).

32. Cic. *Tusc.* 2.52: "cave turpe quicquam, languidum, non virile."

33. Cf. Cic. *Fin.* 2.45 (where *ratio* is said to be the crowning and distinctive glory of humanity, from which spring the four Platonic virtues, the greatest of which is *sophrosyne*, which is in turn opposed to *temeritas, protervum,* and *quod parum virile videatur*) and *Fin.* 2.47 (where *continentia* consists in avoiding behavior that is *parum virile*). For the general theme of exercising *imperium* over oneself or one's desires, cf. also Publ. Syr. *Sent.* A50 ("animo imperato ne tibi animus imperet") and A51 ("animo ventrique imperare debet qui frugi esse vult").

34. Cf. Sen. *Dial.* 1.2.5–6 (discussed by Edwards 1993: 78–81), where mothers are said to be indulgent toward their children, while fathers show a tough love (*fortiter*).

35. Vir. *Aen.* 1.279: "imperium sine fine dedi"; 6.851: "tu regere imperio populos, Romane, memento." If, as I am arguing, Roman *imperium* is conceptualized as masculine, it is interesting to compare what Richlin 1993: 553 calls "the Roman projection of Rome as a male fucking the rest of the world."

36. Nepos, *Hannibal* 1: "si verum est, quod nemo dubitat, ut populus Romanus omnes gentes virtute superarit"; Plin. *N.H.* 7.130: "gentium in toto orbe praestantissima una omnium virtute haud dubie Romana extitit." The hegemonic tone of these comments is noteworthy: the assertions that the Romans' unique claim to *virtus* is beyond a doubt tend to silence opposing views, representing them as virtually unthinkable. See also the discussion of Roman virtue and *virtus* at Edwards 1993: 20–2.

37. Hor. *Epist.* 1.1.64: "et maribus Curiis et decantata Camillis"; Pers. 6.4: "atque marem strepitum fidis intendisse Latinae."

38. Cf. Balsdon 1979: 61 on East vs. West; Herter 1959: 622 and Edwards 1993: 92–7. Relevant sources include Nepos, *Paus.* 3.2 ("epulabatur more Persarum luxuriosius quam qui aderant perpeti possent") and *Alcib.* 11.5 ("venisse ad Persas, apud quos summa laus esset fortiter venari, luxuriose vivere"); Val. Max. 9.1.5 ("non in Graecia neque in Asia, quarum luxuria severitas ipsa corrumpi poterat, sed in horrida et bellicosa provincia [sc., Spain]"); Juv. 8.113–24 (where luxurious Corinth is contrasted with the hairy, brave, and manly men of Spain, Gaul, and Illyria), 15.47–51 (an incident in Egypt, with men dancing amidst perfumes and flowers), and 14.187–8 (on the olden days: "peregrina ignotaque nobis / ad scelus atque nefas, quaecumque est, purpura ducit").

39. The use of the verb *pati* may add the insinuation that they are, or have been, sexually penetrated (perhaps as *eromenoi* in a pederastic relationship); for a discussion of the verb, see chapter 5.

40. Hor. *Sat.* 2.2.10–3: "vel si Romana fatigat / militia adsuetum graecari, seu pila velox / molliter austerum studio fallente laborem, / seu te discus agit, pete cedentem aera disco"; cf. Porph. *ad Sat.* 2.2.11 (where *graecari* is glossed as "aut luxuriari aut Graeco more ludere") and Hor. *C.* 3.24.51–8.

41. Val. Max. 2.6.1: "ut primum se Asiae moribus permisit, fortitudinem suam effeminato eius cultu mollire non erubuit." In the same section, Valerius praises Sparta in passing as being second only to Rome in its implicitly masculine traditions of austerity ("proxima maiorum nostrorum gravitati Spartana civitas").

42. Vir. *Aen.* 4.215–7, 9.598–620, 12.97–100 (discussed later in this chapter); Cic. *Mur.* 31: "verum haec Cato nimium nos nostris verbis magna facere demonstrat et oblitos esse bellum illud omne Mithridaticum cum mulierculis esse gestum." Cicero himself vehemently rejects this view: "atqui si diligenter quid Mithridates potuerit et quid effecerit et qui vir fuerit consideraris, omnibus quibuscum populus Romanus bellum gessit hunc regem nimirum antepones" (32).

43. Livy 34.1.5: "matronae nulla nec auctoritate nec verecundia nec imperio virorum contineri limine poterant."

44. Livy 34.7.12–3: "numquam salvis suis exuitur servitus muliebris, et ipsae libertatem quam viduitas et orbitas facit detestantur . . . et vos in manu et tutela, non in servitio debetis habere eas et malle patres vos aut viros quam dominos dici."

45. Sen. *Contr.* 9.2.17: "si praetor ius in veste servili vel muliebri dixerit, violabit maiestatem."

46. We do not have a Latin version of Cato's phrase, but Plutarch provides a Greek translation (*Cato Maior* 8.4): πάντες ἄνθρωποι τῶν γυναικῶν ἄρχουσιν, ἡμεῖς δὲ πάντων ἀνθρώπων, ἡμῶν δὲ αἱ γυναῖκες. It is certainly likely that Cato used the verb *imperare*.

47. Juvenal 6.224: "imperat ergo viro."

48. Tac. *Ann*. 6.25: "aequi impatiens, dominandi avida, virilibus curis feminarum vitia exuerat"; 12.7: "adductum et quasi virile servitium."

49. Hor. *Epod*. 9.12–4: "emancipatus feminae / fert vallum et arma miles et spadonibus / servire rugosis potest" (cf. *C*. 1.37 and see in general Griffin 1985: 32–47).

50. Cic. *Fin*. 2.94: "fortitudinis quaedam praecepta sunt ac paene leges quae effeminari virum vetant in dolore." Cf. Cic. *Off*. 1.71 (*in dolore molliores*); Livy 25.37.10 (*muliebris fletus*); Hor. *C*. 3.2 (*virtus* entails bravely facing death; cf. *C*. 3.5 on Regulus), *Epod*. 1.9–10 (the ability to endure hardship is opposed to *mollitia*: "mente laturi decet / qua ferre non mollis viros"), *Epod*. 10.17 ("et illa non virilis eiulatio" in a storm at sea), *Epod*. 16.39 (*muliebris luctus* is opposed to *virtus*); Sen. *Ep*. 99.17: "videt aliquem fortem in luctu suo: impium vocat et efferatum; videt aliquem conlabentem et corpori adfusum: effeminatum ait et enervem"; Sen. *Dial*. 12.16.1: "non est quod utaris excusatione muliebris nominis, cui paene concessum est immoderatum in lacrimis ius"; Stat. *Theb*. 497 (*molles lacrimae*); Tac. *Ann*. 16.10 (Antistia Pollitta, one of Nero's victims, pleads for her father "modo muliebri eiulatu, aliquando sexum egressa voce infesta clamitabat").

51. Sen. *Epist*. 67.4: "si aegrotandum fuerit, ut nihil intemperanter, nihil effeminate faciam optabo"; cf. ibid. 78.17: "si illum [sc., dolorem] muliebriter tuleris."

52. Hor. *C*. 1.37.21–4: "quae generosius / perire quaerens nec muliebriter / expavit ensem nec latentis / classe cita reparavit oras."

53. Tac. *Ann*. 15.49: "mollitia corporis infamis"; ibid. 15.70: "non ex priore vitae mollitia."

54. It is interesting to note that here *patientia*, most often a markedly effeminate trait ("submissiveness"), and in sexual terms often a code word for the receptive role in a penetrative act, is here given a positive and explicitly masculine spin (cf. Caes. *B.C*. 1.45.6 ["virtute et patientia nitebantur"] and see *OLD* s.v. *patientia* 1 and 2 for other texts in which *patientia* is represented as a positive quality). This text serves as a reminder that the language of Roman masculinity was not always as cut and dry as it might at first seem.

55. Sall. *Cat*. 11.3: "corpus animumque virilem effeminat"; Sen. *Epist*. 51.10: "effeminat animos amoenitas nimia."

56. Sen. *Ben*. 4.2.4: *virtus* is "labori ac dolori familiarior, virilibus incommodis, quam isti effeminato bono"; *Epist*. 104.34: "in primis autem respuendae voluptates; enervant et effeminant."

57. Caes. *B.G*. 1.1.3: "minimeque ad eos mercatores saepe commeant atque ea quae ad effeminandos animos pertinent important." Elsewhere, describing the Suebi, a German tribe, Caesar notes that they are a strong and disciplined people who have not imported wine, "quod ea re ad laborem ferendum remollescere homines atque effeminari arbitrantur" (*B.G*. 4.2.5).

58. See Edwards 1993: 98–136 and Edwards 1997 for general discussion.

59. Dio 62.6.3: ὄνομα μὲν γὰρ ἀνδρὸς ἔχει, ἔργῳ δὲ γυνή ἐστι – σημεῖον δέ, ᾄδει καὶ κιθαρίζει καὶ καλλωπίζεται. In his biography of the emperor, Suetonius cites Nero's singing and acting first in his catalog of monstrous acts (Suet. *Nero* 19-20). Cf. Tac. *Ann*. 14.15 ("quominus Graeci Latinive histrionis artem exercerent usque ad gestus modosque haud virilis") and *Hist*. 3.2 (a follower of Vespasian, speaking of the supporters of Vitellius: "circo quoque ac theatris et amoenitate urbis emollitos aut valetudinibus fessos").

60. Sen. *N.Q*. 7.31.3: "cotidie comminiscimur per quae virilitati fiat iniuria, ut traducatur, quia non potest exui; alius genitalia excidit, alius in obscenam ludi partem fugit et, locatus ad mortem, infame armaturae genus in quo morbum suum exerceat legit." See chapter 5 for further discussion.

61. Ralph Hexter has suggested to me some further factors in the denigration of gladiators: unlike soldiers, they risked their lives not for Rome but for the sake of trivial

entertainment; and there is surely also an element of class consciousness when Seneca and Juvenal's speaker profess horror at (implicitly free) Roman men descending to the world of actors and gladiators, many of whom were slaves or non-citizens. Another problem, as Daniel Selden has suggested to me, may have been that gladiators were subservient or beholden to their owners, promoters, and even the audience, and thus did not exercise their own *imperium*. See Barton 1993: 11–46 for discussion of "the scandal of the arena" and Edwards 1997 for an overview of the disrepute of gladiators, actors, and prostitutes.

62. See Gilmore 1990 esp. 9–28 for an introductory discussion. Cf. Kenneth E. Read, "The *Nama* Cult Recalled," in Herdt 1993: 220–1, speaking of a Melanesian culture: "'Girls *will* be women' but 'boys *will not* necessarily be men' . . . Men are a cultural artifact and women (in a far more fundamental sense) are simply what they were born to be. This contrast provides the tension and the dilemma in these highly masculine, male-dominated and -oriented societies; for men's image of themselves . . . is built on unstable sands and therefore requires the excessive props of ritual, secrecy, and, in a sense, duplicity to maintain it . . . 'It is hard work to make a man,' Gahuku often said to me; 'it's a big work'; and I gathered it was not a 'big work' to make a woman, indeed, no work at all: they had a natural advantage over men." Fausto-Sterling, in Berger et al. 1995: 129–30, observes a strikingly similar ideology at work in much contemporary medical writing on sex and gender: "Medical texts offer the presence/absence hypothesis. Maleness requires the presence of special hormones; in their absence, femaleness just happens . . . The male is in constant danger. At any point male development can be derailed . . ."

63. See, for further discussion of these and related issues, Herdt 1981 and 1993, Gilmore 1990, Cornwall and Lindisfarne 1994, Berger et al. 1995.

64. Gleason 1995: 59, 81.

65. The notion of gender as "performance" in contemporary Western cultures is most notably explored in Judith P. Butler, *Gender Trouble: Feminism and the Subversion of Identity* (New York, 1990); see Gleason 1995 for discussion of what might be called the balancing act of masculinity in late antiquity.

66. I suggest in chapter 5 that men who displayed a desire to be penetrated by women would have been liable to a charge of effeminacy as well.

67. While Edwards 1993: 63–97 advances similar arguments regarding effeminacy, her analysis at times appears to use homosexuality as a meaningful conceptual category (e.g., p. 91: "Uncontrolled sexuality, as manifested in both adultery and homosexual activity, was felt to pose a threat to the moral order of the state").

68. Mart. 7.58 (*cinaedi* are contrasted with *veri viri*); Catull. 25.1 ("cinaede Thalle, mollior cuniculi capillo"); Mart. 1.96.10 (a man who longingly gazes upon other men's penises in the baths is called *mollis*); Phaed. 4.16 (*molles mares* with a pseudo-vagina) and Cael. Aurel. *Morb. Chron.* 4.9 (*molles* who desire to be penetrated); D. 3.1.1.6 and Tac. *Ann.* 11.36 (*muliebria pati*).

69. Varr. *Menipp.* 205.3: "hic ephebum mulieravit."

70. Curt. Ruf. *Alex.* 10.1.26: "respondit amicos regis, non scorta se colere, nec moris esse Persis mares ducere qui stupro effeminarentur" (though Curtius is describing an incident among foreigners, he is a Roman writing for a Roman audience in Latin, and draws on the Roman language of sexual insults); Apul. *Apol.* 74 (*emasculatores*: see discussion later in this chapter).

71. Juv. 10.304–9: "non licet esse viro; nam prodiga corruptoris / improbitas ipsos audet temptare parentes: / tanta in muneribus fiducia. nullus ephebum / deformem saeva castravit in arce tyrannus, / nec praetextatum rapuit Nero loripedem nec / strumosum atque utero pariter gibboque tumentem."

72. The implication that women might be attracted to soft, effeminate males is ex-

plored in several ancient texts (in Hor. *C.* 1.13, Lydia praises the pink neck [*cervicem roseam*] and smooth arms [*cerea bracchia*] of Telephus; at Juv. 6.63–5, two women are imagined as having orgasmic responses to the soft [*mollis*] Bathyllus as he dances the role of Leda). Of course, the textual tradition only gives us a glimpse into *men's* notions of "what women want."

73. Cf. *Truc.* 658–9 for a country man's point of view: "ne ego urbanos istos mundulos amasios / hoc ictu exponam atque omnis eiciam foras." Elsewhere Stratophanes attacks yet another rival as being at the other extreme, a hirsute country bumpkin ("hominem . . . tam horridum ac tam squalidum," 933); his rhetoric implies that his own desirable masculinity resides somewhere in between the two extremes of Diniarchus and Strabax, between *cincinnatus* and *horridus*. For the gendering of hairiness, see discussion earlier in this chapter.

74. Opelt 1965: 42–8 includes this passage in her discussion of "Die Beschimpfung des Rivalen oder der Rivalin in der Liebe," noting that Stratophanes' attack on his rival, focusing as it does on his appearance and his morality, is characteristic of men's insults as opposed to women's; she also observes that in effect the insult likens his opponent to a *cinaedus* or even a *gallus* (cf. *tympanotribam*, and see further discussion of these terms in chapter 5).

75. Prop. 2.1.2; Catull. 16. Cf. Richlin 1992a: 39, Cantarella 1992: 121–8. See discussion later in this chapter for the gender-reversal inherent in this kind of love poetry.

76. See Segal 1968: 111–6 for antecedents in comedy (e.g., Plaut. *Most.* 144–5: when *amor* takes over, "nunc simul res, fides, fama, virtus, decus / deseruerunt"); cf. Hor. *Sat.* 2.7, esp. 46–94, and see the discussion of the motif of *servitium amoris* later in this chapter.

77. Tac. *Hist.* 3.40: "Fabius interim Valens multo ac molli concubinarum spadonumque agmine segnius quam ad bellum incedens . . ." (cf. 3.62: "procax moribus neque absurdus ingenio in famam urbanitatis per lasciviam petere. ludicro Iuvenalium sub Nerone velut ex necessitate, mox sponte mimos actitavit, scite magis quam probe.")

78. See, e.g., Cic. *Verr.* 2.4.144: "cuius omnis vigilias in stupris constat adulteriisque esse consumptas"; 2.4.83: "domum suam plenam stupri, plenam flagiti, plenam dedecoris . . . in qua semper meretricum lenonumque flagitia versantur"; 2.1.101, "cum meretricibus lenonibusque vixisset"; 2.3.6, "cotidiana adulteria, meretriciam disciplinam, domesticum lenocinium."

79. Cic. *Att.* 1.12.3, 1.13.3, 1.18.2–3; Liv. *Per.* 103; Vell. *Pat.* 2.45.1; Sen. *Epist.* 97.2–8; Suet. *Jul.* 6.2, 74.2; Plut. *Caes.* 9–10, *Cic.* 28–9; App. *B.C.* 2.14, *Sic.* 7; Dio 37.45–6. See Gonfroy 1978 for further discussion of Cicero's portrayal of Clodius.

80. Cic. *Har. Resp.* 44: "P. Clodius a crocota, a mitra, a muliebribus soleis purpureisque fasceolis, a strophio, a psalterio, a flagitio, a stupro est factus repente popularis"; cf. Cic. *Orat. Fragm.* 14.22 (*In Clodium et Curionem*): "nam rusticos ei nos videri minus est mirandum, qui manicatam tunicam et mitram et purpureas fascias habere non possumus. tu vero festivus, tu elegans, tu solus urbanus, quem decet muliebris ornatus, quem incessus psaltriae, qui effeminare vultum, attenuare vocem, levare corpus potes. o singulare prodigium atque monstrum. nonne te huius templi, non urbis, non vitae, non lucis pudet?"

81. Cic. *Planc.* 86: "furialis illa vox nefariis stupris, religiosis altaribus effeminata"; *Mil.* 89: "homo effeminatus."

82. Cic. *Mil.* 55: "quia, quamquam paratus in imparatos Clodius, ipse Clodius tamen mulier inciderat in viros."

83. Bona Dea: *Pis.* 95; *Mil.* 72; *Har. Resp.* 8; *Prov. Cons.* 24; *Dom.* 105; *Sest.* 116; having been penetrated in his youth: *Har. Resp.* 42, 59; incest: *Sest.* 16; *Pis.* 28; *Cael.* 32; *Mil.* 73; *Har. Resp.* 9, 39; *Dom.* 92. At one point he manages to take a swipe at all three simultaneously (*Sest.* 39: "cum scurrarum locupletium scorto, cum sororis adultero, cum

stuprorum sacerdote"). See Santoro L'Hoir 1992: 22–5 for a discussion of Cicero's presentation of Clodius in conjunction with the language of *vir/homo*.

84. Juv. 2.25–7: "quis caelum terris non misceat et mare caelo / si fur displiceat Verri, homicida Miloni, / Clodius accuset moechos . . . ?" Cf. also Juv. 6.345: "sed nunc ad quas non Clodius aras?"

85. Indirectly at 46.22.2 (τὴν μαλακίαν τῆς ψυχῆς καὶ τοῦ σώματος, where μαλακία is a close equivalent to *mollitia*); directly at 46.22.3 (δειλός τε οὕτω καὶ γύννις ὤν, where γύννις is an equivalent to *effeminatus*) and 46.28.1 (καὶ σοὶ δέ, ὦ Κικέρων, παραινῶ μήτε γυναικείως θρασύνεσθαι μήτε τὸν Βαμβαλίωνα μιμεῖσθαι, where γυναικείως is an equivalent to *muliebriter* or *effeminate*).

86. 46.18.1–3 (flowing tunic and perfume); 46.18.4 (Caerellia); 46.18.6(τήν τε γυναῖκα προαγωγεύειν καὶ θυγατέρα μοιχεύειν).

87. See discussion earlier in chapter 4 for effeminacy and the East; for clothing (especially sleeved tunics), the *mitra*, and dancing, see Herter 1959: 629–32, 638.

88. For further discussion of the workings of gender in this scene and indeed throughout Book 9, see Hardie 1994: 14–8 (where he suggests that the experiences of Nisus and Euryalus, Ascanius, and the brothers Pandarus and Bitias, evoke the "trial . . . of surviving childhood through a perilous transitional period in order to enter their full maturity," that is, manhood).

89. As parallels for these insults against Aeneas as effeminate womanizer, Opelt 1965: 45 adduces passages from Valerius Flaccus' *Argonautica* that no doubt display Virgilian influence: Medea's betrothed Styrus insults Jason as *Haemonius adulter* (8.338) and *semivir Achivus* (8.347).

90. Vell. Pat. 2.88.2: "simul vero aliquid ex negotio remitti posset, otio ac mollitiis paene ultra feminam fluens."

91. Porph. *ad* Hor. *Sat*. 1.2.25: "sub Maltini nomine quidam Maecenatem suspicantur significari. ab re tamen nomen finxit. Maltha enim malacos dicitur. porro autem tunicis demissis ambulare eorum est, qui se molles ac delicatos velint haberi."

92. Macrob. *Sat*. 2.4.12: "vale mi ebenum Medulliae, ebur ex Etruria, lasar Arretinum, adamas Supernas, Tiberinum margaritum, Cilniorum smaragde, iaspi Iguvinorum, berulle Porsenae, carbunculum Hadriae, ἵνα συντέμω πάντα, μάλαγμα moecharum." Much of Augustus' language has to do with jewels and precious gems; Gelsomino 1958 offers a rather different text and interprets the last comment to mean not that Maecenas is the "delight" of *moechae* but rather that he is so soft that *moechae* could use him as an "emollient." Cf. also Suet. *Aug*. 86.2: Augustus poked fun at Maecenas' *myrobrechis cincinni*.

93. For this notion, see Sen. *Contr*. 1.pr.8–10 and the discussions in Selden 1992: 476–7, Edwards 1993: 93 with n. 97, and Richlin 1997.

94. Cf. Griffin 1985: 13 and Gleason 1995: 113. For Maecenas' irregular marriage, see D. 24.1.64 with Treggiari 1991: 450, 456; consider also the general comment offered at Publ. Syr. *Sent*. 260 ("habent locum maledicti crebrae nuptiae").

95. Juv. 12.38–9: "vestem / purpuream teneris quoque Maecenatibus aptam"; cf. Mart. 10.73, Juv. 1.66. For Maecenas and women see Hor. *Epod*. 3.21 (a *puella*), *C*. 2.12 (Licymnia), Plut. *Amat*. 760A, Dio 54.30.4–5. At Tac. *Ann*. 1.54 and Dio 54.17.5 (and perhaps implicitly in Hor. *Epod*. 14: see Griffin 1985: 12–3, 25) he is associated with the actor Bathyllus.

96. For walking and masculinity see Gleason 1995: 60–2.

97. *Pace* Cantarella 1992: 192 ("for the ancient world, an effeminate person only meant a passive adult male") and Corbeill 1997: 109 ("in late Republican oratory, effeminate qualities imply passive homoerotic activity").

98. See Richlin 1997 for a general discussion of gender and Roman rhetoric.

99. *Rhet. Her.* 4.52: "suae pudicitiae proditor est, insidiator alienae"; Cic. *Cael.* 42: "parcat iuventus pudicitiae suae, ne spoliet alienam"; Vell. Pat. 2.48.3: "suae alienaeque et fortunae et pudicitiae prodigus"; Suet. *Cal.* 36.1: "pudicitiae <neque suae> neque alienae pepercit"; cf. Sen. *Epist.* 49.12: "de pudicitia utraque, et illa cui alieni corporis abstinentia est, et hac cui sui cura." See also Livy 39.15.14 ("hi cooperti stupris suis alienisque") with 39.15.9 ("stuprati et constupratores") and Sen. *Epist.* 99.13 ("qui suam alienamque libidinem exercent mutuo impudici").

100. Later Postumius returns to the theme of effeminacy: "minus tamen esset si flagitiis tantum effeminati forent—ipsorum id magna ex parte dedecus erat—a facinoribus manus, mentem a fraudibus abstinuissent: numquam tantum malum in re publica fuit, nec ad plures nec ad plura pertinens" (39.16.1). Again the implication is that the men are effeminate because of the entire range of hedonistic, uncontrolled behaviors in which they have engaged.

101. 17: "quid palluisti, femina"; 35: "cinaede Luci" (thus his name may be Lucius, although there is a textual problem here); 9–16: "quid, impudice et improbande Caesari, / si furta dicantur tua, / et helluato sera patrimonio / in fratre parsimonia, / vel acta puero cum viris convivia, / udaeque per somnum nates, / et inscio repente clamatum insuper / Talasio, Talasio?"; 30–2: "obesam ad uxorem redis, / exaestuantes dote solvis pantices, / os crusque lambis saviis." See further discussion of this difficult poem in chapter 5; the text given here is that of Ellis' 1907 OCT.

102. For example, instead of *os crusque lambis saviis*, Salvatore 1964 reads *os usque lambis saviis*. While this reading removes an insinuation of cunnilinctus, there remains a reference to the addressee's wife and a crude allusion to the physical relationship between the two. In line 6, *lingua, qua mas sim tibi* is R. Ellis' emendation (printed in his 1907 Oxford Classical Texts edition) of the manuscript reading *lingua qua adsim tibi*: "my tongue, with which I can be at your side [to assail you]." See Salvatore 1964: 122–3 for a defense of the manuscript reading.

103. Apul. *Apol.* 74–5: "iam inde ab ineunte aevo cunctis probris palam notus, olim in pueritia, priusquam isto calvitio deformaretur, emasculatoribus suis ad omnia infanda morigerus . . . olim sollers suo, nunc coniugis corpore vulgo meret; cum ipso plerique, nec mentior, cum ipso, inquam, de uxoris noctibus paciscuntur." For *morigerus* see especially Gordon Williams 1958.

104. Suet. *Galba* 22 (see chapter 2).

105. See especially Suet. *Galba* 12, 16.

106. Juv. 2.99-109; Suet. *Otho* 6.3: *muliebri sella*; ibid. 12.1: "munditiarum vero paene muliebrium, vulso corpore"; Plut. *Galba* 25.1: τὴν τοῦ σώματος μαλακίαν καὶ θηλύτητα (cf. Plut. *Otho* 4.3, 9.2).

107. Juv. 2.99: "pathici . . . Othonis"; Suet. *Otho* 2.2: "consuetudine mutui stupri" with Nero; ibid. 3.2: "cur Otho mentito sit, quaeritis, exsul honore? / uxoris moechus coeperat esse suae." For the Poppaea affair, see also Tac. *Ann.* 13.45.

108. Tac. *Hist.* 1.30: "habitune et incessu an illo muliebri ornatu mereretur imperium? . . . stupra nunc et comissationes et feminarum coetus volvit animo." For Otho's association with adultery, cf. ibid. 1.22.

109. Tac. *Hist.* 1.74: "muliebribus blandimentis infectae."

110. Tac. *Hist.* 1.22: "non erat Othonis mollis et corpori similis animus."

111. Suet. *Otho* 12.2.

112. Edwards 1993: 85–6.

113. Consider the myth of Teiresias as related by Ovid (*Met.* 3.316–38), as well as the opinions of ancient medical writers that the uterus required frequent irrigation (see, e.g., Ann Ellis Hanson, "The Medical Writers' Woman," in Halperin, Winkler, and Zeitlin 1990: 309–38).

114. Compare Caelius Aurelianus' argument that *molles mares*, who may play both the insertive and the receptive role in penetrative encounters, act out of an excessive lustfulness (*Morb. Chron.* 4.9.137: see chapter 5).

115. The essays in Cornwall and Lindisfarne 1994 ask just this question regarding contemporary cultures.

116. Gleason 1995: 75.

117. Hallett 1973.

118. Griffin 1985: 32–47.

119. Cantarella 1992: 120–36.

120. Barbara K. Gold, "'But Ariadne Was Never There in the First Place': Finding the Female in Roman Poetry," Rabinowitz and Richlin 1993: 91–2.

121. Cf. Prop. 3.25.3 ("quinque tibi potui servire fideliter annos"), the complaint of a slave to his ungrateful owner. Ovid gives a characteristically whimsical touch to this motif: just as Hercules obeyed the *imperium* of his *domina* Omphale, so his male readership should not be embarrassed to serve their mistresses by, for example, holding up a mirror for them (*Ars* 2.215–22).

122. See, e.g., Lyne 1980: 78–81; Griffin 1985: 42–5; Veyne 1988: 132–50. The metaphor of domination and servitude could be applied to various other erotic configurations. Martial occasionally uses *dominus* to refer ironically to slave-boys who exercise a sexual dominion over their male masters: 11.70.2 ("plorantis dominos vendere, Tuccas, potes?"), 12.66.8 ("stant pueri dominos quos precer esse meos"), 13.69.2 ("mavult haec domino mittere dona Pudens": here some manuscripts read the feminine *dominae* instead of the masculine *domino*, but note that Pudens appears in 1.31 as the lover of a slave named Encolpos). At Ov. *Am.* 3.7.11, a woman refers to the poet as her *dominus*, and at Ov. *Met.* 9.466, Byblis calls her brother, for whom she has conceived a sexual desire, her *dominus*.

123. Catull. 10.12–3: "quibus esset irrumator / praetor"; 28.9–13: "o Memmi, bene me ac diu supinum / tota ista trabe lentus irrumasti. / sed, quantum video, pari fuistis / casu: nam nihilo minore verpa / farti estis."

124. Catull. 11.21–4: "nec meum respectet, ut ante, amorem, / qui illius culpa cecidit velut prati / ultimi flos, praetereunte postquam / tactus aratro est." See Skinner 1997: 131.

125. Kennedy 1993: 61–3 concludes a stimulating discussion of "Love's figures and tropes" by offering a reading of Ovid, *Amores* 1.1 that suggests that "the poem offers the frisson of finding out what terms of literary analysis feel like when experienced *a posteriori*."

126. See Gleason 1995: 103–30 for an extended discussion of the opposition between "rough, manly" and "soft, effeminate" styles of delivery in ancient rhetorical writers.

127. See LSJ s.v. II, where the meaning is related to the proverb οὐδὲν πρὸς τὸν Διόνυσον. For the sarcastic use of a woman's name, cf. Cic. *De Orat.* 2.277 (Egilia).

128. Other discussions of the anecdote regarding Hortensius include Richlin 1992: 226, Edwards 1993: 96–7, Gleason 1995: 74–6. As Ralph Hexter has reminded me, this anecdote also encapsulates an inner tension in the world of rhetoric: to the extent that it is artful, it can be criticized as too artful or too "Greek," yet without art there could be virtually no success.

129. See H. Schoonhoven, *Elegiae in Maecenatem: Prolegomena, Text, and Commentary* (Groningen, 1980).

130. *Eleg. Maec.* 1.13–6: "regis eras, Etrusce, genus; tu Caesaris almi / dextera, Romanae tu vigil urbis eras. / omnia cum posses tanto tam carus amico, / te sensit nemo posse nocere tamen." Seneca's unyielding criticism extends even to this point: Maecenas, he claims, showed himself not to be "gentle" (*mitis*) but rather "soft" (*mollis*): *Epist.* 114.8.

131. *Eleg. Maec.* 1.17–20: "Pallade cum docta Phoebus donaverat artes: / tu decus et laudes huius et huius eras, / vincit vulgares veluti beryllus harenas, / litore in extremo quas simul unda movet."

132. *Eleg. Maec.* 1.38–48: note that *fortis* occurs four times in these ten lines.

133. *Eleg. Maec.* 1.49–102, e.g. 93–4 ("sic est: victor amet, victor potiatur in umbra, / victor odorata dormiat inque rosa . . ."). One may contrast these statements, as well as the argument that "when Mars quiets down, everything is fitting for the victors" (1.49–50: "pax erat: haec illos laxarunt otia cultus: / omnia victores Marte sedente decent"), with Sallust's moralizing argument that the problem brought by Roman military victories, and particularly the final defeat of Carthage, was precisely that the subsequent leisure encouraged luxury, avarice, and ambition (Sall. *Cat.* 10).

134. *Eleg. Maec.* 1.51–92.

135. Val. Max. 3.5.4 (discussed in chapter 5).

136. Gleason 1995: 162.

Chapter 5

1. Housman 1931: 408 n. 1 (where he draws an intriguing comparison to the southern Italy of his own day); Gonfroy 1978: 219–62; Veyne 1978, 1985; Boswell 1980: 74–6; Lilja 1983; Kay 1985: 127; Wiseman 1985: 10–1; Richlin 1992a and 1993; Cantarella 1992; Edwards 1993: 70–3. I first advanced the arguments presented in this chapter in Williams 1992: 206–320. Apparently unfamiliar with my earlier work, Parker 1997 offers a number of similar arguments. I have unfortunately not yet been able to consult Eckhard Meyer-Zwiffelhoffer, *Im Zeichen des Phallus* (Frankurt-am-Main, 1995) or Hans Peter Obermayer, *Martial und der Diskurs über männliche 'Homosexualität' in der Literatur der frühen Kaiserzeit* (Tübingen, 1998).

2. Edwards 1993: 73 makes the point in similar terms. For penetrative sexual relations between women, see (e.g.) Sen. *Contr.* 1.2.23, Mart. 1.90, 7.67, with discussion in Hallett 1989 and Brooten 1996.

3. See Adams 1982, index s.vv. on these verbs; for *cevere*, see also Fraenkel 1920. Parker 1997 offers a different chart: see Williams 1998 for the serious problems in Parker's grid. Even the schematization that I offer here obscures certain aspects of ancient usage. First, *crisare* and *cevere* seem not to have been obscene in the way that the other verbs are (Adams 1982: 137); second, in the surviving sources *crisare* is limited to women and *cevere* to men, but if the former simply means "to move the haunches as in coitus" (*OLD*) and the latter "to move the buttocks" (cf. the grammarian Probus [*GLK* 4.37.8]: "cevere est clunes movere, ut in canibus videre est, qui clunes agitando blandiuntur"), it is possible that *crisare* and *cevere* might have been used to describe the motions of either a female or a male, depending on the position and movements of the parties involved. One intriguing graffito from Pompeii reads "Quintio(s) hic futuit ceventes" (*CIL* 4.4977). Commentators have assumed that the *ceventes* are male and that *futuit* stands for *pedicavit* (so Adams 1982: 119, 121), but I see no reason to reject the possibility that the *ceventes* are, or include, women being penetrated *a tergo* either anally or vaginally. And since *futuere* could be used in a transferred sense to refer to the penetration of males (Adams 1982: 121), it is possible that in other graffiti now lost to us, *crisare* might have been applied to males who were penetrated. In short, the schematization I offer cannot represent with complete accuracy the complexities of usage or the slipperiness of colloquial speech.

4. With regard to *irrumare*, Adams 1982: 126 is unnecessarily cautious: "Languages do not necessarily make such a lexical distinction. While *fellatio* is a widely recognised form of sexual behaviour, *irrumatio* is not universally seen as a positive sexual act." The noun φιλυβριστής is used at *A.P.* 5.48 in such a way as to suggest that it is an equivalent for *irrumator*, "a man who orally penetrates others." But this is the only attestation of the Greek word, and it appears to be an ad hoc creation on the model of the Latin.

5. *CIL* 4.10030, which Varone 1994: 76 calls a "frase proverbiale," reads as follows: "Malim me amici fellent quam inimici irrument" ("I would rather that my friends suck me than that my enemies mouth-fuck me"). Whether we take the verbs literally or metaphorically, the point of this dictum seems to be that it is better to sacrifice one's friends' masculine integrity than one's own.

6. See Richlin 1981b, Richlin 1992a: 69, and Adams 1982: 125–30.

7. Sen. *Contr.* 1.2.22 (Seneca himself soundly condemns Murredius for his inappropriate obscenity, and tells us that Scaurus pointed a finger in the direction of Greece, but the fact remains that some Roman rhetoricians felt free to speak of such matters with a frankness unparalleled in extant Greek speeches or rhetorical exercises); Cic. *Red. Sen.* 11, *Phil.* 13.24, etc.; Ov. *Her.* 16.161–2 ("vel mihi virginitas esset libata, vel illud / quod poterat salva virginitate rapi"); Sen. *N.Q.* 1.16 (discussed later in this chapter).

8. Suet. *Gramm.* 23, *Tib.* 45.

9. Richlin 1992a: xvi. Another aspect of this phallic fixation, namely a broadly attested interest in penises of unusual size, is explored in chapter 2.

10. It deserves reiteration that I am speaking of public representations of sexual practices rather than the subjective experience of individual Romans. As discussed in chapter 4, the poetry of Catullus among others shows that the rigid ideology outlined here was in fact capable of being manipulated in complex ways. In poem 28, for example, Catullus plays with the metaphor of *irrumator* (one who compels others to fellate him, thus metaphorically one who arrogantly abuses others): instead of simply saying that Memmius acted like an *irrumator* toward him, the poet imagines a literal enactment of the metaphor, thereby placing himself in an extremely compromising position with regard to his masculine status.

11. Sen. *Epist.* 95.21: "pati natae."

12. "Être actif, c'est être un mâle, quel que soit le sexe du partenaire passif" (Veyne 1978: 50; cf. Veyne 1985: 29). So too Richlin 1993: 538: "what defines the *vir* is penetration." For similar applications of the insertive/receptive dichotomy to masculine ideologies in contemporary cultures, see, among many other studies, Tomás Almaguer, "Chicano Men: A Cartography of Homosexual Identity and Behavior," Abelove et al. 1993: 255–73; Andrea Cornwall, "Gendered Identities and Gender Ambiguity among *travestis* in Salvador, Brazil," Cornwall and Lindisfarne 1994: 111–32; Peter Loizos, "A Broken Mirror: Masculine Sexuality in Greek Ethnography," Cornwall and Lindisfarne 1994: 66–81; and cf. Chauncey 1994 for evidence of a similar ideology in early-twentieth-century New York City.

13. See Santoro L'Hoir 1992 for a review of the various implications of *vir* (mostly in nonsexual senses) in Latin prose.

14. Both Dio Cassius (60.29.6a) and Tacitus (*Ann.* 11.1) tell us that Messalina was in fact covetous of Asiaticus' property (he owned the famous Gardens of Lucullus on the Pincian Hill) and that the charges leveled against him were merely a pretext. In any case, Messalina got what she wanted, at least for the time being: both Valerius and Poppaea committed suicide, and the Gardens of Lucullus became hers. But it was in those very gardens that she was to die only a year later (Tac. *Ann.* 11.37). As for Suillius, he was an experienced accuser who had been exiled by Tiberius but afterward returned to Rome, where he enjoyed the friendship of Claudius. Tacitus provides a characteristically trenchant summary of the man's character: "praepotentem, venalem et Claudii principis amicitia diu prospere, numquam bene usum" (*Ann.* 4.31). After Claudius' death and Nero's accession to power, Suillius came to be widely hated and eventually was convicted on a number of charges and banished (*Ann.* 13.42–3).

15. For the identity of these sons, see discussion later in this chapter. Kroll 1988: 92 understands *corruptionem militum* in a sexual sense ("man machte ihm u.a. Verkehr mit seinen Soldaten, aber auch passive Unzucht zum Vorwurf"), but it seems more likely that

Valerius was accused of corrupting his soldiers by means of monetary and sexual bribes (*pecunia et stupro*), that is, by offering them money and such sexual partners as *virgines, pueri*, or *matronae* (cf. Cic. *Cat.* 2.8, cited in chapter 2).

16. In a speech delivered the following year whose text is preserved on bronze tablets found in Lyons, the emperor Claudius disparagingly refers to Valerius as a *latro* and *palestricum prodigium* (*CIL* 13.1668; cf. Tac. *Ann.* 11.3 for his fondness for gymnastic exercises). But Valerius' undeserved fate was not forgotten; eleven years later, in the reign of Claudius' successor Nero, Suillius himself fell from favor, and among the accusations leveled against him was that he had brought about the destruction of a number of eminent men and women, Valerius Asiaticus being one of them (Tac. *Ann.* 13.43).

17. Tac. *Ann.* 11.3: "fraude muliebri et impudico Vitellii ore"; compare the insult, cited later in this chapter, hurled at Nero's crony Tigellinus (Tac. *Ann.* 14.60).

18. With regard to Catullus' phrase "milia multa basiorum," Quinn 1973 ad loc. implies that only the poems on Juventius are meant, but most other commentators rightly discount such a specific reference. All of Catullus' love poetry is *mollis*: cf. Propertius 2.1.2 ("unde meus veniat mollis in ore liber"), Richlin 1992a: 39, and the discussion in chapter 4.

19. For bibliography on this poem, see Arkins 1982: 242. More recent discussions include Lilja 1983: 55–6, Cantarella 1992: 123–4, Richlin 1992a: 145–7, and Selden 1992: 476–89.

20. Suet. *Jul.* 51: "urbani, servate uxores: moechum calvom adducimus. / aurum in Gallia effutuisti, hic sumpsisti mutuum"; 49.4: "Gallias Caesar subegit, Nicomedes Caesarem: / ecce Caesar nunc triumphat qui subegit Gallias, / Nicomedes non triumphat qui subegit Caesarem." For *subigere*, see Adams 1982: 155–6.

21. Suet. *Jul.* 49.2: "missa etiam facio edicta Bibuli, quibus proscripsit collegam suum Bithynicam reginam, eique antea regem fuisse cordi, nunc esse regnum. quo tempore, ut Marcus Brutus refert, Octavius etiam quidam valitudine mentis liberius dicax conventu maximo, cum Pompeium regem appellasset, ipsum reginam salutavit." The gossip concerning Nicomedes seems to have made a lasting impression: the anonymous work *De Viris Illustribus*, whose composition has been dated to anywhere from the first to the fourth century A.D., refers to the Nicomedes affair in the opening sentence of its discussion of Julius Caesar (*Vir. Illustr.* 78.1: "Gaius Iulius Caesar, veneratione rerum gestarum Divus dictus, contubernalis Thermo in Asiam profectus, cum saepe ad Nicomedem regem Bithyniae commearet, impudicitiae infamatus est").

22. On the other hand, Suetonius reports an occasion on which Caesar, having been insultingly likened to a woman, retorted by observing that Semiramis and the Amazons exercised power in their own day (Suet. *Jul.* 22.2: "ac negante quodam per contumeliam facile hoc ulli feminae fore, responderit quasi adludens in Syria quoque regnasse Sameramin magnamque Asiae partem Amazonas tenuisse quondam"). But Caesar was a powerful man who could afford to engage in such teasing; it is not coincidental that this incident allegedly occurred a few days after the senate had given Caesar control over all of Gaul—a major victory and a significant turning point in his political career. Cantarella 1992: 162–4 may be interpreting the banter of the powerful too literally, I would suggest, and generally oversimplifying matters when she suggests that Caesar's example may have encouraged more ordinary men who had played "the woman's role" in sexual acts to "come out of the closet."

23. Dio 43.20.4: οὐ μέντοι καὶ ἐκεῖνος ἤχθετο ταῦτα αὐτῶν λεγόντων, ἀλλὰ καὶ πάνυ ἔχαιρεν ὅτι τοσαύτη πρὸς αὐτὸν παρρησία, πίστει τοῦ μὴ ἂν ὀργισθῆναί ποτε ἐπ' αὐτῇ, ἐχρῶντο, πλὴν καθ' ὅσον τὴν συνουσίαν τὴν πρὸς τὸν Νικομήδη διέβαλλον – ἐπὶ γὰρ τούτῳ πάνυ τε ἐδυσκόλαινε καὶ ἔνδηλος ἦν λυπούμενος, ἀπολογεῖσθαί τε ἐπεχείρει καὶ κατώμνυε, κἀκ τούτου καὶ γέλωτα προσεπωφλίσκανεν. Cf. Suet. *Jul.* 49.1: "gravi tamen et perenni opprobrio et ad omnium convicia exposito." Cantarella 1992: 221 argues that Caesar "was . . .

a real man, and could afford to be passive if that was what he wanted," but the testimony of both Dio and Suetonius suggests that matters were somewhat more complex.

24. For the use of *Venus* (more often a metonym for "sexual intercourse") to refer to the penis, see Adams 1982: 57. Ralph Hexter has suggested to me that it may not be coincidental that the impotent member is here feminized (*Venus quieta*).

25. Ov. *Am.* 2.15.25–6: "sed, puto, te nuda mea membra libidine surgent, / et peragam partes anulus ille viri."

26. Sen. *Epist.* 47.7: "in cubiculo vir, in convivio puer est."

27. In addition to this secondary sense of "real (i.e., penetrating) man," the noun *vir* can always be used in its primary sense of "biological male." Thus penetrated, effeminate, and even castrated men can still be called *viri*, albeit in a qualified way (Mart. 1.96.10: *virum mollem*; 3.73.4: *mollem virum*; 3.91.5: *steriles viri*; Phdr. *App.* 10.21 (of a *cinaedus*): *virum*.

28. See the passages cited in *OLD* s.v. (1.b), to which Mart. 9.5.5 should be added. Also pertinent is the use of *virilia* as a euphemism for the male genitalia (Adams 1982: 69–70), just as *muliebria* is used of the female genitalia (Adams 1982: 93). See also Ov. *Ars* 1.689–90: "Achilles / veste virum longa dissimulatus erat"; Petr. *Sat.* 129.1 (the impotent Encolpius laments his plight): "non intellego me virum esse."

29. *Semivir* referring to eunuchs (often *galli*, or castrated priests of Cybele): Sen. *Epist.* 108.7; Val. Flacc. 6.695; Mart. 3.91.2; Sil. Ital. 17.20; Juv. 6.513. Martial writes of a *ménage à trois* involving a woman named Aegle, an old man, and the eunuch Dindymus, and as both of her partners prove to be ineffectual, Aegle prays that Venus might make the old man young and the eunuch a *vir*: "hunc iuvenem facias, hunc, Cytherea, virum" (Mart. 11.81.6). Also relevant are Catullus 63.6 ("ut relicta sensit sibi membra sine viro"), Lucan 10.133–4 ("infelix ferro mollita iuventus / atque exsecta virum"), and Tac. *Ann.* 6.31, where a Parthian eunuch named Abdus is described as being "ademptae virilitatis." Pliny (*N.H.* 11.263), discussing the testicles, distinguishes among hermaphrodites (*hermaphroditi*), eunuchs (*spadones*), and *semiviri*, the last being those whose testicles were destroyed by injury or natural causes rather than by a deliberate surgical procedure ("homini tantum iniuria aut sponte naturae franguntur, idque tertium ab hermaphroditis et spadonibus semiviri genus habent"). But his distinctions do not seem to reflect ordinary language, which was certainly capable of describing surgically castrated eunuchs as *semiviri*.

30. Mart. 1.90.8: "mentiturque virum prodigiosa Venus" (cf. Hallett 1989: 215–7, Brooten 1996: 47). *Venus* here seems to be a metonymy for her genitalia; cf. Mart. 1.46.1–2: ("languet / protinus et cessat debilitata Venus") and the phrase from the Priapic poem quoted above ("Venus fuit quieta, nec viriliter / iners senile penis extulit caput"). Later commentators on Martial have tried to draw out his implications, suggesting that Bassa is imagined to penetrate her female partners with her clitoris (see Howell ad loc.). Cantarella 1992: 167 translates "your portentous lust imitates the man," but the 1988 Italian original (p. 215) is more concrete: "la tua Clitoride meravigliosa ha il ruolo dello sposo." Martial's language certainly encourages such an interpretation (the alternative being that Bassa penetrates her female partners with some such artificial device as a dildo: cf. Sen. *Contr.* 1.2.23, ἐγὼ δ᾽ ἐσκόπησα πρότερον τὸν ἄνδρα, εἰ ἐγγεγένηταί τις ἢ προσέρραπται). *Venus* might also be used metonymically of the genitalia in Martial 1.102 ("qui pinxit Venerem tuam, Lycori, / blanditus, puto, pictor est Minervae"), although Howell is singularly unimpressed by the idea.

31. Suet. *Vesp.* 13: "Licinium Mucianum notae impudicitiae, sed meritorum fiducia minus sui reverentem, numquam nisi clam et hactenus retaxare sustinuit, ut apud communem aliquem amicum querens adderet clausulam: 'ego tamen vir sum.'" For *impudicitia*, see discussion later in this chapter.

32. Cic. *Cat.* 2.4: "utinam ille omnis secum suas copias eduxisset! Tongilium mihi eduxit quem amare in praetexta coeperat, Publicium et Minucium quorum aes alienum

contractum in popina nullum rei publicae motum adferre poterat: reliquit quos viros, quanto aere alieno, quam valentis, quam nobilis!" The dynamics are revealing: as he fled Rome, Catiline was accompanied by Publicius and Minucius, whose pathetic little debts could not possibly motivate revolution, but he left behind men whose debts are truly dangerous; so too he was accompanied by Tongilius, but he left behind real men.

33. Ov. *Ars* 1.523–4: "cetera lascivae faciant concede puellae / et si quis male vir quaerit habere virum"; Plaut. *Poen.* 1318: "nam te cinaedum esse arbitror magis quam virum." A contrast between *viri* and men who have been penetrated also underlies Mart. 2.84, 6.16, 7.58 (*cinaedi* are not *veri viri*); Petr. *Sat.* 81.4–5; Quint. *I.O.* 5.9.14 ("parum viri"); Calp. Flacc. *Decl.* 3; Gellius 1.5.1 ("parum vir et ore quoque polluto").

34. There is one text that at first seems to suggest otherwise: Martial's epigram on Victor (11.78), who has never known sexual experience with a woman. As he is about to be married, he is told to see a prostitute, who will teach him what he needs to know: "she will make you a man" ("illa virum faciet," 12). But the point of this epigram is decidedly not to suggest that only heterosexuality will make Victor a man, for if (as he would prefer: 5–8) he anally penetrates his new bride, he will apparently still not be his bride's *vir*. The logic of this piece is based on the concept that the vagina and the penis are made for each other and in some sense define each other (Richlin 1984), and thus Victor will not be a proper *vir* for his wife until he makes her vagina fulfill the role for which it was intended. (I would emphasize the relative rather than the absolute sense of *vir*, as well as the fact that *vir* can often be translated as "husband"; thus perhaps "she will make you *her* 'man' [or 'her husband']" rather than "she will make you a man"). Note, too, Martial 11.22 (discussed further in Appendix 1), where we read that nature has designated boys' penises for girls and their anuses for men. The first statement sounds similar to the advice given to Victor: the penis and vagina are "meant" for each other. But what seems to be an absolute proclamation is of course contradicted by what follows: that nature has designed boys' anuses for men. If a boy's anus is meant to be penetrated by a man's penis, then how can it be said that all penises are meant for vaginas? Of course the poem is a joke, designed to dissuade a man from stimulating a boy's penis and instead to channel his desires into their proper receptacle, namely the boy's anus. But the joke also shows the cultural contingencies lying behind any such apparent proclamations: a belief that penises were meant by nature to penetrate vaginas *exclusively* was clearly not tenable in Martial's Rome. The usual understanding is clear: *real men* can penetrate anuses or vaginas, males or females, indiscriminately, without effect on their masculine status. We might compare 9.41, where Martial teases Ponticus for his insistent avoidance of vaginal intercourse ("numquam futuis") and indulgence in masturbation. Imagine, he says, that nature herself is complaining: "What you are wasting with your fingers is a human being" ("istud quod digitis, Pontice, perdis, homo est," 10). This hardly reflects the usual Roman view (for ancient references to masturbation, see Krenkel 1979a): in that case every sexual act other than vaginal intercourse with an ovulating woman would be condemned. Indeed, Martial himself projects a persona directly at odds with this preachy sentiment, constantly and gleefully "wasting a human being." Both epigrams (the one to Ponticus and the one to Victor) need to be seen as very specifically designed to make an argument against a particular man's refusal to engage in vaginal intercourse; in the interests of persuading someone to change his practices, they make extreme statements.

35. For the two forms see Adams 1982: 123–4. *Pedico* seems to have been the more common form, *pedicator* having only two attestations (Suet. *Jul.* 49.1 and *CIL* 4.4008).

36. So too one might argue that such terms as *moechus* and *pullo/pullarius* (for the latter, see chapter 1) are functional equivalents of "heterosexual man" and "active" (i.e., insertive) "homosexual man" respectively. But *moechus* specifies only a man who pursues inappropriate women (such as other men's wives) and *pullo* only a man who pursues boys,

not males in general. I would argue, moreover, that the Roman terms are not mutually exclusive. We will see in this chapter that one and the same man can be described as simultaneously *moechus* and *cinaedus* or as both *fututor* and *pedico*; I would suggest that in the same way one man could have been called both a *moechus* and a *pullo*, although this last combination is nowhere attested.

37. Once again, it deserves emphasis that I am not speaking of the individual subjective experience of Roman men. It would be absurd to argue that those men who were labeled *fututores* were only interested in penetrating a vagina, and that the fact that their partners were women was irrelevant to them. But this study is primarily concerned with linguistic and conceptual apparatuses available to Roman men as they exchanged representations of their own and others' sexual experience, and these apparatuses are structured around specific acts rather than the opposition between same-sex and different-sex.

38. On this use of compelled fellatio as punishment, see Catullus 21; Mart. 3.82; *Priap.* 13, 22, 35, 74; and Richlin 1981b. The joke in Mart. 3.96 hinges on *tacebis*, for, as Adams 1982: 126–7 notes, "it was a standard joke to speak of *irrumatio* as a means of silencing someone."

39. Or, as David Halperin suggests to me, Martial may even be denying that Gargilius is a *moechus*.

40. Martial 6.26 (Sotades can no longer achieve an erection, but still practices cunnilinctus), 11.47 (Lattara practices cunnilinctus but not vaginal intercourse), 11.85 (Zoilus' tongue has become useless and he will now have to resort to vaginal intercourse).

41. The specifically physical reference contained in the word is emphasized by a graphic joke from the *Carmina Priapea*: "The dick of *pedicones* is shitté" (*Priap.* 68.7–8: "μερδαλέον certe si res non munda vocatur / et pediconum mentula merdalea est"; the otherwise unattested adjective *merdalea* is punning on the Greek (σ)μερδαλέον). For the notion that anal penetration defiles the penis with excrement, see chapter 1. Weeks 1989: 209 cites a late nineteenth-century English male prostitute who seemed to use the term *sodomite* with a similarly specific reference to the act of anal intercourse, speaking of one his clients who was "not an actual sodomite. He likes to play with you and then 'spend' on your belly." As Weeks observes, for this speaker, at least, "sodomite" was "not necessarily coextensive with 'homosexual.'"

42. Mart. 11.78.5–6, 11.99.1–2, 11.104.17–20; *CIL* 10.4483. For other references to the anal penetration of women, see Sen. *Contr.* 1.2.22, *Priap.* 3.7–8, 31 (though cf. Parker 1988: 116–7), 50.2 (*ficosissima puella*: cf. Parker 1988: 145), Ov. *Her.* 16.161–2, Mart. 9.67.3–4, Apul. *Met.* 3.20.

43. *CIL* 4.2210 (*pace* Boswell 1990: 86 n. 49: "clear evidence of preference for male sexual partners" and Varone 1994: 121, who translates "ho voglia di un fanciullo"). For this brothel, decorated with images of male-female copulation, see Clarke 1998: 196–206. Cantarella 1992: 147 observes that this graffito "is the elementary crude expression of a desire to gain the upper hand, expressed (in words in this case) by means of an act which, by subjecting another person—woman or man—to the type of penetration considered most outrageous, confirms that the person doing it, or capable of threatening it, is a real man." She is right to stress the fact that either a female or a male could be the object of *pedicatio*, but there is no evidence that anal penetration was considered more "outrageous" than vaginal penetration; on the contrary, I will argue below that *irrumatio* was held to be more degrading than *pedicatio*. Parker 1988: 37 suggests that the graffito is a quotation of *Priap.* 38.3, just as he argues that *Priap.* 35.2 ("si prensus fueris") is quoted at *CIL* 4.7038 ("si prensus fueris [pueris] poenam patiare necesse est"), but the two phrases (especially *pedicare volo*) seem so general that their appearance in both the graffiti and the Priapic poetry is most likely a coincidence. Indeed, Parker himself later

(1988: 129) notes that *pedicare volo* is "a phrase incidentally found as an inscription at Pompeii."

44. It is just possible that these graffiti do not refer to the same man, but their location in the same brothel, two of them in the same room, argues strongly for an identity, as does the parallel with Martial 11.45.

45. One could in fact, if one were so inclined, apply precisely these labels to the personae of Catullus, Horace, Tibullus, and Martial. The last poet, while never referring to himself directly with either of these coarse words, does have an interlocutor indirectly describe him as *pedico* in 12.85: "Pediconibus os olere dicis. / hoc si, sicut ais, Fabulle, verum est: / quid tu credis olere cunnilingis?" The opening line is directed specifically at Martial just as it is in 11.30 ("Os male causidicis et dicis olere poetis. / sed fellatori, Zoile, peius olet"), and the parallels between the two pieces are striking and illuminating. In 11.30 Zoilus begins with a generalized insult (*os male olere*) with a potential for being taken both literally and metaphorically (imputing fellatio and/or cunnilinctus; cf. Richlin 1992a: 26); but the insult has a specific application to the poet (*poetis*), and in the pentameter Martial simultaneously casts the insult back on to Zoilus and draws out the metaphorical meaning, in the process achieving a characteristically precise jab by insinuating that Zoilus is a *fellator*. So in 12.85 the poet clearly understands a reference to himself in Fabullus' apparently general observation regarding *pedicones*, for he replies with the insinuation— wickedly conveyed by means of the final question, posed with an air of cool detachment— that Fabullus is a *cunnilingus*. In other words, just as Zoilus' *causidicis et poetis* serves to point the insult in Martial's direction, so Fabullus' *pediconibus* must signal the poet. (Taylor 1997: 356–7, ignoring the significant qualification "hoc si, sicut ais, Fabulle, verum est," suggests that "Martial is astutely acknowledging a generalizing trend in everyday usage of the verb [*pedicare*] and its nominalization" and that *pedico* here refers to a man who has both been anally penetrated and performs fellatio. This seems quite unlikely to me.)

46. Thus when Pompeiians read the words "Epagathus fututor" on a wall of the same brothel (*CIL* 4.2242), they would not have understood the message to mean that Epagathus was oriented exclusively or even predominantly to women, but instead that at least one of the activities he enjoyed performing was vaginal penetration. There might well have been another graffito, now lost, that read "Epagathus pedico."

47. Note that the pair of conjunctions *vel . . . vel . . .* (as opposed to *aut . . . aut . . .*) is regularly used in Latin to indicate two alternatives that are not mutually exclusive.

48. Boswell 1990: 79 with n. 41, understands the poem differently, taking "irrumat aut futuit" to be Martial's way of saying that the husband's tastes are exclusively heterosexual. He considers the interpretation advanced here to be "highly unlikely" since it would be "counterintuitive to suggest *irrumo* as a pejorative alternative to anal penetration." But, as we will see, performing fellatio was capable of being understood as more demeaning than being anally penetrated. On Boswell's interpretation the poem loses its point. We might compare 2.60, where a boy called Hyllus is engaged in an affair with a married woman and, like Gallus, is willing to undergo the *supplicium puerile*; but again the poet warns that worse is in store for him, in this case not compelled fellatio but castration.

49. See Halperin 1994 for an elaboration of this point.

50. Suet. *Claud.* 33.2: "libidinis in feminas profusissimae, marum omnino expers."

51. Mart. 11.87.1–2: "sed tunc pedico fuisti, / et tibi nulla diu femina nota fuit."

52. Plin. *N.H.* 28.99: "venerem stimulare genitalia ad sexus suos in melle sumpta, etiamsi viri mulierum coitus oderint" (Richlin 1993: 549–50 understands Pliny to be referring to "passive homosexuality" rather than, as I suggest, to men who play the insertive role with male partners only). Firm. Matern. *Math.* 3.6.6 ("facient steriles et circa venerios actus inefficaces et qui numquam ducant uxores et qui semper puerorum amoribus

implicentur"), 3.6.9 ("faciet steriles et qui filios creare non possint et qui se numquam velint coniugalibus affectibus copulare et qui puerorum semper coitu gaudeant"), and 7.15.2 ("puerorum amatores . . . sed tales qui numquam feminarum coitus †velint . . .").

53. Schalow 1989: 119–20.

54. Firm. Matern. *Math.* 3.6.20: "faciet steriles sine semine, puerorum amatores libidinosos et propter haec vitia in homicidiis aut periculis aut criminibus constitutos." Cf. Jean Rhys Bram, trans., *Ancient Astrology: Theory and Practice* (Park Ridge, N.J., 1975), p. 3: "The ideology is a mixture of Neo-Platonic and Stoic with a high moral tone, for this is an ascetic century among pagans as well as Christians."

55. For *amatores mulierum*, see, e.g., Firm. Matern. *Math.* 4.13.8; for *amatores puerorum*, see, e.g., 3.6.20, 3.6.23, 7.15.

56. Firm. Matern. *Math.* 3.6.23: "faciet steriles et qui generare non possint et qui difficile nuptias adipiscantur; et frequenter puerorum amatores facit aut mulierum scaenicarum, vel qui publicis mercimoniis praesint."

57. Firm. Matern. *Math.* 3.6.4 (innkeepers, and those who marry early), 3.6.28 (men inclined to incest), 3.6.25 (men attracted to female slaves or prostitutes).

58. See Brooten 1996: 132–41. On the one hand she argues that "contrary to the view [associated particularly with Foucault] that the idea of sexual orientation did not develop until the nineteenth century, the astrological sources demonstrate the existence in the Roman world of the concept of a lifelong erotic orientation" (140). This is presumably what Brooten means when, in her introduction, she notes that "like Richlin, I present non-Christian material in this book for a category of persons viewed in antiquity as having a long-term or even lifelong homoerotic orientation" (8–9). There are difficulties created by citing Firmicus Maternus as a typical example of beliefs characterizing "the Roman world" *tout court*; but, apart from this problem, Brooten herself phrases her conclusion in slightly but significantly different terms: "Astrologers in the Roman world knew of what we might call sexual orientation, but they did not limit it to two orientations, homosexual and heterosexual. Instead, these ancient writers believed that configurations of the stars created a broad range of sexual inclinations and orientations. Their framework for classifying human sexual behavior took account of factors that most persons of the twentieth century would see as irrelevant for determining sexual orientation" (Brooten 1996: 140). In the end one is left wondering what the value is of arguing that ancient astrologers "knew of what we might call sexual orientation."

59. Suet. *Galba* 22.1: "libidinis in mares pronior"; ibid. 5.1.

60. Don. *Vita Verg.*: "libidinis in pueros pronioris"; "vulgatum est consuesse eum et cum Plotia Hieria."

61. Ov. *Ars* 2.683–4: "odi concubitus qui non utrumque resolvunt; / hoc est cur pueri tangar amore minus." It will be seen later in this chapter that this conventional belief regarding the pleasure felt (or not felt) by boys in their sexual contacts with men is exploded even in some Roman sources.

62. Boswell 1990: 81.

63. For Roman allusions to men's tastes or preferences for various physical traits in women, including different hair colors, see, e.g., Prop. 2.25.41–2 and Ov. *Am.* 2.4.

64. Halperin 1990: 26–7.

65. Schmitt and Sofer 1991: 5, 19.

66. Here it is worth recalling the basic meanings of the related term *pudor*: "decency; modesty; sense of shame." Tacitus and Martial attribute *impudicitia* to Nero's unsavory crony Tigellinus and, far from having the reputation for enjoying the receptive role, Tigellinus is represented as being fond of the company of women; as we will see, he is accused of a penchant for oral sex (presumably cunnilinctus) as well (Tac. *Ann.* 14.51, 15.50, 15.59;

Mart. 3.20.16; Dio 59.23.9 reports that he had been exiled by Caligula on a suspicion of adulterous relations with Agrippina; at Tac. *Hist*. 1.72 we read that Tigellinus died a disgraceful death in the company of his *concubinae*). Seneca writes disparagingly of certain young men who "exercise their own and others' lust reciprocally" ("qui suam alienamque libidinem exercent mutuo impudici"), suggesting the insertive and receptive role respectively, and he calls them *impudici* (Sen. *Epist*. 99.13). So too *impudicus* can be an epithet hurled at pimps (Plaut. *Pseud*. 360; Cic. *Red. Sen*. 12). The legendarily pure Hippolytus is given the epithet *pudicus* by both Horace (*Odes* 4.7.25) and Seneca (*Phaedra* 1196), while the legendarily impure Nero is reported to have opined that no one is truly *pudicus* (Suet. *Nero* 29.1).

67. Suet. *Jul*. 2.1: "stipendia prima in Asia fecit Marci Thermi praetoris contubernio; a quo ad accersendam classem in Bithyniam missus desedit apud Nicomeden, non sine rumore prostratae regi pudicitiae"; *Jul*. 49.1: "pudicitiae eius famam nihil quidem praeter Nicomedis contubernium laesit, gravi tamen et perenni opprobrio et ad omnium convicia exposito."

68. Cic. *Phil*. 2.3: "ne tu, si id fecisses, melius famae, melius pudicitiae tuae consuluisses. sed neque fecisti nec, si cuperes, tibi id per C. Curionem facere licuisset."

69. See Gonfroy 1978; Lilja 1983: 95–6; Richlin 1992a: 101, 283; Richlin 1993: 538 with n. 37, for a survey of other Ciceronian insinuations that various men had been penetrated, especially in their youth (a rhetorical commonplace for which Richlin coins the helpful term *locus de aetate*).

70. The *tympanum* is a type of drum associated with Eastern dancers and *cinaedi*; see discussion later in this chapter and in chapter 4. Seneca's point is that Epicureans advocate pleasure in theory yet claim (some of them, at least) to keep themselves pure in practice.

71. *Priap*. 59.2: "si fur veneris, impudicus exis."

72. See especially *Priap*. 13, 22, 74. Other sources that imply such a meaning of *(im)pudicus* include Catull. 29.9–10 ("cinaede Romule, hoc videbis et feres? / es impudicus et vorax et aleo"); Cic. *Cat*. 2.23, *Phil*. 3.12, 3.15 (cf. 2.3–4, 45), *Cael*. 15 (cf. Gell. 17.1.9–11, Quint. *I.O*. 4.2.27); [Cic.] *Sall*. 7, 9, 13 (cf. [Sall.] *Inv. in Cic*. 2); [Cic.] *Ep. Oct*. 9.12; Hor. *Sat*. 1.6.82, *Epist*. 1.20.3; Suet. *Aug*. 71.1 (cf. 68.1); Sen. *Contr*. 4.pr.10, 5.6.pr. and 5.6.1 (a young man who on a wager dressed in women's clothes was raped and successfully prosecuted his rapists *de vi*; but he was subsequently prohibited from addressing a *contio* under a rule prohibiting *impudici* from doing so), 10.4.17 ("exoletos suos ut ad longiorem patientiam impudicitiae idonei sint amputant"); Tac. *Ann*. 6.9 (a certain Sextus Vistilius was denounced by Tiberius for having written about the future emperor Caligula as *impudicus*; cf. ibid. 6.5, where Cotta Messalinus was similarly denounced for having insulted Caligula *quasi incestae virilitatis*); Juvenal 3.111; [Quint.] *Decl. Maior*. 3.2, 3.12, 3.16, and 3.17; Calp. Flacc. *Decl*. 3; Rutil. Lup. *Schem*. 2.6 (the orator Hyperides, speaking "de adulescente impudico," asks "quid si . . . ego hunc ostenderem muliebri ritu esse suo corpore abusum?"); Gell. 18.3 ("quid Aeschines rhetor in oratione qua Timarchum de impudicitia accusavit"); D. 1.6.2.pr., 27.2.5, 47.10.1, 47.10.9.4.

73. D. 3.1.1.6: "qui corpore suo muliebria passus est"; Tac. *Ann*. 11.36: "tamquam . . . passus muliebria."

74. Festus 100.24: "intercutitus: vehementer cutitus, hoc est valde stupratus." For the language of *skinning*, see Richlin 1992a: 288, where it is also noted that Festus cites the phrase *inter cutem flagitatus* as an ancient euphemism for a man who had been subjected to *stuprum* (Festus 98.22–3: "mares qui stuprum passi essent").

75. *CGL* 4.xviii: "scultimidoni qui scultimam suam quod est podicis orificium gratis largiantur. dicta scultima quasi scortorum intima." By the standards of modern historical linguistics, the derivation of *scultima* from *scortorum intima* seems absurd, but the fact

that an ancient lexicographer made the connection reveals some interesting conceptual habits, among which is the awareness that prostitutes (implicitly of either sex) might be anally penetrated. Marx, following Baehrens, attributes the word *scultimidoni* to Lucilius (1373M) at least partially because of its dactylic shape.

76. Ernout-Meillet s.v. *patior*: "Dans le sens obscène 'pédéraste passif', les Latins ont purement et simplement transcrit παθικός"; Walde-Hofmann s.v. *patior*: "*pathicus* seit Catull ist direkte Übertragung aus gr. °παθικός, vgl. παθικεύομαι". The *TLL* s.v. *pathicus*, while observing "παθικός (quae vox apud Graecos non legi videtur)," adds a reference to an entry in Philoxenus' Latin-Greek *glossarium*: "morbosus: παθικός" (*CGL* 2.130.58).

77. See Adams 1982: 189–90.

78. Quinn (*ad* Catullus 16.2) claims that "*pathicus = is qui irrumatur*" and "*cinaedus = is qui pedicatur*" and that consequently Catullus 16.1–2 form a chiasmus (so, too, Arkins 1982: 13, 36), but that *pathicus* refers specifically to a man who is orally penetrated is nowhere suggested in the sources. *Pathicus* is sometimes anglicized by scholars into *pathic*, but it seems to me that to do so is to construct a sanitizing distance between the "pathic" (an exotic creature who lives in the pages of scholarship) and real-life men who enjoyed being penetrated. The use of the Romans' own words (*pathicus, cinaedus*, and the like) maintains, on the other hand, the right kind of distance between ancient and modern concepts of sexual agents. Scholars also occasionally use the phrase *pathic sex* to describe the assumption of the receptive role in anal intercourse (e.g., "Romans mocked men who engaged in pathic sex"). The language is odd: since by definition one engages in pathic sex with someone who is not a pathic, the appellation thus suggests a certain objectification of the receptive partner (and not his insertive partner) in a way that adds further support to the misleading representation of the receptive partner as passive.

79. Catullus 16.2: "Aureli pathice et cinaede Furi"; 57.1–2: "pulchre convenit improbis cinaedis / Mamurrae pathicoque Caesarique." See Ellis 1889 and Quinn 1973 ad loc. for the syntax of the first *-que*; Ellis concludes that "the *que* joined as it is with *pathico*, and thus standing between *Mamurrae* and *Caesarique*, distributes the vice equally to both." This seems right, given the plural *improbis cinaedis* in the preceding line.

80. Juv. 9.130–1: "ne trepida, numquam pathicus tibi derit amicus / stantibus et salvis his collibus." The phrase *pathicus amicus* is particularly striking in view of the fact that *amicus* is a key term in the language of social relations among Roman men. (I thank Ralph Hexter for the observation.)

81. See Kroll 1921 for a thorough (if often neglected) review of the evidence. Besides the Roman evidence surveyed below, Kroll points to two inscriptions found at the temple to Isis at Philae: Στρούθειν ὁ κίναιδος ἥκω μετὰ Νικόλα and Τρύφων Διονύσου τοῦ νεοῦ κίναιδος ἥκω παρὰ τὴν Ἰσιν (*CIG* 4926). It is highly improbable that the men in question would have identified themselves as *kinaidoi* if this noun had the primary meaning "penetrated male"; the genitive Διονύσου κίναιδος is also difficult to understand unless the noun means "dancer." See also Françoise Perpillou-Thomas, "Artistes et athlètes dans les papyrus grecs d'Egypte," *ZPE* 108 (1995): 228–9 for lists of artists including some who are identified as *kinaidoi*: dancers with cultic functions (I thank Alan Cameron for the reference). As for the origin of the word, one ancient etymology derives it from κινεῖσθαι τὰ αἰδοῖα (*Et. Gud.* 322.13; cf. Nonius' κινεῖν τὸ σῶμα), but modern linguists are troubled by the fact that *kinaidos* has a short and *kinein* a long iota (see Chantraine and Frisk s.v.); Kroll 1921: 459 suggests that the word may be of Asian origin.

82. For the bird *kinaidion/seisopugis*, see Hesych., Σ Theocr. 2.17; for the fish *cinaedus* see Pliny, *N.H.* 32.146, 37.153.

83. Nonius 5.16–7M: "cinaedi dicti sunt apud veteres saltatores vel pantomimi ἀπὸ τοῦ κινεῖν τὸ σῶμα" (he then cites Lucil. 32M: "stulte saltatum te inter venisse cinaedos"); *CGL*

5.654.7: "cinaedi qui publice clunem agitant, id est saltatores vel pantomimi"; Firm. Matern. *Math*. 6.31.39: "cum effeminati corporis mollitie cinaedos efficient, qui veterum fabularum exitus in scaenis semper saltantes imitentur" (cf. 8.20.8: "erunt pantomimi sed cinaedi").

84. See Edwards 1993: 98–136, especially 129–31, and Edwards 1997.

85. Plaut. *Aul*. 422: "ita fustibus sum mollior magis quam ullus cinaedus"; *Mil*. 668: "ad saltandum non cinaedus malacus aequest atque ego"; *Poen*. 1317–8: "†qur non† adhibuisti, dum istaec loquere, tympanum? / nam te cinaedum esse arbitror magi' quam virum"; *Stich*. 772: "omnis voco cinaedos contra" (cf. 769, *Ionicus aut cinaedicus*). The joke at *Asin*. 627–8 revolves around the double meaning of *verberare*, literally "to beat" but also a handy image for penetration (cf. Adams 1982: 149): "Who would believe this of you, you curly-haired *cinaedus*? That you should 'beat' someone, when you make a living by being 'beaten'?" ("quisnam istuc adcredat tibi, cinaede calamistrate? / tun verberes, qui pro cibo habeas te verberari").

86. Scipio, fr. 30 Malcovati (Macr. *Sat*. 3.14.6): "cum cinaedulis et sambuca psalterioque eunt in ludum histrionum, discunt cantare, quae maiores nostri ingenuis probro ducier voluerunt; eunt, inquam, in ludum saltatorium inter cinaedos virgines puerique ingenui"; fr. 17 (discussed in chapters 1 and 4): "eumne quisquam dubitet, quin idem fecerit, quod cinaedi facere solent?"

87. The epithets are strikingly reversed: one might have expected something like *dextra voraciore* and *culo inquinatiore* ("greedier right hand" and "filthier asshole"). Martial also makes use of the metaphor of the anus "devouring" a penis, writing that Hyllus has spent his last dime on hiring well-endowed men, leaving no money for food. While his belly goes hungry, his anus has a feast (2.51.5–6: "infelix venter spectat convivia culi / et semper miser hic esurit, ille vorat"). *Culus* refers specifically to the anus: see Adams 1981.

88. Mart. 6.37.4–5: "o quanta scabie miser laborat! / culum non habet, est tamen cinaedus."

89. Juv. 2.10: "inter Socraticos notissima fossa cinaedos." See Adams 1982: 151–2, 154–5, for metaphors involving digging, plowing, and the like, and pp. 85–6 for *fossa*.

90. Mart. 9.90.7–8: "sic uni tibi sit puer cinaedus / et castissima pruriat puella"; 12.16: "Addixti, Labiene, tres agellos; / emisti, Labiene, tres cinaedos; / pedicas, Labiene, tres agellos"; 2.43.13: "grex tuus Iliaco poterat certare cinaedo"; 10.98.1–2: "addat cum mihi Caecubum minister / Idaeo resolutior cinaedo."

91. Plin. *Epist*. 9.17: *scurrae, cinaedi,* and *moriones* (see especially 2: "nequaquam me ut inexspectatum festivumve delectat, si quid molle a cinaedo, petulans a scurra, stultum a morione profertur"). Though Livy does not use the word *cinaedus*, he describes the same phenomenon in a Greek context (33.28.2): "prosequentibus mollibus viris qui ioci causa convivio celebri interfuerant."

92. Suet. *Aug*. 68. After reporting some of those rumors, Suetonius notes the following: "sed et populus quondam universus ludorum die et accepit in contumeliam eius et adsensu maximo conprobavit versum in scaena pronuntiatum de gallo Matris Deum tympanizante: 'Videsne ut cinaedus orbem digito temperat?'"

93. Since the noun *spatalium* refers to some kind of jewelry, possibly a bracelet (see *OLD* s.v.), the compound *spatalocinaedi* seems to designate *cinaedi* fond of wearing such adornment. Interestingly, the meter is called Sotadean (see discussion of Sotades the *kinaidologos* later in this chapter): cf. Slater 1990: 184 (with some bibliography). One thinks also of the grammarian Sacerdos' reference to *cinaediambicum tetrametrum brachycatalectum* (*GLK* 6.526.4).

94. Petr. *Sat*. 23–4: "mox et super lectum venit atque omni vi detexit recusantem. super inguina mea diu multumque frustra moluit . . . equum cinaedus mutavit transituque ad comitem meum facto clunibus eum basiisque distrivit."

95. For thighs in a sexual context, see, e.g., Hor. *Sat.* 1.2.80–82. As for *manu procaces*, one might compare Martial's allusion to the manual stimulation of a boy's penis in 11.22 (*fututrici manu*). The reference to buttocks needs no further explanation.

96. For the *galli* see, most recently, Roscoe 1996, Lane 1996, and Taylor 1997: 330–7. Ancient references include Lucr. 2.600–80; Sen. *Dial.* 7.13.3; Mart. 1.35, 2.45, 3.24, 3.73, 3.81, 3.91, 5.41, 7.95, 11.72, 11.74, 13.63, 14.204; and Juv. 6.511–6.

97. This usage was not unparalleled: cf. Mart. 9.2.13, Apul. *Met.* 8.24, 26.

98. Juvenal 2.115–6: "quid tamen expectant, Phrygio quos tempus erat iam / more supervacuam cultris abrumpere carnem?"

99. Apul. *Met.* 8.24–30.

100. Winkler 1990: 45 describes the Greek *kinaidos* as "the unreal, but dreaded, anti-type of masculinity behind everyone's back," a "scare-image standing behind the more concrete charges of shaming one's integrity as a male citizen by hiring out one's body to another man's use."

101. I thank James Zetzel for helping me to formulate this point. It is interesting to note similar associations of gender deviance with the receptive role in intercourse and with dancing in the traditions of certain Polynesian societies, where males who can be described as gender-liminal (called *mahu* in Tahiti and Hawaii and *fa'afafine* in Samoa) are often skilled dancers as well (Besnier 1994). A further and even closer parallel to the *cinaedus* can be seen in the *hijra* of northern India: renouncing their maleness by castrating themselves and becoming "neither men nor women" whose lives are devoted to the mother goddess, they function as entertainers, dancers, and prostitutes paid by men who penetrate them (see especially Nanda 1990 and 1994). Roscoe 1996 and Taylor 1997 explore the parallels and possible historical connections between the *hijra* and the *galli*. Sullivan 1968: 49 n. 2 offers an unsatisfactory explanation of the semantics of the term *cinaedus*: "The earliest meaning of *cinaedus* (literally *one who moves the genitals*) seems to have been a lover of boys (in a bad sense). The name was then applied to a dancer of obscene ballet accompanied by highly indecent songs . . . The term gradually became a nickname for effeminate men who indulged in facepainting and other feminine arts . . ." The term is nowhere used of a lover of boys, neither indeed is there any term of abuse denoting such a man, and the semantic shift that he describes (from "lover of boys" to "effeminate men") makes little sense in ancient terms; furthermore, Sullivan seems to be assuming that the ancient etymology of *cinaedus* cited in n. 81 is correct.

102. Mart. 12.95.1–2: "Musseti pathicissimos libellos, / qui certant Sybariticis libellis"; Mart. 2.86.2: "nec retro lego Sotaden cinaedum"; Varro, *Menipp.* 353.1 (Nonius, p. 176M): "comici cinaedici scaenatici" (but the reading is not entirely secure); Varro, *Epist. Caes.* 1 (Nonius, p. 56M): *cinaedologos*. Lucilius 680 Marx reads "coniugem infidamque placitam familiam, impuram domum?" but some editors emend *placitam* to *pathicam* (see Marx ad loc. and Warmington's 1938 LCL edition.)

103. Martial's Mussetius is otherwise unknown; his lewd poetry is compared to the work of Hemitheon of Sybaris (cf. Ov. *Tr.* 2.1.417), a writer of obscene verse who is himself called a *kinaidos* by Lucian (*Adv. Indoctum* 23; cf. *Pseudolog.* 3). For Sotades, see Athen. 14.620ff.; his verses were called *Kinaidoi*. In contrast, Ralph Hexter has made the intriguing suggestion that there may be a pun in Martial's *retro lego* that argues for an association of the term *cinaedus* with the receptive role in anal intercourse: Does one, as it were, read Sotades *a tergo*? From yet another perspective, Selden 1992 argues that such language exemplifies the appropriation by poets of certain terms relating to gender and sexuality as tropes for processes inherent in the acts of writing and reading.

104. *Priap.* 25.3: "sceptrum quod pathicae petunt puellae"; 40.4: "hoc pathicae summi numinis instar habent"; 73.1–2: "obliquis quid me, pathicae, spectatis ocellis? / non stat in inguinibus mentula tenta meis"; at 48.3–5 the god wryly explains the moisture that has

appeared on his penis: it is neither dew nor frost, but rather a spontaneous ejaculation prompted by fond memories of a *pathica puella* ("non ros est, mihi crede, nec pruina, / sed quod sponte sua solet remitti, / cum mens est pathicae memor puellae"); Catull. 10.24–5: "hic illa, ut decuit cinaediorem, / 'quaeso,' inquit mihi, 'mi Catulle. . . .'"

105. According to one manuscript reading, *Priap*. 50.2 refers to a *ficosissima puella*; given ancient beliefs associating hemorrhoids (colloquially called *fici/ficus* or "figs") with excessive anal penetration (cf. Juv. 2.13 and Mart. 1.65, with Howell ad loc.), the phrase would seem to refer to a woman who enjoys being anally penetrated. Parker 1988: 145 takes it to be "merely a term of abuse, not literal," but prefers it to the alternative reading *fucosissima*, which would, he argues, have "a derogatory sense unsuited to this context."

106. They are, in other words, *protervae* (*Priap*. 58.3–4; cf. 26.4 [*vicinae prurientes*] and 80.3, where we read of *cupidae puellae* who handle Priapus' sizeable member just as the *pathicae* of *Priap*. 73 are interested in gazing upon it). One of the poems that speaks of *pathicae* also mentions *Suburanae puellae* (40.1), or girls from the red-light district of Rome. Parker 1988 variously translates "girls in rut" (25.3), "whores" (40.4), "lusty wench" (48.5), and "wanton girls" (73.1).

107. Ellis explains *cinaediorem* as meaning "impudent," but professes uncertainty; Kroll notes "hier ganz abgegriffen 'frech'"; Quinn translates "a particularly shameless hussy"; and Syndikus 1984: 119 paraphrases "eine schamlose Person." Skinner 1989, following the *TLL*, takes *cinaedus* to be a word for a male prostitute, but I can find no ancient sources to support that interpretation.

108. There is of course the unverifiable possibility that some men who were insulted as *cinaedi* may have used the term among themselves as a positive, self-affirming label.

109. One should also consider the possibility that *cinaedus* was sometimes a dead metaphor or empty insult, as καταπύγων and κίναιδος could be in ancient Greek (cf. Dover 1978: 142–3, Gleason 1995: 65). Romans who wrote graffiti identifying certain men as *cinaedi* might in fact have been deploying the word as a nonspecific insult (like "bastard" or, as Kroll 1988: 90 suggests, "Schweinehund"). Still, in the literary sources at any rate, references to *cinaedi* are nearly always specifically linked to gender deviance often embodied in inappropriate sexual practices.

110. A selection from Martial: 1.65, 2.51, 2.54, 2.62, 3.71, 3.95, 4.48, 4.52 (cf. 9.57), 6.37, 6.54, 7.58, 11.88; Juvenal 2 and 9.

111. Vir. *Ecl*. 3.8: "novimus et qui te—".

112. Juv. 4.106: "improbior saturam scribente cinaedo." In his 1895 Leipzig commentary, Ludwig Friedlaender notes that Juvenal's phrase might refer to a specific *cinaedus* who took up satire: "falls hier eine bestimmte Person gemeint ist (was zweifelhaft ist), kennen wir sie nicht." But, as he observes, we cannot know; in any case, the image of a *cinaedus* taking an active role in criticizing or attacking those around him clearly constitutes a paradox for Juvenal's speaker. Moreover, as Braund (*ad* Juv. 4.106) puts it, "the fleeting self-referentiality here in 'writing satire' affirms the robust masculinity of the speaker, who evidently regards 'a sodomite writing satire' as far removed from his self-image."

113. Pers. 1.87: "an Romule ceves?"; 1.20–1: "cum carmina lumbum / intrant et tremulo scalpuntur ubi intima versu"; 1.103–4: "haec fierent, si testiculi vena ulla paterni / viveret in nobis?" Daniel Selden reminds me that both here and with Juvenal's *cinaedus* who writes satire (4.106: see previous note), we see the appropriation of the language of gender and sexuality to describe the processes of reading, writing, and rhetoric: see discussion of Martial's *pathicissimi libelli* earlier in this chapter.

114. Mart. 4.48.3, 6.50.3.

115. Discussions of Cicero's use of this technique include Gonfroy 1978; Lilja 1983: 88–97; Richlin 1992a: 96–104, 220–1, 282–4.

116. Suet. *Aug.* 68.1, *Cal.* 36.1, *Nero* 29.1, *Otho* 2.2, *Vit.* 3.2, *Dom.* 1.1.

117. See, for example, Diehl 648: "Cosmus Equitiaes magnus cinaedus et fellator est suris apertis"; *CIL* 6.248: "Orfite cinaede, qui bis promisi(s)ti pedicare et non bitidare" (= *vis te dare*, according to *TLL* s.v. *cinaedus* 70).

118. Huelsen 1896 suggests that the tiles belonged to a game whose rules are now lost to us, observing that the tiles with lower numbers bear for the most part "voci ingiuriose" and tiles with higher numbers "appellazioni di buono augurio" (pp. 236–7); but, as he admits, this scheme is not without its problematic exceptions. Other scholars have suggested that the tiles were used as tickets for gladiatorial shows or at *sparsiones*. See Bücheler, *Kleine Schriften* III.245 and *RE* 13 (1927): 2026–7.

119. Juv. 2.45–7: "sed illos / defendit numerus iunctaeque umbone phalanges. / magna inter molles concordia." See Konstan 1993 for a discussion of the sexual dynamics of this satire as a whole.

120. The gesture of scratching the head with one finger will be discussed later in this chapter.

121. I thank David Halperin for reminding me of this point.

122. Taylor 1997:331–2 assumes that they are castrated.

123. Apul. *Met.* 8.24: "cinaedum et senem cinaedum, calvum quidem sed cincinnis semicanis et pendulis capillatum, unum de triviali popularium faece, qui per plateas et oppida cymbalis et crotalis personantes deamque Syriam circumferentes mendicare compellunt" (cf. 8.28 for a scene of self-mutilation); 8.26 (*puellae*); ibid. (the *concubinus'* complaint): "venisti tandem miserrimi laboris vicarius: sed diu vivas et dominis placeas et meis defectis iam lateribus consulas"; 8.29: "passimque circumfusi nudatum supinatumque iuvenem execrandis oribus flagitabant." While this novel is set in the Greek East, it clearly speaks to a Roman readership (in this very episode, for example, the narrator exclaims "porro Quirites!" [8.29]—using the traditional form of addressing the Roman citizenry— and there is a reference to the Roman *lex Cornelia* [8.24]). These considerations, combined with the parallels from Juvenal and Petronius, suggest that the narrative of the *puellae* would not have been perceived by Roman readers as portraying an entirely exotic, alien world.

124. *Priap.* 46.1–5: "o non candidior puella Mauro: / sed morbosior omnibus cinaedis, / Pygmaeo brevior gruem timenti, / ursis asperior pilosiorque, / Medis laxior Indicisve bracis."

125. Cael. Aurel. *Morb. Chron.* 4.9.131–7: see discussion later in this chapter.

126. Sen. *Epist.* 83.20: "tunc impudicus morbum profitetur ac publicat"; Juv. 2.17: "qui vultu morbum incessuque fatetur"; Juv. 2.50: "Hispo subit iuvenes et morbo pallet utroque." In the last passage, the concept surely refers to a preference both for being penetrated anally and for performing fellatio: so also Richlin 1993: 552 (*contra* Courtney ad loc.). Taylor 1997: 354 claims, without supporting evidence, that *subire* can also mean "to enter" or "to assault" (the latter meaning is attested, but not in a sexual sense), and thus that "Hispo's two illnesses are the compounded results of the active and passive roles."

127. Plin. *N.H.* 28.106: "eiusdem loci pilorum cinerem ex oleo inlitum viris, qui sint probrosae mollitiae, severos, non modo pudicos, mores induere."

128. Richlin 1993: 549–50.

129. Plin. *N.H.* 28.106: "eiusdem caverna in sinistro lacerto alligata si quis mulierem prospiciat, amatorium esse tam praesens ut ilico sequatur."

130. *Pace* Arkins 1982: 13 (on Catullus 57, discussed later in this chapter) and Braund 1996 *ad* Juv. 2.17 and 2.50.

131. Plaut. *Cas.* 810: "illo morbo quo dirrumpi cupio, non est copiae." MacCary and Willcock, in their 1976 Cambridge commentary, gloss *illo morbo* as "'that complaint,' i.e. sexual activity."

132. Plaut. *Cist.* 71: "ad istam faciem est morbus qui me, mea Gymnasium, macerat"; *Mil.* 1272: "levandum morbum mulieri video."

133. Cic. *Tusc.* 4.25: "similiterque ceteri morbi, ut gloriae cupiditas, ut mulierositas, ut ita appellem eam quae Graece φιλογυνία dicitur, ceterique similiter morbi aegrotationesque nascuntur" (on this vice see also Cic. *De Fato* 10); *Verr.* 2.4.1: "venio nunc ad istius, quem ad modum ipse appellat, studium, ut amici eius, morbum et insaniam, ut Siculi, latrocinium; ego quo nomine appellem nescio."

134. Sen. *Suas.* 2.17; Hor. *Sat.* 2.3.27 (cf. 64, 77–81, 254); Sen. *N.Q.* 7.31.3. For further nonsexual applications of the concept of *morbus*, see Catull. 39.7, 76.25; Petr. *Sat.* 90.3; Mart. 1.89.5.

135. See most recently Joan Booth, "All in the Mind: Sickness in Catullus 76," in Braund and Gill 1997: 150–68.

136. For example, a sexual act between a fully-gendered man (*vir*) and a *cinaedus* would not have been represented as potentially transmitting any kind of disease to the man (I thank Ralph Hexter for pointing this out to me). Thus even the contagion hysterically imagined by the speaker in Juvenal's second satire (Juv. 2.78–81: "dedit hanc contagio labem / et dabit in plures, sicut grex totus in agris / unius scabie cadit et porrigine porci / uvaque conspecta livorem ducit ab uva") is not spread from *cinaedi* to their sexual partners, but rather from one *cinaedus* to another; cf. 9.130–3 (discussed above), where it is imagined that throngs of *pathici* will flock to Rome.

137. Richlin 1993: 533.

138. Apul. *Met.* 8.26, 8.29.

139. Juv. 9.27–101.

140. Cf. Richlin 1992a: 131: "the speaker scorns what he boasts of using" (cf. 113 on old women). Richlin 1993 further develops this parallel.

141. See Halperin 1990: 30 and Winkler 1990: 40 for the ways in which Artemidoros of Daldis' interpretations of sexual dreams reveal a tendency to conceptualize sexual acts as something done by a man *to* rather than *with* someone else.

142. I owe thanks to an anonymous reader for the Oxford University Press for emphasizing this point.

143. Winkler 1990: 54, citing Halperin 1990: 133. An especially bold statement of the ideology of "losing" can be found in Ovid's advice to his male readership: using force to obtain a woman can be useful, for while she may resist, in the end she will willingly "be defeated" (*Ars* 1.666: "pugnando vinci se tamen illa volet").

144. Winkler 1990: 45–70 makes similar arguments regarding the Greek *kinaidos*, the "scare-image" of masculinity that stood in contrast with the figure of the hoplite. Compare the description of the figure of the "fairy" in early-twentieth-century New York City working-class society offered by Chauncey 1994: 57: the fairy was "regarded as an anomaly, certainly, but as more amusing than abhorrent, and only rarely as a threat to the gender order. He was so obviously a 'third-sexer,' a different species of human being, that his very effeminacy served to confirm rather than threaten the masculinity of other men, particularly since it often exaggerated the conventions of deference and gender difference between men and women. The fairies reaffirmed the conventions of gender even as they violated them: they behaved as no man should, but as any man might wish a woman would."

145. See Richlin 1992a: 34–44, 136–9 for discussion of the ways in which the Roman sources treat adult men who seek to be penetrated far more harshly than they treat boys. Richlin 1984: 76 maintains that while boys' anuses are often praised, adult *cinaedi* "are the male equivalent of old and/or repulsive women, and the anal orifice of such men is often attacked in terms similar to those used of repulsive female genitalia."

146. On *cinaedi* as boys who failed to make the expected transition to manhood, cf.

Richlin 1993: 534 and Skinner 1997: 135–6. For the normative distinction between *pueri* and *viri*, consider Mart. 4.7, where Hyllus tries to argue that he should no longer be penetrated because he has a full beard and body hair, and is thus no longer a boy but a *vir*. Cf. Richlin 1992a: 289 ("Roman citizen males as well as slave boys passed through a stage in life in which they would be viewed as sex objects") and Schalow 1989: 120 on early modern Japan: "At some level, adult men distinguished preadult youths from themselves as occupying a different social category: not women, but not yet men either. That is to say, both *wakashu* [preadult youth] and *yaro* [adult male] were of the male sex (*otoko*), but there was a clear distinction made between the two based on age and/or sexual role."

147. For the rhetoric of *nature* in this passage, see appendix 1.

148. Juv. 9.46–7: "sed tu sane tenerum et puerum te / et pulchrum et dignum cyatho caeloque putabas"; 2.112–3: "crine senex fanaticus albo / sacrorum antistes."

149. Mart. 1.41.13 (a *vetulus cinaedus*, in the company of street-vendors, bad poets, and owners of dancing-girls from Cadiz).

150. Hor. *Epod.* 11.23–4: "nunc gloriantis quamlibet mulierculam / vincere mollitie amor Lycisci me tenet."

151. See Adams 1982: 72, 138 and Richlin 1992a: 41–2.

152. Mart. 9.67.3 (*illud puerile*); 2.60.2 (*supplicium puerile*); Apul. *Met.* 3.20 (*puerile corollarium*).

153. Livy 39.13.14: "aetates et erroris et stupri patientes."

154. Ralph Hexter has suggested to me that the inscription dedicated to Priapus cited in chapter 1, in which the dedicator prays that he may "please good boys and girls with my naughty prick" (*CIL* 14.3565.3–4: "da mihi ut pueris et ut puellis / fascino placeam bonis procaci") may make a similar point in a teasing way. In that case, the description of the boys and girls as "good" (*bonis*) would be naughtily ironic.

155. Cael. Aurel. *Morb. Chron.* 4.9.137: "hinc denique coniciunt plurimi etiam pueros hac passione iactari; similiter enim senibus virili indigent officio, quod in ipsis nondum <est> et illos deseruit."

156. Although Caelius' *plurimi* might possibly refer to his colleagues in the medical profession, it reads more naturally as an allusion to popular beliefs.

157. Livy 39.15.13–4: "hoc sacramento initiatos iuvenes milites faciendos censetis, Quirites? his ex obsceno sacrario eductis arma committenda? hi cooperti stupris suis alienisque pro pudicitia coniugum ac liberorum vestrorum ferro decernent?"

158. For similar conventions in Greek ideologies, see Dover 1978 and Halperin 1990. Arist. *N.E.* 7.5 (1148b15–1149b20) and [Arist.] *Probl.* 4.26 offer speculations on why some males enjoy being penetrated that reveal an awareness that some boys at least derive pleasure from the act (cf. Winkler 1990: 67–9).

159. Martial 2.43.13: "grex tuus Iliaco poterat certare cinaedo"; 10.98.1–2: "addat cum mihi Caecubum minister / Idaeo resolutior cinaedo."

160. Scipio fr. 17 Malcovati: "qui in conviviis adulescentulus cum amatore cum chirodota tunica inferior accubuerit, qui non modo vinosus sed virosus quoque sit, eumne quisquam dubitet quin idem fecerit quod cinaedi facere solent?"

161. Giton is called Encolpius' *frater* (9.2, 24.6, 79.9, 97.9, 127.2, 3, 7), but Encolpius is likewise Giton's *frater* (91.2). For this usage of *frater*, see discussion later in this chapter.

162. Sen. *Contr.* 4.pr.10: "impudicitia in ingenuo crimen est, in servo necessitas, in liberto officium."

163. Apul. *Apol.* 10: "eadem igitur opera accusent C. Catullum, quod Lesbiam pro Clodia nominarit, et Ticidam similiter, quod quae Metella erat Perillam scripserit, et Propertium, qui Cynthiam dicat, Hostiam dissimulet, et Tibullum, quod ei sit Plania in animo, Delia in versu."

164. Cf. Hor. *C.* 4.1.37–40: "nocturnis ego somniis / iam captum teneo, iam volucrem sequor / te per gramina Martii / campi, te per aquas, dure, volubilis."

165. See the discussion in Maurin 1975.

166. For men whose austere appearance is contradicted by their sexual practices see, e.g., Mart. 1.24 (cf. 12.42), 1.96, 7.58 ("habet tristis quoque turba cinaedos," 9), 7.62 (discussed below), 9.27, 9.47, 11.88 (Charisianus complains that he cannot practice anal penetration [*pedicare*], but when he reveals that he is suffering from diarrhea, he makes clear which role he wants to play); and Juvenal 2.

167. Firm. Matern. *Math.* 7.25.7, 9, 12, 18, 21, 23; 8.29.7; discussed in Gleason 1995: 67 and Brooten 1996: 132–7.

168. Förster, *Scriptores Physiognomonici* 2.96.4–6: "qui cinaedi quidem certa fide sunt, verum suspicionem a se removere conantes virilem sumere speciem sibimet laborant." See Gleason 1995: 77 for discussion of the ways in which physiognomists claimed to be able to recognize a *cinaedus* despite his outwardly virile appearance (Förster 2.20.8–9; Diogenes Laertius 7.173; Dio Chrysostom 33.53–4).

169. Richlin 1993; Gleason 1995: 55–81.

170. Quint. *I.O.* 5.9.8–16 (12: "quod si receperimus, vereor ne omnia quae ex facto ducuntur signa faciamus"; 14: "nam si est signum adulterae lavari cum viris, erit et convivere cum adulescentibus, deinde etiam familiariter alicuius amicitia uti; fortasse corpus vulsum, fractum incessum, vestem muliebrem dixerit mollis et parum viri signa, si cui cum signum id proprie sit quod ex eo de quo quaeritur natum sub oculos venit ut sanguis e caede, ita illa ex impudicitia fluere videantur"). Cantarella 1992: 178 unfortunately leaves one with the impression that Quintilian endorses the view he criticizes: "Quintilian writes, for example, that dressing as a woman betokens a lack of virility, just like having a body which is *vulsum* (plucked hairless) and a gait which is *fractum* (effeminate); these habits and these attitudes, he writes, derive from *inpudicitia.*"

171. Phdr. 5.1.12–8: "unguento delibutus, vestitu fluens, / veniebat gressu delicato et languido. / hunc ubi tyrannus vidit extremo agmine / 'Quisnam cinaedus ille in conspectum meum / audet venire?' responderunt proximi / 'hic est Menander scriptor.' mutatus statim / 'homo' inquit 'fieri non potest formosior.'"

172. Phdr. 5.pr.8–10: "adeo fucatae plus vetustati favet / Invidia mordax quam bonis praesentibus. / sed iam ad fabellam talis exempli feror."

173. Suet. *Jul.* 22.2: "ac negante quodam per contumeliam facile hoc ulli feminae fore, responderit quasi adludens in Syria quoque regnasse Sameramin magnamque Asiae partem Amazonas tenuisse quondam." See discussion of this passage earlier in chapter 5, where it was argued that Caesar could get away with things that less powerful men could not.

174. Tac. *Ann.* 16.20: "agitur in exilium tamquam non siluisset quae viderat pertuleratque, proprio odio."

175. Juv. 9.86: "dedimus quod famae opponere possis"; 9.92–103.

176. Cf. Richlin 1992a: 83–6 for a discussion of the role of gossip (particularly that of a sexual nature) in Cicero.

177. Mart. 3.73.5: "rumor negat esse te cinaedum."

178. Mart. 4.43.1–3: "non dixi, Coracine, te cinaedum: / non sum tam temerarius nec audax / nec mendacia qui loquar libenter."

179. Mart. 6.56.2: "verba putas famae te, Charideme, dare?"; 5–6, "scis multos dicere multa: / fac pedicari te, Charideme, putent."

180. There is a pun here on *testis*, meaning either "witness" or "testicle": what Amillus does without witnesses does not involve the exercise of his manhood. This awareness that people do things in private that they wish to be kept secret gives meaning to a couplet that

Martial composes to accompany the gift of a lamp for the bedroom (14.39): "dulcis conscia lectuli lucerna, / quidquid vis facias licet, tacebo." ("I, a lamp, witness to the sweet bed, will keep silent even if you do whatever you want.")

181. Other epigrams on Olus (either a pseudonym for a real man or an entirely fictitious character) mock him for a pretentious lifestyle that is at odds with his actual financial situation (2.68, 3.48, 4.36, 10.54).

182. Schmitt and Sofer 1991: 8. See Winkler 1990 (esp. 1–70) for a discussion of ancient and modern Greek cultural traditions that illustrate the same point.

183. Phdr. *App.* 10.12–4: "tum vir animi simplicis / id dedecus castrorum propelli iubet, / nec cadere in illum credit tantam audaciam."

184. Ibid. 23–5: "hunc ego committi satius fortunae arbitror, / in quo iactura levis est, quam fortem virum, / qui casu victus temeritatis te arguat."

185. Ibid. 30–4: "'corona, miles, equidem te dono libens, / quia vindicasti laudem Romani imperi; / sed exstillescant oculi sic' inquit 'mei,' / turpe illud imitans ius iurandum militis, / 'nisi tu abstulisti sarcinas nuper meas.'"

186. Before we place too much emphasis on Pompey's readiness to sacrifice the man, we should remember that the Roman army prided itself on maintaining a discipline that some might consider ruthless: one need only think of the practice of decimation, whereby a commander might punish a breach of discipline by summarily putting to death every tenth soldier.

187. It has been estimated, for example, that in the second half of the eighteenth century, 31 percent of all executions within the British Navy followed upon sodomy convictions: see Besnier 1994: 294 with n. 27. See Gleason 1995: 134 for a slightly different approach to Phaedrus' poem.

188. Gleason 1995: 67 with n. 60.

189. It is as revealing as it is depressing to contrast the situation I have just outlined with the later situation described by Cantarella 1992: 175–210. Between the fourth and sixth centuries A.D., a series of Christian emperors issued decrees that were shockingly punitive of men who sought to be penetrated. In A.D. 390 Valentinian, Arcadius, and Theodosius issued a constitution that stipulated death by flames as punishment for men who were penetrated in brothels (*virorum lupanaria*; *Coll.* 5.3; cf. Cantarella 1992: 177–80). In A.D. 438 Theodosius II stipulated that *all* men who were caught having been penetrated should be so executed (*Cod. Theod.* 9.7.6; cf. Cantarella 1992: 180–1). Finally, in A.D. 559 Justinian imposed the death penalty on any man who engaged in sexual relations with another male, regardless of the role he played (*Nov.* 141 pr.; cf. Cantarella 1992: 181–6).

190. D. 3.1.1.6: "removet autem a postulando pro aliis et eum, qui corpore suo muliebria passus est. si quis tamen vi praedonum vel hostium stupratus est, non debet notari, ut et Pomponius ait." At D. 3.1.1.2 Ulpian defines *postulare* as "desiderium suum vel amici sui in iure apud eum, qui iurisdictioni praeest, exponere; vel alterius desiderio contradicere."

191. This of course entails some interesting complexities (see discussion later in this chapter); for now it is worth noting that the specified exception meant that men who had been raped by pirates or wartime enemies were exempted even from arguing the tricky point of desire.

192. D. 3.1.1.3–4.

193. Cf. Cantarella 1992: 260 n. 85: "Only some capacities that women lacked were also removed from the *molles:* political capacity, which women never had, was never brought into question in their case." See Gardner 1993: 149–52 for discussion of this provision in the context of a more general treatment of *infamia* (110–54).

194. Here I follow Gardner 1993: 117, who argues that exclusion from the form of

"networking" that *postulatio* represented "was a handicap, and one whose effect would be greatest among the elite. . . . Even these, however, were not dependent on this activity for a living. As a social handicap, it may be compared with that imposed by the Augustan adultery law on adultresses, who were forbidden marriage with the freeborn." It might be argued, though, that convicted adultresses, severely limited in their choice of husbands, suffered from a greater social handicap than men who had "submitted to womanly things."

195. D. 3.2.1.

196. See Edwards 1997: 69–76 for a discussion of *infamia* and sexual practices. Richlin 1993: 560, citing Greenidge, suggests that the very fact of being forbidden to represent others before a magistrate eventually came to be "itself used as a mark of *infamia*," and thus that men who had "played the woman's role" could become legally *infames* by virtue of their sexual practices. But Greenidge's suggestion is only speculative and has no direct ancient evidence to support it; see Gardner 1993: 215 n. 4, where it is also observed that a censorial *nota* "in itself did not necessarily produce any effect on the individual's exercise of his rights." In any case, Gardner argues (154) that "being *infamis* would have made little impact on the ordinary lives of most citizens" and that "the non-criminal *infamis* is not a complete social pariah."

197. Gardner 1993: 112 points to another difficulty inherent in all such disqualifications: "If the magistrate himself knew that an individual was disqualified, he would no doubt refuse to accept him as a contestant in an action; otherwise it was apparently up to the adversary (if he knew of the disqualification) to challenge by an objection . . . No doubt it was possible for some people who were technically disqualified nonetheless to slip through the net."

198. See, for example, Besnier 1994: 293–5 for an overview. MacMullen 1982: 495, referring to the law recorded on the *Tabula Heracleensis* (see chapter 1), claims that Romans "protected decent citizens (as they would have called themselves) against finding a known homosexual sitting next to them in public gatherings," but this is a skewed reading of the text, which specifically addresses only those men who had prostituted themselves ("quei corpore quaestum fecit fecerit").

199. Richlin 1993 (esp. 523–4).

200. Suet. *Dom.* 10.5: "satisque constat duos solos e notioribus venia donatos, tribunum laticlavium et centurionem qui se, quo facilius expertes culpae ostenderent, impudicos probaverant et ob id neque apud ducem neque apud milites ullius momenti esse potuisse."

201. Dio 67.11.4: κατ' ἐρωτικὴν χρείαν αὐτῷ συγγεγονέναι. Dio adds the revealing comment that Calvaster's claim was believable because he was young and desirable: καὶ γὰρ ἦν οἷος ἐρᾶσθαι δύνασθαι.

202. Lateranus was expelled from the Senate, but later readmitted by Nero in a show of clemency (Tac. *Ann.* 13.11). Later still he became involved in the conspiracy of Piso against Nero and was executed (Tac. *Ann.* 15.49, 60). The uncle whose services saved Lateranus' life was A. Plautius Silvanus, who had led a Roman invasion of Britain (see Furneaux *ad* Tac. *Ann.* 11.36).

203. Tac. *Ann.* 11.36: "Suillio Caesonino et Plautio Laterano mors remittitur, huic ob patrui egregium meritum: Caesoninus vitiis protectus est, tamquam in illo foedissimo coetu passus muliebria."

204. Tac. *Ann.* 11.2 (discussed earlier in this chapter). Furneaux asserts that Caesoninus was indeed one of the elder Suillius' sons (so too *RE* s.v.), noting that he was named after his father's half-sister Caesonia (*ad* 11.36; see also his note *ad* 11.2); but he makes no further comment on the sexual dynamics implied in these passages. In his 1967 commentary, Erich Koestermann, discussing Valerius Asiaticus' allegations regarding Suillius' sons, notes that one of those sons was "wahrscheinlich Suillius Caesoninus," and that the later

incident (regarding Messalina's orgy) "ein bezeichnendes Schlaglicht auf unsere Stelle wirft" (*ad* 11.2, thus apparently assuming that Suillius Caesoninus was in fact P. Suillius Rufus' son). I take the identification as almost certain, and here offer a more explicit description of that "bezeichnendes Schlaglicht."

205. At least with regard to one of Suillius' sons: the other son, M. Suillius Nerullinus, seems not to have suffered any damage to his reputation. He went on to become consul three years later (A.D. 50; see Tac. *Ann.* 11.25 with Furneaux ad loc.). Eight years after that, his father fell from grace and was exiled, and certain accusers, relying on ill-will against the elder Suillius, charged Nerullinus with extortion, but Nero intervened (Tac. *Ann.* 13.43). Yet Tacitus gives no hint that Nerullinus' accusers made any charges of a sexual nature against him. Consequently, either Valerius was using the plural "sons" for effect, really directing his accusation at only one son, or he was implying that he had had sexual relations with both, but, unlike his brother, Nerullinus managed to steer clear of further public accusations of this nature.

206. Of course, it is just possible that the revelation was actually made by someone else, as a piece of malevolent tattle. But if so, it backfired, and the irony is delicious: Caesoninus' sexual experiences were once again publicized by a hostile party, but this time it ended up saving Caesoninus' life.

207. As opposed to his brother Nerullinus (see n. 205), we never hear of Caesoninus again; but he survived the crisis of Messalina's downfall, and that was a feat in itself.

208. It is just possible, as David Halperin has reminded me, that Valerius Asiaticus' insinuation concerning Suillius' sons was a desperate insult with no basis in fact, and that Suillius Caesoninus' self-accusation (if such it was) was an equally desperate fabrication by a man who decided to accept the lesser of two evils: a reputation as a *cinaedus* as opposed to execution. In that case these texts would tell us little about the real experiences of *cinaedi*, but they still would illustrate ways in which the system could be manipulated. One graffito presents a drawing of a penis and the words "I shat this out," or perhaps "I shat on this" (*CIL* 10.8145: "hanc ego cacavi"); for the application of the language of defecation to the activity of the receptive partner in anal intercourse, see the discussion in chapter 1. Housman 1931: 404 dryly comments, "scripsit impudicus εὐρυπρωκτία sua gloriatus." Perhaps, then, we hear the voice of a man who has been penetrated. Alternatively, though, this graffito might be *mocking* that voice: a bit of unflattering ventriloquism.

209. Cf. Boswell 1980: 162; Krenkel 1980a; Adams 1982: 211–3; Richlin 1992a: 26–9, 69, 150–1. Adams 1982: 131 and Krenkel 1980a: 85 suggest that it was worse for a man to be thought a *fellator* than for a woman to be thought a *fellatrix*, but the sources never seem to make this distinction. *Fellatores* and *fellatrices* are represented as equally dirty.

210. See Richlin 1992a: 26–30; Adams 1982: 199, 213 with n. 1. Cf. Sen. *N.Q.* 1.16.2 and Mart. 1.83 (see J. P. Hallett, "Puppy Love," *Hermes* 105 [1977]: 252–3, for a different interpretation), 1.94, 2.15, 2.21, 3.17, 3.87, and 9.63, where (*pace* Krenkel 1980a: 83 and Adams 1982: 199) the reference is most likely to fellatio: for the pun on *pascit*, compare the conceit in the Pompeiian graffito "qui verpam vissit, quid cenasse illum putes?" (*CIL* 4.1884).

211. See, e.g., *Priap.* 35.5: "pedicaberis irrumaberisque" (clearly echoing Catull. 16.1); 70.13: "custodes . . . irrumatos."

212. Catull. 21.12–3: "quare desine, dum licet pudico, / ne finem facias, sed irrumatus."

213. Cic. *Red. Sen.* 11: "quis enim ullam ullius boni spem haberet in eo cuius primum tempus aetatis palam fuisset ad omnis libidines divulgatum? qui ne a sanctissima quidem parte corporis potuisset hominum impuram intemperantiam propulsare?" For the phrase "sanctissima parte corporis," see Adams 1982: 212 n. 1 (a list of euphemisms for the mouth). Cicero's harsh invective against Gabinius in this speech and elsewhere includes the insinu-

ation that he had been penetrated by none other than Catiline (*Red. Sen.* 10: "Catilinam amatorem suum"; ibid. 12: "eius vir Catilina"; *Dom.* 62: "Catilinae delicias"); in another speech (*Sest.* 18) he makes a broad swipe by referring to "veteres vexatores aetatulae suae." See Gonfroy 1978: 255–7 for a full listing of Cicero's attacks on Gabinius.

214. Cic. *Att.* 1.18.5: "Auli autem filius, o di immortales! quam ignavus ac sine animo miles! quam dignus qui Palicano, sicut facit, os ad male audiendum cotidie praebeat!" Shackleton Bailey ad loc. observes, "possibly there is an underlying *sensus obscenus*; Afranius seems to have had a character for *mollitia*." But the double entendre is fairly clear: for the phrase *os praebere* cf. *caput praebere* at *Priap.* 22.2 and consider Donatus' misplaced prudishness in his interpretation of the phrase *os praebui* at Ter. *Adelph.* 215 as a κακέμφατον.

215. E.g., *CIL* 4.1969 (Lachis for two *asses*), 2028 (Libanis for three), 5408 (Felix at the reduced rate of one *as*).

216. *CIL* 4.4185: "Sabina, felas; non belle faces." Varone 1994: 75 translates, "Sí, Sabina, tu lo succhi, ma non lo sai far bene," but this seems an unlikely meaning of *belle facis* (cf. Cic. *Att.* 5.17.6: "illum fecisse non belle"). Other graffiti describing men or women as fellators include *CIL* 4.1253 (Lemnius), 1284 (Secundus), 1388 (Timele), 1389 (Nymphe), 1427 (Salvia), 1510 (Amarillis), 1631 (Restitutus), 1651 (Rufilla), 1666 (Genialis, with an illustration), 1708 (Victor), 1825 (Cosmus, "magnus cinaedus et fellator"), 1850 (Phoebus, with an illustration), 1852a ("filius felat"), 1869 (Felix), 2169 and 2170 (Ismenus), 2259 (Fortunata), 2268 (Myrtale), 2275 (Fortunata), 2278 (Nike), 2292 (Myrtis), 2402 (Ionas and Philetus), 3968 (Secundus), 4156 (Lucius Albucius), 4192 (Egidia), 4434 (Methe), 4580 (Amilatus), 4652 (Lucius), 4997 (Coresus), 7057 (Fyllis), 7243 (Iarinus), 7497 (Spuncles), 8307 (Navius), 8329 (Severa), 8361 (Ianuaria), 8413 (Valentinus), 8449 (Camudia), 8461 (Regulus), 8465 (Ianuaria again), 8512 (Ianuarius), 8711 (Felicula), 8844 (Martialis, with specification of the recipient of his services, Proculus), 8959 (Pyralis, with an illustration). Occasionally we encounter a compliment (2273 ["Myrtis bene felas"], 2421 ["Rufa ita vale quare bene felas"], 9027 ["Secundus fellator rarus"]) or a demand: 760 ("obli(n)ge mea(m) fela mentulam elinges"). 3494h ("Orte, fellator eco fui"), accompanied by a sketch of a man, seems at first glance to be a confession; but, as with *CIL* 10.8145 ("hanc ego cacavi," discussed earlier in this chapter), it is also possible that the words are not a first-person confession but are teasingly attributed to the man represented by the sketch.

217. There may be an amusing twist on this theme in *CIL* 4.1623: "et qui scribit felat." Was this a tag added by another hand to an insult of the type "fellat qui legit," now lost? On *CIL* 4.2360, see Housman 1931: 406–7.

218. I thank David Halperin for reminding me of this aspect of the graffiti.

219. *CIL* 11.6721.9: "(s)alve Octavi felas"; 34: "esureis et me felas."

220. Only the agent noun *cunnilingus* (and possibly *cunnio*, cited later in this section) is attested in the ancient sources; no *nomen actionis* has come down to us. In contemporary English, "cunnilingus" has taken over that role, but I prefer to adhere to ancient usage, reserving the Latin *cunnilingus* for the person and using "cunnilinctus" to refer to the action (this word, too, is unattested in the ancient sources, but cf. *linctus*, denoting the act of licking, at Plin. *N.H.* 31.104, 36.133). See Krenkel 1981 for a useful compilation of both Greek and Roman references to cunnilinctus.

221. Mart. 1.77 (see Howell and Citroni ad loc. on the notion of pallor) and 9.92.11.

222. Mart. 9.67 (see Adams 1982: 199 and Richlin 1993: 53 with n. 34). A similar scenario appears in 3.54: "cum dare non possim quod poscis, Galla, rogantem, / multo simplicius, Galla, negare potes." In 9.4 we read that Galla charges two *aureoli* (gold pieces) to be vaginally penetrated (*futui*) and another two "to be more than fucked" (*plus quam futui*; i.e., anally penetrated?). Yet Aeschylus paid her ten *aureoli*, and Martial is puzzled:

"Galla doesn't charge that much for giving head. What is she doing then? She's keeping quiet." ("non fellat tanti Galla. quid ergo? tacet.") Howell *ad* 1.83 explains that Galla "is paid an extra large fee not just to do it [sc., fellatio] but to keep quiet about it." But there would be no reason for Aeschylus to pay her off if she were merely fellating him; rather, he must be buying her silence because he is performing cunnilinctus. For the shame attaching to a man who performed the act, cf. Juvenal 9.3–4, where the speaker compares Naevolus' dejected expression to that of a certain Ravola who was caught in the act of orally gratifying his girlfriend: "quid tibi cum vultu, qualem deprensus habebat / Ravola dum Rhodopes uda terit inguina barba?"

223. Cic. *Phil*. 13.24: "in lustris, popinis, alea, vino tempus aetatis omne consumpsisses, ut faciebas, cum in gremiis mimarum mentum mentemque deponeres." Thus when Cicero elsewhere (*Phil*. 11.5) speaks of Antony's *incestum os*, the reference is most probably to cunnilinctus (Krenkel 1980a: 84 suggests fellatio, but there is not a hint of this in the *Philippics*).

224. Cic. *Dom*. 25: "qui sua lingua etiam sororem tuam a te abalienavit"; ibid. 47: "hanc tibi legem Clodius scripsit spurciorem lingua sua . . . ? Sexte noster, bona venia, quoniam iam dialecticus <es> et haec quoque liguris . . ."; ibid. 83: "invenient hominem apud sororem tuam occultantem se capite demisso" (for *capite demisso*, Adams 1982: 192 compares Catull. 88.8 and Sen. *N.Q.* 1.16.4); *Cael*. 78: "ore, lingua, manu, vita omni inquinatum"; *Har. Resp*. 11: "ore tincto"; *Sest*. 111: "in quo tamen est me ultus, cum illo ore inimicos est meos saviatus."

225. Val. Max. 3.5.4: "omnibus scortis abiectiorem et obsceniorem vitam exegit, ad ultimumque lingua eius tam libidini cunctorum inter lupanaria prostitit quam avi pro salute civium in foro excubuerat." While I am interpreting this as a reference to cunnilinctus, it might possibly signal fellatio, and the disagreement among modern commentators (Krenkel 1981: 50 assumes that specifically cunnilinctus is at stake here, whereas Richlin 1993: 539 understands the reference to be to fellatio) stems from a Roman tendency to blur the distinction between *fellator* and *cunnilingus* to which we will return later in chapter 5. The problem in interpreting Valerius Maximus' reference stems from the combination of the term *lupanaria* and the masculine *cunctorum*. Since *lupa* is an established euphemism for a female prostitute, but *lupus* is never used of male prostitutes (see *OLD* and *TLL* s.vv.), one might think that *lupanaria* were staffed exclusively by women; if so, the masculine *cunctorum* is generic. (Or did Valerius write *cunctarum*? The Teubner editor approvingly cites the conjecture *cunnorum* in his apparatus, but the appearance of such an obscenity in this text is unthinkable.) On the other hand, an imperial *constitutio* from A.D. 390 speaks of *virorum lupanaria* (*Coll. leg. Mos. et Rom.* 5.3, discussed at Cantarella 1992: 177–80), and if this reflects earlier usage, then Hortensius may have been said to practice fellatio.

226. Suet. *Gramm.* 23: "vis tu, magister, quotiens festinantem aliquem vides abligurire?" (In the biographer's decorous but unambiguous phrase, "he especially burned with lusts for women, to the point of disgracing his mouth": "sed maxime flagrabat libidinibus in mulieres usque ad infamiam oris.") The unnamed man's question earns Suetonius' praise ("dicto non infaceto") because of its pun on *festinantem*, which has the secondary meaning "approaching orgasm." See Adams 1982: 144–5 and Housman 1931: 412. One might reproduce the pun by translating "everyone you see coming," but the sense of haste present in *festinantem* would be lost, and the man is not coming toward Remmius but trying to avoid him.

227. An audience watching an Atellan farce reacted en masse to a line concerning an old goat who licked the genitals of does (Suet. *Tib*. 45). In the same passage Suetonius also gives us a glimpse at a fascinating possibility, namely that the bias against cunnilinctus was

so strong as to provoke disgust even in the women who might have been pleasured thereby. A woman named Mallonia, having refused to fellate the emperor, killed herself instead of facing the emperor's revenge; but before stabbing herself she cursed Tiberius not for attempting to force her to perform fellatio but for his own predilection for cunnilinctus ("donec ea relicto iudicio domum se abripuit ferroque transegit, obscentitate oris hirsuto atque olido seni clare exprobrata").

228. When, at Poppaea's instigation, Octavia was falsely accused of having had sexual relations with a slave, a number of her slave-women were interrogated and tortured. One of them responded to Tigellinus' threats by retorting that her mistress's private parts were more chaste than his mouth (Tac. *Ann.* 14.60: "castiora esse muliebria Octaviae respondit quam os eius"; cf. Dio 62.13.4, καθαρώτερον, ὦ Τιγελλῖνε, τὸ αἰδοῖον ἡ δέσποινά μου τοῦ σοῦ στόματος ἔχει). Veyne 1985: 29–30 takes the reference to be to fellatio, but Tacitus associates Tigellinus only with women, as does Plutarch, whose language directly implies that Tigellinus had performed cunnilinctus (*Otho* 2.2: αὐτάς τε τὰς ἀνοσίους καὶ ἀρρήτους ἐν γυναιξὶ πόρναις καὶ ἀκαθάρτοις ἐγκυλινδήσεις; for "doing the unspeakable" as Greek code for oral sex, see Winkler 1990: 38 with n. 20).

229. *CIL* 4.4995: "Sulemnis, cunu linge"; 4.8419: "cunum linge Stabili"; 4.8698: "Vettius cunnum linget. Optatus."; 4.8877: "Secundus cunnum linget"; 4.8939: "Maritimus cunnum linget assibus quattuor"; Diehl 649: "Centius cunnu lingit, Dionusia linget (mentulam?)"; Diehl 649a: "Martialis cunuligus." In two graffiti, "Priscus Extalio cunnum" (8834), and "Popilus (ut) canis cunnum linget Reno" (8898), it appears that males are said to have *cunni*. Krenkel 1980a: 86 translates *cunnum* as "private parts" in both instances, claiming (n. 52) that *cunnus* stands for *mentula*, but the reference could be to anilinctus (cf. 1261, where *cunnus* might be an equivalent for *culus* [so Adams 1982: 121]).

230. Huelsen 1896, nos. 20, 35, 38. The *OLD* contains an entry for *cunnio* (with this *tessera* as the sole source), which is tentatively identified as a synonym for *cunnilingus*, in turn explained as "a type of sexual pervert (see etym.)." Adams 1982: 116, comparing a graffito in which *cunnus* is "apparently used *pars pro toto*, of a *cinaedus*," seems to suggest that *cunnio* may be an insulting reference to a male who is penetrated.

231. Mart. 11.45. See Kay ad loc. for the allusion to "mixoscopy" (cf. Sullivan 1968: 244).

232. There are, of course, logically two other possibilities. First, he could be anally receptive, but Martial's point that he exhibits such extreme modesty with both male and female prostitutes makes this implausible. Second, he could be an *irrumator*, compelling his hired companion to fellate him, but there is no evidence that being caught in this role would cause a man to feel shame. Such a man could be accused of mistreating others (e.g., Suet. *Tib.* 45, Sen. *N.Q.* 1.16.7), but that is another matter.

233. SHA *Comm.* 5.11: "omni parte corporis atque ore in sexum utrumque pollutus"; ibid. 10.8: "habuit in deliciis homines appellatos nominibus verendorum utriusque sexus, quos libentius suis osculis applicabat."

234. Auson. *Epigr.* 78, p. 341 Peiper: "Lambere cum vellet mediorum membra virorum / Castor nec posset vulgus habere domi, / repperit ut nullum fellator perderet inguen: / uxoris coepit lingere membra suae."

235. Diehl 501 offers a slightly different reading of the second sentence: "rogat te Arpogra, ut sibi lingas mentula."

236. *CIL* 4.8380: "Onesime xurikilla dos labii (tui). Onesimus. Onesime qunu(m) li(n)ge." The *CIL* editor suggests that *curicilla* is an equivalent of *mentula* with no further comment. Is *curicilla* a corrupt diminutive of *curculio* or *gurgulio* (for which see Adams 1982: 33–4)? Adams 1982: 65, not making that connection, suggests that *xurikilla* may be a "nonsense word"; he also points out that the reading has been challenged (instead of *xurikilla*, one scholar has read *Auricilla*). For a man who is both *cunnilingus* and *fellator*, we might

also compare *CIL* 4.1331 ("Martialis cunuli(n)gus") with 8841 ("Martialis fellas Proculum"). Although these two insulting graffiti were found in different parts of the town (1331 in Reg. VI, 8841 in Reg. III), it is just possible that they refer to one and the same Martialis, notorious for his penchant for oral sexual acts.

237. Cf. Mart. 12.59.10, where among the unpleasant characters who greet the addressee with a kiss are "fellatorque recensque cunnilingus." Mart. 3.88 reads as follows: "Sunt gemini fratres, diversa sed inguina lingunt. / dicite, dissimiles sunt magis an similes?" One of the twin brothers performs fellatio and the other cunnilinctus, and the question is raised: are they dissimilar or similar? The epigram has the pointed ending so important to Martial only if we understand him to be suggesting that they are really more alike than not. The chiastic ordering also suggests this conclusion: they are twins (thus *similes*) yet they "lick different groins" (*diversa*); but instead of being dissimilar (*dissimiles*) they are similar (*similes*) after all. The implication is that their like indulgence in oral sexual acts unites them in more important ways than their involvement with partners of different genders separates them.

238. *Priap.* 28, 35 (for *irrumatio* as a harsh punishment in general, cf. 13, 22, 44, 56, 74); Mart. 2.47 (cf. 2.60, where instead of *irrumatio* the ultimate penalty is said to be castration).

239. Mart. 12.35: "Tamquam simpliciter mecum, Callistrate, vivas, / dicere percisum te mihi saepe soles. / non es tam simplex quam vis, Callistrate, credi. / nam quisquis narrat talia plura tacet." For *tacet* (i.e., he is silent because he has a penis in his mouth), see above. For *percisum*, see Adams 1982: 146–7. In 12.42, Callistratus is said to have married a bearded man named Afer, taking the role of the bride (see Appendix 2).

240. Mart. 6.56.5–6: "'quae ratio est?' inquis. scis multos dicere multa: / fac pedicari te, Charideme, putent." For hairiness as manly and depilation as the mark of an effeminate, see chapter 4. In another epigram from the same book, we read that Charidemus has dirtied the public bathwater by washing first his genitals and then (even worse) his head (6.81). Both poems might very well constitute an insinuation of oral sex in general; but if we assume a continuity in Martial's characters (not necessarily a safe assumption to make), an epigram published nearly seven years later, in which Charidemus is said not to have been interested in sexual relations with women until poverty forced him to seek out a rich widow (11.87), suggests that in the poems from Book 6, Charidemus has dirtied his mouth specifically by performing fellatio.

241. Mart. 2.84: "Mollis erat facilisque viris Poeantius heros: / volnera sic Paridis dicitur ulta Venus. / cur lingat cunnum Siculus Sertorius, hoc est: / abs hoc occisus, Rufe, videtur Eryx." Martial's description of Philoctetes directly implies that he was a *cinaedus* (for *facilis*, see Howell *ad* Mart. 1.57.2). He is drawing on the same tradition that is recorded by the scholia on Thucydides 1.12.2: Φιλοκτήτης, διὰ τὸν Πάριδος θάνατον τὴν θήλειαν νόσον νοσήσας καὶ μὴ φέρων τὴν αἰσχύνην, ἀπελθὼν ἐκ τῆς πατρίδος ἔκτισε πόλιν ἣν διὰ τὸ πάθος Μαλακίαν ἐκάλεσε. ("On account of Paris' death, Philoctetes became ill with the female disease and, unable to endure the shame, left his homeland and founded a city which he named Malakia ['Softness'] after his suffering.")

242. In 6.55 Martial implies that Coracinus' breath is offensive; cf. 12.85 on the breath of *cunnilingi*.

243. A poem addressed to Phoebus, who enjoys the company of well-endowed boys, is himself incapable of an erection, but is said not to be a *cinaedus*, constitutes a similarly mischievous riddle; the solution must be that Phoebus fellates his boyfriends (Mart. 3.73).

244. Cf. Kay 1985 *ad* Mart. 11.61.13 and Richlin 1992a, general index s.v. "Genitalia, female."

245. To describe the act Romans resorted to the periphrasis *cunnum lingere*. Occa-

sionally *lingere* alone ("to lick") is used of cunnilinctus, but as the verb can also take *culum* ("ass") and *mentulam* ("cock") as its object (Adams 1982: 134–5), we cannot consider it to be a *vox propria* for cunnilinctus.

246. Parker 1997: 51–3 argues for a different understanding of the "ontological status of cunnilingus" (namely, that the act "corresponds to a man being used vaginally"), but see Williams 1998 for the serious problems with that argument. It is instructive to contrast the considerable bias against cunnilinctus displayed in both Roman and Greek sources (for the latter, cf. Henderson 1991: 185–6) with the traditions of medieval Japanese erotic paintings, many of which depict cunnilinctus in loving detail; see Theodore Bowie, "Erotic Aspects of Japanese Art," in Theodore Bowie and Cornelia V. Christenson, eds., *Studies in Erotic Art* (New York, 1970), pp. 171–239.

247. Mart. 7.67.1–3, 14–17: "Pedicat pueros tribas Philaenis / et tentigine saevior mariti / undenas dolat in die puellas . . . / non fellat—putat hoc parum virile—/ sed plane medias vorat puellas. / di mentem tibi dent tuam, Philaeni, / cunnum lingere quae putas virile."

248. Hallett 1989: 216 and Brooten 1996: 47 understand the epigram similarly. The Greek medical writer Galen makes the general observation that "among those who perform oral sex, we are more disgusted by those who perform cunnilinctus than by those who perform fellatio" (vol. 12 p. 249 Kühn: ἀλλὰ καὶ τῶν αἰσχρουργῶν μᾶλλον βδελυττόμεθα τοὺς φοινικίζοντας τῶν λεσβιαζόντων; cf. Kay 1985 *ad* Martial 11.61).

249. For the role played by the narrative of Hostius Quadra in Seneca's treatise, see Franz Peter Weiblinger, *Senecas Naturales Quaestiones: Griechische Wissenschaft und römische Form* (Munich, 1977), pp. 69–70, and Citroni Marchetti 1991: 153–61. Nothing else is known of Hostius Quadra.

250. Sen. *N.Q.* 1.16.2: "non erat ille ab uno tantummodo sexu impurus, sed tam virorum quam feminarum avidus fuit"; 3: "foeda dictu sunt quae portentum illud ore suo lancinandum dixerit feceritque"; ibid.: "non in os tantum sed in oculos suos ingereret"; 4: "cum caput merserat inguinibusque alienis obhaeserat."

251. The point of the phrase "admissos sibi pariter in omnia viros" is that he was both orally and anally penetrated. Seneca had earlier made this quite clear, informing us that while Hostius was being penetrated from behind he stimulated his lust by looking into a magnifying mirror that reflected his "stud" (*admissarius*; see Adams 1982: 206–7) and by imagining that the man's penis was really as prodigious as it seemed in the mirror. (See discussion in chapter 2.)

252. Housman 1931: 405–6 understands the scenario similarly: "Hostius pedicatori substratus et feminam lambens pene tamen mare, hoc est virilitatem, exercet . . . iam *contumelia alicuius* virilitatem exercet qui viri feminaeve ore abutitur . . ."

253. Suet. *Nero* 29: "suam quidem pudicitiam usque adeo prostituit, ut contaminatis paene omnibus membris novissime quasi genus lusus excogitaret, quo ferae pelle contectus emitteretur e cavea virorumque ac feminarum ad stipitem deligatorum inguina invaderet et, cum affatim desaevisset, conficeretur a Doryphoro liberto; cui etiam, sicut ipsi Sporus, ita ipse denupsit, voces quoque et heiulatus vim patientium virginum imitatus." For *conficere*, see Adams 1982: 159. It is intriguing, and in keeping with tendencies evident throughout the sources, that in a passage apparently deriving from Suetonius, Aurelius Victor (*Caes.* 5.5–6) opines that Nero's oral proclivities were more repugnant even than his playing the role of bride in his marriage to Doryphorus (for which see Appendix 2), and that his fondness for performing castrations was worse still: ". . . cunctis festa more celebrantibus in manum conveniret lecto ex omnibus prodigiosis. quod sane in eo levius aestimandum. quippe noxiorum vinctis modo pelle tectus ferae utrique sexui genitalia vultu contrectabat; exsector marium maiore flagitio."

254. Cic. *Cat*. 1.26, 2.4, 2.9; *Tog. Cand*. fr. 7, 23 Schoell.

255. Cic. *Cat*. 2.8: "qui alios ipse amabat turpissime, aliorum amori flagitiosissime serviebat." The notion of subjection inherent in the verb *servire* is significant (cf. Gonfroy 1978).

256. Cic. *Cat*. 1.13: "quae libido ab oculis, quod facinus a manibus umquam tuis, quod flagitium a toto corpore afuit?"

257. For similar accusations, cf. Cic. *Har. Resp*. 59 (of Clodius): "quis minus umquam pepercit hostium castris quam ille omnibus corporis sui partibus?" (cf. ibid. 42); [Sall.] *Cic*. 5: "cuius nulla pars corporis a turpitudine vacat"; Catull. 110.8: "quae sese toto corpore prostituit"; SHA *Comm*. 5.11: "omni parte corporis atque ore in sexum utrumque pollutus"; SHA *Elag*. 5.2: "quis enim ferre posset principem per cuncta cava corporis libidinem recipientem?"

258. Cic. *Phil* 2.77: "ergo, ut te catamitum, nec opinato cum te ostendisses, praeter spem mulier aspiceret, idcirco urbem terrore nocturno, Italiam multorum dierum metu perturbasti?"

259. It is even possible that *te catamitum* is "you, her catamite": in Apul. *Met*. 1.12 a woman speaks of her male lover as "carus Endymion, catamitus meus." One commentator on the *Philippics* passage (W. K. Lacey, 1986) translates *catamitum* as "pretty boy," claiming that this "insinuat[es] that Fulvia was boss, rather than sexual perversion."

260. Cic. *Phil*. 13.24: "cum in gremiis mimarum mentum mentemque deponeres."

261. Cic. *Phil*. 2.48: "intimus erat in tribunatu Clodio qui sua erga me beneficia commemorat: eius omnium incendiorum fax, cuius etiam domi iam tum quiddam molitus est. quid dicam ipse optime intellegit"; *Phil*. 2.50: ". . . advolasti egens ad tribunatum, ut in eo magistratu, si posses, viri tui similis esses."

262. Cic. *Sest*. 39: "cum scurrarum locupletium scorto, cum sororis adultero, cum stuprorum sacerdote." *Scurrae* are specifically men (see *OLD* s.v.). Cf. *Har. Resp*. 59: "quae navis umquam in flumine publico tam vulgata omnibus quam istius aetas fuit? quis umquam nepos tam libere est cum scortis quam hic cum sororibus volutatus?"

263. Mart. 7.58.3–5 (Galla has married six or seven *cinaedi*, but has divorced them after finding them unable to achieve an erection): "deinde experta latus madidoque simillima loro / inguina nec lassa stare coacta manu / deseris imbelles thalamos mollemque maritum."

264. Ov. *Am*. 1.8.68: "amatorem flagitet ante suum"; *Ars* 3.437–8: "femina quid faciat, cum sit vir levior ipsa, / forsitan et plures possit habere viros?" The poetry of Tibullus constructs a complex relationship between himself, the boy Marathus, and the woman Pholoe (1.8), as well as an even more complex situation in which he is involved with a boy (*puer*) who has another, even older male lover (*senex*) who is married to a woman (*uxor*) who has a younger male lover (*iuvenis*) on the side (1.9). While these scenarios do not include the figure of the womanizing *cinaedus*, they do demonstrate a notable fluidity with respect to sexual object-choice.

265. Lucil. 1058 Marx: "inberbi androgyni, barbati moechocinaedi."

266. The so-called Oxford fragment of Juvenal 6 (which might be a later, even medieval, interpolation) also evokes the stereotype: "oculos fuligine pascit / distinctus croceis et reticulatus adulter. / suspectus tibi sit, quanto vox mollior et quo / saepius in teneris haerebit dextera lumbis" (Juv. 6.O.21–4).

267. Suet. *Aug*. 68–9: "sed et populus quondam universus ludorum die et accepit in contumeliam eius et adsensu maximo comprobavit versum in scaena pronuntiatum de gallo Matris Deum tympanizante: 'videsne, ut cinaedus orbem digito temperat?' adulteria quidem exercuisse ne amici quidem negant . . ."

268. As Arkins 1982: 13 asserts ("they suffer from the disease of homosexuality").

269. There may be an ambiguity in the Latin phrase *rivales socii puellularum*: Ellis in

his 1876 commentary translates "rival partners in the company of the fair," but notes (only to reject) Haupt's alternative interpretation: "rivals and lovers of women at once" ("qui et socii sint amatoresque puellarum et rivales earundem tanquam pathici"). In other words, Mamurra and Caesar might be rivals of girls for men as well as rivals for girls' affections. Even so, the fact remains that they are called *adulteri*.

270. Mart. 6.39.12–4: "quartus cinaeda fronte, candido voltu / ex concubino natus est tibi Lygdo: / percide, si vis, filium: nefas non est."

271. Mart. 2.51; the poet's crass joke is that Hyllus satisfies the hunger of his anus at the expense of his stomach.

272. For this formulaic phrase, see the earlier discussion of *pudicitia* and cf. Cic. *Cael.* 42, *Rhet. Herenn.* 4.52, Sen. *Contr.* 1.pr.9, Vell. Pat. *Hist.* 2.48.3.

273. Suet. *Cal.* 36: "pudicitiae neque suae neque alienae pepercit. M. Lepidum, Mnesterem pantomimum, quosdam obsides dilexisse fertur commercio mutui stupri. Valerius Catullus, consulari familia iuvenis, stupratum a se ac latera sibi contubernio eius defessa etiam vociferatus est. super sororum incesta et notissimum prostitutae Pyrallidis amorem non temere ulla inlustriore femina abstinuit. quas plerumque cum maritis ad cenam vocatas praeterque pedes suos transeuntis diligenter ac lente mercantium more considerabat . . ."

274. For commentary and bibliography on this poem, see Westendorp Boerma 1963: 73–92, who calls it "non minus obscenum quam obscurum" (76) and is plainly unamused by the poem's bluntness: "quamquam Scaliger poema *elegans et eruditum* vocavit, mea opinio fert id obscenissimum esse et vero poeta indignum" (77). See also Salvatore 1964, who by contrast sees "una certa misura (quanto all'uso dei vocaboli) nell'accennare ad alcune situazioni scabrose." For the man's name, see Westendorp Boerma 1993: 75, 91.

275. [Vir.] *Cat.* 13.13–6: "vel acta puero cum viris convivia / udaeque per somnum nates / et inscio repente clamatum insuper / 'Thalassio, Thalassio'"; 17: *femina*; 35: *cinaede*; 19–21: "non me vocabis pulchra per Cotytia / ad feriatos fascinos, / nec deinde te movere lumbos in †ratulam . . ." (cf. Juv. 2.83–116).

276. 7–8: "prostitutae turpe contubernium / sororis"; 29–32: "quibus repletus et salivosis aquis / obesam ad uxorem redis / exaestuantes dote solvis pantices, / os crusque lambis saviis." See discussion of this poem in chapter 4 for the textual problems.

277. Taylor 1997: 330 n. 35. Taylor suggests that the poem "associates the *cinaedus* with the transvestism and pathic sexual behavior of an urban subculture of sailors and *fratres.*" See discussion later in this chapter for my arguments against speaking of such a "subculture."

278. Nor is it unheard of in the Greek sources (see Gleason 1995: 64–5).

279. Perhaps it deserves reiterating that when I speak of "identities" and of how the *cinaedus* was "defined," I am speaking of the social roles lying behind labels assigned to men in the arena of public discourse; I am not addressing the issue of how such men understood themselves or constructed their own subjective identities.

280. Richlin 1993 (e.g., 526, 530).

281. Fantham 1991: 286.

282. Fantham 1991: 279 with n. 31.

283. Brooten 1996: 159.

284. Taylor 1997: 322. The qualifications ("primary" and "at times") reveal the difficulties created when we try to fit the ancient *cinaedus* into the modern category of the "homosexual." In the same article Taylor speaks of men who "openly flaunt their homosexuality" in the ancient texts, "confessing their homosexual inclination," and of a "gradual recognition of male homosexuality as an institution and lifestyle rather than simply an aberrant act" (Taylor 1997: 326, 327, 348–9).

285. Compare this prefatory remark in Richlin's groundbreaking *Garden of Priapus*, originally published in 1983 (Richlin 1992a: vii–viii): "Roman invective assumed that there was only one main kind of male homosexual, pathic (those who were penetrated); these are often identified as effeminate. Men who penetrated other males (usually boys) were generally assumed to be bisexual; free men who penetrated adult males were either punishing them or engaging in a rare form of homosexuality."

286. Foucault 1978: 43.

287. Winkler 1990: 45–6.

288. Maud Gleason, "The Semiotics of Gender: Physiognomy and Self-Fashioning in the Second Century C.E.," Halperin, Winkler, and Zeitlin 1990: 411–2.

289. Halperin (forthcoming).

290. Cf. Halperin 1990: 24 for similar arguments regarding the Greek *kinaidos*. Chauncey 1994: 48 describes a stereotype in early-twentieth-century New York City, that of the *fairy*, in closely similar terms as well: "The fairies' sexual desire for men was not regarded as the singular characteristic that distinguished them from other men, as is generally the case for gay men today. That desire was seen as simply one aspect of a much more comprehensive gender role inversion (or reversal), which they were also expected to manifest through the adoption of effeminate dress and mannerisms; they were thus often called *inverts* (who had 'inverted' their gender) rather than *homosexuals* in technical language." In general, Chauncey argues, "one had an identity based on one's gender rather than on one's 'sexuality,' which was not regarded as a distinct domain of personhood but as a pattern of practices and desires that followed inevitably from one's masculinity or femininity."

291. Besnier 1994.

292. For other perspectives on Phaedrus' poem, see Hallett 1989 and Brooten 1996: 41–50. For the language of "softness" (*mollitia*) and men, see chapter 4. The word *tribas* is apparently derived from the Greek verb *tribein* ("to rub"): see Brooten 1996: 4–8 for a thorough discussion.

293. See Schrijvers 1985, Halperin 1990: 22–4, and Brooten 1996: 146–62 for more detailed discussions of this text.

294. I here reproduce the text offered by Schrijvers 1985 in his commentary, with one exception: instead of *timentes* he prints the manuscript variant *tumentes*.

295. Cf. Schrijvers 1985: 28: "Die Gedankengang scheint sich folgendermassen weiterzuentwickeln: beim Zuschaustellen typisch-männlicher Verhaltensweisen können sie kein Mass halten und durch ein Übermass (der *cupiditas* oder der Überkompensation) hingerissen (*nimietate sublati*), verstricken sie sich in ihren heterosexuellen Aktivitäten in noch grössere Untaten (Ehebruch, Unzucht/Hurerei mit Frauen)."

296. See Schrijvers 1985: 32–3 and Brooten 1996: 151, 157 with n. 43.

297. Cael. *Morb. acut.* 3.18.180–1, noted by Schrijvers 1985: 7–8, followed by Halperin 1990: 22–3, and Brooten 1996: 148 with n. 15. Schrijvers' title ("Eine medizinische Erklärung der männlichen Homosexualität aus der Antike") is thus quite inaccurate.

298. Brooten 1996: 148, 151. And yet Brooten occasionally uses the language of "homoeroticism" (e.g., 156: "one major area of debate regarding homoerotic sexual behavior was and continues to be its origins"). Moreover, citing Caelius' reference to boys who are afflicted with the desire to be penetrated (*hac passione iactari*), Brooten argues (against Halperin 1990) that in Caelius' terms "there exists no same-sex encounter in which both partners are disease-free, which means that the same-sex factor is an important classificatory principle." But Caelius finds disease only in a male's *desire* (*passio*) to be penetrated. He does not address penetrative same-sex encounters in which the receptive partner does not actually desire to be penetrated (not an unheard-of occurrence, especially in a slave-owning society). In fact, by Caelius' standards, a situation in which a master penetrated his

male slave who derived no pleasure from the act but who was merely doing what he was told would be entirely "disease-free."

299. Following Schrijvers 1985, I offer here the text of Drabkin; the crucial phrase "nunc faciendo nunc patiendo" is in fact a scholarly conjecture for manuscript readings that make no sense.

300. Mart. 1.41.13 (*vetulus cinaedus*); Apul. *Met*. 8.24: "scitote qualem: cinaedum et senem cinaedum, calvum quidem sed cincinnis semicanis et pendulis capillatum"; ibid. 8.26: "'puellae, servum vobis pulchellum en ecce mercata perduxi." sed illae puellae chorus erat cinaedorum . . .'"

301. Sen. *Epist*. 95.20–1: "non minus pervigilant, non minus potant, et oleo et mero viros provocant, aeque invitis ingesta visceribus per os reddunt et vinum omne vomitu remetiuntur, aeque nivem rodunt, solacium stomachi aestuantis. libidine vero ne maribus quidem cedunt: pati natae (di illas deaeque male perdant!) adeo perversum commentae genus impudicitiae viros ineunt." Edwards 1993: 88 euphemistically translates "viros ineunt" as "when they are with men they play the man's part"; more strangely, Robert 1997: 270 takes the passage to be an allusion to cunnilinctus. The verb *inire* bluntly refers to penetration (cf. Suet. *Aug*. 69.2: "reginam ineo"; "tu deinde solam Drusillam inis?").

302. Mart. 7.67.1–3: "pedicat pueros tribas Philaenis / et tentigine saevior mariti / undenas dolat in die puellas."

303. I thank Randolph Trumbach for drawing my attention to this question.

304. These scenarios remind us of the inadequacy of any system of pigeonholing human sexual desires and experiences: How would such men (whom Romans might call *molles* or *impudici*) be labeled today? Unorthodox, even "queer," in their desires, they nonetheless would not be called homosexual. Their practices are heterosexual, but do they really belong in the same category as men dedicated to playing the insertive role with women, preferably their wives, in the missionary position? (Cf. Halperin 1990: 44: "Is a gay woman into S/M more like a gay woman who is not or a straight woman who is?")

305. Halperin 1990: 24 makes precisely this point in his discussion of Caelius Aurelianus.

306. Gellius obviously translates the story in the expectation that the joke will make sense to his Roman audience; the anecdote does not read like an example of "foreign humor."

307. Gell. 3.5.1–2: "Plutarchus refert Arcesilaum philosophum vehementi verbo usum esse de quodam nimis delicato divite, qui incorruptus tamen et a stupro integer dicebatur. nam cum vocem eius infractam capillumque arte compositum et oculos ludibundos atque inlecebrae voluptatisque plenos videret, 'nihil interest,' inquit, 'quibus membris cinaedi sitis, posterioribus an prioribus.'"

308. Plut. *Quaest. Conviv*. 705E, *De Tuend. San*. 126A: μοιχικούς and ἀκολάστους. A graffito from Pompeii may also suggest that a man could be called a *cinaedus* even if he played the insertive role with a male partner: "Vesbinus the *cinaedus* butt-fucked Vitalius" ("Vesbinus cinaedus Vitalio(m) pedicavit," *CIL* 4.2319). Of course we have no way of knowing who wrote the graffito or why, but the possibilities are intriguing. Was it Vesbinus, trying to counter rumors about himself (Vesbinus, though called a *cinaedus*, actually penetrated Vitalius)? Was it a third party, trying to denigrate Vitalius as being so unmanly as to be penetrated even by a *cinaedus* (a possibility suggested to me by Ralph Hexter)? Taylor 1997: 351–7, observing that "whether this is a boast or a taunt is impossible to tell, but it does apparently place the *cinaedus* in the active role," cites this graffito as evidence for "an acknowledgement (though not acceptance) of reciprocal roles in homosexual relationships as a Roman subculture of homosexuality became well established." This seems to me to stretch the evidence; see my arguments later in this chapter against the notion of a "Roman subculture of homosexuality." Varone 1994: 126 understands *Vesbinus cinaedus* as a nomi-

native functioning as a vocative, and *Vitalio* as a third-declension nominative: "Vesbino cinedo, Vitalione ti ha sodomizzato."

309. Scipio fr. 17 (Gell. 6.12.5).

310. Plut. *Pomp.* 48.7; cf. Dio 39.19.1, where the questions are summarized thus: τίς ὁ ποιῶν ἢ καὶ λέγων τοιόνδε τι ἦν.

311. Quoted at Sen. *Contr.* 7.4.7: "digito caput uno / scalpit. quid credas hunc sibi velle? virum." For the gesture of scratching the head with one finger, see the discussion of "subculture" later in this chapter.

312. Ov. *Ars* 1.524: "si quis male vir quaerit habere virum."

313. Juv. 2.129: "traditur ecce viro clarus genere atque opibus vir."

314. Richlin 1993 (e.g., 544: "The homophobia of this poem [Juvenal 2] is undeniable").

315. Indeed, the open interest displayed by *cinaedi* in penises as penetrative instruments is one telling sign of their anomalous nature. Cf. *Priap.* 25.5, 64.1–2 ("quidam mollior anseris medullae / furatum venit huc amore poenae"); Mart. 1.96, 6.16, 6.37.

316. Thus in the pointed question directed against Pompey (τίς ἀνὴρ ἄνδρα ζητεῖ;) the anomaly lies not in the sameness of the sex of the two parties involved (note the somewhat tendentious addition of "another" into Richlin's translation of the question as "Who is the man who seeks another man?" [Richlin 1993: 523] and into Edwards' as "Who is the man who runs after other men?" [Edwards 1993: 85]) but rather in the fact that the one who is the subject of desire for a "man" is biologically male (τίς ἀνήρ). Cf. Juv. 2.129 ("traditur ecce viro clarus genere atque opibus vir") with Braund ad loc.: "The shocking effect of *viro . . . vir* is fuelled by postponement of *vir* to the end and the disruptive impact of the single final monosyllable." The emphasis is not on the combination of subject and object but on their hierarchical, even grammatical, relationship. In the case of Pompey, for example, the question τίς ἀνὴρ παῖδα ζητεῖ; ("Who is the man who is looking for a boy?") would not have been an effective weapon.

317. So, too, Seneca has this question to ask concerning a man who refuses to assume his masculine identity as penetrator: "Will he never be a *vir*, so that he can submit to a *vir* for a long time?" (Sen. *Epist.* 122.7: "numquam vir erit, ut diu virum pati possit?"). This question derives its pointedness from the normative paradigm of non-*vir* submitting to *vir*.

318. I thank David Halperin for helping me formulate this point.

319. This might seem hair-splitting or special pleading; but it is, I hope, neither. At the very least I would say that to speak of *homophobia* in Roman culture creates more problems than it solves. The qualifications that Richlin makes when laying down her introductory arguments reflect, it seems to me, the unavoidable conceptual difficulties entailed by speaking of homosexuals and homophobia in antiquity. In the space of one page we read the following: "it ['homosexual'] is *partly* adequate to describe the adult male who preferred to be penetrated"; "there was a concept of sexual deviance in Roman culture, which was not homologous with the modern concept 'homosexuality' but partook of *some* of the same homophobic overtones our nineteenth-century coinage owns"; "mainstream Roman culture was severely homophobic, *at least* where passives were concerned"; "legal restrictions on *some* male-male sexual activities"; "a social identity and a social burden *much like* the one that Foucault defined for the modern term 'homosexual'" (Richlin 1993: 530, emphases added).

320. Cf. Edwards 1993: 66: "There is little to suggest that Romans ever saw people with exclusively homosexual preferences as a distinct social group."

321. As discussed earlier in this chapter, the terms *pedico* and *pedicator* could be used to designate men who anally penetrated *cinaedi*, boys, or women indifferently.

322. Cf. Halperin 1990: 15–40 for extensive arguments along the same lines for classical Greece, and Herdt 1993: xiii–xiv for Melanesia.

323. Richlin 1993: 541. Cf. ibid.: "though largely hostile, the extant sources give tantalizing hints that Roman culture may have included a subculture that substituted norms associated with passive homosexuality for the norms of the mainstream culture."

324. Clarke 1993: 289; he repeats the argument at Clarke 1998: 83.

325. Taylor 1997: 320.

326. Chauncey 1994: 43.

327. Trumbach 1989: 136.

328. See, e.g., Richard K. Herrell, "The Symbolic Strategies of Chicago's Gay and Lesbian Pride Day Parade," in Gilbert Herdt, ed., *Gay Culture in America: Essays from the Field* (Boston, 1992), p. 248: "The difference between the gay and other American 'subcultural' communities is that, for gays and lesbians, the experience of community derives, not from parents and peers during childhood, but from adult participation in a network of institutions and from shared responses to the pervasive denial of social personality itself"; Carol A. B. Warren, "Homosexuality and Stigma," in Judd Marmor, ed., *Homosexual Behavior: A Modern Reappraisal* (New York, 1980), p. 139: "The single most important factor about homosexuality as it exists in this culture is the perceived hostility of the societal reactions that surround it. From this one critical factor flow many of the features that are distinctive about homosexuality. It renders the business of becoming a homosexual a process that is characterized by problems of access, problems of guilt, and problems of identity. It leads to the emergence of a subculture of homosexuality."

329. See, e.g., Weeks 1989: 202–4; Trumbach 1989: 135–40; and the bibliographical survey at Rocke 1996: 301 n. 4.

330. Trumbach 1989: 136.

331. Weeks 1989: 202.

332. Chauncey 1994: 41–5.

333. Juv. 9.130–3 (*pathici* flocking to Rome in droves); Martial 6.50, 9.63 (poor men improve their lot in life by courting, and sexually servicing, wealthy *cinaedi* who invite them to dinner); Petr. *Sat.* 21–3 (the *cinaedus* at Quartilla's party); Phdr. *App.* 10.1 (the man in Pompey's army reputed to be a *cinaedus*).

334. Plut. *Sert.* 26.

335. Rocke 1996: 191; cf. ibid. 15, 26–7, 149–51.

336. Cf. Edwards 1993: 71: speaking of legal restrictions on men who were penetrated (discussed earlier in this chapter), she points out that "they do not necessarily mean men who enjoyed being penetrated were any more of a social group than, for instance, adulteresses." The case of slaves and prostitutes is different, since they constituted classes of persons that were in general quite clearly defined, and marginalized, by society at large. See Rocke 1996: 302 n. 7 for bibliography on the "important distinction between networks of shared activities and subculture as a source of collective and personal identity."

337. Taylor 1997: 341.

338. Taylor 1997: 357 n. 131.

339. Ov. *Ars* 1.89–134.

340. *Coll. leg. Mos. et Rom.* 5.3; see Cantarella 1992: 177–80.

341. Petr. *Sat.* 7.3–4 (Encolpius' narrative of his arrival at the brothel): "cum ego negarem me agnoscere domum, video quasdam inter titulos nudas meretrices furtim spatiantes. tarde, immo iam sero intellexi me in fornicem esse deductum . . ."); 8.3–4 (Ascyltus' description of what happened to him): "per anfractus deinde obscurissimos egressus in hunc locum me perduxit prolatoque pecunio coepit rogare stuprum. iam pro cella meretrix assem exegerat, iam ille mihi iniecerat manum, et nisi valentior fuissem, dedissem poenas."

342. Clarke 1991 argues that a private home in Ostia decorated with an image of

Ganymede was converted in the first century A.D. into a "gay hotel for wealthy patrons" interested in meeting male partners (the quotation is from p. 101; cf. ibid., "a hotel for homosexual men"). But at Clarke 1998: 88 he acknowledges that "the very notion of a 'gay hotel' is, I now realize, naively anachronistic." Taylor argues that "the evidence of Petronius and other sources further suggests that brothels and wharves were fairly comfortable environments for homosexual fraternizing and soliciting," yet he also observes that the House of Jupiter and Ganymede in Ostia "seems to have been a brothel specializing in same-sex services to males, but some women left their names on the walls as well" (Taylor 1997: 341 n. 68). One can just as well say that the establishment in Ostia, like the one imagined in Petronius, provided a "fairly comfortable environment for heterosexual fraternizing and soliciting."

343. Richlin 1993: 543: "This culture can only be described as passive homosexual rather than 'gay,' since Juvenal 2 is devoted strictly to accounts of adult males who allow themselves to be penetrated by other males." The title of Taylor 1997 speaks of "pathic subcultures in ancient Rome."

344. Juv. 2.45-7: "sed illos / defendit numerus iunctaeque umbone phalanges. / magna inter molles concordia"; 2.78-81; 2.83-116. Of course, as Ralph Hexter reminds me, satiric hyperbole must be taken into account here: Laronia, and the satiric persona himself, may well be stretching the truth as a scare tactic ("they are everywhere").

345. Richlin 1993: 541-3. As she observes, Maecenas "is also a prime example of a *mollis* man notorious for heterosexual exploits" (542 n. 45).

346. Cic. *Cat.* 2.22-3.

347. Lucil. 883 Marx; Sen. *Epist.* 52.12; Juv. 9.133; Licinius Calvus *FPL* 18 Morel (*apud* Sen. *Contr.* 7.4.7); Plut. *Pomp.* 48.7, *Jul.* 4.9; Lucian, *Rhetoron Didaskalos* 11.

348. Taylor 1997: 339. Cf. Richlin 1993: 542-3: "It seems at least possible that some of these characteristics . . . formed part of a self-presentation used for sexual signals and group cohesion."

349. So too Herter 1959: 632: "Die Frisur war so künstlich, daß man sich nur mit einem Finger kratzen konnte." See also Edwards 1993: 63 and Corbeill 1997: 121.

350. Plut. *Jul.* 4.9: ἀλλ' ὅταν ἔφη τὴν κόμην οὕτω διακειμένην περιττῶς ἴδω, κἀκεῖνον ἑνὶ δακτύλῳ κνώμενον, οὔ μοι δοκεῖ πάλιν οὗτος ἄνθρωπος εἰς νοῦν ἄν ἐμβαλέσθαι τηλικοῦτον κακόν, ἀναίρεσιν τῆς Ῥωμαίων πολιτείας.

351. Taylor 1997: 327-8, citing Williams 1992.

352. See Williams 1992: 321-67 for some preliminary discussion; see also Boswell 1994: 75-80 and Ellen Oliensis, "The Erotics of *amicitia*: Readings in Tibullus, Propertius, and Horace," in Hallett and Skinner 1997: 151-71.

353. Taylor 1997: 328. For this usage of *frater* and *soror*, see Williams 1992: 332-67 (where I try to place it in the context of more general overlaps between concepts of brotherly love, love between male friends [*amici*], and love between sexual partners) and Boswell 1994: 67-71. Taylor 1997: 330 interprets [Vir.] *Cat.* 13 (discussed earlier in this chapter and in chapter 4) as evidence for "an urban subculture of sailors and *fratres*." But he may be mistranslating "olentis nauticum" (23)—literally "those who stink of things pertaining to ships," in Taylor's version "men reeking sailor-stench"—and it is not certain in any case that the poem imagines these men to be sexually involved with the *cinaedus*. Nor need Luccius' "idle brothers" (*ignavos fratres*, 37-8) be his "male lovers" (Taylor 1997: 330)—they could be his biological brothers, or indeed his brothers and sisters (as Westendorp Boerma 1963: 91 reminds us). After all, the poem opens with insulting references to Luccius' sister ("prostitutae sororis," 7-8) and brother ("et helluato sera patrimonio / in fratre parsimonia," 11-2), and, in view of the solid tradition in invective of insinuating both incest and the consumption of one's inheritance, these are most naturally interpreted as his biological siblings.

354. Mart. 2.4 (cf. 10.65, 10.89, 12.20); [Tibull.] 3.1.23–8.
355. Taylor 1997: 337.

Conclusions

1. As for the intermediate category of former slaves (*libertini*), a man could generally get away with making sexual use of his own freedmen or freedwomen, but other men's ex-slaves, since they were now of free status, were protected by the same traditions that pertained to the freeborn.

2. When ancient writers moralize about such couplings, they tend to be quite negative in tone—negative, that is, with regard to the man's partner, who is represented either as a whore (as in Cicero's vicious depiction of Clodia but indulgent approach to the young Caelius: see chapter 1) or as an effeminate *cinaedus* (as in Juvenal's savage attacks on aristocratic male brides, but not their husbands: see Appendix 2).

3. I thank Randolph Trumbach for directing my attention to the latter question.

Appendix 1

1. Important discussions include Boswell 1980: 11–5, 49–50, 119–66; Foucault 1986: 150–7, 189–227; and Winkler 1990: 20–1, 36–7, 114–8.

2. Boswell 1980: 129, 149. Cf. ibid. 15: "The objection that homosexuality is 'unnatural' appears, in short, to be neither scientifically nor morally cogent and probably represents nothing more than a derogatory epithet of unusual emotional impact due to a confluence of historically sanctioned prejudiced and ill-formed ideas about 'nature.'"

3. Winkler 1990: 20.

4. For this important distinction between the morality espoused by philosophers and what we might call *popular morality*, see the introduction and chapter 1.

5. Richlin 1993: 533 n. 25.

6. In other words, I would like to go a step or two beyond the observation that "'nature' is generally used by Roman moralists to justify what they approve of" (Edwards 1993: 88 n. 87).

7. See, for example, Boswell 1980: 137–43, 152–6, and Winkler 1990: 23 (on Philo's description of crocodiles mating).

8. Such an argument does occasionally appear in Greek texts, such as Plato, *Laws* 836c(μάρτυρα παραγόμενος τὴν τῶν θηρίων φύσιν καὶ δεικνὺς πρὸς τὰ τοιαῦτα οὐχ ἁπτόμενον ἄρρενα ἄρρενος διὰ τὸ μὴ φύσει τοῦτο εἶναι) and [Lucian], *Amores* 36. To be sure, Musonius Rufus' condemnation of sexual practices between males as παρὰ φύσιν (see below) might imply a reference to animal practices, and it is possible that in some work now lost to us the Roman Stoic followed in Plato's footsteps in being explicit on the point.

9. This is obvious to anyone who has spent time with dogs. With regard to the academic study of the question, the remarks of Linda D. Wolfe, "Evolution and Female Primate Sexual Behavior," in James D. Loy and Calvin Peters, eds., *Understanding Behavior: What Primate Studies Tell Us about Human Behavior* (New York and Oxford, 1991), p. 130, are as illuminating as they are depressing: "I have talked with several (anonymous at their request) primatologists who have told me that they have observed both male and female homosexual behavior during field studies. They seemed reluctant to publish their data, however, either because they feared homophobic reactions ('my colleagues might think that I am gay') or because they lack a framework for analysis ('I don't know what it means')." On the latter point, Wolfe insightfully comments that the same problem affects our attempts to understand *any* sexual interactions among primates: "Because the

alloprimates do not possess language, it is impossible to inquire into their sexual eroticism. In other words, homosexual and heterosexual behaviors can be observed, recorded, and analyzed, but we cannot infer either homoeroticism or heteroeroticism from such behaviors" (p. 131).

10. An epigram by the Greek poet Strato gives the latter point an interesting twist. We human beings, he writes, are superior to animals in that, in addition to vaginal intercourse, we have discovered anal intercourse; thus men who are dominated by women are really no better than mere animals (*A.P.* 12.245: Πᾶν ἄλογον ζῷον βινεῖ μόνον – οἱ λογικοὶ δὲ / τῶν ἄλλων ζῴων τοῦτ᾽ ἔχομεν τὸ πλέον, / πυγίζειν εὑρόντες. ὅσοι δὲ γυναιξὶ κρατοῦνται, / τῶν ἀλόγων ζῴων οὐδὲν ἔχουσι πλέον.)

11. Ov. *Met.* 10.83–5: "ille [sc., Orpheus] etiam Thracum populis fuit auctor amorem / in teneros transferre mares citraque iuventam / aetatis breve ver et primos carpere flores." The stories that Orpheus proceeds to relate include those of the young Cyparissus, once loved by Apollo (*Met.* 10.106–42), and the tales of Zeus and Ganymede, Apollo and Hyacinth (*Met.* 10.155–219). Consider also the beautiful sixteen-year-old Indian boy Athis and his Assyrian lover Lycabas (*Met.* 5.47–73; a passage with echoes of Virgil's lines on Nisus and Euryalus, discussed in chapter 2); and the remark that the stunning but haughty young Narcissus, also in his sixteenth year, had many admirers of both sexes (*Met.* 3.351–5).

12. Gell. 6.8.3: "neque hi amaverunt quod sunt ipsi genus, sed pueros forma liberali in naviculis forte aut in vadis litorum conspectos miris et humanis modis arserunt." Cf. Athen. 13.606C-D and Plin. *N.H.* 8.25–8 for this and other tales of male dolphins falling in love with human boys.

13. Plin. *N.H.* 8.1: "maximum est elephans proximumque humanis sensibus, quippe intellectus illis sermonis patrii et imperiorum obedientia, officiorum quae didicere memoria, amoris et gloriae voluptas . . ."; 8.13–4: "nec quia desit illis amoris vis, namque traditur unus amasse quandam in Aegypto corollas vendentem . . . alius Menandrum Syracusanum incipientis iuventae in exercitu Ptolemaei, desiderium eius, quotiens non videret, inedia testatus"; 10.51: "quin et fama amoris Aegii dilecta forma pueri nomine Olenii Amphilochi, et Glauces Ptolemaeo regi cithara canentis quam eodem tempore et aries amasse proditur."

14. Foucault 1986: 215–6. See also the discussions in Boswell 1980: 11–5 (where he distinguishes between "realistic" and "ideal" notions of nature), Beagon 1992, and Carlos Levy, ed., *Le concept de nature à Rome: La physique* (Paris, 1996).

15. Anon. *De Differentiis* 520.23 ("monstrum est contra naturam, ut est Minotaurus"); Serv. *Aen.* 6.286 (centaurs); Suet. *Prata* fr. 176.113–5 (snakes with feet, birds with four wings); Serv. *Aen.* 1.235.11 (Pasiphae and the bull).

16. Plin. *N.H.* 7.45–6: "in pedes procidere nascentem contra naturam est"; "ritus naturae capite hominem gigni, mos est pedibus efferri."

17. Quint. *I.O.* 11.3.160: "capillos a fronte contra naturam retro agere."

18. Sen. *Epist.* 55.1: "labor est enim et diu ferri, ac nescio an eo maior quia contra naturam est, quae pedes dedit ut per nos ambularemus."

19. Celsus, *Medic.* 3.21.15 (on fluids that are retained in the body *contra naturam*); Cic. *Off.* 3.30 (*morbus* is *contra naturam*); Gell. 4.2.3 (Labeo defines *morbus* as "habitus cuiusque corporis contra naturam, qui usum eius facit deteriorem"; cf. D. 21.1.1.7); D. 42.1.60.pr. ("motus corporis contra naturam, quem febrem appellant"); Quint. *Decl. Min.* 298.12 (weak and malformed bodies are implicitly *contra naturam*).

20. Quint. *Decl. Min.* 246.3 (the plaintiff refers to a substance as a *venenum* "quoniam medicamentum sit et efficiat aliquid contra naturam"); Sen. *Epist.* 5.4 (to torment one's own body and to eat unhealthy food is *contra naturam*).

21. Winkler 1990: 17. In the same way Edwards 1993: 87–8 discusses a passage from Seneca (*Epist.* 95.20–1) discussed in chapter 5, having to do with women who violate their

"nature." She concludes that "Seneca was not reacting to naturally anomalous behaviour. He was taking part in the reproduction of a cultural system." So, too, Veyne 1985: 26: "When an ancient says that something is unnatural, he does not mean that it is disgraceful [*monstrueuse*], but that it does not conform with the rules of society, or that it is perverted or artificial."

22. Serv. *Comm. Art. Don.* 444: "Plinius autem dicit barbarismum esse sermonem unum, in quo vis sua est contra naturam"; Serv. *Aen.* 4.427: "'revelli' non 'revulsi': nam 'velli' et 'revelli' dicimus; 'vulsus' vero et 'revulsus' usurpatum est tantum in participiis contra naturam"; cf. Sen. *Contr.* 10.pr.9 (of the rhetorician Musa): "omnia usque ad ultimum tumorem perducta, ut non extra sanitatem sed extra naturam essent."

23. D. 41.2.3.5: "contra naturam quippe est, ut, cum ego aliquid teneam, tu quoque id tenere videaris." Interestingly, another jurist argues that the principle underlying the institution of slavery—that one person can be owned by another—is actually "unnatural" (D. 1.5.4.1: "servitus est constitutio iuris gentium, qua quis dominio alieno contra naturam subicitur"). In a Horatian satire we read that *natura* sees to it that no one is ever truly the "master" of the land that he legally owns, and *natura* puts a limit on how much one can inherit (Hor. *Sat.* 2.2.129–30, 2.3.178).

24. Sall. *Cat.* 2.8: "quibus profecto contra naturam corpus voluptati, anima oneri fuit."

25. Cic. *Fin.* 5.35: "corporis igitur nostri partes totaque figura et forma et statura quam apta ad naturam sit apparet . . ."

26. Similar condemnations of inappropriate bodily comportment, marked as effeminate, abound: walking daintily, scratching the hair delicately with one finger, and so on (see chapter 4 in general, and see Gleason 1995 for a general discussion of physiognomy and masculinity in antiquity).

27. Taylor 1997: 325.

28. This is indeed the way Pliny uses the phrase elsewhere, noting that we ought to call earthquakes "miracles of the earth rather than crimes of nature" (*N.H.* 2.206: "ut terrae miracula potius dicamus quam scelera naturae"); see Beagon 1992: 49. In other words (*pace* Taylor 1997 and H. Rackham's 1940 LCL translation), I take the genitive *naturae* to be subjective rather than objective; I have not found any parallels for such an objective use of a genitive noun dependent upon *scelus*.

29. Plin. *N.H.* 8.13–4, 10.51.

30. Juv. 2.139–40: "sed melius, quod nil animis in corpora iuris / natura indulget: steriles moriuntur . . ." For further discussion, see Appendix 2.

31. Sen. *Contr.* 10.4.17: "principes . . . viri contra naturam divitias suas exercent: castratorum greges habent, exoletos suos ut ad longiorem patientiam impudicitiae idonei sint amputant."

32. Cael. Aurel. *Morb. Chron.* 4.9.137: "naturalia veneris officia."

33. Hor. *Sat.* 1.2.111: "nonne cupidinibus statuat natura modum quem . . ." (see chapter 1 for further discussion of this poem); cf. *Sat.* 1.4.113–4: "ne sequerer moechas concessa cum venere uti / possem."

34. Sen. *Epist.* 122.2: "sunt qui officia lucis noctisque perverterint nec ante diducant oculos hesterna graves crapula quam adpetere nox coepit. . . ."

35. Comparing them to the Antipodes, mythical beings who live on the opposite side of the globe, he asks, "Do you think these people know *how* to live when they don't even know *when* to live?" (122.3: "hos tu existimas scire quemadmodum vivendum sit, qui nesciunt quando?").

36. Sen. *Epist.* 122.6: "non videntur tibi contra naturam vivere <qui> ieiuni bibunt, qui vinum recipiunt inanibus venis et ad cibum ebrii transeunt?"

37. Sen. *Epist.* 122.6: "atqui frequens hoc adulescentium vitium est, qui vires excolunt

<ut> in ipso paene balinei limine inter nudos bibant, immo potent et sudorem quem moverunt potionibus crebris ac ferventibus subinde destringant. post prandium aut cenam bibere vulgare est; hoc patres familiae rustici faciunt et verae voluptatis ignari."

38. Cf. Boswell 1980: 29, 81.

39. Cf. Winkler 1990: 21: "'Contrary to nature' means to Seneca not 'outside the order of the kosmos' but 'unwilling to conform to the simplicity of the unadorned life' and, in the case of sex, 'going AWOL from one's assigned place in the social hierarchy.'"

40. Sen. *Epist.* 122.8: "non vivunt contra naturam qui fundamenta thermarum in mari iaciunt et delicate natare ipsi sibi non videntur nisi calentia stagna fluctu ac tempestate feriantur?"

41. Sen. *Epist.* 122.9: "cum instituerunt omnia contra naturae consuetudinem velle, novissime in totum ab illa desciscunt. 'lucet: somni tempus est. quies est: nunc exerceamur, nunc gestemur, nunc prandeamus.'"

42. Foucault 1986: 170.

43. Cic. *Tusc.* 4.71: "atque, ut muliebris amores omittam, quibus maiorem licentiam natura concessit, quis aut de Ganymedi raptu dubitat, quid poetae velint, aut non intellegit, quid apud Euripidem et loquatur et cupiat Laius?"

44. I thank Gordon Williams for helping me to formulate this point.

45. Cic. *Tusc.* 4.76: "If love were natural, everyone would love, they would always love, and would love the same thing; one person would not be deterred [from loving] by a sense of shame, another by rational thought, another by his satiety" ("etenim si naturalis amor esset, et amarent omnes et semper amarent et idem amarent, neque alium pudor, alium cogitatio, alium satietas deterreret").

46. Similarly the passage from Phaedrus' *Fables* (4.16) discussed in chapter 5 implies, without actually using the word *natura*, that males who desire to be penetrated (*molles mares*) and females who desire to penetrate (*tribades*) have a flawed design: when Prometheus was assembling these people's bodies from clay, he attached the genital organs of the opposite sex in a drunken slip-up. But this more popularizing account only specifies that those males who *desire* to be penetrated are anomalous; it does not designate those men who seek to penetrate other males as unnatural. On this model, a sexual act in which a master penetrated his unwilling male slave was not unnatural; by contrast, according the philosophers discussed here (Musonius most explicitly) this act would be unnatural.

47. Note the logical contradiction that this playful invocation of nature creates: if the penis was designed by nature for girls and the anus for men, how can a man use a boy's anus in the way nature intended (i.e., to be penetrated by men) and at the same time use his own penis in the way nature intended (i.e., by penetrating a girl)? See chapters 1 and 5 for further discussion of this epigram together with Martial's humorous invocation of the paradigm of nature with regard to masturbation (9.41).

48. Cf. Boswell 1980: 149: "Lucretius' *De rerum natura* dealt with the whole of 'nature,' but it was the 'rerum'—'of things'—which suggested to Latin readers what modern speakers mean by 'nature.'"

49. Winkler 1990: 21.

50. As Ralph Hexter reminds me, Cicero proposes many different rhetorical and philosophical positions in his speeches, letters, and dialogues, and Seneca's epistles to Lucilius offer a tentative and experimental mixture of Stoicism and other philosophical schools (many of his earlier letters end with quotations from Epicurus, for example). In any case, Boswell 1980: 130, citing ancient sources claiming that the very founder of Stoicism, Zeno, engaged in sexual practices with males (perhaps even exclusively), notes that many ancient Stoics actually seem to have considered the question of sexual practices between males to be ethically neutral.

51. Dio 61.10.4: τὰς τε ἀσελγείας, ἃς πράττων γάμον τε ἐπιφανέστατον ἔγημε καὶ μειρακίοις ἐξώροις ἔχαιρε, καὶ τοῦτο καὶ τὸν Νέρωνα ποιεῖν ἐδίδαξε. The historian goes on to insinuate that Seneca fellated his partners, speculating on the reason why he refused to kiss Nero: one might imagine, Dio notes, that this was because he was disgusted by Nero's penchant for oral sex, but that makes no sense given Seneca's own relations with his boyfriends (61.10.5: ὃ γάρ τοι μόνον ἄν τις ὑποπτεύσειεν, ὅτι οὐκ ἤθελε τοιοῦτο στόμα φιλεῖν, ἐλέγχεται ἐκ τῶν παιδικῶν αὐτοῦ ψεῦδος ὄν).

52. Plin. *Epist.* 7.4.

53. For Cicero and Tiro, see McDermott 1972 and Richlin 1992a: 34, 223. Cantarella 1992: 97, 103 assumes that they actually enjoyed a sexual relationship.

Appendix 2

1. The *stola* was the characteristic garment of the Roman matron. There is no way of precisely converting this slur into contemporary English, although "as if he had given you a ring" comes close.

2. While the phrase *tamquam stolam dedisset* makes it clear that a *stola* was not in fact given, the indicative main verb *conlocavit* might be taken to mean that the marriage is represented as actually having taken place (cf. Boswell 1980: 82: "Cicero regarded the younger Curio's relationship with another man as a marriage"). I would argue instead that the *tamquam* colors the whole sentence: Cicero's rhetoric would not have us believe that Antony and Curio literally entered into a *matrimonium*. Boswell is harshly criticized on this point by MacMullen 1982: 496 n. 43; Richlin 1992a: 221 is more temperate. Boswell 1994: 80 acknowledges Cicero's sarcasm, but still considers as "open to speculation" the possibility that Cicero "felt that there was some de facto comparability between this sort of same-sex relationship and established heterosexual unions."

3. Suet. *Nero* 28–9; Tac. *Ann.* 15.37; Dio 62.28, 63.13, 63.22; Aurel. Vict. *Caes.* 5.5.

4. SHA *Elagab.* 10.5, 11.7; Dio 79.5, 14–6; cf. the discussion at Boswell 1994: 83–5.

5. *Codex Theodosianus* 9.7.3 (a *constitutio* of the emperors Constantius and Constans from the year 342): "cum vir nubit in feminam, femina viros proiectura quid cupiat, ubi sexus perdidit locum, ubi scelus est id, quod non proficit scire, ubi Venus mutatur in alteram formam, ubi amor quaeritur nec videtur, iubemus insurgere leges, armari iura gladio ultore, ut exquisitis poenis subdantur infames, qui sunt vel qui futuri sint rei." (I here provide the text of Mommsen [Berlin, 1905]; see discussions in Dalla 1987: 167–70, Cantarella 1992: 175–6, Boswell 1994: 85–7.) The phrase following *cum vir nubit in feminam* is very difficult to construe and has been interpreted in various ways. Cantarella punctuates with a question mark after *cupiat*, and translates: "When a man couples [literally 'marries'] as though he were a woman, what can a woman desire who offers herself to men?" ("Quando un uomo si accoppia [letteralmente, 'sposa'] come se fosse una donna, una donne che si offre agli uomini che cosa può desiderare?") But *viros proiectura* cannot mean "who offers herself to men," and must be something like "who will abandon men" (cf. *OLD* s.v. 8). Thus Dalla translates "Quando un uomo si sposa a mo' di femmina, la 'donna' che sta per abbandonare gli uomini cosa può desiderare . . ." He thus understands the second *femina* to refer metaphorically to the feminized man, who will "abandon men" (i.e., I assume, give up his identity as a man); this seems the only way to understand the text as printed above. An alternative reading to *femina viros proiectura* is *viris porrecturam* (omitting the *femina*). Adopting this reading, a translation published by the Department of Classics of Vanderbilt University (2nd ed., 1947) renders the opening phrase thus: "When a man marries in the manner of a woman with the purpose of offering himself to men, what does he wish, when sex has lost its significance . . . ?" Boswell 1994: 85–6 accepts this reading and translates,

"When a man marries [a man] as if he were a woman [literally, 'as a woman offering herself to men'], what can he be seeking, where gender has lost its place?" But I do not see how *viris porrecturam* can have the reflexive sense "offering herself to men." Gordon Williams has suggested to me the emendation *viro porrecturam quod cupiat* ("When a man marries in the manner of a woman who is going to offer a man what he desires . . ."), a brilliant solution to the problem.

6. So Dalla 1987: 169–70 ("questa è clausola per indicare chi si sottomette in un rapporto omosessuale, non per evidenziare un reale rapporto matrimoniale, che il diritto romano non ha mai preso in considerazione"), Cantarella 1992: 175–6, and apparently also Treggiari 1991: 281 (where the *constitutio* is said to have established the death penalty for "homosexuality"). Cantarella claims that the metaphorical use of the verb *nubere* to refer to "the behaviour of a man who takes up a sexually passive role" is "frequent," but cites Martial 1.24 (which surely imagines an actual wedding between males—"evidence of which," Cantarella herself notes, "does survive in the sources") and, oddly, Mart. 8.12, where the speaker notes that he does not want to be financially dependent upon his wife because *uxori nubere nolo meae*. The phrase is ironic—he does not want to be his wife's "wife"—and is not a metaphor for a sexual act. In fact, Adams 1982: 159–61 cites only one example of the use of *nubere* to refer to a sexual act: Plaut. *Cist.* 43–4 ("haec quidem ecastor cottidie viro nubit, nupsitque hodie, / nubet mox noctu: numquam ego hanc viduam cubare sivi"). This refers to a prostitute, and the verb is used for humorous effect (the repetition is notable) in a way that suggests that it is an ad hoc euphemism motivated by the use of the verb in its literal sense in the preceding line ("at satius fuerat eam viro dare nuptum potius"). R. Pichon, *De sermone amatorio apud Latinos elegiarum scriptores* (Paris, 1902), p. 217, understands *nubere* at Catull. 70.1–2 ("nulli se dicit mulier mea nubere malle / quam mihi") metaphorically (glossing "de amore non coniugali"), as does John Kevin Newman, *Roman Catullus and the Modification of the Alexandrian Sensibility* (Hildesheim, 1990), pp. 248–9 (translating "mate with"), but Quinn 1973 more reasonably observes that "the fact that *nubere* occurs in colloquial or euphemistic contexts should not cause us to suppose that C.'s tone is other than sober and serious." Kroll 1959 ad loc. professes uncertainty ("die Tragweite des Wortes ist kaum zu ermitteln, zumal es sich um ein Scherzwort handelt").

7. Cf. the phrase "virile corpus muliebriter constitutum alieni sexus damnare patientia," from a constitution of A.D. 390 quoted at *Coll. leg. Mos. et Rom.* 5.3 and reissued in abbreviated form in A.D. 438 (*Cod. Theod.* 9.7.6).

8. Note the tone of *quid quaeris?* ("Why are you asking?" Juv. 2.134). Boswell 1994: 81 with n. 140 translates, "Nothing special," observing that this indicates that "to Juvenal's disgust, those invited to the ceremony are not in any way fazed by it." Braund 1996 ad loc. similarly observes: "The casualness of the question (no more emphatic than Eng. 'Oh, . . .') suggests that what follows will be run-of-the-mill, ordinary, conventional. What follows is therefore the more shocking."

9. Boswell 1994: 80 n. 135 cites the specificity of the ancient historians' accounts as itself being substantiating evidence.

10. Cf. Treggiari 1991: 1–13; for the phrase *liberorum quaerundorum causa*, see p. 8 with n. 37.

11. See Treggiari 1991: 5–11 for an overview of the Roman language of matrimony. An important point is that instead of a single verb "to marry," of which either the husband or the wife might be the subject, the vocabulary was usually differentiated along the lines of gender: the husband was normally said to "lead" a woman "into matrimony" (*in matrimonium ducere*), while the wife was said to "be veiled [as a bride]" (*nubere*). Treggiari 1991: 251–61, discussing the ideal of *concordia*, offers the hypothesis, by her own admission "controversial" (p. 261 n. 232), that "subordination of the wife . . . was not essential or

important by the time of Cicero." But she is mostly concerned with ideologies of marriage as they related to the emotional relationship between spouses ("conjugal love") rather than with broader issues of power.

12. I thank David Halperin and Ralph Hexter for helping me formulate this point.

13. For this use of *lex* ("term, condition" rather than "law"), see *OLD* s.v. 12 and *TLL* 7.1242.75–1243.69, 1246.33–1247.72; especially apposite are *Priap.* 5.1–2 ("quam puero legem fertur dixisse Priapus, / versibus haec infra scripta duobus erit . . .") and Mart. 11.23.1–2 ("nubere Sila mihi nulla non lege parata est; / sed Silam nulla ducere lege volo"). Boswell (1980: 82 and 1994: 80) takes *lex* to mean "law."

14. See *OLD* s.v. *nubo.* Two exceptions, in which the verb is used of a man who marries a woman, are cited there (Pompon. 88–9 Ribbeck, "frater . . . nupsit . . . dotatae vetulae" and Val. Max. 4.6.ext.3, "dignas fuisse quibus Minyae nuberent"), but in the two epigrams cited here Martial is obviously making a special point by using the verb of males: they are playing the role of the bride. Adams 1982: 160 dilutes the meaning of Mart. 1.24.4, explaining, "presumably 'he had (homosexual) intercourse yesterday.'" He does admit to the possibility that "Martial is thinking of a mock marriage ceremony of the type submitted to by homosexuals," but his notion that men "submitted to" such marriages, the qualification that they were only "mock" marriages, and indeed his use of the term "homosexuals," are all objectionable.

15. Cf. Braund 1996 ad loc.: "Both words [*dotem* and *cornicini*] are postponed for maximum impact . . . It is surprising to learn that Gracchus 'gave a dowry' for this apparently combines the roles of the bride and bride's father; the enjambment of *cornicini* is still more surprising, for trumpeters were generally slaves." Both Braund *ad* 2.118 and Boswell 1994: 81 n. 143 point to the double entendre in the image of the "straight horn," although neither of them openly states the odd implication: that the trumpeter fellates his "bride." Boswell 1994: 81 with n. 144 raises the possibility that the dowry was only four hundred sesterces, but that would be an absurdly small figure for an aristocrat such as Gracchus, who is portrayed as being completely ostentatious in his indulgence in traditionally frowned-upon behaviors; the omission of *milia* in descriptions of amounts of money (sesterces in particular) is quite standard (see *OLD* s.v. *sestertius* 3b).

16. For Juv. 2.129 ("traditur ecce viro clarus genere atque opibus vir"), see chapter 5.

17. For the pun in *concide*, see Adams 1982: 147 (discussing the use of verbs of "striking" and the like to denote penetration): "the double entendre here is from the language of butchering."

18. Dio 79.14.4: γυνή τε καὶ δέσποινα βασιλίς τε ὠνομάζετο; 79.15.1: ὁ δὲ δὴ ἀνὴρ αὐτῆς Ἱεροκλῆς ἦν; 79.16.4: μή με λέγε κύριον – ἐγὼ γὰρ κυρία εἰμί. The writer of the *Historia Augusta* biography states that Elagabalus' husband was Zoticus, not Hierocles; Boswell 1994: 84 n. 155 suggests that the biographer may have confused the two.

19. Henry Furneaux, ed., *The Annals of Tacitus*, 2nd ed. (Oxford, 1907), *ad* Tac. *Ann.* 15.37.10, followed by Howell *ad* Martial 1.24.4, suggest that Suetonius' "Doryphoros" is an error for "Pythagoras," but there is no reason to exclude the possibility that Nero was married (or was thought to have been married) to different grooms on two different occasions. On the other hand, Dio mentions only Pythagoras (62.28.3 and 63.13.2), and an epigram of Martial's (11.6.10) implies that Pythagoras was a fairly well-known servant of Nero: "misce dimidios, puer, trientes, / quales Pythagoras dabat Neroni."

20. For Nero's marriage with Sporos, see Suet. *Nero* 28, Dio 62.28.2–3a, 63.13. The joke is reported at Dio 62.28.3a: "εὖ γε" ἔφη "ποιεῖς, ὦ Καῖσαρ, τοιαύταις συνοικῶν. αἴθε γὰρ ὁ σὸς πατὴρ τὸν αὐτὸν ζῆλον ἔσχεν καὶ τοιαύτη συνῴκησε γαμετῇ," δεικνὺς ὡς εἰ τοῦτο ἐγεγόνει, οὐκ ἂν οὗτος ἐτέχθη καὶ μεγάλων κακῶν ἠλευθεροῦτο ἡ πολιτεία.

Suetonius records the joke without explaining it (*Nero*. 28: "exstatque cuiusdam non inscitus iocus bene agi potuisse cum rebus humanis, si Domitius pater talem habuisset uxorem").

21. Plut. *Galba* 9.3: ἆθλα δὲ αὐτῆς οὐ νομίζων ἱκανὰ καρποῦσθαι τὰς τιμὰς καὶ τὰ χρήματα καὶ τὸ Σπόρῳ τοῦ Νέρωνος συγκαθεύδειν, ὃν εὐθὺς ἀπὸ τῆς πυρᾶς ἔτι καιομένου τοῦ νεκροῦ μεταπεμψάμενος ἐκεῖνος ἐν γαμετῆς εἶχε τάξει καὶ Ποππαίαν προσηγόρευεν, ἐπὶ τὴν διαδοχὴν παρεδύετο τῆς ἡγεμονίας; Dio 64.8.3 (on Otho): τό τε τῷ Σπόρῳ συνεῖναι καὶ τὸ τοῖς λοιποῖς τοῖς Νερωνείοις χρῆσθαι πάνυ πάντας ἐξεφόβει. Dio later reports Sporos' sad fate: Otho's successor Vitellius intended to make Sporos appear in the arena in the form of a maiden who was being raped, but Sporos killed himself before suffering such a disgrace (65.10.1).

22. For the biases against actors pervading the Roman tradition, see chapter 4.

23. MacMullen 1982: 496 n. 43 misleadingly represents this passage as offering evidence "for Nero's relationship with Sporus seen as a cause for revolution."

24. Aurel. Vict. *Caes*. 5.5: "quod sane in eo levius aestimandum." Dio 63.13.2 implies a similar ranking: καὶ τί τοῦτο [sc., that he married Pythagoras and Sporos] θαυμάσειεν ἄν τις, ὁπότε καὶ μειράκια καὶ κόρας σταυροῖς γυμνὰς προσδέων θηρίου τέ τινος δορὰν ἀνελάμβανε καὶ προσπίπτων σφίσιν ἠσέλγαινεν ὥσπερ τι ἐσθίων;

25. Suet. *Nero* 28: "puerum Sporum exsectis testibus etiam in muliebrem naturam transfigurare conatus." MacMullen 1982: 495 not implausibly takes this to refer to "surgical tinkering" (*natura* could be used euphemistically to refer to the genital organs: see *OLD* s.v. 15, Adams 1982: 59–62, and Winkler 1990: 217–20). Aurelius Victor's language even more directly implies some kind of physical reshaping (*Caes*. 5.16: "spadone quem quondam exsectum formare in mulierem tentaverat"), while Dio is rather vague on the point (62.28.3): τά τε ἄλλα ὡς γυναικὶ αὐτῷ ἐχρῆτο καὶ προϊόντος τοῦ χρόνου καὶ ἔγημεν αὐτόν.

26. Boswell 1994: 80–1 ignores this consideration when he translates Suet. *Nero* 28 ("puerum Sporum . . . cum dote et flammeo per sollemnia nuptiarum celeberrimo officio deductum ad se pro uxore habuit") as "married a man [named Sporus] in a very public ceremony with a dowry and veil [*flammeum*], with all the solemnites of matrimony, and lived with him as his spouse." It is misleading to call Sporos simply "a man," and translating *uxore* ("wife") as "spouse" misses Suetonius' point: Nero erased Sporos' masculinity.

27. Dio's comment that Elagabalus played both the "male" and the "female" role in his marriages "most lasciviously" (Dio 79.5.5: καὶ περὶ μὲν τῶν γάμων αὐτοῦ, ὧν τε ἐγάμει ὧν τε ἐγήματο, αὐτίκα λελέξεται – καὶ γὰρ ἠνδρίζετο καὶ ἐθηλύνετο καὶ ἔπραττεν καὶ ἔπασχεν ἑκάτερα ἀσελγέστατα) is probably not relevant, since the allusion is to his overall licentiousness and likely points to marriages with *women* in which Elagabalus played the role of husband (for his wives, with whom he was certainly thought to have had sexual relations, cf. SHA *Elagab*. 24.2, 31.2 and Dio 79.9, where we read of five different wives, one of whom, Aquilia Severa, he violated when she was a Vestal Virgin). Unfortunately the text of Dio becomes fragmentary at this very point, and as a result we cannot know if Dio reported any marriages to *men* in which Elagabalus played the role of husband.

28. While Boswell 1994: 83 alludes to this conceptual difficulty, some of the implications of his discussion (e.g., when he speaks of "publicly recognized relationships entailing some change in status for one or both parties, comparable in this sense to heterosexual marriage," 80) are not, I think, supported by the evidence. The situation in antiquity may have been rather more comparable to the contemporary situation in the United States than Boswell's discussion suggests: while formalized same-sex unions exist, and mainstream culture is becoming increasingly aware of them, it cannot be claimed that they have gained a "publicly recognized" status as marriages.

Appendix 3

1. Quint. *I.O.* 10.1.93: "satura quidem tota nostra est."

2. Cf. Kroll 1988: 92: "Wenn die Satiriker voll davon [sc., of references to "Päderastie"] sind, so mag man darin vielfach Übertreibung sehen wollen; immerhin hätten ihre unzähligen Anspielungen kein Verständnis gefunden, wenn die Sache nicht allgemein verbreitete gewesen wäre."

3. And yet, as we saw in chapter 4, Catullus for one is capable of playing with his masculine self-image.

4. An important difference lies in the fact that the first-person narrator of Petronius or Apuleius is clearly himself an object of satiric humor; here the distinction between the author and the narrative voice is as clear as it could be.

5. Dover 1974: 1–45.

6. Beagon 1992: 14. See also the detailed discussion in Citroni Marchetti 1991.

7. Cf. the similar remarks at Winkler 1990: 18–20 regarding Greek philosophers.

8. Consider the conservative estimates of William Harris, *Ancient Literacy* (Cambridge, Mass., 1989), p. 329, where it is suggested that "the combined literacy level in the period before 100 B.C. is unlikely to have much exceeded 10%," but that the level may have increased somewhat over the subsequent centuries.

9. Contrast Kroll 1988: 90 on Pompeiian graffiti: "Daß wir uns in den untersten Regionen der Gesellschaft befinden, beweisen außer der Sache die meist auf Sklaven hinweisenden Namen und die Orthographie." But there is no reason to think that only the "lowest regions of society" represented their views in this medium, nor need we believe, as Kroll argues, that only men of the lower classes visited the brothels of Pompeii ("nur von Männern der niedersten Stände," 97). See Varone 1994 for a wide selection of graffiti with discussion.

WORKS CITED

The texts of ancient authors are regularly taken from the Oxford Classical Texts edition when that exists, and otherwise from the Teubner edition, with the following exceptions.

Fragments of the Republican orators (except for Cicero):
Malcovati, Enrica, ed. 1955. *Oratorum Romanorum fragmenta liberae rei publicae*, 2nd ed. Turin.
Lucilius:
Marx, Friedrich, ed. 1904. *C. Lucilii carminum reliquiae*. Leipzig.
Republican comedy:
Ribbeck, Otto, ed. 1898. *Comicorum Romanorum praeter Plautum et Syri quae feruntur Sententias fragmenta*, 3rd ed. Leipzig.
Fragments of Cicero's speeches:
Schoell, F., ed. 1918. *Orationum deperditarum fragmenta*. In *M. Tulli Ciceronis scripta quae manserunt omnia*, edited by A. Klotz *et al.* (vol. 8, pp. 391–494). Leipzig.
Priapea:
Baehrens, Emil, ed. 1879. *Poetae Latini minores* (vol. 1, pp. 54–87). Leipzig.
Petronius:
Müller, Konrad, ed. 1961. *Petronii Arbitri Satyricon*. Munich.
Digest:
Mommsen, Theodor, and Paul Krueger, eds. 1985. *The Digest of Justinian* (with a translation edited by Alan Watson). Philadelphia.

The following are works of modern scholarship to which reference is made more than once in the notes, or those which are of fundamental importance.

Abelove, Henry, Michèle Aina Barale, and David M. Halperin, eds. 1993. *The Lesbian and Gay Studies Reader*. New York.

Adams, J. N. 1981. "*Culus, clunes* and Their Synonyms in Latin." *Glotta* 50: 231–64.

———. 1982. *The Latin Sexual Vocabulary*. Baltimore.

Anderson, William S. 1993. *Barbarian Play: Plautus' Roman Comedy*. Toronto.

Ariès, Philippe, and André Béjin, eds. 1985. *Western Sexuality: Practice and Precept in Past and Present Times*. Translated by Anthony Forster. Oxford.

Arkins, Brian. 1982. *Sexuality in Catullus*. Hildesheim.

Balsdon, J. P. V. D. 1979. *Romans and Aliens*. London.

Barton, Carlin A. 1993. *The Sorrows of the Ancient Romans: The Gladiator and the Monster*. Princeton.

Beagon, Mary. 1992. *Roman Nature: The Thought of Pliny the Elder*. Oxford.

Berger, Maurice, Brian Wallis, and Simon Watson, eds. 1995. *Constructing Masculinity*. New York.

Besnier, Niko. 1994. "Polynesian Gender Liminality Through Time and Space." Herdt 1994: 285–328.

Blümner, H. 1911. *Die römische Privataltertümer*. (Handbuch der klassischen Altertumswissenschaft 4:2:2). Munich.

Boswell, John. 1980. *Christianity, Social Tolerance, and Homosexuality: Gay People in Western Europe from the Beginning of the Christian Era to the Fourteenth Century*. Chicago.

———. 1982/83. "Revolutions, Universals, and Sexual Categories." *Salmagundi* 58–59: 89–113.

———. 1990. "Concepts, Experience, and Sexuality." *Differences* 2: 67–87.

———. 1994. *Same-Sex Unions in Premodern Europe*. New York.

Braund, S. H. 1988. *Beyond Anger: A Study of Juvenal's Third Book of Satires*. Cambridge.

———. 1995. "A Woman's Voice? Laronia's Role in Juvenal Satires 2." In B. Levick and R. Hawley, eds., *Women in Antiquity*, 207–19. London.

———, ed. 1996. *Juvenal: Satires Book I*. Cambridge.

Braund, Susanna Morton, and Christopher Gill, eds. 1997. *The Passions in Roman Thought and Literature*. Cambridge.

Bremmer, Jan. 1980. "An Enigmatic Indo-European Rite: Pederasty." *Arethusa* 13: 279–98.

Brendel, Otto J. 1970. "The Scope and Temperament of Erotic Art in the Greco-Roman World." In Theodore Bowie and Cornelia V. Christenson, eds., *Studies in Erotic Art*, 3–107. New York.

Brooten, Bernadette J. 1996. *Love between Women: Early Christian Responses to Female Homoeroticism*. Chicago.

Buchheit, Vinzenz. 1962. *Studien zum Corpus Priapeorum*. Munich.

Cantarella, Eva. 1992. *Bisexuality in the Ancient World*. Translated by Cormac Ó Cuilleanáin. New Haven.

Caplan, Patricia, ed. 1987. *The Cultural Construction of Sexuality*. London.

Chauncey, George. 1994. *Gay New York: Gender, Urban Culture, and the Making of the Gay Male World, 1890–1940*. New York.

Citroni, Mario. 1975. *M. Valerii Martialis epigrammaton liber primus*. Florence.

Citroni Marchetti, Sandra. 1991. *Plinio il Vecchio e la tradizione del moralismo romano*. Pisa.

Clarke, John R. 1991. "The Decor of the House of Jupiter and Ganymede at Ostia Antica: Private Residence Turned Gay Hotel?" In Elaine K. Gazda, ed., *Roman Art in the*

Private Sphere: New Perspectives on the Architecture and Decor of the Domus, Villa, and Insula, 89–104. Ann Arbor.

———. 1993. "The Warren Cup and the Contexts for Representations of Male-to-Male Lovemaking in Augustan and Early Julio-Claudian Art." *Art Bulletin* 75: 275–94.

———. 1996. "Hypersexual Black Men in Augustan Baths: Ideal Somatotypes and Apotropaic Magic." In Kampen 1996: 184–98.

———. 1998. *Looking at Lovemaking: Constructions of Sexuality in Roman Art 100 B.C.– A.D. 250*. Berkeley.

Cody, Jane M. 1976. "The *senex amator* in Plautus' *Casina*." *Hermes* 104: 453–76.

Cohen, David. 1991. *Law, Sexuality, and Society: The Enforcement of Morals in Classical Athens*. Cambridge.

Corbeill, Anthony. 1997. "Dining Deviants in Roman Political Invective." In Hallett and Skinner 1997: 99–128.

Cornwall, Andrea, and Nancy Lindisfarne, eds. 1994. *Dislocating Masculinity: Comparative Ethnographies*. London.

Courtney, Edward. 1980. *A Commentary on the Satires of Juvenal*. London.

Crook, J. A. 1967. *Law and Life of Rome, 90 B.C.–A.D. 212*. Ithaca.

Dalla, Danilo. 1987. *Ubi Venus mutatur: omosessualità e diritto nel mondo romano*. Milan.

Davidson, Arnold I. 1987/88. "Sex and the Emergence of Sexuality." *Critical Inquiry* 14: 16–48.

DeVries, Keith. 1997. "The 'Frigid Eromenoi' and Their Wooers Revisited: A Closer Look at Greek Homosexuality in Vase Painting." In Duberman 1997: 14–24.

Diehl, Ernst, ed. 1930. *Pompeianische Wandinschriften und Verwandtes*, 2nd ed. Berlin.

Dover, K. J. 1974. *Greek Popular Morality in the Time of Plato and Aristotle*. Berkeley.

———. 1978. *Greek Homosexuality*. London.

Duberman, Martin, et al., eds. 1989. *Hidden from History: Reclaiming the Gay and Lesbian Past*. New York.

———, ed. 1997. *Queer Representations: Reading Lives, Reading Cultures*. New York.

Earl, Donald. 1967. *The Moral and Political Tradition of Rome*. Ithaca.

Edwards, Catharine. 1993. *The Politics of Immorality in Ancient Rome*. Cambridge.

———. 1997. "Unspeakable Professions: Public Performance and Prostitution in Ancient Rome." In Hallett and Skinner 1997: 66–98.

Ellis, Robinson. 1889. *A Commentary on Catullus*. 2nd ed. Oxford.

Epstein, Steven. 1987. "Gay Politics, Ethnic Identity: The Limits of Social Constructionism." *Socialist Review* 93/94: 9–54.

Eyben, E. 1972. "Antiquity's View of Puberty." *Latomus* 31: 677–97.

Fabre, Georges. 1981. *Libertus: Recherches sur les rapports patron-affranchi à la fin de la république romaine*. Rome.

Fantham, Elaine. 1991. "*Stuprum*: Public Attitudes and Penalties for Sexual Offences in Republican Rome." *Echos du Monde Classique/Classical Views* 35: 267–91.

Fedeli, Paolo. 1983. *Catullus' Carmen 61*. Amsterdam.

Fehling, Detlev. 1974. *Ethologische Überlegungen auf dem Gebiet der Altertumskunde*. Munich.

Ferrary, J.-L. 1988. *Philhellénisme et impérialisme*. Paris.

Foucault, Michel. 1978. *The History of Sexuality*. Vol. 1: *An Introduction*. Translated by Robert Hurley. New York.

———. 1985. *The History of Sexuality*. Vol. 2: *The Use of Pleasure*. Translated by Robert Hurley. New York.

———. 1986. *The History of Sexuality*. Vol. 3: *The Care of the Self*. Translated by Robert Hurley. New York.

Fraenkel, Eduard. 1920. "*Cevere* im Plautustext." In *Kleine Beiträge zur klassischen Philologie* (Rome, 1964) 2: 45–52. (Originally published in *Sokrates, Zeitschrift für das Gymnasialwesen* 74 [1920]: 14–9.)

———. 1960. *Elementi Plautini in Plauto.* Translated by Franco Munari. Florence.

Friedlaender, Ludwig. 1922. *Darstellungen aus der Sittengeschichte Roms in der Zeit von Augustus bis zum Ausgang der Antonine*, 10th ed. Leipzig.

Friedländer, P. 1912. "Ganymedes." *RE* 7: 737–49.

Furneaux, Henry, ed. 1907. *The Annals of Tacitus.* 2nd ed. Oxford.

Gardner, Jane. 1986. *Women in Roman Law and Society.* London.

———. 1993. *Being a Roman Citizen.* London.

Garthwaite, John. 1984. "Statius, *Silvae* 3.4: On the Fate of Earinus." *ANRW* II.32.1: 111–24.

Gelsomino, Remo. 1958. "Augusti Epistula ad Maecenatem." *Rheinisches Museum* 101: 147–52.

Gillis, Daniel. 1983. *Eros and Death in the Aeneid.* Rome.

Gilmore, David D. 1990. *Manhood in the Making: Cultural Concepts of Masculinity.* New Haven.

Gleason, Maud W. 1995. *Making Men: Sophists and Self-Presentation in Ancient Rome.* Princeton.

Gonfroy, Françoise. 1978. "Homosexualité et idéologie esclavagiste chez Cicéron." *Dialogues d'histoire ancienne* 4: 219–62.

Greenberg, David F. 1988. *The Construction of Homosexuality.* Chicago.

Greenidge, A. H. J. 1894. *Infamia: Its Place in Roman Public and Private Life.* Oxford.

Griffin, Jasper. 1985. *Latin Poets and Roman Life.* London.

Grimal, Pierre. 1963. *L'amour à Rome.* Paris.

Gruen, Erich S. 1990. *Studies in Greek Culture and Roman Policy.* Leiden.

———. 1992. *Culture and National Identity in Republican Rome.* Ithaca.

Gurlitt, Ludwig. 1921. *Erotica Plautina: Eine Auswahl erotischer Szenen aus Plautus.* Munich.

Hallett, Judith P. 1973. "The Role of Women in Roman Elegy: Counter-Cultural Feminism." In John Peradotto and J. P. Sullivan, eds., *Women in the Ancient World: The Arethusa Papers*, 241–62. Albany.

———. 1977. "*Perusinae glandes* and the Changing Image of Augustus." *American Journal of Ancient History* 2: 151–71.

———. 1988. "Roman Attitudes toward Sex." In M. Grant and R. Kitzinger, eds., *Civilization of the Ancient Mediterranean*, 2: 1265–1278. New York.

———. 1989. "Female Homoeroticism and the Denial of Roman Reality in Latin Literature." *Yale Journal of Criticism* 3: 209–227.

———. 1993. "Feminist Theory, Historical Periods, Literary Canons, and the Study of Greco-Roman Antiquity." In Rabinowitz and Richlin 1993: 44–72.

Hallett, Judith P., and Marilyn B. Skinner, eds. 1997. *Roman Sexualities.* Princeton.

Halperin, David M. 1990. *One Hundred Years of Homosexuality, and Other Essays on Greek Love.* New York.

———. 1994. "Historicizing the Subject of Desire: Sexual Preferences and Erotic Identities in the Pseudo-Lucianic *Erotes*." In Jan Goldstein, ed., *Foucault and the Writing of History*, 19–34, 255–61. Oxford.

———. 1997. "Questions of Evidence." In Duberman 1997: 39–54.

———. Forthcoming. "Forgetting Foucault: Acts, Identities, and the History of Sexuality." In *What Men Call Love: Ancient Texts, Modern Readings.* Chicago.

Halperin, David M., John J. Winkler, and Froma I. Zeitlin, eds. 1990. *Before Sexuality: The Construction of Erotic Experience in the Ancient Greek World.* Princeton.

Hamblenne, P. 1984. "*Cura ut vir sis!* . . . ou une *vir(tus)* peu morale." *Latomus* 43: 369–88.

Hardie, Philip, ed. 1994. *Virgil,* Aeneid *Book IX.* Cambridge.

Henderson, Jeffrey. 1991. *The Maculate Muse: Obscene Language in Attic Comedy.* Rev. ed. New York.

Herdt, Gilbert. 1981. *Guardians of the Flutes: Idioms of Masculinity.* New York.

———, ed. 1993. *Ritualized Homosexuality in Melanesia.* Berkeley.

———. 1994. *Third Sex, Third Gender: Beyond Sexual Dimorphism in Culture and History.* New York.

Herter, Hans. 1932. *De Priapo.* Giessen.

———. 1954. "Priapos." *RE* 44: 1914–42.

———. 1959. "Effeminatus." *RAC* 4: 620–50.

———. 1960. "Soziologie der antiken Prostitution im Lichte der heidnischen und christlichen Schriftum." *Jahrbuch für Antike und Christentum* 3: 70–111.

Hexter, Ralph, and Daniel Selden, eds. 1992. *Innovations of Antiquity.* New York.

Housman, A. E. 1930. "*Draucus* and Martial XI.8.1." *Classical Review* 44: 114–6.

———. 1931. "Praefanda." *Hermes* 66: 402–12.

Howell, Peter. 1980. *A Commentary on Book One of the Epigrams of Martial.* London.

Huelsen, C. 1896. "Miscellanea epigrafica: *Tessere lusorie*." *MDAI(R)* 11: 227–57.

Jocelyn, H. D. 1985. "Concerning an American View of Latin Sexual Humour." *Echos du monde classique/Classical Views* 29 [n.s. 4]: 1–30.

Johns, Catherine. 1982. *Sex or Symbol: Erotic Images of Greece and Rome.* Austin.

Joshel, Sandra R. 1992. *Work, Identity, and Legal Status at Rome: A Study of the Occupational Inscriptions.* Norman.

Kampen, Natalie Boymel, ed. 1996. *Sexuality in Ancient Art: Near East, Egypt, Greece, and Italy.* Cambridge.

Katz, Jonathan Ned. 1995. *The Invention of Heterosexuality.* New York.

Kay, N. M. 1985. *Martial Book XI: A Commentary.* London.

Kempter, Gerda. 1980. *Ganymed: Studien zur Typologie, Ikonographie und Ikonologie.* Cologne.

Kennedy, Duncan F. 1993. *The Arts of Love: Five Studies in the Discourse of Roman Love Elegy.* Cambridge.

Keuls, Eva C. 1985. *The Reign of the Phallus: Sexual Politics in Ancient Athens.* New York.

Kleijwegt, Marc. 1991. *Ancient Youth: The Ambiguity of Youth and the Absence of Adolescence in Greco-Roman Society.* Amsterdam.

Koehl, Robert B. 1986. "The Chieftain Cup and a Minoan Rite of Passage." *Journal of Hellenic Studies* 106: 99–110.

———. 1997. "Ephoros and Ritualized Homosexuality in Bronze Age Crete." In Duberman 1997: 7–13.

Konstan, David. 1983. *Roman Comedy.* Ithaca.

———. 1993. "Sexuality and Power in Juvenal's Second Satire." *Liverpool Classical Monthly* 18: 12–4.

Krenkel, Werner. 1970. *Lucilius: Satiren.* 2 vols. Leiden.

———. 1978. "Männliche Prostitution in der Antike." *Das Altertum* 24: 49–55.

———. 1979a. "Masturbation in der Antike." *WZR* 28: 159–72.

———. 1979b. "Pueri meritorii." *WZR* 28: 179–89.

———. 1980a. "Fellatio and irrumatio." *WZR* 29: 77–88.

———. 1980b. "Sex und politische Biographie." *WZR* 29: 65–76.

———. 1981. "Tonguing." *WZR* 30: 37–54.

———. 1982. "Libido im Griechischen und Lateinischen." *WZR* 31: 39–41.

————. 1988. "Prostitution." In M. Grant and R. Kitzinger, eds., *Civilization of the Ancient Mediterranean*, 2: 1291–7. New York.

Kroll, Wilhelm. 1921. "Kinaidos." *RE* 11: 459–62.

————. 1924. "Lesbische Liebe." *RE* 23: 2100–2.

————, ed. 1959. *C. Valerius Catullus*. 4th ed. Stuttgart.

————. 1988. "Römische Erotik." In Siems 1988: 70–117. (Originally published in *Zeitschrift für Sexualwissenschaft und Sexualpolitik* 17 [1930]: 145–78.)

Kytzler, Bernhard. 1978. *Carmina Priapea: Gedichte an den Gartengott*. Zurich.

Lambert, Royston. 1984. *Beloved and God: The Story of Hadrian and Antinous*. New York.

Lane, Eugene N., ed. 1996. *Cybele, Attis, and Related Cults: Essays in Memory of M. J. Vermaseren*. Leiden.

Lilja, Saara. 1983. *Homosexuality in Republican and Augustan Rome*. Helsinki.

Lutz, Cora E. 1947. "Musonius Rufus: 'The Roman Socrates.'" *Yale Classical Studies* 10: 3–147.

Lyne, R. O. A. M. 1980. *The Latin Love Poets from Catullus to Horace*. Oxford.

————. 1987. *Further Voices in Vergil's 'Aeneid'*. Oxford.

MacCary, W. Thomas. 1975. "The Bacchae in Plautus' *Casina*." *Hermes* 103: 459–63.

MacMullen, Ramsay. 1982. "Roman Attitudes to Greek Love." *Historia* 31: 484–502.

————. 1991. "Hellenizing the Romans (2nd Century B.C.)." *Historia* 40: 419–38.

Makowski, John F. 1989. "Nisus and Euryalus: A Platonic Relationship." *Classical Journal* 85: 1–15.

Marcadé, Jean. 1965. *Roma Amor: Essay on Erotic Elements in Etruscan and Roman Art*. Geneva.

Marquardt, Joachim. 1886. *Das Privatleben der Römer*. 2nd ed. Leipzig.

Martin, R. 1978. "La vie sexuelle des esclaves, d'après les Dialogues rustiques de Varron." In *Varron: Grammaire antique et stylistique latine—Receuil offert à Jean Collart*, 113–26. Paris.

Maurin, J. 1975. "Remarques sur la notion de 'puer' à l'époque classique." *BAGB* 2: 222–30.

McDermott, William C. 1972. "M. Cicero and M. Tiro." *Historia* 21: 259–86.

McGinn, Thomas A. J. 1989. "The Taxation of Roman Prostitutes." *Helios* 16: 79–110.

McIntosh, Mary. 1968. "The Homosexual Role." *Social Problems* 16: 182–92.

Moorton, Richard F. 1990. "Love as Death: The Pivoting Metaphor in Vergil's Story of Dido." *Classical World* 83: 153–66.

Morabito, Marcel. 1981. *Les réalités de l'esclavage d'après le Digeste*. Paris.

Murray, Stephen O., and Will Roscoe, eds. 1997. *Islamic Homosexualities: Culture, History, and Literature*. New York.

Myerowitz, Molly. 1992. "The Domestication of Desire: Ovid's *Parva Tabella* and the Theater of Love." In Richlin 1992b: 131–57.

Nanda, Serena. 1990. *Neither Man nor Woman: The Hijras of India*. Belmont, Calif.

————. 1994. "Hijras: An Alternative Sex and Gender Role in India." In Herdt 1994: 373–417.

Neudling, Chester Louis. 1955. *A Prosopography to Catullus*. Oxford.

O'Connor, Eugene Michael. 1989. *Symbolum Salacitatis: A Study of the God Priapus as a Literary Character*. Frankfurt.

Opelt, Ilona. 1965. *Die lateinischen Schimpfwörter und verwandte sprachliche Erscheinungen: Eine Typologie*. Heidelberg.

Ortner, Sherry B., and Harriet Whitehead, eds. 1981. *Sexual Meanings: The Cultural Construction of Gender and Sexuality*. Cambridge.

Padgug, Robert A. 1979. "Sexual Matters: On Conceptualizing Sexuality in History." *Radical History Review* 20: 3–23.

Parker, Holt N. 1997. "The Teratogenic Grid." In Hallett and Skinner 1997: 47–65.

Parker, W. H., ed. and trans. 1988. *Priapea: Poems for a Phallic God*. London.

Petrochilos, Nicholas. 1974. *Roman Attitudes to the Greeks*. Athens.

Putnam, Michael C. J. 1985. "Possessiveness, Sexuality, and Heroism in the *Aeneid*." *Vergilius* 31: 1–21.

———. 1995. "Ganymede and Virgilian Ekphrasis." *American Journal of Philology* 116: 419–40.

Quinn, Kenneth. 1972. *Catullus: An Interpretation*. London.

———, ed. 1973. *Catullus: The Poems*. 2nd ed. London.

Rabinowitz, Nancy Sorkin, and Amy Richlin, eds. 1993. *Feminist Theory and the Classics*. New York.

Raditsa, L. F. 1980. "Augustus' Legislation concerning Marriage, Procreation, Love Affairs and Adultery." *ANRW* II.13: 278–339.

Rawson, Beryl. 1974. "Roman Concubinage and Other *De Facto* Marriages." *Transactions of the American Philological Association* 104: 279–305.

———, ed. 1986. *The Family in Ancient Rome: New Perspectives*. Ithaca.

———, ed. 1991. *Marriage, Divorce, and Children in Ancient Rome*. Canberra.

Richardson, T. Wade. 1984. "Homosexuality in the *Satyricon*." *C&M* 35: 105–27.

Richlin, Amy. 1981a. "Approaches to the Sources on Adultery at Rome." In Helene P. Foley, ed., *Reflections of Women in Antiquity*, 379–404. New York.

———. 1981b. "The Meaning of *irrumare* in Catullus and Martial." *Classical Philology* 76: 40–6.

———. 1984. "Invective against Women in Roman Satire." *Arethusa* 17: 67–80.

———. 1991. "Zeus and Metis: Foucault, Feminism, Classics." *Helios* 18: 1–21.

———. 1992a. *The Garden of Priapus: Sexuality and Aggression in Roman Humor*, rev. ed. New York.

———, ed. 1992b. *Pornography and Representation in Greece and Rome*. New York.

———. 1993. "Not Before Homosexuality: The Materiality of the *Cinaedus* and the Roman Law against Love between Men." *Journal of the History of Sexuality* 3: 523–73.

———. 1997. "Gender and Rhetoric: Producing Manhood in the Schools." In William J. Dominik, ed., *Roman Eloquence: Rhetoric in Society and Literature*, pp. 90–110. New York.

Robert, Jean-Noël. 1997. *Eros romain: Sexe et morale dans l'ancienne Rome*. Paris.

Rocke, Michael. 1996. *Forbidden Friendships: Homosexuality and Male Culture in Renaissance Florence*. New York.

Roscoe, Will. 1991. *The Zuni Man-Woman*. Albuquerque.

———. 1996. "Priests of the Goddess: Gender Transgression in Ancient Religion." *History of Religions* 35: 195–230.

Rousselle, Aline. 1988. *Porneia: On Desire and the Body in Antiquity*. Translated by Felicia Pheasant. Oxford.

Rudd, Niall. 1986. *Themes in Roman Satire*. London.

Saikaku, Ihara. 1990. *The Great Mirror of Male Love*. Translated by Paul Gordon Schalow. Stanford, Calif.

Salvatore, Armando, ed. 1964. *Appendix Vergiliana*. 2 vols. Naples.

Santoro L'Hoir, Francesca. 1992. *The Rhetoric of Gender Terms: 'Man', 'Woman', and the Portrayal of Character in Latin Prose*. Leiden.

Schalow, Paul. 1989. "Male Love in Early Modern Japan: A Literary Depiction of the 'Youth.'" Duberman et al. 1989: 118–28.

Schievenin, Romeo. 1976. "Trimalcione e il puer non inspeciosus." *BStudLat* 6: 295–302.

Schmitt, Arno, and Jehoeda Sofer, eds. 1991. *Sexuality and Eroticism among Males in Moslem Societies*. New York.

Schrijvers, P.H. 1985. *Eine medizinische Erklärung der männlichen Homosexualität aus der Antike*. Amsterdam.

Segal, Erich. 1968. *Roman Laughter: The Comedy of Plautus*. Cambridge, Mass.

Selden, Daniel. 1992. "*Ceveat lector*: Catullus and the Rhetoric of Performance." In Hexter and Selden 1992: 461–512.

Sergent, Bernard. 1986. *Homosexuality in Greek Myth*. Translated by Arthur Goldhammer. Boston.

Sichtermann, Hellmut. 1953. *Ganymed: Mythos und Gestalt in der antiken Kunst*. Berlin.

———. 1988. "Ganymedes." *Lexicon Iconographicum Mythologiae Classicae* 4: 154–69.

Siems, Andreas Karsten, ed. 1988. *Sexualität und Erotik in der Antike*. Darmstadt.

Skinner, Marilyn. 1989. "*Ut decuit cinaediorem*: Power, Gender, and Urbanity in Catullus 10." *Helios* 16: 7–23.

———. 1997. "*Ego mulier*: The Construction of Male Sexuality in Catullus." In Hallett and Skinner 1997: 129–50.

Slater, Niall. 1985. *Plautus in Performance: The Theatre of the Mind*. Princeton.

———. 1990. *Reading Petronius*. Baltimore.

Solin, Heikki. 1981. "Un epigramma della Domus Aurea." *Rivista Filologica* 109: 268–71.

Stevenson, Walter. 1995. "The Rise of Eunuchs in Greco-Roman Antiquity." *Journal of the History of Sexuality* 5: 495–511.

Sullivan, J. P. 1968. *The Satyricon of Petronius: A Literary Study*. Bloomington.

———. 1979. "Martial's Sexual Attitudes." *Philologus* 123: 288–302.

———. 1991. *Martial: The Unexpected Classic. A Literary and Historical Study*. Cambridge.

Syndikus, Hans Peter. 1984. *Catull: Eine Interpretation. Erster Teil: Einleitung; Die kleine Gedichte (1–60)*. Darmstadt.

Taylor, Rabun. 1997. "Two Pathic Subcultures in Ancient Rome." *Journal of the History of Sexuality* 7: 319–71.

Thomsen, Ole. 1992. *Ritual and Desire: Catullus 61 and 62*. Aarhus.

Tong, Rosemarie. 1989. *Feminist Thought: A Comprehensive Introduction*. Boulder.

Treggiari, Susan. 1969. *Roman Freedmen during the Late Republic*. Oxford.

———. 1991. *Roman Marriage: "Iusti Coniuges" from the Time of Cicero to the Time of Ulpian*. Oxford.

Trumbach, Randolph. 1989. "The Birth of the Queen: Sodomy and the Emergence of Gender Equality in Modern Culture, 1660–1750." In Duberman et al. 1989: 129–40.

Vanggaard, Thorkil. 1972. *Phallós: A Symbol and Its History in the Male World*. New York.

Varone, Antonio. 1994. *Erotica Pompeiana: Iscrizioni d'amore sui muri di Pompei*. Rome.

Vermeule, Cornelius. 1963. "Augustan and Julio-Claudian Court Silver." *Antike Kunst* 6: 33–40.

Verstraete, Beert C. 1980. "Slavery and the Social Dynamics of Male Homosexual Relations in Ancient Rome." *Journal of Homosexuality* 5: 227–36.

———. 1982. *Homosexuality in Ancient Greek and Roman Civilization: A Critical Bibliography with Supplement*. Toronto.

Veyne, Paul. 1978. "La famille et l'amour sous le Haut-Empire romain." *Annales (E.S.C.)* 33: 35–63.

———. 1985. "Homosexuality in Ancient Rome." In Ariès and Béjin 1985: 26–35.

———. 1988. *Roman Erotic Elegy: Love, Poetry, and the West*. Translated by David Pellauer. Chicago.

Walters, Jonathan. 1997. "Invading the Roman Body: Manliness and Impenetrability in Roman Thought." In Hallett and Skinner 1997: 29–46.

Waters, Sarah. 1995. "'The Most Famous Fairy in History': Antinous and Homosexual Fantasy." *Journal of the History of Sexuality* 6: 194–230.

Weeks, Jeffrey. 1977. *Coming Out: Homosexual Politics in Britain from the Nineteenth Century to the Present*. London.

————. 1989. "Inverts, Perverts, and Mary-Annes: Male Prostitution and the Regulation of Homosexuality in England in the Nineteenth and Early Twentieth Centuries." In Duberman et al. 1989: 195–211.

Westendorp Boerma, R. E. H. 1963. *P. Vergili Maronis libellus qui inscribitur Catalepton*. Assen.

Whitehead, Harriet. 1981. "The Bow and the Burden Strap: A New Look at Institutionalized Homosexuality in Native North America." In Ortner and Whitehead 1981: 80–115.

Wilkinson, L. P. 1974. *The Roman Experience*. New York.

————. 1978. *Classical Attitudes to Modern Issues*. London.

Williams, Craig A. 1992. "Homosexuality and the Roman Man: A Study in the Cultural Construction of Sexuality." Ph.D. diss., Yale University.

————. 1995. "Greek Love at Rome." *Classical Quarterly* 45: 517–39.

————. 1997. "*Pudicitia* and *Pueri*: Roman Concepts of Male Sexual Experience." In Duberman 1997: 25–38.

————. 1998. Review of Hallett and Skinner 1997. *Bryn Mawr Classical Review* 98.10.16.

Williams, Gordon. 1958. "Some Aspects of Roman Marriage Ceremonies and Ideals." *Journal of Roman Studies* 48: 16–29.

————. 1968. *Tradition and Originality in Roman Poetry*. Oxford.

————. 1983. *Technique and Ideas in the 'Aeneid.'* New Haven.

Williams, Walter L. 1986. *The Spirit and the Flesh: Sexual Diversity in American Indian Culture*. Boston.

Winkler, John J. 1990. *The Constraints of Desire: The Anthropology of Sex and Gender in Ancient Greece*. New York.

Wiseman, T. P. 1985. *Catullus and His World: A Reappraisal*. Cambridge.

Zwierlein, Otto. 1990. *Zur Kritik und Exegese des Plautus I: Poenulus und Curculio*. Mainz.

————. 1991. *Zur Kritik und Exegese des Plautus III: Pseudolus*. Mainz.

INDEX OF PASSAGES CITED

GENERAL INDEX

Achilles and Patroclus: 313n.89, 314n.92
active and passive sexual roles: 18 with
  n.16
actors and acting, biases against: 70–1,
  139–40, 175
adultery (*adulterium*): 32, 43, 51–2, 62,
  96–7, 113–24, 165, 206–8, 217–8, 237,
  308n.23, 310n.57, 344n.194. *See also*
  Lucretia; *stuprum*
Aelius Verus: 51
Aeneas as effeminate: 145–7
Alexis. *See* Virgil
anal intercourse: and hemorrhoids,
  338n.105; and imagery of defecation,
  24, 28–30, 331n.41, 342n.166; with
  women, 27, 50–1, 57, 168–9, 331n.42.
  See also boys; *cinaedi*
animal behavior: 54, 114, 232–4,
  303n.140
Antinous: 60–1. *See also* Hadrian
  (emperor)
Antonius, Lucius: 104, 129
Antonius, Marcus (Mark Antony): 21, 41,
  42, 51, 55–6, 57, 129, 137, 154, 173–4,
  199, 205–6, 245–6, 248, 275n.115,
  286n.223, 297n.66. *See also* Cleopatra;
  marriage between males

appearances, importance of: 10–1, 18,
  188–93
army, Roman: *See miles Marianus*; military
  discipline; Pompey the Great; wartime
  rape
Augustus (Octavian): 34, 51, 55–6, 57, 81,
  94, 129, 157–9, 176, 199, 207,
  275n.115, 286n.223

Bacchanalian scandal (186 B.C.): 42, 67,
  74, 108, 111–2, 150–1, 185
baths: 69–70, 89–90, 219–21, 238
beards: 19, 26, 73–4. *See also* hair, bodily
berdache. *See* Native American cultures
bisexuality. *See* homosexuality,
  heterosexuality, and bisexuality
Boudicca: 82, 85, 140
boys: 19, 73–5; and anal intercourse,
  50–1, 76, 185–8, 242, 333n.61;
  compared to women, 23–6; desirability
  of, 19–28, 183–8, 238–9; and
  effeminacy, 183–8; and male teachers,
  75–6, physical traits of, 19–28; and
  pleasure felt in anal intercourse, 185–7;
  puberty in, 25–6, 269n.51. *See also*
  cinaedi; effeminacy; hair, bodily;
  pedicare

391